INTERNATIONAL RELATIONS

The Global Condition in the Twenty-First Century

INTERNATIONAL RELATIONS

The Global Condition in the Twenty-First Century

FOURTH EDITION

Frederic S. Pearson

Wayne State University

J. Martin Rochester

University of Missouri–St. Louis

The McGraw-Hill Companies, Inc.

New York   St. Louis   San Francisco   Auckland   Bogotá   Caracas
Lisbon   London   Madrid   Mexico City   Milan   Montreal   New Delhi
San Juan   Singapore   Sydney   Tokyo   Toronto

Preface

When we began the first edition of this textbook over a decade ago, the immediate question we faced was: Does the world really need another international relations text, given the many books already available on this subject? We answered in the affirmative, convinced we could write a book that would be somewhat distinctive in content as well as style. In particular, we were seeking to write a book that would somehow appeal to beginning students—its primary audience—as well as to more advanced readers, a book that would combine in a balanced fashion the traditional as well as the new approaches to the study of international relations. We believe that we succeeded in this goal, as judged by our readership, enough to warrant a second, third, and now a fourth edition.

Although the fourth edition differs significantly from the others, in that it is truly a "*post–Cold War*" edition that has undergone major revisions (see below), our core philosophy behind the text remains unchanged. In terms of *content*, we have tried to give comprehensive coverage to the major topics in the field. The general theme of the book can be summarized as the need for scholars, policymakers, and laypersons to take into account the complex variety of relationships that exist today—among more than 5 billion people, 180 countries (nation-states), and 10,000 international organizations—in order to understand the contemporary "global condition" and to make intelligent judgments about international affairs. Although nation-states remain the key actors in the arena of world politics, and national security a fundamental concern, other actors and issues are competing for attention, with these forces containing the seeds of both increased conflict and increased cooperation among peoples. The organization of this text carefully reflects this theme. Part I introduces international relations as a field of study and provides *historical* background for contemporary world politics. Part II focuses on *states* as actors and examines the determinants of foreign policy, international bargaining and diplomacy, and war. Part III focuses on *international institutions*, including international law and international organizations. Part IV examines the congeries of forces involved in *global problem solving*, with separate chapters devoted to arms races, terrorism, coordination of the world economy, economic development, and the management of renewable and nonrenewable resources. Part V contains a concluding chapter that looks to the *future*—the year 2001 and beyond—and offers an analysis of alternative world order models.

In terms of *style*, we have sought to combine high scholarly standards with readability. The text discusses the latest theoretical ideas and research findings in a lively, readable manner—complete with photographs, cartoons, tables, graphs, case studies, and vignettes. We believe that these "supplementary" materials do not in any way compromise academic integrity but, instead, add another dimension to the text. For the beginning student, we have employed several pedagogical aids, including a summary of important points, suggested readings at the end of each chapter, and a glossary of terms. For the more scholarly reader, an extensive notes section appears at the end of the book.

Admittedly, it is often difficult to find a lighter side to a world in which several million people lack access to drinkable water and in which the stockpile of nuclear weapons still amounts to roughly ten tons of TNT for every man, woman, and child on earth. Notwithstanding the cartoons and sidelights, the reader will find that the authors consider international relations a deadly serious subject—a subject where the ability to develop and communicate sound knowledge has much bearing on humanity's future prospects for survival and prosperity. We hope this book makes at least some small contribution in this regard.

This latest edition of the text appears at a special, millennial moment, as the twentieth century is passing into history and giving way to a new century. The fourth edition, aside from incorporating substantial updating of textual material, figures, and tables, aims to capture the mounting turbulence and complexity surrounding international relations in the post–Cold War era. Taking into account the latest developments, this edition shows how the trends discussed in the earlier editions are becoming even more pronounced and accelerated, including the growing diffusion of power, the growing fluidity of alignments, ever more intricate patterns of interdependence associated with an expanding agenda of concerns, and the growing role of nonstate actors and the increasing linkages between subnational, transnational, governmental, and intergovernmental levels of activity. In short, this new edition attempts to come to grips further with the major dramas now being played out between the forces of globalism and regionalism, nationalism and transnationalism, security and welfare, and order and change.

On the subject of order and change, we have found in our own teaching that it can be extremely difficult to explain to students how, on the one hand, the key concepts that have helped to define international relations as a field of inquiry over the past century and longer—national sovereignty, national interests, national citizenship, and the like—remain of utmost importance in understanding how the world works, and yet, on the other hand—given the proliferation of multinational corporations and related phenomena—seem to be losing some of their cogency. Put another way, how does one grasp the fact that we still obviously live in a world of states (as reflected in the powerful images projected by the dark boundaries surrounding the entities found on a map of the world), while such a conception is becoming increasingly inadequate to comprehending what is going on "out there." It is said that an educated person is one who can cope with ambiguity. There is much to cope with today! This book does not seek to make the ambiguous simple but rather a bit more fathomable.

As with any project that has consumed several years of effort, we are indebted to many people. At the very top we must acknowledge the special contribution of the two research centers with which we have been affiliated. In the Center for International Studies at the University of Missouri–St. Louis, we wish to thank its former director, Professor Edwin Fedder, whose support was critical to the birth of this book, as well as staff members Robert Baumann, Gordon Bardos, Mary Hines, Pat Mulligan, and Mickey Williams. In the Center for Peace and Conflict Studies at Wayne State University, we must thank Adam Avrushian, Thomas Tarnow, Jeffrey Wiegand, Rachel Brickner, Joyce Hudson, and Darlene Brownlee. We greatly appreciate the cooperation of the many publishers who granted us permission to use copyrighted material. We also owe considerable thanks to the many reviewers who have offered helpful critiques along the way. For reviewing the third edition, we would like to thank Ronald Francisco, University of Kansas; Larry George, California State University–Long Beach; Ghulam Haniff, St. Cloud State University; Margaret Karns, University of Dayton; Vincent Khapoya, Oakland University; Richard Siegel, University of Nevada–Reno; Charles Stevens, Western Carolina University; and Sandra Wurth-Hough, East Carolina University. For this fourth edition, we would like to thank the following reviewers: Mario Carranza, Indiana University of Pennsylvania; Terry Clark, University of Illinois; Cynthia Combs, University of North Carolina–Charlotte; Roxanne Lynn Doty, Arizona State University; Martin David Dubin, Northern Illinois University; Jeffrey Obler, University of North Carolina–Chapel Hill; Henry Shockley, Boston University; and Timothy White, Xavier University. A long-standing intellectual debt must be acknowledged to our "mentors," William Coplin at Syracuse University and J. David Singer at the University of Michigan, both of whom in their own way taught us the importance of sound scholarship in collecting evidence and of sound pedagogy in presenting it. Finally, our acknowledgments would be incomplete without expressing gratitude to Bert Lummus, our original editor, and Lynn Uhl and Leslye Jackson, who shared editorship of this edition, and to the superb staff at McGraw-Hill—particularly Katy Redmond, Monica Freedman, Larry Goldberg, and Stephanie Capiello—who all contributed greatly to the final product.

For our families who have had to live with us for the past several years during the life of this project, amid the conflict that always attends collaboration, we reserve a well-earned dedication.

Frederic S. Pearson
J. Martin Rochester

INTERNATIONAL
RELATIONS

The Global Condition
in the Twenty-First Century

PART
I

Introduction

An introduction to the study of international relations in our time is an introduction to the art and science of the survival of mankind. KARL W. DEUTSCH, *The Analysis of International Relations*

This is a book about contemporary international relations. The quotation from Deutsch suggests both the importance of studying international relations and the immensity of the task. Albert Einstein was once asked, "Why is it that when the mind of man has stretched so far as to discover the structure of the atom we have been unable to devise the political means to keep the atom from destroying us?" Einstein reputedly responded, "That is simple, my friend, because politics is more difficult than physics."

The moral of this story, of course, is not that introductory physics courses are the easy courses at universities, only that getting a handle on international relations phenomena and bringing them under control can in some ways be more vexing than conquering the mysteries of the physical universe. In exploring a wide range of international relations phenomena in this book, we will be attempting to show the complexity of the world today at the same time that we are trying to unravel that complexity.

Before this exploration can begin, it is necessary first to provide some intellectual and substantive background for the study of contemporary international relations. Hence, in Part I we will discuss the development of international relations as a field of study, the various approaches that students of international relations have used through the years, and the differing concerns of scholars, policymakers, and laymen (Chapter 1). We will also present a brief *historical* look at the evolution of international relations over the last four centuries (Chapter 2) as well as a bird's-eye view of the planet *today,* comparing the environment of contemporary international relations with that of the past (Chapter 3).

The Study of International Relations, or Getting a Handle on the World

It is that time again—*fin de siècle,* the end of a century. Such moments are generally cause for celebration, greeted with much pageantry and fanfare. They also offer an occasion for more serious soul-searching and deep reflection about the human condition. In any century one can identify defining events. The first half of the twentieth century was marked particularly by two world wars, the second half by a global geopolitical struggle that came to be called the Cold War. What awaits us in the next century?

As an old Roumanian proverb says, "It is always hard to predict anything, especially the future."[1] For proof, one need only look at the events that have transpired since the late 1980s. Few, if any, observers can claim to have anticipated the Cold War ending as abruptly and peaceably as it did.[2] On September 26, 1988, speaking before the United Nations General Assembly in one of his last addresses as President of the United States, Ronald Reagan confessed to his own astonishment, stating that "a change that is cause for shaking the head in wonder is upon us, . . . the prospect of a new age of world peace."[3] Reagan, who had waged a crusade against communism and had called the Soviet Union the "evil empire" earlier in his administration, was alluding to the startling changes underway in the Soviet Union, Eastern Europe, and elsewhere as nondemocratic regimes were experiencing pressures to liberalize their political systems, and peace seemed to be "breaking out" in various parts of the world. Still more dramatic developments followed. The Berlin Wall, since 1961 a symbol of the post–World War II ideological struggle between East and West, started to come down in November 1989 as the East German government allowed its citizens to cross into West Germany and began reunification talks leading to the restoration of a single German state. In December 1989, during a whirlwind round of diplomacy, Soviet Foreign Minister Eduard Shevardnadze made the first visit of an East bloc minister to the headquarters of the Western alliance in Brussels and announced that the Soviet Union sought to become part of "a common European house." Just before New Year's Eve ushered in the 1990s, the Soviet Red Army Chorus appeared at a Kennedy Center gala in Washington, D.C., honoring several Americans with artistic achievement awards and, in a grand finale, led President George Bush and a throng of dignitaries in a stirring rendition of "God Bless America." Bush proclaimed a "New World Order," one in which by the end of his tenure in office the Soviet Union itself no longer existed, having been dismembered and replaced by a set of new entities on the world map.

President Bill Clinton, addressing the UN General Assembly on September 27, 1993, attempted to capture the millennial mood of the post–Cold War era:

> It is clear that we live at a turning point in human history. Immense and promising changes seem to wash over us every day. The Cold War is over. The world is no longer divided into two armed and angry camps. Dozens of new democracies have been born.
>
> It is a moment of miracles. We see Nelson Mandela stand side by side with President de Klerk, proclaiming a date for South Africa's first nonra-

EAST AND WEST GERMANS MEET AT THE BERLIN WALL IN NOVEMBER 1989, CELEBRATING THE END OF SEPARATION AND THE BEGINNING OF GERMAN UNIFICATION.

cial election. We see Russia's first popularly elected President, Boris Yeltsin, leading his nation on its bold democratic journey. We have seen decades of deadlock shattered in the Middle East, as the Prime Minister of Israel and the Chairman of the Palestine Liberation Organization reached past enmity and suspicion to shake each other's hands and exhilarate the entire world with the hope of peace.[4]

As humanity proceeded to negotiate its way through the last decade of the twentieth century, one had to be cautious in interpreting these events as signaling a "new age of world peace." For one thing, history was littered with similar pronouncements that proved to be premature, including some earlier in this century, such as on the eve of World War I, when Norman Angell in 1910, in *The Great Illusion*, claimed that war had become a relic of the past insofar as it was no longer profitable even to the victors,[5] and on the eve of World War II, when Prime Minister Neville Chamberlain of the United Kingdom returned from a 1938 meeting with Germany's Adolph Hitler in Munich, reassuring the world of "peace for our time."[6] The happenings that occasioned much euphoria at the outset of the 1990s remained fragile developments capable of being reversed or evolving in a manner that could replace the old post–World War II order rooted in the American-Soviet rivalry with an even more unstable international order. Indeed, a shattering reminder of the fleeting nature of peace was the Iraqi invasion of neighboring Kuwait in August 1990, leading to over 500,000 American troops together with forces from several other coalition partners being dispatched to the Middle East to punish "naked aggression" and at the same time protect the oil interests of the United States and its allies. Other reminders were provided by daily headlines reporting on what seemed a growing number of smaller conflicts, predominantly ethnopolitical in nature, being waged in the former Yugoslavia and assorted other locales around the world. As the 1990s progressed, some observers were relabeling the new world order "the new world disorder."[7]

Juxtaposed against democratization and other promising trends were some more ominous conditions forming a larger backdrop on the global scene: a continued high level of world military expenditures, hovering around $1 trillion annually, tied to concern over ABC (atomic, biological, and chemical) weapons proliferation; a serious security threat in the form of terrorism and drug trafficking; stubborn problems of poverty in less developed countries, aggravated by a "debt bomb" that, though defused somewhat since the 1980s, still amounted to their aggregately owing some $2 trillion to foreign financial institutions and by a "population bomb" that resulted in these societies adding 200,000 people a day to the planet; the specter of possible trade wars and renewed economic nationalism among the richer developed countries such as the United States and Japan; a series of shocks in international financial markets, including in 1990 an unprecedented panic on the Tokyo stock exchange (shortly after the worst stock market crash in American history as the Dow Jones Average plunged 508 points in a single day) and in 1995 a 28-year-old stock trader in the Singapore office of Baring Bros. losing a billion dollars on the Nikkei exchange and in the process not only single-handedly bankrupting the 232-year-old British firm that had once financed the Louisiana Purchase but also sounding alarm bells throughout the world banking system; the spread of the acquired immune deficiency syndrome (AIDS) virus, affecting one of every four males in parts of Africa and threatening to become a worldwide "pandemic"; and mounting anxiety over a variety of environmental problems, such as a predicted increase in the earth's temperature of a magnitude to cause massive flooding and other side effects, a concern heightened by the fact that the ten hottest years on record in the twentieth century all were registered since 1980.

Amid this volatile, uncertain melange of events and conditions, one could discern at least one feature of international life that seemed a given. For better or worse, human beings generally were experiencing a steady, almost inexorably increasing interconnectedness across geographical, cultural, and other divides even as they sought to maintain the distinctiveness and separateness of their individual communities.

From Poughkeepsie to Peoria to Portland: The Relevance of International Relations

Picture yourself sitting in front of a television set viewing the world, national, and local news on a typical evening. Increasingly individuals around the globe are receiving news in this fashion, through the electronic mass media, which are capable of transmitting instantaneous reports and images about events close to home as well as in distant reaches of the world. There are now more TV sets in the United States than there are toilets, and they are relied on for news by the general public far more than newspapers. Even in a low-income country such as China, most peasant communes and virtually all urban households have access to television, which is looked to as an important source of data about the outside world despite heavy government control over programming. It is estimated that almost half of humanity now is able to watch television.[8] An especially influential source of news for publics and leaders alike is the Cable News Network (CNN), the Atlanta-based network that broadcasts to more than 140 countries and that used satellite technology to bring live coverage of the 1990 Gulf War into living rooms around the world.

The specific bits of information to which one is likely to be exposed while viewing the evening news will of course vary from place to place and moment to moment. However, on almost any given day, whether in Poughkeepsie, New York, or Peoria, Illinois, or Portland, Oregon—or, for that matter, in Tokyo, Sydney, Paris, or Mexico City—one basic thread can be found among the daily occurrences reported: Although they might appear to be removed in various degrees from the immediate concerns of the average man or woman on the street (or student in the classroom), all such events are bound to have some interrelatedness and potential implications for each of us. At first glance some events may seem to fall neatly into the category normally labeled "international" (involving foreign concerns), whereas others seem to fall equally neatly into the category normally labeled "domestic" (involving national or local concerns). On further reflection, one would discover that the "international" events are not so far removed from one's particular locality, and the "domestic" events even of a local nature are not unconnected with world affairs.

LINKAGES IN AN INTERDEPENDENT WORLD

As a concrete illustration of these linkages, let us consider a newscast presented on the evening of May 8, 1995, in St. Louis, Missouri, in the American heartland. The program contained some standard elements one would expect to find in a nightly newscast (or, for those inclined toward more in-depth coverage, a daily newspaper) in most communities—a review of major stories abroad, a crime report, an economic and business survey, and a weather forecast. Among the particular news items that evening were the following:

> American, French, British, Russian, and German leaders meet in Berlin to mark the fiftieth anniversary of V-E Day, the end of World War II in Europe . . . The Nuclear Non-Proliferation Treaty (NPT) Conference continues in New York City as 170 nations seek to reach agreement on a pact that would permanently limit the spread of nuclear weapons . . . The annual United Nations Human Development Report finds economic progress slow in most less developed countries . . . On Wall Street, the Dow Jones Industrial Average is up forty points to a new high . . . Locally, Anheuser-Busch stock is up two points . . . General Motors and Chrysler report that their sales plunged in April, marking four consecutive monthly declines . . . Five homicides occurred over the weekend in St. Louis . . . The winter of 1994–1995 was officially the second warmest on record here.

One of the most important domestic concerns in the United States is the high crime rate. It has been well documented that as much as one-third of violent crime occurring in large cities such as St. Louis is related to drug usage and can be traced to narcotics traffic from other countries.[9] Most heroin consumed in the United States comes from opium production in Southwest Asia (including Iran and Afghanistan), Southeast Asia (including Myanmar, Laos, and Thailand), and Mexico. Peru, Bolivia, and Colombia are the chief suppliers of cocaine, and Mexico the primary source of marijuana. Americans spend over $30 billion annually on cocaine and heroin. Many third world economies facing severe unemployment might be even worse off were it not for the lucrative drug trade. For example, in Bolivia over 5 percent of the population are directly employed in the cocaine industry, whereas in the "Golden Triangle" of Myanmar, Laos, and Thailand, which accounts for 75 percent of the world opium supply, the heroin industry engages several hundred thousand peasants in cultivation and thousands more in the refining process.[10]

News of the V-E Day celebration in Berlin brought back memories to many St. Louis families touched by World War II; few families anywhere were unaffected. The NPT conference underway in New York at that same moment was one of several arms control efforts being made in the post–Cold War era by a new generation of leaders hoping to enhance the prospects of averting World War III. Although the relaxation of East-West tensions was much welcomed, at least one St. Louis–based company, McDonnell-Douglas—one of the largest defense contractors in the United States—had to feel somewhat concerned about the latest peace offensives. The company had been instrumental in keeping the United States a close competitor with the Soviet Union as the premier "arms merchant" in the world in the 1980s, with U.S. sales totaling over $100 billion, and then helping the United States to overtake the Soviet Union in the 1990s and to capture half the world market by 1995.[11] McDonnell-Douglas, whose F-15 Eagle was the most advanced fighter plane in the world and much in demand—Saudi Arabia had recently placed a $9 billion order for 72 aircraft—was the single biggest employer in the state of Missouri and vital to the local economy, employing 23,000 workers in the St. Louis area.[12] A less hostile international environment, with the accompanying opportunities for the U.S. government and other governments to produce a "peace dividend" for their citizens by reducing military expenditures and shifting resources into education and other sectors, could be at least in the short run economically harmful to the St. Louis region in terms of weapons production cutbacks and the resultant loss of jobs. Other localities heavily dependent on munitions factories or military installations for their prosperity likewise were experiencing some ambivalence over the latest trends. Some defense industry layoffs attributable to a reduced Department of Defense budget were already taking their toll. Over 1 million jobs had already been lost nationwide since the late 1980s. One study found that, among states in the United States, Missouri would be the most severely impacted by further U.S. government cutbacks in defense spending, with Massachusetts, California, New York, Ohio, Minnesota, Connecticut, Kansas, Washington, and Michigan not far behind.[13]

The economic well-being of communities can be affected substantially by international developments ranging from increases or decreases in the incidence of war to increases or decreases in trade barriers. For example, the problems of the American automobile industry reported in the newscast had been a recurrent story since the early 1980s. Those problems could be traced partly to the flood of foreign imports—led by the Japanese—that had claimed over 20 percent of the domestic car market in the United States by 1995, and partly to the growth of foreign "transplants" in the United States—foreign-based firms such as Honda and Toyota producing cars in Marysville, Ohio, Georgetown, Kentucky, and elsewhere on American soil—that further eroded the market share held by the "Big Three" (General Motors, Ford, and Chrysler).[14] Detroit could hardly complain about foreign penetration of the American market. After all, Ford in the 1990s was the biggest automaker in the United Kingdom, Australia, Mexico, and Argentina; the second largest in Canada; and the third largest in Brazil and Spain. GM was the second largest auto producer in western Europe.[15] With the growing internationalization of automobile production, including the forging of "strategic alliances" between American companies and their foreign competitors aimed at mutual survival (see the Sidelight on pages 12–13), some communities may find themselves winners and others losers. The St. Louis metropolitan area, the second largest auto-manufacturing center in the United States (outside of Detroit), recently suffered the loss of 3,000 jobs when Chrysler decided to follow the path of Ford and General Motors by moving more production overseas, opening a new minivan factory in Austria. (However, St. Louis figured to benefit from the globalization of the international economy in other sectors. Witness, for example, the continuing growth of Anheuser-Busch, the St. Louis–based company whose status as the world's largest brewery was owed in part to its sizable foreign operations, including the production of Budweiser beer in Europe under agreement with a Czech firm as well as new arrangements concluded with Chinese and Japanese distributors to tap into the vast Asian market.)

Even the local and national weather has international dimensions. The mild winter experienced in St. Louis and much of the United States in 1995 was seen by some as part of a larger global climatic pattern in recent years. Some experts trace the record heat waves to the "greenhouse effect" (the accumulation of carbon dioxide and other gases in the atmosphere caused primarily by the burning of fossil fuels). Other experts have raised an opposite concern about a coming ice age, as the suspension of trillions of dust and smoke particles in the atmosphere or an increase in cloud cover conceivably block the sun's rays; in fact, the 1991 eruption of Mt. Pinatubo in the Philippines, the largest volcanic eruption in a century, blanketed the planet with volcanic ash and in the process seemed to have partially offset the greenhouse effect for a couple of years until the ash dissipated and the warming trend resumed.[16] Although climatologists remain uncertain about the long-term consequences of all this pollution, there is no question that the problem is a global one that spills over national boundaries. Missouri's environmental policy decisions have potential implications not only for neighboring Cairo, Illinois, but—in combination with countless decisions made in other localities—for Cairo, Egypt, and other parts of the globe as well. Despite political opposition by critics lamenting the economic costs of environmental regulations, the celebration of "Earth Day 1995" on April 22 by more than 300 million people in 140 countries testified to the growth of the "Green Movement" in world politics. Increasingly such networks are being mobilized along the "communications superhighway" through the expansion of the Internet, "connecting 42,000 computer networks sprawled across 84 countries" and currently serving "32 million users, with a million more people becoming 'netizens' every month."[17]

The fact that the term **interdependence** has become a cliché does not make it any less real a phenomenon. One can debate the exact definition of the term and the extent to which interdependence has actually increased—for example, whether it has reached the point where one can consider the world a "global village" as Marshall McLuhan suggested or "Spaceship Earth" as Barbara Ward suggested—but it is hard to dispute the essential validity of the following observation: "What happens far away matters much more now. Aerosol use in Europe can cause skin cancers in South America. A crop failure in Russia can mean more hunger in Africa. Conflict in Africa can bring more asylum-seekers to Europe. Economic difficulties in Eastern Europe can lead to xenophobia in Western Europe. By the same token . . . industrial restructuring in the North can reduce poverty in the South, which in turn can enlarge markets for the North."[18] This is not mere "globaloney," as some would say. The most dramatic aspect of interdependence, of course, is the fact that global annihilation can occur today in a matter of minutes through the use of thermonuclear weapons.

MAKING THE PUBLIC MORE WORLDLY

Judging from the results of numerous public opinion surveys taken in the United States, it would appear that the average American is not very aware of the relevance of the outside world. For example, just as the great national energy debate was heating up in the United States in the late 1970s, at a time when the United States imported almost 50 percent of its oil needs from abroad, half of the American people did not know that the United States imported *any* foreign oil,[19] a knowledge gap that had renewed implications in the 1990s as American dependence on foreign oil was again rising. Over half the Americans interviewed in polls taken throughout the 1980s were not sure whether it was the United States or the Soviet Union that was a member of the North Atlantic Treaty Organization (NATO) alliance.[20] A 1995 Gallup poll revealed that 25 percent of the American public could not name the country that had been the target of the first atomic bomb dropped fifty years earlier.[21] Closer to home, in a recent survey of 5,000 high school seniors in Dallas, 25 percent could not identify the foreign country that bordered Texas.[22] In another poll, only 2 percent of the public could identify the president of Mexico, and only 1 percent the prime minister of Canada, despite the fact that the United States had just concluded the North American Free Trade Agreement (NAFTA), designed to promote closer economic integration of the three nations' economies.[23] In the 1990s, with the U.S. government spending little more than 1 percent of the federal budget on foreign aid, the public assumed the figure was close to 20 percent.[24]

Numerous other examples of the American public's lack of information about international affairs, past and present, can be cited.[25] Although the pub-

SIDELIGHT

A STUDY IN INTERDEPENDENCE

If you drive a Ford Escort, chances are that your transmission was made in Japan, your wiring in Taiwan, your door lift assembly in Mexico, your shock absorber struts in Spain, your rear brake assembly in Brazil, your steering gears in Britain, and assorted other parts elsewhere. Since 1980, when the introduction of the Escort trumpeted the arrival of the "world car," the automobile industry has gotten only more globalized and more complicated. As the article below shows, "car wars" and other battles for global market share in everything from washing machines to robotics are heating up, with "alliances" among giant corporations across national boundaries making it difficult to keep track of the nationality of many products. Whether these trends continue will depend on the willingness of governments to promote an open world economy.

[Former Chrysler Chairman] Lee Iacocca's television ads blared, "Here's to You, America," as jet planes streaked red, white, and blue exhausts across the sky. There is no subtlety in the appeal: buying from Chrysler is your patriotic duty. But the pitch is more than normally disingenuous. For behind the smoke and clamor of the trade wars, Chrysler and the rest of the world's automotive majors are frantically forming engineering, production, and marketing alliances, literally carving up the world, to buttress their positions in the struggle for global car-sales supremacy. Who the eventual winners will be is far from certain, but what is clear is that only a small number of global companies will survive, and it is increasingly meaningless to speak of them as "American" or "Japanese" or "European" companies. (Even in Iacocca's ad the planes are French.) . . .

Take Chrysler itself: For all of Iacocca's red, white, and blue bunkum, auto-industry analysts say that Chrysler has the lowest percentage of American-made parts in its cars of any of the Big Three. It also owns 24 percent of Mitsubishi Motors and, through Mitsubishi, a share of the South Korean upstart Hyundai. Mitsubishi has long made cars under Chrysler's label, and the two companies run a fifty-fifty joint venture in Normal, Illinois, which will be producing 240,000 vehicles under both nameplates by the end of next year.

Ford, with one third of its sales outside the United States, owns 25 percent of Mazda. Mazda makes cars in America for Ford; Ford will reciprocate by making compact trucks for Mazda; and the two companies trade parts. Each owns a piece of Korea's Kia Motors, which produces the Ford Festiva for export to the United States. Ford and Nissan, Japan's No. 2, swap vehicles in Australia and are planning a joint minivan program in America.

Ford and Volkswagen have merged into a single company in Latin America, which exports trucks to the United States.

General Motors holds a 41.6 percent stake in Isuzu, which is starting a joint venture in America with Subaru, which is partly owned by Nissan. GM also owns half of Daewoo Motors, Hyundai's competitor in Korea. Daewoo makes Nissan cars for Japan and Pontiacs for America; soon it will be selling cars that were primarily designed by GM-Europe to Isuzu in Japan. GM has also teamed with Japan's No. 1, Toyota, to produce cars under both companies' labels in America and Australia.

Europe is laced with partnerships, joint ventures, and production agreements. Honda America sells more cars in America than its parent does in Japan . . . and some analysts see the power balance within the company shifting to the American subsidiary. Honda plans to be exporting 70,000 cars from the United States by 1991. . . . In a year or so global Japanese companies will be turning out two million high-quality *American* cars a year, with American workers, in American plants.

The automobile industry is not the only one to have felt the competitive lash. . . . Whirlpool has joined with the Dutch electronics giant Philips to operate six major appliance factories in the Common Market [the European Union]. Philips has also joined with a group of American executives and the Taiwanese government to create an advanced semiconductor-fabrication plant in Taiwan, where Texas Instruments is also building an advanced chip factory with a Taiwanese partner. Ball, of Muncie, Indiana, has entered into a series of joint ventures around the world to market and manufacture its lightweight containers for soft drinks. The list goes on and on—USX and Kobe Steel, Armco and Kawasaki Steel. The misnamed National Steel Company is a fifty-fifty joint venture between an American and a Japanese company. . . . Japan's robotics leader, FANUC, has partnerships with General Motors in robots, with General Electric in computerized factory control devices, and with the German firm Siemens in electronics.

The drive for global market share is forcing what Stanley Feldman, of Data Resources, calls the Third Industrial Revolution. A wholesale reordering of production technology is under way—computerized factory schedules and inventory controls to cut costs, intelligent production machinery that can shift processes in the middle of an assembly line. The object is to produce local products adapted to local markets, but reap world economies of scale in research and development, raw-materials sourcing, and production balancing.

Source: Excerpted from Charles R. Morris, "The Coming Global Boom," *The Atlantic Monthly,* 264 (October 1989), pp. 51–53. Reprinted by permission of Russell & Volkening as agents for the author. Copyright © 1989 by Charles R. Morris.

lic in other countries, particularly in Western Europe, often seems to be better informed than the American public, there is much evidence to suggest that even in these countries a sizable segment of the population has only marginal interest in and knowledge about international affairs despite the implications of interdependence.[26] In all countries, many people seem to adopt the attitude of the student who was asked, "Which is worse, ignorance or apathy?" The response: "I don't know and I don't care!"

Even those individuals who are interested in international affairs and do attempt to become informed often find it difficult to comprehend the myriad events that are reported daily and to fit these events into any kind of coherent framework. How are U.S.–China relations affected by the actions of American-based multinational corporations that do business in China, or U.S.–Saudi Arabian relations affected by the giant multinational oil companies operating in the Middle East? Can the sale of the U.S. government's most sophisticated military aircraft to Israel and Saudi Arabia be expected to promote peace in the Middle East, or war? In the United Nations, why is Cuba entitled to the same voting power as the United States in the General Assembly, when the United States is twenty-five times bigger in population and pays 200 times more money into the UN budget? In a showdown with the Russian Federation, should tensions resume, is it possible that the United States has the capability to kill every Russian twenty-seven times but can still "lose" a nuclear war? And to what extent do American (or French or Russian) foreign policymakers, while pondering the potential consequences of their decisions for the nation and the world, ask the question: "How will it play in Peoria (or Marseilles or Vladivostok)?"

The basic purpose of this book, aside from generating increased *interest* in international relations, is to contribute to some *understanding* of a broad range of contemporary international phenomena and what could be called the "global condition" as we face the twenty-first century. In other words, we shall attempt to make sense out of what may at times appear to be chaos and, indeed, "cause for shaking the head in wonder."

The "What" Question:
Defining International Relations

As a starting point, let us try to define as precisely as possible what we mean by the term **international relations.** Trying to define international relations reminds one of the judge in the obscenity case who said, "I can't define it, but I know it when I see it." A dictionary provides us with some guidance, defining international relations as "a branch of *political science* concerned with relations between political units of *national* rank and dealing primarily with *foreign policies* [italics ours]."[27]

DEFINITIONAL PROBLEMS

That seems to be a reasonable enough definition of international relations—except for at least three problems that arise immediately. First, where does an actor such as Colombia's Cali drug cartel fit in, with its links to an international narcotrafficking network? What about multinational corporations, or the private Western banks owed huge sums of money by heavily indebted poor countries, or the Islamic Resistance Movement (HAMAS), which has complicated Israeli attempts to resolve the Palestinian question? None of these are "national political units," nor are they entirely subsumed by the latter; they seemingly are excluded from the dictionary definition, yet they are not exactly irrelevant to relations between nations. Second, in an interdependent world, is it as easy as the dictionary definition suggests to separate "foreign" policy decisions from "domestic" policy decisions? A decision by the U.S. government to legalize certain drugs may be a purely domestic matter, but it is likely to be accompanied by changes in U.S. foreign policy regarding international narcotics control as well. Likewise, arms control may be purely a foreign policy concern, but such decisions can have important domestic fallout. The blurring of domestic and foreign policy concerns becomes all the more problematical in other areas, such as energy, economic, and agricultural policy. Third, although the dictionary cites international relations as a "branch of political science," the field clearly encompasses not only political but also economic and other relations, being multidisciplinary in scope.

We are not arguing here that the field of international relations has no boundaries, only that the boundaries are perhaps harder to identify than in other fields of study. However, if one is to develop an understanding of international relations, then clearly there is a need to establish *some* boundaries at the outset, granted that "the effort to draw them with any great precision is at best arbitrary and at worst futile."[28] Over the years the "boundary" question in the international relations field has occasioned almost as much conflict among academics as other sorts of boundary questions have caused among nations.[29] We have no desire here to add to this great debate about the essence of international relations. We want only to make sure that students have a grasp of what the field is all about.

As an alternative to the dictionary definition, consider for a moment a second, much broader definition of international relations: the study of all human interactions across national borders and the factors that affect those interactions. Figure 1.1 indicates the various kinds of interactions that are possible.

Examples of the first type of interaction (line A) would be a meeting between the President of Colombia and the President of the United States, or a communication from the Chinese government warning the U.S. government not to meddle in any internal Chinese affairs, or U.S.-Japanese negotiations regarding the imposition of tariff barriers and quotas against Japanese cars imported into the United States. What do all of these situations have in com-

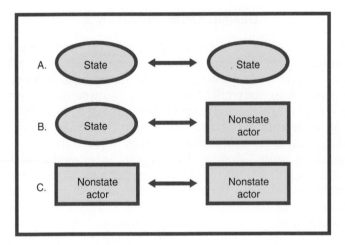

Figure 1.1
KINDS OF INTERNATIONAL INTERACTIONS

mon? They all involve interactions between *national governments*—more specifically, between official representatives of national political units we call **nation-states.** (Such interactions can, of course, be greatly affected by pressures exerted by domestic interest groups and private citizens on their national governments.)

Examples of the second type of interaction (line B) would include talks between the Oil Minister of Saudi Arabia and the representatives of a multinational oil company, or a raid by Israeli troops against HAMAS commando bases in Lebanon, or a visit by the head of Chase Manhattan Bank to Brazil to discuss rescheduling of loans with the Brazilian Finance Minister. **Nonstate actors** such as multinational corporations or HAMAS may initiate international interactions or they may be the targets of them, but in either case their activities are a part of international relations.

Examples of the third type of interaction (line C) could conceivably include the Texas Rangers playing the Toronto Bluejays in an American League baseball game in Toronto, a meeting of labor-union representatives from a variety of countries, or an exchange of letters between pen pals in England and Mongolia. Although many of these kinds of interactions are quite far removed from the weighty concerns of statesmen, even the travels of Ping-Pong teams between New York and Beijing (the much-publicized U.S.-China "Ping-Pong diplomacy" of 1971) can on occasion be an important form of international relations.

Broadly speaking, all of the above interactions constitute international relations. Obviously though, not all of these lines of interaction are equally important and deserve equal treatment. It is safe to say that when most people think of international relations, they think in dictionary terms of relations between national governments that act on behalf of nation-states, as typified by the first set of examples. This preoccupation is justified, because it is true that only national governments are in a position to make foreign policy and only national governments ultimately have the legal authority to control all inter- actions across national boundaries. In this book, we, too, will primarily be concerned with relations between national governments. But we will also be concerned with the other two types of interactions and the role of nonstate ac- tors, particularly insofar as they affect the relations between governments and have an impact on world affairs. Increasingly, such actors, whether subna- tional or transnational in nature, are competing with national governments as players on the world stage.

THE SUBSTANCE OF INTERNATIONAL RELATIONS

What are we finally left with, then, as a definition of international relations? The working definition that we have decided to adopt in this book is one that is borrowed from political science and reflects the authors' primary concern with the political dimension of international relations. Hence, we will be using the terms "international *relations*" and "international *politics*" inter- changeably and examining economic and other relations in their political con- text. If "politics" is "the study of who gets what, when, and how,"[30] then *in- ternational politics is the study of who gets what, when, and how in the international arena.* This is a somewhat narrower and more focused defini- tion than the one offered initially as an alternative to the dictionary defini- tion, but it seems to capture better what the field of international relations— and this book—are most about.

As this definition suggests, politics has to do with the way in which a group of people living together govern their affairs. In the case of international poli- tics, we are interested in how over 5 billion human inhabitants of the planet do so. To the extent that one can think of the world's roughly 5 billion people as constituting a single political entity, the most striking and fundamental feature of this polity is that it is a highly *decentralized* one, with the members organized in more than 180 territorially based units—nation-states—recogniz- ing no higher authority than their own individual governments. As we have noted, notwithstanding the existence of nonstate actors, the nation-state re- mains the primary form of political organization and locus of authority in the world. In other words, international politics occurs in an arena in which there is no set of central authoritative institutions (no world government) to regu- late the behavior of the members, in contrast with *intra*national politics, which is regulated to some extent by courts, legislatures, and other authorita- tive bodies. The United Nations is at best a primitive attempt at creating a world government out of a system of formally independent states.

The decentralized nature of the international polity, in the eyes of many ob- servers, makes the body politic inherently prone to disorder and violence, so that its members tend to be obsessed with feelings of insecurity and the need to arm themselves, if only for self-protection. Although many national societies experience similar problems of violence and instability in the form of civil wars—indeed, a much-discussed phenomenon in the 1990s has been the growing number of "failed states"[31] that have collapsed into anarchy, such as Rwanda and Somalia—it is true that such problems seem built-in and endemic to international society because of the very structure of relationships among the constituent units. Nonetheless, the international community is not eternally at war; humanity has often been able to overcome these deficiencies and achieve some peace and order in international relations even without authoritative institutions. *Cooperation* occurs amid *conflict*. As John Stoessinger has expressed it: there is in international relations an "ever-present tension between the struggle for power and the struggle for order,"[32] the drive for more national resources being tempered by the mutually felt need for at least some modicum of stability.

This central concern of international relations is not new; it has existed as long as there have been nation-states. However, it has taken on greater urgency today not only because humankind has the capability for total global destruction but also because of the emergence of a truly global society in which the proliferation of economic, social, and other transactions across national boundaries is straining the capacities of national governments to regulate these relations.[33] Whereas some see the "shrinking and linking" of the world as marking progress toward fulfillment of the historic dream of a harmonious world community,[34] others see it as sowing the seeds for possibly even greater conflicts among nations and people than in previous eras.[35] The mere three-and-one-half-hour time span it now takes to travel from London to New York aboard the Concorde airliner is exceeded in earthbound travel efficiency only by the thirty-minute ride that can be taken by a nuclear warhead aboard an intercontinental ballistic missile between Moscow and New York.

It is, indeed, somewhat paradoxical that at the same time that humanity has the potential for unparalleled conflict, there is also the potential for unprecedented cooperation. There have been more international agreements signed since 1945 than were negotiated in the previous 2,000 years. The growth of international organizations in recent years and the ongoing attempts to formulate "regimes" or "rules" in various problem areas[36]—nuclear weapons proliferation, control of the oceans, management of the international economy, and other areas—represent the latest, most ambitious efforts yet to deal with the age-old concern of maintaining order in the absence of a world government. Increasingly, too, there is a call not only for order but for a *just* order based on an equitable distribution of resources. One can see in all this a "political system" at work, with global problem-solving processes operating, albeit in a decentralized fashion.

It should be added that international relations can be studied at several levels, with some concerns directly involving only a few countries or a single geographical region, although ultimately all international relations can be fitted into a larger global context. A recurrent theme of this book is that a variety of actors and a complicated network of relationships must be taken into account in any attempt to fully understand contemporary international politics. See the box on pages 20–22 for some further thoughts on "Human Governance in the Post–Cold War Era."

The "How" Question: Alternative Approaches

Just as the "what" question has produced much debate within the international relations field, so also has the "how" question. How should one go about studying international relations in terms of the various approaches that might be used? Actually the "what" and "how" questions have never been completely distinguishable, as will be seen in the following discussion, which briefly traces the development of international relations as a field of study. We will examine two aspects of the "how" question: (1) the various *paradigms* that have guided theory and research in the field over the years and (2) the various *methodologies* that have been utilized.

ALTERNATIVE PARADIGMS

A **paradigm** is an intellectual framework that structures one's thinking about a set of phenomena.[37] Paradigms are nothing more than "cognitive maps" that help to organize reality and to make some sense out of the multitude of events that occur in the world each day.[38] Different paradigms offer different models of reality or views of the world, and thus have the effect of focusing attention toward some things and away from others. There are four major paradigms that have structured thinking about international relations in this century: (1) the *idealist* paradigm, (2) the *realist* paradigm, (3) the *globalist* paradigm, and (4) the *Marxist* paradigm.

The **idealist paradigm** can trace its roots at least as far back as Dante, the Italian poet of the fourteenth century who wrote of the "universality of man" and envisioned a unified world-state.[39] In the twentieth century this paradigm has been most closely associated with Woodrow Wilson and other thinkers around the time of World War I, when international relations was just emerging as a distinct academic field in the United States.[40] The idealists were prominent in the interwar period—between the end of World War I in 1918 and the beginning of World War II in 1939—and are still an active school of international relations as represented by the World Federalists and similar groups. Like many observers of international affairs, idealists are attracted to the challenge of minimizing conflict and maximizing cooperation among na-

HUMAN GOVERNANCE IN THE POST–COLD WAR ERA

This book is about the governance of human affairs. As our discussion up to now has suggested, we can rightly speak today of a global economy, a global society, and a global ecosystem, yet there is no global government. Whereas some individuals call for world government or at least improved "central guidance" mechanisms—to cope with nuclear proliferation and other planetary concerns—and although one can see possible stepping stones in that direction now being laid in the form of increased intergovernmental institution building beyond the nation-state at both the regional and global levels, one can also find trends occurring in the opposite direction.

In the post–Cold War era, many observers have noticed a schizophrenic quality that characterizes the "new world order." As former UN Secretary-General Boutros Boutros-Ghali has noted:

> We have entered a time of global transition marked by uniquely contradictory trends. Regional and continental associations of states are evolving ways to deepen cooperation and ease some of the contentious characteristics of sovereign and nationalistic rivalries [referring to such collaborative interstate efforts as the North American Free Trade Agreement (NAFTA) and the European Union (EU)]. . . . At the same time, however, fierce new assertions of nationalism and sovereignty spring up, and the cohesion of states is threatened by ethnic, religious, social, cultural, or linguistic strife [exemplified by the recent breakup of Yugoslavia and the problems experienced by "failed states"].[1]

Likewise, Benjamin Barber has pointed to the twin tendencies of "Jihad vs. McWorld," that is, "a threatened Lebanization of national states in which culture is pitted against culture, . . . tribe against tribe" alongside "MTV, Macintosh, and McDonald's pressing nations into one commercially homogeneous global network. . . . The planet is falling precipitately apart *and* coming reluctantly together at the very same moment."[2]

These competing forces of integration and disintegration, of centralization and decentralization, can be seen at work in the ongoing governance debates occurring in the United States. The United States has recently entered into a three-nation economic integration process through NAFTA that will likely require strengthening of joint decision-making institutions among the member countries at the regional level, perhaps extending eventually throughout the Western hemisphere; the United States has also entered the World Trade Organization, established to promote improved governance of interstate economic relations at the global level. Conversely, there is a growing "grassroots" movement in the United States to shift some power and authority in nondefense matters (ranging from setting highway speed limits to setting environmental standards) away from the federal government in Washington back to the fifty states (most of which, by the way, maintain their own overseas trade offices, which are only loosely co-ordinated with the U.S. Department of Commerce). In the case of the European Union (formerly the European Community), a collection of more than a dozen Western European countries involved in an even more ambitious regional integration process than NAFTA, the member states are building what appear to be almost supranational institutions at the same time that they are promoting the "subsidiarity" principle, whereby most policies are to be decided at national and perhaps local levels whenever possible. Trying to capture the complexity of the EU's evolving governance structure, *The Economist* envisions "a Europe of many spires," as "Eurocrats speak of overlapping layers of European economic and political 'spaces,' tied together . . . by the community's 'spiderlike strategy to organize the architecture of a Greater Europe.'"[3]

Everywhere governments are struggling to meet the rising expectations of mass publics, with variable success. Two main questions arise. First, what should be the proper role of government; that is, what matters should be handled by government, and what should be left to the private sector ("civil society")? Second, to the extent government should concern itself with some set of issues, what level of government is best equipped to address the problem? With regard to the first question, there has been a growing trend toward deregulation, privatization, and reliance on markets, voluntary associations, and nonstatist approaches; the stress here is on reinvigorating civil society, including what some see as an emergent "global civil society" of transnational interest groups and movements of various sorts.[4] In answer to the second question, it has been noted that "the state [the nation-state] has become too big for the small things [such as overseeing education], and too small for the big things [such as controlling greenhouse warming]. The small things call for delegation downwards to the local level. . . . The big things call for delegation upwards, for coordination between national policies, or for transnational institutions."[5] A favorite phrase today is "think globally, act locally."

But where does all this leave the nation-state? For the moment at least, as Boutros Boutros-Ghali reminds, "the foundation-stone of this work [global governance] is and must remain the State."[6] We will be discussing governance questions throughout this book. In Chapter 2, we will see that the contradictory trends that Boutros-Ghali called "unique" to the post–Cold War era are not entirely so, because much of human history can be read as an ongoing tension between centripetal and centrifugal forces. In Chapter 3, we will focus on how these forces are operating in the contemporary international system, and in Chapter 16, on how they might play out in the more distant future during the twenty-first century.

[1] *An Agenda for Peace,* Report of the Secretary-General on the Work of the Organization, UN Doc. A/47/277 and S/24111, June 17, 1992, p. 3.
[2] Benjamin Barber, "Jihad vs. McWorld," *The Atlantic* (March 1992), p. 53. Also, see Barber's book-length *Jihad vs. McWorld,* New York: Times Books, 1995.
[3] Cited in John G. Ruggie, "Territoriality and Beyond," *International Organization,* 47 (Winter 1993), p. 140.
[4] Ronnie D. Lipschutz, "Reconstructing World Politics: The Emergence of Global Civil Society," *Millennium,* 21, no. 3, 1992, pp. 389–420.
[5] Paul Streeten, monograph on International Governance, IDS, University of Sussex, Silver Jubilie Papers (1992), p. 2; cited in Erskine Childers, *Renewing the United Nations System,* Dag Hammarskjold Foundation, Uppsala, Sweden, 1994, p. 17. A similar remark was made by Daniel Bell in "The World of 2013," *New Society* (December 8, 1987), p. 35.
[6] *An Agenda for Peace,* p. 5.

tions. What distinguishes the idealists, however, is their tendency to focus attention on legal-formal aspects of international relations, such as international law and international organization, and on moral concerns such as human rights. It was out of the ashes of World War I that idealists claimed to have learned certain lessons about the workings of international relations and what had to be done to prevent another catastrophe like that war. In their minds, a new world order had to be constructed based on a respect for law, the acceptance of shared universal values, and the development of international organizations such as the League of Nations.

Idealists tend to be most interested in how the world *ought* to be, rather than necessarily in how it actually *is.* The idealist would argue that the reality of the moment is not the only possible reality. The idealist mode of thinking is perhaps best captured in the statement by President Wilson when questioned by his advisers about the practicality of his League of Nations idea: "If it won't work, it must be made to work."[41]

It was the very failure of the idealists to anticipate and prevent World War II that gave rise to the dominance of the **realist paradigm** in the immediate postwar period after 1945. Whereas the idealists argued that their ideas had not been fully implemented in the interwar period and hence had not been fairly tested, realists such as E. H. Carr contended that they *had* been tested but could not stand up against armies marching across Europe and halfway around the world.[42] Hans Morgenthau, in his classic work *Politics Among Nations,* became identified as the "father" of realism, even though Carr had been writing a few years earlier and the roots of realist thought could in fact be traced as far back as the sixteenth century to Machiavelli's *The Prince* and even to Thucydides' accounts of the Peloponnesian War between Athens and Sparta in ancient Greece.[43] Realists are just as interested as idealists in the problem of conflict management, but they are less optimistic about the effectiveness of international law and organization and about the extent of international cooperation that is possible. Realists tend to view international relations almost exclusively as a "struggle for power" (rather than as a "struggle for order") among nation-states. To the realist, the ultimate goal of all countries is security in a hostile, anarchic environment. Their policies are determined by power calculations in pursuit of national security. Countries that are satisfied with their situation are inclined to pursue status quo foreign policies, whereas countries that are dissatisfied are inclined to pursue expansionist foreign policies. Alliances are made and broken, old friends are rejected and old enemies embraced, all depending on the requirements of "realpolitik."

It is not surprising that realists have tended to focus on such topics as military strategy, the elements of national power, diplomacy and other instruments of statecraft, and the nature of national interests rather than such subjects as international law and organization. The realists claimed to have learned their own lessons from World War II, namely, that the way to prevent future wars was to rely not on formal-legal institutions or moral precepts but on a "balance of power" capable of deterring would-be aggressors, or on a "concert of powers" willing to police the world. The realist paradigm has dominated the thinking of an entire generation of international relations observers since World War II—scholars, practitioners, and laymen alike—and

What paradigm makes sense for the post–Cold War era?

continues to exert a powerful hold on many. Contemporary realists, often referred to as "neorealists," incorporate more economics into their analyses and seek to extend knowledge about the basic structure of international relations and the underlying dynamics of interstate conflict.[44]

The third paradigm, the **globalist paradigm** (sometimes called the pluralist paradigm), approaches the study of international relations from a somewhat different perspective than either the idealist or realist paradigms.[45] Led in 1971 by a groundbreaking volume edited by Robert Keohane and Joseph Nye entitled *Transnational Relations and World Politics*, the globalists have focused their criticism on the realist paradigm in particular, arguing that the latter has never entirely corresponded with reality and is especially inadequate in comprehending contemporary events in an age of interdependence.[46] Most globalists have not rejected the realist paradigm totally but have sought to refine and amplify it, their premise being that the dealings between national governments are only one strand in the great web of human interactions. Rather than viewing international relations through realist lenses as simply a contest between national units driven by the dominant concern of national security, the globalists perceive a more complex set of relationships between not only national governments (which are themselves composed of often competing bureaucracies) but also nonstate actors, involved not only in war and peace issues but in economic and social welfare issue-areas as well.[47] For example, in the air safety issue-area, globalists point to the role of such entities as the International Civil Aviation Organization, the International Air Transport Association, the International Federation of Airline Pilots Associations, and the airline interests and transportation ministries within various countries. Whereas the world of the realist is populated primarily by soldiers, diplomats, and foreign policy strategists, the world of the globalist includes multinational corporation executives, transnational labor union leaders, international organization officials, and skyjackers.

In short, globalists choose to consider a much wider range of actors and concerns than do realists in their study of international relations. Because of their emphasis on the need for cooperative institution building to help manager interdependence, globalists are considered in some ways the heirs of the idealist tradition and are at times referred to as "neoliberals."[48] Some scholars have argued that recent history, notably the peaceful end of the Cold War, has vindicated the Wilsonian liberal–idealist vision.[49] Other scholars have suggested that complex interdependence and the blurring of domestic and foreign affairs have accelerated to the point where an entirely new "postinternational politics" paradigm is called for.[50]

Somewhat related to but distinct from the globalist paradigm is the **Marxist paradigm.** Marxists trace their intellectual roots to Karl Marx, the nineteenth-century German philosopher who wrote *Das Kapital* and (with Friedrich Engels) *The Communist Manifesto.* Marx argued that **capitalist** economic systems, which stressed private property and the accumulation of private wealth, produced a "bourgeois" ruling class that exploited a "proletarian" working class. He indicated that once class distinctions and private property were eliminated in a worldwide workers' revolution, there would be no further need for national governments and nation-states. A harmonious global **communist** society would result, with each person receiving wealth according to need rather than privilege.

Latter-day Marxists have added some new wrinkles to these theories, because capitalism has proved to have more staying power than Marx predicted. In particular, Marxists maintain that capitalist states have been able to relieve their inner class tensions by exploiting other, less developed countries—utilizing cheap foreign labor and captive foreign markets to avoid economic collapse. Marxists, like the globalists, point to the spreading tentacles of multinational businesses and transnational coalitions of elite groups but find much more harmful effects of such actors than do globalists. Wealthy elites in developed capitalist states supposedly are linked with counterparts in less developed states and are together responsible for enormous rich-poor gaps. The proliferation of multinational corporations is placed in a broad historical context as the latest stage in the centuries-long institutional development of the "world capitalist system."[51] Marxists, then, tend to view international relations more as a struggle between rich and poor classes than as a contest between national governments or nation-states. What is needed, according to this view, is for leaderships to emerge that are capable of replacing "laissez-faire" (free market) capitalist economies with more mass-oriented, centrally planned and managed economies, which will supposedly result in more harmonious social relations both domestically and internationally. Clearly, though, Marxist analysts have suffered setbacks recently with the nearly universal bankruptcy of Marxist economies from the Soviet Union to Mozambique and the experimentation with capitalist ideas from Cuba to China.

We shall draw on all these different perspectives in this book. They represent very general orientations toward international affairs. Few people are in actuality pure realists or pure idealists, although many lean strongly in one direction or the other. Keeping in mind the role of paradigms in structuring one's view of the world, it is important to understand that there are often conflicting interpretations of international relations because different peoples and cultures, based on their historical and recent experiences, often have different lenses through which they see things. For example, many people in Africa and Asia who have experienced colonialism start with a somewhat different set of assumptions about the world than, say, Americans. Whereas many Americans are inclined to interpret international affairs in terms of the realist or perhaps the idealist paradigm, observers in less developed countries might be more inclined to view events in the context of the Marxist paradigm. As for the globalist paradigm, it may offer an increasingly compelling framework for anyone trying to understand political outcomes in a world in which linkages between subnational, transnational, governmental, and intergovernmental levels of activity are becoming ever more intricate. In addition to the paradigms we have just mentioned, other approaches can be noted as well, such as "postmodern" and "feminist" perspectives.[52] We should stress that even though certain scholars have been identified with a specific paradigm, their research does not always fall neatly into one pigeonhole or another, as the international relations field today is increasingly characterized by eclectic approaches.

ALTERNATIVE METHODOLOGIES

The second aspect of the "how" question has to do with methodologies. Although there is considerable overlap between the methodological debate and the paradigm debate, somewhat different issues are involved in each. The great debate in the area of methodology has boiled down to the "traditionalists" versus the "behavioralists."[53] Until the 1960s, the international relations field was dominated methodologically by the **traditionalists,** for whom knowledge was something that could be arrived at only through firsthand participant observation and practical experience or secondhand immersion in the great works of diplomatic history and related library resources. In addition to diplomatic histories, the literature consisted largely of statesmen's memoirs, international law treatises, and philosophical writings.

During the 1960s, traditionalists were challenged by an increasing number of **behavioralists** such as Karl Deutsch, J. David Singer, and James Rosenau, who sought to make the international relations field more *scientific.* Hence, their goal was to build a cumulative body of knowledge based on more sophisticated and rigorous methods borrowed from the biological and physical sciences.[54] The tools of the trade for the behavioralists were aggregate data, quantitative analysis techniques, mathematical modeling, and computers.[55] The behavioralist literature consisted of writings that emphasized the systematic development and testing of *theories* that could *explain* the dynamics of international relations.

Today, traditionalists and behavioralists remain divided over various methodological issues and the extent to which the international relations field can approach the scientific level of the biological and physical sciences. Each side is interested in many of the same questions: Under what circumstances do wars tend to occur? What is the impact of domestic politics on foreign policy? Under what conditions is deterrence likely to succeed, or to fail? What is the relationship between foreign aid and political influence? What effect does increased interdependence between nations have on relations between governments? And so forth. Whereas behavioralists believe their methods will ultimately enable them to answer such questions with a high degree of precision and confidence, even to the point of being able to predict various international occurrences, the traditionalists argue that the complexities of the international environment and the limits of quantification are such that reasonably educated guesses (along the lines of the local weather forecaster rather than the nuclear physicist) are the most we can ever hope for. Actually, most behavioralists would be willing to settle for the predictive powers of meteorologists, who deal in probabilities and tendencies and whose only certainties are that mistakes will occur; as Charles McClelland has said, "the goal is not to foretell exactly what events will take place in China [in, say, 2002]" but rather "to develop skill in showing 'which way the wind is blowing' and, therefore, what might well happen under stated circumstances."[56]

Despite continued disagreement among traditionalists and behavioralists, an uneasy truce has been declared between the two camps in the last several years. The discipline is now in the "postbehavioral" era, with both sides recognizing that neither has a monopoly on wisdom (or knowledge) in this field and that the "science" of international relations is still in its infancy. In the same spirit of humility, we will refrain from taking methodological sides in this book, and we will make use of both traditional and quantitative research in our study of international relations.

The Concerns of Policymakers, Scholars, and Laymen

All of us—policymakers, scholars, and laymen alike—have some need for knowledge about international relations, although not all of us have exactly the same needs. All of us want to have a handle on the world, although some of us are content with a looser grip than others. The scholar would generally like to know everything there is to know; the policymaker, whatever it takes to keep the country going from one day to the next (or, if you are President of the United States, from one 4-year term to the next); and most laymen, only whatever it takes to enable them to make at least roughly informed judgments about how well the policymakers have been doing. Let us look first at the relationship between policymakers and scholars and then relate their concerns to those of the average person.

QUESTIONS FOR SCHOLARS AND POLICYMAKERS

Thinkers and writers from the times of Plato and Machiavelli to the present have always sought to influence the actions of policymakers.[57] Indeed, some have gone beyond mere influence to actual policy-*making*. Henry Kissinger and Jeane Kirkpatrick are two contemporary examples. For the most part, however, international relations scholars do not have as much influence as they would like.

The world of the scholar is somewhat different from the world of the practitioner. The scholar tends to be more concerned about long-term trends, hypothetical relationships, and general patterns ("theory"), whereas the practitioner tends to deal more with specific cases and immediate situations that seem to have unique characteristics ("practice").[58] As you recall from our discussion of methodology, scholars are interested in the following kinds of theoretical questions: Under what circumstances do wars tend to occur? What is the impact of domestic politics on foreign policy? Under what conditions is deterrence likely to succeed, or to fail? What is the relationship between foreign aid and political influence? What effect does increased interdependence between nations have on relations between governments? In contrast, although policymakers may have some intellectual curiosity about theoretical questions, they tend to be preoccupied with more concrete matters: Will the sale of several sophisticated military aircraft to Saudi Arabia aggravate hostilities in the Middle East? What is the impact of far left-wing or right-wing groups on foreign policy in, say, Russia? What conditions are necessary to deter a nuclear strike against the United States, or deter terrorism against Americans abroad? Can a $150 million aid package buy North Korean friendship toward the United States? How will the imposition of a 2 percent higher quota on Japanese car imports into the United States affect U.S.-Japanese relations, as well as the price American consumers will pay for automobiles? Scholars, too, may address these questions, but only as slices of a broader set of phenomena to be investigated.

Notwithstanding these differences, scholars and policymakers do share one common goal: to understand how the world operates. Plato himself suggested that each had something to offer the other and that the ideal ruler was a combination thinker and doer, a "philosopher-king." There is nothing more practical than a good theory that can order reality for policymakers and help them to anticipate the possible consequences of their decisions.

QUESTIONS FOR LAYMEN

To the extent that laymen are interested in international relations, they tend to be more intrigued by the concrete questions that preoccupy policymakers than by the abstract, theoretical ones that concern scholars. Yet laymen, like policymakers, can benefit from answers to the theoretical questions. The same general knowledge that can help policymakers deal more intelligently with the problems that cross their desks can also help laymen in their roles as citizens more intelligently evaluate the soundness of the decisions made by their government. Although policymakers and laymen are inclined to dismiss theoretical concerns, it should be noted that they cannot escape them entirely. Even if they are not fully conscious of it, their judgments are ultimately based to some degree on "theories"—a variety of personal assumptions about how the world works—however undeveloped (and unfounded) those theories may be. To see how the concerns of policymakers, scholars, and laymen intertwine, let us briefly examine the different *modes of analysis* that people engage in when they think about social phenomena in general and international relations phenomena in particular.

Modes of Analysis

At least four modes of analysis can be identified: (1) description, (2) explanation, (3) normative analysis, and (4) prescription.[59] *Description* is the most basic type of analysis: One simply tells what reality looks like or has looked like. When one indicates how many wars have occurred in the world in the last twenty years and whether dictatorships have been more war-prone than democracies, one is making descriptive statements, which may be true or false. *Explanation,* though based on description, requires one to go beyond merely reporting a fact and to account for its existence. The ability to explain some past or present set of phenomena can imply the ability to predict the future as well, although not necessarily. *Normative analysis* entails making value (moral) judgments about some reality thought to exist or thought to be possible. When one laments the fact that the United States has no greater voting power than Cuba in the United Nations, despite contributing a much larger share of the UN budget, one is making a normative statement that is cast in "good-bad" rather than "true-false" terms. Finally, *prescription* involves offering recommendations as to a future course of action or policy, given some goal to be achieved (which itself may involve prior value judgments). One engages in prescriptive analysis when trying to solve the world's problems—for example, when purporting to have a solution to the conflict between the Israelis and the Arabs. Although these four modes of analysis constitute distinct intellectual tasks reflecting different purposes of inquiry, they are all somewhat interrelated.

The relationship between these modes of analysis—and how policymakers, scholars, and laymen use them—can best be illustrated by a single example. Suppose you are interested in the distribution of wealth in the world. An example of a descriptive statement would be the following: One-half of the world's people live in countries with a per capita gross national product (PGNP) of under $500, roughly 30 percent live in countries with a PGNP between $500 and $5,000, and roughly 20 percent live in countries with a PGNP above $5,000.[60] This statement, which happens to be true, simply indicates what the world looks like. It says nothing about why it looks this way, nor does it assume any moral judgments about whether this is good or bad, nor does it suggest what, if anything, might be done to deal with this situation. If you were to inquire why this condition exists—because of climatic differences

THE CONVENTIONAL WISDOM: A SAMPLER

A key objective of this book is to give students a more sophisticated understanding of international relations phenomena. The following quotations are representative of a number of ideas about international relations that have rolled off the tongues of practitioners and the pens of philosophers over the years. Do *you* accept the validity of the propositions embodied in these statements, or do they appear somewhat simplistic?

On the types of countries that are war-prone:

"A tyrant . . . is always stirring up some war or other, in order that the people may require a leader."—Plato, *The Republic,* 4th century, B.C.

"Of all nations, those most fond of peace are democratic nations. . . ." —Alexis de Tocqueville, *Democracy in America,* 1835

On the prevention of war:

"To be prepared for war is one of the most effectual means of preserving peace."—George Washington, first annual address to Congress, January 8, 1790

". . . only when our arms are sufficient beyond doubt can we be certain beyond doubt that they will never be employed."—John F. Kennedy, inaugural address, January 20, 1961

"History has shown us all too well that weakness promotes aggression and war, whereas strength preserves the peace."—Ronald Reagan, paid political announcement, 1980 presidential election campaign

"I've often wondered what would have happened if we [the U.S., Japan, and Germany] had the same bonds of trade and commerce before 1939 and before 1941 [as we have today]. That's why I'm such a staunch advocate of global commerce."—Jimmy Carter, Twenty-sixth World Conference of the International Chamber of Commerce, October 1, 1978

On winning wars:

"It is said that God is always for the biggest battalions."—Voltaire, quoting Frederick the Great, in a letter to M. Riche, February 6, 1770

On the virtues of the "carrot" (nice guy) versus the "stick" (tough guy) approach to exercising influence in international affairs:

"Speak softly and carry a big stick; you will go far."—Theodore Roosevelt, Minnesota State Fair, September 2, 1901

"If the adversary feels that you are unpredictable, even rash, he will be deterred from pressing you too far."—Richard M. Nixon, *The Real War,* 1980 (because most of the poorer countries are located in the Southern Hemisphere), or technological differences (because most of the poorer countries are underdeveloped technologically), or racial differences (because most people in the poorer countries have black, brown, or yellow skin), or colonial heritage (because most of the poorer countries have only recently gained independence), or whatever—you would be shifting from description to explanation and would be engaged essentially in what we have called theoretical pursuits. If you decide that, regardless of causes, the existing distribution of wealth is bad in terms of being unethical and also fostering resentment and international conflict, then you would be engaging in normative analysis. And if you were to seek to alter this situation and were to recommend economic development strategies aimed at redistributing wealth in the world, then you would be playing problem solver and engaging in prescription.

The reader may recognize that many people engage in all of these modes of analysis, often all at once. There is a tendency to make a "mesh" of things, blending the four types together without being fully aware that what passes for factual description may only be wishful thinking and what passes for an explanation may be merely a rationalization for policies one espouses. Most of us prefer to concentrate on normative and prescriptive analysis more than the other two modes, because debating the great moral issues of the day and solving the world's problems seem inherently more interesting than examining a set of tables and graphs. Applying knowledge somehow seems more fun than acquiring it in the first place. For policymakers, normative and perscriptive analysis is their main job; for the layman, they lend themselves more easily to discussion over a glass of beer after a hard day's work.

However, the trouble is that one cannot properly perform normative and prescriptive analysis *until* one has done serious descriptive and explanatory analysis, that is, until one has as accurate a picture as possible of what the world looks like and why it is the way it is. Without a handle on the world, moralizing is reduced to pontification and prescriptions are doomed to failure. As we suggested earlier, practitioners and laymen often act on the basis of a certain set of assumptions about the world that are not very well spelled out or tested out, leading at times to unforeseen and disastrous results. It is only fair to add that professors can be equally guilty of not doing their "homework." (The box on page 30 lists a few samples of some popularly held notions about international relations that have been found by researchers to be of questionable validity or for which the evidence is at best mixed.)

The reason we have bothered to devote space to these rather abstract matters is to alert readers at the outset that they will be disappointed if they expect to find in the pages that follow a solution to conflicts in the Middle East and other problems in the world or a polemical attack on the evildoers responsible for these problems. The emphasis in this book is on basic description and explanation—with important bits of information provided along with a conceptual framework for digesting them—which is in keeping with our stated purpose of contributing to some *understanding* of international phenomena as we begin a new century. In the process of imparting a better understanding, we hope to arouse further curiosity about international relations. We also hope to sharpen the reader's ability to analyze problems and, ultimately, to propose or evaluate remedies for them. A careful diagnosis of the "global condition" is necessary before one can ascertain what cures might be applied.

The Plan of This Book

In the remaining chapters in Part I, we will further set the stage for the study of international relations by briefly examining the historical development of the international system up to the present. We will trace the roots of the global condition and provide an overview of the environment in which contemporary international relations occur, going beyond our initial observations and sketching in greater detail some of the trends mentioned in Chapter 1. In Part II we will focus on nation-states and national governments as actors in world politics, examining their foreign policy behavior and official interactions and the kinds of phenomena (such as the use of economic and military power) that many consider the "real stuff" of international relations. This section of the book will thus tend to deal with some of the more conflictual aspects of international politics. In Part III we will shift our attention to attempts to develop international law, which are designed to facilitate the routine flow of economic and other transactions across national boundaries and to provide conflict-management mechanisms when disagreements occur; we will focus here more on the cooperative impulse in international politics and the search for some degree of order in a decentralized world. Then, after having exposed students to the rudiments of world politics in the previous sections, in Part IV we will pull things together by treating the international system as a global polity in which there is at work a political process consisting of (1) a number of issues or problems on the agenda, (2) a number of different demands made by a variety of actors (both state and nonstate) in these issue areas, and (3) a series of outcomes or outputs ("regimes") produced by the interactions of these actors in the different issue-areas; by focusing on the congeries of forces at work in five selected issue-areas—arms control, control of terrorism and unorthodox violence, coordination of the international economy, economic development, and the management of resources—we hope to illustrate in a holistic fashion the rich dynamics of contemporary international relations and how the current generation of *Homo sapiens* is coping with the historic tension between order and disorder. In a concluding chapter, in Part V, we look ahead beyond the year 2001 and well into the twenty-first century.

SUMMARY

1. Today we are living in an interdependent world. The well-being of all communities can be substantially affected by international developments ranging from increases or decreases in the number of wars to increases or decreases in tariff barriers.

2. International politics can be defined as the study of who gets what, when, and how in the international arena.

3. Unlike domestic politics, international politics occurs in a decentralized fashion, with no world legislature or other central authoritative institutions to regulate the members of the international community—the more than 180 nation-states in which people are organized around the world.

4. Although there is potential for unparalleled conflict today, represented by nuclear weapons, there is also potential for unprecedented cooperation, represented by the growth of international organizations.

5. The idealist (liberal) school is one of the four major paradigms that have structured thinking about international relations in the twentieth century. This school emphasizes the importance of international law and organization, as well as moral concerns such as human rights, in the hope of maximizing cooperation between states.

6. The realists are less optimistic about the potential for international cooperation, viewing international relations primarily as a power struggle between nation-states in the pursuit of national security. Realists focus on military strategy, the elements of national power, and the nature of national interests rather than on international law and organization. Contemporary realists (neorealists), like classical realists, focus on the behavior of states in an anarchical environment, but see themselves as more rigorous in their pursuit of knowledge.

7. The globalist (pluralist) paradigm views international relations in more complex terms, as consisting not only of war and peace issues but also of economic and social welfare issue-areas and involving not only national governments but multinational corporations and other nonstate actors caught in a web of interdependence.

8. The Marxist paradigm views international relations as a class struggle between the world's rich and poor rather than a contest between nation-states.

9. There are two general methodological approaches to the study of international relations. Traditionalists seek knowledge through participant observation, practical experience, and the careful understanding of diplomatic history. Behavioralists take a more scientific approach, using aggregate data, quantitative analysis techniques, and computers to systematically develop and test theories that could explain the dynamics of international relations.

10. Despite differing orientations, scholars, policymakers, and laymen all share an interest in understanding how the world works. There is nothing more practical than a good theory.

11. At least four modes of analysis are used in examining international relations: (a) description, which simply declares what reality looks like; (b) explanation, which accounts for the existence of that reality; (c) normative analysis, which makes ethical or value judgments; and (d) prescription, which offers recommendations for a future course of action or policy. Although these various modes constitute distinct intellectual tasks reflecting different purposes of inquiry, they are all interrelated.

SUGGESTIONS FOR FURTHER READING AND STUDY

Much has been written in recent years about interdependence. See the works cited in Note 33. On the implications of interdependence for statehood and nationhood, see Joseph A. Camilleri and Jim Falk, *The End of Sovereignty? The Politics of a Shrinking and Fragmenting World* (London: Edward Elgar, 1992); and Robert H. Jackson and Alan James, eds., *States in a Changing World: A Contemporary Analysis* (Oxford: Clarendon Press, 1993). The trends relating to the disintegration and integration of nation-states are elucidated in K. J. Holsti, "Change in the International System: Interdependence, Integration, and Fragmentation," in Ole R. Holsti et al., eds., *Change and Continuity in the International System* (Boulder, Colo.: Westview Press, 1980), pp. 23–53, which comments on this developing puzzle well before the end of the Cold War; and the writings in Ernst-Otto Czempiel and James N. Rosenau, eds., *Global Changes and Theoretical Challenges* (Lexington, Mass.: Lexington Books, 1989), written as the Cold War was ending. The "role of science and technology in the evolution of world affairs," and particularly their "implications for the processes of national and international governance" in the post–Cold War era, is discussed in Eugene B. Skolnikoff, *The Elusive Transformation* (Princeton: Princeton University Press, 1993).

For an excellent discussion of the "what" question, see Patrick M. Morgan, *Theories and Approaches to International Politics*, 4th ed. (New Brunswick, N.J.: Transaction Books, 1986), ch. 1. The author examines the boundary question as well as other problems in studying international relations, including the so-called levels of analysis problem. For the distinction between domestic policy and foreign policy, see James N. Rosenau, "Foreign Policy as an Issue-Area," *The Scientific Study of Foreign Policy*, 2d ed. (London: Frances Pinter, 1980), pp. 461–500; and Eugene J. Meehan, "The Concept 'Foreign Policy,' " in Wolfran F. Hanrieder, ed., *Comparative Foreign Policy* (New York: David McKay, 1971), pp. 265–294. The nature of nation-states and the nation-state system is treated in Barry Buzan, *People, States, and Fear: An Agenda for International Security in the Post-Cold War Era*, 2d ed. (Boulder, Colo.: Lynne Rienner, 1991), and Hedley Bull, *The Anarchical Society* (London: Macmillan, 1977).

For the "how" question, in addition to ch. 2 of the Morgan book, see James E. Dougherty and Robert L. Pfaltzgraff, *Contending Theories of International Relations*, 3d ed. (New York: Harper and Row, 1990); Paul R. Viotti and Mark V. Kauppi, *International Relations Theory*, 2d ed. (New York: Macmillan, 1993); and John A. Vasquez, ed., *Classics for International Relations*, 2d ed. (Englewood Cliffs, N.J.: Prentice Hall, 1990), all of which offer a wide-ranging examination of competing paradigms. Klaus Knorr and James N. Rosenau, eds., *Contending Approaches to International Politics* (Princeton: Princeton University Press, 1969), focuses more on methodological issues. The neoliberal challenge to realism in the post–Cold War era is discussed in Charles W. Kegley, Jr., ed., *Controversies in International Relations Theory: Realism and the Neoliberal Challenge* (New York: St. Martin's, 1995); and David A. Baldwin, ed., *Neoreal-*

ism and Neoliberalism: The Contemporary Debate (New York: Columbia University Press, 1993). Also, see Joseph S. Nye, "Neorealism and Neoliberalism," *World Politics,* 40 (January 1988), pp. 235–251.

Among the classic realist works are E. H. Carr, *The Twenty Years' Crisis, 1919–1939* (London: Macmillan, 1939), and Hans J. Morgenthau, *Politics Among Nations* (New York: Knopf, 1948). In addition to Woodrow Wilson's writings, idealist thought can be found in Grenville Clark and Louis B. Sohn, *World Peace Through World Law: Two Alternative Plans,* 3d ed. (Cambridge, Mass.: Harvard University Press, 1966). Among works that exemplify the globalist perspective, in addition to the ones cited in Note 45, is Richard W. Mansbach and John A. Vasquez, *In Search of Theory: A New Paradigm for Global Politics* (New York: Columbia University Press, 1981). A concise treatment of the Marxist world view can be found in Keith L. Nelson and Spencer C. Olin, *Why War?* (Berkeley: University of California Press, 1979), pp. 69–74; for the related "world systems" approach, beyond the works cited in Note 51, see Robert Cox, *Power, Production, and World Order* (New York: Columbia University Press, 1987); Ronen Palan and Barry Gills, eds., *Transcending the State-Global Divide* (London: Lynne Rienner, 1994); and Andre Gunder Frank, "A Plea for World System History," *Journal of World History* (Winter 1991). A "postmodernist" dialogue appears in James N. Rosenau, ed., *Global Voices: Dialogues in International Relations* (Boulder, Colo.: Westview Press, 1993); a feminist theory of international relations is the basis for V. Spike Peterson and Anne Sisson Runyan, *Global Gender Issues* (Boulder, Colo.: Westview Press, 1993).

For examples of specific studies that use quantitative techniques to examine international relations phenomena, see J. David Singer, ed., *Quantitative International Politics: Insights and Evidence* (New York: Free Press, 1968), and Dina A. Zinnes, *Contemporary Research in International Relations* (New York: Free Press, 1976). The problems involved in scientific inquiry in the international relations field are discussed in Benjamin A. Most and Harvey Starr, *Inquiry, Logic, and International Politics* (Columbia: University of South Carolina Press, 1988).

An extensive discussion of the various modes of analysis and the role of theory in the international relations field is furnished by David Edwards, *International Political Analysis* (New York: Holt, Rinehart and Winston, 1969); also, see Alexander L. George, "Theory for Policy in International Relations," *Policy Sciences,* 4 (December 1973), pp. 387–413. Three writings that examine a variety of themes discussed in Chapter 1 and provide an overview of the development of international relations as a discipline are William Olson's "Growing Pains of a Discipline: Its Phases, Ideals, and Debates," in Olson et al., eds., *The Theory and Practice of International Relations,* 6th ed. (Englewood Cliffs, N.J.: Prentice-Hall, 1983), pp. 391–401; K. J. Holsti, *The Dividing Discipline: Hegemony and Diversity in International Theory* (London: Allen and Unwin, 1985); and Joseph Kruzel and James N. Rosenau, eds., *Journeys Through World Politics* (Lexington, Mass.: Lexington Books, 1989), a compendium of the "autobiographic reflections" of several major scholarly figures in the post–World War II period. Also, see Jim George, *Discourses of Global Politics: A Critical (Re)Introduction to International Relations* (Boulder, Colo.: Lynne Rienner, 1994).

A Glimpse into the Past: The Historical Development of the International System

In examining the evolution of international relations over the years, some observers are struck by the degree of *change* that has occurred and others are struck by the degree of *continuity*. The former lean toward the *sui generis* school of history, which argues that history never repeats itself because each historical event is unique ("one of a kind"); the latter lean toward the *déjà vu* school of history, which argues that the more things change the more they stay the same ("I've seen it all before").

Representative of the first view are the following statements, one by Barbara Tuchman, a historian, and one by Alvin Toffler, a futurologist. Consider the comments by Tuchman, comparing the circumstances surrounding the Soviet invasion of Afghanistan in 1979 with those existing on the eve of World War I in 1914:

> Events in history do not—I would venture to say cannot—repeat themselves; nor can they be acted out in the same pattern as before because circumstances are never the same as before. They alter as the years pass, and the longer the elapsed time, the more new factors enter the situation. When the pace of change, as in the twentieth century, is rapid, the change can be immense.[1]

Similarly, consider Toffler's comments on the futility of comparing the present with the past, whether with regard to international relations or any other phenomena:

> The final, qualitative difference between this and all previous lifetimes is the one most easily overlooked. For we have not merely extended the scope and scale of change, we have radically altered its pace. We have in our time released a totally new social force—a stream of change so accelerated that it influences our sense of time, revolutionizes the tempo of daily life, and affects the very way we "feel" the world around us. We no longer "feel" life as men did in the past. And this is the ultimate difference, the distinction that separates the truly contemporary man from all others. For this acceleration lies behind the impermanence . . . radically affecting the way we relate to other people, to things, to the entire universe of ideas, art and values. . . .[2]

In contrast, consider the remarks of Kenneth Waltz, one of the more prominent members of the second school:

> International politics is sometimes described as the realm of accident and upheaval, of rapid and unpredictable change. Although changes abound, continuities are as impressive, or more so. . . . In the two world wars of this century [for example] . . . the same principal countries lined up against each other, despite the domestic political upheavals that took place in the interwar period. The texture of international politics remains highly constant,

patterns recur, and events repeat themselves endlessly. The relations that prevail internationally seldom shift rapidly in type or in quality.[3]

Perhaps the most well-known and oft-quoted statement reflecting the *déjà vu* school of history belongs to the philosopher George Santayana, who cautioned that "those who cannot remember the past are condemned to repeat it."[4]

Change and Continuity in International Relations: Sui Generis *or* Déjà Vu?

Are international relations characterized mostly by change, or by continuity? As suggested in Chapter 1, the authors would argue that elements of both change *and* continuity can be identified in international relations, that the truth lies somewhere between the *sui generis* view of history and the *déjà vu* view.

SUI GENERIS

It is obvious that, strictly speaking, events never repeat themselves exactly in the same manner; as the ancient Greek philosopher Heraclitus noted, one can never step in the same stream twice. At the very least, the particular personalities involved in shaping events change. More important, it is also obvious that the environment in which international relations are conducted itself undergoes change. Clearly, there have been countless developments in international relations over the years that would make today's world unrecognizable at first glance to the statesman of the eighteenth or nineteenth century or even the early twentieth century—the invention of weapons of mass destruction capable of leveling entire countries, the negotiation of a treaty to avoid a shoot-out in outer space, environmental crises and population explosions, skyjackings by revolutionaries, the "Coca-Colanization" of the world, instantaneous satellite communication of happenings in one corner of the globe to the opposite corner, the growth of multinational corporations, to name but a few developments.

DÉJÀ VU

Even though the particular personalities and conditions surrounding various international events may change over the years, however, some commonalities and parallels can still be found throughout different periods of international relations history. Although events may never repeat themselves exactly, they may nonetheless share some rough similarities. Indeed, it is the assumption that individual events are not wholly unique and that there are identifiable patterns of international behavior that enables us to develop useful knowledge about international relations; otherwise, there would be no lessons to be learned from the study of international relations and no perspective to be derived from history.

Wars continue to be fought, even if the nature of the weapons changes drastically. The process of diplomacy goes on, even if the territory being negoti-

SIDELIGHT

HISTORICAL FACTS

- *The total world population in* A.D. 1:
  Approximately 250 million people

- *The longest reign of a major European monarch:*
  Louis XIV of France, who ascended the throne in 1643 at age four and reigned until his death seventy-two years later in 1715

- *The longest tenure in office by a democratically elected head of government:*
  Tage Erlander, Swedish Prime Minister for twenty-three years between 1946 and 1969

- *The first resident embassy established abroad:*
  Accredited to the court of Cosimo de Medici by the Duke of Milan in 1450 (in the Italian city-state system)

- *The first peace treaty (based on written evidence):*
  An agreement between Egypt and the Hittite Kingdom (situated in present-day Turkey), circa 1270 B.C., after some twenty years of war

- *The first intergovernmental international organization:*
  The Central Commission for the Navigation of the Rhine, created in 1815

- *The inventor of dynamite:*
  Alfred Nobel (initiator of the Nobel Peace Prize), in 1866

- *The first tank used in battle:*
  "Mother," produced by the British and used at the Battle of Flers in 1916, during World War I

- *The first air force:*
  Created in 1794 by the French government, which used balloons for reconnaissance purposes during the Napoleonic Wars

- *The first "great power" war to result in one million battle deaths:*
  The Thirty Years' War, involving most parts of Europe in the seventeenth century

ated happens to be in outer space. Pressures caused by population pushing against resources have regularly been a source of friction in international relations, even though they may now be of a different kind and magnitude than in the past. If skyjackings are a fairly recent phenomenon, international terrorism is not. Societies have always experienced "cultural diffusion" of ideas and tastes across national boundaries—whether in the form of Coca-Cola or beer or more revolutionary innovations—despite frequent attempts by governments to limit "foreign" influences. In this sense, interdependence is not altogether new today—only more intricate, more accelerated, and more difficult to prevent or undo. Nations and peoples still manage to misunderstand and misperceive each other's actions even as advanced communications technology provides greater and faster information about the world than ever before. And new forms of human organization may develop, but old ones—such as nation-states—persist alongside them.

In short, some features of international relations are more enduring and less given to change than other features. Change is not as all-pervasive as the *sui generis* school might suggest, nor is it as insignificant and superficial as it might be depicted by the *déjà vu* school. There are important *continuities* to be observed in international relations, but there are also important *changes* as well. "New generations take up the story, the grass grows again over concentration camp and battlefield, new divisions spring up between old wartime comrades while scars of conflict heal and the children of enemies marry and produce new generations with their own affinities and differences, loves and hates."[5]

THE INTERNATIONAL SYSTEM IN FLUX

It is this history that we wish to trace in this chapter. In discussing the evolution of international relations, our concern is not to provide a detailed chronology of events but rather, in the space of a few pages, to provide some sense of how certain essential aspects of international relations have changed significantly over the years while others have remained relatively constant. Such historical perspective can enable us to understand better the *current* global condition.

To furnish a thumbnail sketch of several hundred years of history in a single chapter, it is helpful to utilize the concept of **international system,** which can be defined as the general pattern of political, economic, social, geographical, and technological relationships that shape world affairs or, more simply, as the general setting in which international relations occur at any point in time. At times, the basic fabric of international relations seems to change so much, not necessarily in all its parts but in many key elements, that one can say the international system has been "transformed." There is disagreement among scholars as to how often international system transformation has occurred and one distinct era of international politics has given way to another era.[6]

For purposes of discussion, we will divide the last several centuries of international relations history into four periods: (1) the Classical International System (1648–1789), (2) the Transitional International System (1789–1945), (3) the Post–World War II International System (1945–1989), and (4) the Contemporary (Post–Cold War) International System. Some observers might take exception to this compartmentalization of history.[7] However, these chronological boundaries are not offered as the definitive mileposts in the life of the international system but only as rough markers that can serve as a basis for organizing our historical discussion and comparing the past with the present. We will examine the first three systems in this chapter and leave the contemporary international system for closer scrutiny in Chapter 3.

To compare different eras of international politics, it is necessary to identify those elements of the international system that are potentially subject to change and that seem to be most worthy of comparison. An examination of the scholarly literature suggests that among the most important characteristics ("variables") of the international system are the following: (1) the nature of the *actors* (nation-states and nonstate actors); (2) the *distribution of power* (equilibrium among several major actors or dominance by one or two actors); (3) the *distribution of wealth* (the extent of the "rich-poor gap" between actors); (4) the *degree of polarization* (flexibility or rigidity of alignment); (5) the *objectives* of the actors (preoccupation with territorial acquisition or some other objective); (6) the *means* available to actors for pursuing their objectives (the nature of weapons technology, for example); and (7) the *degree of interdependence* (in terms of both "interconnectedness"—the raw volume of goods and services, people, and communications flowing across national boundaries—and "mutual sensitivity and vulnerability"—the potential effects of one country's actions on other countries).[8] We now examine how and to what extent these features of international relations have changed over the years.

The Classical International System (1648–1789)

By most accounts, the "story" of international relations begins in 1648, with the **Peace of Westphalia** ending the Thirty Years' War. This date is widely accepted as marking the origin of the international system because it was only in the mid-seventeenth century that the world began to witness the emergence of actors called *nation-states*, cited in Chapter 1 as the primary units of political organization on the globe. That is to say, it was only then that there appeared on the scene certain entities having the following characteristics: (1) a single *central government* exercising **sovereignty** over (2) a relatively fixed *population* within (3) a relatively well-defined *territory*. Such entities were said to be "sovereign" in terms of there being a government that had supreme decision-making authority within the boundaries of the territorial unit and that acknowledged no higher authority outside those boundaries. Sovereignty did not mean that the state was necessarily able to control all the actions of its members at all times, only that internally it could claim a monopoly on the legitimate use of physical force as a possible tool in seeking to compel their obedience and externally it could claim a monopoly right to act on their behalf vis-à-vis other states. (See the box on pages 44–46 for a discussion of definitional problems surrounding such terms as **state, nation,** and **nation-state.** These terms are worth examining in some detail, because they are essential to the study of international relations and can be a source of much confusion.)

THE BIRTH OF THE NATION-STATE

It is important to keep in mind that from a long-term historical perspective, the nation-state is a relatively young institution in human affairs. It is not even 400 years old—which is not very old when compared to at least 5,000 years of recorded history. Human beings had been on the earth for roughly a million years before the mid-seventeenth century. However, they had been organized in other kinds of political units, such as tribes, city-states, and empires, rather than nation-states. One can read Thucydides' accounts of the city-state system of ancient Greece (which lasted from 800 B.C. to 322 B.C.), Kautilya's writings on the ancient Hindu state system under the Mauryan Empire (325 B.C.–183 B.C.), and Machiavelli's accounts of the city-state system of Renaissance Italy (during the fifteenth century). The history of humanity could be read as the search for the optimal political unit, with the pendulum seemingly swinging between two extremes: almost a single universal political order (e.g., the world empires of Rome and Alexander the Great) and a set of much smaller, highly fragmented polities (e.g., the series of walled cities and other entities that typified the Middle Ages).[9]

In Europe, for example, even as late as 1600, there were elements of both fragmentation (manifested by the semi-sovereign political jurisdictions presided over by various feudal lords and princes) and universalism (manifested by the Pope and the Holy Roman Emperor, who claimed supreme spiritual and secular authority). In short, the political landscape of Europe consisted of a crazy-quilt pattern of duchies, independent cities, feudal manors, kingdoms, ecclesiastical territories, and assorted other units tied together in a complicated hierarchy. While kings and queens sat on thrones in England and France, their authority was contested by both local princes and papal powers in Rome.[10]

However, as 1648 approached, the political landscape was changing. Gunpowder was making the walled cities of the past no longer viable as units of political organization capable of protecting their populations. In addition, the growing merchant capitalist class was finding the feudal system, with its chaotic set of juridical relationships, dysfunctional in terms of facilitating ex-

NATIONS, STATES, AND NATION-STATES: SOME PROBLEMS IN DEFINING TERMS

In everyday conversation, people tend to use a number of terms interchangeably—"nations," "states," "countries"—to refer to those entities that are distinguished by thick boundary lines on world maps. Although one might casually interchange these terms, they are not exactly synonymous. Technically speaking, "state" refers to a *legal-political* entity, "nation" refers to a *cultural* or social entity, and "country" refers to a *geographical* entity. In defining "state" and "nation," the distinction is not merely technical; it has real importance for international relations scholars as well as policymakers and lawyers.

When we say that "state" refers to a legal-political entity, we mean an entity that has a sovereign government exercising supreme authority over a relatively fixed population within well-defined territorial boundaries and acknowledging no higher authority outside those boundaries. Today, there are well over 180 such territorial units considered by most observers to be states. Such entities have "international legal status," which enables them to enter into treaties, join intergovernmental organizations such as the United Nations, exchange ambassadors, and engage in other "official" international activities. In short, whether one uses the term or not, "states" are the main reference points one sees on a world map. Some states, such as the United States and Japan, are obviously well known, but other states, such as Palau and Nauru, are less so. No matter how tiny or inconspicuous a state is, its sovereignty gives it at least formal equality with all other states.

A "nation," however, is conceptually and legally different. When we say "nation" refers to a cultural or social entity, we mean a group of people having some sense of shared historical experience (generally rooted in a common language, ethnicity, or other cultural characteristics) as well as shared destiny. A nation may constitute part of a state (e.g., the Timorese constituting a distinct cultural group within the state of Indonesia), may be coterminous with the state (e.g., the American people and the United States), or may spill over several different states (e.g., the Palestinians in Israel, Lebanon, Jordan, and several other states). As one can imagine, there are many more "nations" than "states" in the world.

These distinctions are not always clear-cut. In the case of the United States, the society is composed of many nationality groups claiming different national origins (Irish-Americans, Polish-Americans, and other "hyphenated Americans"); but because these groups over time have for the most part become assimilated into American society and have come to identify themselves as "Americans," one can say that the state and nation are practically one in the United States. The oneness of the state and nation is also the case in many other established states such as France. Although various groups in France quarrel vociferously, sometimes violently, over the political institutions of the state, they nonetheless generally consider themselves "French" and do not speak of seceding to form a new state. In contrast, the Timorese in Indonesia tend not to consider themselves Indonesians; the Palestinians in Israel, Jordan, and Lebanon tend not to think of themselves as Israelis, Jordanians, or Lebanese; the Kurds in Iran and Iraq tend not to identify themselves as Iranians or Iraqis. In all the latter cases, the states in question are plagued by culturally diverse populations that include separatist movements intent on establishing their own independent statehood. In the early 1990s, the breakup of the Soviet Union (into the Russian Federation, Ukraine, Armenia, and a dozen other "successor states") and Yugoslavia (into Serbia and Montenegro, Croatia, Slovenia, Bosnia, and Macedonia) owed to ethnic faultlines that could not be contained within existing states. Many of these successor states themselves continue to experience internal ethnopolitical conflict because they still have sizeable minority groups disaffected from the general population.

It has often been noted that in the early development of the international system, during the seventeenth and eighteenth centuries, it was the state that created the nation. That is, the states were ones in which the central political authorities gradually managed to forge a sense of national identity among a group of people who happened to find themselves living within the same set of borders but who had not previously thought of themselves as "French" or "English." In the nineteenth and early twentieth century, however, the nation often created the state. Groups sharing common linguistic and other cultural bonds eventually united into single states, with the prime examples being the loose confederation of German-speaking territories forming Germany in 1870 and the various Italian-speaking territories forming Italy around the same time. The pattern after World War II was more like that in the seventeenth and eighteenth centuries insofar as many of the societies in Africa and Asia that achieved independence from colonial powers after 1945 became states whose borders did not correspond to any natural cultural groupings but were the artificial product of imperialist rivalries and colonial mapmaking; hence, in countries such as Indonesia and Uganda, the leaders who had led the independence movement were faced with the problem of getting diverse and often historically hostile tribal units to identify with the new state in which they were situated. As evidenced by the recent breakup of the Soviet Union and Yugoslavia, the latest trend may be a return to nationalism energizing the creation of new states. An important aspect of world politics over the years has been this search by culturally distinct nations for statehood and by polyglot states for nationhood.

In the course of this book we will follow the literary convention of using various terms—states, nations, countries—interchangeably; unless otherwise specified, we will be using these terms to refer to the political-legal entities known as "states." There is one other term, which we have already mentioned, that requires some explanation, namely "nation-state." This term is used by scholars as a synonym for "state," not to add confusion to an already confusing terminology but rather to connote the fact that over the last three centuries there has been a persistent impulse to achieve some congruence between state and national boundaries, to make the state and nation one in the minds and hearts of its people.

panded commerce; traders were attracted to the idea of a single ruler presiding over a specified territory in which a common set of laws would apply, including a standardized currency and standard weights and measures conducive to reducing the transaction costs of doing business. This small but rising bourgeois commercial middle class began casting its lot with kings and queens against the prerogatives of the landed nobility. And the authority of the Pope and Holy Roman Emperor, always existing more in theory than in reality, became even more marginal. The feudal order was dying.[11]

These trends culminated in the Peace of Westphalia in 1648, symbolizing a fundamentally new set of political arrangements based on the sovereignty of the nation-state. In consolidating their power against local princes and repudiating any allegiance to higher religious or other authorities outside their territory, national monarchs seemed to be rejecting the forces of both fragmentation and universalism that had characterized previous eras. As we will see, the development of nation-states has been an uneven phenomenon, with the first ones appearing in the seventeenth century, others (such as Germany and Italy) not materializing until the mid-nineteenth century, and still others (such as many societies in Africa and Asia) appearing only in the mid-twentieth century. As we will also see, the nation-state has managed to survive despite both centrifugal forces (tending toward fragmentation) and centripetal forces (tending toward universalism). But that is getting ahead of the story.

ACTORS IN THE CLASSICAL SYSTEM

When one examines the international system that existed in the seventeenth and eighteenth centuries, commonly referred to as the "classical" era of international relations, one finds a relatively small number of actors involved in international politics—namely, the heads of royal families of England, France, and other European nation-states along with their aristocratic elites. The claim by King Louis XIV of France that *"l'état c'est moi"* ("I am the state") was applicable to his fellow monarchs as well, and derived from the "divine right of kings" or some other such rationale. Only toward the very end of the eighteenth century was *dynastic nationalism* to give way to *democratic nationalism* whereby sovereignty derived from the will of the people who inhabited the state. Indeed, throughout much of this period, the average peasant in the village still did not identify wholeheartedly with the state and was not inclined to respond emotionally to flag-waving and other national symbols. (It was hard for Louis XIV to wave the banner of French nationalism when his wife was Spanish, his chief adviser was from the Italian peninsula, and his army consisted largely of foreign mercenaries.) Patriotism had not yet become a major impulse in the affairs of state.

POWER AND WEALTH

Although there existed independent entities outside of Europe, such as China and Japan, and later the United States, international politics in this period was essentially *European* politics. Power (in terms of military capability and related factors) was distributed roughly evenly among several dominant European states, including England, France, Austria, Sweden, Spain, Turkey, and (as the era progressed) Prussia and Russia. (**Power** is as important a concept in the study of international relations as the concepts *state* and *nation* and can be just as much a source of confusion. See the box on pages 48–50 for a focused look at problems in assessing national power, both historically and in contemporary times.)

The European states were similar not only in power but also in wealth. The two tended to go hand in hand insofar as power was exercised mainly through military prowess, which in turn required economic resources for support. At a time when the Industrial Revolution was not yet fully underway, all states had similar sources of wealth, and the differences between them were not nearly as great as the disparities that were to develop later.

There was always the possibility that a given state might not be satisfied with its power or wealth position and might threaten the sovereignty of other states and upset the equilibrium by engaging in empire building. In the absence of any centralized political authority in the international system, order among states was to be maintained primarily through the so-called **balance of power.** Any aggressively minded states intent on hegemony would, it was hoped, be deterred by the prospect of coming up against a coalition of states having equal or superior power; if deterrence failed and an attack occurred, the latter coalition could be expected to fight to defeat the aggressor. Throughout much of the classical era, France was viewed as the major threat to the stabil-

POWER: SOME PROBLEMS OF DEFINITION AND MEASUREMENT

Power has been variously defined—by Hans Morgenthau as "man's control over the minds and actions of other men," by Karl Deutsch as "the ability to prevail in conflict and overcome obstacles," and by Robert Dahl as the ability of one actor "to get [another actor] to do something that [the latter] would not otherwise do."[1]

The concept of power has taken on different meanings in international relations, depending on the context in which the term has been used. In the context of national actors, it normally refers to a country's existing strength (a commodity a state possesses in some amount) or a goal (something a state wants more of). In the context of interactions between states, it normally refers to their relative capabilities and the manner in which one state seeks to control the behavior of another state, i.e., the economic, military, or other tools of influence used. In the context of the international system, as treated in this chapter, it normally refers to the stratification pattern formed by the global power distribution among states.

It is one thing to define power; it is another thing to try to measure it so that one can make accurate statements about which states are powerful and which states are not so powerful. One encounters measurement problems no matter what the context within which one is analyzing power. In regard to the actor context, many classic works have attempted to identify the "bases" of national power—certain national attributes on which a state's capacity to influence others presumably depends. Almost invariably the list includes geography (territorial size, location, and natural resources), population (size, homogeneity, and level of education), economic capability (gross national product and degree of industrialization), and military capability (quantity and quality of weaponry and troops). Countries possessing a sizable land area and population, economic and military capability, and natural resource endowment, along with a high level of economic and technological development, have traditionally been considered "powerful" by definition, whether or not they take advantage of these assets.

Aside from the measurement problem of deciding what weight to assign each of these factors, there is always some analyst who argues that some attribute has been erroneously omitted from the list, so that the list can become endless. Also, there are analysts who argue for the inclusion of such "soft" and less measurable factors as national character and morale. Others have noted, too, that the importance of these factors can vary from one historical period to another. For example, territorial features such as a large land mass or insular location or mountainous topography may have conferred power (at least in terms of invulnerability to attack) in the eighteenth century but may be somewhat less significant in an age of intercontinental ballistic missiles. Similarly, a large population may have been the *sine qua non* needed in the nineteenth and early twentieth centuries to produce tons of weapons and bodies for the armed forces but may be somewhat less crucial in an age of automated industry and warfare. One could argue differently, though, that a rough terrain and large population can still pose formidable obstacles to a would-be aggressor even in modern times, as in the case of guerrilla warfare.

Although a country's power may be closely associated with its human and material resource base, power and resources are not exactly the same. Here is where the interaction context must be taken into account. As in other areas of life, the "underdog" sometimes wins in international relations because the country in a seemingly favored position is unable to translate its resources into domination of another country. The "paper tiger" is a well-known phenomenon in international relations. Also related to the interaction context, the exercise of power can take many different forms, ranging from moral suasion to economic coercion to the threatened or actual use of military force. Certain national attributes may be relevant to certain modes of statecraft but not to others. And certain modes of statecraft may be common to some historical eras more than to others.

In regard to the systemic context, scholars have tended to characterize the global distribution of power in terms of either equilibrium among several major powers or hegemony by only one or two, depending on the historical era. Often the major powers are referred to as "poles" toward which other lesser states gravitate for protection; and the system itself is classified as to "polarity," i.e., the concentration of power in a few or several countries (unipolarity meaning one power center, bipolarity two, and multipolarity several such centers). Polarity here is distinguished from "polarization," which refers to the rigidity or flexibility of alliances among states in the system.

Further distinctions are made between "great powers," "middle powers," and "small powers," usually based on possession of the aforementioned national attributes assumed to be associated with power. However, countries designated as "powerful" do not necessarily act powerfully at all times. It is often difficult to determine where to draw the line between, say, a "middle power" and a "small power" and which states belong in which categories. One is on much safer ground attempting to ascertain the general power structure of the international system rather than attempting to identify an exact ranking of states. Indeed, despite all the measurement problems and disagreements cited here, a fairly broad scholarly consensus exists on the nature of the power structure in the three international systems discussed in this chapter.

Our point in making these comments is to emphasize that power is a more complex concept than is sometimes suggested by the way the term is bandied about in everyday discourse. The kinds of problems noted here not only complicate efforts by scholars to analyze power but also complicate the power calculations of policymakers as well. As we will see in Chapter 3, power is especially difficult to assess with precision in contemporary international relations.

[1] Hans J. Morgenthau, *Politics Among Nations,* 5th ed. (New York: Knopf, 1973), p. 28; Karl W. Deutsch, "On the Concepts of Politics and Power," *Journal of International Affairs,* 21 (1967), p. 334; Robert A. Dahl, "The Concept of Power," *Behavioral Science,* 2 (July 1957), p. 203.

ity of the system, with England assuming the chief "balancer" role, even though the latter's own hegemonic ambitions were somewhat suspect as well.

DEGREE OF POLARIZATION

For the balance of power to operate as intended, it required a low level of polarization, i.e., a high degree of alignment flexibility, whereby countries could shift their power quickly from one side to another as a counterweight against would-be aggressors. The international system in this period was, indeed, flexible, in the sense that the European powers and other actors in the system did not fall into rigid armed camps at opposite poles poised against each other but rather were amenable to making and breaking alliances frequently as the situation warranted. Although there was enormous palace intrigue, wheeling and dealing, and military maneuvering associated with the balance of power at this time, the classical system worked fairly effectively, if imperfectly, as at least a crude vehicle for maintaining stability in the international system— not necessarily out of any conscious attempt by states to keep order but out of their mutual security concerns.[12]

Two factors in particular contributed to the flexibility of the system and the operation of the balance of power mechanism. One was the concentration of decision-making competence in the hands of a few rulers so that decisions about alliance making and breaking could be made swiftly without need for consultation or popular approval. The second was the absence of any major ideological cleavages among the main actors. Had such differences existed, certain potential alliance partners might have been somewhat incompatible, which might have inhibited the shifting of alliances called for by the balance of power calculus. Not only were the leaders of European states all conservative monarchs steeped in similar cultural traditions, but in many instances they were also related by marriage. The combination of multiple power centers together with flexibility of alignments made for an international system that scholars have labeled **multipolar**.[13]

OBJECTIVES AND MEANS

The European monarchs spoke the same "language" in more ways than one. In particular, they shared to some extent a common understanding of the "rules of the game" surrounding international politics at the time: (1) not to interfere in the internal affairs of another country in any way that might destabilize monarchical institutions, and (2) not to allow any one state to achieve dominant power in the system (unless it happened to be one's own state). The objectives of states in the classical era were not so much national objectives as personal objectives of the various rulers, namely, to enhance dynastic wealth, power, and prestige.

The royal houses of Europe shared common bloodlines and values, but they also had conflicts of interests. All rulers experienced the **security dilemma** that statesmen in later generations were to experience as well—the felt need for more national power to increase national security, although the quest for power merely tended to increase feelings of insecurity. Although some rulers may have harbored hegemonic aspirations, the objectives they usually sought were relatively limited, partly because the available means of pursuing national objectives were also relatively limited. The stakes over which wars were fought consisted mostly of a few patches of real estate—Alsace or some other province—several of which changed hands frequently without their inhabitants having much opportunity to develop a clear national identity. The classical era, then, was not known as an era of peace, but rather one in which the violent international conflicts that occurred were fairly small affairs between monarchs, resembling blood feuds or gentlemanly rivalries in contrast to the total wars among whole societies that were to be waged in subsequent eras.

As much as one national leader might wish to crush and eliminate another, the niceties of palace etiquette and the realities of limited military power tended to dictate otherwise. For firepower, monarchs relied on small, expensive professional armies, often consisting of foreign mercenaries whose loyalty was questionable and whose desertion rate was high. The military technology they were armed with—muskets and cannon loaded with gunpowder—was deadly enough but relatively crude and applicable only on a small scale compared with the state of the art that was to be developed in the nineteenth and, of course, the twentieth century. The masses were largely innocent bystanders during wartime, being raped, plundered, and pillaged but not having any vested interests in the outcome of most conflicts; their political and economic lot was not likely to change very much no matter what the fate of their sovereign was or even who their sovereign happened to be.

DEGREE OF INTERDEPENDENCE

All of this made for an international system that had a curious blend of parochialism and cosmopolitanism. Whereas the elites of Europe traveled and conversed freely across national boundaries, the masses knew little of the world outside their towns and villages, much less outside their national borders. Whereas monarchs were reliant to some extent on gold and other resources from the New World beyond the oceans to help finance their professional armies, nation-states in this period were still fairly self-contained and self-sufficient economic units only minimally dependent on international commerce. Whereas diseases could have contagious effects spreading across national boundaries, cultural and other kinds of diffusion processes occurred slowly; the still primitive communications technology kept one corner of the globe insulated from developments in another corner, so that there was little likelihood of revolutions and terrorist activities becoming immediate worldwide epidemics. Whereas balance of power considerations created mutual concerns in the military sphere, the primitive nature of weapons technology meant that—in contrast to later periods—allies were not linked together by any need for coordinated military planning and training, and enemies did not share the common bond of knowing that a fatal decision by one side could mean annihilation for both. In short, the classical international system was characterized by a relatively low degree of interdependence among states, in terms of "interconnectedness" (the raw volume of transactions across national boundaries) as well as "mutual sensitivity and vulnerability" (the potential effects of one country's actions on other countries).

However, many of these conditions were already starting to change toward the end of the eighteenth century. The French Revolution that occurred in 1789 not only ushered out the monarchy in France but also set in motion certain forces that were to usher in a new era of international politics.

The Transitional International System (1789–1945)

Although the French Revolution was preceded a decade earlier by the American Revolution, the "shot heard around the world" that started the thirteen colonies' revolt against the British was neither as loud as the storming of the

Bastille in Paris nor as revolutionary a turning point in the development of the international system. The reason was simply that France was an integral part of the European state system that dominated world politics at the time, while the fledgling United States remained on the periphery. The distinctiveness of the "transitional" international system that emerged at the end of the eighteenth century and was to last until 1945 lay precisely in the fact that it constituted a bridge between the classical and post–World War II eras, retaining certain features of the former while also introducing new features presaging the latter. The transitional era was like a "prism" through which passed certain elements of the past that were refined and reshaped and out of which emerged a new ambience—a new environment—surrounding international relations.[14]

ACTORS

With the French Revolution that ultimately brought Napoleon Bonaparte to power, an age of **nationalism** began that was to carry over into the late twentieth century. The new nationalism was based on a firmer relationship between the central government of the state and the people over which it presided, particularly a greater emotional bond between the two created by the greater involvement of the masses in the political life of the country. It was the new nationalism that enabled Napoleon—posing as a man of the people while wearing emperor's clothing—to recruit a mass citizen army through nation-wide conscription of young Frenchmen and to mobilize the French *nation* in support of France's military activities abroad. French nationalism had the unintended effect of provoking nationalism in other states that felt threatened. In Britain and other societies, rulers found that once they appealed to a sense of nationalism, they had opened the door to democratic pressures, with the loyalty and support of the middle class and general populace likely to be solidified the more the government could project an image of being responsive to popular demands. If the rise of mass democracy meant that leaders might have to become more sensitive to public opinion in formulating foreign policy, it also meant that they potentially could count on the total military and economic capabilities that their societies had to offer in international politics. Although full-scale democratic institutions developed only gradually and unevenly in Europe and elsewhere during the transitional era, rulers could increasingly claim to be acting on behalf of a mass, nationalistic following in a way that their predecessors in the classical period could not.[15]

Nationalistic impulses led to the appearance of new states on the map. Some gained their independence from colonial masters (e.g., the Latin American states in the early nineteenth century revolting against Spain), and others emerged through the political unification of culturally similar groups that had previously been only loosely affiliated (e.g., the confederations of German-speaking and Italian-speaking peoples forming the modern states of Germany and Italy in the mid-nineteenth century). Although nationalistic impulses led to the liberation of some peoples, such as the independence of the Romanians from Turkish rule in 1878, the same impulses touched off a new wave of European imperialism that resulted in the subjugation of other peoples in Africa and elsewhere. Pressures for national "self-determination" grew stronger, especially after World War I when Poland and Hungary became independent along with several other states. Although a considerable increase in the number of independent national actors occurred during the transitional era, with more than fifty nation-states existing in the world by 1945, this was only the prelude to a much more explosive proliferation of nation-states that was to take place in the subsequent era, particularly in Africa and Asia. (See Fig. 2.1 for historical trends in the growth of nation-states, which shows the pivotal character of the transitional era.)

Aside from the proliferation of nation-states, the transitional era also witnessed the proliferation of other kinds of actors as well, notably *individual human beings*. It was during this time, in 1830, that world population reached 1 billion, with the second billion coming only 100 years later in 1930. Through most of this period the world population boom was caused primarily by lower death rates in Europe and North America, which was the result of major medical and health care advances that accompanied industrialization in the northern part of the globe. However, just as the proliferation of nation-states was to be even more explosive in the post–World War II period and was to be concentrated in the southern part of the globe, so also was humanity to multiply in even greater numbers after World War II—reaching the 4 billion mark by 1975 and 5 billion a decade later—largely as a result of the transfer of medical technology to the peoples of Africa, Asia, and Latin America. (See Fig. 2.2 for world population trends, which also shows the pivotal character of the transitional era.)

POWER AND WEALTH

The increased industrialization that occurred in Europe and America in the nineteenth and early twentieth centuries contributed to a growing disparity in wealth between societies in the Northern Hemisphere and those in the Southern Hemisphere. Although a "rich-poor gap" had historically always existed *within* societies, the gap that started to form *between* them during the transitional era was virtually unprecedented. In the past, the masses in one national society were roughly as well off as their counterparts in any other society. The Industrial Revolution was to spread far from Europe but it bypassed the southern half of the globe, thus leaving some societies with rapid income growth and markedly improved living standards for their rich and poor citizens alike, while other societies were practically untouched. The widening rich-poor gap, which had produced a 2:1 ratio between incomes in industrial and nonindus-

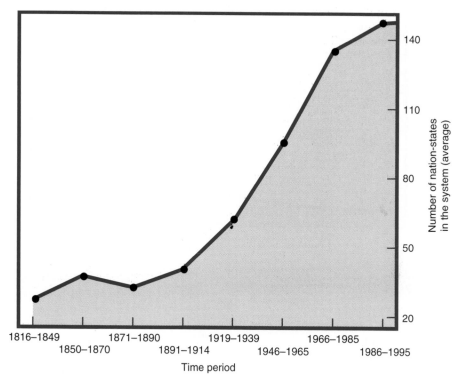

Figure 2.1

THE GROWTH OF NATION-STATES IN THE INTERNATIONAL SYSTEM
The numbers represent "average system size" for a given period. For the periods
from 1816 to 1919, "nation-states" were defined as territorial units having at least
500,000 population and recognized as states by England and France; for the periods
from 1919 to the present, they were defined as territorial units having at least
500,000 population and recognized by any two major powers or holding membership in the League of Nations or United Nations. Because of the 500,000 population
threshold, roughly thirty "ministates" are not counted in the 1986–1995 period.
Based on data from J. David Singer et al., *Explaining War* (Beverly Hills, Calif.: Sage,
1979), p. 65; and Arthur S. Banks, *Political Handbook of the World 1992* (Binghamton, N.Y.: CSA Publications, 1992).

trial societies by 1850, was to become even more accentuated in the
post–World War II system, by the end of which some societies had a per capita
income exceeding that of other societies by a factor of almost 500 to 1.[16]
Industrialization not only skewed the distribution of wealth in favor of certain states but it also further skewed the distribution of power in their favor,
because the new economic technology was readily convertible into military
advantage. As in the classical system, power throughout the transitional era

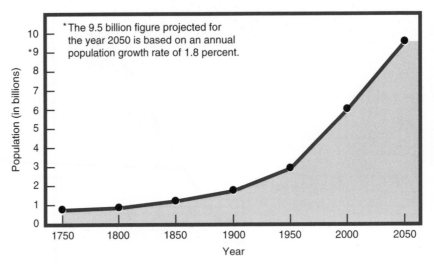

Figure 2.2
THE GROWTH OF WORLD POPULATION

was distributed fairly evenly among several states that dominated the rest of the system, although Great Britain was considered the "first among equals" during the nineteenth century and the identity of the other "great powers" changed in some cases between the two centuries. (See Table 2.1 for a listing of "great powers" from the classical system to the post–World War II system.)[17]

In particular, the transitional era witnessed the emergence of two highly industrialized non-European states as major world powers by the beginning of the twentieth century—the United States (with the defeat of Spain in 1898) and Japan (with the defeat of Russia in 1905). Russia, itself a semi-European state (straddling Eurasia) and a semipowerful member of the international system throughout the nineteenth century, was to take on special significance as a world actor after the Bolshevik Revolution of 1917 created the Soviet Union. Indeed, it was the gradual passing of European domination of the state system that was perhaps the most salient feature of the transitional era. At the turn of the century, European powers controlled over 80 percent of all territory on the globe. As historian Geoffrey Barraclough observed, the year 1900 represented both the peak of the European-centered world and the beginning of its decline: "[While] by 1900 European civilization overshadowed the Earth," the period between 1900 and 1945 was "a period of utmost confusion in which a new system was struggling to be born and the old system fighting hard for its life."[18] By the end of the transitional era, not only had Britain and the continental European states been eclipsed by the United States and the Soviet Union,[19] but other non-European power centers such as China were already looming on the horizon as well.

Table 2.1

GREAT POWERS IN THE INTERNATIONAL SYSTEM, 1700–1945

	1700	*1800*	*1875*	*1910*	*1935*	*1945*
Turkey	X					
Sweden	X					
Netherlands	X					
Spain	X					
Austria (Austria-Hungary)	X	X	X	X		
France	X	X	X	X	X	
England (Great Britain)	X	X	X	X	X	
Prussia (Germany)		X	X	X	X	
Russia (Soviet Union)		X	X	X	X	X
Italy			X	X	X	
Japan				X	X	
United States				X	X	X

The last column relates to the post–World War II period.
Source: Kenneth Waltz, *Theory of International Politics,* Table 8.1. © 1979, Addison-Wesley, Reading, Mass. Reprinted by permission of The McGraw-Hill Companies. Adapted with permission, from Quincy Wright, *The Study of War,* Appendix 20, Table 43, 1965, University of Chicago Press.

DEGREE OF POLARIZATION

In addition to bringing non-European powers to the fore in world politics, the transitional era injected **ideological** conflict—the competition between rival political philosophies—into international relations for the first time and portended the extreme polarization that was to occur in the post–World War II period. It was in the mid-nineteenth century that Karl Marx wrote his treatises urging the working classes of the world to unite under the banner of **communism** against their "bourgeois" rulers. Although Marx envisioned ultimately a single classless and stateless world society, history ran counter to his predictions. Combined with the forces of nationalism, the forces of ideology created some further hardening of relations among states. At the beginning of the transitional era, the international system was polarized between Napoleon's armies seeking to export the French Revolution across Europe and the armies of the conservative European monarchs seeking to stem the revolutionary tide. Toward the end of the era, the United States under Woodrow Wilson and the Soviet Union under Lenin exchanged diatribes on the relative merits of democratic capitalism as opposed to communism, followed by Benito Mussolini in Italy and Adolf Hitler in Germany lecturing both Wilson's and Lenin's successors about the supremacy of **fascism** and **national socialism.**

Throughout most of the transitional era, however, alignments in the international system were still fairly flexible, as neither newly developed national rivalries nor ideological differences prevented states from keeping their options open as to prospective alliance partners. In other words, the system was still multipolar in terms of both power and alignment. Although ideological conflict occurred within countries between liberal democratic and conservative monarchical forces, it was not fought out on the international plane. The battle lines in the few wars that were waged in the period were not drawn clearly along ideological lines (e.g., the democracies of Britain, France, and the United States joining arch-conservative Russia against other conservative countries such as Germany and Austria in World War I). Indeed, the jockeying for position by the European states on the eve of World War I in 1914 resembled the balance of power machinations engaged in by European monarchs in the classical system, except that the advent of mass democracy and modern military technology had partially lessened decision-making flexibility in the transitional era.[20]

OBJECTIVES AND MEANS

The 100 years between the Congress of Vienna, which ended the Napoleonic Wars in 1815, and the beginning of World War I in 1914 have been recorded as a period of relative peace in international relations, with several minor but no major wars occurring in the interval. Although the nationalistic fervor of the time threatened to unleash violent conflict, the major powers were usually able to avoid direct military confrontation partly by sublimating chauvinistic energies through a collective carving up of territory in Africa and elsewhere. **Imperialism** was a response to a dual need to pacify a restless public at home and to ensure access to raw materials and markets associated with growing industrialization in the late nineteenth century. The objectives of the major powers—consisting primarily of territorial land-grabbing—were not unlike those pursued in the classical era, although more highly expansionist and defined more in terms of the greater glory and well-being of the nation rather than of any individual ruler. Imperialist objectives could be accommodated without major conflict as long as there was enough colonial territory to go around, a condition that had evaporated by 1914.

Not only had available territory disappeared by 1914, but so also had the memory of the horrors of the Napoleonic Wars, during which the involvement of the entire French nation in the war effort had resulted in the death of massive numbers of French citizens. New generations were more impressed by the swift and painless fruits of victory won by the Prussians in their seven-week war with Austria in 1866. However, the "century of peace" between 1815 and 1914—including the "cheap" Prussian victory achieved through the innovative use of the railroad, telegraph, and breechloading rifle—disguised the growing and more deadly military arsenals that were increasingly available to states as potential means for pursuing foreign policy.[21] The mobilization of mass armies combined with the application of science and technology to warfare ultimately produced an unparalleled world war, which was to end formally in 1918—four autumns after the German Kaiser had promised that his troops would be back home "before the leaves fall."[22]

The *total* war that World War I became—fought with poison gas, machine guns, submarines, and biplanes in addition to rifles and bayonets—was to pale in comparison with World War II, less than a generation later. It lasted six autumns, from 1939 until 1945.[23] Although the horror of World War I had failed to leave a lasting imprint on the minds of the leaders of the day, the globe-encircling weapons of World War II were to leave a somewhat more indelible impression. A historical era that began with the new importance of the mass foot soldier was giving way to the atomic age. (See Fig. 2.3 for trends in the range and destructiveness of weaponry.)[24]

DEGREE OF INTERDEPENDENCE

While the transitional era saw the arrival of total war, it also saw the arrival of increasing interdependence among states, particularly in the economic sphere—a development that was to be interrupted by the two world wars but was to be resumed in the post–World War II era. The emergence of total war alongside economic interdependence seemed a paradoxical phenomenon at first, but the two proved they could exist together in the same system. Although trade interdependence among European states had become so great by the end of the nineteenth century that many observers at the time assumed war between them unthinkable lest it totally disrupt their economies, World War I demonstrated that political impulses could be stronger than economic imperatives. In the interwar interval between 1919 and 1939, the very economic interdependence of the industrialized states made the Great Depression a global one, adding to the tensions that resulted in World War II.

The point here is that interdependence is not something that appeared just yesterday. It was rather a process already well underway at the turn of this century and was already having uncertain implications for world order. As Kenneth Waltz has argued, in some respects economic interdependence was greater before World War I (particularly if one uses "exports plus imports as a percentage of gross national product" as an indicator of interdependence and if one focuses on the extent of economic ties among the major powers).[25] Some analysts even called the late nineteenth and early twentieth centuries "the *belle époque* [beautiful epoch] of interdependence,"[26] whereas others at the time recognized interdependence as a mixed blessing, observing that "the world is, more than ever before, one great unit in which everything interacts and affects everything else, but in which also everything collides and clashes."[27] (See the Sidelight on pp. 62–63, which suggests some parallels that can be found between the current "globalization" of the international economy and transnational economic activity in the nineteenth century.)

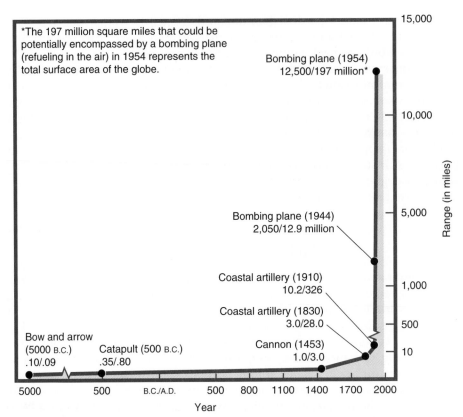

*The 197 million square miles that could be potentially encompassed by a bombing plane (refueling in the air) in 1954 represents the total surface area of the globe.

Bombing plane (1954)
12,500/197 million*

Bombing plane (1944)
2,050/12.9 million

Coastal artillery (1910)
10.2/326

Coastal artillery (1830)
3.0/28.0

Cannon (1453)
1.0/3.0

Bow and arrow
(5000 B.C.)
.10/.09

Catapult (500 B.C.)
.35/.80

Range (in miles)

15,000

10,000

5,000

1,000

500

10

5000   500   B.C./A.D.   500 800 1100 1400 1700 2000

Year

Figure 2.3
TRENDS IN RANGE AND DESTRUCTIVENESS OF WEAPONS DELIVERY VEHICLES
The first number indicated beneath each weapon on the graph represents its maximum range in miles; the second number represents the "killing area" (in square miles)—the maximum area within which lives and property may be destroyed by such projectiles. Based on data from Harold and Margaret Sprout, *Toward a Politics of the Planet Earth* (New York: Van Nostrand, 1971), p. 403.

Although international interdependence was growing in the nineteenth century, it is misleading to suggest that the phenomenon peaked in the years preceding World War I and went downhill thereafter. Quite to the contrary, in many ways it was only the tip of the iceberg. For one thing, although it is true that in most countries foreign trade as a percentage of gross national product (GNP) was to decline from record pre–World War I levels, the *total volume* of world trade in absolute terms was to expand enormously in the twentieth century, increasing from $15.6 billion in 1880 to over $3 trillion by 1990.[28] In addition, regarding many other dimensions of "interconnectedness," such as flows of people and communications across national boundaries, one likewise finds that the trends begun in the transitional era did not peak in that period but instead foreshadowed even greater interdependence that was to follow after World War II.[29] As for other, more fundamental aspects of interdependence—such as "mutual sensitivity and vulnerability" regarding military-strategic and ecological concerns—the conclusion appears even more inescapable that the transitional era marked the historic but only bare beginning of a truly interdependent world.

THE RISE OF NONSTATE ACTORS: INTERNATIONAL ORGANIZATIONS

Finally, one other phenomenon, closely related to interdependence, developed significantly during the transitional era and was to become an even more important feature of the international system after World War II. This was the growth of **international organizations** as nonstate actors in world politics. In particular, *intergovernmental organizations* (IGOs) appeared on the scene, ranging from the modest creation of the Central Commission for the Navigation of the Rhine in 1815 to the Universal Postal Union and International Telegraph Union in the mid-nineteenth century to the League of Nations and ultimately the United Nations in the twentieth century. A variety of such organizations were to be established on both a regional and global basis by member *governments* in response to problems that transcended national boundaries and seemed to call for institutional responses.

In addition, there was the growth of another type of nonstate actor, *nongovernmental organizations* (NGOs), formed among *private* groups of individuals sharing specialized interests across national borders, also on both a regional and global basis. Although a few such organizations had existed from the beginnings of the nation-state system (e.g., the Rosicrucian Order in the seventeenth century), they were to proliferate in the transitional era (e.g., the International Red Cross and the Salvation Army in the 1860s) and—as with IGOs—increase even more dramatically after World War II. A special subcategory of NGO, the *multinational corporation* (MNC) was to become especially significant as an actor in world affairs.[30] (See Figs. 2.4 and 2.5 for trends in the growth of IGOs and NGOs.)[31] The IGO and NGO phenomena were interrelated. For example, in the economic sphere, just as the birth of the nation-state was partly a response to the failure of the feudal mode of organization to accommodate growing intertown economic activity spawned by a new entrepreneurial class, IGOs developed partly in response to the limited capacity of nation-states to accommodate growing interstate commerce dominated by ever-expanding commercial enterprises that were outgrowing national borders; national governments and economic elites alike viewed IGOs as hopefully facilitating uniform rules and orderly economic relations in an emergent world capitalist economy. Thus, just as total war existed alongside interdependence, the age of nationalism was accompanied by the rise of "transnationalism" as nonstate actors were becoming more organized across national boundaries.

SIDELIGHT

ECONOMIC INTERDEPENDENCE: A HISTORY LESSON

The article below, comparing the world economy of the nineteenth century with the world economy today, should clear up any illusions one might have that economic interdependence is a wholly new phenomenon. Although the author might be accused of understating the accelerated pace and complexity of transnational economic processes in the contemporary international system, his analysis nonetheless provides a useful historical perspective in understanding the roots of the modern global economy.

The laying of the first trans-Atlantic telegraph cable in 1866 did not just allow people to send last-minute birthday greetings or pleas for cash. The cable let them move money from New York to London and back in a few minutes rather than waiting for steamships to make the 12-day crossing.

More than a century later, communications are only slightly faster but governments are still struggling to cope with the problems that have accompanied the high-speed international financial deals that the cable made possible. These deals have [recently] swamped the dollar, sunk the Mexican peso, wrecked a 232-year-old British bank and pushed the [U.S.] Administration to propose lifting Depression-era American banking regulations.

The swift transactions permitted by the undersea cable helped generate a surge of worldwide financial and economic ties that peaked on the eve of World War I. Two world wars, the Great Depression and the massive confiscation of foreign investments that accompanied the rise of Communism and the decline of colonialism all combined to reverse the trend for several decades. But during the 1970s, most controls on the movement of money across national borders were phased out. Capitalism is once again tying more and more countries more and more tightly together.

"To a significant extent, the industrialized nations of the world only recently reattained the levels of economic integration that they had reached at the eve of World War I," said Alan S. Blinder, the vice-chairman of the Federal Reserve. . . .

Yet the financial ties of today are still only a pale shadow of the links that spanned the globe at the start of this century. The billions of dollars that now slosh from country to country at the touch of a button are not as big—compared to the size of the economies involved—as the immense flow of money among countries before 1914.

To summarize, a metamorphosis in international relations occurred between 1789 and 1945. Out of the shadows of the transitional system, the outlines of contemporary international relations were coming more into view. Most notably, an international system that at the beginning of the era was es-

Massive Japanese investments in everything from air-conditioner factories in Malaysia to car assembly lines in Tennessee are overshadowed by the scale of British overseas investment a century ago. During the four decades preceding World War I, the British invested a quarter of their savings overseas, mainly in railroads and mines in their colonies and in the United States. By contrast, Japanese companies created fears here that they were "buying America," when they invested 10 percent of their savings outside Japan during the 1980s. Japan's foreign investment has slowed since then. . . .

Two weeks ago Barings P.L.C., the 232-year-old British investment bank, failed because of poor bets in Singapore on the direction of the Japanese stock market. Yet in 1890 the Bank of England had to rescue Barings after a wrong bet on the prices of bonds in Argentina. And Singapore is 152 miles closer to London than Argentina is.

The remarkably steep decline of Mexico's currency and economy in the last several months, after foreign investors pulled out their money in response to its chronic trade deficits and political instability, has parallels in the 1870s. Then, it was the United States that depended on foreign investment money. . . . The collapse of the biggest American investment bank, J. Cooke & Company, in 1873 stopped British bankers from investing in this country. Railroad construction, which had employed a tenth of the American non-farm work force, almost ground to a halt during the six-year recession that followed.

To be sure, computerization accelerated international financial dealings somewhat since the days of telegraph cables. And when markets move especially swiftly, governments find it hard to respond.

A broader question is whether close economic and financial ties make countries less likely to fight wars. Lawrence Summers, the [U.S.] Under Secretary of the Treasury for International Affairs, contends . . . "I think you will find that successful economic growth and economic integration is the best way mankind has yet found to produce stability." While many political scientists and economists agree, the argument is familiar. A British author, Sir Norman Angell, wrote early in this century that the economies of Europe's great powers had become so interdependent that war was impossible. His book appeared in 1910, four years before World War I broke out.

sentially a European state system had gradually expanded to become a European-centered world by the late nineteenth century and a global system no longer anchored to Europe by the end of the era.[32] It was still a "lopsided" world,[33] in the sense that three-fourths of the sovereign states were located in

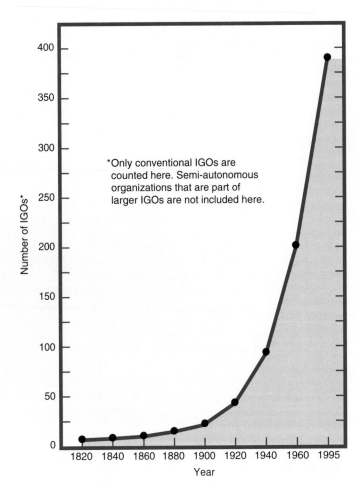

*Only conventional IGOs are
counted here. Semi-autonomous
organizations that are part of
larger IGOs are not included here.

Figure 2.4
**TRENDS IN THE GROWTH OF INTERGOVERNMENTAL ORGANIZATIONS (IGOS) IN
THE INTERNATIONAL SYSTEM**
Based on data from Michael Wallace and J. David Singer, "Intergovernmental Orga-
nization in the Global System, 1815–1964," *International Organization,* 24 (Spring
1970), p. 277; and Union of International Associations, *Yearbook of International
Organizations, 1995* (Brussels: UIA, 1995).

Europe or the Western Hemisphere. Moreover, patterns of interdependence
and international organization membership were very uneven, with the rich
industrialized states being far more enmeshed in these processes than the poor
less-developed states. As we will see, the uneven nature of such phenomena
was to continue after World War II, as the roots of the current "global condition" were becoming ever more noticeable.

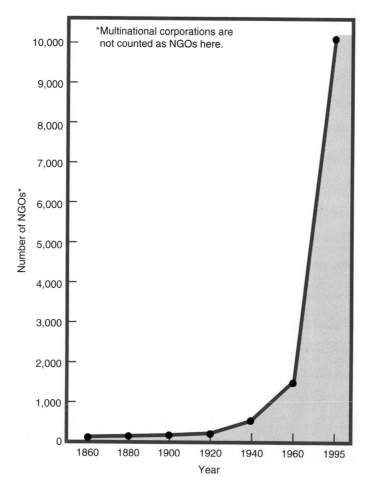

*Multinational corporations are not counted as NGOs here.

Figure 2.5
TRENDS IN THE GROWTH OF NONGOVERNMENTAL ORGANIZATIONS (NGOS) IN THE INTERNATIONAL SYSTEM
Based on data from Werner J. Feld, *Nongovernmental Forces in World Politics* (New York: Praeger, 1972); and Union of International Associations, *Yearbook of International Organizations, 1995* (Brussels: UIA, 1995).

The Post–World War II International System (1945–1989)

There is almost total agreement among scholars that the two atomic bombs that were dropped by the United States on Hiroshima and Nagasaki in 1945 marked the beginning of a new era of international politics that, though foreshadowed by the previous era, was distinctive in many ways. There is also general agreement that the international system born out of the cauldron of World War II saw some of its most salient features begin to break down by the 1970s, eventually leading by the late 1980s to the transformation of the postwar system itself into yet another, newer structure, which can be said to exist in the contemporary period. In our discussion of the postwar system, we will not treat actors, power and wealth, and other variables as separate subtopics but will examine more general developments during this era.

DISTINCTIVE FEATURES OF THE POSTWAR SYSTEM: SUPERPOWERS AND BIPOLARITY

The arrival of the atomic age and weapons of mass destruction in 1945 was an occurrence that from the start had profound consequences for world politics.[34] Initially, it fostered two related developments that were virtually unprecedented in international politics and that, more than anything else, distinguished the post–World War II system from previous international systems. One of these developments was the emergence of only two states as the dominant powers in the international system—the United States and the Soviet Union. The two were labeled "superpowers" to distinguish them from the second tier of powers (including Britain and France, which had experienced economic devastation in World War II, Germany and Japan, which had experienced military defeat, and China, which had yet to industrialize) and the bottom tier of states. What particularly separated the United States and the Soviet Union from all the rest were the enormous nuclear arsenals the two states built after World War II, although the Soviet Union was not to achieve full nuclear parity with the United States until the 1970s.[35] Of the two giants, the United States was "first among equals," accounting in 1950 for 50 percent of the world's military spending and financial reserves as well as two-thirds of the world's industrial production, giving it virtual hegemony in the economic sphere.[36]

The second related development was the emergence of a highly polarized system in terms of alignment configurations, i.e., the appearance of the **East-West conflict** and "Cold War" waged between two cohesive blocs organized around competing ideologies and led by the two superpowers. One bloc, the so-called "First World" (or the "West"), consisted of the United States along with the economically developed capitalist democracies of Western Europe, Japan, Canada, Australia, and New Zealand. The other bloc, the "Second World" (or the "East"), consisted of the Soviet Union along with the relatively developed communist states of Eastern Europe as well as Communist China. Accusing each other of seeking global dominance, the Americans and Soviets organized the two blocs into opposing alliances, with the members within each bloc becoming closely linked not only militarily but also economically.

Dependent on the United States and the Soviet Union for both military and economic support, the members of the respective coalitions adhered rigidly to the policies established by the bloc leaders, at least initially. The other states in the system tended, also, to gravitate toward the two "poles." This system was labeled **bipolar,** to refer to both the power and the alignment structures.

FISSURES IN THE POSTWAR SYSTEM

In the early postwar period, there were few parts of the globe that were not tied to one or the other bloc. Much of Asia and Africa remained Western-controlled colonial possessions in the first decade after World War II, whereas the Latin American countries became part of the U.S. alliance network and the Soviets brought a few other states outside Europe into their orbit. Hence, only a handful of states, notably Yugoslavia, India, and Egypt, occupied the middle ground between Eastern and Western camps in the late forties and early fifties. However, as the postwar era progressed, "bipolarity" gave way to "tripolarity" in terms of alignment patterns if not in actual power distribution, with the middle ground becoming more crowded by the proliferation of newly independent nation-states in Africa and Asia, many of which tended to adopt a "nonaligned" stance in the East-West conflict. Strictly speaking, these countries did not constitute a third "pole" or rival "bloc" in the system—no alliance was formed among them—but they did represent a third element to be reckoned with in world politics. The so-called **Third World,** consisting of less developed countries found mostly in the Southern Hemisphere, was not to become a major force in world politics until later; but it had already started materializing as a distinct entity when twenty-nine Afro-Asian nations met in Bandung, Indonesia, in April 1955 to call for an end to all colonialism.[37]

The "decolonialization" process itself, which introduced unparalleled cultural diversity into the international system, was a major development in the postwar era. Between 1945 and 1975, the number of nation-state actors more than doubled from roughly 60 to more than 130. Whereas in 1945, almost a quarter of the world's people and its land area remained under colonial rule, by 1975 less than 1 percent of the world's population and territory were still without self-government. In the span of a single generation, some 1 billion people and eighty nations achieved independence—a dramatic revolution in human affairs.

Although both the United States and the Soviet Union sought to recruit the new nations into their respective blocs, their efforts were only mildly successful, not only because the two giants tended to neutralize each other in many areas but also because the new third world nationalism placed limits on what even superpowers could do to cajole or coerce midsized or tiny states into line. In particular, because of the widespread aversion to foreign rule, the two superpowers—more than "great powers" in the past—were inhibited from expanding their influence in the world through direct territorial annexation or occupation.[38] Instead of acquiring territory, the object of superpower competition was to gain *influence* over the foreign policies of individual third world states. The time-honored balance of power "game" continued to be played but in a somewhat different manner than in the past. If the world map had previously resembled a gigantic Monopoly board on which the players competed for property, the map in the post–World War II era looked more like a chessboard on which two players attempted to manipulate a set of "pawns" for maximum advantage. Third world leaders increasingly learned to play off both superpowers against each other in this game.

LARGER CRACKS IN THE POSTWAR SYSTEM

The development of an independent, "nonaligned" third world movement in the late fifties and sixties was symptomatic of a larger phenomenon that was becoming apparent yet not fully appreciated at the time—namely, the growing fragmentation of both the power structure and the alliance structure of the postwar international system. The very factor that had fostered a world of dual superpowers and bipolarity at the outset of the postwar era—the advent of nuclear weaponry—was, along with other factors, increasingly contributing to a diffusion of power and alliance disintegration as the postwar system wore on.

Regarding the disintegrative tendencies within the Western and Eastern blocs, what were initially minor disagreements eventually became major ones. On the Western side, for example, the Suez crisis of 1956 saw the United States essentially siding with the Soviet Union against America's own allies, admonishing the British and French for their military aggression against Egypt and pressing for their withdrawal from Egyptian territory. The "Atlantic alliance" survived, but the incident left its members with strained feelings and lingering suspicions about the worth of American alliance commitments.[39] Almost at the same moment, on the Eastern side, the Hungarian Revolution occurred and threatened to remove Hungary from the Soviet orbit; although revolt was frustrated and Hungary was forced back into the Soviet sphere, the episode left a legacy of doubts among members of the "communist commonwealth" regarding the true nature of Soviet fraternal feelings toward them.[40] Finally, also in 1956, the Soviet leadership—mindful of the mutual devastation that could be caused by the escalation of conflict into nuclear war between the United States and Soviet Union—called for "peaceful coexistence" between the two superpowers.

By the 1960s, some observers already were prophesying "the end of alliance," due to the uncertainty of superpower defense guarantees in an age of intercontinental ballistic missiles and the difficulty of maintaining bloc cohesion in the face of what seemed to be lessening tensions and security threats accompanying a partial "thaw" in the Cold War.[41] The Europeans, in particular, were growing less concerned about military aggression and, also, less confident of superpower assistance should such aggression somehow arise. The result was a gradual loosening of unity within both blocs, with the French under Charles de Gaulle becoming the main mavericks in the Western bloc and the Rumanians under Nicolae Ceausescu, along with the Chinese under Mao Tse-tung, becoming the chief mavericks in the Eastern bloc. Just as de Gaulle was proclaiming that "France has no permanent friends, only permanent interests," Ceausescu and other Communist party leaders in Europe and elsewhere were urging "polycentrism" in place of a single party line emanating from Moscow.[42] Indeed, at times—for example, when Greece and Turkey, two members of the Western alliance, went to war over Cyprus in the late sixties and early seventies—there appeared to be more fighting going on *within* the blocs than between them.

The fragmentation of the alliance structure in the postwar system tended to coincide with the fragmentation of the power structure. Not only had the "nuclear club" expanded to five members by the early 1970s,[43] but more importantly, nuclear arsenals that were once thought to confer superpower status were increasingly proving to be unusable and of questionable relevance to the day-to-day exercise of power in international relations. If anything, the existence of nuclear weapons and the fear of escalation seemed to make military giants such as the United States and the Soviet Union more gun-shy and less inclined to risk confronting each other directly in a crisis than had traditionally been the case with "great powers." The "superpower" label itself was becoming something of a misnomer as the United States experienced humiliation at the hands of two small Asian countries—North Korea during the *Pueblo* incident of 1968[44] and Vietnam during the disastrous Indochina war that ended in 1972—while Soviet advisers were being rudely evicted from Egypt in 1972.[45]

Insofar as the United States and the Soviet Union remained powerful actors, it was their economic clout—the ability to provide foreign aid and trade benefits to client states—as much as military prowess that gave them leverage in world politics, although economic influence, too, was beginning to erode as the American and Soviet economies were beset with increasing problems. The "gold and dollar standard," which since 1945 had been founded on American economic hegemony and the assurance that "the dollar was as good as gold," was allowed to lapse in 1971, to avoid a drain on U.S. gold supplies and to let the dollar "float" to more normal values based on the need to export competitively priced products. Other states, including economically revived West Germany and Japan and even some less developed countries, were at the same time learning how to use economic resources to their advantage in the international arena.

Perhaps nothing better illustrated the growing complexity and changing nature of the postwar system than the oil embargo episode of 1973. By the 1970s, the major industrialized countries had become heavily dependent on oil imports to meet not only their oil consumption needs but also their overall energy requirements. The **Organization of Petroleum Exporting Countries (OPEC)**—a group of thirteen less developed countries spanning four continents, accounting for over 85 percent of world oil exports—had been trying for some time to acquire greater direct control over their own oil resources from the multinational corporations (the "Seven Sisters," such as Exxon and Shell) and the governments of oil-consuming industrialized countries.[46] During the Yom Kippur War in 1973–1974 between Israel and three Arab states, an oil embargo was launched by Libya, Saudi Arabia, and other Arab members of OPEC aimed at pressuring the United States and its oil-thirsty Western allies to withdraw support from Israel. The cutoff of key energy supplies not only caused some Western states to rethink their Middle East foreign policy, producing discord in the Western camp, but also emboldened OPEC to quadruple the price of oil in what was an almost unprecedented exercise of power and act of defiance by a group of less developed countries. Although the Arabs derived more mileage out of a general atmosphere of panic and *perceived* economic deprivation in the West than out of any actual damage incurred—the West was able to find creative ways to limit the adverse effects of the embargo—there was little question that they had the capability to disrupt economies in the industrialized world if they chose to make full use of the oil "weapon," especially when backed by fellow OPEC members. At the very least, the petroleum price increases sent a shock wave through the world (the industrialized and nonindustrialized parts alike). OPEC's power was to wax and wane after the early 1970s, as the organization experienced difficulty in maintaining unity of action among its members and coordinating production and pricing policies with non-OPEC producers.[47]

THE COLLAPSE OF THE POSTWAR SYSTEM

By the late 1970s, the "superpower" status of the United States and the Soviet Union had become further tarnished and thrown into question, especially by two debacles in 1979. The Soviets experienced their own "Vietnam" when they sent 100,000 troops into Afghanistan that year to support a client Marxist regime against Muslim rebels seeking to replace the latter with an Islamic republic; the undermanned rebel *fedayeen* guerrilla fighters, aided by arms from the West, were able to defeat the Soviet military machine and, in the process, contributed heavily to domestic political unrest in the Soviet Union that was eventually to lead to the toppling of the Soviet regime itself. Meanwhile, in 1979, the United States experienced its own frustrations in the exercise of power when fifty-two American embassy personnel in Tehran were held as hostages by the newly installed militant Islamic government of Iran, which attempted to coerce Washington into meeting several demands, including surrendering the Western-backed deposed Shah, who had fled the country;

although the Shah was never returned to Iran, the United States suffered through humiliation for over a year, including an abortive rescue mission, before the episode finally ended with the release of the hostages. Both episodes confirmed the changing power calculus in international relations—particularly, the seeming inadequacy of traditional military power in many situations—and also demonstrated the resistance of non-Western cultures to the westernization (modernization) of the world.

The 1970s and 1980s also saw a more complicated picture evolve in terms of the distribution of wealth. One of the immediate side effects of the OPEC price decisions in 1973 was the further widening of the rich-poor gap among countries. Although the gap in the seventies was closed somewhat between the rich developed states and a few less developed states (a handful of OPEC members), it became even more accentuated between the developed states and many other less developed ones (the poorest ones that could least afford to absorb the oil price shocks). The result was the creation of a **Fourth World** of countries pejoratively referred to as international "basket cases." During the 1980s, conditions in these latter countries generally worsened as their population growth in most cases outpaced economic growth; in the words of the World Bank, conditions "turned from bad to worse," with per capita incomes falling and the poor getting poorer relative not only to the rich but also to their previous experience.[48] Even the OPEC states saw the gap between themselves and the rich developed states widening again as declining oil revenues in the 1980s translated into negative economic growth. However, there were at least a few striking success stories in the developing world, notably an expanding group of so-called newly industrializing countries (**NICs**), predominantly in East Asia, experiencing rapid economic growth.

The whole concept of a bipolar world, as understood by policymakers and scholars after World War II, had assumed not only the existence of two superpowers but also that East-West issues were *the* all-consuming issues in international politics. At the very least, the oil embargo episode and other subsequent events showed how other sets of issues could vie for attention and how fluid and complicated alignments could be on such issues.[49] Some started labeling the international system **bimultipolar** as a way of characterizing the growing complexity of alignment patterns along with power configurations.[50] For most countries in the world—those situated near or beneath the equator— the **North-South** confrontation, pitting the rich against the poor, came to take on greater importance in the postwar system than the East-West axis of conflict. Throughout the 1970s the "Group of 77" less developed states made strident demands for a "New International Economic Order," using their large majority in the United Nations General Assembly to push through a "Charter on the Economic Rights and Duties of States" and other measures designed to give themselves more economic and political clout.[51] As we just noted, they did not succeed very well in redistributing wealth and narrowing disparities. Although a depressed world economy put calls for a New International Eco-

SIDELIGHT

THE END OF THE COLD WAR

There tends to be a strong element of inertia and resistance to change in human affairs, including international affairs. However, as we have seen, change does occur, often at a glacial pace but at times quite rapidly and unexpectedly—as in the case of the whirlwind events in Eastern Europe during the late 1980s. Describing the movement of the Soviet Union's Eastern European satellites away from strict Marxis-Leninist doctrine and out of the Soviet orbit in the 1980s, the *Los Angeles Times* noted, "it took ten years for the revolution to occur in Poland, ten months in Hungary, ten weeks in Czechoslovakia, ten days in East Germany, and ten hours in Rumania."

Although this was an exaggerated, flippant depiction of the pace of change—pressures in fact had been building for some time throughout Eastern Europe—few if any observers were prepared for the suddenness with which events unfolded in 1989, sweeping across national boundaries in an almost "epidemic" fashion. A few key moments of 1989 are worth noting as a way of illustrating the nature of the changes in Eastern Europe and, in a larger sense, the rate of change possible in world affairs:

■ *June 5, Warsaw:*
Solidarity, the once banned independent trade union that had been granted legal status in April, ousts the Communists from power in Poland in the first freely contested election in the East bloc in over 40 years.

■ *September 20, Budapest:*
After paying belated tribute a few months earlier to former reformist prime minister Imre Nagy—slain in the abortive Hungarian Revolution of 1956—Hungary opens its borders to the West, allowing thousands of vacationing East Germans to cross into West Germany to seek asylum.

■ *October 7, Budapest:*
The Hungarian Communist Party repudiates Marxism, manifested by the order to remove the Red Star from all government buildings.

■ *November 9, East Berlin:*
After the resignation of the long-time Communist leadership, a caretaker East German government authorizes the gates to West Berlin to be opened and demolition to begin on the Berlin Wall that had been constructed in

nomic Order on hold in the 1980s, the North-South conflict continued to fester and remained a major source of international tensions. Increasingly, a new agenda of other issues was competing for attention—such as ecology, population, trade, and women's rights—which did not have clear East-West or North-South dimensions to them. An interesting phenomenon that became com-

1961 to prevent access to the West. East and West Berliners come together in a massive celebration.

- *November 10, Sofia:*
Communist leader Todor Zhivkov, in power in Bulgaria since 1954, resigns.

- *November 24, Prague:*
Half a million people rally in Wenceslas Square and hear Alexander Dubcek, the liberal reformer who had led the unsuccessful "Prague Spring" movement in 1968, call for an end to Communist rule in Czechoslovakia. Later that day the Jakes regime surrenders power, paving the way for a new constitution to be written.

- *December 25, Bucharest:*
Communist dictator Nicolae Ceausescu is executed as a violent revolution ends his twenty-four-year rule.

IN NOVEMBER 1989, MEMBERS OF THE SOVIET RED ARMY CHORUS MEET WITH PRESIDENT BUSH AT THE WHITE HOUSE.

monplace over time was the United Nations' sponsoring of global conferences on these various concerns, meetings that not only involved official governmental representatives of nation-states (whose numbers had increased to over 150 by the 1980s) but also permitted participation by the representatives of many NGOs (whose numbers had exceeded 10,000 by the 1980s).

**IN MAY 1990, MARCHERS PROTESTING COMMUNIST RULE
PASS THROUGH MOSCOW'S RED SQUARE DURING THE
ANNUAL MAY DAY CELEBRATION, HURLING INSULTS AT THE
ONLOOKING SOVIET LEADERSHIP.**

The East-West axis of conflict itself remained an important element of world politics in the 1980s. However, despite increased hostility between the United States and the Soviet Union in the first half of the decade, the battle lines between the Western and Eastern blocs were becoming less clear-cut and more tangled; this was reflected in America's Western European allies rejecting Washington's pleas to limit their growing energy imports from the Soviet Union and choosing instead to collaborate with Moscow by providing relatively cheap loans and advanced technology to build a natural gas pipeline connecting the rich fields of Siberia with the heart of Western Europe. West-West disputes (over trade and other issues) threatened to overshadow East-West conflict. By 1989, the muting of ideological differences and the disintegration of the rival alliance systems had progressed to the point where the Eastern European states had vacated the Soviet orbit and were considering applying for entry into the European Community, and the Soviet Union itself was proclaiming its desire to be part of "a common European house," leaving one alliance—the Warsaw Pact—moribund and its Western counterpart—the North Atlantic Treaty Organization—in search of a new rationale and mission. (The fall of the Berlin Wall and the related events we described at the very outset of this book, marking the end of the Cold War, are examined in greater detail in the Sidelight on pages 72–73.) The post–World War II era had come to a close.

Conclusion

We have seen how the international system has undergone some profound changes over the centuries, but also how there have been some basic continuities. Continuity and change mark world politics even today.

Citing the forces of democratization at work in Eastern Europe and elsewhere at the end of the Cold War, some observers found 1989 as revolutionary a year as when the French Revolution occurred 200 years earlier, and at least one commentator equated it with the Reformation in the 1500s:

> One thing is certain: we have never seen a year like 1989. Only the Reformation is remotely comparable to today's gale-force intellectual winds and loud cracking of institutional foundations. No year, even in the 16th century, ever swept so many people or such complex societies into a vortex of change. Nineteen eighty-nine has been the most startling, interesting, promising, and consequential year ever.[52]

Still others went so far as to proclaim "the end of history," the final triumph of western liberal-democratic, capitalist values in a global society.[53]

However, historians would have to wait many years before they would be able to put these events in true perspective and judge with any certainty their place in history. Rather than the "end of history," 1989 seemed instead to mark the beginning of the next chapter in history, one that might well usher in a new millennium in the form of a more peaceful and prosperous "new world order" or—on the other hand—might resemble a return to world politics as it looked before 1945 or perhaps a return to a pre-Westphalian "new feudalism,"[54] and might even be so disorderly as to cause us to "miss the Cold War."[55] The complex character of the post–Cold War order will be delineated in the next chapter as we move on to an examination of the *contemporary* international system.

SUMMARY

1. One can identify elements of both change and continuity in international relations over the years.

2. International relations as we know it today can trace its roots to the Peace of Westphalia in 1648, when in place of the walled cities of the feudal era there emerged

political units called nation-states that had central governments exercising sovereignty over a fixed territory and population.

3. International relations history since 1648 can be divided into four periods: (a) the classical system, (b) the transitional system, (c) the post–World War II system, and (d) the contemporary (post–Cold War) system. These systems differ in a number of ways, including the nature of the actors, the distribution of power and wealth, the degree of polarization, the objectives of the actors and the means available to them, and the degree of interdependence.

4. The classical international system (1648–1789) was characterized by a fairly even distribution of power and wealth among several European states ruled by monarchs who shared common values and understandings of the "rules of the game." These actors dominated the state system. Other features of the system included a high degree of alliance flexibility, limited objectives and means, and a relatively low level of interdependence.

5. The transitional international system (1789–1945) constituted a bridge between the classical and the post–World War II eras, in that it saw the beginning of (a) a world population boom; (b) a proliferation in the number of nation-states, brought on by increased nationalism; (c) a rich-poor gap between states, brought on by the Industrial Revolution that spread throughout the North but bypassed the South; (d) ideological conflict in international politics; (e) total war and weapons of mass destruction; (f) an economically and otherwise interdependent world; and (g) international organizations, both IGOs and NGOs, as nonstate actors in world politics.

6. Power continued to be distributed fairly evenly among several states in the transitional era, with Britain "first among equals." However, it was this era that saw the gradual passing of European dominance of the state system and the emergence of the United States, the Soviet Union, and Japan as world powers.

7. Despite ideological cleavages between states, there remained a high degree of alliance flexibility, and states of all types engaged in imperialism.

8. Imperialist objectives could be accommodated without major conflict as long as there was enough colonial territory to go around. This condition had evaporated by 1914, by which time the world powers had also acquired the military means to fight total wars.

9. The post–World War II international system (1945–1989) was called a bipolar system because, unlike the previous eras that featured multiple power centers and flexible alignments, this era was mostly characterized by two relatively rigid blocs of states organized around competing ideologies and led by two dominant "superpowers." The Western bloc, led by the United States and its nuclear arsenal, consisted of the developed capitalist democracies. The Eastern bloc, led by the Soviet Union and its nuclear arsenal, consisted of the developed communist states. Through much of this period, the United States was the "first among equals" and enjoyed virtual hegemony over the world economy.

10. Bipolarity loosened somewhat with the emergence of the third world, consisting of the less developed countries, which tended to adopt a nonaligned stance in the East-West conflict. The proliferation of newly independent third world countries in the 1950s and 1960s reflected the growing fragmentation of both the power structure and the alliance structure of the postwar international system.

11. By the 1970s, power had become still more diffuse, alliances less unified, interdependence ever more intricate and complicated. The postwar pattern of international relations was in flux, with a new and more complex environment emerging.

12. By the late 1980s, the latter trends had culminated in the end of the Cold War and the passage of the post–World War II era into the contemporary era of international relations.

SUGGESTIONS FOR FURTHER READING AND STUDY

For a general discussion on the utility of history in the study of international relations, see Raymond Aron, "Evidence and Inference in History," *Daedalus*, 87 (Fall 1958), pp. 11–39. Regarding the application of "systems" analysis to international relations, see Charles A. McClellan, "On the Fourth Wave: Past and Future in the Study of International Systems," in James N. Rosenau et al., eds., *The Analysis of International Politics* (New York: Free Press, 1972), pp. 15–37. As discussed in Note 6, many scholars have attempted to demarcate distinct international systems that have existed at various points in history; for example, Stanley Hoffmann, in "International Systems and International Law," *World Politics*, 14 (October 1961), pp. 205–237, identifies three international systems similar to those discussed in this chapter. Also, see Seyom Brown, *New Forces, Old Forces, and the Future of World Politics*, post–Cold War ed. (New York: Harper Collins, 1995), chs. 1–4.

The significance of the Peace of Westphalia is discussed in Leo Gross, "The Peace of Westphalia, 1648–1948," *American Journal of International Law*, 42 (January 1948), pp. 20–41. The beginnings of the Westphalian system are explained in Charles Tilly, "Reflections on the History of European State-Making," in Tilly, ed., *The Formation of National States in Western Europe* (Princeton, N.J.: Princeton University Press, 1975), pp. 3–83; Henrik Spruyt, "Institutional Selection in International Relations," *International Organization*, 48 (Autumn 1994), pp. 527–557; and Stephen Krasner, "Westphalia and All That," in Judith Goldstein and Robert Keohane, eds., *Ideas and Foreign Policy* (Ithaca, N.Y.: Cornell University Press, 1993), pp. 235–264.

There are a number of excellent narrative histories that provide detailed chronologies and analyses of events in various historical periods. For the classical period, see Leo Gershoy, *From Despotism to Revolution, 1763–1789* (New York: Macmillan, 1944). For the nineteenth and early twentieth centuries, see Edward V. Gulick, *Europe's Classical Balance of Power* (Ithaca, N.Y.: Cornell University Press, 1955), and F. S. Northedge and M. J. Grieve, *A Hundred Years of International Relations* (New York: Praeger, 1971). For the post–World War II era, see Peter Calvacoressi, *World Politics Since 1945*, 6th ed. (New York: Longman, 1991); T. E. Vadney, *The World Since 1945* (New York: Penguin, 1987); and William G. Hyland, *The Cold War: Fifty Years of Conflict* (New York: Random House, 1991). A helpful, concise chronology of events during the Cold War is provided in John W. Young, *Cold War and Detente 1941–91* (New York: Longman, 1993). Hedley Bull and Adam Watson, eds., *The Expansion of International Society* (Oxford: Oxford University Press, 1985), examines the incorporation of the third world into the state system after World War II. In chs. 1 and 2 of *Gulliver's Troubles, or The Setting of American Foreign Policy* (New York: McGraw-Hill, 1968), Stanley Hoffmann discusses developments in the late 1960s that started to change the postwar pattern of international relations.

A number of writings can be cited that focus on specific aspects of international politics discussed in the chapter. On the historical development of nationalism, see C. J. H. Hayes, *The Historical Evolution of Modern Nationalism* (New York: Macmillan, 1945), as well as Rupert Emerson, *From Empire to Nation* (Cambridge, Mass.: Harvard University Press, 1960). On the concept of "nation-state," see Alan James, *Sovereign Statehood* (London: Allen and Unwin, 1986); Mostafa Rejal and Cynthia H. Enloe, "Nation-States and State-Nations," *International Studies Quarterly*, 13 (June 1969), pp. 140–158; and Gideon Gottlieb, *Nation Against State* (New York: Council on Foreign Relations Press, 1993), and Gottlieb, "Nations Without States," *Foreign Affairs*, 73 (May/June 1994), pp. 100–112. On the historical operation of the balance of power (along with a conceptual treatment), see Inis Claude, *Power and International Relations* (New York: Random House, 1962). On the history of weapons technology and military strategy, see George H. Quester, *Offense and Defense in the International System* (New York: John Wiley, 1977), and Jack S. Levy, "The Offensive/Defensive Balance of Military Technology: A Theoretical and Historical Analysis," *International Studies Quarterly*, 28 (June 1984), pp. 230–235. On the development of economic inequalities, see Paul Bairoch, *The Economic Development of the Third World Since 1900* (Berkeley: University of California Press, 1975). On the historical relationship between power and wealth, see Paul Kennedy, *The Rise and Fall of the Great Powers* (New York: Random House, 1987). On the historical development of both intergovernmental and nongovernmental international organizations, see Harold K. Jacobson, *Networks of Interdependence*, 2d ed. (New York: Knopf, 1984), chs. 2 and 3. On historical trends relating to interdependence, see James A. Field, "Transnationalism and the New Tribe," in Robert O. Keohane and Joseph S. Nye, eds., *Transnational Relations and World Politics* (Cambridge, Mass.: Harvard University Press, 1971), pp. 3–22.

On the general theme of "continuity and change" in international relations, and history repeating itself, see interesting perspectives provided by Yale Ferguson and Richard Mansbach, "The Past as Prelude to the Future," in *The Return of Culture and Ideology in International Relations Theory*, ed. by Yosef Lapid and Friedrich Kratochwil (Boulder, Colo.: Lynne Rienner, 1994); Janice Thomson, *Mercenaries, Pirates, and Sovereigns* (Princeton: Princeton University Press, 1993); and Henrik Spruyt, *The Sovereign State and Its Competitors* (Princeton: Princeton University Press, 1994). A good overall treatment of the roots of the Westphalian state system and the challenges confronting it throughout the twentieth century is offered by Lynn Miller, *Global Order*, 3d ed. (Boulder, Colo.: Westview Press, 1994).

A Bird's-Eye View of the Present: The Contemporary International System

Like the passengers on a large ship, humanity currently seems to be undergoing passage through unfamiliar and somewhat treacherous straits. We have left one international system behind and are seeking to establish our bearings in a new system, embarking on a new epoch with great uncertainty. One is reminded here of remarks once uttered by former British Prime Minister Harold Macmillan near the beginning of the Cold War: "As they left the Garden of Eden, Adam turned to Eve and said, 'we live in an age of transition.' "[1]

As suggested in Chapter 2, history is an unfolding process, and the world in a sense is forever in transition. However, we have also noted that, in the study of international relations, one can identify certain critical moments that seem to mark a special watershed in terms of breaks with the past. Just as there is general agreement that 1945 was one such moment, so also is it commonly understood that 1989 marked an important turning point in human affairs, at the very least the end of a half-century pattern of world politics. The 1990s have seen a flurry of scholarly articles on "lessons to be learned from the end of the Cold War" and what they portended for the "new world order."[2]

As the post–Cold War order takes shape, certain elements are coming more clearly into focus. Trends in the direction of a more complicated international system, which were already discernible toward the later stages of the Cold War, are becoming more pronounced and accelerated. First, there exists a growing ambiguity and diffusion of power. Second, there exists a growing fluidity of alignments. Third, there exist ever more intricate patterns of interdependence, associated with an expanding agenda of concerns (economics, ecology, etc.) and a broadening conception of "national security" beyond traditional military considerations. Fourth, related to the latter trend, there exists a growing importance of nonstate actors (multinational corporations and the like) along with increasing linkages between subnational, transnational, and intergovernmental levels of activity, even as nation-states and their national governments remain at the center of world politics.

The question remains whether we are witnessing today merely the *déjà vu* transformation of the international system from bipolarity back to the more normal historical pattern of full-blown multipolarity that had characterized international relations between 1648 and 1945, or whether we are on the brink of a much more profound and epic transformation in the very fabric of the Westphalian state system itself. Some seize on the first two trends (the increased diffusion of power and flexibility of alignments) and suggest that the *déjà vu* scenario is the correct one; these observers see the continued relevance of the realist paradigm—with its emphasis on the classic concerns of power politics, war, and statecraft among statesmen—and a few predict the post–Cold War system will be more dangerous than its predecessor.[3] Others seize on the other two trends (relating to interdependence, transnationalism, and intergovernmentalism) and see things quite differently, i.e., the rising importance of new issues and new actors is eroding sovereignty and (along with the war-inhibiting effects of nuclear weapons) is fundamentally altering the way in which states relate to each other, making the international system "messier" and less readily manageable but not necessarily more dangerous; these observers find the globalist paradigm more compelling, with some arguing that, at least among highly developed societies, the Wilsonian liberal-idealist vision of a world at peace that was articulated at the beginning of the twentieth century may finally be materializing.[4] One bit of evidence relied on by the latter analysts is the fact that, despite enormous superpower tension and competition during the Cold War, never once (other than a few isolated incidents) did the two major actors directly engage in actual physical hostilities between each other, and they were able to end their competition without a shot being fired; as one writer describes this so-called "long peace" that continues into the post–Cold War period, "never since the Treaty of Wesphalia in 1648 . . . have great powers enjoyed a longer period of peace than we have known since the Second World War."[5]

There are reasons to be both hopeful and pessimistic about the "new world order." Clearly, peace does not prevail everywhere on the planet. Even where the long peace seems to be holding, is it perhaps making us "blindly optimistic" about the implausibility of resumption of hostilities among major actors, conjuring up parallels with the mood on the eve of World War I, when few could remember the last time all-out war had occurred among great powers?[6] We noted in Chapter 1 the competing forces of integration and disintegration that can be seen today. Our purpose in this chapter is to give an overview of the general setting in which international relations currently occur, examining the fourfold trends we have identified as well as other features of the post–Cold War system. Before providing this "bird's-eye view" of the contemporary international system, we first look briefly at the disintegration of Yugoslavia in the 1990s, because it makes a useful case study for demonstrating the growing complexity of international politics.

The Disintegration of Yugoslavia in the 1990s

In the 1990s, what was once a single state, Yugoslavia, became five states (shown in Fig. 3.1). The story of how this happened is told below.

BACKGROUND

Yugoslavia was created in 1918, at the end of World War I, fashioned out of a religiously and ethnically diverse set of peoples who had previously inhabited Serbia (which fought on the victorious side during the war) and the Austria-Hungary and Ottoman empires (which fought on the losing side and were dismembered). It was never truly a "nation"; instead, it was a crazy-quilt, jerry-

Figure 3.1
THE FORMER YUGOSLAVIA—THE NEW STATES OF CROATIA, SLOVENIA, SERBIA AND MONTENEGRO, BOSNIA AND HERZEGOVINA, AND MACEDONIA
Source: U.S. Central Intelligence Agency, *The Former Yugoslavia: A Map Folio* (July 1992).

built state, consisting mainly of Serbs, Croats, Slovenes—all Slavic-speaking but nonetheless culturally distinct populations—plus Hungarians, Albanians, Turks, Gypsies, and assorted other nationality groupings. The central government in Belgrade, under a monarchy, faced an enormous challenge in seeking to cultivate a common identity in such a polyglot society. In the words of one scholar, Yugoslavia was "a patchwork of territories and peoples who were at the same time both united and divided by language, religion, culture, history, and political tradition."[7]

Between World War I and World War II, Yugoslavia was a unitary state in which the Serbs, as the largest single ethnic group, dominated. Throughout the interwar period, animosities flared between the Serbs and other groups who felt subjugated by them, especially the Croats, leading to the assassination of King Alexander in 1934 by Croatian extremists who wanted Croats to have their own state. During World War II, the Croats supported Nazi Germany and committed numerous atrocities against the Serbs as the Germans occupied Yugoslavia and controlled a puppet state of Croatia; some 700,000 Serbs, 60,000 Jews, and 20,000 Gypsies were murdered.[8] Hence, the conflict between Serbia and Croatia that was to erupt in the 1990s had long historical roots, particularly in the perceived mistreatment of Croats by Serbs in the interwar period and the Croat collaboration with the Nazis against Serbs during World War II.

Josip Broz Tito, leader of the resistance against German occupation during World War II (and himself a Croat), came to power in 1945 and was able to bring a degree of unity and cohesion to Yugoslav politics in the postwar period. He was a communist, but one who internally sought to apply a somewhat less centralized, more pluralistic brand of socialism than that practiced by the Soviet Union and who externally resisted Moscow's efforts at domination in Eastern Europe. He refused to take sides in the East-West Cold War struggle and helped found the Nonaligned Movement. The Tito regime succeeded in not only providing order to Yugoslav politics but also modernizing the economy and improving the standard of living of the entire population.

Tito relied heavily on a federal system of government whereby Yugoslavia was divided administratively into six republics: Serbia, Croatia, Bosnia-Herzegovina, Slovenia, Montenegro, and Macedonia. With the Serbs having the potential to dominate the federation because of their superior numbers, Tito purposely tried to dilute their power in a variety of ways. Within Serbia itself, two autonomous provinces were created. One was Kosovo, considered the "cradle of the Serbian nation," which until the Ottoman conquest in the fourteenth century had been predominantly Serbian but by the 1970s was almost 80 percent ethnic Albanian; a second was Vojvodina, having a large Hungarian minority. In the republic of Bosnia-Herzegovina that Tito had created, he helped cultivate a sense of strong "Muslim" cultural identity among the descendants of Slavs who had been converted to Islam under Turkish rule centuries earlier but who had never felt any special emotional bond apart from their Slavic heritage. By the 1970s, the Bosnian Muslims were the single largest demographic group within the Bosnian republic, followed closely by the Bosnian Serbs (who were mostly Orthodox Christians) and the Bosnian Croats (predominantly Catholic), with no one group constituting an overall majority; because they were widely dispersed in rural areas rather than being concentrated in urban centers, the Serbs actually occupied 60 percent of the Bosnian landscape despite being fewer in number than the Muslims. The republic of Croatia was almost 80 percent Croat, although it had a sizable Serb minority, especially in the Krajina region, where they were a majority. Slovenia was fairly homogeneous, with 90 percent of its population ethnic Slovenes. Macedonia had some Serbs, but two-thirds of the population was Macedonian (of Greek and Bulgarian extraction) and 20 percent was Albanian. The sixth republic, Montenegro, consisted mostly of Serbs and persons close to Serbs in their cultural features.[9] By the mid-1970s, much of the power had shifted from the central institutions in Belgrade to the constituent republics, as elites and masses were coming to identify more with their regional and ethnic enclaves than with the country as a whole.[10] The more that the dominant ethnic group in a republic voiced its own nationalist, separatist aspirations, the more alienated the minorities within those boundaries felt and the more they sought to forge stronger ties to their brethren in other republics.

With Tito's death in 1980, Yugoslavia lost the one figure who was able to hold the fragile union together. The federation remained intact for another decade, with its high-water mark coming when it hosted the 1984 Winter Olympics in Sarajevo, Bosnia. The festival-like atmosphere and the outward appearances of a highly developed, progressive society that greeted foreign visitors were in stark contrast to the ethnic cleansing and mass destruction that was soon to occur. While long-dormant ethnic hatreds were resurfacing throughout the 1980s, Susan Woodward notes that Yugoslavia still had the potential to remain a viable state even after Tito:

> Despite the claims made by nationalist leaders [leaders of the individual republics who were promoting parochialism], the reality of multi-national Yugoslavia still existed in the lives of individual citizens . . .—in their ethnically mixed neighborhoods, villages, towns, and cities; in their mixed marriages, family ties across republic boundaries, and second homes in another republic; in their conceptions of ethnic and national coexistence and the compatibility of multiple identities for each citizen. . . .[11]

However, in addition to Tito's death, other factors were working against the union in the late 1980s and early 1990s. These were (1) the end of the Cold War and with it the movement of communist states in Eastern Europe toward market economies, producing major economic dislocations, bringing high unemployment and internal political instability to Yugoslavia and other states attempting to make the difficult transition to capitalism; (2) the rupture of traditional trade and other economic relationships that Yugoslavia, despite its nonaligned posture, had developed during the Cold War with the Soviet bloc through its associate membership in the Council for Mutual Economic Assistance (the East bloc counterpart to the European Community in Western Europe), further aggravating economic conditions; (3) the rise to power in Yugoslav politics of ex-communists who sought to solidify their position by engaging in scapegoating and chauvinistic appeals to their respective disaffected ethnic constituencies wanting somebody to blame for the deteriorating economic climate in the country; (4) the example of the Baltic states (Lithuania, Estonia, and Latvia), which reasserted their right to self-determination in 1990, seceded from the Soviet Union in 1991, and gained instant recognition of their sovereignty by the international community; (5) the further inspiration taken from the successful independence movements of other Soviet republics, which likewise rejected their minority status within the Soviet Union and achieved independence around the same time as the Baltic states; and (6) with the disintegration of the Soviet Union, the removal of what had been for many Yugoslavs a common external rival and, hence, part of the glue holding them together.

On the eve of the breakup of Yugoslavia, the federation was functioning with a collective presidency that rotated among the different republics. The ethnic makeup of the country was the following: 36 percent were Serbs, 20 percent were Croats, 10 percent were Bosnian Muslims, 8 percent were Slovenes, 6 percent were Macedonians, and 20 percent were of other ethnic stock. Bosnia, in particular—with its geographical interspersing of Muslims (44 percent of the population), Serbs (over 31 percent), and Croats (almost 18 percent)—reflected the rich mosaic of Yugoslav culture that was to shatter into brutal ethnopolitical warfare. What was about to transpire was a gradual process of fragmentation leading from the feeble attempt to salvage the union in a weaker confederal arrangement, to one republic after another opting for secession, to the final dissolution of the country—with the entire outside world watching almost helplessly as the tragedy unfolded.[12]

THE SEQUENCE OF EVENTS

Although all of the Yugoslav republics in the late 1980s were experiencing economic problems, Serbia was having particular difficulties. In addition to increased unemployment (among the highest in Yugoslavia), Serbia saw its annual rate of inflation jump to 1,200 percent by 1988. The end of the Cold War only aggravated the economic woes, as the pressure to move from communism to capitalism was accompanied by painful "shock therapy"—a radical weaning of the economy from reliance on state enterprises and subsidies—administered by Western financial advisors and the International Monetary Fund. A stagnant economy helped bring to power Slobodan Milosevic, a former communist who assumed the leadership of the republic of Serbia and proceeded to fan the flames of Serbian nationalism not only within Serbia but also among ethnic Serbs in Bosnia, Croatia, and the other republics as he called for recentralization of federal authority in Belgrade under Serb domination. He exploited Serb frustrations over their being denied their own state after World War I and World War II, and over the mistreatment of Serb minorities in the various republics and especially at the hands of the Albanian majority in Kosovo province who were making demands of their own for self-determination.

Milosevic's attempt to assert Serbian hegemony over the Yugoslav federation ran counter to the desire of Slovenia and Croatia for still greater autonomy and "sovereignty" within a weaker confederation. Slovenia was the most economically prosperous of all of the republics and was the furthest along in the transition to Western-style capitalist democracy. By the time the Berlin Wall fell in 1989, Slovenia had already increased its economic ties to the West considerably (for example, with Austria opening up four bank affiliates in the Slovene capital city of Ljubljana) and was envisioning one day possibly going it alone and becoming associated with the European Community.[13] The Slovenian parliament demanded that Slovene youth in the all-Yugoslav armed forces be stationed in Slovenia rather than scattered among the republics and be permitted to use the Slovene language. In Croatia, which likewise was more affluent and Western-oriented than Serbia and did not wish to have to bail out the less developed regions of the federation, the parliament similarly attempted to assert greater control over economic and security affairs. Rumblings of discontent were being heard in Bosnia and the other republics as well.

These developments came to a head in mid-1990, with the flashpoint being Milosevic's attempt in July to suspend Kosovo's status as an autonomous province within Serbia, to dissolve the Kosovo parliament, and to transfer Albanian-controlled enterprises to Serb ownership. Fearing that Milosevic might try to impose similar rule over them, the Slovene parliament declared that its laws took precedence over those of the Yugoslav federation; the Slovene foreign minister went so far as to state "Yugoslavia no longer exists."[14] Croatia followed suit in declaring sovereignty over Croatian territory and proceeded to adopt the flag of the Croatian puppet fascist state that had existed during World War II. Slovenia and Croatia both called for Yugoslavia to become a loose confederation of sovereign states, each with its own armed forces and overseas embassies. Whereas Milosevic could ignore Slovenia's act of defiance, because there were few Serbs living in Slovenia, Croatia was another matter. More than 500,000 Serbs lived in Croatia, including 200,000 in the Krajina region. When the Croatian parliament in Zagreb issued decrees requiring all public employees to take a loyalty oath and replacing Serb police with Croatians in those localities having mixed Serb-Croat populations, Milosevic called for Krajina to become a Serbian autonomous region tied to Belgrade. The momentum toward the dissolution of Yugoslavia was gaining speed as "all factions . . . pursued the same objective—avoiding minority status in Yugoslavia or any successor state."[15] As one diplomat put it, the operative question driving events was, "Why should I be a minority in your country when you can be a minority in mine?"

When last-gasp negotiations to save the Yugoslav federation failed, Slovenia and Croatia formally declared their complete independence in June 1991. The federal government in Belgrade responded to the two secessions by dispatching troops from the Serb-dominated all-Yugoslav Army to put down the rebellions. Full-scale civil war erupted in Yugoslavia. Macedonia around the same time declared its independence as well. The bloodiest fighting was in Croatia, where Serb forces were able to occupy one-third of the territory. The United Nations Security Council acted in September 1991 to institute a total ban on the outside shipment of arms to any of the republics and by January 1992 had established an uneasy truce to be policed by 14,000 blue-helmeted United Nations soldiers (the UNPROFOR peacekeeping mission).

The international community was slow to respond to the evolving Yugoslav crisis. The end of the Cold War meant that Yugoslavia had lost the pivotal geopolitical strategic importance it had enjoyed during the East-West conflict. The Soviet Union, faced in the early 1990s with its own internal problems and imminent disintegration, was hardly in a position to act even if it had believed major interests were at stake. The United States, which was retrenching somewhat from global commitments in the face of severe budget deficits at home and was rethinking its own role in the "new world order," was inclined to treat Yugoslavia as mainly a European concern to be dealt with by its NATO allies. The European institutions (IGOs) left over from the Cold War—NATO, the European Community, the Conference on Security and Cooperation in Europe, and other regional organizations—were also searching for their proper place in the post–Cold War era and were ill equipped to respond to what seemed a series of civil wars within a larger civil war in the Balkans. In addition, all eyes were focused in late 1990 and early 1991 on the Gulf War in the Middle East—the so-called first post–Cold War crisis—as Western access to oil was threatened by Iraq's invasion and attempted annexation of Kuwait, leading to a United States–led multinational force of 500,000 troops being sent to the Persian Gulf under UN auspices. Finally, there was a sense of disbelief in the United States and elsewhere that the Yugoslav conflict would turn very deadly and required immediate, concerted attention. The Gulf War aside, there was "general euphoria and self-confidence in the West based on the belief that threats to international security were truly on the decline [at least in the developed world, as in Europe] and that peace dividends and economic interests would define the next period of global order."[16]

By the time the United Nations acted in 1991–1992, it was too late to restore Yugoslavia, especially after the European Community (led by Germany) voted in December 1991 to formally recognize Croatia and Slovenia as sovereign states.[17] Many believed the German recognition was premature. Croatia, Slovenia, as well as Macedonia, were subsequently recognized by the United States and other countries and were admitted into the United Nations, with Serbia and Montenegro merging together to form what was essentially the successor state to Yugoslavia (although the UN General Assembly voted to suspend its membership because of alleged atrocities committed by the Milosevic government against non-Serbs). As for Bosnia-Herzegovina, with its volatile mix of Serbs, Croats, and Muslims—none of which constituted a majority in the Bosnian republic—it became a microcosm of the Yugoslav conflict and the locale of the most brutal warfare. Bosnia initially had preferred remaining within a multi-ethnic Yugoslavia, but saw this option foreclosed by the secession of other republics. The Bosnian government then held a referendum on independence that was boycotted by most Bosnian Serbs, who feared living in a state where the largest single ethnic group was Muslim and where Islamic law might prevail. The referendum passed, Bosnia-Herzegovina declared its sovereignty in April 1992, and the new state was immediately admitted into the United Nations.

While the UN truce in Croatia separating the Serbs from Croats was holding, the Serbs in Bosnia—aided by arms and other support from the Milosevic government in Belgrade—rejected Bosnian authorities and announced their intention to form their own state and to join it to Serbia. Adding to the complex nature of the fighting was the attempt by Bosnian Croats to forge their own ties with the Croatian government in Zagreb. Massive bombings of towns and villages occurred. Horror stories appeared in the world press depicting various incidents of "ethnic cleansing," whereby the members of one ethnic group reportedly murdered or evicted masses of people of other ethnic groups to create ethnically homogeneous enclaves that could more easily be annexed to their "mother republic." More UN troops were dispatched to Bosnia in the name of "humanitarian intervention," to insure food supplies to starving refugees and to provide neutral "safe havens" for civilian populations. The UN, assisted by NATO, banned all military aircraft in a "no-fly" zone over Bosnia. The Bosnian Serb leaders, Radovan Karadzic and his chief military commander Ratko Mladic, linked to Serbian President Milosevic, increasingly came under criticism from the UN for permitting the rape and murder of civilians and condoning **genocide,** although there was evidence of atrocities committed by all sides. To punish the Serb republic for its "aggression" in Bosnia, the UN ordered an economic embargo against Serbia, hoping the latter would bring pressure to bear on Karadzic to end the fighting. A "war crimes" tribunal was organized by the UN to bring Karadzic and others to trial for violation of human rights, assuming they could be apprehended. However, the war raged on, with the UNPROFOR peacekeeping mission exceeding 40,000 troops by 1995 and costing over $1 billion annually.

Between 1992 and 1995, numerous diplomatic efforts were made to bring a halt to the fighting in Bosnia. Proposals included the partition of the country into a tripartite confederation organized along ethnic lines, but it was hard to get agreement, especially because Serbs, Croats, and Muslims—even with the attempts at ethnic cleansing—were not concentrated in distinct areas.[18] Negotiations were also complicated by disagreements among foreign governments. In the UN, the United States, backed by the Organization of the Islamic Conference (consisting of Saudi Arabia and other Muslim states), tended to take the side of the Bosnian Muslims, whereas Russia tended to be more sympathetic to the Serbs based on their common Slavic heritage. The West Europeans, notably France and Britain, whose soldiers made up the bulk of UNPROFOR ground forces and were most at risk from an escalating conflict, were reluctant to follow a "lift and strike" strategy that many U.S. officials were urging; the latter strategy would have lifted the UN-imposed arms embargo and enabled heavier arms to get through to the Muslims so that they could better defend themselves

SERB SOLDIERS ON HILLSIDE OUTSIDE SARAJEVO, SITE OF THE 1984 WINTER OLYMPICS.

against the Bosnian Serbs (who had been getting arms from the well-equipped Serbian military), and would have relied on NATO airstrikes to punish Serb artillery attacks against population centers, such as the 1994 mortar attack that killed and wounded over 200 men, women, and children in the central marketplace of Sarajevo, the Bosnian capital.[19]

The marketplace massacre spurred the United States to become more intensely involved in the peace process, as Washington increased its rhetoric against the Serbs in the hope that it would bring them to the bargaining table. President Clinton offered to put 25,000 American troops into the former Yugoslavia to assist in the UN "peace enforcement" operation, a proposal that worried members of Congress who envisioned a war of attrition fought on difficult terrain that conjured up memories of Vietnam. In 1995, action on the diplomatic front was further complicated by a resumption of hostilities in Croatia, where Croat forces succeeded in not only removing Serb troops that had earlier occupied the Krajina region but also driving thousands of Croatian Serbs off their centuries-old land holdings, forcing them to flee to Serbia, where the Belgrade government made room for them by in turn evicting Albanians from their homes in Kosovo. Some observers believed a denouement to the entire Yugoslav tragedy, including Bosnia, was made more possible by the increasingly weakening position of the Serbs, who were reeling from both military losses and UN-imposed economic sanctions and might finally be ready to make major concessions in the peace talks. These talks produced a fragile agreement on Bosnia in November 1995, at Wright-Patterson Air Force Base in Dayton, Ohio, brokered by the United States and signed by the presidents of Serbia, Croatia, and Bosnia, which provided for (1) a single confederal state of Bosnia-Herzegovina that would be divided into two entities called the Federation of Bosnia and Herzegovina (primarily comprising Muslims and Croats, who would control 51 percent of the territory) and the Serb Republic (primarily comprising Bosnian Serbs), (2) a distribution of powers whereby the central government in Sarajevo would have responsibility for foreign policy, foreign trade, customs and immigration, monetary policy, and transportation, whereas the two constituent entities would control all other functions, and (3) the imposition of a ceasefire to be policed by several thousand troops drawn mainly from the United States and other NATO countries. The Dayton agreement did not address the larger issues beyond the Bosnian conflict. As of this writing (spring 1997), it remains to be seen when the final chapter will be written on this affair and what the final outcome might look like. The only universal agreement that existed was the understanding that the war had exacted terrible human costs. As one commentator said:

> How bad has this war been? When one drives past the destroyed speed-skating rink and the Olympic stadium in Sarajevo, the eye involuntarily turns to row upon row of markers atop fresh graves dug in the new and largest cemetery in the capital. Clearly, thousands have died in Sarajevo. How many people have died in this war overall? Nobody knows.[20]

Among the other, larger costs of the war was the very credibility of the so-called new world order. Many questions were raised by the Yugoslav crisis relating to the shape of the post–Cold War international system. How much damage was done to the principles embodied in the United Nations Charter that aggression and genocide would not be tolerated and that they would be punished rather than rewarded? Were the United States and its allies, along with regional and global institutions such as the European Community and the United Nations, up to the task of providing leadership that could foster a more peaceful, democratic, and prosperous planet? Were traditional military-security concerns, rather than economic concerns, still paramount in international relations? At what point does "humanitarian intervention" by external actors become interference in the domestic affairs of a sovereign state? How much importance should the international community attach to supporting the territorial integrity of states (such as Yugoslavia), as opposed to self-determination for minority nationality groups within those states (such as Croatians and Slovenes), and should the international community recognize a new state in which a majority of the population is alienated from the government (as in Bosnia)? If Croatia can create a state, then why not the Krajina Serbs or the Albanians in Kosovo? What about Scotland, Catalonia, and other distinctive ethnic communities, however small they might be? Diplomats and scholars will be puzzling over these questions for years to come. We will puzzle over these and other questions as well as we now provide a capsule overview of the contemporary international system.

Characteristics of the Contemporary International System

The breakup of Yugoslavia symbolized the "new international politics." The new international politics was actually not altogether new, because some of its features were an extension of long-term trends that had simply become more accentuated (for example, the growing role of interdependence in affecting relations between countries). Other features, however, represented a clearer break with the patterns that had characterized much of post–World War II international relations (for example, the absence of sharply defined, bipolarized conflict). Above all else, the Yugoslav episode seemed to highlight the increasingly untidy nature of world politics, with localized ethnopolitical conflicts vying for attention with the globalization of the international economy and other systemwide phenomena.

DISTRIBUTION OF POWER

We noted in Chapter 2, in the discussion of the Arab oil embargo and OPEC price increases, that "superpower slippage" was already noticeable by the 1970s, as a group of less developed countries, many of which were tiny "statelets" (e.g., Qatar and the United Arab Emirates, each with less than a million people) and all of which were devoid of the assets traditionally associated with power, seemed to demonstrate that power was becoming more diffuse and ambiguous in world affairs. The Yugoslav crisis in the 1990s raised deeper questions about whether any pecking order at all still existed among the countries of the world in terms of power rankings, because neither the United States nor the Russians and the Europeans seemed able to influence the course of events in bringing the conflict to a speedy conclusion. In the case of the Soviet Union, having been unable to keep its own house in order—by 1992, the USSR had disintegrated into more than a dozen independent republics—it could hardly be expected to keep Yugoslavia together. In the case of the United States, one commentator blamed the failure not so much on a lack of resources but on a lack of resolve on the part of the White House, which "turned a superpower into a subpower."[21] Others, however, argued that the United States—no less than a truncated and weakened Russia—needed to resign itself to the realities of "a post-superpower age."[22]

"The decline of American hegemony" had already become a familiar theme in the international relations literature by the 1980s.[23] The United States, between 1950 and 1980, saw its share of world military spending decline from 50 percent to 25 percent, its share of world monetary reserves drop from 50 percent to less than 7 percent, and its share of world industrial output fall from two-thirds to less than one-third.[24] During the 1980s and 1990s, the U.S. share of both global military spending and the global economic product did stabilize and even increase somewhat.[25] Some scholars argued that the American "decline" was greatly exaggerated and had to be put in proper perspective, noting it was mainly a case of the war-ravaged economies of Western Europe and Japan rebuilding and partially catching up to what had been in the immediate aftermath of World War II an extraordinary lead enjoyed by the United States.[26] Indeed, the current U.S. position in the international hierarchy would appear to be superior to the status it enjoyed during the Cold War, given the dismemberment of its chief rival and the absence of any clear challenger for the top spot. However, the U.S. claim to dominance is problematical for a variety of reasons. The twenty-first century poses special challenges to the exercise of American power, given the "triple deficits" the United States was saddled with at the end of the 1990s, namely, an almost $200 billion annual

Is the United States still a superpower, and can it alone handle all the "911" calls for help?

federal government budget deficit, a $100 billion yearly trade deficit, and over $1 trillion of debt owed to foreigners.[27]

The United States still accounts for one-third of world military spending. The Russian Federation, even in its weakened condition, still possesses almost as much firepower as the United States (in addition to vast natural resources it inherited as the major successor state to the Soviet Union). However, American and Russian military might has been less readily usable than the military prowess enjoyed by great powers in the past, mostly because of mutual fear of escalation and nuclear holocaust. The huge nuclear arsenals of both countries, amounting to 95 percent of the global stockpile of 36,000 nuclear weapons (as of 1997), are the shadow that continues to hover over the fate of humanity. But it is only a shadow—always lingering in the background though not coming directly into play. One cannot say for certain that these arsenals will never be used in the future, only that there are enormous constraints on their use.

Moreover, several other countries are gradually developing this "life and death" power. At least a dozen states—including several less developed ones—are considered on the brink of joining the "nuclear club," which currently consists of the United States and Russia along with its "lesser" members, China, Britain, and France (with the former Soviet republics of Ukraine, Kazakhstan, and Belarus having agreed to transfer nuclear weapons on their soil to Russia); India, Israel, and Pakistan are thought to be de facto members already, unofficially in possession of nuclear weapons.[28] Smaller states also are acquiring increasingly sophisticated and deadly conventional weaponry along with biological and chemical war capabilities. The American Ambassador to the United Nations reported to the U.S. Congress in 1995 that Iraq, even though it did not have substantial delivery capabilities, had produced "enough biological warfare agents to kill every man, woman, and child on Earth."[29]

What is especially striking about the contemporary era is that countries find themselves in possession of certain nonmilitary resources that in the past did not translate directly into power but that today can provide considerable leverage in world politics. One cannot discount military power, as seen in the success of the United States–led coalition during the 1990 Gulf War; Kenneth Waltz is among those scholars who still believe in the primacy of military power even in the post–Cold War era, noting that "no state lacking in military ability to compete with other great powers has ever been ranked among them."[30] However, the contemporary era may mark the acceleration of a process underway for some time, namely the eclipse of military potential as the main source of control in the international system. At the same time that such resources as oil and food grain along with investment capital have become a part of the currency of power, traditional military resources generally have become somewhat devalued.[31] Even a realist such as Henry Kissinger has commented that "the issues susceptible to solution by military action are in

"And as a last resort in hand-to-hand combat, you can always strike the enemy with your wallet."

Dugan's People by Ralph Dunagan. © 1975 Field Enterprises, Inc., courtesy of Field Newspaper Syndicate.

Petropower: How important will it be in the future?

decline" and that military power "is less and less relevant to most foreseeable international crises."[32]

One could argue that in addition to traditional military power potential, a particularly important alternate form of usable power today is "technopower." Here a state's economic assets come into play, but mainly as they are harnessed to the creation of innovative modes of production and new knowledge on which other states come to depend heavily. For example, Japan has been able to create such dependencies peacefully through trade and investment relations with Asian states, such as Malaysia, which it had tried to capture by force in the 1930s and 1940s. In the process, Japanese enterprises make use of markets, resources, and populations (workers) that would otherwise have been unavailable to them. Although at some point in the future Japan may feel a need to back up its economic prowess with added military prowess (including possibly developing nuclear weapons), current trends seem to point in a different direction. One measure of technopower is the development of new patents and scientific breakthroughs. The United States still leads the world in these categories, but Japan and Western Europe have closed the gap. A premium is now put on control of information, mediated through instantaneous world communications networks, on matters as varied as crop failures in South America to corporate mergers and acquisitions in London.

Despite the increased diffusion and ambiguity of power in the contemporary world, observers of international relations continue to engage in one of the favorite pastimes of the field: rank-ordering states according to their power and fitting them into a neat pecking order. Some observers still refer to the United States as a "superpower" at the top, trailed by all the rest, in what they see as a "unipolar" system; although some such analysts see the United States as capable of dealing with threats to international order through its own unilateral action, many believe Washington cannot afford to be the lone "global policeman" and must settle for the role of "sheriff of the posse."[33] Many others have noted the emergence of at least five world power centers: the United States, Russia, Japan, China, and the European Union members, led by Germany, Britain, France, and Italy.[34] Still others speak of the growing importance of "middle powers," such as Brazil, Argentina, Turkey, Indonesia, Nigeria, India, Algeria, Canada, the Nordic countries, and Australia.[35]

As noted earlier, most attempts to construct such pecking orders assume that there are certain national attributes that constitute "elements" or "bases" of national power and that, when added together, provide a summary index of a given state's power. *Size*—in terms of population, land area, gross national product, or military resources—has been traditionally considered an important determinant of power. If size were the only important determinant of power, then it would not be difficult to produce an accurate power ranking. Certainly, there are vast disparities among countries in the international system in terms of size, differences that are likely to become even more accentuated as more "mini-states" or "micro-states" enter the community of nations as the decolonialization process winds down and—if disintegration trends persist—ethnopolitical conflict produces secessionist movements wanting their own statehood. Thirty-five countries, one-fifth of the membership of the contemporary international community, have less than 1 million people, and more than half of these—the micro-states—are under 300,000; half of the "family of nations" are less populous than the state of Tennessee. The sovereign equality of nations cannot disguise the fact that they come in many different sizes and shapes, as indicated in Table 3.1.

Although Table 3.1 shows the wide differences between countries in size characteristics, it also illustrates the limited utility of trying to construct a meaningful power ranking of countries based on size criteria alone. Pakistan and Bangladesh are among the most populous countries in the world (the seventh and the ninth largest, to be exact); yet it is questionable whether their ability to affect international relations is greater than that of much smaller oil-rich states. Realizing the simplistic nature of looking only at size features, many analysts also try to take into account *qualitative* elements of national power—such as level of economic and technological development—which may confer added stature on some smaller states such as Israel. In one recent study, for example, power is defined as the capacity of a state both to exercise influence and to resist influence attempts. Therefore, it is said to depend on factors such as a state's geographical position, political organization and gov-

Table 3.1
SIZE CHARACTERISTICS OF SELECTED COUNTRIES

Country	Population (in millions)	Land Area (in sq. miles)	Gross National Product (U.S. $ millions)	Total Armed Forces
Bangladesh	116.7	55,598	25,882	107,000
Barbados	0.3	166	1,620	1,000
Brazil	156.4	3,286,487	471,978	296,000
Canada	27.8	3,830,840	574,884	76,000
China (PRC)	1,175.4	3,696,100	581,109	3,031,000
Croatia	4.8	21,829	26,300	103,000
Egypt	55.7	386,900	36,679	424,000
Gambia	1.0	4,125	372	1,000
Haiti	6.8	10,700	2,200	8,000
Indonesia	187.2	741,098	136,991	271,000
Israel	5.3	8,017	72,662	181,000
Japan	124.8	142,705	3,926,660	242,000
Kuwait	1.5	6,880	34,120	12,000
Malta	0.4	122	1,940	1,500
Nigeria	104.9	356,669	32,988	76,000
Pakistan	122.8	307,293	53,520	580,000
Russia	148.5	6,582,811	348,413	2,250,000
Saudi Arabia	17.4	848,400	95,830	172,000
Seychelles	0.07	175	440	1,000
Sri Lanka	17.6	325	10,658	22,000
Sweden	8.7	173,620	216,294	44,000
Switzerland	7.0	15,943	254,066	31,000
Tajikistan	5.7	55,240	2,686	3,000
Turkey	59.5	300,947	126,330	686,000
United Kingdom	58.0	94,475	1,042,700	271,000
United States	258.1	3,614,170	6,387,686	1,815,000

Source: Population and GNP data are for 1993, and were obtained from *World Bank Atlas, 1995* (Washington, D.C.: World Bank, 1995). Data on armed forces are for 1993, and were obtained from *World Military Expenditures and Arms Transfers, 1993–1994* (Washington, D.C.: U.S. Arms Control and Disarmament Agency, 1995). Data on land size are for 1995, and were obtained from *The Statesman's Yearbook, 1995–96* (New York: St. Martin's Press, 1995).

ernmental legitimacy, and leadership competence, as well as material capabilities. The latter capabilities then are classified along three "dimensions": demographic capabilities (represented by an educated urban population); industrial capabilities (reflected in the society's consumption of energy supplies); and military capabilities (indicated by the size of its armed forces).[36]

Although these national attributes are measurable and countries can be ranked by them, the utility of pecking order exercises remains questionable for a variety of reasons, many of which were alluded to in our initial discussion of power in the previous chapter. One problem is that today so many societal variables are relevant to the exercise of power that it is difficult to obtain agreement on a single set of criteria, much less on what weight should be assigned to each individual criterion. We have suggested, for example, that the kind of "high-tech" technological prowess possessed by the Japanese today may be more crucial to exercising power in the future than the more traditional economic bases of power such as coal and steel production. A second problem is that power may be based as much on intangibles such as *will* as it is on paper counts of tons of steel or numbers of rifles and riflemen. The latter may be more measurable but not necessarily more important.[37] Although all the will in the world cannot compensate for a lack of resources, all the resources in the world may be meaningless without the will to use them.

The example that is commonly cited to illustrate the role of "will" was the unwillingness of the United States during the early 1970s to use more than a small fraction of its military arsenal against North Vietnam, a country that managed to win the Vietnam War even though it was far inferior to the United States on almost any conventional measure of power. One could argue that the United States lacked the necessary resources to achieve its goals 10,000 miles away from home. In any case, what was thought by some to be "the greatest power in the world" was unable to defeat "a band of night-riders in black pajamas."[38] Similar questions about American "will to lead" were raised during the Yugoslavia civil war. It has been said that the United States suffers from a "weak state" syndrome; i.e., compared with say, Japan, the United States has a domestic political culture that tends to place substantial limits on the capacity of central governmental decision makers and bureaucracies, including the foreign policy establishment, to act on behalf of the state and, hence, often produces governmental paralysis.[39] At the same time, some scholars have suggested that another key intangible is the capacity to lead by example based on the admiration and respect one commands abroad. Joseph Nye has argued that the United States enjoys an edge over Japan and other states because of this sort of "soft" or "co-optive" power, what some have referred to as "the projection of a set of norms [e.g., a commitment to pluralistic democracy] and their embrace by leaders in other nations."[40]

Even if one can somehow overcome the above analytical problems, the notion of an international pecking order makes sense only if one thinks of power as some gross societal capability or set of resources that can be hypothetically mobilized and employed. However, today especially it is more helpful to think of power as an influence *relationship* in which the capacity of one country to exert influence on another ultimately depends not only on the sum of their respective potential resources ("raw" factors), but also on several relative factors: (1) whether a country actually has the right resources to apply to the particular situation, (2) whether a country attaches the same importance or salience to the situation as an adversary country, and (3) how many other demands are being made on a country's resources at that moment. In short, power is best viewed as *situation-specific* or *issue-specific.*[41]

The OPEC countries are still potentially powerful in affecting world energy politics, but much less so in other issue-areas. As a member of the Group of Seven (the seven leading industrialized democracies, which hold annual economic summit meetings), Japan is a major actor in the international economy but, with a smaller army than Indonesia, plays a relatively minor role in the area of arms control and other military-strategic concerns. Canada, whose vast real estate dwarfs its population, contains valuable raw materials that make the country influential in global mineral politics. Malta, with its 1,500-strong army, has played a key role in the politics of the law of the sea; this is beyond anything one would expect from a quick glance at its resource base and more prominent than any role it has played in any other issue-area. The Vatican City-State, the smallest state in the world in both population (1,000) and territory (.17 square mile) and without any army divisions, has exercised far more influence on the politics surrounding the world population issue than most states considerably larger in size, although it has had little effect in persuading states to abide by its "commandments" in areas other than birth control.

We do not wish to imply that all countries are equal in power today and that power is now so elusive a concept that it is just as reasonable to rank the United States as number 185 and Malta as number 1 as the other way around in the international hierarchy. The contemporary international system *is* stratified in terms of power, but the stratification does not lend itself to predicting "winners" and "losers" quite so easily as in the past. Some countries such as The Gambia—"mini-states" without any vital natural or other resources that can currently be used as bargaining chips—can be safely assigned to the bottom of the international ladder; other countries such as the United States—states that potentially can influence events over a wide geographical area and over a wide range of issues—can be safely placed toward the top of the ladder. A pecking order of sorts may be said to exist, but it is one that is given to frequent collapse. If one must be careful not to underestimate the power of the United States today, one must also be careful not to exaggerate it.

DISTRIBUTION OF WEALTH

The contemporary international system is stratified in terms not only of power but also of *wealth*, although here, too, the stratification pattern is complicated. We noted in Chapter 2 that the post–World War II system was characterized by a growing rich-poor gap between developed and developing countries, notwithstanding the fact that at least a few of the latter states made impressive strides.[42] Some observers see this gap growing still bigger in the post–Cold War era as some societies use cutting-edge twenty-first century technologies to expand their economies while technologically backward societies become even more marginalized.[43] The globalization of the international economy also may add to rich-poor disparities *within* societies as well, with uncertain implications for international politics (as seen in the Yugoslav case study, in which uneven levels of development between Slovenia and Croatia and the rest of Yugoslavia contributed to the breakup of the country).[44]

The "less developed countries" (LDCs) today include a wide assortment of states: the "nouveau riche" but still in many ways economically underdeveloped and politically fragile OPEC nations such as Saudi Arabia; the "NICs" that are becoming increasingly industrialized and are classified by the World Bank as "upper middle-income" or in some cases "high-income" economies, such as Brazil, Mexico, South Korea, and Singapore; another group referred to as the "next NICs," including Thailand, Malaysia, and Indonesia; more than forty faltering "Fourth World" countries, typified by Bangladesh and Ethiopia; and others that do not quite fit any of these categories.[45] The "developed" countries themselves range from the most highly developed and wealthiest market economies such as the United States, Japan, and most members of the European Union to the less wealthy economies of Eastern Europe currently seeking to make the difficult transition from centrally planned, communist systems to market-oriented, capitalist systems. Some observers believe the former communist systems are experiencing such severe economic problems that they should be relabeled "developing" and that there are now two broad categories of states: the first world and the "two-thirds world" (the third world combined with the former second world).

Two authors have suggested that "the world's work is divided up according to a more complex pattern among seven groups of nations":

> Almost four-fifths of the measured economic activity on earth is still generated by two dozen richer countries: the United States, Canada, Japan, Australia, New Zealand, South Africa, and the nations of Western Europe. All but a handful of the world's top corporations are based here. . . .
>
> Eight countries, though still poor by many measures, have entered the industrial age to become large-scale manufacturers of a broad range of products. This second group is made up of nations aspiring to become the middle class in the global economic hierarchy: Brazil, Mexico, Argentina, India, and especially the so-called Asian tigers [particularly Singapore and South Korea]. . . .
>
> A third group of nations has achieved some limited industrialization but they are still predominantly dependent on agriculture. . . . But only a very few have any real prospects of becoming members of the industrialized world soon. Among two dozen aspiring nations, China, Thailand, Indonesia, and Malaysia appear to have the best chances, especially China. . . .
>
> The former communist countries of Eastern Europe make up a fourth group of producers for the global market. Despite the relatively high state of industrialization some of them had achieved before World War II, . . . most are finding it difficult to compete for foreign investment with the industrializing enclaves of Asia and Latin America. . . .

Most of the dozen oil-exporting countries belonging to OPEC constitute a fifth set of countries. . . . A sixth set of countries is made up of forty or so poor countries that are situated just above the bottom of the global economic pyramid [countries that rely on the production and export of primary commodities, such as Bolivia, Ghana, and Zambia]. . . .

The poorest of the poor are forty-seven so-called "least developed countries," almost all of them in Africa, and these make up the seventh group. They are so poor that their economic connection with the rest of the world is pretty much limited to cashing relief checks and opening bags of food from government and private relief agencies.[46]

As noted in Chapter 1, one-half of the world's people live in fifty countries with a per capita gross national product (PGNP) under $500; roughly 30 percent live in 93 countries with PGNP between $500 and $5,000; and roughly 20 percent live in forty-six countries with PGNP over $5,000.[47] Table 3.2 indicates how wealth, population, and nation-states are distributed in the world according to region.

As this table shows, both population and poverty (defined in terms of PGNP, the most commonly used indicator of standard of living and level of economic development) tend to be concentrated in the southern part of the

Table 3.2
DISTRIBUTION OF WEALTH, POPULATION, AND NATION-STATES BY REGION

Region	Population (in millions)	Number of Countries with PGNP Less than $500	Number of Countries with PGNP $500–$5,000	Number of Countries with PGNP Greater than $5,000
Sub-Saharan Africa	640	30	14	1
Middle East and North Africa	291	1	12	8
East and South Asia	2,963	12	7	5
Latin America	458	6	26	4
Oceania	26	1	7	3
Western Europe	451	0	1	22
Eastern Europe and Central Asia (including former Soviet republics)	495	0	26	1
North America	286	0	0	2
TOTAL	5,610	50	93	46

Source: Adapted from World Bank, *World Development Report, 1995* (New York: Oxford University Press, 1995) and *World Bank Atlas 1995* (Washington, D.C.: World Bank, 1995).

globe. This fact is made even plainer when one adds that of the twenty-two countries with PGNP greater than $15,000, all are situated in the higher northern latitudes except for Australia, Singapore, and a few small oil-rich states. We live in a world in which per capita gross national product ranges from an average of $380 per year in "low-income" Fourth World countries (located primarily in Sub-Saharan Africa and South Asia) to more than $20,000 per year in "high-income" developed states with market economies.[48] To put this disparity more concretely, a comparison of PGNP for Switzerland and Mozambique gives a ratio of 408:1.[49]

One can perhaps see the differences between states more vividly if one examines the developmental characteristics of some selected countries. Table 3.3 shows that the poorer countries in PGNP terms tend to have relatively low literacy rates, high infant mortality rates, and short life expectancies. However, the pattern is complicated by the fact that low PGNP does not always correlate exactly with such characteristics. In particular, it is clear that a number of countries that on paper appear to be very rich, based on a high PGNP produced suddenly by an oil bonanza or some other good fortune, have in fact not yet attained a level of economic development commensurate with their PGNP. Other countries that on paper appear to be poor still manage through imaginative government planning and societal resourcefulness to stretch their resources to produce what seems to be a surprisingly high standard of living.

Saudi Arabia, for example, is a relatively rich country, yet has a literacy rate of 62 percent, life expectancy of 69 years, and fairly high infant mortality rate. Sri Lanka, one of the poorest countries in the world, has a literacy rate of 88 percent, life expectancy of 72 years, and roughly half the infant mortality rate of Saudi Arabia. Many factors account for these discrepancies. One that is especially significant is the inability of societies, even those blessed with the huge financial resources of some Arab oil sheikdoms, to modernize overnight and to produce all of the benefits associated with a high level of economic development, such as sophisticated transportation, health care, and educational systems. Another factor is the unwillingness of many societies to distribute economic benefits broadly across their population rather than confining them to a narrow stratum at the top. Hence, some analysts have argued that PGNP is a misleading indicator of national wealth, and they have suggested another measure, the physical quality of life index (PQLI), which combines literacy rate, infant mortality rate, and life expectancy.[50] The United Nations Development Program annually publishes a ranking of states according to a "Human Development Index," which includes literacy rate and average years of schooling among the population, life expectancy, and per capita income.[51]

Regardless of what indicators are used, it is clear that the contemporary international system is divided into "haves" and "have-nots." Some countries rank high on almost every measure of national well-being, some rank uniformly low, and others show uneven developmental characteristics. Even in

Table 3.3

THE RICH-POOR GAP AMONG SELECTED COUNTRIES

Country	PGNP (U.S. $)	Literacy (%)	Infant Mortality (per 1,000 Live Births)	Life Expectancy at Birth (Years)
Bangladesh	220	35	91	55
Barbados	6,240	99	10	75
Brazil	3,020	81	58	66
Canada	20,670	99	7	78
China (PRC)	490	73	31	69
Croatia	5,600	93	12	73
Egypt	660	48	57	62
Gambia	360	27	132	45
Haiti	370	53	93	55
Indonesia	730	77	66	60
Israel	13,760	95	9	76
Japan	31,450	99	5	79
Kuwait	23,350	73	14	75
Malta	7,630	84	9	76
Nigeria	310	51	84	52
Pakistan	430	35	95	59
Russia	2,350	99	20	69
Saudi Arabia	7,780	62	32	69
Seychelles	6,370	58	16	71
Sri Lanka	600	88	18	72
Sweden	24,830	99	5	78
Switzerland	36,410	99	6	78
Tajikistan	470	90	49	69
Turkey	2,120	81	54	67
United Kingdom	17,970	99	7	76
United States	24,750	99	9	77

Source: Data on PGNP, infant mortality rates, and life expectancy are the latest available estimates as of 1996, and were obtained from *World Development Report, 1995* (New York: Oxford University Press, 1995) and *World Bank Atlas, 1995* (Washington, D.C.: World Bank, 1995). Data on literacy rates, based on percent of population fifteen years of age or older able to read and write, are the latest available estimates as of 1996, and were obtained from *World Bank Atlas, 1995,* supplemented by *The World Factbook, 1995–1996* (Washington, D.C.: U.S. Central Intelligence Agency, 1995).

the case of such oil-rich countries as Nigeria and Indonesia, efforts to develop an improved standard of living are hampered by huge populations, political upheavals, and the unpredictability of oil revenues. A large population often may be an asset in terms of power, but it can be a liability in terms of economic development. As less developed countries have gained greater access to advanced medical technologies, life expectancy has been increasing considerably, in the process contributing to the enormous population growth that has outstripped economic growth in may cases. We discuss these problems and the politics associated with them in Chapter 14.

DEGREE OF POLARIZATION

We noted in the previous chapter that the alignment picture had become more complicated as the Cold War neared its conclusion, with the East-West axis of conflict increasingly having to share the spotlight with the North-South axis of conflict and with the East-West battlelines themselves becoming less neatly drawn. Still, if there was one thing that most defined world politics in the half-century after World War II, it was the ideologically tinged superpower competition and bloc structure, which seemed to give a certain "order to the anarchy of international relations,"[52] or at least an element of clarity. As a former Israeli foreign minister put it: "The Cold War, with all its perils, expressed a certain bleak stability: alignments, fidelities, and rivalries were sharply defined. . . . Nationalist rivalries, religious fanaticism, unsolved territorial disputes, ancient prejudices and enmities [and other conflicts suppressed below the surface of the Cold War system] . . . had all been squeezed into a Pandora's box. The end of the Cold War set these tensions free; they can now explode in their own right and seek their own horizons."[53]

We saw how such an explosion materialized in Yugoslavia. With the end of their global geopolitical struggle, neither the United States nor Russia believed they had critical interests at stake and hence were content for the most part, at least initially, to leave the Yugoslavs to sort out their own difficulties. The West Europeans, who were closer to the conflict, were in disarray over how to handle the crisis; for example, on the issue of whether to recognize Slovenia and Croatia as independent states, the German foreign minister, based partly on German economic interests, told his fellow ministers from other European Community countries in 1991 that "we will move ahead whether any, all, or none of the European states joint us."[54] Most other states outside Europe had equal difficulty choosing up sides. As the Yugoslav case illustrates, the polarizing tendencies of the Cold War have been replaced by a far more complex alignment pattern, with many sources of conflict and cross-cutting cleavages to be found in the post–Cold War world.

It is, of course, possible that the East-West conflict could be revived and the Cold War ideological battles resumed. Not only do a few orthodox Marxist regimes still exist in Cuba and elsewhere, but China also remains officially a communist system, whereas capitalist reforms have yet to prove successful in the former Soviet republics and in Eastern Europe, where former communists have even regained power through elections in some cases. However, a resurrection of the East-West conflict is unlikely, given popular revulsion regarding a return to one-party totalitarian dictatorship throughout the former Soviet bloc, the current weakened condition of Russia, and the changed foreign policy orientations of Vietnam, Syria, and other former Soviet clients who have been seeking to open up political and economic ties to the West to replace the diplomatic and financial support Moscow once provided.[55]

Still, it does seem premature to declare, as some did when the Berlin Wall fell in 1989, that "the end of history" has come, with laissez-faire capitalism's "victory" over communism.[56] In addition to the fact that some Marxist states exist, some of the most productive parts of Western economies, such as agriculture, have involved substantial government intervention and subsidies rather than reliance purely on free enterprise and the marketplace. Some Western capitalist states (e.g., the United States) have stressed "market" approaches (private sector initiatives) as opposed to "statist" approaches (public sector initiatives) far more than others (e.g., Sweden and France). Whether Russia and other former Marxist societies might follow a "mixed economy" orientation or some other model remains to be seen. (China's current experimentation with capitalism under a communist regime has been called "Market-Leninism," as opposed to Marxist-Leninism.[57])

Just as the East-West conflict has diminished as East bloc states have moved ideologically toward the West, the North-South conflict also shows signs of possibly losing its defining character despite the persistence of the rich-poor gap. Here, too, it is possible that the North-South axis of conflict left over from the Cold War could heat up again, especially if Western preoccupation with helping Poland and other Eastern states convert to capitalism results in transference of foreign aid and investment from the South to the East, thereby fueling racially tinged feelings of betrayal and resentment on the part of nonwhite peoples. However, the one factor (other than opposition to colonialism) that in the past allowed the "South" to maintain a relatively high degree of cohesion on a broad range of issues despite many rivalries and even hostilities between coalition members was the recognition of shared economic problems and interests vis-à-vis the North. Given the growing diversity within the "developing" world we have alluded to, Southern solidarity likely will be increasingly difficult to maintain as some of the more industrialized members gravitate toward the North, or at least no longer perceive themselves as part of the third world. Indeed, the "third world" nomenclature—owing its origins to the notion of a "third pole" situated between the first and second worlds in the East-West conflict—has in many ways become an anachronism in the analysis of international relations, even though it is still commonly used.[58] When 108 members of the Non-Aligned Movement (NAM) met in 1992 in Bandung—the place where the movement had first begun, under the banner of anticolonialism—they had to search hard for a rationale for their continued existence.

As for the "North," increasing economic competition between technologically advanced states threatens to make West-West conflict almost as volatile an arena as East-West conflict had been. Witness, for example the report in *L'Express* in May 1990 that government intelligence services in France were trying to penetrate American corporate technological secrets, as the CIA was attempting to counter such espionage by its own NATO ally.

If the East-West and North-South conflicts were, in the words of one commentator, "the two dominant struggles of our time"[59] in the last half of the twentieth century, what then might replace them as the central global dramas in the twenty-first century? What new divisions and descriptive categories in the post–Cold War era might replace the vernacular of first, second, and third worlds and other such terminology that dominated discourse during the Cold War? Some see the world already dividing into continental blocs built around economic relationships, with the emergence of a Japanese-led Pacific Rim bloc pitted against an American-led North American entity (eventually extending throughout the Western Hemisphere) and an increasingly integrated European Union—all sharing common Western values of capitalist democracy but nonetheless engaged in intense competition.[60] Others envision a "clash of civilizations" based on competing cultural values, arguing that "the paramount axis of world politics will be the relations between 'the West and the Rest' . . . ; a central focus of conflict for the immediate future will be between the West and several Islamic-Confucian states."[61] Still others see the kind of Moslem-Serb-Croat conflict that occurred in Yugoslavia as the harbinger of a series of isolated, localized conflicts that will increasingly define international politics and that will not necessarily fit into any larger global axis of conflict.[62]

This book is about the "global condition" and, as such, assumes that all international relations ultimately can be placed into a global context. At the same time, the richness and complexity of international politics can be lost sight of if one fails to note that below the global level lies a number of *regional subsystems.* Each regional subsystem, although touched by global concerns, exhibits a life of its own in certain respects. One can, for example, talk about the politics of the Middle East or Latin America or Western Europe or Asia. (Depending on how complicated one wants to get, one can distinguish between East Asian, South Asian, and West Asian subsystems within Asia.) Although the rivalry between Pakistan and India, say, may not be particularly visible at the global level, it may reveal more about and have greater bearing on the politics of South Asia than larger East-West, North-South, or other global-level conflicts do. It also may be of greater interest to the average Indian or Pakistani. Even the Middle East, although central to global energy politics, can be treated in some respects as a distinct subsystem, with its own peculiar dynamics based on local or regional issues and rivalries. Numerous other examples of "discontinuities" in the international system can be cited that illustrate the oversimplifications that are necessarily made when one attempts to treat the international system as a coherent whole.

Especially with the weakening of global superpowers and of global, systemwide axes of conflict such as the East-West and North-South constellations, regional politics may well be given greater play in the future, as regional powers attempt to push more localized agendas. Still, given the globalization of the international economy and the inherently global character of such issues as nuclear weapons proliferation and ozone layer deterioration, there are limits to the extent to which action can be expected to move from the global arena to the regional level. Considering the trends we have described and the myriad of concerns facing humanity, one would expect the alignment patterns in the international system to be marked increasingly by new and shifting coalitions of actors across more than two sets of issues. As one scholar has said, we may have entered an era of "unalignment."[63]

OBJECTIVES AND MEANS

In the contemporary international system, "national security" has become a more ambiguous concern than in the past, no longer equated almost exclusively with military issues. Although it may remain the overriding goal of nation-states, "security" has been broadened to include economic, ecological, and other dimensions that have gained rising visibility and salience on the agendas of governments.[64]

As mentioned in Chapter 2, this trend was already apparent by the 1970s, when Stanley Hoffmann noted that we were witnessing

> the move from a world dominated by a single chessboard—the strategic-diplomatic one (which either eclipsed or controlled all others)—to a world dispersed into a variety of chessboards. This is partly the result of the nuclear stalemate (which has somewhat neutralized the strategic chessboard and reduced, if not its fundamental importance, at least its daily saliency), partly the product of economic and social processes and scientific invention in a world obsessed by the quest for economic growth.[65]

Likewise, Henry Kissinger, another realist thinker writing at the same time, acknowledged that the traditional notion of international relations as a geopolitical "balance of power" struggle waged primarily in military terms did not quite square with the emerging new reality; he noted that "the problems of energy, resources, environment, population, the uses of space and the seas now rank with questions of military security . . . and territorial rivalry which have traditionally made up the diplomatic agenda."[66]

Clearly, economic prosperity, and "welfare" concerns generally, have become even more important as national goals in the post–Cold War era. We have noted throughout this chapter that economic phenomena (e.g., the use of economic levers of influence, the debate over market and nonmarket approaches to the welfare state, and the rise of continental trade blocs) are increasingly competing for attention with military phenomena. There is disagreement among scholars as to whether welfare issues have now achieved primacy over military issues. Some observers so argue, pointing out that finance ministers are now getting the kinds of front-page newspaper headlines that were once reserved for defense ministers and foreign ministers. Economics is being called "the continuation of war by other means,"[67] particularly among highly developed societies, which may well intensify their economic competition but, presumably, are unlikely to wage shooting wars against each other given the destructiveness of armed combat in the nuclear age. At the outset of this chapter we referred to the "long peace"—the absence of great power war since 1945; some analysts, grounded in the idealist paradigm, have suggested that industrialized societies now constitute a "zone of peace" that eventually will encompass even Africa and other "developing" parts of the globe that currently represent a "zone of turmoil," leading to "the end of war."[68] It is said that most people on the planet are less likely to be affected by military-strategic issues today than by "developments in trade, immigration, or international health policy."[69]

However, others point to the Yugoslav conflict as evidence that war in its most savage form can still occur even between people living in relatively highly developed societies; the contestants in the Yugoslav conflict had, before the war, enjoyed a per capita income of roughly $3,000, life expectancy of over 70 years, and a literacy rate of over 90 percent. The Yugoslav case also shows how convulsions in international economic relations can contribute to escalation of tensions, possibly culminating in violent conflict. Peter Rodman argues that not only will the world continue to be faced with a proliferation of wars such as Bosnia—"teacup wars"[70] in which major actors are only peripherally involved—but one also cannot rule out larger wars between great powers themselves:

> If relations among the major powers go sour, the world's ability to collaborate on any of the more ambitious challenges will evaporate instantly. If we take for granted today's relatively benign relations among the big powers, we will lose them. It is obvious that economic trends are fundamental. But if trade disputes among the major economic powers are not contained and resolved . . . they will indeed unravel the international order.[71]

We will discuss the "long peace" and trends in warfare in greater depth in Chapter 8.

Moreover, classic "security dilemmas" and territorial disputes persist. One need only cite growing apprehension felt by Japan and other states in Southeast Asia over the recent arms buildup by China, as well as China's pressing of claims to the Spratlys, some sixty rocky atols in the South China sea that are thought to sit near as much as $1 trillion in oil and gas deposits and that are also claimed by five other states.[72] Although such disputes are less likely to eventuate in war today than, say, a century ago, they are still a source of con-

THE CHINESE NAVY PATROLLING THE SOUTH CHINA SEA IN 1995.

cern.[73] So also is the fact that, despite a decline in the actual use of force by states in recent years, levels of world military expenditures, military manpower, and arms imports remain high. Indeed, many believe humanity needs to move beyond the concept of national security altogether to embrace the concept of "international security"; i.e., "global security must be broadened from its traditional focus on the security of states to the security of people and the planet."[74]

DEGREE OF INTERDEPENDENCE

The oil embargo of 1973 (discussed in Chapter 2), probably more than any other single episode during the post–World War II period, popularized the notion that the world had become highly interdependent. There was a good deal of hard evidence to back up this general feeling. Based on an extensive study of international transaction trends in such areas as trade, investment, tourism, and mail and phone communications, Alex Inkeles concluded that over

> a wide range of systems of exchange we find evidence for rapid acceleration
> in the development of ties linking nations, their institutional components,

and the individuals who populate them. The abundance and complexity of the networks which interconnect the world's population are, and have been for some time, growing at a phenomenal rate. With some variation according to the specific indicator used, recent decades reveal a general tendency for many forms of human interconnectedness across national boundaries to be doubling every ten years.[75]

These trends have only accelerated since the 1970s. We noted just a few manifestations of interdependence in the 1990s at the very beginning of this book. We could have added countless other examples. "Sesame Street" and Coca-Cola are now available in more than 160 countries; the international financial market has been called "a global marketplace that never sleeps";[76] and so on. Numerous data can be cited that demonstrate the spreading web of human contacts as the twentieth century draws to a close.[77] Despite the attempts by some national governments to set up barriers to international flows of goods (through tariffs and quotas), people (through immigration and travel restrictions), and ideas (through jamming radio signals or banning TV satellite transmissions), modern communications and travel technology have made borders extremely "permeable."[78]

One needs to keep interdependence in proper perspective, however. For example, even though the number of university students studying abroad has been increasing in recent years by almost 10 percent per year, 98 percent of the world's total student body remains at home to receive schooling.[79] This reflects the fact that international transactions are still merely a tiny fraction of all human interactions in relative terms. One study finds that although certain kinds of transactions, such as telephone calls, are increasing more rapidly internationally than domestically, this is less true for other categories, such as mail flows and air travel; in the case of air travel, for example, the authors note: "Although the number of international travelers leaving the United States in 1980 was almost six hundred times what it was in 1930, the number of domestic air travelers has increased even more rapidly. In fact, [in terms of the foreign component of air travel] the postwar high for the United States, 11 percent in 1970, was still less . . . than it was in 1930. Neither U.S. nor world air traffic demonstrates any [increased] trend in the ratio of international to domestic travel."[80]

Then, too, the growth of international transactions is only one aspect of the interdependence phenomenon. Increasing human interconnectedness across national boundaries may or may not affect a second, more important aspect of interdependence—the mutual sensitivity and vulnerability nation-states and national governments experience with regard to each other's actions. The fact that more and more people around the world may be watching "Sesame Street" while drinking Coca-Cola is not necessarily relevant to world politics. Some kinds of international flows (e.g., trade) obviously have the potential to create greater sensitivities and vulnerabilities than other types (e.g., pen pal correspondence). We saw how, with the end of the Cold War, the rupture of traditional trade relationships that Yugoslavia had once enjoyed with the Soviet bloc aggravated economic and political conditions within Yugoslavia.

Interdependence is a very *uneven* phenomenon, in terms of both patterns of interconnectedness and patterns of sensitivity and vulnerability. Regarding interconnectedness, it is clear that goods and services, people, and communications do not flow evenly around the world. In the trade sector, for example, the advanced industrialized countries account for 70 percent of total exports worldwide; three states alone (the United States, Japan, and Germany) account for a third of all exports. The bulk of world trade, particularly in manufactured goods, continues to occur among well-established, highly developed capitalist countries (e.g., Canada and Japan are the United States' first and second leading trade partners), although trade winds are beginning to shift somewhat as NICs and other developing countries, along with China and the former communist states of the East bloc, become further enmeshed in the global economy.[81]

Very similar patterns can be found with regard to the flow of foreign investment funds, tourists, and communications, with the highest levels of interdependence observed among the industrialized democracies. The industrialized democracies in recent years have accounted for well over half of all memberships in the more than 10,000 international nongovernmental organizations (NGOs) and have been headquarters for a vast percentage of all of these organizations; they likewise have accounted for well over half of all memberships in the more than 300 intergovernmental organizations (IGOs).[82] Here, too, though, as the former East bloc states open their borders and assume a larger role in the world economy, they along with developing states are gradually increasing international organization membership and are becoming more "deeply entangled in this expanding web."[83]

Not only are interconnectedness patterns uneven in the contemporary international system but so also are sensitivity and vulnerability patterns. If by "sensitivity" and "vulnerability" one means the general tendency today for many problems, such as pollution and inflation, to spill over national frontiers and defy unilateral national solutions, then it is true that all states are interdependent. Certainly, on *some* dimensions of interdependence (e.g., ecological concerns relating to climatic change), it would seem that everybody has an equal stake in the matter. However, on other dimensions (e.g., economic), some countries are less sensitive and vulnerable to external actions than are other countries.

Much interdependence is *asymmetrical* in nature, with dependencies being one-sided. Many relationships that the United States enters into with another country tend to be asymmetrical; i.e., the United States tends to attach less importance to the relationship than does its counterpart. For example, to the extent that the United States and Zaire are interdependent, it is Zaire that "needs" the United States more than the United States "needs" Zaire. However, even here, the United States has some dependency, because

Zaire is a chief source of cobalt, a mineral that is found practically nowhere in the United States and is essential for making certain communications equipment as well as aircraft engines. If no substitute could be found for cobalt, if no alternative supplies were available, and if Zaire were able to reduce its own import and export dependence on the United States, then the United States indeed would not only be "sensitive" but "vulnerable" in this area. Another example of asymmetrical interdependence is the American dominance in the North American economy; in the 1990s, less than 25 percent of total U.S. exports went to Canada, and less than 10 percent to Mexico, whereas over 70 percent of all Canadian and all Mexican exports went to the United States.

Countries can try to minimize their dependence on other countries by reducing their permeability and erecting various barriers, although "undoing" interdependence can be extremely difficult and costly. Among the countries that have felt especially "penetrated" and have made special efforts in the past to lessen this condition—with only modest results—are Burma, Iran, Tanzania, and Canada (whose resentment over perceived U.S. economic and cultural domination did not prevent it from deciding in 1992 to join the North American Free Trade Agreement). Suffice it to say that interdependence is very real but also very complicated.

SOME FURTHER COMPLICATIONS: NONSTATE ACTORS

If the reader does not find the contemporary international system complicated enough, there are other complications that might be noted that have only been hinted at in our discussion up to now. In particular, in offering a bird's-eye view of the international system, we have been looking at the world essentially through **state-centric** lenses. That is, we have examined such things as the distribution of power and wealth, degree of polarization, and interdependence largely in the traditional context of relationships between nation-states. Our picture of contemporary international relations would be incomplete, however, if we failed to acknowledge the fact that nation-states, acting through national governments, are not the only actors in international relations and that *nonstate* actors—such as intergovernmental and nongovernmental organizations and multinational corporations—have some effect on international relations.

We noted earlier that these kinds of actors have existed on the world scene for a long time and that they proliferated in the twentieth century, particularly after World War II. We have not discussed their importance in international relations. Nonstate actors are worth examining only if one can demonstrate that they are to some extent autonomous agents in international politics—that they have their own distinct objectives apart from national governments, that they actively pursue these objectives in the international arena, and that they have some impact on world politics and relations between states.

For example, one cannot fully understand the dynamics of the 1992 United Nations Conference on Environment and Development held in Rio de Janeiro (the "Earth Summit," to be discussed in Chapter 15) unless one takes into account, in addition to the interplay between Northern and Southern governments, the variety of nonstate actors involved: the secretariats of the UN, World Bank, and other IGOs, scientific research bodies and global environmental advocacy groups, multinational companies with a stake in ecological issues, and a host of other players. Although state-centric analysts would contend that IGOs are little more than fragile collections of states that tend to be dominated by a few national capitals, and that NGOs are no match for the power of governments, our point is not that nonstate actors played the decisive role in this conference, only that they were a not insignificant part of the equation that produced several new environmental agreements.

As another example, consider the power of private bankers and currency traders who, in the course of transacting business in the multibillion dollar "Eurocurrency market" and other international financial markets, have the capacity to frustrate attempts by national governments through their central banks to regulate exchange rates and interest rates and shape trade, monetary, and other economic policies. It may be true that "the Euromarkets are not stateless; they rest on the implicit and sometimes explicit support of major western governments. . . . At any point in the last thirty years, the U.S. government could have put a stop to much Euromarket activity by prohibiting American banks from participating and by blocking the use of the U.S. dollar offshore."[84] However, the fact is that there are costs involved in government intervention in capital markets—for example, business expansion worldwide could be dampened—which may explain why these markets have been allowed to operate freely despite at times playing havoc with efforts by states individually and collectively to control economic forces.[85]

Many other examples can be cited of nonstate actors, organized either *subnationally* (within national boundaries) or *transnationally* (across national boundaries), competing with national governments in affecting world politics. World politics can be seen as a series of issue-areas in which outcomes are determined by a congeries of forces, including both state and nonstate actors. Case studies have suggested the relevance of nonstate actors to many different sets of issues.[86] Even in the war-peace area, traditionally considered to be the exclusive domain of national governments, one may choose to ignore the role of nonstate actors such as the United Nations and the International Red Cross, but one cannot ignore the substantial capacity of actors such as the Popular Front for the Liberation of Palestine and the Irish Republican Army to generate violence in the international system. In our examination of the Yugoslavia case study, we made mention of numerous nonstate actors (e.g., the European Community, NATO, the UN, the International Monetary Fund, and assorted ethnic groups organized across state boundaries) that played some role in the affair.

Many observers have associated the nonstate actor phenomenon with what they perceive to be the decline of the nation-state as a political, economic, and social unit. One noted scholar, reflecting on the growth of multinational corporations in particular, has observed that "the state is about through as an economic unit."[87] Another observer, formerly a high-level U.S. policymaker, has said that "the nation-state is a very old-fashioned idea and badly adapted to serve the needs of our present complex world."[88] Still another observer, who has had his feet in both the academic and policymaking sectors, has commented that "transnational ties are gaining in importance, while the claims of nationalism, though still intense, are nevertheless becoming diluted. . . . The consequence is a new era—an era of the global political process."[89] This theme is best summarized in the following remarks:

> At present what seems to be at work is a complex interaction between a much more dynamic . . . international system and the individual nation-states that we have traditionally viewed as relatively autonomous. Sovereignty still prevails . . . but a host of international or transnational forces are simultaneously at work, affecting how people act in what were once considered to be domestic affairs, and above all, impinging on the priorities of government. All governments are put under pressure by the increasingly significant flows of international trade, finance, and communications; by the effects of contemporary science and technology; and by all the other elements that make up what we imprecisely called modernization.[90]

There is some disagreement among those who envision the possible demise of the nation-state as to whether the primary threat to its viability comes from *integrative* tendencies (i.e., the transnational links referred to above) or *disintegrative* tendencies (i.e., the proliferation of many small marginally self-sustaining polities, fueled especially by the revival of ethnic conflict and separatist movements on the part of minorities within existing states, as evidenced by the breakup of Yugoslavia),[91] or both. We alluded to these competing integration and disintegration trends—what one writer calls "powerful tensions, profound contradictions, and perplexing paradoxes"[92]—in the box on "Human Governance in the Post–Cold War Era" in Chapter 1. Some analysts go so far as to speak of a "new feudalism" (see box on pp. 115–117). Others speak of just the opposite, an emergent "global village." In either case, if these observers are correct, the world is witnessing the most significant and sweeping change the international system has experienced in the last 400 years, namely the transformation of the very structures in which human beings are organized and around which their political lives revolve.

However, it needs to be emphasized that for every observer who sees the imminent demise of the nation-state, there are at least three other observers who argue that the nation-state is alive and well. The latter are quick to re-

Globalization: The new patriotism?

mind the former that the twentieth century has been the century of "the state"—that is, the seemingly universal tendency in all modern societies, democracies and nondemocracies alike, is for national governments to become bigger and more heavily involved in the lives of their citizens. If the nation-state is withering away, someone has forgotten to tell the leaders in Washington and other national capitals. In nondemocratic societies especially, which include over half the world's people,[93] there are severe constraints on what individuals can do internally as well as externally. Although it is true that there has been a dramatic democratization process at work lately in Eastern Europe, Latin America, and elsewhere—with increasing acceptance of liberal democratic political principles and free-market economic principles—along with a "deregulation" and "privatization" movement in many Western circles, there remains almost everywhere a generalized commitment to both the "national security state" and the "welfare state" and to the notion that governments have a right to exercise control over the amount and type of transnational activity in which citizens can engage outside national boundaries.[94] Given these facts, prognostications about the demise of the nation-state do seem quite premature.

James Rosenau suggests we think of world politics today as "bifurcated," in terms of a "state-centric system" existing alongside a "multicentric actor system."[95] We would argue that there is a global political process at work today, but that nation-states remain at the core of this process. They remain the key actors in the drama of contemporary world politics, although they are being

THE "NEW FEUDALISM"

It has been said that the nation-state came into being largely because the previous unit of human organization—the walled city or moated castle of the feudal era—no longer could provide for the protection and security of its population in an age of gunpowder. An added impetus for the nation-state was the felt need for clearer lines of authority within larger territorial jurisdictions over which a common set of laws would apply, so as to enhance enforcement of contracts, standardization of currency, and other elements critical to facilitating and expanding commerce. Some scholars have argued that the nation-state today can no longer perform the security function and is as much an anachronism as the walled fortress of yore, given the ease with which national boundaries can be penetrated by nuclear weapons. Likewise, it is argued that the nation-state is no longer able to meet human needs in the economic realm, as commerce has outgrown national boundaries (because of the growth of international currency speculators, transnational business enterprises, and other such actors), producing an incongruity between economic and political-legal space and leading to "loss of control" over fiscal and monetary policy levers national governments have normally used to provide for the welfare of their citizens. From "failed states" in Africa where authority has collapsed totally (e.g., Somalia) to established states in the developed world where the unity of the state is being challenged (e.g., Canada), people appear to be uneasy with the way existing institutions are working.

It seems the nation-state has never been more vibrant as a human institution, given the desire of Serbs, Croats, and others to have their *own state* modeled after the modern Westphalian polity; yet in many respects it has never been more at risk. Susan Strange, echoing Hedley Bull and others, speaks of the "new medievalism," i.e., "the state is coming to share authority in economy and society with other entities [IGOs, NGOs, MNCs]. . . . Within the state the authority of central government is increasingly shared with local and regional authorities. . . . [In other words,] state authority has leaked away, upwards, sideways, and downwards." She adds: "I am not arguing that states themselves are obsolete. Collectively they are still the most influential and therefore critical sources of authority in the world system. But they are increasingly becoming hollow or defective institutions."[1]

In the excerpt below, Vincent Cable elaborates on how new forms of political organization are evolving that might replace, or at least substantially modify, the nation-state:

As the global system becomes more integrated, there is a demand for international public goods that neither markets nor nation-states will provide. . . . These are roughly as follows: systemic financial stability; the rule of law and dispute settlement needed for an open system of trade and investment; common standards for weights and measures; management of global communications networks like aviation, telecommunications, and sea-lanes to prevent congestion and disasters; management of environmental concerns like Antarctica, the atmosphere, and oceans. . . .

All of these require some form of institutional development beyond the nation-state. Some of these activities are largely self-regulating, since the main commercial users have a collective interest in providing the public good, as is the case with bond markets (International Securities Markets Association) and many industrial standards (the International Standards Organization). . . . In some cases, there is mixed public/private sector participation, as in the International Telecommunications Union. But, mostly, there is sovereignty pooling by governments through new institutions (the European Union; the World Meteorological Organization). . . . There is a complex but rich system of governance growing up to manage globalization. . . .

The most obvious consequence of globalization is that forces of international competition, and the mixture of opportunity and personal risk that they represent, affect a widening spectrum of the population. Not just steel and textile workers, but bank clerks, journalists, creative artists, shopkeepers, employees of public utilities, and doctors operate increasingly in a global as well as a local marketplace. . . .

Globalization may be squeezing the wages and job prospects of the more unskilled workers [and organized labor generally] in rich countries. At the same time, for the educated and moneyed section of the population, the opportunities presented by globalization—travel, wider experience, promotion—are great. We thus have one, potentially large, disadvantaged, alienated, and powerless element in society and another which is flourishing but has less of a stake in the success of any particular country.

Such tendencies might lead to a loss of authority of those who govern in the name of the nation-state . . . where the state cannot any longer rely on the loyalty of its citizens. . . . There is a chain of cause and effect which links economic globalizing forces to contemporary expressions of "tribalism." . . .

[One approach] for small and medium-sized countries is to try to recreate a sense of national identity and cohesion through larger units. . . . Certainly for European "federalists," the goal of a United States of Europe has been a guiding vision. . . .

It is possible in the very long term to envisage a world of large entities, "supernations"—the United States, the EU [European Union], Russia, Greater China, India, Brazil—which capture many of the economies of scale and scope that globalization offers and manage to create an overarching sense of "national" identity to encompass many nationalisms within a federal structure. One problem, however, is that even the largest nation-states are having to respond to globalization by opening their economies to trade and foreign investment (as China, Russia, and India are doing) or by building yet bigger structures (the United States and NAFTA). And, as the EU is discovering through its enlargement, the bigger the structure the smaller the sense of identity. . . .

Another, and perhaps complementary, development is the growth of subnational identities within federal structures. Many [governmental roles] . . . can be dealt with at the level of Wales rather than Britain, California rather than the United States, Quebec rather than Canada. Indeed, the move to larger units gives the new "nationalisms"—of Scotland, the Italian and Spanish regions, Flanders, and Wallonia [in Belgium]—space to operate within a loose European federal structure (which is why Scottish Nationalists . . . favor the vision of EU federation). In China, much economic decision-making is now devolved at the level of the province and city. In India, central government is delegating a wider range of investment promotion, regulatory, and fiscal powers to the states. . . . In these cases, there is a recognition that multilayered forms of identity and responsibility have to be created around (above and below) the nation-state.

Source: Vincent Cable, "The Diminished Nation-State: A Study in the Loss of Economic Power," reprinted by permission of *Daedalus,* Journal of the American Academy of Arts and Sciences, from the issue entitled, "What Future for the State?" Spring 1995, Vol. 124, No. 2, pp. 23–53.

[1] Susan Strange, "The Defective State," *Daedalus,* 124 (Spring):56–57, 1995. Also, see the other articles in this volume, which featured a symposium on "What Future for the State?," especially Vivien Schmidt's "The New World Order Incorporated: The Rise of Business and the Decline of the Nation-State," pp. 75–106.

buffeted by both centrifugal and centripetal forces, which in the short run may undermine the ability of national governments to control events fully in international relations and in the long run may pose challenges to their very existence. In terms of world order, these forces contain the seeds of both increased conflict and increased cooperation. In the latter part of this book, we will explore the relationships that exist between the various nation-states and nonstate actors in the global political process.

Conclusion

The international system in the post–Cold War era remains a decentralized system, even if, as some say, some sort of "central guidance" mechanism is needed more than at any time previously. Nation-states are still legally and formally sovereign—independent—but are behaviorally interdependent to a greater degree than in the past. Nationalism persists alongside transnationalism, regionalism alongside globalism. National governments in many cases (judging by their budgets) are bigger than ever but less able by themselves to deal with problems that spill over national boundaries. National security continues to be a paramount concern but must vie for attention increasingly with welfare concerns. The international system remains stratified in terms of power and wealth, although the patterns are complex, with once "superpowers" often frustrated by "mini-states" and with some developing countries beginning to join the ranks of the advanced industrialized states while others fall further behind. East-West and North-South conflicts linger, but are being overshadowed by West-West, South-South, and other permutations of conflicts, many of which are highly localized. And if communications and travel technology has produced a "shrinking and linking" of the world and a nascent "world society," it has also made individuals in some cases even more aware of the differences that exist between peoples within that global society.

We have attempted in this chapter to provide an overview of the general setting in which international relations occur as a new century begins. We obviously live in complicated and tumultuous times, although the world has never been an uncomplicated place. Having provided a broad-brush portrait of the contemporary international system, we are now ready to examine it in greater detail and in more dynamic perspective. In later chapters we will focus on specific elements of the international system and we will see how the interactions of roughly 6 billion people, 190 nation-states, and 10,000 international organizations are determining "who gets what, when, and how" in the global polity.

SUMMARY

1. The Yugoslav conflict in the 1990s illustrated the growing complexity of international relations in the post–Cold War era. As reflected by this episode, the contemporary international system is characterized by (a) increased ambiguity in the measurement and exercise of power, (b) decreased cohesion of alliances and blocs, along with multiple axes of conflict, (c) complicated patterns of interdependence, and (d) challenges to the nation-state from both within and without.

2. Regarding the distribution of power in the contemporary system, it is more difficult to identify a meaningful "pecking order" among states today than in the past. The two postwar "superpowers" (the United States and the Soviet Union) have given way to multiple "power centers," all of which can find themselves frustrated even by "mini-states."

3. In the past, power—although dependent on economic strength—was exercised mainly through military means and was measurable mainly in military terms. Today economic resources can have more direct effects apart from military factors and can be at least as important in influencing international relations. Although military power clearly cannot be discounted, the nuclear weaponry concentrated in the hands of a few states is less readily usable than the more conventional military prowess enjoyed by the great powers of the past.

4. There are vast differences between states today in terms of size. However, power is based on a wide variety of societal variables, not only on raw size but also on many qualitative or intangible factors, and it can best be viewed as situation-specific or issue-specific.

5. Regarding the distribution of wealth, one can distinguish between the advanced industrialized democracies (the "first world") and the rest of the states in the system (the "two-thirds world"), which includes great variety: the developed former Soviet bloc states attempting the transition from communism to market economies, the NICs and next NICs, oil-rich but still underdeveloped OPEC countries, and impoverished third world and even "Fourth World" countries. Some countries in the world rank high on almost every measure of national well-being, others rank low on almost every measure, whereas others have uneven development characteristics.

6. The international system has moved further away from the bipolarity of the Cold War era in terms of not only power distribution but also alignment patterns. Although some vestiges of the East-West and North-South axes of conflict linger, they have been replaced by a far more complex alignment picture, with many sources of conflict and cross-cutting cleavages occurring around varied sets of issues. Where the ideological struggle between the United States and USSR dominated the post–World War II period, some see the post–Cold War period dominated by either a cultural struggle between "the West and the rest" or an economic struggle between continental trade blocs. Others see the end of the Cold War as giving greater play to local and regional rivalries that had long simmered beneath the surface of the global system, such as those unleashed in the Yugoslav conflict. Still others find the relationships so fluid today as to suggest we are living in an era of "unalignment."

7. Traditional military-security issues, although remaining the highest priority of states, now have to compete increasingly for attention with economic, environmental, and other issues that have been added to the international agenda.

8. Interdependence is clearly increasing. However, it is very uneven, in terms of both interconnectedness and patterns of sensitivity and vulnerability. Some countries are relatively independent and others relatively dependent in their relations with each other.

9. International relations are further influenced by nonstate actors, such as IGOs and NGOs and multinational corporations. These groups at times can pursue objectives apart from national governments and compete with the latter in affecting world politics. Although transnationalism is an important trend in contemporary world politics, it is premature to speak of the demise of the nation-state, given the continued attachment to nationalism felt throughout the world and the continued role of the state in regulating human activity within and across national boundaries. To the extent the nation-stage is under siege, it is as much from subnational ethnopolitical and other tensions as from globalizing forces, although these disintegrative and integrative phenomena may all be interrelated.

SUGGESTIONS FOR FURTHER READING AND STUDY

Among the many works dealing with the Yugoslavia conflict, Susan Woodward's *Balkan Tragedy* (Washington, D.C.: Brookings Institution, 1995) is especially useful in examining the roots of the conflict and the complex dynamics involving both state and nonstate actors. Also see Misha Glenny, *The Fall of Yugoslavia: The Third Balkan War* (London: Penguin, 1992); and Mark Thompson, *A Paper House: The Ending of Yugoslavia* (New York: Pantheon, 1992).

On the general shape of the "new world order" in the post–Cold War era, many provocative and conflicting views can be seen in John J. Mearsheimer, "Why We Will Soon Miss the Cold War," *The Atlantic Monthly* (August 1990), pp. 35–50, along with his "Back to the Future: Instability in Europe After the Cold War," *International Security*, 15 (Summer 1990), pp. 5–56; Max Singer and Aaron Wildavsky, *The Real World Order* (Chatham, N.J.: Chatham House, 1993); Mark Zacher, "The Decaying Pillars of the Westphalian Temple: Implications for International Order and Governance," in James N. Rosenau and Ernst-Otto Czempiel, eds., *Governance Without Government: Order and Change in World Politics* (Cambridge, Eng.: Cambridge University Press, 1992); Seyom Brown, *New Forces, Old Forces and the Future of World Politics*, post–Cold War edition (New York: Harper Collins, 1995), part 3; the symposium on "The Quest for World Order," in *Dadealus*, 124 (Summer 1995); and the symposium on "Shaping the New World Order," in *International Security*, 17 (Summer 1992).

On the distribution of power in contemporary world politics, see Joseph S. Nye, *Bound to Lead: The Changing Nature of American Power* (New York: Basic Books, 1990), which argues that the United States may still be the preeminent world power, but that power is not what it used to be. Three excellent articles that point out the complexity of power in the contemporary international system, focusing on the relationship between economic and military power, are Theodore Moran, "An Economic Agenda for Neorealists," *International Security*, 18 (Fall 1993), pp. 211–215; Robert Jervis, "International Primacy: Is the Game Worth the Candle?," *International Security*, 17 (Spring 1993), pp. 52–67; and Samuel Huntington, "Why International Primacy Matters," in *International Security*, 17 (Spring 1993), pp. 68–83; also, see Kenneth Waltz, "The Emerging Structure of International Politics," *International Security*, 18 (Fall 1993), pp. 44–79. On the distribution of wealth in the contemporary international system, see *World Bank Atlas, 1995* (Washington, D.C.: World Bank, 1995); Lester R. Brown et al., *State of the World 1990* (New York: W. W. Norton, 1990), ch. 8; and Lester R. Brown et al., "Income Gap Widens," in *Vital Signs 1995* (New York: W. W. Norton, 1995), pp. 144–145.

On alignment configurations and what categories might replace East vs. West and North vs. South in the post–Cold War era, see Samuel P. Huntington's "The Clash of Civilizations," *Foreign Affairs*, 72 (Summer 1993), pp. 22–49 and the accompanying forum in the September/October 1993 issue of *Foreign Affairs* as well as *The Clash of Civilization and the Remaking of World Order* (New York: Simon and Schuster, 1996); the articles cited in Note 58, which discuss the future of the "third world" and the "South"; Myron Weiner, "Peoples and States in A New Ethnic Order?," *Third World Quarterly*, 13 (1992), pp. 317–333; Francis Fukuyama's controversial article "The End of History?" in *The National Interest*, (Summer 1989), pp. 3–16; and Charles W. Kegley, Jr. and Gregory Raymond, *Multipolar Peace?: Great-Power Politics in the Twenty-First Century* (New York: St. Martin's Press, 1994).

For a discussion of the new agenda of issues, including a broadened view of "national security," see Sean M. Lynn-Jones and Steven E. Miller, eds., *Global Dangers: Changing Dimensions of International Security* (Cambridge, Mass.: MIT Press, 1995), especially Part I on "Rethinking Security"; and Michael T. Klare and Daniel C. Thomas, eds., *World Security: Challenges for A New Century* (New York: St. Martin's Press, 1994). A good overview of the interdependence phenomenon, along with "techno-power" issues, is provided by Dennis Pirages, *Global Technopolitics* (Pacific Grove,

Calif.: Brooks/Cole, 1989). On the role of nonstate actors in world politics, see Philip Taylor, *Nonstate Actors in International Politics* (Boulder, Colo.: Westview Press, 1984); and Ronnie D. Lipschutz, "Reconstructing World Politics: The Emergence of Global Civil Society," *Millennium,* 21, no. 3 (1992), pp. 389–420.

The somewhat paradoxical trends and countertrends relating to nationalism and transnationalism and the disintegration and integration of nation-states are treated in Benjamin Barber, *Jihad vs. McWorld* (New York: Random House, 1995), as well as his article by the same title in *The Atlantic Monthly* (March 1992). The erosion of sovereignty and the mounting pressures on the nation-state as an institution, particularly in meeting the economic needs of its citizens, are examined in the symposium on "What Future for the State?" in *Daedalus,* 124 (Spring 1995); and Walter Wriston, *Twilight of Sovereignty* (New York: Scribner's, 1992). An interesting counterpoint is provided in Janice E. Thomson and Stephen D. Krasner, "Global Transactions and the Consolidation of Sovereignty," in James N. Rosenau and Ernst-Otto Czempiel, eds., *Global Changes and Theoretical Challenges* (Lexington, Mass.: Lexington Books, 1989), pp. 195–219.

PART II

National Actors and International Interactions

I only regret that I have but one life to lose for my country.
NATHAN HALE, UTTERED ON THE GALLOWS, SEPTEMBER 22, 1776

Our country: in her intercourse with foreign nations may she always be in the right; but our country, right or wrong.
STEPHEN DECATUR, A TOAST OFFERED IN APRIL OF 1816

Nationalism is an infantile disease. It is the measles of mankind.
ALBERT EINSTEIN

For better or worse, nationalism has been a powerful force in world affairs. It continues to be so today, even though it is being diluted somewhat by a variety of other forces. There is hardly a place on the planet other than the high seas and the airspace above them that does not fall within the sovereign jurisdiction of some nation-state. Even if one adopts what we have called a "globalist" perspective—acknowledging the existence of a variety of actors in world politics—it is hard to dispute the assertion that "the starting point of international relations is the existence of states, of independent political communities."[1]

Part II focuses on *nation-states* as actors in world politics, i.e., the formulation and conduct of foreign policy by national governments and the dynamics of their interactions. One manifestation of the decentralized nature of the international system is the absence of any single, universally recognized, definitive list of nation-states in the world. Some policymakers and scholars would include such places as the Vatican City, Puerto Rico, Monaco, Taiwan, and Bophuthatswana, whereas others might omit these, depending on the political and analytical criteria being employed.[2] Allowing for some disagreement, there are well over 180 entities today that are widely viewed as nation-states.

In this section we will examine the kinds of foreign policy behavior that countries in general and four countries in particular (the United States, Russia, China, and Japan) display (Chapter 4). We will also investigate the different sets of factors that affect such behavior (Chapter 5), including a look inside the foreign policy decision-making process itself (Chapter 6). Hence, our discussion of foreign policy is aimed at both description and explanation. In addition, we will examine how countries interact with each other, and how international relations can be treated as a "game" (or a series of "games") in which nations seek to influence each other through various modes of statecraft (Chapter 7). Finally, we will discuss the occasional breakdowns in the "game" of international politics and examine the circumstances under which violence occurs and the different forms it can take (Chapter 8).

Describing Foreign Policy Behavior: What Is It Nation-States Do?

The 1991 breakup of the Soviet Union, one of the key international actors of the post–World War II system, raises fascinating questions about foreign policy, especially questions pertaining to change versus continuity. Is there something immutable about foreign policy behavior that characterizes a state no matter what changes occur in its internal and external environment, or do states evolve new ways of relating to each other over time and under new circumstances? In other words, can we expect the Russian Federation, the main successor state to the Soviet Union, to behave in world politics much as its predecessor did, or are there new conditions present that predict a fundamentally different foreign policy? Does it matter, for example, that communist ideology has been replaced by a more capitalist system?

In this chapter we examine the foreign policy behavior of nation-states. We focus particularly on the United States, Russia, China, and Japan, not simply because they are highly influential and visible states—smaller states can have important impacts in world politics, as already noted—but because their contrasting historical experiences have produced certain distinctive (albeit changeable) behavior patterns the study of which can provide insights into the conduct of foreign policy generally. In many ways their behavior illustrates the range of options open to all countries in international relations, and their interactions run the gamut of international cooperation and conflict from economic questions to territorial disputes. Although some states may enjoy wider latitude of maneuver than others, all face similar kinds of decisions about how to act toward friends and foes on the world stage.

The Nature of Foreign Policy

The Soviet Union was not the first state to undergo fundamental transformation. Many others, of course, have experienced major reordering of their boundaries. For example, Pakistan, which had become a sovereign state in 1947 when the Indian subcontinent achieved independence from Britain and was partitioned into the Hindu-dominated Republic of India and the Moslem-dominated Islamic Republic of Pakistan, originally consisted of two noncontiguous territorial areas separated by part of India. In addition to having different religious orientations, India and Pakistan also had a diversity of ethnic groups. In Pakistan's case, a rift developed between the largely Punjabi population of West Pakistan and the predominantly Bengali population of East Pakistan, with both of these ethnic groups having their counterparts across the border in India. When, by 1971, the Bengalis were in open revolt over the failure of the Pakistan government to meet their demands, they received cross-border assistance from India, which saw an opportunity to weaken its neighboring rival and to avert the influx of thousands of Bengali refugees.[1] This situation soon degenerated into a full-scale Indo-Pakistani war, which Pakistan lost, leading to the formation of the new state of Bangladesh in what had been East Pakistan.

The truncated Pakistani state continued its regional rivalry with India over other issues, particularly the disputed possession by India of the Kashmir border area and the perceived threat that India posed as an aspiring regional hegemon in South Asia. Seeking outside sources of help, Pakistan maintained a security alliance with the United States, formed during the Cold War as a bulwark against the Soviet Union, and also continued friendly relations with China, which shared Pakistan's concern over India's intentions. The end of the Cold War, however, brought U.S.-Pakistan frictions, as the smaller ally discovered it was no longer vital to the West; Washington denied Pakistan foreign aid and arms in efforts to get both India and Pakistan to renounce development of nuclear weapons. Nevertheless, despite its changed circumstances and resultant adjustments in its foreign relations, there was also a certain degree of continuity in Pakistani foreign policy.[2] The latter suggests that policies need not change with changes in leadership and other conditions, as long as the situations or interests that they were meant to address are still relevant.

We need to distinguish here between foreign policy and foreign policy behavior. **Foreign policy behavior** refers to the actions states take toward each other. The formation of alliances is one type of foreign policy behavior. Other types include the establishment or suspension of diplomatic relations, the threatened or actual use of armed force, the giving or withdrawal of foreign aid, voting in international organizations, concluding trade agreements, and countless other acts. It is important to note that these actions usually are not taken as ends in themselves but are tied in some way to larger purposes—from long-run aspirations, such as regional dominance, to more immediate aims, such as acquisition of a specific slice of territory. **Foreign policy** refers to the set of priorities and precepts established by national leaders to serve as guidelines for choosing among various courses of action (behaviors) in specific situations as they strive to achieve their goals.

Notwithstanding the growing influence of IGOs and NGOs, foreign policy remains ultimately the province of governments, emanating from duly appointed, if not elected, officials. Although foreign policy is the set of authoritative pronouncements and guidelines for action adopted by official national decision makers, various factors can cause a nation-state's behavior to depart substantially from these official doctrines. Policy can become muddled if the government does not speak with one voice, as frequently happens. Different governmental entities (the legislative as opposed to executive branch, or the central as opposed to regional or local authorities) as well as interest groups, ethnic groups, or political parties at times compete over the right to speak for the country. We have noted the growing phenomenon of failed states and states experiencing severe civil war, such as Lebanon and Somalia. Knowing the precise foreign policies of such states may be difficult; it may be difficult to determine even who, if anyone, is ruling.

Even in the case of nation-states in which there is a relatively unified body politic and a foreign policy consensus exists, there may still seem a disjuncture between policy and actual behavior. After all, governments are concerned with various types of issues, and policy is devised to meet different sets of interests, ranging from the security domain to economic and other domains. Policies that relate to, say, economic priorities such as trade might conflict with policies meant to address certain ideological concerns such as promoting democracy or human rights. A government might have to decide whether it values trade or human rights more highly in dealing with another state that is an important trade partner but also represses its own population.

We can try to discern the policies that inform the relations between any two states by observing both their actions and their statements toward each other. Usually words and deeds roughly correspond, in patterns of friendship or hostility. Sometimes, however, rhetoric and action diverge; critical statements might accompany cooperative behavior, or vice versa. The divergence might be accidental, as when an American U-2 spy plane mistakenly overflew Cuba at the height of the Cuban missile crisis in 1962, despite President Kennedy's clear orders banning such flights. Occasionally, the discrepancy can reflect conflicting policy priorities. During the 1980s, Iran's new Islamic government preached a very militant line against the "three great Satans" in world politics—the United States, the Soviet Union, and Israel—blaming them for most of the problems plaguing the Middle East. At the same time, the Iranian government, engaged in a fierce war against neighboring Iraq, relied heavily on arms imports from all three. The security threat posed by Iraq proved to be a more compelling concern to Iranian rulers than the ideological-based crusade of opposing the great Satans.

States often shift gears in determining with whom they wish to have diplomatic relations. We have noted that establishment of diplomatic relations is one type of foreign policy behavior. Although "recognition" of new governments by other states is normally a routine, legal formality, at times it is used as a political tool to signal approval or disapproval of the regime in question. For example, it was not until 1933, sixteen years after the Bolshevik Revolution in Russia, that the United States agreed to formal diplomatic recognition of the Soviet Union. Similarly, it was not until 1979, thirty years after the Communist Revolution in China, that the United States agreed to formal diplomatic recognition of the People's Republic of China (PRC). On the eve of recognition by Washington, the Soviets in the 1930s and the Chinese in the 1970s had not suddenly changed from untrustworthy enemies to loyal friends of the United States. Instead, Washington, Moscow, and Beijing discovered that they needed each other. The United States and the Soviet Union were brought together by growing concern over Japanese power in the Pacific, and the United States and China found common ground at the end of the Vietnam War in mutual anxiety about the Soviet Union. Likewise, the decision by a number of Arab leaders to enter into partial peace agreements with Israel in the 1990s—in the process finally recognizing Israel's right to exist as a sovereign state after more than forty years of nonrecognition—was a response to not only Israeli concessions on the issue of a Palestinian homeland but also mutual security and economic needs. Growing Arab recognition of Israel led many other states in the world to follow suit, resulting in Israeli diplomatic relations mushrooming from 74 to 146 states, meaning, among other things, more trade and investment opportunities for the Jewish state.[3]

What may appear, then, to be erratic behavior on the part of a state in the international arena—in terms of an abrupt shift in foreign relations, or discrepancies between words and deeds or between one set of actions and another set of actions—may have a certain logic to it that is grounded in broader policy considerations. To those who would criticize the United States for hypocrisy in mobilizing the international community in 1990 to punish Iraqi aggression against Kuwait and genocidal treatment of its Kurdish population while being far more reluctant to get involved in the Bosnian conflict, where comparable violations of international norms occurred, the realist would only remind that more clear-cut American interests were at stake in the former case than in the latter. In particular, Iraq's potential stranglehold on a substantial percentage of the world's oil reserves directly threatened American energy security. In contrast, with the end of the superpower competition in Europe and elsewhere in the post–Cold War era, the United States felt less compelled to take an active leadership role and commit itself to large-scale military involvement in the Balkans in support of an ill-defined "new world order." In a revealing comment uttered in 1994, former U.S. Secretary of State Lawrence Eagleburger noted that "if the Soviet Union still existed, we would have done more in Yugoslavia."[4]

We are mainly interested here in delineating patterns of foreign policy behavior. Explanations of *why* states behave as they do—including whether domestic, internal developments are as important as external factors—will be more fully explored in Chapter 5.

Patterns of Foreign Policy Behavior

The nature of foreign policy is such that one can expect to find double standards and inconsistencies in the records of all countries. It is not easy to label countries as simply "peace-loving" or "warlike" or to use other such categorizations. Nevertheless, predominant or recurring patterns of foreign policy behavior can be identified. Arnold Wolfers, an astute observer of international relations, suggested that all foreign policy behavior ultimately boils down to three possible patterns: (1) self-preservation (maintaining the status quo); (2) self-extension (revising the status quo in one's favor); and self-abnegation (revising the status quo in someone else's favor).[5] Realists assume that the first two of these dominate and that the third, self-sacrifice, is rare. However, the three need not be mutually exclusive. When one country provides expensive foreign assistance to another, as in the U.S. Marshall Plan aid to Europe during the 1940s or Soviet support for Egypt's Aswan High Dam on the Nile River in the 1950s, it may indeed forego other potentially desirable projects to do so (self-abnegation), but it also may reap important political benefits in the aid recipient's region and through a return on money invested (self-extension).

Although all international relations may be reducible to Wolfer's trio of patterns, there are other, more elaborate ways of describing foreign policy behavior. That is, one can attempt to classify a nation-state's foreign policy behavior along a number of specific dimensions, keeping in mind that behavior can change over time and with different sets of leaders and conditions.

ALIGNMENT

One can first speak of *alignment* tendencies, in particular whether national leaders choose to ally with certain countries or to remain neutral. Our focus here is not on the alignment configurations in the international system as a whole (i.e., bipolarity and multipolarity as discussed in Chapters 2 and 3) but the alignment decisions of individual governments. A country's alignment behavior can vary from time to time during its history in response to changing circumstances and policy decisions. For example, partly because a neutrality policy had failed to shield Holland from Germany's attack and occupation in 1940, the Dutch government joined the North Atlantic Treaty Organization alliance soon after World War II. The shifting nature of alignments is vividly recalled in the World War II coalition of the United States, Britain, Soviet Union, and China against three states that would subsequently in the postwar period become America's allies—Germany, Italy, and Japan.

Alliances are formal agreements to provide mutual military assistance; as such, they carry legal weight and certain benefits as well as risks.[6] Allied countries can pool their military resources, acquire access to foreign bases, and stake out territories that enemies are on notice will be denied them by force if necessary. Yet an allied state also risks interference by allies in its domestic affairs, the possibility of being dragged into another ally's quarrels, and the ultimate danger of a sell-out if war begins. Table 4.1 indicates the general likelihood of such sell-outs, as well as trends in the formation of alliances and other types of alignment agreements. Although the historical record suggests a high degree of alliance fidelity, many observers have questioned the reliability of alliance guarantees, especially in the nuclear age.[7]

Neutrality is a stance of formal nonpartisanship in world affairs. By keeping a low profile, neutrals may avoid some of the problems associated with alliances, particularly the generating of potential enemies and counter-alliances.[8] However, neutrals also must be aware that if war clouds gather,

Table 4.1

ALIGNMENT TENDENCIES

Nineteenth-century alliances were mainly military pacts with allies promising to help defend each other, whereas in the twentieth century, states have opted more often for promises not to attack each other. Pacts formed during years in which major wars were occurring were mainly mutual defense agreements. During years of peace a wider variety of alignment pacts were formed. The threat of war seems to lead to more explicit promises of mutual defense. Alliances and other alignment pacts were honored most of the time in both the nineteenth and twentieth centuries, and the threat of war occurring in the year of alignment generally increases only slightly the probability that the pact would be honored.

	Historical Era		*Formed in Year of War or Peace*	
Type of Alignment	*1815–1919*	*1919–1945*	*War*	*Peace*
Military pacts[a]	38 (60%)	18 (27%)	32 (54%)	24 (34%)
Nonaggression pacts[b]	8 (13%)	37 (56%)	20 (34%)	26 (37%)
Ententes[c]	17 (27%)	11 (17%)	7 (12%)	21 (30%)
Effectiveness of Pacts	*1815–1919*	*1919–1945*	*War*	*Peace*
Invoked and honored	33 (89%)	9 (82%)	24 (92%)	18 (82%)
Invoked and not honored	4 (11%)	2 (18%)	2 (8%)	4 (18%)

[a]Military pact: Promise to intervene with force on behalf of allies (what we here include as an "alliance").
[b]Nonaggression pact: Promise not to intervene with force against a state or states involved in war that are parties to the pact.
[c]Entente: Promise to consult together in time of threat (what we here include as an "alliance").
Source: Ole R. Holsti, P. Terrence Hopmann, and John D. Sullivan, *Unity and Disintegration in International Alliances: Comparative Studies,* Tables 12 and 14. © 1973. Adapted with permission from John Wiley and Sons, Inc.

there may be no one committed to providing a protective military umbrella. Switzerland is one country that has carried neutrality to an extreme, even refusing membership in the United Nations lest it involve the Swiss in controversial "collective security" military or economic sanctions against states accused of violating the UN charter.[9]

Although the term "alignment" as used above refers to formal agreements on alliance or neutrality, it also can describe the general affective orientation of a country, i.e., which nation or nations it tends to side with on issues. Countries can tilt toward one side or another in a conflict without necessarily becoming part of a formal alliance. For example, we have noted that during the Cold War there existed a group of third world countries taking a stance of **nonalignment**—siding with the United States on some issues and with the Soviet Union on other issues but refusing to become locked into either camp in the East-West conflict. As the Cold War blocs themselves dissolved in the 1990s, some of the options open to weaker states to play off alliances against each other for increased foreign aid also evaporated. The third world "non-aligned" movement became progressively less cohesive and searched for new issues around which to revive their coalition.[10]

In the contemporary era, in particular, governments often have to make alignment decisions with regard to not one but several axes of conflict. The choices are becoming increasingly complicated. For example, Sweden, a staunch traditional neutral much like Switzerland, moved to join the European Union for economic benefits in the mid-1990s. As it did so, it faced the difficulty of picking and choosing types of commitments, debating whether to commit to European military groupings as well, such as the Western European Union. For Sweden, the question was whether alignment in the economic policy domain could remain separated from nonalignment in the security domain.

SCOPE

A second foreign policy dimension is the *scope* of a country's activities and interests. Some countries have extensive, far-reaching international contacts, and other countries have more limited activities abroad. A country's scope of contacts can affect the outcome of disputes and crises, for instance, if worldwide connections are needed (as was the case during the 1991 Gulf War, when the United States was able to engineer a coalition against Iraq that included its European allies, the former Soviet Union, and key Arab states such as Saudi Arabia, Egypt, and Syria). Major powers in international relations have historically been those that have defined their interests in **global** terms, interacting regularly with countries in nearly every region of the world. Although so-called "great" or "super" powers can fail in their attempts to influence or control events, what distinguishes them from other countries is the scope of their interests and the panoply of means available to them to pursue those interests even at a distance.

Most countries in the world are essentially **regional actors,** interacting primarily with neighboring states in the same geographical area except for contacts, frequently concerning economic issues such as trade, with major actors like the United States outside their region. For example, Guatemala in Latin America does not interact much with Malawi in Africa. Admittedly, the foreign policy scope of some states defies easy categorization. Even poor or militarily limited states can have a few important extraregional interests (e.g., Cuban military adventures in Africa during the 1970s and 1980s to defend Marxist Ethiopian and Angolan regimes from pro-Western rebel forces, or worldwide petroleum contacts maintained by the Dutch through the Shell Oil Corporation). Indeed, in an age of interdependence, all countries are to some extent concerned about the politics of both their neighbors and distant regions. However, states such as the United States and Russia, even with recent budgetary pressures to scale back overseas commitments, can more accurately be labeled "global actors" because of the comprehensive nature of their concerns and contacts—political, economic, military, and diplomatic. For example, Washington and Moscow maintain embassies in almost every country in the world, whereas many other states can afford embassies in only a few countries and so rely on the United Nations and international organizations for the bulk of their formal diplomatic contacts. Roughly two-thirds of the nations of the world maintain diplomatic missions in fewer than sixty countries, with the most diplomatically pervasive actors being located in North America and Europe.

At some moments in history, factors such as military weakness or geographic remoteness may cause the scope of a country's foreign policy to become so narrow that **isolationism** results. This was the case with Myanmar (formerly Burma) in the 1960s and 1970s.[11] However, by the 1990s, even Myanmar had joined in the globalization of the international economy, becoming the source of much of the heroin flowing into the United States and—based on a plentiful supply of cheap labor and natural resources—being touted as "the latest darling of (foreign) investors."[12] Few countries ever have been totally cut off from the outside world, and in an age of interdependence, isolationism becomes an increasingly less viable foreign policy orientation.

MODUS OPERANDI

In addition to the alignment and scope dimensions of a nation's foreign policy, we can speak of foreign policy "m.o." (*modus operandi*, or method of operation). Just as police have noted recurrent patterns in the behavior of criminals and have used such patterns to identify suspects, so also states evidence characteristic behavior patterns and favored methods of pursuing goals. We do not mean to imply that international relations resemble crime (though there are those who would make the argument), only that the notion of *modus operandi* can be useful in describing foreign policy behavior. Such patterns can change over time, sometimes quite quickly with dramatic leadership changes; as we have cautioned, it is not easy to fit multifaceted foreign policies into neat pigeonholes. Yet certain actors leave characteristic imprints, and we can classify these along at least two dimensions: (1) degree of *multilateralism* and (2) degree of *activism*.

The more **multilateralist** a state, the greater its tendency to seek joint solutions to problems through diplomatic forums in which several states participate—such as the United Nations—rather than using purely **bilateral** (country to country) approaches. During the Cold War, the United States and the Soviet Union pursued arms control both multilaterally (through the 40 Nation Conference on Disarmament) and bilaterally (through the Strategic Arms Reduction Treaty—START—talks and other such discussions between the two superpowers). The General Agreement on Tariffs and Trade (GATT), a global body which spawned the World Trade Organization (WTO) in 1995, was created after World War II as a multilateral approach to reducing trade barriers among countries through periodic rounds of negotiations and joint dispute settlement procedures. U.S.-Japanese trade talks, however, represent a bilateral forum focused on the relations of these two states only, although their separate agreements are expected to conform to GATT rules.[13] As these examples indicate, countries do not rely exclusively on one or the other mode of diplomacy. However, some states seem to devote considerably more resources and energies than other states to international organizations and multilateral action. Table 4.2 lists the states with the highest number of intergovernmental

Table 4.2
STATES WITH THE HIGHEST NUMBER OF IGO MEMBERSHIPS

Rank Order	State	Full and Associate Memberships in All Categories of IGOs
1	Denmark	164
2	France	155
3	Norway	154
4	Sweden	153
5	United Kingdom	140
6	Finland	139
7	Federal Republic of Germany	135
8	The Netherlands	131
9	Belgium	127
10	Italy	124
11	United States	122
12	Spain	113
13	Canada	110
14	Japan	106
15	Iceland	105
16.5	Australia	104
16.5	Soviet Union	104
18	India	102
19	Brazil	100
20	Poland	99
21	Algeria	96
22.5	Austria	95
22.5	Yugoslavia	95
25	Egypt	94
25	Mexico	94
25	Switzerland	94

Source: Harold K. Jacobson, William M. Reisinger, and Todd Mathers, "National Entanglements in International Governmental Organizations," *American Political Science Review,* 80 (March 1986), p. 149. Used by permission of the American Political Science Association and the authors.

organization (IGO) memberships in the world at the outset of the 1990s, with Scandinavian states occupying three of the top four positions. Among less developed states, India ranked first.

In the area of foreign aid, in particular, Canada and the Scandinavian states have channeled a large percentage of their contributions (roughly half) through international organizations such as the World Bank. In so doing, these countries give up some control over the ultimate disbursement of the funds. In contrast, the United States, France, and many other countries, evidently more protective of their purse strings, have traditionally provided the bulk of their foreign aid in bilateral form through their own governmental agencies. Although the amount of foreign aid given multilaterally by the United States through the UN has been substantial, it has been proportionally lower than that supplied by the Scandinavians and many other countries, especially in terms of ability to pay (i.e., foreign aid as a percentage of gross national product). In 1988, Japan, seeking an enlarged international role, began to challenge the United States as the chief aid donor in overall bilateral and multilateral assistance and made special efforts to upgrade its funding of UN programs, including peacekeeping operations. The United States did regain the lead in the 1990s.

The more *active* a state, the more likely it is to initiate actions in international relations or to resist initiatives taken by others. Acts of resistance can range from protests, threats, and warnings to the actual use of force. This dimension is partly related to scope and alignment. For example, it has been suggested that certain leaders define their country's role in world affairs as "bastions of revolution," as "defenders of the faith," and as "regional leaders or protectors" or "active independents," whereas others have styled themselves as "isolates," as "protectees," or as "faithful allies."[14] Without stereotyping any government's overall policy, one might argue that Iran, both before and after the overthrow of the Shah in 1979, has more resembled the former pattern than the latter; after becoming an Islamic republic, it especially projected the image of defender of the faith and bastion of revolution.

Activism can include a tendency toward **intervention** in the internal affairs of other countries. Such action is viewed generally as a violation of state sovereignty and of the rules governing international behavior. However, intervention also can be invited by a government to gain outside support against internal insurgencies. Interventions can be military (e.g., sending troops across a border), economic (e.g., sending financial aid to an opposition group that might overthrow a government), or diplomatic (e.g., advising a government on how to deal with a rebellion).

Interventionism is not a new phenomenon; interventionist behavior can be found in ancient civilizations as rulers sought to subvert one another. In the early nineteenth century, Napoleon Bonaparte attempted to export the French Revolution to other countries, while the conservative monarchs of Europe responded by attempting to suppress democratic uprisings in Greece, Spain, and elsewhere. Although intervention is not new, it has become an especially prevalent form of foreign policy behavior since World War II. As seen in Figure

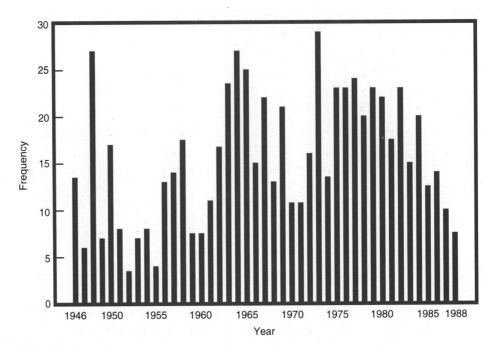

Figure 4.1
ANNUAL FREQUENCIES FOR OVERT MILITARY INTERVENTION INITIATION
Source: Frederic S. Pearson, Robert A. Baumann, and Jeffrey J. Pickering, "Military Intervention and Realpolitik," in Frank W. Wayman and Paul F. Diehl, eds. *Reconstructing Realpolitik* (Ann Arbor: University of Michigan Press, 1994), p. 210. Copyright © 1994 University of Michigan Press.

4.1, the frequency of *military* interventions varied during the Cold War period, with peaks in the late 1940s, 1960s, and mid-1970s, and a moderate decline in the 1980s as various regional conflicts were settled or ran their course. Most of these interventions were located in the third world, with the United States, Britain, and France among the most frequent interveners (more than thirty interventions each), seeking to prop up pro-Western governments or topple pro-Soviet governments. Israel, with a much smaller resource base, intervened at roughly the same rate. The Soviet Union, China, and South Africa exceeded twenty interventions each. Iraq, Syria, Egypt, and India were among the next most active interveners, closely followed by Libya, Vietnam, Morocco, and Jordan.[15]

Although intervention continues to be a means whereby states pursue their perceived interests inside other states, the types of interests at stake and expectations about permissible intervention have changed over time:

States used to intervene militarily to collect debts from foreign governments; they no longer do so. States have intervened for humanitarian reasons for centuries but who is "human," deserving of protection, and how states can legitimately intervene to protect people has changed. . . . Changing international understandings about state sovereignty, human equality, and international order have shaped the pattern of military intervention, not just by changing the political costs of different kinds of interventions, but more fundamentally by making some kinds of military action conceivable or inconceivable where it might not previously have been so. Military intervention to protect starving Muslim Africans [as in Somalia in 1992] was simply not on the political agenda in the nineteenth century. Similarly, marriages of rulers is not a matter of international concern or cause for intervention today.[16]

During the 1990s, without the impetus of the Cold War, a number of states, including the United States, have appeared increasingly reluctant to become excessively involved in foreign crises. As the United States undertook military interventions in Somalia (attempting to deliver emergency food supplies in a civil war involving rival clans and hoping to promote a ceasefire, but ultimately departing before order could be restored), Bosnia (flying NATO air strikes, but refusing to dispatch ground troops to enforce United Nations ceasefire agreements until late in the conflict), and Haiti (sending 20,000 American troops under a United Nations mandate to oust a military dictatorship and restore the previously deposed President Jean Bertrand Aristide, but then removing the troops while the political system remained highly unstable), Washington was criticized by some for intervening in "low-priority" states and by others for not more resolutely sticking by its intervention commitments. Other previously interventionist states, such as the former Soviet Union, France, South Africa, Vietnam, Libya, and Iraq, appeared to be ambivalent about their foreign involvements as well, in many instances because of domestic preoccupations, although some degree of interventionist behavior persisted (as with Russia dispatching troops to neighboring Georgia and France to Rwanda).

The rationale for military intervention has evolved from debt collection and other economic concerns in the early twentieth century, to ideologically based geopolitical moves during the Cold War, to a more recent trend of humanitarian or peacekeeping missions aimed at addressing the breakdown of order in countries wracked by civil war and ethnic violence. As the Somalian, Bosnian, and Haiti cases illustrate, intervention in the 1990s has often been multilateral in character (authorized by the United Nations or a regional organization, such as the Organization of American States or Organization of African Unity) rather than undertaken unilaterally.[17] Multilateral intervention can be a preferred mode of intervention insofar as it confers on the military action greater legitimacy, permits burden sharing among the participants, and tends to reassure various parties that no single state is seeking its own advantage. Unilateral military intervention, however, offers the intervener greater potential control over the operations, including when to attack and when to leave.[18] Conceivably, if regional and global institutions are strengthened as part of a "New World Order," and if new norms of "humanitarian intervention" take firmer root in the international community, the frequency of unilateral intervention as a mode of foreign policy behavior could decline significantly. However, even "humanitarian intervention" authorized by the international community—on behalf of starving refugees in Somalia, fleeing tribesmen in Rwanda, an oppressed Kurdish minority in Iraq, or other disadvantaged groups elsewhere—raises troubling questions regarding external interference in the domestic affairs of a sovereign state.[19]

Four Case Studies

We have identified several dimensions of foreign policy that we consider suggestive, although certainly not exhaustive, of the kinds of behavior patterns nation-states display. We have also noted that foreign policy often appears "schizophrenic"; i.e., there are notable disparities between the officially proclaimed doctrines of some countries, such as support for nonintervention, and their actual behavior. This dualism is evident in the history of U.S., Russian, Chinese, and Japanese foreign affairs, a history we will review in the remainder of this chapter. An examination of these four states provides a portrait of the workings of international politics at the global and regional levels, and the manner in which foreign policy behavior can vary in terms of alignment, scope, methods of operation, and other features.

American Foreign Policy: A Profile

The United States has been called the world's first "new nation."[20] From the beginning, Americans reacted against the outside world and particularly the world of traditional European powers. With great commercial zeal, America's founders envisioned a unique society practicing a different form of relations with other countries. They would not reestablish monarchy and engage in foreign conquests but would concentrate on exploiting the advantages of a practically private continent. Although there would be the need to dispose of a few obstacles on the continent posed by native American Indian tribes and foreign empires, and although slavery would underwrite the southern economic system, the new nation generally saw itself behaving in a nobler fashion than the already established states.

   To protect and nurture the young republic, early American foreign policy was neutral in terms of alignment tendencies and mainly regional in scope. Americans also came to see themselves as somewhat isolationist—insulated from European affairs by vast oceans and preoccupied with taming the frontier. Indeed, after alliance with France during the Revolutionary War, the United States, on George Washington's advice in his Farewell Address in 1796, chose to avoid such "entangling alliances" over the next two centuries until the signing of several security pacts after World War II. However, even in the early nineteenth century, America's aloofness from the world was not complete, as traders, adventurers, and religious missionaries traveled far and wide. As seen in the Sidelight on page 140, the new nation's rather inexperienced leaders did not fully understand the foreign cultures they encountered. Promising not to interfere in European affairs, American leaders called on Europeans not to meddle in the Western Hemisphere. The **Monroe Doctrine** officially established the United States as an aspiring regional power with an activist "protector" role, although its behavior was frequently more accommodative than its rhetoric might have suggested, given the nation's relatively limited military power.

As a dynamic new republic with the "manifest destiny" to fill a continent—interrupted by a civil war in mid-century—the United States was unlikely to cease its westward push to the Pacific coast. Few Americans wanted to build an Old World–style empire, but many wanted to find wealth and influence in places controlled by foreign powers, places as far away as China. On the continent itself, Texas and California were "liberated" in the mid-nineteenth century through war against Mexico, a conflict largely provoked by Presidents Tyler and Polk. In a similar vein overseas, Spanish possessions ranging from Puerto Rico to the Philippines were garnered in a war at the turn of the century. Without a formal empire, the United States obtained dependencies, bases, and considerable prestige as a growing—if seemingly reluctant—world power.[21]

In the process of nineteenth-century expansion, U.S. policy reflected a characteristic dualism. As a fresh new state free of the taint of colonialism, Americans could speak of high principles, of promoting democracy abroad, of favoring revolutionaries in Latin America and the Philippines while seeking to overthrow Spanish "despots." Americans could denounce exclusive spheres of influence in Asia, which benefited the rich European powers. Yet in defending such noble causes, American leaders sometimes worked in common purpose with European empires (as in U.S.-British opposition to the Spanish) and also served the interests of various domestic groups in the United States such as those wishing a share of the China trade (hence, the famous "Open Door" Notes on China in 1900). The pursuit of U.S. influence was reflected, for example, in President Theodore Roosevelt's turn-of-the-century "gunboat diplomacy" in Asia and "big stick" policy in Latin America, and his dispatch of the U.S. Navy on an around-the-world excursion to "show the flag."

The need to apply moral sugarcoating to self-interested actions has been a frequent and recurring feature of the U.S. foreign policy style. Although not unique in this, American leaders have tended to couch their actions in terms of morality more than most leaders.[22] This is different from the mere manipu-

SIDELIGHT

THE "CLASH OF CIVILIZATIONS": EARLY U.S. ENCOUNTERS WITH THE ISLAMIC WORLD

We have noted Samuel Huntington's thesis regarding the coming "clash of civilizations." Cultural differences have long been a source of conflict in relations between states. In particular, American foreign policy behavior toward the Islamic world has long been rooted in a degree of misunderstanding.

By the eighteenth century, established Arab rulers in North Africa and the Middle East had been used to dealing with Old European powers such as Britain. Islamic views of international law and custom contrasted somewhat with Western notions on such issues as conditions of peace and recognition. In the West, it was generally assumed that states were at peace unless a state of war was declared; under Islamic law, though, peace prevailed only if formal agreements were signed giving due recognition and respect to the Islamic states. The older European powers, and particularly the English, had come to understand these expectations, even if they did not always agree with them.

When the Islamic rulers inquired of London as to whether the new U.S. republic was indeed independent after 1789, and were told it was, they assumed that a state of war existed with America because no formal mutual recognition or peace treaties had been signed. U.S. leaders were shocked, therefore, when their clipper ships sailing the Mediterranean were attacked by "Barbary coast pirates," or hired navies working for North African princes. Americans considered this unprovoked aggression, and gave the Marines their first taste of action in the Middle East at the "shores of Tripoli." It was to be several years before leaders such as Adams and Jefferson came to realize that piracy was not the issue; rather the North Africans were waiting for Americans to come to their senses and offer the proper gifts, including transportation for princes on U.S. ships, that would signal true recognition. Eventually Washington got the idea and formal treaties were worked out, though several mini-wars and clashes from 1796 through the early nineteenth century showed Washington's confusion about dealing with the status and pecking order among Muslim rulers in North Africa.

Source: Based on Pramila Hemrajani and Alexis Manaster Ramer, "Beyond 'Barbary': A Reappraisal of War and Peace Between the United States and the Maghrib, 1776–1826," Working Papers, Program on Mediating Theory and Democratic Systems, Wayne State University, 1993.

lation of rhetoric and propaganda so familiar in world politics and reflects a tendency to treat international relations as a morality play—the struggle of the good against the bad, seen in our time, for example, in President Reagan's Hollywoodesque description of the "evil empire." Although idealistic tendencies can be refreshing, they can also lead to policy confusion and charges of hypocrisy when morality loses out, as it so often does, to concrete interests.[23]

Reflecting both high principles and pragmatism, President Woodrow Wilson took the lead at the Versailles Peace Conference after World War I in urging the creation of a League of Nations and a new world order based on law and democratic values, such as "national self-determination" for former German and Austrian colonies in east-central Europe. Wilson believed that both peace and prosperity would be promoted by accentuating principles of democracy and free trade. The appeal of Wilsonian thinking has persisted for various American presidents of both political parties.[24]

America had grown economically and militarily powerful by the early twentieth century, but was slow to take on all the responsibilities of a great power; the myth of American "exceptionalism" persisted. In the postwar period, Americans sought a return to "normalcy," rejecting Wilson's multilateralist plea for League of Nations membership and in the process leaving European powers to their own unsuccessful balancing act. U.S. leaders did try in the 1920s to preserve commercial order and relieve the great financial burdens on Germany. But when the Great Depression hit, Presidents Herbert Hoover and Franklin Roosevelt turned protectionist, greatly restricting U.S. trade in a short-term effort to protect jobs. With the world's greatest trading nation withdrawing, total world trade dried up and unemployment spread, contributing to the rise of fascism and militarism in Europe and Japan.

Once again the dualism of American policy was exhibited in dealing with China and Japan during the 1930s. Japan invaded northern China in 1931, setting up a puppet state of Manchukuo. Secretary of State Stimson, concerned about China's survival, Japanese power, and potential threats to the Philippines, announced that the United States would not diplomatically recognize new states created by conquest. However, the nonrecognition policy, a policy without teeth, merely inflamed U.S.-Japanese relations without ousting Japan from China and without settling U.S.-Japanese differences in the Pacific. Many historians trace the road to Pearl Harbor from this point.[25]

When in the late 1930s it again seemed that Berlin was intent on dominating Europe, this time with Adolf Hitler at the controls, President Roosevelt tried to ease a war-shy America toward a firmer commitment to Britain. While promising to keep America out of war, Roosevelt pressed successfully for suspension of neutrality legislation on trade and for massive aid to Britain and the Soviet Union once World War II began in Europe.[26] With public opinion running against involvement, it was the shock of Japan's attack on Pearl Harbor in December of 1941 that finally brought the United States into the war.

A generation of American leaders grew to political maturity with the "lessons" of World War II fresh in their minds. These impressions were to affect strongly the scope, alignment, and *modus operandi* of U.S. policy after 1945. Emerging from the war as the world's leading military and economic power, challenged only by the Soviet Union, the United States would never again sit by and allow "aggressors" to go unchecked. The luxury of isolationism, always more a myth than a reality in U.S. policy, could no longer be afforded. America became a chief architect and key member of the League of Nations' successor, the United Nations. More fundamentally, there was national consensus that the United States would have to play a permanent, active world role to prevent states hostile to U.S. interests from dominating key regions.[27]

It may have been inevitable that the two most powerful wartime allies, the United States and the Soviet Union, surviving a grueling conflict with Germany and Japan and emerging relatively intact, would turn suspicious eyes on each other in 1945 as they surveyed the postwar wreckage. From the Soviet point of view, it was necessary and legitimate for Moscow to have friendly regimes along the potential invasion routes into Russia, especially in Poland and Czechoslovakia.[28] Many Americans, however, had been struck by the memory of the **Munich Pact** of 1938, when Britain and France abandoned their Czech allies and appeased Hitler's territorial demands. For Americans, it was easy to perceive any Soviet moves toward increased control in Eastern Europe

THE JAPANESE ATTACK ON PEARL HARBOR, HAWAII, ON DECEMBER 7, 1941. IN THE FOREGROUND IS THE BATTLESHIP USS *WEST VIRGINIA* AND IN THE BACKGROUND THE USS *TENNESSEE*.

or the Mediterranean as analogous to German drives in 1938. U.S. leaders interpreted civil wars and local disputes involving communist parties as part of a global challenge spearheaded by the regime of Josef Stalin in Moscow, even though in Greece, for instance, the Russians held back from fully supporting the communist cause, partly out of deference to prior agreements with Britain.[29]

The Cold War was ushered in in March of 1946, with Winston Churchill's "Iron Curtain" speech, in which he warned of the political and military wall that Moscow was building around Eastern Europe.[30] This was followed by two actions in the spring of 1947—the enunciation of the **Truman Doctrine** warning the Soviets against aggression in Greece and Turkey, and the launching of the **Marshall Plan** to rebuild the war-torn economies of Western Europe. It was hoped that revived prosperity would keep communist parties from victory at the polls in France and surrounding countries and would reconstitute markets for the vigorous U.S. economy. By the time the Soviets absorbed Czechoslovakia as a communist satellite in 1948, U.S. diplomat George Kennan had already written his famous *Foreign Affairs* article under the pseudonym "Mr. X," urging the **containment** of communism that was to become the major theme running through American policy during the Cold War era.[31] For the first time since the nation's early days, the United States in 1949 entered into a peacetime military alliance—the **North Atlantic Treaty Organization (NATO)**—and agreed to station troops overseas.[32] It was hoped that the U.S. policy of alliance commitments backed by American nuclear superiority would contain further communist advances outside Eastern Europe and ultimately would cause the Soviet system to collapse internally.

Moves to demobilize the U.S. army were reversed by new challenges, such as North Korea's attempt in 1950 to reunify Korea by force. Korea, an area not previously included in descriptions of U.S. security interests, suddenly seemed crucial to the defense of the newly pro-Western Japan, and hence, seemed to require broadening the scope of American military commitments. U.S. leaders, viewing North Korea as a Soviet puppet, came to the defense of South Korea. Although the Truman administration did not wish to become involved in a land war against neighboring China, the Korean War brought U.S. troops to China's doorstep. Mao Zedong's communist government had achieved control of the Chinese mainland only in 1949, pushing Chiang Kai-shek's Nationalist forces onto the small island of Taiwan. Communist Chinese leaders were very sensitive to potentially hostile major power forces on their border. After repeated warnings to the Americans, Chinese troops entered the Korean War, inflicting heavy losses on U.S. forces. Thus, American neutrality in the Chinese civil war gave way to intervention and defense commitments to both South Korea and Taiwan.

Other challenges confronting American leaders included a series of crises over Berlin and the future of Germany, which had been divided into U.S., Soviet, British, and French occupation zones after World War II. The Soviet

Union, stung by Hitler's invasion, wanted a permanently weakened Germany, whereas the Western allies opted to rebuild an economically viable Germany that would not require permanent occupation. When the Western powers went ahead with currency reform in their zones in 1948 over Soviet objections, the Soviets blockaded land and canal access to Berlin, a city 100 miles inside the Russian occupation zone (later East Germany) but within which the Allies had occupation rights. However, Stalin left air routes open, and thus Truman was able to supply West Berlin for a year by air until the crisis subsided.

In the 1950s, trouble brewed again in divided Germany as the Soviets sought unsuccessfully to discourage the United States from including West Germany in NATO. Premier Nikita Khrushchev, Stalin's successor, attempted to force the Western powers to recognize the East German state or be forced out of Berlin. During the summer of 1961, NATO nations were shocked to find the Russians and East Germans building a fortified wall in Berlin to separate East from West and stem the outflow of skilled workers fleeing to the West. President Kennedy accepted that wall and, many believe, paved the way for an eventual agreement on the status of Germany, which was to come a decade later when East and West Germany were officially recognized as sovereign states. The famous Berlin Wall itself was to come tumbling down in 1989 as East German protesters forced the resignation of the communist regime and the two Germanys became unified.

In the 1950s the Soviet Union and the United States also began to compete for influence in the newly emerging less developed countries of Asia, Africa, and Latin America—the "third world." Washington had great difficulty coming to grips with third world nationalism as more and more countries achieved independence from colonial rulers. During the Eisenhower administration, Secretary of State John Foster Dulles wanted further allies in America's efforts to resist communism and Soviet expansion. However, third world leaders, such as Jawaharlal Nehru of India, saw colonial rule and economic backwardness as greater problems than communism. Hence, Dulles's appeals for alliance were resisted in much of the third world.

As noted earlier, the object of the superpower competition in the third world was not to acquire territory but to gain influence over the foreign policies of third world states, entailing at times intervention in their internal affairs to determine the makeup of their governments. The regimes that one side tried to topple, the other side generally tried to prop up. In addition to periodic direct military intervention (as in U.S. excursions to Lebanon in 1958, the Dominican Republic in 1965, Southeast Asia in the 1960s and 1970s, Grenada in 1983, and Panama in 1989, and Soviet involvements in Hungary in 1956, Czechoslovakia in 1968, Ethiopia in 1977, and Afghanistan in the 1980s), the two superpowers frequently relied on more subtle forms of intervention, including supplying arms to local forces, transmitting propaganda, and plotting rebellions or assassinations. Because of mutual restraint in the nuclear age, certain "rules of the road" were developed, notably a tacit understanding that direct confrontation between American and Soviet forces was to be avoided.[33]

Nothing reflected U.S. frustrations in the third world more than the Vietnam War. John Kennedy had assumed the presidency in 1961, urging democratic reform abroad. But Kennedy also had a set of priorities typical of a number of U.S. administrations, i.e., a willingness to opt for right-wing dictatorship in preference to left-wing dictatorship along the lines of Fidel Castro's Cuba. Kennedy's advisers developed doctrines of "nation-building," which called for development of third world economies to win peasants' loyalty to pro-Western leaders while keeping Communist insurgents at bay with U.S. Green Berets and other special counterinsurgency forces. Theories about nation-building were tested in the laboratory of Vietnam and were found wanting. In the words of journalist I. F. Stone, it proved difficult to win a war in a "peasant society on the side of the landlords."[34] What was at first a modest American counterinsurgency force would become an army of 500,000 by the mid-sixties after Lyndon Johnson succeeded Kennedy. President Johnson struggled for the "hearts and minds" of the Vietnamese people; but the bombings, defoliations, and search and destroy missions of the Johnson administration, and later the Nixon administration, failed to win America's longest war against a regime that enjoyed great nationalist support.

The Vietnam experience was to reverberate through American foreign policymaking circles, in much the same way the Munich experience had, for the next two decades. Among the lingering questions were: when, for what purposes, and to what extent might U.S. military intervention be warranted or prudent in world troublespots, especially if goals were not clear-cut and involvements were potentially prolonged? The Vietnam War's immediate "lessons" caused President Richard Nixon and Secretary of State Henry Kissinger to conclude in the early 1970s that the United States no longer could police the world alone. The mission of maintaining U.S. influence in distant regions remained the same, but the techniques were modified with the **Nixon Doctrine,** another in a long series of presidential foreign policy doctrines, which stressed "self-help" by pro-American regional powers in the third world. Washington would supply the weapons and advice to enable powers such as Iran under the Shah to resist revolutionaries and preserve regional stability, especially in areas such as the Middle East, where vital resources were at stake. Ultimately, this approach too was found wanting, for example, when the Shah and his army, among the best equipped in the world, were unable to suppress a popular domestic revolution fueled by anti-American resentment that brought a militant Islamic regime to power in Tehran.

Kissinger also sought to forge a "structure of peace" through a more pragmatic, less ideological approach toward the Soviet Union. The result was a relaxation in American-Soviet tensions that came to be known as **détente,** based on the recognition that the Soviets had finally achieved true nuclear parity with the United States and that both sides had a vested interest in world stability. A series of arms control agreements were concluded, most notably the Strategic Arms Limitation Agreement of 1972 (SALT I).[35] Washington also established a dialogue with Communist China, which had grown apart from Moscow. The exchange of table-tennis teams, termed "ping-pong diplomacy," ultimately led to President Nixon's trip to Beijing to visit with Chairman Mao in 1971.[36] Despite these efforts, major power disagreements persisted.[37]

During the Nixon administration, America's predominance in the global economy began to erode visibly. The Vietnam years and resulting inflation, together with higher oil prices and stiff overseas competition from a fully recovered Europe and Japan, took their toll on U.S. trade. As exports declined, imports increased, and domestic industries shut down, Washington wrestled with its commitments to free trade and investment. As in the 1930s, considerable domestic political support developed for trade protectionism in the form of tariffs and other barriers against foreign imports. During the 1990s, this debate would flash again over the creation of a North American Free Trade Agreement (NAFTA) and a World Trade Organization (WTO).

After the Kissinger era in the Nixon and Ford administrations, Jimmy Carter arrived in Washington in 1977 and attempted to revise certain central elements of U.S. foreign policy, playing down the necessity for Soviet "containment," for U.S. interventionism and support of leaders with poor human rights records, and for an expanding nuclear arms race and global arms trade. Instead, President Carter brought human rights issues to global prominence and proposed significant nuclear arms reductions, arms trade restrictions, lessened dependence on foreign oil, and greater stress on conflict settlements—as in the Camp David agreement he brokered between Israel and Egypt in 1978.[38]

The dualism of American foreign policy was particularly evident in the Carter years as idealism contended with realism. By the end of President Carter's term, a harder line toward the Soviet Union was reemerging, driven by the Soviet invasion of Afghanistan. Eventually, human rights violations, such as those by China, South Korea, the Philippines, and Pakistan, were ignored to improve relations with these regionally influential actors who were in the anti-Soviet camp.[39] The imperatives of American influence, oil supplies, and trade seemed to require increased arms exports to countries such as Israel, Egypt, and Saudi Arabia. American armed forces were restructured for rapid projection of power overseas, and new nuclear armaments were developed.

When the Reagan administration assumed office in 1981, it threatened to return to the policy of containment with all the shrill rhetoric that had accompanied that policy in earlier years. The Soviets were accused of terrorism, of involvement in Central America and Africa, and of seeking nuclear superiority in the arms race. With a multiyear, multibillion-dollar defense budget increase, the Reagan administration sought to reassert American military power, which had been maligned since Vietnam. President Reagan also moved toward a somewhat expanded interventionism, enunciating a **Reagan Doc-**

trine, which argued for weakening and undermining third world Soviet clients, such as Angola, Libya, Vietnam, and Nicaragua. In most cases, intervention was limited to covert action, with direct military force used only against small states such as Grenada and Libya. The limits of American power could be seen in the ill-fated U.S. intervention in the Lebanese civil war in 1983, as 241 Marines were killed by a terrorist truck bomb.

The Reagan administration was accused of engaging in "global unilateralism," flouting international law and refusing to take seriously the United Nations and multilateral institutions. However, toward the end of his term, Reagan entered into a dialogue with the new reformist-minded Soviet leader, Mikhail Gorbachev, who was seeking a change in priorities in the direction of greater concern over economic, technological, and environmental matters. A series of cordial summit meetings was held between the two leaders resulting in important arms reduction initiatives in the areas of long-range and intermediate-range nuclear weapons. Against this background, the startling events in Eastern Europe unfolded as the Cold War drew to a close in the late 1980s. Succeeding Ronald Reagan, President George Bush presided over the transition from the postwar era to the post–Cold War era, calling for a "new world order" with a revitalized role for the United Nations. In the face of dramatic political and economic upheaval, the Soviet Union itself disintegrated in the early 1990s. With the elimination of America's major rival, Washington's political leaders and policy planners had a difficult time making sense of the new international environment and adjusting to it.

The end of the Cold War spurred demands within the United States for scaling down the massive defense budget and addressing domestic policy concerns through the "peace dividend."[40] President Bill Clinton came to office in 1993, stressing the theme of economic redevelopment at home. However, the Clinton administration found that the press of foreign challenges and crises would not abate—in the Balkans (the former Yugoslavia), the former Soviet Union (continued economic and political turmoil), the Middle East (Iranian and Iraqi military moves), Asia (North Korean nuclear arms developments and Chinese human rights violations), Africa (bloody civil wars), and Latin America (Mexican financial and political crises). The decline of Soviet power left regional actors and armed groups more able than before to assert their claims and exploit ethnic tensions for political gain, and left Washington without a clear opponent on which to focus. Themes of promoting democracy abroad ("enlargement" of the area of the globe under democratic rule), of safeguarding access to vital resources, of resolving ethnic conflict, of promoting favorable trade terms, and of halting the spread of nuclear and other weapons of mass destruction were sounded; but getting the priorities straight among these sometimes conflicting aims proved difficult. The role of the United Nations was hotly debated, as America's first attempt to put its troops under a foreign commander leading a UN peacekeeping operation (in Somalia in 1993) turned into a fiasco and raised questions about the U.S. commitment to the organization.

One troubling contrast was evident between American policy at the Cold War's beginning and at its end. Whatever one thought of the wisdom of policy-making in the immediate aftermath of World War II, it was characterized by a firm bipartisan commitment, rather careful planning, and clear, well-supported goals and strategies: containment, the Marshall Plan, the Truman Doctrine, NATO, and other major initiatives. The post–Cold War period, however, began with American leaders seemingly baffled as to the required initiatives, and discouraged about the American public's willingness to pay for them.[41] The United States was uncertain about the extent to which it could or should continue to play a lead role in world affairs, either bilaterally or multilaterally. Former Secretary of State Kissinger, commenting in 1993 on the road the United States had traveled over two hundred years from isolationism to superpower global engagement, perhaps put the issue most squarely: "The challenge for American foreign policy today is to define a role for the United States in a world which for the first time in our history we can neither withdraw from nor dominate."[42]

Russian Foreign Policy: A Profile

On Monday, August 19, 1991, at approximately 5:00 P.M. Moscow time, a group of advisors close to Soviet President Mikhail Gorbachev, calling themselves the State Committee for the State of Emergency, held a press conference to announce that Gorbachev was ill and had turned over all of his powers to then Vice President Gennadi Yanayev. This coup attempt by communist hardliners in the Red Army and KGB (the security and intelligence service) against Gorbachev and his fellow reformers propelled the world's second superpower, a vast state composed of twelve time zones and more than 100 distinct ethnic groups, to the brink of civil war. A Soviet civil war was averted at that moment by the strength of Russian Republic leader Boris Yeltsin, who mobilized opponents of the coup in the armed forces and government. However, the Soviet Union was to dissolve in December, the Communist Party was swept from power, and several new independent nation-states—Ukraine, Kazakhstan, and others—were formed from what had been the Soviet Union's constituent republics. (See the map in Fig. 4.2.) A "Union Treaty" was signed among a loosely structured Commonwealth of Independent States (CIS), with the largest among them—the Russian Federation—itself containing many diverse ethnic groups and nationalities (although 80 percent of the population was Russian).

Since the time of its founding in the ninth century at Kiev in what is now Ukraine, Russia (then known as "Kievan Rus") has tended to pursue certain recurring foreign policy objectives. First and foremost among these has been the concern to protect and enhance the security of the Russian people within

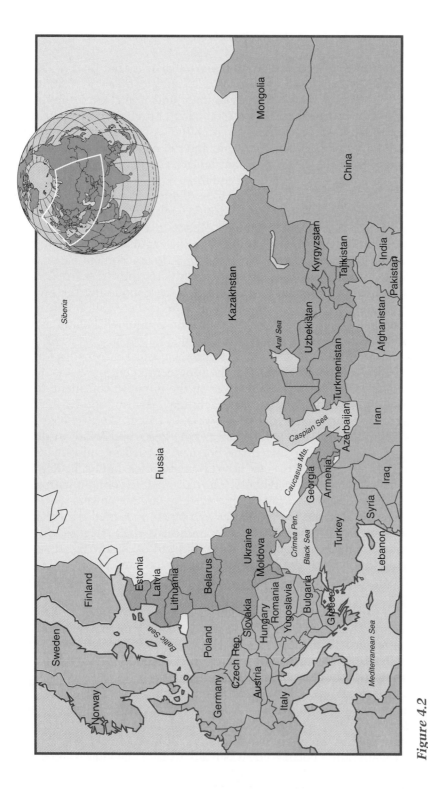

Figure 4.2
RUSSIA AND ITS NEIGHBORS.
Source: From *Great Decisions 1997*, p. 27. © Foreign Policy Association 1997. Reprinted with permission.

a large area interspersed with non-Russians. As a basis for national consciousness, Russian rulers have used various proselytizing campaigns to unite the
vast Russian homeland. Under the aristocracy and czars, for example, the
state was firmly linked to the Eastern Orthodox church to help consolidate
power. Later, under the Bolshevik Party after the Communist Revolution in
1917, the unifying principle was "socialism and the new Soviet man"—a principle that sought to create a new popular identity and to overcome ethnic differences through promises of economic equality.[43]

Russian leaders have indulged in periods of territorial expansion, sometimes, as in the thirteenth century, to be driven back and invaded in return (in
1240 by the Mongol leader Batu, Ghengis Khan's grandson). The rise of the
first czar, Ivan the Terrible, in 1547 resulted in the expulsion of foreign rulers,
in this case the Tartars, and the extension of Russian borders eastward to
Siberia and southward to the Caspian Sea. Under Peter the Great (1682–1725),
Russian forces moved westward in numerous wars, conquering the Swedish
and Finnish kingdoms and extending the realm to St. Petersburg. During the
reign of Catherine the Great (1762–1796), Russia conquered Poland and the
Crimean and Black Sea regions. After turning back Napoleon's invasion, Russian czars advanced toward the Dardanelles and the Caucasus, Muslim Kazakh,
and Central Asian regions by the end of the nineteenth century. Thus, Russia
established itself as the greatest land power on the Eurasian continent, but alternated between expansionism and retrenchment, desiring foreign territory
partly as a shield against hostile outside powers.

Marxists-Leninists rose to power on slogans of "Peace and Bread" at the end
of World War I. On assuming power, the Bolsheviks tried to consolidate control through policies designed to seize strategic territories, but backed off from
confrontations with powerful neighbors. They also had to contend with a civil
war against "White Russian" armies supported by outside powers. Several of
these powers, including the United States and Japan, mounted a military intervention in northern Russia in 1918, only to retreat when effective anti-Bol-
shevik domestic opposition could not be mobilized. A legacy of alienation,
mutual fear, and resentment had begun to separate East and West.

With the "reactionary forces" defeated at home, the USSR went on to absorb the southern republics of Georgia, Armenia, and Azerbaijan, where the
czars had made significant inroads earlier. States bordering Russia had long
been conscious of the need to conform to policies favorable to Moscow or risk
Russian interference or annexation. In the process, some minority ethnic
groups were able to retain autonomy while others lost out.

Despite rhetoric about the international brotherhood of the working class
and the need to spread revolution, pragmatism was evident as Vladimir Lenin,
father of the Bolshevik Revolution, sought to nurture the fledgling Soviet republic during the 1920s, especially in the central "heartland" of Russia and
Ukraine. Lenin pushed forcefully when he thought he could get away with it,
as in an early war against Poland, but was ready to take one or two steps back-

ward if necessary. Revolutionary action was put on the backburner, in much the same way that U.S. leaders frequently downplayed democracy and human rights when such concerns conflicted with state security and other more practical matters.[44]

In a way, Moscow offered an alternative to Woodrow Wilson's advocacy of national self-determination for the European states that acquired independence from the German and Austrian empires. Wilson had little to offer leaders in other regions who wanted independence from the British and French empires. One such aspiring leader was the young Vietnamese Ho Chi Minh, whose country was refused independence by the French in 1919 at the Versailles Peace Conference. Wilson could not force his allies to dismantle their empires, so young Ho, who remained a strong Vietnamese nationalist, turned to Moscow for guidance and training. It was the beginning of a fifty-five-year struggle for the Vietnamese, and foretold the appeal that the Soviet Union was to have in some parts of the third world.

Even though Ho was not alone in his conversion to communism in the early part of the twentieth century, Soviet leaders at the time continued to behave quite conservatively, not wanting to risk their newly established state in foreign wars and not fully trusting national liberation leaders in Asia and elsewhere. In its early days the Soviet state was relatively isolated from world affairs. It did not take up membership originally in the League of Nations, nor did it even enjoy diplomatic recognition from many countries. This isolation eased somewhat in 1922 with the signing of the Rapallo treaty for commercial and diplomatic relations with Germany. Both Germany and Russia could play off each other against Britain and France and did so frequently during the 1930s.

As we have noted, power considerations were a primary Soviet concern, even at the expense of ideology. When Stalin succeeded Lenin in the 1920s, his primary aim was to restore Soviet industry and build the military. He justified the sacrifices that were extracted from the Russian people by articulating an ideology that emphasized the happiness of future generations at home as long as outside threats and "capitalist encirclement" could be withstood. Socialism had to be built first and protected in one country. The interests of communist parties around the world had to bow to Russian interests as interpreted by Moscow. Ideology was tailored to fit the interests of the moment. Stalin, like Lenin, was a realist-opportunist, but with an added element of paranoia. He purged or executed thousands of political opponents (over six million by some estimates) and exiled leaders such as Trotsky who favored the interests of the international communist movement over Soviet national interests.

The limited role of ideology is perhaps best illustrated by Soviet reactions to Mao Zedong's attempted revolution in China during the 1930s. Seeing Mao both as an uncontrollable communist upstart and as too weak to win, Moscow continued to recognize non-Communist Chiang Kai-shek's government. In many ways the seeds of the Sino-Soviet split, which nearly brought China and Russia to war in the late 1960s, were sown well before Mao assumed power in China; the split could even be traced to traditional rivalries that predated the advent of the Russian Revolution itself.

In August of 1939, dedicated revolutionaries throughout the world were shocked to learn that Hitler and Stalin, Europe's archenemies, had signed a nonaggression pact. Germany and the Soviet Union had agreed not to oppose each other in war; in fact, secret understandings allowed them to share in an attack on Poland. Disillusioned communists in Europe and America left the Party, bewildered at such an unlikely turn of events. Stalin, interested above all in the survival of the Soviet state in a sea of hostile powers, had witnessed the weak British-French response to Hitler at Munich and concluded that if Britain and France would not protect an ally in Czechoslovakia, they could hardly be expected to fight against Nazi Germany to protect a communist regime in Moscow. A time-saving nonaggression pact with Hitler seemed the best security alternative. Confident that the Allies would still fight to save Poland and perhaps overestimating British and French firepower, Stalin assumed that Germany might at least be turned away from Poland, the doorstep to the Soviet Union,[45] while Moscow consolidated territory in Poland, Finland, and the Baltic states (Lithuania, Latvia, and Estonia—independent of Russia only since 1918).

For all his calculations, Stalin could not change Hitler's unlimited and unreasonable goals. In June of 1941, German troops came smashing into the Soviet Union, and none of the time or good will Stalin had tried to buy kept the Germans from reaching the gates of Stalingrad and Moscow. The Soviet army, relying on slogans of Russian nationalism rather than communism and aided with military equipment from Great Britain and the United States, fought a bitter rear-guard resistance. In all, an estimated twenty million Russian soldiers and civilians died in a war the Soviet government labeled the "Great Patriotic War."[46] The trauma of such losses was to have profound effects on Soviet postwar policy.

After World War II and throughout most of the Cold War, Soviet leaders concentrated primarily on controlling as much of the immediate border area as possible in Central and Eastern Europe, South Asia, and East Asia. Hindered by an inferior nuclear arsenal, Stalin's successor, Nikita Khrushchev, was careful to repudiate the doctrine on the "inevitability of war" between communist and capitalist camps and to substitute "peaceful coexistence" in its place.[47] Khrushchev called for economic and political competition rather than military confrontation; but the Soviet economic system, cut off from international trade and investment and hampered by inflexible planning, was not up to the task. Under the Soviet-sponsored economic zone for eastern Europe (the Council on Mutual Economic Assistance, or COMECON), there was a forced exchange of goods and raw materials at artificial prices, resulting in few of the East bloc states developing high-quality products desired on world markets or being able to support convertible currencies (i.e., those that could be exchanged for Western currencies and thus used to purchase needed goods abroad).

Within their sphere of influence, particularly in Eastern Europe, the Soviets showed a willingness to act ruthlessly to maintain control, which included direct military intervention in East Germany in 1953, Hungary in 1956, and Czechoslovakia in 1968, when domestic political uprisings threatened to move those satellites out of the Soviet orbit. In the latter two cases, the Soviets tried to justify their behavior by claiming they were fullfilling obligations toward fellow members of the **Warsaw Pact,** an alliance formed in 1955 by the Soviets and their satellites after West Germany's entry into NATO.[48]

As with the United States, Soviet leaders had difficulty adjusting to the meaning of third world nonalignment. Gradually, however, they became interested in inserting themselves in distant third world struggles where they felt such intervention could weaken Western powers' regional influence. For example, they distrusted early postwar Arab leaders as "tools of Britain," because many Arab monarchs owed their thrones to the British. Oddly enough (in view of later conflicts), the Soviet Union was one of the first states to recognize and supply arms to Israel in 1948, viewing the Jewish state as a foe of Britain. Only in the mid-fifties, with the emergence of Egyptian President Nasser's opposition to Western and particularly British influence, did Soviet leaders begin to see the usefulness of third world leaders in the East-West conflict. Moscow frequently put aside ideology to aid such leaders, looking the other way, for example, while Nasser jailed Egyptian Communists.

U.S. and Soviet forces nearly collided over third world politics in 1962, during the Cuban missile crisis. The crisis was spawned partly by Khrushchev's desire to deploy offensive nuclear missiles ninety miles from U.S. shores as a counterweight to overall American strategic superiority and threats to Fidel Castro's Cuba. President Kennedy's response to the discovery of the missiles was to institute a naval blockade of Cuba to force Soviet withdrawal of the missiles. The crisis proved a disaster for Soviet foreign policy, even if it was not as great a success for the Americans as the press claimed.[49] Confronted with U.S. naval superiority in the Caribbean, Khrushchev had to back down. Khrushchev's recklessness opened him to such ridicule inside and outside the Kremlin that, at least partly as a result, in 1964 he was quietly removed from his leadership position in favor of Leonid Brezhnev and Aleksei Kosygin, with the former emerging as the new head of the Soviet Communist Party.

The Cuban missile crisis had a major effect on American-Soviet relations. Several agreements were reached, including the establishment of a "hot line" to improve communications in future crises. At the same time, assessing their own naval and nuclear inferiority, the Soviets embarked on a crash armaments program that was to produce virtual parity with the United States in many defense areas by the mid-1970s.

With this increased power came increased Soviet activity in the third world, including the Middle East and Africa. Under the **Brezhnev Doctrine** the Soviet Union claimed the right to intervene in those states where "capitalist circles" threatened an established Marxist government. In 1979, the Soviets sent 100,000 troops into Afghanistan, creating what President Carter dramatically called "the greatest threat to peace since World War II." The invasion was generally attributed to the need by the Soviets to maintain dominant influence in a neighboring country where Muslim tribal forces were attempting, with outside help from the United States, China, and Pakistan, to topple a pro-Soviet regime. Soviet forces became bogged down in a "counterinsurgency" conflict with Afghan rebels that was reminiscent of U.S. involvement in Vietnam and that had a similarly ignominious conclusion.

Leonid Brezhnev's death in 1982 brought to power a series of physically infirm leaders who in their brief tenure did little to alter hard-line domestic and foreign policies. The object of ridicule about their aging leadership, the Soviets attempted to project a more youthful and vigorous international image with the appointment of Mikhail Gorbachev as General Secretary of the USSR Communist Party in 1985. Gorbachev attracted worldwide attention and popularity with his call for superpower summits and arms reductions. During his tenure, the Soviet government moved away from foreign adventures and in a sense turned inward, desperately seeking a viable model of reform for its creaky economy. Clearly unable to compete with the likes of the United States and Japan in the areas of international trade and technology, Moscow adopted the twin principles of *glasnost* (political openness) and *perestroika* (economic restructuring). Hoping to retain socialist precepts of equity, but adding a humane political face (permitting the expression of opposition viewpoints) and market incentives (permitting managerial autonomy and the possibility of leasing or owning land), the Soviet leadership talked of emulating a country such as Sweden.

However, it proved impossible to reform the economy in time to save the state. As the Baltic republics declared their independence from Moscow in 1991, Gorbachev—in remarkable contrast to Khrushchev in the 1950s—decided not to try to retain them through massive military intervention. Meanwhile, with negotiations taking place between Moscow and West Germany over the future of East Germany, communist regimes were removed from power in Eastern Europe. Long dormant political views, ranging from democracy to Christianity to fascism, along with ugly reminders of ethnic hatred, surfaced again throughout the former Soviet bloc.

Russia was restored to the world stage as the Soviet Union's successor and, with the reform-minded Boris Yeltsin at the helm, sought to forge closer ties with the United States and the West. However, Washington had to be careful not to appear too eager a suitor in assisting Moscow along the path to democracy and capitalism, because Russian nationalists—remembering the Cold War vividly—were all too ready to condemn President Yeltsin for being a puppet of the West and for selling out the Soviet state that millions had died defending in World War II. Still, American economic advisors flocked to Moscow in the early 1990s, counseling the new government and business leaders on how to establish a "free-market economy." Loans and foreign aid

THE LEGACY OF LENINISM WEIGHED HEAVILY ON SOVIET REFORMER MIKHAIL GORBACHEV IN 1989.

were made available through the International Monetary Fund and other channels. The difficulties of attempting a quick transition from communism to capitalism proved immense, and resulted in increased corruption, crime, and ethnic unrest. Yeltsin's poor health further complicated matters.

Moscow developed numerous new trade and financial links with the West, including a free trade agreement with the European Union in 1994. Because of need for trade, Russian arms, previously distributed for political purposes to friendly client states in the third world, now were sold widely in global arms markets. Though Moscow continued to collaborate with the West in efforts to control nuclear and chemical weapons, frictions developed with Washington over proposed nuclear and submarine sales to Iran. Despite lingering tensions and at times disagreements, Russia and the United States also consulted closely on UN peacekeeping efforts in the former Yugoslavia and elsewhere.

As probably the greatest symbol of change in the post–Cold War era, in 1994 the Russian government signed the Clinton administration's "Partnerships for Peace" initiative, thereby following their former Warsaw Pact allies in linking themselves loosely to NATO. This arrangement did not afford actual NATO membership, as Hungary, Poland, Ukraine, and the Baltic states—anxious for Western defense commitments against possible Russian revanchism—had hoped, but it did constitute a creative compromise; for the East Europeans there was the promise of joint military training exercises and other "confidence-building" measures designed to alleviate their security anxieties, and the Russians were promised special and close consultation as a leading military power.[50] Russia continued to bridle at the prospect of Washington eventually extending explicit defense guarantees to former East bloc states bordering Russia.

Russian foreign policy, both before and after the dismemberment of the Soviet Union, defies simple pigeonholing. Moscow has displayed a variety of behavior modes over the years, some "dovish" and some "hawkish." At times Russian leaders have operated out of what appeared to be defensive instincts, and at other times they seemed to act on opportunistic impulses. Russia has continued to be concerned primarily with the status of states and groups along its long borders, what Russian leaders euphemistically refer to as "the near abroad." Indeed, many Russian nationalists do not recognize the loss of regions such as Ukraine, Kazakhstan, and Belarus. One of Moscow's foreign policy frustrations has been its inability to win full, unconditional acceptance as a global power among the economic elite of the Group of Seven. Russia often is invited as an observer to their annual summit meetings, representing as much an aid problem for the Seven as a partner.[51]

Aside from the ongoing challenge of economic reform, among Moscow's key preoccupations in the 1990s were the gradual settlement of disputes with the Baltic republics over treatment of ethnic Russians still living in those territories; accords with Ukraine over control of the former Soviet navy, nuclear weapons, and the Crimean area; the status of Islam, oil, and nuclear weapons in such southern neighbors as Kazakhstan; and the reinstatement of Belarus as a Russian dependency. Russian forces also interceded in ethnic conflicts within and between neighboring republics such as Georgia, Armenia, and Azerbaijan. Within Russia itself, Moscow unleashed its armed forces in 1995 to crush the independence movement of Chechnya, in the Caucasus region, in an effort to avoid further fragmentation of the Russian Federation.[52] Historical disputes with Japan over island territories persisted and complicated efforts to pursue joint economic projects with Tokyo. As a vast state with wide geographic interests, there is naturally a tendency to pursue an array of concerns and to do so with a variety of strategies.

We began this chapter asking whether Russian foreign policy was likely to change from that of the Soviet Union. Our historical review indicates that the answer is "yes and no." Certainly Russia's interest in association with NATO, its opening to the global economy, and other recent developments mark a significant departure from the Soviet, and even the czarist, past. Conversely, Moscow's continued preoccupation with border security and its interest in the fate of fellow Slavs in the former Yugoslavia correspond to age-old behaviors. Whether, as many geostrategists have argued for centuries, Russian leaders desire warm water ports to the south, or simply want influence in security zones around their borders, Moscow continues to seek recognition of its concerns and of its status in the councils of major powers.[53]

Chinese Foreign Policy: A Profile

As Russia experimented in the 1990s with simultaneous political and economic reforms and found them an explosive brew, China sought to confine its modernization process mainly to the economic arena. China's aging leadership banked heavily on its ability to provide enough economic opportunity—enough business outlets, motorbikes, Walkmans, and color TVs—to satisfy the huge Chinese population without the necessity of political reform, which would threaten the single-party communist state. In other words, communists hoped to hang onto power through rapid economic development, including the manufacture and import of consumer goods and the development of market-oriented enterprises. The hope was to make China another of the Asian "miracle states" able to compete effectively on the world market.[54] How the above scenario will play out remains uncertain. In any case, China remains a formidable regional military power and the most populous state on earth, one thought capable of emerging as a true world power in the twenty-first century.

As with the United States and Russia, a dualism is apparent in Chinese foreign policy. China is both an ancient society and a new state.[55] The Chinese people can point to a civilization that has flourished and has absorbed invaders and conquerers for thousands of years (see Fig. 4.3). Outsiders were, and in some ways still are, considered barbarians; this was natural for a society that in its early days encountered no dynamic civilizations and considered itself the "Middle Kingdom" around which the rest of the world was organized.

It has always been difficult to identify the boundaries separating China's foreign and domestic policies. Traditionally, the Chinese considered themselves more a civilization than a state or nation as known in the West. The

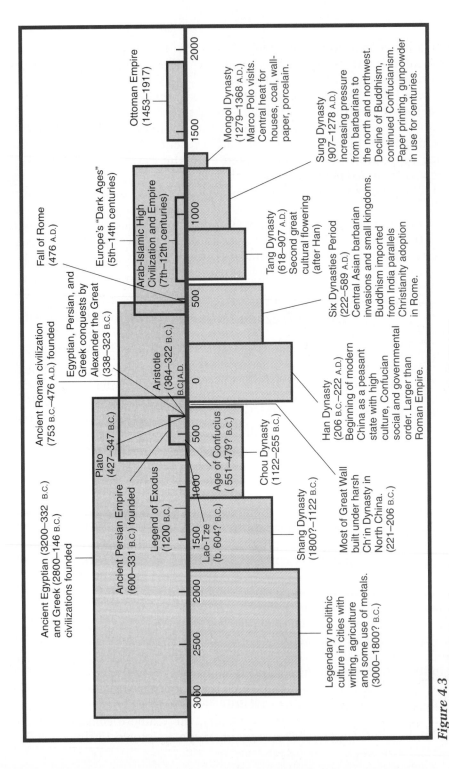

Figure 4.3
HISTORICAL DEVELOPMENT OF CHINESE AND WESTERN CIVILIZATIONS

Empire included surrounding peoples from whom the Emperor, the Son of Heaven, was prepared to receive tribute and commerce. The tributary states, which for the Chinese included even England and Holland at one time, were expected to conform to civilized Chinese behavior and to accept the harmony and hierarchies of Chinese life. China dominated nearby lands, but the Koreans, the Indochinese in Southeast Asia, the Japanese, and others generally ruled themselves within the accepted standards. On the whole, the self-contained Chinese civilization had little need for and was expected to have little to do with foreigners; it was isolated and yet sublimely confident.

When Westerners arrived, therefore, the Chinese were slow to react to a potential threat.[56] Although Marco Polo had shown great deference to the Khan during his visit in 1275 and was dutifully impressed by the use of paper money and the burning of coal, later generations of Westerners were not to be intimidated. By the mid-nineteenth century, the British had already introduced the opium trade and in the Opium War forced the Chinese to continue opium imports. Other major powers, including Russia and the United States, joined in efforts to carve out exclusive trade concessions and territory. Frustration over foreign domination led to the Boxer Rebellion in 1900, which saw the storming of foreign embassies in Peking by Chinese militants. The Boxers were crushed by the combined forces of the "civilized" nations of the West and Japan. However, the Boxer Rebellion shook China out of its complacent Middle Kingdom mentality and forced the Chinese to recognize the need for some change.

After the democratic-minded Nationalist Revolution led by Sun Yat-sen in 1911, marking the end of the Manchu Empire, the fight for the succession to Chinese power raged between one of Sun's Nationalist disciples, Chiang Kaishek, and a young Communist named Mao Zedong. It resembled the feuds that had been fought among warlords in ancient Chinese history, except that there was need for some degree of accommodation between the two factions to deal collectively with the Japanese invasions of 1931 and 1937. Once the long struggle against the Japanese ended with the termination of World War II, Chiang and Mao concentrated on the unfinished business of determining who would govern the Chinese people. The United States attempted a mediating role in the civil war initially but bowed out after failing to achieve peace. Mao ultimately achieved victory in 1949; Chiang fled to the island of Taiwan with the remnants of his army, and the Truman administration was saddled with blame for the "loss of China" even though it was never Truman's to lose.[57]

Mao faced an enormous rebuilding task in a country that remained a largely rural peasant society. A history of foreign exploitation also made the Beijing leadership highly suspicious of and resistant to foreign powers. China's identification with the third world was partly a function of its underdeveloped status and partly a function of its need for ideological justification in its opposition to potentially harmful world powers. In signing a security treaty with the Soviets in 1950, Beijing entered into an uneasy relationship with Moscow.[58]

The Chinese began to press long-standing grievances over "unfair and unequal" nineteenth-century treaties. Although reluctant to risk military action far from their territory, Chinese leaders were quite willing to use force closer to home, to keep foreign powers away from the borders, and to incorporate parts of "ancient China." Tibet was invaded and subdued in the 1950s; China risked a war in Korea, despite American atomic weapons, to push U.S. forces away from the Chinese border; China attacked and routed Indian forces in 1961 to quiet Indian border claims along the Himalayan frontier; and Beijing harassed the Taiwan government when it appeared that Chiang Kai-shek might launch an attack against the mainland, and reminded the United States that Taiwan was part of a single Chinese state. (Indeed, the Communists and Nationalists agreed that Taiwan, Tibet, and the border areas were rightfully part of "one China"; they simply disagreed on who should rule China.)

When it came to promoting revolution and pursuing ambitions in the far reaches of the third world, the Chinese leadership exercised caution, relying mostly on rhetoric and moral support. Even when the Chinese developed nuclear weapons in the 1960s, they were not in a very good position to help third world countries materially, either in military or economic terms. Although they undertook certain projects, such as building railroads in Tanzania and other black African states, the Chinese Communists, like their predecessors, remained reluctant to involve China too deeply in world affairs. During the Vietnam War, the Chinese condemned U.S. imperialism and called for peasant uprisings against capitalist societies; but Mao's regime became too preoccupied in the late sixties and early seventies with its own internal upheaval—the so-called **Cultural Revolution**—to cultivate revolutions elsewhere.

During the Cultural Revolution, Mao attempted to instill revolutionary fervor in a generation of Chinese that had not experienced the "Long March" that had enabled the communists to survive the civil war in the thirties. The Red Book containing Chairman Mao's sayings became the bible of Chinese society—a dramatically transformed society in which schools and universities were closed for several years, people were removed from positions of authority and forced, often by groups of zealous youths, to repent their past "sins," and highly trained scientists and professionals were made to work among peasants on farms and in villages. This severely damaged the Chinese economy. As for its international relations in this period, China virtually withdrew from world affairs—retaining only *one* ambassador in a single foreign country (Egypt). This episode in Chinese history called to mind an order in the ancient Chinese Book of Rites that "the officials of the Empire shall have no intercourse with foreigners."[59]

The Cultural Revolution had been at least partly motivated by Mao's desire to distinguish the Chinese model of communism from the Soviet model, which had resulted in a rather rigid government with a central bureaucracy, inflexible planning, and privileged party and professional elites. Mao argued that a classless society along Marxist lines could never be achieved through a

Soviet-style system. He also observed that the Soviets had become "bourgeois" themselves and had acted in no less an imperialistic fashion than the United States in the third world, thereby relinquishing their leadership role in the international communist movement.

The Sino-Soviet split became evident only in the mid-sixties and seemed to be mainly a battle over ideological purity—but in fact the split could be traced to long-standing concerns of security and prestige. Mao's deep-seated hostility toward the Soviets was based on historical rivalries over territorial and other issues, together with Stalin's initial indifference to the Chinese Communist revolution. The Soviets likewise harbored deep-seated animosity toward the Chinese—the potential "yellow peril" represented by almost a billion "peasants" poised along their 4,500-mile border. The Soviets had denied Chinese access to nuclear secrets in 1958, a harbinger of the withdrawal of Soviet technicians and equipment in 1961. Mao countered with blistering criticism of the Soviet backdown in the Cuban missile crisis. The 1950 security treaty became a dead letter and the Sino-Soviet relationship deteriorated rapidly, despite periodic attempts at reconciliation.

China's successful nuclear explosions in 1964, together with the unpredictable, almost self-destructive tendencies of the Cultural Revolution and growing friction over border questions, alarmed the Soviet leadership in the late 1960s. Moscow responded by building up its forces along the Chinese border, so much so that rumors circulated about planned Soviet attacks on the nuclear test grounds in Xinjiang Province; in fact, it has been noted that China is the only country to have been threatened, at different times, with nuclear attack by both the United States and Russia.[60] Beijing enlarged its border forces, and what had been mainly a Sino-Soviet political propaganda fight became a military confrontation. In 1969, two clashes occurred along the Ussuri River, scene of Sino-Russian skirmishes even at the turn of the century.

With Sino-Soviet tensions high, Beijing's foreign policy began to shift toward the West. It seemed imperative that Beijing respond to American initiatives and improve relations with Russia's opponents in Washington. After the deaths of Chou En-lai in 1975 and Mao in 1976, the new Communist Chinese regime headed by Deng Xiaoping stepped up its wooing of Washington, looking not only for military support against the Soviets but advanced technology for modernizing a Chinese economy that had been set back at least a decade by the Cultural Revolution. The Chinese Communists showed they could be as pragmatic as their Soviet counterparts. Under Deng, the Chinese pursued "four modernizations" in agriculture, industry, science, and defense.

The prospect of breaking into a market of over a billion people made American business interests highly supportive of the opening to China; the manufacturers of farm machinery and computers were especially intrigued by the size of the market, not to mention the makers of soft drinks and deodorants. In the process many American as well as European and Asian corporations established joint ventures with Chinese firms, and the United States became one of the largest markets for Chinese products ranging from silks to shoes. Beijing saw advantages in learning, even copying, Western technology, making itself more self-sufficient and ultimately less dependent on foreign powers. These evolving relationships led to trade frictions, as the Chinese rather liberally "borrowed" Western products and technology, including pirated CD music and computer software, without paying royalties or recognizing patents and copyrights. Gradually the United States accumulated a considerable trade deficit with Beijing, importing far more than it exported.

During the 1980s, China became more active diplomatically both inside and outside the United Nations, as evidenced in Table 4.3.[61] China's expanding international ties produced domestic fallout. As Chinese students increasingly went overseas for higher education and as radio and television brought news of political change in the rest of the world, word filtered back to the ambitious youth in major Chinese cities, those who had not yet benefited significantly from expanded commerce, that a hopeful future could only be achieved through a greater share of political power. This was vividly illustrated when students erected a statue representing democracy during massive demonstrations in Beijing's Tiananmen Square in June 1989, a statue bearing similarity to Liberty in New York harbor. The statue along with the revolution proved short-lived, however, as government tanks violently terminated the uprising. During the 1990s, China was frequently criticized, especially in the United States, for its suppression of dissent, use of prison and child labor to produce goods for export, denial of women's rights, and other human rights abuses. With the return of the British Crown Colony of Hong Kong to Chinese rule in 1997 (under a 1984 agreement with Britain), it was unclear whether Beijing's

Table 4.3

CHINA'S GROWING LINKAGES TO THE INTERNATIONAL SYSTEM

	1949–65	*1966–77* *(UN Entry, 1971)*	*1978–88*
IGO Memberships	1	21	37 (including global financial institutions such as World Bank and IMF)
International Conventions (Multilateral Treaties)	8	15	103 (including seven on arms control)
NGO Memberships	0	71	574 (including 250 in the science and technology field)

Source: Adapted from Samuel S. Kim, "Thinking Globally in Post-Mao China," *Journal of Peace Research,* 27 (May 1990), pp. 192–193, and 196.

A LONE CHINESE STUDENT FACING THE CHINESE ARMY TANKS THAT ROLLED INTO BEIJING'S TIANANMEN SQUARE IN JUNE 1989 TO SUPPRESS MASS DEMONSTRATIONS URGING DEMOCRATIC REFORM.

pledge to preserve Hong Kong's vibrant capitalist commercial system would extend to keeping democracy alive in that city.

In the military sphere, Chinese forces had invaded Soviet-backed Vietnam in 1979 and continued skirmishing with the Vietnamese for a decade over the latter's occupation of Kampuchea before the conflict finally subsided. Some of China's other neighbors, such as Thailand and Singapore, who had previously feared revolutionary expansionism under Mao, opted for improved economic relations in later years. Other neighbors, such as the Indonesian and Malaysian governments, still feared Chinese dominance through links with sizable overseas Chinese communities living throughout Southeast Asia. Malaysia, along with Vietnam and several other states, found themselves in the 1990s contesting China's claim to the oil-rich Spratly Island chain in the South China Sea. States throughout the region watched with some anxiety as Beijing moved to modernize its armed forces, acquiring long-distance naval capabilities (aircraft carriers and submarines) for the first time. In fact, with the fall of the Soviet Union, China became the number one market for arms exports from its former adversaries in Russia.[62]

As an aspiring world power, China is beset by a number of problems—growing environmental concerns related to a rapidly industrializing economy and still burgeoning population pressures, gaps in living standards among classes and between the relatively prosperous export-oriented coastal cities (some of which have been designated "special economic zones" to facilitate access to foreign trade and investment) and more remote regions, difficulties in trying to convert state-owned enterprises to more efficient management, persistent troubles with leadership succession (following Deng's death in 1997) and domestic political unrest, and the unresolved matter of whether Taiwan should be permitted to assume its place as a recognized state in its own right entitled to UN membership.[63] Notwithstanding these problems, China continues to claim the singular distinction of speaking for more than one-fifth of humanity.

Japanese Foreign Policy: A Profile

We complete our foreign policy review by examining Japan, a nation only recently reemerging as a significant world power, and one doing it by stressing economic and technological over military instruments. Like the others we have discussed, Japan evidences great foreign policy variability. The same nation that in the first part of the twentieth century spent the most years at war, in the latter half of the century prospered under a constitution renouncing war as an instrument of policy. A formerly isolated state, Japan has become the hub of a worldwide network of trade and investment links. Dependent on U.S. security guarantees, yet frequently conflicting with Washington over trade policy, Japan has been able to exert important influence on the world economy and, in the process, the world polity as well.

As with China, Japanese civilization is very old, tracing its roots to clan kingdoms well before the sixth centuryA.D. There followed a period of cultural borrowing from and dependency on China, with a more autonomous Japanese civilization emerging in the tenth and eleventh centuries, centered on the samurai aristocratic warrior class. In 1185, the first of a series of feudal military dictatorships, or shogunates, was established, a system that persisted for seven centuries, gradually obscuring the political role of Japan's emperors. Trade with foreign states grew during much of this period, though it was confined to certain ports and zones of the country. Foreign influences, such as various forms of Buddhism and Christianity, also penetrated the society, to mix with native Japanese Shinto beliefs.[64]

The Japanese state was finally unified under the strong Tokugawa shoguns beginning in the 1600s, as the national capital was moved to Edo, later to be called Tokyo. These rulers also adopted a modified version of Chinese Confucian thought, with well-defined social class hierarchies and complex notions of mutual social roles and responsibility—a pattern that still typifies Japan in contrast to more individualistic societies. A key feature of Tokugawa policy was the closing of Japan to foreign commerce in 1638, a move somewhat similar to China's radical closure during the Cultural Revolution. In Japan's case, fear of increased penetration by Christian missionaries and potential European colonization led to the reaction, but it is somewhat typical of societies that fear loss of national identity to foreign influences and powers.[65]

A further turning point in Japanese history and foreign policy came about in the mid-nineteenth century with the forced reopening of Japan to international commerce. Complete isolation proved impractical in the industrial age. After numerous polite refusals of foreign trade requests, Japan was forced to accede in 1853 by the arrival of an American naval armada under Commodore Matthew Perry. The Japanese refer to this traumatic event as the coming of the "black ships," and it was a less than auspicious beginning to a complex and intimate U.S.-Japanese relationship.

Realizing their abject weakness in the face of foreign industrial powers, the Tokugawas went on to accept commercial treaties with a number of European states as well. Firmly embracing the need for major economic and political reform, Japanese leadership replaced the shoguns in 1868 with a coalition of court aristocracy and young samurai, proclaiming the Meiji Restoration, or "Enlightened Rule," and using the emperor once more as the national symbol. In addition, these young modernizers, under the slogan "enrich the country and strengthen the military," went about the task of copying Western industrial, financial, military, and educational techniques in a full-speed attempt to overcome Western advantages.[66]

Aiming to beat the foreigners at their own game, the new Japanese government sought to link economic interests to foreign policy. By the 1890s, while China languished under foreign domination, Japan was able to reverse the unequal treaties and high tariff rates imposed by foreign powers. Styling themselves as the first modern and autonomous Asian state, Japanese leaders sought to open markets and establish colonies of their own in both nearby Korea and China. Tokyo proceeded to defeat Russia in 1905 in a war over territorial disputes—a striking demonstration of Asia's new power to compete with European empires.[67]

Thus, Japan has oscillated between assertiveness and nonprovocation in world politics. For example, their policy shifted in reaction to World War I; while accepting the supposed virtues, standards, and practices of Western "civilization," many Japanese were shocked and horrified at the war's carnage and cruelty. Tokyo felt increasingly distrusted and rejected by European powers, evidenced in Britain's failure to renew its early twentieth century alliance with Japan. Post–World War I arms control agreements allotted the Japanese an inferior quota of naval battleships. Washington was increasingly callous about trade agreements and imposed limits on Japanese immigration. Thus, Tokyo turned to a more assertive "Orientalization" of its foreign policy—a self-styled role as a militant, self-reliant, and race-conscious Asian power resisting white imperialism.

Given the country's near total lack of natural resources, it was difficult to carry on a productive industrial policy and remain a world power without either an empire or free trade. The more Japan pressed for dominance and empire in Asia to obtain needed rubber, tin, coal, oil, iron ore, and other raw materials, the more resistance it met from Washington, London, the Hague, and other capitals with interests in the Pacific. Under the army's influence, Japan intervened to take what it needed militarily by invading first Manchuria (in 1931) and then China itself (in 1937), using the term "Greater East-Asian Co-Prosperity Sphere" as a cover for conquest. The League of Nations and Western powers responded with a series of economic sanctions, ultimately leading to a trade embargo over Japanese occupation of China.

Perhaps the U.S.-Japanese clash at Pearl Harbor could have been avoided if bilateral negotiations in 1940–1941 had produced agreement to guarantee Japan access to resources in Southeast Asia and territorial control of China, but the Roosevelt administration judged this too great a price. Thus, Japan's preemptive attack on Hawaii, meant to weaken the U.S. presence in the Pacific at least temporarily, provoked American involvement in a war that ended in humanity's first use of atomic weapons, on Hiroshima and Nagasaki, in 1945.

Japan took the nuclear age as a signal that war was an ineffective approach to power and that economic expansion in an atmosphere of peace was the only way forward after World War II. General Douglas MacArthur, in charge of American occupation forces, framed a "peace constitution," with democracy and free press guarantees. Under the constitution, there was to be no army as such, only "self-defense" forces designed for immediate defense of the islands. The Japanese public developed a firm aversion to nuclear weapons but at the same time failed to come to terms fully with the ruthlessness and brutality of Japan's military forces in World War II. This record was, however, well remembered by the victims throughout Asia. (On the way in which the Japanese have viewed their history, as compared with the Germans, see the box on pages 167–168).

Adopting "export-led" economic policies, and exhibiting a tendency to stay out of major international political disputes, Japan ultimately won—through peaceful means—the Asian "co-prosperity" sphere it had failed to conquer by force. With a defense budget limited to roughly 1 percent of its gross national product (still enough to equip a considerable army and navy because of the growing size of the GNP), Japan during the Cold War relied on American security and nuclear guarantees while nevertheless resisting the stationing of nuclear weapons on its soil. With Washington willing to open its market to stimulate Japanese recovery, Tokyo invested in modern consumer goods production for export, whereas consumer spending at home was limited through high prices. Japan went from exporting toys and dinnerware to booming multinational automotive, optics, and electronics industries.

As a vibrant, mid-sized power, Tokyo in a sense could play on Washington's desire for a stable, strong, but peaceful ally, and could "move with the power-

WAR GUILT: A TALE OF TWO COUNTRIES

In recent years, Japanese nationalists, as well as some American strategists hoping to shore up a strong ally on Russia's borders, have argued that someday the country will have to be "normal" again, with a complete array of foreign policy options including the existence of regular armed forces. However, because those responsible for education in Japan could not agree on how to approach the subject, the postwar generation learned relatively little about the history of Japanese militarism and wartime atrocities such as forced "death marches" and executions of prisoners, the massacre of civilians, and the enslavement of women to serve as prostitutes.

In 1995, during commemorations of the 50th anniversary of the end of World War II, Japanese leaders stated regrets about various incidents involving Filipinos, Chinese, Koreans, Westerners, and others, and proceeded to use the term "apology" forthrightly in this context for the first time. Japanese political parties have been divided over this issue, with the Socialist Party generally supporting apologies and recognition of guilt, and members of the dominant Liberal Democratic Party generally unwilling to apologize unless Japan's sacrifices (as in the atomic bombings) also draw Western apologies. The result during 1995 was a parliamentary resolution promising "national self-reflection." Resistance to governmental payments of war damages to Asian and Western victims also has remained strong, though encouragement has been given to private fundraising. Despite the opposition of Chinese and Korean opinion, many Japanese still see the war effort as their effective resistance to Western domination of Asia.[1]

The comparison between Germany and Japan on this score is instructive. West Germany also suffered severe war guilt and likewise carved out a rather nonprovocative, economically oriented foreign policy that stressed multilateralism, under a new constitution that barred war-making. Like Japan, the Federal Republic became an American ally and developed a considerable "defensive" military establishment. The younger postwar generation in West Germany discovered that they, too, were learning little about World War II history. However, they pressed their parents for answers about the Nazi past. West German educational curricula, therefore, began to dwell extensively on the wartime period, especially on the Holocaust against the Jews, Gypsies, the infirm, and other minorities. The West German government agreed to pay reparations to Israel for the Holocaust. East German curricula under the Marxist state, however, emphasized mainly the struggle against fascism as the last stage of capitalism.

When the two Germanies merged in 1991, historical shocks awaited residents of the East. They were somewhat more prone than the majority in the West to blame continued harsh economic conditions on foreigners and minorities. Even in the West, though, by 1995 there were influential groups advocating less concern with collective guilt, less recollection of the Holocaust, and more emphasis on German "heroism" in struggles against enemies such as the Soviet Union. In the aftermath of the 1990–1991 Gulf War, the German constitution was amended to allow potential use of troops in UN peacekeeping missions outside the NATO area; a debate ensued about the permissibility of combat forces being dispatched to crisis zones such as Bosnia, where German World War II atrocities were recalled. Similar debates were held in Japan in the 1990s concerning possible Japanese participation in peacekeeping operations in Asia.

[1] National Public Radio report, June 3, 1995; and Cameron Barr, "How Japanese 'Reflect,' Not Apologize, on WWII," *Christian Science Monitor* (June 13, 1995), pp. 1 and 8.

ful" to surpass them.[68] For example, during the many years the United States boycotted trade with China, Japan was allowed to maintain commercial ties to Beijing by arguing that it could help moderate China's policies as well as weaken Russian influence in Asia. The United States encourged Japan to join the General Agreement on Tariffs and Trade (GATT), a free trade arrangement, yet looked the other way when Japan erected numerous indirect trade barriers against foreign goods and manipulated the value of its currency to protect domestic producers.

After 1970, however, a series of external shocks jarred this comfortable foreign policy, causing Japanese leaders to reevaluate their rather passive foreign policy stance. In 1971, the Nixon administration, stung by its growing trade imbalances, took the dollar off fixed exchange rates and allowed it to float in value (downward) on currency markets, thereby making U.S. products cheaper to foreigners and impeding Japanese reliance on a "cheap yen" export strategy. Nixon and Secretary of State Kissinger also engineered their own surprise opening to China without informing their Japanese allies, thus shattering Tokyo's sense of a special relationship with Washington, particularly as a conduit to China. Finally, the increased oil prices caused by the Arab oil embargo during the 1973 Arab-Israeli war delivered a sharp blow to Japanese economic expansion. Inflation and fear of energy shortages created a renewed sense of vulnerability in a country at that time nearly 90 percent dependent on Middle Eastern oil.

Japanese leaders thus concluded that a more active and purposeful foreign policy would again be necessary to preserve economic prosperity and stability.

They moved toward what was called "comprehensive security," i.e., a broad economic and strategic initiative to assure national well-being. They diversified raw materials sources so as to minimize vulnerability and sought cleaner, more abundant energy, including nuclear power, for industry. In turn, they tried even harder to make foreign resource centers dependent on Japanese capital, goods, technology, and services. Foreign aid was centered on countries such as oil-rich Indonesia, and Japan became mineral-rich South Africa's chief trade partner despite that country's human rights violations.[69] Slowly Tokyo began to take positions on controversial subjects such as the Arab-Israeli and Persian Gulf disputes, becoming more critical of Israel and attempting, unsuccessfully, to mediate between Iraq and Iran during their war of the 1980s, all in the interest of assuring more secure access to Middle Eastern oil.

By the 1990s, amid considerable national debate, the government decided that Japanese forces could be used overseas in strictly humanitarian relief and peacekeeping roles under UN auspices; they were dispatched to Cambodia, where they stayed in relatively isolated locations so as not to revive anti-Japanese feelings in Southeast Asia.[70] Tokyo, still valuing its partnership with Washington, continued to help pay for U.S. military bases on Japanese territory after Washington was forced by Philippine nationalism to close its bases in that country. The American presence, it was hoped, would provide stability in nearby Korea and reassure anxious Asian neighbors that Japanese foreign policy would continue to be multilateralist and democratically oriented. Indeed, in 1994 the first steps were taken, despite a lingering territorial dispute over Russian-occupied islands, toward a three-way U.S.-Japanese-Russian strategic consultation on Northeast Asian security.

Although Japan has come to play a more assertive role in world affairs, and has moved closer to a permanent seat on the UN Security Council, certain problems have persisted. Japan's economy alone is not large enough for the yen completely to displace the dollar as the premier world currency for commerce. As downturns in the 1990s showed, Japan's domestic economy is highly subject to global economic forces such as recession, poor overseas investment strategies, and fluctuations in foreign currencies (notably the devaluation of the dollar). The country remains virtually devoid of indigenous sources of raw materials. Despite its peaceful and cooperative orientation, Tokyo is viewed with lingering mistrust on the part of many industrialized democracies that are its trade partners, Russia (where territorial conflict has persisted), and some countries in Asia. Some developing countries resent the flood of Japanese consumer goods, which squeezes out local investors and fosters dependence on Tokyo.[71]

Perhaps Japan's chief irritation is the ongoing trade friction with Washington despite their close security partnership. During the 1990s, the ongoing U.S.-Japanese trade imbalance, whereby Americans annually imported billions of dollars worth of goods more than they exported to Japan, caused the Clinton administration to "get tough" with Tokyo. In 1995, the United States went so far as to announce stiff tariff penalties (high import taxes) on Japanese luxury cars if Tokyo did not agree specifically to greater purchases of U.S. auto parts. The Japanese, however, resented being blamed for U.S. trade problems, noting that they remained one of America's leading export markets and that much of the U.S. trade deficit was caused by structural weaknesses in the American economy. A showdown was avoided over the auto parts issue, but Japanese leaders resolved to get tougher themselves in resisting Washington's trade demands, urging that disputes be settled multilaterally through the new World Trade Organization.

Thus, Japan over time has modified its foreign policy considerably to adjust to changing conditions in its international environment. Among Tokyo's current

Table 4.4
FOREIGN POLICY PROFILES

Country	Alignment	Scope	Methods
United States	Neutrality between 1800 and 1945, with exception of world war participation. Alliance network after 1945 as West bloc leader. Continued security treaties as blocs and hegemony decline in post–Cold War era.	Mainly regional in 19th century. Scope expanded gradually and became global by 1945.	Mainly bilateral though willing to use multilateral means when serving U.S. purposes. Active regional intervenor becoming global intervenor after 1945.
Russia	European balance of power alliances through 1917. Shifting informal alignment until 1941. Alliances during and after World War II. Bloc leader until 1990. Shifting informal alignment after Cold War.	Mainly Eurasian regional until 1955. Third world competitive and increasingly global after 1955, mainly on political and military rather than economic issues. Restrained somewhat by economic and other factors in the 1990s.	Mainly bilateral, though increasingly willing to use multilateral organizations as Western dominance in them decreased. Regionally interventionist in Eurasia.
China	After 1949, alliance with USSR. Alliance lapsed with informal membership in nonaligned movement after 1955. Tilt toward West in 1970s and 1980s. Nonaligned in 1990s.	Mainly Asian regional; increasing third world involvement after 1955. Highly restricted during Cultural Revolution. Renewed global contacts after mid-1970s.	Bilateralist until late 1970s. Regional interventionist in Asia. Aspirant for leadership among developing countries.
Japan	Failed early 20th century alliances. Axis member in World War II; U.S. ally since 1945.	Mainly Asian and Pacific regional, with global economic influence. Slowly reemerging political influence.	Mainly bilateralist prior to World War II. Increasingly multilateralist after World War II.

guiding principles, one could identify the following: (1) avoid military involvements if possible; (2) keep good ties to key supplier and transit countries; (3) diversify trade partners to avoid commodity dependence; (4) maintain sufficient stockpiles of materials and supplies; (5) exploit technology, such as instantaneous worldwide communications and information gathering, to reduce dependency and increase bargaining leverage; and (6) promote multinational enterprises and joint ventures to sustain Japanese influence at the center of the global economy.[72]

Conclusion

The United States, Russia, China, and Japan each have journeyed through periods of relative isolation, regional preoccupation, and global involvements; of alliance and neutrality; of foreign war and intervention; and of civil war. In their foreign relations, these states have employed varied tactics: trade restrictions as well as trade concessions; diplomatic nonrecognition and strategically timed recognition; Olympic boycotts and table-tennis competitions; covert intelligence and propaganda activities along with cultural exchanges; and the threatened or actual use of armed force along with ringing support for the peaceful settlement of disputes. Given their importance in world politics, experts have tried to forecast the future of the four countries' mutual relations. For example, some have noted Japanese concerns that China will surpass Japan as an Asian power in the twenty-first century, attracting greater attention from the United States, Russia, and other actors.[73] Others argue that all of these states will become preoccupied mainly with economic growth and will seek mutual collaboration. Such speculation aside, in Table 4.4 we summarize the main historical tendencies in the foreign policy behavior of these four countries.

Our synopses, of course, cannot possibly do complete justice to the subject. Although our analysis here might suggest that nation-states are driven by fairly simple motives, such as the pursuit of power or territorial defense and expansion, a closer look at the *determinants* of foreign policy behavior in the next chapter will indicate that a number of other factors also are evident. Accounting for foreign policy is becoming a more complex task, especially as subnational (domestic) and transnational forces take on greater importance in an increasingly interdependent international system. We have seen some of the things nation-states do—the record of their policy shifts and turns. We now turn to a fuller consideration of *why* they behave as they do.

SUMMARY

1. Foreign policy is a set of priorities and guides for action in certain circumstances that underlies a country's behavior toward other states, and includes both the basic goals a national government seeks to pursue in the international arena and the instruments used to achieve these goals. Inconsistencies can develop because of various "policy domains" and other factors.

2. Foreign policy behavior can generally be classified along three dimensions: (a) alignment, (b) scope, and (c) *modus operandi* (methods of operation). Countries have different alignment tendencies, with some choosing to ally with other countries and others remaining neutral.

3. Major powers have historically defined the scope of their interests in global terms, whereas most other countries are essentially regional actors, and a few even isolationist.

4. Countries also demonstrate a characteristic *modus operandi*. Some countries tend to operate multilaterally, whereas others use primarily bilateral approaches. Similarly, some states are more active and willing to use force than others in world affairs. With the end of the Cold War, the nature of interventionism has changed somewhat.

5. Like most countries, the United States, Russia, China, and Japan demonstrate significant disparities between their officially proclaimed principles and their actual behavior. These countries have also gone through significant changes or fluctuations in alignment, scope, and methods of operation and have used a variety of political, economic, and military tools of foreign policy.

6. The United States in its early history maintained a foreign policy that was neutral in terms of alignment behavior and mainly regional in scope. By the turn of the twentieth century, however, the United States had become a world power with global interests. A recurring feature of U.S. foreign policy had been the need to find moral justification for self-interested actions.

7. The containment of communism became a major theme in American foreign policy after World War II, with the United States organizing a global alliance network against the Soviet Union. Relations between the two countries during the Cold War alternated between periods of détente and episodes of hostility. Both countries actively intervened in the internal affairs of third world countries, but they avoided direct military confrontation with each other. With the Cold War's end, Washington has had difficulty formulating a clear foreign policy in a world in which the United States lacks an obvious singular enemy.

8. Before the Bolshevik Revolution in 1917, Czarist Russia had engaged in territorial expansion for centuries. The new Soviet regime, after an early period of relative isolationism, resumed an assertive policy, though one concerned mostly with securing border areas. During the Cold War, the Soviet Union's foreign policy became increasingly global in scope as the leader of the Communist bloc. Like the United States, the Soviet Union frequently showed a gap between its rhetoric and its actions, with ideology often sacrificed to practical interests. In the post–Cold War era, Russia is seeking to continue to project itself as a world power while coping with internal problems of economic restructuring, political reform, and ethnic strife.

9. Throughout much of its long history, the self-contained Chinese civilization had little to do with foreigners, remaining relatively isolated. Ultimately, however, it suffered exploitation and attack by surrounding major powers. Nationalists and revolutionaries sought to reverse these unequal relations. Under Mao Zedong,

China became regionally active and challenged the Soviet Union for leadership of the international Communist movement. The post-1949 alliance between Communist China and the Soviet Union was uneasy. China's overall foreign policy began to shift in the 1970s, as Chinese leaders began to criticize the Soviet threat and to improve relations with the United States, reaching out to the West and becoming more involved in the global economy and the UN. Subsequently, Chinese leaders sought to bring about a rapid modernization of the country's economy while still preserving the single-party communist state. The result has been increased ties to but also increased frictions with other economically ambitious states and regional neighbors.

10. Japan is a country particularly subject to external shocks and the necessity of overcoming resource scarcities and other forms of dependence. During the first half of the twentieth century, Japan was frequently at war, seeking to offset the regional dominance of other major powers and obtain its own empire. Chastened by the World War II experience, especially its being targeted by atomic weapons, the Japanese government during the postwar period attempted to produce prosperity by keeping a low profile in international affairs and developing a foreign policy focused on economic concerns. More recently, Japan has demonstrated willingness to take positions on controversial political questions and to become more involved in multilateral organizations such as the UN.

SUGGESTIONS FOR FURTHER READING AND STUDY

In addition to the sources on U.S., Russian, Chinese, and Japanese foreign policy cited in the notes for this chapter, those interested in profiling a given country's policies can make use of the following types of information sources: (1) major national and international newspapers and periodicals, such as the *World Press Review, Times* (London), *New York Times, Wall Street Journal, Le Monde, Christian Science Monitor, Economist, Jerusalem Post, Japan Times, Beijing Review,* and *German Tribune;* (2) on-line electronic news sources such as those accessed through the World Wide Web and Internet; (3) specialized journals such as *Foreign Affairs, Foreign Policy, International Security, Current History, World Policy,* and *International Affairs;* (4) regional journals, such as *African Affairs, Journal of Modern African Studies, Africa Research Bulletin, Asian Survey, Far Eastern Economic Review, Journal of Asian Studies, Journal of Latin American Studies, Latin American Research Review, Middle East Economic Digest, Middle East Journal,* and *Middle East Monitor;* (5) chronologies and news compilations, such as *Facts on File,* Lexis-Nexis (on computer), and *Keesing's Contemporary Archives;* (6) statistical abstracts and yearbooks, such as the *Yearbook of World Affairs, Europa Yearbook, Statesman's Yearbook, Americana Annual,* and *Whitaker's Almanac;* and (7) scholarly and news indexes, such as the *International Political Science Abstracts, Social Science Index,* and *New York Times Index.* In addition, the U.S. Department of State publishes periodic "country studies" on most large and regional powers.

Good comparative studies of foreign policy can be found in Laura Neack, Jeanne A. K. Hey, and Patrick Haney, *Foreign Policy Analysis: Continuity and Change in Its Second Generation* (Englewood Cliffs, N.J.: Prentice-Hall, 1995); Gavin Boyd and Gerald W. Hopple, eds., *Political Change and Foreign Policies* (London: Frances Pinter, 1987);

Alan C. Lamborn, *The Price of Power: Risk and Foreign Policy in Britain, France, and Germany,* Studies in International Conflict, vol. 4 (Boston: Unwin Hyman, 1991); Roy C. Macridis, ed., *Foreign Policy in World Politics: States and Regions,* 7th ed. (Englewood Cliffs, N.J.: Prentice-Hall, 1989); Edward J. Lincoln, *Japan's New Global Role* (Washington, D.C.: Brookings Institution, 1993); James P. Nichol, *Diplomacy in the Former Soviet Republics* (Westport, Ct.: Praeger, 1995); Bernard Reich, *Securing the Covenant: United States-Israeli Relations after the Cold War* (Westport, Ct.: Greenwood Press, 1995); James E. Winkates, J. Richard Walsh, and Joseph M. Scolnick, Jr., *U.S. Foreign Policy in Transition* (Chicago: Nelson-Hall, 1994); Nicholas D. Kristof and Sheryl WuDunn, *China Wakes: The Struggle for the Soul of a Rising Power* (New York: Times Books/Random House, 1994); Jan F. Triska, ed., *Dominant Powers and Subordinate States: The United States in Latin America and the Soviet Union in Eastern Europe* (Durham, N.C.: Duke University Press, 1986); *South Asia and the United States After the Cold War* (New York: The Asia Society, 1994); Douglas J. Murray and Paul R. Viotti, *The Defense Policies of Nations: A Comparative Study,* 2nd ed. (Baltimore: Johns Hopkins University Press, 1989); Edward E. Azar and Chung-In Moon, eds., *National Security in the Third World: The Management of Internal and External Threats* (College Park, Md.: Center for International Development and Conflict Management, University of Maryland, 1988); Graham Allison and Gregory F. Treverton, eds., *Rethinking America's Security: Beyond Cold War to New World Order* (New York: W. W. Norton, 1992); Jarel A. Rosati, Joe D. Hagan, and Martin W. Sampson III, *Foreign Policy Restructuring: How Governments Respond to Global Change* (Columbia: University of South Carolina Press, 1994); Marshall D. Shulman, ed., *East-West Tensions in the Third World* (New York: W. W. Norton, 1986); and Peter Zwick, *Soviet Foreign Relations: Process and Policy* (Englewood Cliffs, N.J.: Prentice-Hall, 1990).

For a sampling of writings that focus on specific countries not examined in this chapter, see Nelson Mandela, "South Africa's Future Foreign Policy," *Foreign Affairs,* 72 (November-December 1993), pp. 86–97; Hans-Dietrich Genscher, "The Foreign Policy of a United Germany," *The Fletcher Forum of World Affairs,* 15 (Summer 1991), pp. 87–94; Pierre Lellouche, "France in Search of Security," *Foreign Affairs,* 72 (Spring 1993), pp. 122–131; Walter Carlsnaes and Steve Smith, eds., *European Foreign Policy: The EC and Changing Foreign Policy Perspectives in Europe* (London: Sage, 1994); Syed Ali Mujtaba and Bruce Vaughan, "South Asia and the Emerging New World Order," *Strategic Analysis,* 15 (October 1992), pp. 669–682; N. Ganesan, "Singapore's Foreign Policy Terrain," *Asian Affairs,* 19 (Summer 1992), pp. 67–79; R. K. Ramazani, "Iran's Foreign Policy: Both North and South," *The Middle East Journal,* 46 (Summer 1992), pp. 393–412; M. E. Ahrari, "Rational Foreign Policy Behavior of A Weak State: The Case of Kuwait," *Australian Journal of International Affairs,* 47 (May 1993), pp. 131–148; Dewi Fortuna Anwar, "Indonesia's Foreign Policy After the Cold War," *Southeast Asian Affairs* (1994), pp. 146–163; and Charles F. Furtado, "Nationalism and Foreign Policy in Ukraine," *Political Quarterly,* 109 (Spring 1994), pp. 81–104.

Explaining Foreign Policy Behavior: Why Do Nation-States Do What They Do?

We have seen that it is possible, at least in general terms, to describe patterns of foreign policy behavior. Not all countries act in the same manner. The next question is *why*? Why do some countries seek global or regional influence, whereas others are relatively isolationist? Why do countries ally with or intervene inside other countries? Why are some countries more inclined to use force or multilateral diplomacy in certain circumstances than other states?

These and similar questions have perplexed policymakers as well as scholars and average citizens. For example, Winston Churchill, as British prime minister, grappled with the same sorts of questions and offered his own answer concerning Soviet behavior: "I cannot forecast to you the action of Russia. It is a riddle wrapped in a mystery inside an enigma; but perhaps there is a key. That key is Russian national interest."[1]

It is impossible to know all the "why's" of international relations. Leaders themselves often are not fully conscious of precisely which pressures exert

HANDSHAKE ON WHITE HOUSE LAWN BETWEEN ISRAELI PRIME MINISTER YITZHAK RABIN AND PALESTINE LIBERATION ORGANIZATION CHAIRMAN YASSIR ARAFAT, WITH U.S. PRESIDENT BILL CLINTON BETWEEN THEM, IN 1993.

the greatest influence on their own behavior. When we see evening news coverage of an Israeli prime minister, Yitzhak Rabin—a lifelong soldier who fought against Arab enemies—reluctantly offering his hand to an old nemesis, Yassir Arafat, leader of the Palestine Liberation Organization (as was done on the White House lawn in Washington in 1993), one can appreciate the often tortuous decision making that produces certain happenings in world politics. However, as we saw in the last chapter, seemingly perplexing behavior, such as a trip by one of America's foremost anti-Communists, Richard Nixon, to meet one of the world's most dedicated revolutionaries, Mao Zedong, can have a certain underlying logic. One would hope that political scientists can do better than *National Enquirer* or *Parade* gossip columnists in elucidating this logic and deciphering affairs of state.

In fact, a serious body of scholarly research on the causes of foreign policy behavior does exist. This body of research, often referred to as **comparative foreign policy analysis,** has provided us with a better understanding of the forces that shape nation-state behavior. We will examine a number of comparative foreign policy theories and research findings in this chapter as we explore the "why" question. As we will see, differences in the foreign policy behavior of countries, as well as changes in any single country's behavior over time, can be attributed to a variety of influences found both within and outside national boundaries.

Determinants of Foreign Policy Behavior: An Explanatory Framework

THE CONCEPT OF NATIONAL INTERESTS

Many people, realists in particular, would argue that international relations is not nearly as complicated as we are making it sound, that *all* foreign policy behavior of any consequence can be traced simply to what Winston Churchill referred to as **national interests.** According to this view, national leaders basically seek to maximize their country's advantages vis-à-vis other states, either in cooperation with or at the expense of such states. The concept of national interests is worth examining because it has been the basis for much speculation about the motives behind state actions. We engaged in such speculation ourselves indirectly in the previous chapter, suggesting that American, Russian, Chinese, and Japanese foreign policy behavior over the years has conformed more to self-interest than to ideological or moral principles. The question remains, however, whether this in itself constitutes a complete explanation of foreign policy behavior.

There are at least three fundamental interests that all nation-states are said to have: (1) ensuring the physical survival of the homeland itself, which includes protecting the lives of its citizens and maintaining the territorial integrity of its borders; (2) promoting the economic well-being of its people; and (3) preserving national self-determination regarding the nature of the country's governmental system and the conduct of its internal affairs. All of these together can be considered a nation's core values or most basic foreign policy goals.[2]

Several problems, however, are associated with such conceptualizations of national interests, problems that partly explain why countries can share similar goals and yet behave quite differently. First, the term "national interest" itself is extremely vague and provides few clues for policymakers to follow in their decision making. For example, does a nation's economic well-being entail economic self-sufficiency, i.e., nonreliance on the outside world for any crucial resources? And does that goal then require territorial expansion beyond one's existing borders? Does the goal require trade protectionism—measures to restrict imports and allow domestic industries to survive even if they are not producing at "world class" standards? As an early foreign policy analyst, Charles Beard, observed:

> The conception of national interest revealed in the state papers is an aggregation of particularities assembled like eggs in a basket. Markets for agricultural produce were in the national interest; markets for industrial commodities were in the national interest; naval bases, territorial acquisitions for commercial support, an enlarged consular and diplomatic service, an increased navy and merchant marine, and occasional wars were all in the national interest. These contentions were not proved; they were asserted as axioms, apparently regarded as so obvious as to call for no demonstration.[3]

Second, related to the first problem, not all states and leaders employ the same criteria for determining when national defense, economic needs, and self-determination are being satisfied. In the last chapter we saw the highly contrasting interpretation of the U.S.-Japanese trade imbalance in Tokyo and Washington during the 1990s; one party thought that the overall trade picture was fair, and the other thought that its trade with its partner was far too unbalanced. Also, as happens frequently in zones of intense conflict such as the Middle East, what are believed to be purely self-defense policies by one country, such as massive arms purchases to upgrade one's deterrent capabilities, can be construed as blatant threats by neighboring states.

Third, the three goals of national defense, economic prosperity, and self-determination often can be incompatible, necessitating trade-off decisions of the "guns or butter" variety. There has long been a scholarly and political debate about whether defense spending is good or bad for a nation's economy, because military hardware is expensive and can only be consumed in warfare. In some quarters it is argued that overreliance on the military can undermine economies (as in the Soviet Union) and democratic forms of government, thus endangering democratic self-determination.[4] It also has been noted that "national security" can be narrowly defined as military defense or can include broad-based policies to improve the educational, health, social, and environmental standards of the population.[5]

Fourth, "national interests," as interpreted by a government, may benefit the nation as a whole or may benefit only privileged, select segments of the nation. Even if everyone has a collective stake, certain working definitions of national interests tend to coincide with the private interests of some groups more than others (e.g., a multibillion dollar U.S. Department of Defense budget would seem to benefit an individual on the welfare rolls less than it would benefit, say, a McDonnell-Douglas Aircraft Company employee).

Fifth, some governments are not content merely to articulate and pursue the three basic goals noted above. Additional interests can be identified, such as commanding prestige or building regional or global communities, which may be only peripherally related to the other three. Indeed, the national interest concept depends on the assumption that the nation-state is the primary unit of world politics; as that assumption has been challenged in recent years with the rise of multinational and nongovernmental actors and the splintering of some nation-states, the national interest becomes further clouded.

The final problem, then, is an issue that runs through all of these concerns, one that we mentioned earlier in our discussion of the contemporary international system: Where do "national interests" end and "international interests" (the interests of the world community) begin, and how does one separate the two? Although few if any foreign policymakers would agree, some people argue that if the chief national goal is the physical safety of one's citizens, nothing short of dismemberment of the nation-state and its replacement by a world government will spare the human race from annihilation in the nuclear age. By the same token, other citizens are suspicious of anything labeled "international" and sometimes even suspicious of national governmental power; they would prefer to see power or sovereignty rest mainly with local communities.[6]

Given the problems and ambiguities we have cited, the national interest concept would seem to raise as many questions as it resolves. The realization that governments generally act in accordance with what they perceive mainly to be in their own interests is an important primary guide for our understanding foreign policy behavior. Governments do seek to achieve basic goals. However, reality is too complicated to be explained by a single factor. It is necessary, then, to go beyond an explanation based solely on national interests and to look more systematically at the welter of factors affecting nation-state behavior.

An Explanatory Framework

It is helpful to have some framework for classifying the various determinants of foreign policy behavior and for organizing a discussion of them. We shall categorize them here according to what foreign policy scholars refer to as "levels of analysis:" (1) **systemic factors**—conditions external to the state that are present in the international system surrounding it; (2) **national attribute factors**—characteristics of the nation-state itself; (3) **idiosyncratic factors**—characteristics of individual national leaders and groups of decision makers.[7]

The Role of Systemic Factors

Systemic factors are closely related to "national interest" explanations of foreign policy, because leaders often define their country's interests in terms of the challenges or opportunities in the world around them. Leaders generally do not have as much control over their external environment as they do over their domestic environment, although domestic events may still get out of control—sometimes because of the impact of external forces. In a remarkable statement in 1995, for example, Bill Clinton admitted that international economic forces made it impossible for the American government fully to control the value of its currency on international markets, a value that affects both jobs and buying power inside the United States.

Hence, foreign policymakers often find themselves reacting to, rather than shaping, unforeseen events or intractable conditions. Among the factors in a country's external environment that can affect its foreign policy are (1) geography, (2) international interactions and links, and (3) the structure of the international system.

In Chapters 2 and 3, we defined an international system as a broad set of relationships among interacting states, and noted that one can talk about the system as a whole (the global system) or about regional subsystems. For example, South Asia (see Fig. 5.1) has several interacting states, some large in terms of land area and population (e.g., India) and some small (e.g., Sri Lanka and Nepal); outside powers such as China, Russia, and the United States may impinge on the regional subsystem. Actions by one state can have momentous implications for, and are monitored closely by, the others in the subsystem. The importance of systemic factors in explaining foreign policy, and particularly in accounting for *alignment* behavior, will become apparent in this discussion.

GEOGRAPHY

Among the more crucial geographical features that can affect foreign policy are, first, conditions along a nation's borders and, second, distances that must be traversed to reach key points of strategic interest. The German resort to armed force in World War I and World War II can be explained at least partly as

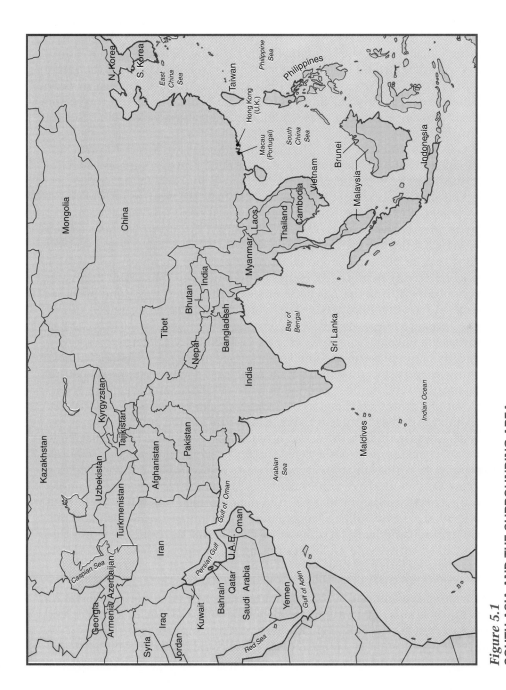

Figure 5.1
SOUTH ASIA AND THE SURROUNDING AREA
Source: From *Maps on File.* Copyright © 1989 Martin Greenwald Associates. Reprinted with permission of Facts On File, Inc., New York.

181

a response to being geographically sandwiched between France on the one side and Russia on the other. German tactics were similar in both wars, even though the German government was led by a traditional autocratic monarch in 1914 and by a modern totalitarian dictator in 1939. In both cases German leaders felt obliged to attack France in a lightning swing from the north to knock the French out of the war quickly. In 1914 the Germans tried to eliminate France so they could turn attention to prolonged warfare with the gigantic Russian army to the east. In 1939 Hitler had concluded a nonaggression pact neutralizing the Russian threat for the time being, but he too wanted no prolonged war in the west that could have left Germany vulnerable to Moscow in the east.

The Germans' reaction to their geographical landscape was not unique and typifies concerns about "two-front" wars in other countries, such as Israel (for many years caught between hostile neighbors Egypt and Syria) and Russia (during the Soviet period, caught between NATO in the west and China in the east). A tendency of "sandwiched" states is to strike first in threatening situations with preemptive attacks to avoid prolonged two-front warfare. Israel's 1967 strategy reflected these concerns, and the 1978 Camp David accords with Egypt are better understood when one notes the fact that the Egyptian front was effectively neutralized. Israeli Prime Minister Menachem Begin told an election rally during the Lebanese crisis of 1981 that "if we did not have the peace treaty with Egypt today, we would already have mobilized the reserves . . . because of the dispute with Syria!"[8]

Some geographical factors, such as the possession of vital natural resources, are basically national attributes and are discussed in the next section. Here we are mainly interested in those geographical factors that are systemic in nature, such as location, the number of borders to be defended, and the degree of access to various points on the globe.[9] Geography can confer on a country certain advantages or disadvantages that can affect its foreign policy behavior in a variety of ways, including the scope of its interests as well as the degree of conflict or cooperation experienced. Among possible advantages a country might enjoy are control of strategic waterways (for example, Turkey's position along the Dardanelles) or remoteness from warring powers (for example, American and Australian insulation from major foreign foes for much of their history). By the same token, geographical disadvantages can include landlocked territory, a problem faced by more than thirty states in the world that lack coastlines, or extreme proximity to warring powers (Poland's historic position in the cockpit of Europe).

It is important to realize, however, that advantages at one moment can soon turn to disadvantages. Control of waterways can attract foreign envy, resentment, or attack. Insulation can mean that long distances must be traversed to reach key world regions (witness America's difficulties with its 10,000-mile supply line to Vietnam that complicated its war effort there). Advantages can also be quickly erased by technological and other circumstances;

for example, the Panama Canal and the Suez Canal, although still significant waterways, have diminished in importance somewhat as they have been hard-pressed to compete economically with other shipping routes and unable to accommodate some of today's larger tankers and warships.

Just as advantages can evaporate because of technological changes, so also can technology be employed to overcome disadvantages. At least as far back as Hannibal's elephantine crossing of the Alps, leaders have devised ingenious ways of circumventing geographical barriers. In the contemporary age in particular, technology can neutralize geographic factors to some extent; the development of intercontinental and intermediate-range missiles, for example, has lessened the value of neighboring territories as protective buffers, although countries still squabble over ownership of mountaintop fortresses and other geographical assets.[10]

Borders continue to be of utmost importance to leaders of nation-states.[11] Chinese sensitivity to the approach of American forces during the Korean War, American sensitivity to the placement of Soviet offensive missiles in Cuba in 1962, and Soviet sensitivity over the intrusion of the ill-fated Korean airliner KAL 007 into Soviet airspace in 1984 all testify to the nearly universal concern states have about border security. Although all states share such concerns, varying geographical locations can ease the degree of anxiety. As seen in our four case studies, the United States has not been confronted by major nearby hostile powers, as have Russia, China, and Japan. Table 5.1 shows the great variation among states in terms of the number of borders that must be defended. (The box on page 185 suggests some ways that geography impacts on policy.)

International relations research has revealed some uncertainty about the overall importance of geography in predicting conflict or cooperation among countries. Earlier philosophers such as Kautilya and Machiavelli argued that states that border each other tend to be natural rivals. Some contemporary analysts also have concluded that geographical proximity increases *conflict,* and others argue that it increases various forms of interstate *cooperation,* from trade and tourist traffic to diplomatic contacts.[12] The equivocal role of geographical proximity in promoting conflict or cooperation is exemplified by two cases: the 5,500-mile undefended frontier between the United States and Canada (each being the other's major trading partner) and the 4,500-mile Russo-Chinese border that at various times has been manned on each side by up to one million troops.[13]

INTERNATIONAL INTERACTIONS AND LINKS

Some writers have argued that countries can be close or far apart not only in a geographical sense but in other ways as well. There is evidence that the degree of similarity or difference between countries—the "distance" between them in

Table 5.1
THE NUMBER OF NEIGHBORS OF SELECTED COUNTRIES

Country	Number of Contiguous Countries*
China	16
Russia	14
Brazil	10
Germany	9
Zaire	8
Sudan	8
Turkey	8
Saudi Arabia	7
Hungary	7
Serbia/Montenegro	7
Ukraine	7
Iran	6
Iraq	6
India	6
Libya	6
South Africa	5
Laos	5
Argentina	5
Croatia	5
Peru	4
Nigeria	4
Pakistan	4
Armenia	4
Tajikistan	4
Rwanda	3
Mexico	3
Egypt	3
Vietnam	2
Bangladesh	2
USA	2
Canada	1
United Kingdom	1
Australia	0
Philippines	0
Japan	0

*Note that contiguity alone does not give a complete picture of a country's neighbors. For example, Russia, Poland, France, Italy, and Turkey all have more than 20 countries within 1,000 km of their borders; Japan has four, and Australia two. On the other hand, a true geographical isolate, New Zealand, has none.
Sources: U.S. Central Intelligence Agency, *World Factbook 1993* (Washington, DC: 1993); J. P. Cole, *Geography of World Affairs,* 6th ed. (London: Butterworths, 1983), Table 3.2.

terms of political, cultural, and other characteristics—can be a key to the volume and kinds of transactions between them.[14] Generally speaking, the more similar countries are in political, economic, and cultural features, the greater their level of mutual trade, communications, and other forms of interaction.

THE INTERPLAY OF GEOGRAPHY AND POLICY

The Netherlands exemplifies how geography can affect the foreign policy behavior of a small country. Located at the mouths of three major European rivers and facing the sea, Holland has always been a transportation center, with canals designed to carry goods into the heart of Europe, and especially into Germany.

This location has meant that, throughout history, neighbors such as Britain, France, and Germany, as well as seafaring rivals such as Spain during the "age of exploration," have been vitally interested in who exercises control over Dutch territory. The Netherlands has oscillated in policy between neutrality and alliance with these powers to preserve independence and prevent attack. Until World War II, tiny Holland also attempted to maintain a worldwide empire of 100 million people in the Pacific (what is now mostly Indonesia) and Latin America (Surinam and the Antilles).

Not only did Netherlands geography bring about certain policies, but Dutch policies themselves also came to define the importance of geography. As long as the Netherlands attempted to maintain its empire, the country's geographical remoteness from both the Pacific and Central America was a problem. When—because of growing opposition to colonization and the inability to control distant lands—the empire was dismantled, Pacific and Latin American access quickly receded in importance.

The Netherlands is not the only country to have encountered the interaction effects of geography and policy. As states develop alternate fuel and energy policies and sources, their concerns about the "intrinsic" strategic importance of the Persian Gulf may well diminish. The Netherlands itself has enjoyed a period of relative immunity to energy crises since the 1970s, when North Sea oil and gas became available. Someday the exhaustion of these supplies could renew Dutch concerns about a "global" energy strategy.

One of the most striking findings reported recently in the scholarly literature focuses on the political distance between states and the likelihood of hostilities occurring between them. Democracies, though they are involved in conflict and warfare about as often as other types of states, are extremely unlikely to fight *each other,* as compared with their willingness to fight nondemocracies and the willingness of nondemocracies to fight each other.[15] The explanation offered for this pattern is that it is difficult to convince the public in a democracy to support a war against another open society that shares its values and to incur substantial costs in lives and money in the process; an added explanation is the supposed greater commitment of democracies to the rule of law and the search for compromise, as well as the obstacles to warmaking posed by parliaments and representative bodies.[16] As one author notes:

> Democratic institutions are visible signs that the state in question is likely to face high political costs for using force in its diplomacy. When both sides are democracies, each actor is likely to be dovish, to see the other as dovish, and to be encouraged to pursue negotiated solutions to differences. However, if one party is not a democracy, then the democratic adversary faces a greater danger of being exploited. To avoid this, the democracy is likely to launch a preemptive strike.[17]

As more democracies emerge in the world, therefore, some theorists—particularly those associated with the idealist paradigm—predict an era of "democratic peace." One should be cautious, however, both about the longevity of democratization trends, and their likely implications. Few of the newly democratic governments in regions such as Central Europe, Central America, East Asia, and Africa have deeply entrenched traditions of Western pluralistic democracy and constitutional law, such as protection of civil liberties, press freedom, and minority group rights; prosperous and influential middle classes, thought to be necessary for stable democracy, may or may not exist in some states. Hence, the recent democratization trends may be fragile ones. Even if democratization continues, one cannot presume an altogether peaceful world. Although it has been said that "this absence of war between democratic states comes as close as anything we have to an empirical law in international relations,"[18] one must remember that full-blown democracies did not appear on the Westphalian state system scene until relatively recently, a little over a century ago; and it could be that the sheer probability of hostile encounters among democratic states would rise in a highly democratic world. Moreover, researchers have found that democracies have not been averse to confronting each other in lower levels of conflict short of war.[19]

We noted the "birds of the same feather flock together" phenomenon. However, countries that are dissimilar in many respects can also develop intense interactions and become linked together in a kind of social system. Such a social system can be defined as a set of closely and continuously interacting entities. Continuous interaction affects the entities themselves, engaging most of their energies in the system. For example, because the Americans and Soviets, the Indians and Pakistanis, and Arabs and Israelis confronted each other as competitors for over four decades after World War II, they came to rivet attention on each other, to mimic each other's defense strategies and budgets, to increase their societal reliance on the military, and to base their domestic political choices in large measure on what the other party was doing (e.g., the U.S. interstate highway system was built with Defense Department funds to speed the military from coast to coast). Those caught in such conflict systems can break out of them, however, as demonstrated by evolving U.S.-Russian and Jordanian-Israeli cooperation amidst continued mistrust during the 1990s, and by the 1992 agreement by India and Pakistan not to attack each other's suspected nuclear weapon facilities despite severe political disagreements over issues such as control of the Kashmir territory.

One system described in the previous chapter was the U.S.-Soviet-Chinese triangle. President Nixon and Chairman Mao got together mainly because they shared a mutual interest in balancing the power of the Soviet Union in the 1970s. "Strange bedfellows" in world politics are often accounted for by the old maxim, "My enemy's enemy is my friend."

Interdependencies also can influence foreign policy in a number of respects. Foreign aid to and investment in a country can increase or diminish its foreign policy options, depending on the number of strings attached to the money (for example, insistence that purchases be made in the donor state rather than importing goods from another state). States heavily in debt to foreign powers often lack the finances needed to undertake important projects and can be pressured by their creditors for repayment. Creditors and powerful states also are themselves somewhat bound by interdependencies. Once governments invest heavily in foreign states, they can develop deep stakes in the survival of those governments; as one example, French intervention in Russia after World War I was designed, unsuccessfully, to restore a heavily bankrolled Czarist ally.

When states such as Germany or the United States enter organizations such as the European Union (EU) or NATO, they develop a stake in the organization's survival as well; therefore, they lose a degree of policy flexibility. Berlin could let fellow EU or NATO members go bankrupt or fall victim to domestic disruption, or declare war on each other, but there would be a price to pay in terms of the stability of the organizations on which European, including German, postwar security and prosperity have been built. If intergovernmental organizations provide sufficient benefits, their members may feel compelled to sacrifice for their maintenance.

INTERNATIONAL SYSTEM STRUCTURE

There is considerable debate about how the structure of the global system affects the behavior of the actors. Traditionally, the debate has been about how unipolarity, bipolarity, and multipolarity affect conflict and war. Certain writers argue that with *one* dominant world power or center of alignment, other states are kept in order and few wars occur.[20] Others maintain that with *two* major powers balancing each other, world war is unlikely because neither will have the incentive to confront the other directly, although small-scale fighting between less powerful states can still occur.[21] Still others maintain that the balancing of *several* powerful states in a multipolar system diverts the attention of every power; hostilities cannot be focused in one place very long and war is minimized.[22] Obviously these theories can become quite complex and contradictory. Much research has gone into testing the rival claims, without full consensus emerging except for the general conclusion that bipolarity may produce fewer systemwide (or "world") wars, while allowing for more localized fighting.[23]

Recent analyses of international system structures have come to emphasize dynamic processes—i.e., how systems change and become transformed over time. In particular, much research has delved into the "long-term economic and political trends in the global system," especially as they relate to conflict and cooperation.[24] Discoveries of repeated, "long cycles" of system development, decay, and redevelopment have been identified. According to long cycle theory, dominance by certain powers erodes over time (partly because of the economic costs of attempting to exercise hegemony), leading other states to challenge the latter, sometimes resulting in large-scale systemwide war; the German challenge to the Pax Britannica that culminated in the First World War can be interpreted in this light. As a result of such wars, or of the natural decline and rise of great powers, a new international system is born, with a new hegemon possibly emerging and seeking to define the new rules of expected behavior (system "norms").[25]

There has been growing debate about the future development of the international system regarding its movement toward greater or lesser global order and governance. We have noted that the older power hierarchies and hegemonies are being challenged as leading powers today seem less able to regulate events globally or even in their traditional spheres of influence. Power is becoming a less fungible commodity, because it may be possible to have one or two great military powers yet have several different clusters of influential states constituting "decision-making centers" which change from one issue to another (for example, the key role played by the G-7—Japan, Britain, France, Italy, Germany, Canada, the United States (and conceivably Russia in a G-8)— in shaping the international economy). Because the international system in some ways is becoming more fragmented, with the structure of the system less clear-cut than conventionally described in balance of power theories, the effect of system structure on foreign policy behavior is more difficult to pin down. Theorists have begun to speculate that an international system with a number of shifting power centers may be less stable than past international systems of a bipolar or even multipolar character.[26]

The role of system structure can be examined at the *regional* as well as the global level. In the Middle East, a traditional rivalry dating to ancient times exists between three great Arabic civilizations based in the cities of Baghdad (modern Iraq), Damascus (modern Syria), and Cairo (modern Egypt). Nearby non-Arab powers, such as Iran (formerly Persia) and Turkey (formerly the Ottoman Empire), also have intervened at times in this Arab system. Rivalries persist today in new form and over new issues, with Iraq, Syria, Egypt, along with Iran, Turkey, and Israel, contending for Middle Eastern influence and leadership. The competition has spawned wars, assassinations, summit meetings, interventions, and intrigues—as well as gestures of Arab and Islamic unity.[27]

Global and regional power hierarchies and disputes complicate the policy choices leaders must make. If a region is in a major power's "sphere of influence," that power's government might insist on approving important policy moves of less powerful states in its sphere. Despite the slippage in power we have noted, Russia still has a profound impact on initiatives taken by states such as Ukraine, Georgia, Kazakhstan, Azerbaijan, and Armenia, and the United States continues to seek to control outcomes in such Latin and Caribbean neighbors as Panama and Haiti, where American troops intervened in 1989 and 1994. In Western Europe, however, Washington's allies and client states are relatively stronger and able to resist U.S. pressures, as demonstrated in NATO disagreements over what do about Bosnia. As the nineteenth century German leader Bismarck observed, an alliance is like horseback riding—the struggle is over who must be the horse.

Clearly, then, a country's external environment can affect behavior ranging from war involvement to commercial activity. The direction of international trade, the channeling of international communications, the exchange of diplomatic visits, and the formation and collapse of alliances all reflect to some extent the ebb and flow of systemic forces. The box on pages 190–191 summarizes some research findings on the overall roll of systemic factors in foreign policymaking.

The Role of National Attributes

The presence or absence of various national attributes also can strongly affect a country's foreign policy behavior, particularly in terms of *scope* and *modus operandi*. We saw in the last chapter the effects of Japan's near total lack of natural resources as that rapidly industrializing country embarked on expansionist quests during the 1930s. This example illustrates what some researchers have labeled a "lateral pressure," or tea-kettle effect, in foreign policy. It is argued that as a nation-state grows, either in population or economic output, it experiences new demands for raw materials and other resources, only some of which can be satisfied domestically. The result is similar to pressure building inside a kettle; the expanding pressure can lead to expansionist policies, seeking to obtain the needed resources abroad by either peaceful or violent means. In this way, national attribute scarcities interact with the international system, as the expanding state comes up against resistance from other expanding or declining states.[28]

Clearly, Japan would not have been sensitive to U.S. pressure in 1941, or to Arab pressure concerning petroleum supplies in 1973, if its islands sat atop vast oil deposits. It should be noted, though, that it is not always easy to pre-

ASSUMPTIONS AND RESEARCH FINDINGS ON SYSTEMIC FACTORS AND FOREIGN POLICY

Some common *assumptions* about the effects of systemic factors on foreign policy behavior:

1. The more two states depend on each other economically and socially, and the more democratic their systems, the more peaceful their relations will tend to be.

2. The more often different peoples and cultures interact, the greater the tendency for understanding and friendship to increase between their governments.

3. The more balanced two states are in terms of power, the less likely they are to go to war with each other.

4. The greater the external threat confronting the members of a group of states, such as an alliance, the more cohesion there will be within the group.

5. The greater the hegemonic dominance of a system, the fewer the foreign policy options for weaker states in the system.

Some research *findings* related to the foregoing assumptions[1]:

1. There is no clear relationship between the level of economic, communications, and other transactions between states and their tendency to experience violent conflict with each other (Rummel, 1968); at times, such contacts may even increase the probability of conflict (Wright, 1964; Russett, 1967), although beneficial trade links also have been found to decrease conflict (Gasiorowski, 1986). Pluralistic democracies tend not to fight each other (see notes 14 and 15).

2. The less geographic distance between states, the more interactions between them (Cobb and Elder, 1970; Brams, 1966). Although geographic proximity can increase trade and other cooperative transactions, it is also correlated with interstate wars (Singer, 1972). Some geographic regions appear more conflict-prone than others. More militarized disputes are generated that can escalate to war in such "shatterbelt" regions. Somewhat greater domestic conflicts are seen as well, with more resultant outside intervention (Hensel and Diehl, 1994).

3. The more borders a country has (particularly land borders) with other countries, or the more civil or international wars taking place on a country's borders, the more violent conflicts in which it tends to become involved; the farther away a crisis is from the country it affects, the less likely that country is to use force to deal with the crisis (Weede, 1970; Wright, 1964; Richardson, 1960; Zinnes, 1980; Starr and Most, 1985).

4. Former colonial ties tend to promote trade, foreign aid, and other interactions between states (Brams, 1966; Wittkopf, 1971). The lingering ef-

fect of empire is seen in unresolved ethnic conflicts and national movements, which can result in domestic repression and international intervention in the former colony (Katz, 1993).

5. Although there is evidence of cyclical patterns in the concentration, deconcentration, and re-concentration of international power among system leaders, in the overall period since 1494 a model based on chaos does better at predicting such concentrations than a model based on regular cycles (Richards, 1993).

6. Alliance formation leading to polarization of the international system tends to increase the chances that war will break out in the system (at least in the twentieth century), and to produce major wars of high magnitude, severity, and duration, although systems without alliances also can experience severe wars as the weak are taken over by the strong (Wayman, 1984; Wallace, 1973; Bueno de Mesquita, 1978; Vasquez, 1987; Schweller, 1993). As a system depolarizes, with relaxation in the tightness of alliances, there is a tendency for less warfare (Bueno de Mesquita, 1978).

7. Alliance cohesion tends to increase as an outside threat increases, and to diminish as the threat diminishes; the establishment and maintenance of alliances is based primarily on security concerns rather than ideology (Holsti et al., 1973; Kegley and Raymond, 1990).

8. There is no clear connection between the degree of power parity (equality) among pairs of states and their propensity to go to war with each other (Rummel, 1966; Sullivan, 1976); wars of various types occur between equals as well as unequals. More parity in the distribution of military capabilities in the world tends to open the system to more competing interpretations of treaty commitments and norms (Kegley and Raymond, 1990).

9. A bipolar power distribution in the international system tends to limit the magnitude (nation-months) of wars; multipolar distribution of power makes for wars of greater magnitude; and equal capability between blocs tends to increase the severity (battle deaths) of wars (Levy, 1985; Levy and Morgan, 1984; Wayman, 1984; Thompson, 1983, 1986; Vasquez, 1986, 1987; Kegley and Raymond, 1990).

[1] Full citations for the specific studies noted in parentheses appear at the end of this chapter. Research findings can depend on the measurements used to test relationships. The findings noted should be treated as suggestive rather than as the last word on the subject.

dict the precise policy a state suffering scarcities will adopt; in 1941 Japan forcibly resisted U.S. demands for its withdrawal from China, whereas in 1973 Tokyo modified its previous pro-Israeli line and began to acknowledge the rights of Palestinians. In the first instance Japan was highly resistant to opponents; in the second instance, highly accommodative.

Such variations in foreign policy would appear to be traceable not merely to a country's sheer population size or resource base but also to its other national attributes, including its economic and population growth rates, the technology available to exploit or create substitutes for resources, the extent of its internal political instability, cultural features, and the readiness of its armed forces, together with the nature of its governmental system and public attitudes about the use of force and other tools of foreign policy.[29] As a shorthand way of grouping these characteristics, we will speak of (1) demographic, (2) economic, (3) military, and (4) governmental attributes. Many of these attributes relate to aspects of national power that we discussed earlier in Chapters 2 and 3. If one thinks of power as the capability to *act* (and especially to *influence* others) in international relations, one can readily understand how certain national attributes can contribute to or limit a state's capabilities and, hence, vitally shape its foreign policy behavior.

DEMOGRAPHIC ATTRIBUTES

The size, motivation, skills, and homogeneity of a country's population help determine the foreign policy levers available to its government. Therefore they affect foreign policy scope and *modus operandi,* such as the degree of the state's foreign involvements and its success in influencing others. Population size is an important facet of national power mainly because a large population provides personnel for armed forces and industry. Military force and industrial output allow a government to threaten punishments or offer rewards to other states. A country such as Canada, with its vast territorial size and wealth of natural resources, fails to rival either the United States or even Japan for international influence partly because it has a population of under 30 million. Large populations, however, can be mixed blessings, especially if the state in question lacks resources necessary to feed, educate, and employ the multitudes. On the basis of population alone, India should be a major world power; yet it wrestles with developmental problems in trying to support a huge populace with scarce resources and must devote much of its productive capacity to meeting basic needs.

A society's ethnic divisions also can put its foreign policymakers under pressure. Enemy states might be tempted to support dissident groups to overthrow a rival state's government, and opposition groups within a state might oppose their country's government and its foreign policies if they feel threatened by those policies.[30] India and Pakistan each fear that the other will incite ethnic separatists, India accusing Pakistan, for example, of inciting Kashmiri Muslims. Iran and Iraq share similar reciprocal fears, Iraq worrying particularly about Iranian appeals to Kurds and Shia Muslims. In addition to its geostrategic interests in the Balkan region, Russia had a key role to play in the Bosnian struggle because of its affinity for the Serbs (ethnic, linguistic, and religious cousins of Russia). See the box on page 194 for how ethnicity has affected relations between Lebanon and its neighbors.[31]

Aside from the importance of ethnic divisions, the broader notion of *culture* appears to be gaining researchers' attention as a factor influencing foreign policy behavior.[32] Culture here means the mores, folkways, and belief systems that form a people's distinctive way of life—often expressed in philosophy, the arts, and literature. It may be crucial to tailor one's foreign policy moves in a manner familiar and basically acceptable to a foreign state's cultural "norms." In reviewing U.S. foreign policy in Chapter 4, we noted the repeated troubling encounters with Islamic states and China, raising a question about whether such states view the world fundamentally differently than do Western states. We have also noted Samuel Huntington's thesis about the "clash of civilizations."[33] One relevant question for Israel and her Arab neighbors, for example, is whether either Islamic or Judaic law can ever fully recognize an outsider's sovereignty on land defined as "holy."[34]

Realists tend to argue that a state's ethnic and cultural makeup is far less important in predicting its foreign policy moves than its objective interests and needs. They might predict that Islam, like ideologies such as Marxism, gives way to pragmatism where important issues of state security are concerned. Certainly when revolutionary Iran needed parts for its U.S. military equipment during its long war with Iraq during the 1980s, it had little trouble turning to Israel and even the United States.

Despite such pragmatism, however, the leaders' interpretation of foreign events and their tactics in pursuit of goals still may be highly conditioned by their cultural backgrounds, particularly in situations short of acute crisis and war. It is known that East Asian culture, and particularly the Japanese, put high value on "saving face" in public and not creating embarrassment that would threaten social harmony. Western, and particularly American culture, however, often has been characterized as valuing directness, openness, and individuality. When East meets West at the negotiating table, therefore, over such questions as trade, human rights, the future of Korea, or arms control, the approaches and expectations may be very different and stand as an obstacle to agreement.[35]

ECONOMIC ATTRIBUTES

A state's demography is closely related to its economy. A skilled and technologically advanced population can enable a country to achieve high living standards, to enjoy trade advantages in the international market, and to dominate or assist other states. Conversely, countries that are overpopulated relative to technological skills and available capital and resources are likely to have unstable economies and governments, to be vulnerable to penetration by outside powers, to suffer recurring famine and chronic poverty, and therefore

ETHNIC DIVISIONS AND THE LEBANESE WAR

The mixing of demographic characteristics and international systemic factors can be seen clearly in the tragic events of the Lebanese civil war, which has been an ongoing struggle for the past several decades. Lebanon and, to a lesser extent, Syria have diverse ethnic and religious minorities who frequently are at each other's throats. As in other incidents of ethnic violence, this is often attributable to the influence and interests of opportunistic leaders seeking to take advantage of ethnic distrust for political gain.

Lebanese politics has long been dominated by family clans, some Christian (Roman Catholic "Maronite," Greek Orthodox, or Protestant), some Sunni or Shia Muslim, some Druze (an ethnic offshoot of Islam). The society was ordered along these lines, with strong clan leaders forming the leading political parties. Under the independence constitution of the 1940s, in an effort to preserve stability and political balance among these groups, it was agreed that no further census counts would be made, and certain political offices, such as president, prime minister, and parliamentary speaker, were reserved for specific ethnic communities; different ethnic communities attended different confessional schools, and very little social integration existed. This tended to leave the society highly splintered, with some groups more economically privileged than others, and each suspicious of the other's supposed desired to dominate.

Lebanon's fractured society drew international attention and intervention when civil war erupted in 1958, but the degree of disruption and intervention became far greater in the 1970s and 1980s. Syria, highly sensitive to its immediate neighbors, traditionally has sought to dominate Lebanese politics, both to extend its Arab political influence and territorial control and to put greater pressure on Israel. Syria has taken an interest in the struggles of diverse Lebanese religious and clan groups against each other, and against outsiders who have settled in Lebanon, such as Palestinian refugees from Israel and Jordan. Israel, in turn, has sought to control sections of southern Lebanon, opposing the pro-Palestinian elements that have operated there, and backing Christian and even some Islamic groups in the process.

Syria, therefore, has had to play a tricky balancing act for fear of war with Israel and loss of influence in Lebanon. Damascus has sided first with one and then with another rival Lebanese faction to keep any one of them from becoming too strong and autonomous. In the process, with the added impact of Israeli and Palestinian intrusions, Lebanese society has been torn apart, and innocent civilians on all sides have been killed. The effort to rebuild the country in the 1990s also has depended heavily on Syrian and Israeli input.

to orient their foreign policies toward the pursuit of foreign aid and military protection.[36]

Essentially three types of economic characteristics affect a state's foreign policy behavior: the size and growth rate of a nation's economy, its degree of wealth, and the nature of its economic system (capitalist, socialist, or communist). Economic size and rates of growth are generally measured in gross national product (GNP)—the annually estimated total value of goods and services produced by a nation's economic activities at home and abroad.[37] Industrialization tends to boost GNP, but some predominantly agricultural countries such as India also have relatively large GNPs. A large economy generally increases a country's interests in and means of influencing events abroad but also can lead to vulnerabilities, such as resource dependencies.

Besides economic size, a country's overall wealth (the total amount of income available per person, usually measured as GNP per capita) also influences foreign policy. Rich countries can better afford the expense of participating in international organizations and maintaining embassies abroad than poor countries, for example. In one study of intergovernmental organization membership, it was found that among the twenty states having the most IGO memberships, fifteen were wealthy, developed countries of various sizes (a pattern that could be discerned in Table 4.2 in the preceding chapter).[38] Poor states not only belong to fewer IGOs, they also have fewer overseas embassies and, hence, will be even more reliant on multilateral diplomatic contacts (particularly through the UN) than rich states. The wealth of a country obviously is also the main determinant of whether it is a donor or a recipient of foreign aid. Clearly, it is the sheer size of the U.S. economy and its wealth that has provided the resources necessary for the United States to play a global role in world politics since World War II, whereas it is a series of domestic economic problems that now are occasioning some rethinking of that role.[39]

In addition, the type of economic system is often thought to bear heavily on a country's foreign policy. Capitalist economies (those emphasizing private ownership of wealth and capital) tend to spawn powerful interest groups that seek foreign trade and investment. In protecting overseas assets, capitalist states frequently have tried to resist or to overthrow governments advocating the expropriation of property and radical redistribution of wealth. Lenin predicted early in this century that capitalist states would fall into warfare among themselves over the resources and markets of less developed societies, which capitalists supposedly had to exploit to sustain their economies. World War I could conceivably be interpreted in this light but hardly World War II, which involved the Soviet Union and the capitalists on the same side.[40] There is no evidence that communist states (those advocating state ownership of wealth and capital) have been less war-prone than capitalist states.

It would appear that the effect Lenin claimed to have observed had more to do with economic interdependence of states than with the capitalist nature of their economies per se. As suggested previously, interdependent states, caught

SIDELIGHT

NATIONAL ATTRIBUTES

The following rankings of national attributes are based on the latest available figures as of 1997:

- *The country with the largest Muslim population in the world:*
  Indonesia (approximately 177 million Muslims)

- *The country with the largest Catholic population in the world:*
  Brazil (approximately 140 million Catholics)

- *The richest country in the world among countries with over one million people (based on per capita GNP):*
  Switzerland (approximately $36,000)

- *The country with the second largest land area in the world (after Russia, which spans eleven times zones):*
  Canada (3.9 million square miles)

- *The country that devotes the largest percentage of its GNP to military expenditures:*
  North Korea (over 25 percent)

- *The country with the largest armed forces in the world:*
  China (approximately 3 million)

- *The country with the greatest population density among countries with over 1,000 square miles of territory:*
  Bangladesh (over 2,000 people per square mile)

- *The largest corn producer in the world:*
  United States (accounting for approximately 40 percent of total world production)

- *The largest crude oil producer in the world:*
  Saudi Arabia (trailed by the United States and Russia)

- *The country whose people enjoy the longest life expectancy at birth:*
  Japan (79 years)

up with each other in mutual trade and other forms of exchange, appear to have higher levels of both conflict *and* cooperation.[41] Interdependent communist states, such as China and the Soviet Union, and China and Vietnam, certainly have been known to fight among themselves and with neighbors.[42]

The distinctions between different types of economic systems and the impacts on foreign policy behavior attributed to this variable, figure to become less discernible if ideological convergence continues to occur between market-oriented and planned economies. Economic issues are becoming of increasing importance in foreign policy for all varieties of states. States experiencing trade and international debt problems, undergoing inflation or recession, suffering diminished productivity, or judged undesirable for foreign investment clearly are at a foreign policy disadvantage that can be remedied only with great difficulty.

MILITARY ATTRIBUTES

A country's readiness for war can interact with the factors already discussed, especially with geographic factors, to produce more or less assertive and interventionist foreign policies. A government can be dissatisfied about conditions in the international system, but if its military capability to change the situation is lacking, the resultant foreign policy is likely to remain relatively passive and confined to diplomacy rather than force.

Although ratings of military power are important in predicting relations among states (see Table 5.2), such rankings must be interpreted with care.

Table 5.2
MILITARY RANKINGS OF THE WORLD'S "TOP TWENTY"

	Military Expenditures ($ billions)	Military Expenditures as % of GNP	Regular Armed Forces
1. United States	297.6	4.7	1,837,000
2. Russia	113.8	14.6	2,250,000
3. China	56.2	2.7	3,031,000
4. France	42.6	3.4	506,000
5. Japan	41.7	1.0	242,000
6. Germany	36.7	2.2	398,000
7. United Kingdom	34.7	3.6	273,000
8. Italy	20.6	2.1	450,000
9. Saudi Arabia	20.5	15.8	172,000
10. South Korea	11.9	3.6	750,000
11. Taiwan	10.4	4.7	442,000
12. Canada	10.3	2.0	80,000
13. India	8.5	3.3	1,265,000
14. Spain	8.3	1.8	199,000
15. Australia	7.4	2.6	68,000
16. Turkey	7.1	5.8	811,000
17. Netherlands	7.1	2.4	86,000
18. Israel	6.3	9.1	181,000
19. Brazil	5.9	1.1	296,000
20. Sweden	5.0	2.8	44,000

Source: U.S. Arms Control and Disarmament Agency, *World Military Expenditures and Arms Transfers, 1993–1994* (Washington, D.C., 1994). Data taken from "1993 country rankings" based on statistical tables I and II.

Some countries excel according to some military criteria and fall short on others. Countries can be ranked according to size of armed forces, number of weapons of various types, skill levels, research and development, amount of military expenditures, and military expenditures as a percentage of GNP or per person (indicating degree of effort). The Arab states together have more raw weaponry and larger armed forces than the Israelis, but the Arab states seldom fight as one force, and Israel has enjoyed superior technology, motivation, and levels of mobilization. Also, one must remember that military capability that is effective in one type of situation, such as that shown stunningly by the U.S.-led coalition in the Gulf War "Desert Storm" operations against Iraq, may have little relevance to other types of situations, such as the mountains of Bosnia or the back alleys of Somalia.

Changes in world political and economic relations often are reflected in changing military rankings. For example, if one compares the rankings in Table 5.2 for the mid-1990s with those of a half-decade earlier, one would note that China has risen considerably in military spending though not in overall size of the armed forces. Beijing undertook a major military modernization effort, replacing outdated equipment and establishing a modern arms industry. At the same time, both Russia and the United States have reduced their forces but continue to lead in overall military effort. Britain dropped a few ranks, whereas South Korea and Taiwan surged in both military spending and manpower (though not in spending as a percentage of their fast-growing economies). Japan also maintained quite a high military ranking despite a formal spending limit of about one percent of GNP. One can speculate that economic and financial conditions, economic interests in defense production, the influence of the military on policymakers, and the uncertain future of international tensions have had something to do with all these trends.[43] In China's case, the lessons of a difficult struggle with Vietnam, along with regional security ambitions, competition with the United States, and trade interests, may have spurred the new military spending.

Regionally, the rankings also show the potential for European military power if the European Union is ever extended to form a common defense policy and army (Britain, France, Germany, and Italy have over 1.5 million troops combined, and spend jointly more than Russia). Asia generally, not just China, experienced considerable military buildup in the 1990s, largely through arms acquisition and development. In the Middle East, Saudi Arabia, Israel, and Turkey, with strong interests in local conflicts, made major military efforts as measured in terms of domestic or gross national product. Others, such as the previously ambitious Iraq, fell from the top ranks of military effort because of the pressures of UN sanctions. Some of the relative merits and costs of military preparation in certain circumstances are discussed in the box on pages 199–200.

The level of a country's or bloc's military preparedness is monitored by other interested governments in planning their foreign policies. In the late 1930s, for example, many of the smaller Western European countries that

MILITARY PREPARATIONS AND THE IRAN-IRAQ WAR DURING THE 1980s

Iran's example is instructive about the degree of benefits achieved through military preparations. During the 1970s, vast defense spending under the Shah failed to produce a military capable of keeping him in power—indeed, helped spawn the resentment and revolution that toppled him in 1979—and failed to deter Iraq from launching a war to regain territory during the political chaos that accompanied the revolution. (The loss of the United States as an Iranian ally also emboldened Iraq.) However, Iran's continued allocation of vast sums to its military after the revolution did help to turn the tide of that war and, ultimately, after a ten-year struggle, resulted in the expulsion of Iraqi forces. Often lacking expensive higher technology equipment, Iran sometimes resorted to "human wave" assaults, relying on a combination of population size, Islamic fervor, and Iranian nationalism to motivate young foot soldiers to attack Iraqi tank brigades and mine fields and to carry the war to Iraqi territory.

In examining the military attributes used in the Iran-Iraq war, and the impact such traits had on foreign policy behavior, one must note that capabilities were augmented both by vast arms imports from other countries and by the financial backing of other states, such as Libya for Iran and Saudi Arabia for Iraq. Outside states sought economic returns on arms sales, and also in some cases political advantage through arms assistance, hoping for more regional influence or for trade-offs on other issues, such as oil. Arms transfers also sometimes were aimed at promoting a stalemate so that neither Iran nor Iraq, both feared in the region, would win a clear victory.

As listed below, the outside suppliers constituted "strange bedfellows" and unlikely suppliers on each side, and sometimes on *both* sides. All were guided by their own supposed national interests. Depending on sophisticated weapons to overcome Iranian manpower, Iraq imported higher values of arms than did Iran—in some years as much as $5 billion or more in major equipment. Iran generally imported less than $1 billion worth of such equipment per year, but both states used multiple arms sources to make up for the restrictions imposed by major power arms suppliers. Sometimes the same suppliers sold to both states, and once, surplus Iraqi tanks actually ended up being sold to Iran.

Suppliers to Iran, 1980–1988:

Algeria; Argentina; Brazil; China; East Germany; France; Israel; Italy; Libya; North Korea; South Africa; South Korea; Soviet Union; Syria; Taiwan; the

United States. Britain, West Germany, and Switzerland sold civilian-labeled goods, which were put to military use.

Suppliers to Iraq, 1980–1988:

Austria; Brazil; Britain; China; Czechoslovakia; East Germany; Egypt; France; Italy; North Korea; Poland; Soviet Union; Spain; the United States; West Germany; Yugoslavia.

Iraq subsequently used both the weapons and experience acquired to launch its campaign for regional dominance against neighbors such as Kuwait. Iran continued to import relatively sophisticated weapon systems and to develop basic capabilities to upgrade weapons, though its spending level remained at a moderate 3.5 percent of GNP in the mid-1990s.

Sources: John Turner and SIPRI, *Arms in the 80s* (London: Taylor and Francis, 1985); Michael Brzoska and Thomas Ohlson, *Arms Transfers to the Third World, 1971–85* (Oxford: Oxford University Press and SIPRI, 1987); U.S. ACDA, *World Military Expenditures and Arms Transfers, 1993–1994* (Washington, D.C., 1994); augmented by the authors' files.

might have relied on Britain and France for protection against an expansionist Germany assessed the lack of British-French military readiness and deduced from this that the Western allies were not reliable protectors.[44] However, it can be a mistake to read too much into a state's level of readiness at any particular moment. A country might be ill-prepared at the beginning of a crisis but able to gear up later, as was the case with the United States after Pearl Harbor, when it became the "arsenal of democracy."[45] Relative preparedness and the strain of military competition can strongly affect defense policies and doctrines; as seen in Table 5.2, for example, India fields a quite large army, but can afford only a relatively small spending base for supplying its military, especially in trying to compete with neighbors like China. Hence its evolving policies of mutual border recognition with China and continued development of nuclear weapons potential become more understandable.[46]

GOVERNMENTAL ATTRIBUTES

One view of world politics is that it does not matter whether states are **democracies** or **dictatorships** ("open" or "closed" political systems), because the pressures of the international system or other national attributes largely determine foreign policy. One could predict a hostile response by a major power that had just discovered enemy troops encamped near its borders regardless of whether its leaders were elected or self-appointed. Those taking this position argue that national interests are interpreted by an elite professional foreign policy establishment playing a "fiduciary" role—like a trustee administering a will—aimed at protecting the nation's population and territory.

Others, however, argue that domestic politics and the nature of a country's political system do affect interpretations of national interests and foreign policy. This can be true for both major and minor powers.[47] Perhaps exaggerating a bit, one noted observer has commented as follows about American foreign relations:

> One of the most consistent and incurable traits of American statesmanship [is] . . . its neurotic self-consciousness and introversion, the tendency to make statements and take actions with regard not to their effect on the international scene to which they are ostensibly addressed but rather to their effects on those echelons of American opinion . . . to which the respective statesmen are anxious to appeal.[48]

Foreign policy moves can be used to improve a leader's domestic standing, as when one of President George Bush's advisors characterized his order to intervene in Panama in 1989 as "hitting one over the fence" in terms of boosting the president's public image.

A continuing debate exists in the international relations literature about the importance of "governmental variables," i.e., characteristics of the governmental system, in shaping foreign policy. We noted earlier in the chapter that democracies are no less war-prone than dictatorships but that they rarely fight each other. In addition to effects on war-making, the type of political system is thought to influence policy flexibility, discretion, and efficiency.

George Kennan, among others, has argued that democracies have special problems fighting protracted "limited wars," such as Vietnam, because there is a tendency for a restless public to demand a conclusive outcome: "win or get out."[49] Hence, democracies are seen as subject to relatively inflexible, "all or nothing" types of policies and involvements. Freer from domestic political constraints, dictatorships supposedly are more able to switch policies when necessary. Yet we must note that the authoritarian Soviet Union failed to reappraise its policy of backing Egypt after the latter's humiliating defeat in the 1967 Six-Day War against Israel, a failure that cost millions of rubles in burned-out Soviet-supplied equipment. Moscow immediately poured millions more into rearming Egypt, only to be eventually expelled from the country after the 1973 fighting.[50]

In regard to rigidity, dictators such as Stalin, Hitler, and Saddam Hussein reportedly severely punished advisors who disagreed with their policies, stifling frank advice and policy evaluation. President Johnson showed during the Vietnam War that democratic leaders also can punish advisors considered too critical, although not to the extreme of physical execution or imprisonment. One could argue that the greater potential for careful deliberation, debate, and scrutiny of foreign policy decisions in a democracy gives the latter an advantage over dictatorships, but also that common decision-making pressures can be experienced by both democratic and authoritarian leaders.[51]

We are not arguing that type of governmental system is an irrelevant factor in world politics, only that its importance can be exaggerated. All leaders, whether presiding in open or closed political systems, are concerned to some extent about their domestic political environment.[52] Admittedly, in democratic countries there are greater pressures because of a wider circle of relevant actors, some controlling the purse strings, others seeking out news stories, others evaluating the proper strategy for the next election campaign, and still others complaining about how their taxes are spent or whether their children could be drafted. Even in nondemocratic countries, however, various groups inside and outside the government might express dissent on foreign policy and might have to be placated, as when Russian mothers protested the fate of their sons in the Afghanistan and Chechen wars.

One set of persistent domestic political pressures that can be found in both democratic and authoritarian systems alike are the demands made by various agencies within the government itself. Examples of such *bureaucratic* pressures include the battles that have been fought over the years between various branches of the U.S. armed services over slices of the defense budget pie; decisions on new weapons systems or military base closings can be based as much on political pressures by certain armed services as on battlefield needs.[53] In certain foreign policy domains, particularly those demanding significant technical expertise, such as trade negotiations, heavy reliance may be placed on bureaucratic agencies, as with Japan's Ministry of International Trade and Industry (MITI). These agencies often allow for continuity of policy even while political leaders at the top may topple.[54]

In addition to bureaucratic pressures, *societal interest groups* (based on economic, ethnic, ideological, or other shared concerns) can have an impact on foreign policy, especially in democracies, where they are freer to organize and operate. Interest groups often have close "clientele" relations with specific agencies in the government bureaucracy. In a large country such as the United States, economic interests may vary by region—fishing interests off the east and west coasts, oil and energy interests of the west, agricultural concerns of the midwest, and immigration policy preoccupations of southern border states—and can affect a whole range of policies.[55] Certain American ethnic groups have deep concerns about developments in various foreign countries, such as Cuba, Israel, South Africa, Haiti, Serbia, Greece, Poland, and Ireland. Interest groups clearly have more impact on domestic policy than on foreign policy; within the foreign policy arena, they are likely to have more impact on foreign economic issues than on military-security issues. However, in an age of interdependence, as the domestic and foreign policy arenas along with security and nonsecurity concerns become increasingly blurred, interest groups appear to be playing a greater role generally in foreign policy.[56] We will examine this matter further in the next chapter.

Recalling our earlier discussion, *public opinion* also can limit a leader's freedom of action in foreign policy, especially in democracies (at election time in particular), although leaders in both open and closed political systems can manipulate public opinion to some extent by taking advantage of the public's generally low level of interest in and information about foreign policy. Public opinion has been said to operate in a "cascade" fashion, with "opinion leaders" (media and other elites within a small "attentive public") at the top of a pyramid passing viewpoints to the mass public below.[57] In democracies, public opinion backlash is likely to be greater and more politically costly than in dictatorships if policies fail to produce promised results. Even a popular president such as Franklin Roosevelt was wary of exceeding the tolerance of public opinion for war involvement before Japan's attack on Pearl Harbor in 1941. Before moving against Iraq in defense of Kuwait in 1990, George Bush allowed for a highly visible, open congressional debate and vote on the permissibility of military action, which enabled him to share the blame more widely were defeat to occur on the battlefield.

The Vietnam War provides a good case study in the dynamics of public opinion and how it impacts on foreign policy. Despite telling the American electorate in 1964 that American boys would not be sent to do the fighting that Asian boys should be doing, President Johnson was able to escalate U.S. military involvement in Vietnam for four years, manipulating both public and congressional opinion to support his policies. However, as casualties increased, as middle-class youths were drafted in ever greater numbers, and as the news media brought horrible war scenes and accounts of American failures to family dinner tables each night, public pressures opposing the war mounted among diverse groups—some demanding quick victory, others demanding compromise with the North Vietnamese, and others opting for immediate withdrawal. In such circumstances the President seemed caught in a game of musical chairs; the object was not to be the President when Vietnam fell. Therefore, U.S. bombing targets were sometimes widened, battlefield casualty figures were sometimes doctored, and peace overtures were sometimes offered—frequently all three in combination—at least partly in an effort to convince the public that those in charge knew how to bring peace to Southeast Asia. Arguments were even heard in the Johnson administration, as well as the Nixon administration that followed, that American public opinion was Hanoi's best weapon because dissension supposedly encouraged North Vietnam to fight on. However, public opinion did not cause an American defeat in Vietnam; it merely reflected the concern caused by increasingly bleak events, and it raised the political cost of the war.[58]

Finally, there is one other political factor sometimes thought to affect foreign policy behavior: the amount of domestic political instability experienced by a regime. Internal political instability can diminish the credibility of a country's foreign policy and affect the scope of its foreign involvements. If a national government is fighting a civil war, its promises to pay its bills, to preserve order for foreign investors, to participate effectively in alliances, and to undertake other commitments all become suspect. Some theorists have also speculated that regimes pressured by internal conflict are likely to trump up external conflicts against foreign "scapegoats" to divert public attention from domestic problems and to unify the country. Individual cases can be cited that seem to support this hypothesis, such as the Argentine invasion of the Falkland (Malvinas) Islands against the British in 1982, at a time of mounting domestic unrest and deteriorating economic conditions in Argentina. Britain's forceful response to this South Atlantic invasion also was seen in some quarters as an opportunity for Prime Minister Margaret Thatcher's government to regain popularity lost in a time of soaring unemployment. However, the overall evidence suggests governments seem to be reluctant to risk foreign confrontations in most cases when their own population, and perhaps more importantly their armed forces, are not unified and reliable. If anything, war involvements have historically eroded public unity, especially if the wars are long and costly; foreign conflict involvement can worsen or cause domestic conflict. Domestic conflict may induce foreign conflict, though, if enemy states are tempted to intervene in the unstable state to take advantage of political disruption and gain territory or other concessions. The box on pages 205–206 summarizes some overall research findings on national attributes and foreign policy.

The Role of Idiosyncratic Factors

Until now we have discussed mainly objective factors that affect foreign policy. In this section we examine subjective factors that can have an impact. Those who might be called "environmental determinists" would argue that at least 90 percent of the decisions made by national governments and the results of these decisions would have occurred regardless of the identity of the specific individuals in decision-making positions. Especially in the case of "big" events, it is argued that the objective constraints and historical forces at work are larger than any single individual. For example, environmental determinists would contend that a harsh peace treaty in 1919 and the subsequent economic depression in Germany would have produced a German desire for revenge no matter what leader had come to power in Berlin; in other words, Adolf Hitler did not "cause" World War II.

In contrast, others argue that single individuals ("devils" or "saints") are indeed capable of shaping great events. Those who rely on the **great man (or woman) theory,** or other explanations of foreign policy that focus on individual decision makers, emphasize the role of *idiosyncratic* factors. Here we find the assumption that Charles de Gaulle's presence in the Élysée Palace in Paris, or Stalin's in the Kremlin, or Churchill's in Whitehall, or Mao's in Beijing ma-

ASSUMPTIONS AND RESEARCH FINDINGS ON NATIONAL ATTRIBUTES AND FOREIGN POLICY

Some common *assumptions* about the effects of national attributes on foreign policy behavior:

1. Countries with large populations are more war-prone than countries with small populations, in terms of requiring more living space or having more personnel and economic resources with which to undertake foreign military activity.

2. Large, economically developed countries have a higher level and broader scope of international interactions, including international organization membership, than small, less developed countries.

3. A country's level of economic development is closely related to its voting behavior in international organizations, especially on economic issues.

4. Democracies are less war-prone than dictatorships.

5. Dictatorships' foreign policies are less subject to public opinion and domestic political pressures than is the case with democracies, so that dictatorships tend to enjoy certain advantages in the conduct of foreign policy.

6. Countries experiencing domestic turmoil, including ethnic conflict, are especially likely to become involved in foreign conflict.

Some research *findings* related to the above assumptions[1]:

1. Smallness of population size, as opposed to other measures such as geographic size, seems to be the most relevant size factor impacting on foreign policy adaptation and action. It leads to strategies for preserving political autonomy and maximizing socioeconomic development (Geser, 1992). Big countries tend to become involved in more wars than small countries (Modelski, 1971; Wright, 1964; Small and Singer, 1970) and tend to initiate more conflictual acts (warnings, threats, etc.) in general (Weede, 1970).

2. Economic development seems to lead to a slightly higher percentage of cooperative as opposed to conflictual acts (Salmore and Hermann, 1970; Duval and Thompson, 1980). Economically developed countries tend to belong to more intergovernmental organizations than less developed states (Jacobson, 1979), tend to be more negative in their attitudes toward the United Nations (Vincent, 1968), and tend to utilize the International Court of Justice more (Coplin and Rochester, 1972).

3. Level of economic development is a strong general predictor of UN voting behavior, especially on North-South issues, with less developed countries tending to vote in support of increased multilateral aid. Level of development, however, does not entirely predict behavior in inter-

governmental organizations; as demonstrated by differing U.S., Soviet, French and German actions in the UN Educational, Scientific and Cultural Organization, states tend to pursue their own perceived interests, and these can vary even among developed countries (Billing, 1993).

4. Type of economic system (capitalist, socialist, communist, or mixed) has no overall association with a state's number of involvements in armed conflict, in the 1945–89 period (Kinnucan, 1992).

5. General orientations of public opinion belief systems constrain specific foreign policies; people's general feelings about militarism and containment are more stable than specific preferences about issues such as defense spending or particular foreign interventions (Peffley and Hurwitz, 1993; Blum, 1993).

6. Although democracies tend not to fight each other, there is little overall relationship between type of governmental system and war or conflict involvement (Rummel, 1968; Luard, 1968; Maoz and Abdolali, 1989). Because they fit more readily into the international economic system, democracies find it more feasible to fill their needs through trade than do authoritarian regimes; this also means they need to resort to war less often in their mutual dealings (Brawley, 1993). Because arms transfers tend to facilitate military coups and lengthen military rule in states, military regimes seem to depend heavily on the arms trade (Maniruzzaman, 1992).

7. Nations' domestic and foreign conflict behaviors generally are unrelated, although states in certain regions and with certain forms of government engage in foreign and domestic conflicts simultaneously more than other states. When domestic conflict becomes intense, states tend to retreat from foreign involvements to resolve the situation at home. Severe domestic conflict also can tempt other states to intervene (Tanter, 1966; Rummel, 1963; Wilkenfeld, 1968; Pearson, 1974). Ethnic conflicts aimed at freeing the state from colonialism, at breaking off a portion of a state's territory, or at reuniting a divided population have varying impacts on international interventions and involvements (Carment, 1993; Morgan and Bickers, 1989).

[1] Full citations for the specific studies noted in parentheses appear at the end of this chapter. Research findings can depend on the measurements used to test relationships. The findings noted here should be treated as suggestive rather than as the last word on the subject.

terially changed the course of history.[59] Idiosyncratic accounts have ranged from Pascal's perhaps overstated musings that if Cleopatra's nose had been only slightly shorter, the face of the world would have been changed, to Robert Kennedy's equally dramatic and perhaps overstated observation that if six of the fourteen men in the "Ex Com" decision group formed during the

Cuban missile crisis had been President of the United States, the world would probably have blown up.[60] How different are these approaches from the perspective of a balance of power systems theorist!

The fact is that both objective conditions *and* idiosyncratic factors must be taken into account in seeking a full understanding of foreign policy. Adopting what might be called an "environmental possibilism" approach, we would argue that a decision maker's domestic and international environments (i.e., national attribute and systemic factors) impose limits on the capacity to act, but that individuals can and do exercise some element of free will and do make a difference. It took a Hitler to take full advantage of the possibilities presented by Germany's internal turmoil and international situation. Likewise, without a leader of Nehru's dynamic qualities and neutralist persuasion present at the birth of India in 1947, it is open to question whether India's foreign policy behavior would have taken the turn it did in the postwar period, particularly its active role in the nonaligned movement and its commitment to membership in numerous multilateral international organizations despite scarce resources. In the last chapter we saw the crucial role played by Gorbachev in interpreting changes in the Soviet Union's international and domestic environment and guiding Russia toward fundamental reorientation in its international relations.[61] Yet even Gorbachev could not survive the forces he set in motion. One would expect idiosyncratic factors to be especially important in dictatorships, where one or only a few leaders dominate policymaking,[62] although such factors can be significant in democracies as well; in democracies, idiosyncratic factors are likely to play a larger role in the foreign policy process than in the domestic policy process because leaders generally are given greater leeway in the foreign policy arena.

One reason individuals make a difference is that they do not all see their environment the same way. Harold and Margaret Sprout were among the first to draw attention to the distinction between the decision maker's "objective" and "psychological" environments—the difference between reality and an individual's *perception* or **image** of reality.[63] Kenneth Boulding has likewise noted that

> we must recognize that the people whose decisions determine the policies and actions of nations do not respond to the "objective" facts of the situation, whatever that may mean, but to their "image" of the situation. It is what we think the world is like, not what it is really like, that determines our behavior.[64]

Individuals can differ not only in their worldviews but also in *personality* traits such as temperament. The brashness or impulsiveness of leaders—sometimes equated with what theorists call "risk acceptance"[65]—or the extent to which they are tolerant of opposing viewpoints can have important implications for foreign policy decisions. Some researchers have examined the

ADOLPH HITLER (LEFT) CHATTING WITH HIS AIR FORCE MARSHAL SHORTLY AFTER BECOMING THE LEADER (*DER FÜHRER*) OF GERMANY IN 1934.

impact of early childhood experiences on the adult behavior of leaders. For example, it has been argued that Woodrow Wilson's "authoritarian personality," derived from his strict parental upbringing, affected his dealings with other world leaders and members of the U.S. Senate, and was at least partly responsible for the failure of the Senate to approve U.S. membership in the League of Nations after World War I.[66]

Often far more germane than early childhood experiences are a leader's recent political experiences. For example, in 1961, while still new to the presidency, John Kennedy met Nikita Khrushchev in Vienna. By most accounts of the Kennedy years, that summit meeting was to affect profoundly the young President's decisions in dealing with the Soviets. Kennedy came away from the meeting convinced that he had failed to impress Khrushchev, that the Russian leader considered him weak and immature. At least one former U.S. official has argued that one reason for Kennedy's initial Vietnam commitment in 1961 was a series of early personal setbacks, including his humiliation at Vienna and his failure to respond to Moscow's construction of the Berlin Wall.[67]

One factor that has received increased attention in recent years is the possible impact of *gender* on foreign policy behavior.[68] It has been hypothesized that male aggressiveness, purportedly related to upbringing or socialization patterns, and even perhaps to testosterone levels, is responsible for a certain preoccupation with power, dominance, hierarchies, and the use of force in world politics.[69] It might be claimed, for example, that President Kennedy's preoccupation with his image relative to an older leader such as Premier Khrushchev represents a largely male competitive struggle for dominance, with each party worried about the other misperceiving reasonableness as weakness. It is therefore sometimes argued that if more women were in positions of decision-making responsibility, there would be more negotiated settlements of disputes and fewer wars, and more concern about "humanitarian" issues such as the status of children, poverty, and the global environment rather than "security" as defined by the competition for resources and control of territory.[70] There might be less behavior of the type evidenced by General Ratko Mladic, the military commander of Bosnian Serb forces during the Bosnian civil war, who (along with his civilian superior, Dr. Radovan Karadzic, a psychiatrist by training) was accused by international human rights monitors of committing genocide; Mladic's response to charges that his troops had raped Muslim peasant women was that they would not do so because "we are too picky."[71]

Whether male leaders in fact are inherently more aggressive and insensitive than their female counterparts is an empirical question that could be subject to testing if more women were to assume leadership positions; however, it is difficult to conceive of a perfect laboratory setting, free from other factors, to determine the effects of gender. The overall historical evidence on the role of women in world politics thus far has been mixed. In the entire twentieth century, there have been only eight female presidents and sixteen prime ministers among heads of state.[72] Female leaders such as India's Indira Gandhi, Israel's Golda Meir, and Britain's Margaret Thatcher certainly did not shrink from the use of power, including war-making and political manipulation, where and when they deemed it necessary.[73] Some, such as Isabela Peron of Argentina and Benazir Bhutto of Pakistan, struggled against domestic opponents in the military to maintain power. Eugenia Charles, Prime Minister of the tiny island of Dominica in the 1980s, backed the U.S. military intervention in Grenada. There have been female leaders in other relatively small countries, such as Norway and Iceland, whose governments have not participated in for-

ASSUMPTIONS AND RESEARCH FINDINGS ON IDIOSYNCRATIC FACTORS AND FOREIGN POLICY

Some common *assumptions* about the effects of idiosyncratic factors on foreign policy behavior:

1. Individual leaders—their beliefs, personalities, and ways of thinking—will have a greater impact on foreign policy in economically underdeveloped states than in developed states.

2. Individual leaders will have a greater impact on foreign policy in dictatorships than in democracies.

3. Idiosyncratic factors will have a greater impact on decision making the greater the threat, the shorter the time, and the greater the element of surprise in the decision situation.

4. The more detailed the decision that is required, the less likely will idiosyncratic factors affect decisions. The more ambiguous or uncertain the decision-making situation, the greater the impact of idiosyncratic factors.

5. Although individuals are capable of changing their beliefs, information processing is selective and subject to biases that can produce faulty decisions.

Some research *findings* related to the above assumptions[1]:

1. Although leaders who have "authoritarian personalities" (i.e., feel a need to dominate others) are more likely to approve of highly nationalistic, aggressive foreign policy behavior (Scott 1965), the importance of such personality factors in a country's foreign policy varies and depends at least partly on how much control a leader has over policy (M. Hermann, 1974; Etheredge, 1978; Shepard, 1988; Gerner, 1990).

2. Individuals who favor the use of force in interpersonal relations will tend to favor the use of force in interstate relations (Etheredge, 1978), although the leader's institutional role (senator, president, etc.) often outweighs personal dispositions (Singer and Ray, 1966). Crisis situations tend to lessen the effect of roles (Snyder and Diesing, 1977).

3. The particular images that individual leaders have of the world tend to affect their attitudes toward defense, foreign aid, and other foreign policy concerns; there is evidence that leaders' perceptions change after they decide to change behavior, rather than necessarily before such decisions (Larson, 1988; R. Herrmann, 1986; Gerner, 1990).

4. Women were decidedly less prone to internalize the pattern of the Cold War's competition than were men, and "American men are less likely to acknowledge apprehension over the risk of war than women, and are more prone to accept the strategic uses of wars" (Rosenberg, 1967).

5. Changes in a country's foreign policy are more likely after a change in leadership rather than during the continuation of leadership, particu-

larly in less developed countries (Rosen, 1975). Governments whose top decision-making unit is dominated by a strong individual leader, as opposed to a leadership group or multiple autonomous leaders, appear to adopt relatively moderate, less conflictual foreign policies. Units that are closed off from outside advice and information appear to behave more conflictually than those more open to input (Hermann and Hermann, 1989).

[1] Full citations for the specific studies noted in parentheses appear at the end of this chapter. Research findings can depend on the measurements used to test relationships. The findings noted here should be treated as suggestive rather than as the last word on the subject.

eign wars. The question remains whether the percentage of women leaders refraining from fighting is any higher than the corresponding percentage of male leaders in similar situations. In other words, is it gender, or the state's characteristics or demands of the leadership *role,* that affects policy most?[74]

Idiosyncratic factors can affect foreign policy when the right person, be they male or female, turns out to be in the right place at the right time. Although improvement in U.S.-Chinese relations in the 1970s depended mainly on an end to the Vietnam War and growing worries about the Soviet Union, Richard Nixon was perhaps in a better position to take advantage of the situation than any other American politician would have been. The pro-Taiwan "China lobby" in the United States could not accuse Nixon of being soft on Communism when he traveled to Beijing, because his anti-Communist credentials, fashioned during the McCarthy era of the 1950s, were impeccable. Similarly, Israeli Prime Minister Menachem Begin, a staunch hawk and former terrorist leader in Israel's fight for independence, could hardly be criticized by security-minded Israelis for being overly dovish in 1979 when he agreed with Egyptian President Sadat to return the occupied Sinai territory to the Egyptians.

The example of a Nixon or Begin shows that a country's foreign policy can change in certain circumstances, but one should not lose sight of *continuities.* Whether attributable to bureaucratic inertia or other factors, some countries develop a certain tradition in foreign policy, which tends to be maintained even as national leaders come and go. For example, differences among NATO members on whether to enlarge the alliance and how to deal with Russia are better explained by long-standing differences in their approaches to security matters—based on disparities in size, geographical location, historical experience, and domestic political forces—than by differences in the nature of individual leaders.

Based on our discussion in this section, it would seem, insofar as idiosyncratic factors are important, that they have a special impact on the *modus operandi* of foreign policy, particularly on the degree of assertiveness and propensity to use force displayed by a country. See the box on pages 210–211 for a summary of some research findings on the role of idiosyncratic factors in foreign policy.

Conclusion

All three sets of factors—systemic, national attribute, and idiosyncratic variables—*intermingle* as foreign policymakers consider how their state should relate to others.[75] Systemic factors seem especially important in affecting *alignment* behavior. National attribute factors seem especially important in affecting the *scope* dimension of foreign policy. Idiosyncratic factors can be especially telling in accounting for some aspects of a country's *modus operandi,* the specific tactics adopted to pursue general policy aims.

Although in a given situation one particular set of factors might be the main influence on foreign policy, frequently all three sets operate simultaneously. For example, Soviet foreign policy initiatives toward the West at the end of the Cold War can be understood at several levels of analysis. Mr. Gorbachev's designation as *Time* magazine's "man of the decade" in 1990 is but one testament to the difference people came to believe he made in world politics as the individual widely credited with engineering the end of the Cold War, many citing his case as supporting the "great man" thesis. Yet *glasnost* and *perestroika,* as well as the loosened hold on Eastern Europe, suspension of nuclear testing, and other initiatives, were responses to pressures in the domestic and international environments that had been growing over a period of years and which were beginning to preoccupy Kremlin rulers even before Gorbachev's arrival on the scene (and that still preoccupy his successors). The Soviet Union's move toward rapprochement with the West, although receiving great impetus from Gorbachev's personal leadership qualities (*idiosyncratic* factors), could be attributed also to a stagnant economy and felt need to pursue Western technology and capital transfers (*national attributes*) as well as a recognition that the "correlation of forces" did not favor continued Soviet confrontation with the United States and American allies in light of the huge American defense buildup in the 1980s, joined with the emergent twenty-first century challenge posed by nuclear-armed China to the East (*international system* conditions). Some saw Gorbachev caught up in the vast sweep of Russian history and the unfinished business of Russian modernization; as one scholar phrased it, Gorbachev may have been trying to "direct" and "use" the "major forces of contemporary Russian history."[76]

With all the official speeches and statements pouring out of foreign ministries "clarifying" or "explaining" various actions or inactions, it is often difficult to cut through the verbiage to determine which forces actually are driving a given state's foreign policy at a given moment. For policymakers seeking to make sense of the world, it is difficult enough to come to grips fully with their own motives, much less those of counterparts in other countries. Yet this is precisely what they must try to do if they are to act wisely. Citizens generally have even more trouble deciphering events. As one midwestern American woman put it in struggling to define the appropriate level of U.S. involvement in the Bosnian tragedy of the 1990s:

> I try to follow the war in Bosnia, but it's so confusing. It's been going on for 300 or 400 years. I know there are atrocities going on. I understand Serbs are raping Muslim women, and kidnapping their sons. I think it's sad. I think, 'Golly, is this a similar situation to Nazi Germany?' And everybody ignored that for how many years? [But] I think it would be another Vietnam. I don't think our sons and fathers should be losing their lives over it. I think we should continue the dialogue.[77]

Information streaming in from the "objective" international environment, often screened and filtered by the media, is passed along through government agencies and subjected to a variety of domestic political pressures. Ultimately, the result is some set of judgments about the world, and some set of actions. What is done with the information has an important bearing on the quality of those judgments and the effectiveness of those actions, as we shall see in the next chapter.

SUMMARY

1. Although many people argue that all foreign policy behavior can be traced to national interests, it is necessary to examine a variety of factors found both inside and outside national boundaries to understand why states act as they do. These factors can generally be classified as (1) systemic, (2) national attribute, and (3) idiosyncratic.

2. Systemic factors are those conditions in a country's external environment that can affect its foreign policy. These include geography, international interactions and links, and the international system structure. For example, as the international political environment becomes less threatening, two countries allied militarily may feel less need to continue their alliance relationship.

3. National attributes—demographic, economic, military, and governmental factors— also affect foreign policy behavior. Demography can include the impact of ethnicity and culture, as well as the size and capabilities of a country's population. The more economic assets a country has, the greater its ability to pursue global interests, to use economic tools of influence, and to participate in international organizations. A country's military preparedness, rate of economic growth, and access to resources can affect its propensity to intervene abroad. The type of political system a country has can also shape its foreign policy behavior, with leaders in a democracy having to be more concerned about public opinion than their counterparts in a dictatorship. However, in democracies and nondemocracies alike, foreign policy is shaped by a combination of external forces and domestic political pressures.

4. Those who rely on "the great man/woman theory of history," or other explanations of foreign policy that focus on the role of individual decision makers, emphasize the importance of idiosyncratic factors. Although objective conditions such as national attributes and systemic factors impose limits on a state's capacity to act no matter who is at the helm, differences in leadership personality, temperament, and other personal characteristics can have important impacts on foreign policy, as in the case of such individuals as Hitler, Mao, Thatcher, Gorbachev, and Yeltsin.

5. Generally speaking, systemic factors seem especially important in affecting alignment behavior, national attribute factors especially affect the scope of foreign policy, and idiosyncratic factors affect the *modus operandi* of a state. However, frequently all three sets of factors operate simultaneously, intermingling as foreign policymakers consider how their state should relate to other states.

SUGGESTIONS FOR FURTHER READING AND STUDY

One work that shows how factors operating at the systemic, nation-state, and individual levels of analysis all can affect a state's foreign policy behavior is G. John Ikenberry, ed., *American Foreign Policy: Theoretical Essays* (Glenview, Ill.: Scott, Foresman, 1989), which examines various explanations of American foreign policy behavior, including the role of not only "international sources of foreign policy" but also "bureaucratic politics" and other domestic political influences as well as "social psychology and perceptions." Also, see Charles W. Kegley and Eugene R. Wittkopf, *American Foreign Policy: Pattern and Process*, 5th ed. (New York: St. Martin's Press, 1996); and Howard J. Wiarda, *American Foreign Policy: Actors and Processes* (New York: Harper Collins, 1996).

General works that provide an inventory of theories and research findings on foreign policy determinants include Brian H. Gibbs and J. David Singer, *Empirical Knowledge on World Politics: A Summary of Quantitative Research, 1970–1991* (Westport, Conn.: Greenwood Press, 1993); James E. Dougherty and Robert L. Pfaltzgraff, Jr., *Contending Theories of International Relations*, 4th ed. (New York: Harper and Row, 1993); Lloyd Jensen, *Explaining Foreign Policy* (Englewood Cliffs, N.J.: Prentice-Hall, 1982); and Michael P. Sullivan, *International Relations: Theories and Evidence* (Englewood Cliffs, N.J.: Prentice-Hall, 1976). Also, see Mike Bowker and Robin Brown, eds., *From Cold War to Collapse: Theory and World Politics in the 1980s* (Cambridge: Cambridge University Press, 1993); and Harvey Starr, "Rosenau, Pre-Theories, and the Evolution of the Comparative Study of Foreign Policy," *International Interactions* (1988).

Sources on specific foreign policy approaches and themes include Chris Brown, *International Relations Theory: New Normative Approaches* (New York: Harvester Wheatsheaf, 1992); Michael Clarke and Brian White, eds., *Understanding Foreign Policy: The Foreign Policy Systems Approach* (Aldershot, UK: E. Elgar, 1989); Peter M. Slowe, *Geography and Political Power: The Geography of Nations and States* (London: Routledge, 1990); Gerard Chaliand and Jean-Pierre Rageau, *A Strategic Atlas: Comparative Geopolitics of the World's Powers*, 3rd ed. (New York: Harper Perennial, 1992); Paul Sutton and Anthony Payne, "Towards a Security Policy for Small Island and Enclave Developing States," *Journal of Commonwealth and Comparative Politics*, 31 (July 1993), pp. 93–200; Melvin Small, *Democracy and Diplomacy: The Impact of Domestic Politics on U.S. Foreign Policy, 1989–1994* (Baltimore: Johns Hopkins University Press, forthcoming 1996); Deon Geldenhuys, *Isolated States: A Comparative Analysis* (Cambridge: Cambridge University Press, 1990); Geoffrey Hayes, *Middle Powers in the New World Order* (Toronto: Canadian Institute of International Affairs, 1994); Mark R. Brawley, *Liberal Leadership: Great Powers and Their Challengers in Peace and War* (Ithaca, New York: Cornell University Press, 1993); Stephen Ryan, *Ethnic Conflict and International Relations* (Aldershot, Hunts, UK: Dartmouth, 1990); Charles L. Mee, Jr. *Playing God: Seven Fateful Moments when Great Men Met to Change the World* (New York: Simon and Schuster, 1993); Vivian Green, *The Madness of Kings: Personal Trauma and the Fate of Nations* (New York: St. Martin's Press, 1993); Francine D'Amico and Peter R. Beckman, eds., *Women in World Politics: An Introduction* (Westport, Conn.: Bergin and Garvey, 1995); and J. Ann Tickner, *Gender in International Relations: Feminist Perspectives on Achieving Global Security* (New York: Columbia University Press, 1992).

The following works were cited in boxes in this chapter: Hayward R. Alker and Bruce M. Russett, *World Politics in the General Assembly* (New Haven, Conn.: Yale University Press, 1965); Peter Billing et al., "State Characteristics and Foreign Policy Behavior: Industrialized Countries and the UNESCO Crisis," *Cooperation and Conflict*, 28 (June 1993), pp. 143–180; Douglas W. Blum, "The Soviet Foreign Policy Belief System: Beliefs, Politics, and Foreign Policy Outcomes," *International Studies Quarterly*, 37 (December 1993), pp. 373–394; Mark Brawley, "Regime Types, Markets, and War: The Importance of Pervasive Rents in Foreign Policy," *Comparative Political Studies*, 26 (July 1993), pp. 178–197; Steven J. Brams, "Transaction Flows in the International System," *American Political Science Review*, 60 (December 1966), pp. 880–898; Bruce Bueno de Mesquita, "System Polarization and the Occurrence and Duration of War," *Journal of Conflict Resolution*, 22 (June 1978), pp. 241–267; David Carment, "The International Dimensions of Ethnic Conflict," *Journal of Peace Research*, 30 (May 1993), pp. 137–150; Steve Chan, "Mirror, Mirror on the Wall . . . Are the Freer Countries More Pacific?" *Journal of Conflict Resolution*, 28 (December 1984), pp. 617–648; Roger W. Cobb and Charles Elder, *International Community: A Regional and Global Study* (New York: Holt, Rinehart and Winston, 1970); William D. Coplin and J. Martin Rochester, "The Permanent Court of International Justice, the International Court of Justice, the League of Nations, and the United Nations: A Comparative Empirical Survey," *American Political Science Review*, 66 (June 1972), pp. 529–550; Robert D. Duval and William R. Thompson, "Reconsidering the Aggregate Relationship Between Size, Economic Development, and Some Types of Foreign Policy Behavior," *American Journal of Political Science*, 24 (August 1980), pp. 511–525; Lloyd S. Etheredge, "Personality Effects on American Foreign Policy, 1898–1968: A Test of Interpersonal Generalization Theory," *American Political Science Review*, 72 (June 1978), pp. 435–451; Mark J. Gasiorowski, "Economic Interdependence and International Conflict: Some Cross-National Evidence," *International Studies Quarterly*, 30 (March 1986); pp. 23–38; Deborah Gerner, "Foreign Policy Analysis: Renaissance, Routine, or Rubbish?" in William Crotty, ed., *Political Science: Looking to the Future*, vol. 2 (Evanston, Ill.: Northwestern University Press, 1990); Hans Geser, "Small States in the International System," *Kolner Zeitschrift for Soziologie and Sozialpsychologie*, 44 (1992), pp. 627–654; Michael Haas, "Societal Approaches to the Study of War," *Journal of Peace Research*, 2 (1965), pp. 307–323; Paul R. Hensel and Paul F. Diehl, "Testing Empirical Propositions About Shatterbelts, 1945–1976," *Political Geography*, 13 (January 1994), pp. 33–51; Margaret G. Hermann, "Leader Personality and Foreign Policy Behavior," in James N.

Rosenau, ed., *Comparing Foreign Policies: Theories, Finding, and Methods* (New York: John Wiley, 1974), pp. 201–234; Hermann and Charles Hermann, "Who Makes Foreign Policy Decisions and How: An Empirical Inquiry," *International Studies Quarterly*, 33 (December 1989), pp. 361–387; Richard K. Hermann, "The Power of Perceptions in Foreign Policy Decision Making: Do Views of the Soviet Union Determine the Policy Choices of American Leaders?" *American Journal of Political Science*, 30 (December 1986), pp. 841–875; Ole R. Holsti, et al., *Unity and Disintegration in International Alliances* (New York: John Wiley, 1973); Harold K. Jacobson, *Networks of Interdependence* (New York: Knopf, 1979), chap 3; Mark N. Katz, "The Legacy of Empire in International Relations," *Comparative Strategy*, 12 (October-December 1993), pp. 365–383; Charles W. Kegley, Jr., and Gregory A. Raymond, *When Trust Breaks Down: Alliance Norms and World Politics* (Columbia: University of South Carolina Press, 1990); Michael J. Kinnucan, "Political Economy and Militarism," *PS*, (September 1992), pp. 506–516; Deborah W. Larson, "Problems of Content Analysis in Foreign Policy Research: Notes from the Study of Cold War Belief Systems," *International Studies Quarterly*, 32 (March 1988), pp. 241–255; Jack S. Levy, "The Polarity of the System and International Stability: An Empirical Analysis," in Alan Ned Sabrosky, ed., *Polarity and War: The Changing Structure of International Conflict* (Boulder, Colo.: Westview Press, 1985); Levy and T. Cliff Morgan, "The Frequency and Seriousness of War," *Journal of Conflict Resolution*, 28 (December 1984), pp. 587–615; Evan Luard, *Conflict and Peace in the Modern International System* (Boston: Little, Brown, 1968); Tulukder Maniruzzaman, "Arms Transfers and Military Coups and Military Rule in Developing States," *Journal of Conflict Resolution*, 36 (December 1992), pp. 733–755; Zeev Maoz and Nasrin Abdolali, "Regime Types and International Conflict, 1816–1976," *Journal of Conflict Resolution*, 33 (March 1989), pp. 3–35; George Modelski, "War and the Great Powers," *Peace Research Society Papers*, 18 (1971), pp. 45–60; T. Clifton Morgan and Kenneth N. Bickers, "Domestic Politics and Aggressive Foreign Policy: A Causal Link?" paper presented at annual meeting of American Political Science Association, Atlanta, September 1989, p. 14; Frederic S. Pearson, "Foreign Military Interventions and Domestic Disputes," *International Studies Quarterly*, 18 (September 1974), pp. 259–290; Mark Peffley and Jon Hurwitz, "Models of Attitude Constraint in Foreign Affairs," *Political Behavior*, 15 (March 1993), pp. 61–90; Diana Richards, "A Chaotic Model of Power Concentration in the International System," *International Studies Quarterly*, 37 (March 1993), pp. 55–72; Lewis F. Richardson, *Statistics of Deadly Quarrels* (Pittsburgh: Boxwood, 1960); David Rosen, "Leadership Change and Foreign Policy," CREON Abstract #6 (Columbus: Ohio State University, 1975); and Milton J. Rosenberg, "Attitude Change and Foreign Policy in the Cold War Era," in Rosenau, ed., *Domestic Sources of Foreign Policy* (New York: Free Press, 1967); pp. 111–159.

Also cited in the boxes were Rudolph J. Rummel, "A Social Field Theory of Foreign Conflict Behavior," *Peace Research Society Papers*, 4 (1966), pp. 131–150; Rummel, "Dimensions of Conflict Behavior Within and Between Nations," *General Systems Yearbook*, 8 (1963), pp. 1–50; Rummel, "The Relationship Between National Attributes and Foreign Conflict Behavior," in J. David Singer, ed., *Quantitative International Politics* (New York: Free Press, 1968), pp. 187–214; Rummel, *Understanding Conflict and War*, vol. 4 (Beverly Hills, Calif.: Sage, 1979); Bruce M. Russett, *International Regions and the International System* (Chicago: Rand McNally, 1967); Steven A. Salmore and Charles F. Hermann, "The Effects of Size, Development and Accountability on Foreign

Policy," *Peace Research Society Papers*, 14 (1970), pp. 27–28; Randall Schweller, "Tripolarity and the Second World War," *International Studies Quarterly*, 37 (March 1993), pp. 73–103; William Scott, "Psychological and Social Correlates of International Images," in Herbert C. Kelman, ed., *International Behavior: A Social Psychological Analysis* (New York: Holt, Rinehart and Winston, 1965), pp. 71–103; Graham H. Shepard, "Personality Effects on American Foreign Policy, 1969–1984: A Second Test of Interpersonal Generalization Theory," *International Studies Quarterly*, 30 (January 1988), pp. 91–123; J. David Singer, "The Correlates of War Project: Interim Report and Rationale," *World Politics*, 24 (January 1972), pp. 243–270; Singer and Paul Ray, "Decision Making in Conflict: From Inter-Personal to Inter–National Relations," *Bulletin of the Menninger Clinic*, 30 (1966), pp. 300–312; Melvin Small and J. David Singer, "Patterns in International Warfare, 1816–1965," *Annals*, 391 (1970), pp. 145–155; Glenn H. Snyder and Paul Diesing, *Conflict Among Nations* (Princeton, N.J.: Princeton University Press, 1977); Harvey Starr and Benjamin A. Most, "The Forms and Processes of War Diffusion: Research Update on Contagion in African Conflict," *Comparative Political Studies*, 18 (July 1985), pp. 206–227; Raymond Tanter, "Dimensions of Conflict Behavior Within and Between Nations, 1958–1960," *Journal of Conflict Resolution*, 10 (March 1966), pp. 41–64; William R. Thompson, "Polarity, the Long Cycle, and Global Power Warfare," *Journal of Conflict Resolution*, 30 (December 1986), pp. 587–615; Thompson, "Cycles, Capabilities, and War," in *Approaches to World System Analysis* (Beverly Hills, Calif.: Sage, 1983), pp. 141–163; John A. Vasquez, "Capability, Types of War, and Peace," *Western Political Quarterly*, 39 (June 1986), pp. 313–327; Vasquez, "The Steps to War: Toward a Scientific Explanation of Correlates of War Findings," *World Politics*, 40 (October 1987), pp. 108–145; Jack E. Vincent, "National Attributes as Predictors of Delegate Attitudes of the United Nations," *American Political Science Review*, 62 (September 1968), pp. 916–931; Vincent, "Predicting Voting Patterns in the General Assembly," *American Political Science Review*, 65 (June 1971), pp. 471–498; Michael D. Wallace, "Alliance Polarization, Cross-Cutting, and International War, 1815–1964; A Measurement Procedure and Some Preliminary Findings," *Journal of Conflict Resolution*, 17 (December 1973), pp. 575–604; Frank W. Wayman, "Bipolarity and War: The Role of Capability Concentration and Alliance Patterns Among Major Powers, 1816–1965," *Journal of Peace Research*, 21 (1984), pp. 61–78; Erich Weede, "Conflict Behavior of Nation-States," *Journal of Peace Research*, 7 (1970), pp. 229–235; Weede, "Democracy and War Involvement," *Journal of Conflict Resolution*, 28 (December 1984), pp. 649–664; Jonathan Wilkenfeld, "Domestic and Foreign Conflict Behavior of Nations," *Journal of Peace Research*, 5 (1968), pp. 56–59; Wilkenfeld, "Some Further Findings Regarding the Domestic and Foreign Conflict Behavior of Nations," *Journal of Peace Research*, 6 (1969), pp. 147–156; Eugene R. Wittkopf, "The Distribution of Foreign Aid in Comparative Perspective: An Empirical Study of the Flow of Foreign Economic Assistance, 1961–1967," Ph.D. dissertation (Syracuse, N.Y.: Syracuse University, 1971); Quincy Wright, *Study of War*, 2nd ed. (Chicago: University of Chicago Press, 1964); and Dina Zinnes, "Three Puzzles in Search of a Researcher," *International Studies Quarterly*, 24 (September 1980), pp. 315–342.

The Foreign Policy Process:
A View from the Inside

In the previous chapter, we examined several determinants of foreign policy behavior. We noted that although systemic and national attribute factors tend to place constraints on state action, they alone do not dictate foreign policy behavior but operate in conjunction with other, idiosyncratic factors. In other words, national leaders must still make decisions that involve *choices* among foreign policy ends and means, no matter how much it may seem their hands are tied by "structural" conditions.

In this chapter, we will look more closely at the foreign policymaking *process* itself, including some of the more subtle factors at work. Clearly, the institutions and procedures involved in foreign policymaking differ from country to country. However, we are not interested here in the legal-formal aspects of the foreign policy process but rather in the various factors—intellectual, psychological, and otherwise—underlying the decision process in all political systems. For example, the kinds of information and time constraints that operate on American policymakers in a crisis situation can operate in a similar manner on Russian policymakers or the policymakers of Japan, China, and any other country and produce comparable behavior in like situations, especially if the individuals involved have similar personalities and dispositions in moments of stress.

Much of the discussion in this chapter follows from the Chapter 5 discussion of how individual decision makers relate to their environment. We want to look further *inside* the foreign policy process, seeing how those officials responsible for foreign policy produce decisions under varying circumstances. We especially want to examine whether decisions about foreign policy ends and means (such as using nuclear weapons) are made as carefully and *rationally* as the average citizen might assume or hope. As Graham Allison poignantly notes in his study of the Cuban missile crisis, such concerns are not merely of academic interest:

> The Cuban missile crisis is a seminal event. For thirteen days of October 1962, there was a higher probability that more human lives would end suddenly than ever before in history. Had the worst occurred, the death of 100 million Americans, over 100 million Russians, and millions of Europeans as well would make previous natural calamities and inhumanities appear insignificant. Given the probability of disaster—which President Kennedy estimated as "between one out of three and even"—our escape seems awesome. The event symbolizes a central, if only partially thinkable, fact about our existence. That such consequences could follow from the choices and actions of national governments obliges students of government as well as participants in governance to think hard about these problems.[1]

Does Each Country Have a Foreign Policy?

Six months after an American president assumed office, a newspaper ran the following headline: "Reagan Pressed to Spell Out Foreign Policy."[2] A year into his presidency, Ronald Reagan's successor also was being criticized for passively reacting to events rather than trying to shape them, until at least one headline proclaimed: "A Bolder Bush Foreign Policy Emerges."[3] Likewise, Bush's successor was criticized for lack of foreign policy direction, with one magazine running a story entitled "The Clinton Foreign Policy: Is There a Doctrine in the House?"[4] All of these cases begged the question: foreign policy with regard to *what*—the world, Latin America, Russia, foreign aid, arms sales?

Such headlines conjure up visions of foreign policy as being a single, conscious, overarching "plan"—a master blueprint containing an explicit set of goals and strategies for achieving those goals, into which all other smaller decisions are fitted. References are commonly made to the "architects" of U.S. (or Russian) policy. National leaders themselves like to reassure their citizenry that they have a plan, and they often accuse their counterparts in other states of having their own "grand design." However, to what extent does this square with reality?

Among those who have questioned whether states, particularly those with large government bureaucracies, have such blueprints is Henry Kissinger (at least before he was to become U.S. Secretary of State). The quotation below suggests that any American notions of a tiny clique of Soviet leaders hatching a worldwide conspiracy within the Kremlin walls (or Soviet notions of a cabal of American leaders doing likewise within the Oval Office of the White House), even during the height of the Cold War, might have been the figments of someone's imagination:

> The most frequent question that one is asked when abroad, or by people who are concerned with international affairs and have not seen policy made, is "What is American policy?" . . . [People] attempt to give a rationality and consistency to foreign policy which it simply does not have. I have found it next to impossible to convince Frenchmen that there is no such thing as an American foreign policy, and that a series of moves that have produced a certain result may not have been planned to produce that result.
>
> Foreigners looking at American policy have a tendency to assume that anything that happened was intended and that there is a deep, complicated purpose behind our actions. I wish this were true, but I don't believe that it is. In fact, I think that in any large bureaucracy it probably cannot be true, and this is probably the case with the Soviet Union also. We probably ascribe more consistency to Soviet foreign policy than really exists.[5]

Kissinger may have overstated the case a bit. Franklin Roosevelt, for example, had what he considered a "Great Design" for the post–World War II period, whose centerpiece was an active internationalist role for the United States. As we have noted, later American presidents invoked the "containment doctrine," "détente," or "human rights" as guiding principles of their foreign policy during the Cold War. Searching for new catchwords or phrases to define American foreign policy in the post–Cold War era, George Bush spoke of "the new world order," and Bill Clinton spoke of "enlargement" as a replacement for "containment."[6] These themes represented at least to some extent an attempt to give an overall rationale and sense of direction to U.S. foreign affairs. Indeed, every U.S. president has felt compelled, either in his inaugural address or in his first state of the union address, to announce how the nation's foreign policy would be charted over the next four years. Similar pronouncements can be found in the major addresses of leaders in other countries.

It is not that leaders make no attempt to develop a comprehensive framework for action. The thrust of Kissinger's remarks is that no matter how much a leadership tries to carve out a single, overall foreign policy, it inevitably finds itself having to make decisions about more discrete matters—whether, for example, to grant "most favored nation" trade status to China, whether to sell the latest fighter plane technology to Saudi Arabia, whether to give territorial asylum to a dissident writer and numerous other concerns that do not fit neatly into a "grand plan." As Roger Hilsman has noted: "Very often policy is the sum of a congeries of separate or only vaguely related actions."[7]

Types of Foreign Policy Decisions

Foreign policy should thus be thought of not as a single overall plan but, more realistically, as a series of hundreds of decisions that have to be made, which may hold together in a coherent fashion but which more likely will not. These hundreds of foreign policy decisions confronting a national government can be classified in a variety of ways. One way to categorize foreign policy decisions is according to *issue-area*—national security policy, economic policy, and so forth.[8] Another typology is based more on the *situational* setting in which decisions are made than on the substantive content of the decisions, for instance crisis as opposed to noncrisis decisions.[9] A number of observers have noted that issue-area and situational variables can affect the foreign policy process in important ways. For example, it is frequently argued that in the national security or military-strategic issue-area, and especially in crisis situations, the role of domestic politics tends to be diminished somewhat as leaders seek to behave as "statesmen" rather than "politicians." Let us focus on situational features and examine three categories of foreign policy decisions: macro-decisions, micro-decisions, and crisis decisions.

MACRO-DECISIONS

Some of the most important foreign policy decisions that a government must make relate to such matters as level of defense spending, level and type of foreign aid to be given or sought, arms control policy, and international trade policy. For a country such as the United States, with diverse global interests, decisions also must be made on Middle East policy, Asian policy, Latin American policy, and so forth. Narrower, but still fairly broad decisions might have to be made regarding, say, a reevaluation of relations with China or the terms of peaceful nuclear technology transfer to less developed countries. One can label such decisions **macro-decisions** in the sense that they involve relatively large, general concerns and are designed to establish guidelines or "rules of thumb" to be applied later to specific situations (for example, a request by the Pakistani government for additional uranium from the United States to fuel a nuclear reactor). Some guidelines are formulated in a relatively elaborate and explicit fashion, and others less so. The existence of well-developed general rules can make it easier for decision makers to handle specific problems as they arise. Macro-decisions are the kinds of decisions that conform most closely to what is ordinarily implied by the term "policy."

These decisions normally occur in a setting in which (1) the need to make the decision has been *anticipated* and is not in response to some sudden, surprise occurrence in the environment, (2) there is a relatively *lengthy time frame* in which to reach a decision, and (3) a *large variety of domestic political actors* inside and outside of the government can become involved in the decision process, although the decision is ultimately made by top-level officials. Such decisions may or may not involve serious "high-threat" concerns. Macro-decisions allow for foreign policy *planning* by bureaucratic staffs, although it is commonly noted that policymakers tend to be preoccupied with short-term rather than long-term concerns.

MICRO-DECISIONS

An enormous number of foreign policy decisions can be labeled **micro-decisions** (or, as they are sometimes called, "administrative" decisions). These may or may not involve the element of surprise and may or may not allow for lengthy deliberation. In any case, such decisions by definition normally involve concerns that are (1) relatively *narrow* in scope, (2) *low-threat* in seriousness, and (3) handled at the *lower levels of the government bureaucracy.* Examples might include the authorization of a visa by Austrian officials allowing a particular person to travel in Austria, the response to a request from an embassy in Malawi for additional office supplies, the determination of seating arrangements for visiting dignitaries at a British reception in Whitehall, and the approval of a $5 million credit extension allowing Bangladesh to purchase needed farm equipment.

The bulk of foreign policy decisions made by a government are micro-decisions. "The American State Department on any one day receives about 2,300 cables from American diplomatic and consular officials abroad providing information, requesting directions, or seeking permission to make certain decisions in the field. But . . . the Secretary of State will read only . . . 2 percent of the total. The State Department also sends out approximately 3,000 cables daily; . . . of these, the Secretary of State may see only six, and the President will have only one or two of the most important communications referred to his office."[10]

Micro-decisions are supposed to be based on macro-decisions; i.e., they are made by bureaucrats applying a standard set of guidelines. For example, U.S. officials use the Munitions List and International Traffic in Arms Rules to process 90 percent of the private arms sales license applications they receive. A change of policy at the macro-level associated with a relaxation of tensions with certain adversaries would mean that specific items would be dropped from the "restricted" munitions list and offered more openly for trade. However, administrative decisions are often made independently of, and possibly at variance with, the general policy. Although such decisions by themselves are unlikely to have significant consequences (even if a minor diplomatic incident may be created, for example, by an errant choice of dining utensils, which happened when some "made in Taiwan" chopsticks turned up at a Carter White House dinner honoring officials from mainland China), taken together they can add up to major foreign policy developments.

The relationship between micro- and macro-decisions can be seen in the U.S. handling of the Nelson Mandela affair. The general American policy of opposing communism in the 1950s and 1960s led to opposition to Nelson Mandela, leader of the African National Congress (which had ties to South African leftists) and to support for the *apartheid* policies of the South African government. This reportedly included a CIA tip during the Kennedy administration leading to Mandela's arrest and imprisonment in South Africa. Only with President Carter's new human rights policy in the 1970s, and a decline in the U.S.-Soviet rivalry in the 1980s, did the United States modify its treatment of the African National Congress, putting pressure on Pretoria that contributed to Mandela's release in 1989 after he had become an international *cause célèbre*.

CRISIS DECISIONS

A number of foreign policy decisions fall somewhere between the two types just discussed. Charles Hermann, for example, has identified eight possible decision "situations," each with its own distinct characteristics affecting the dynamics of the decision-making process.[11] One special category of decisions that has attracted the attention of Hermann and many other scholars involves crisis situations. **Crisis decisions** are made in situations normally characterized by (1) a *high degree of threat* and potential gravity, (2) a *finite time frame* in which to reach a decision, and (3) involvement of the *very highest level* of the foreign policy establishment in the decision process (usually in a small group setting). Hermann's initial definition of a crisis situation included the element of surprise, but he has since dropped that requirement from the definition.[12] Although it is possible that decision makers might not be completely surprised, a crisis ordinarily is occasioned by some change or disturbance in a state's environment—a potential turning point in its relationship with other states in the system—that is seen by its policymakers as threatening. Michael Brecher has defined a crisis as a situation entailing perceptions of "threat to basic values, finite time for response, and the likelihood of involvement in military hostilities."[13] Although a crisis is often associated with short response time, some crises can drag on for a long time (e.g., the Iranian hostage "crisis" faced by the Carter administration in 1979 and 1980, which lasted 444 days). At a minimum, a crisis entails a sufficiently serious problem to command the intense, sustained attention of the top leadership. One such situation, the Cuban missile crisis of 1962, may well be the most studied single case in history.

Some argue that much of what passes for foreign policy is really "crisis management," i.e., responding to the latest collapse of the Colombian government on Tuesday, the renewal of civil war in Lebanon on Wednesday, an attempted coup d'état in Liberia on Thursday, the skyjacking of a plane on Friday, and other such events. At times multiple crises can occur simultaneously and compete for attention, as in the case of the bombing of the U.S. Marine headquarters in Beirut and the American invasion of Grenada within the same week in 1983. However, it is a mistake to depict the foreign policy process as consisting of one round after another of crisis management. Foreign policymakers do not spend all their time lurching from one crisis to another any more than they do sitting at their desks pondering grand designs and stratagems. When crises occur, though, policymakers are clearly confronted with some of the most crucial decisions they are called on to make.

In the foreign policy process, the various types of decisions blend together, often imperceptibly. Some decisions, such as the Kennedy administration's commitment of 10,000 American troops to Vietnam as "advisory" counterinsurgency personnel in 1961, can set in motion a myriad of smaller administrative decisions, breed more than one crisis, and even come to dominate a country's foreign policy agenda for a decade—beyond anyone's expectations or intentions.

The Conventional View of Foreign Policy: States as Rational Actors

Those attempting to understand foreign policy—practitioners, scholars, and laymen alike—commonly view foreign policy as the work of a *unitary* actor (a nation-state or national government). Every day we hear references in conversation and news reports that "the United States" or "Washington" (or "Japan"

A WEEK OF CRISIS IN U.S. FOREIGN POLICY—LEBANON AND GRENADA (OCTOBER 22–28, 1983)

(Clockwise from top left)
Saturday, Oct. 22, 5:15 A.M.: President Reagan is briefed in his suite at the Augusta, Ga., National Golf Club by National Security Advisor McFarlane (seated in chair) and Secretary of State Shultz regarding a request by five Caribbean nations for a joint invasion of Grenada in response to a violent coup that had just occurred on the island.
Sunday, Oct. 23, 7:30 A.M.: While en route to Washington on Air Force One, the President confers with Shultz and McFarlane after having learned of the killing of 240 U.S. Marines by a terrorist bombing in Beirut, Lebanon.
9:30 A.M.: The President discusses the Beirut developments in the White House Situation Room with his chief advisors (seated clockwise from the President at the head of the table are Secretary of State Shultz, Deputy CIA Director MacMahon, Presidential Assistant Baker, National Security Advisor McFarlane, White House Counsel Meese, General Vessey of the Joint Chiefs of Staff, Secretary of Defense Weinberger, and Vice-President Bush).

or "Tokyo") has "decided" something or "done" something in the international arena. These are not just convenient shorthand expressions but a reflection of a natural tendency to reify the nation-state, i.e., to attribute human qualities to a collectivity. According to this conventional states-as-actors perspective, which is a hallmark of the realist paradigm, states are treated as "billiard balls"—reacting to each other's moves as billiard balls impact against each other on a pool table—with the resultant interactions constituting international relations.[14] Put another way, states are viewed here as if they were monolithic "black boxes" cranking out foreign policy decisions and behaviors based on national interest calculations, with the observer not having to look beneath the surface at the internal dynamics of the policymaking process.

Much of international relations can be understood in these "billiard ball" or "black box" terms. In this book we, too, at times have resorted to the shorthand notation in describing foreign policy behavior and have said that states acting through their national government are the lead players in the drama of international relations. Associated with this conventional view is the assumption that nation-states and their governments are *rational* actors. Graham Allison has commented that most people tend to explain international events in terms of a "rational actor" model, as the product of deliberate decisions of unified national governments:

> For example, on confronting the problem posed by the Soviet installation of strategic missiles in Cuba [in 1962] . . . [the] analyst frames the puzzle: Why did the Soviet Union decide to install missiles in Cuba? He then fixes the unit of analysis: governmental choice. Next, he focuses attention on . . . goals and objectives of the nation or government. And finally, he invokes certain patterns of inference: if the nation performed an action of this sort, it must have had a goal of this type. The analyst has "explained" this event when he can show how placing missiles in Cuba was a reasonable action, given Soviet strategic objectives. Predictions about what a nation will do or would have done are generated by calculating the rational thing to do in a certain situation, given specified objectives.[15]

THE RATIONAL ACTOR MODEL

Let us examine the assumptions of the **rational actor model** more closely. When faced with a decision-making situation—i.e., with a problem that requires resolution—rational individuals supposedly follow a certain process in which they

1. define the situation that calls for a decision, basing their assessment on an objective consideration of the facts
2. specify the goal(s) to be achieved in the situation (and, if there is a conflict among several goals, rank-order them as to priorities)

3.   consider all possible alternative means of achieving the goal(s)

4.   select the final alternative calculated to maximize achievement of the goal(s)

5.   take the necessary action to implement the decision

One can add a sixth step, evaluation of the consequences of an individual's actions, assuming that a rational actor will want to determine whether the goal in question has been achieved and whether similar actions can be expected to achieve similar goals in similar situations in the future.

This all sounds very simple and obvious, even if somewhat abstract. All of us like to think of ourselves as rational creatures. Yet few if any of us behave in the above fashion when having to make a decision. The rational actor model is essentially an "ideal type" that cannot be fully conformed to in the real world, whether the decisions involve which brand of beer to buy or more sober matters such as those confronting foreign policymakers. How many people are capable of viewing the world in a totally objective, unbiased manner?

"Gentlemen, the fact that all my horses and all my men couldn't put Humpty together again simply proves to me that I must have more horses and more men."

Drawing by Dana Fradon; © 1978 The New Yorker Magazine, Inc.

The rational problem solver at work: policy evaluation

How many undertake the effort to spell out goals and to come to grips with the often agonizing choices between equally desired but mutually incompatible benefits? How many have the time to ponder all conceivable options, or possess the complete information with which to arrive at the very best solution? And when others are being relied on to implement a decision, how many people follow through to ensure that the decision is executed as intended? Finally, how many people bother to review systematically the consequences of their decisions so as to draw proper lessons of possible use in the future?

Although the rational actor model is an ideal type, some decision makers come closer than others to fulfilling the requirements. To the extent that a decision maker approximates the model, that individual can be said to act more or less "rationally." As we have noted, in foreign policymaking rational behavior is associated with the pursuit of national interests, so that the criterion for judging whether a foreign policy decision is a rational one is generally whether it is calculated to promote national goals at reasonable costs or risks.

An Alternative View: States as Collections of Individuals, Groups, and Organizations That May or May Not Act Rationally

As analysis of foreign policy has become more sophisticated in recent years, it has become apparent that many factors can contribute to **nonrational behavior** on the part of states. This is especially so when one takes into account the fact that foreign policy decisions are made and implemented not by mechanistic actors called "the United States" or "Japan" but by specific persons who individually or in combination with each other are subjected to a multitude of societal and extrasocietal pressures when acting in the name of the state. Hence an alternative perspective on foreign policy has developed, which incorporates all of the various factors discussed in the previous chapter and focuses on the human decision makers themselves as actors responding to stimuli from both their external, international environment and their internal, domestic environment.[16] This alternative view is represented in Figure 6.1.

Although the rational actor (state-as-actor) model can provide important insights into nation-state behavior, models that focus on *individuals, groups,* and *organizations* as actors in the foreign policy process allow us to gain a richer, fuller understanding of such phenomena. In his well-known study of the Cuban missile crisis, Graham Allison argues that the best explanation of the U.S. naval blockade decision can be derived by analyzing the decision from several different "cuts," using not only a rational actor model (interpreting it as the outcome of the leadership's collective deliberations and shared view of what was the best way to protect American national security) but also

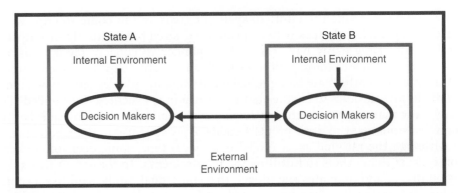

Figure 6.1
AN ALTERNATIVE TO THE "BILLIARD BALL" OR "BLACK BOX" VIEW OF FOREIGN POLICY

a "governmental politics" model (interpreting it as the result of intense bargaining and compromise among a group of different personalities who saw the situation from competing bureaucratic and other viewpoints), and an "organizational process" model (interpreting it as the outcome of various organizational procedures and routines that affected the collection and analysis of intelligence data and other aspects of the decision process).[17]

As we commented in our discussion earlier in this chapter, a country's entire foreign policy establishment does not become mobilized every time there is a decision to be made and implemented. Depending on the nature of the decision—the issue-area or situation—different parts of the foreign policy apparatus (different individuals, groups, and organizations) will become involved. The box on pages 231–233 deals with what one writer calls "intermestic" issues, focusing on the dynamics of U.S. trade policy in the 1970s, a subject that has definite parallels with current debates over U.S.-Japanese trade relations and the North American Free Trade Agreement (NAFTA); if anything, the link between the international and the domestic environment has become more complex and significant in the contemporary era. In the industrialized democracies especially, as "welfare" issues increasingly compete with "security" issues for attention on foreign policy agendas, the number of actors claiming membership in a state's "foreign policy establishment" is expanding accordingly, as is the potential for internal cleavages to affect policy. Executive branch agencies as well as legislative committees dealing with agricultural, energy, transportation, environmental, and other concerns—bodies that previously had little or no connection to the foreign policy arena—now frequently find themselves involved in the foreign policy process. These entities are pressured usually to promote the interests of particular domestic constituencies having the most direct stake in a given sector, reconciling the latter demands with the demands

THE INTERFACE BETWEEN DOMESTIC AND FOREIGN POLICY ISSUES AND PROCESSES: UNDERSTANDING U.S. TRADE POLICY

The United States has been called a "weak state," not in terms of its capability to exercise power internationally but in terms of the capability of its central governmental decision makers to exercise power vis-à-vis internal, societal actors.[1] More so than countries such as France or Japan, the United States has a highly pluralistic, fragmented governmental institutional structure and an historical aversion toward "big government" generally—often making it difficult for the top leadership to ride herd over not only domestic policy but also foreign policy.

It has been possible to overcome this "weak state" syndrome in the past when there have been major security threats presented by the international environment, for example, during World War II and during the Cold War, as conditions encouraged a strong presidency and permitted the White House to mobilize widescale domestic support for many overseas commitments. Indeed, some observers in the postwar period spoke of the American political system as having "two presidencies"—one in the domestic policy arena where the president was just one player among a myriad of political actors, and one in the foreign policy arena where, in contrast—consistent with the rational actor model—"politics stopped at the water's edge" and the president with his chief advisors was given great decision latitude to act on behalf of the state.[2] However, as Ryan Barilleaux shows in the case study below, even during the Cold War the domestic and foreign policy arenas were not always distinguishable, with trade policy being one area in which interest group, bureaucratic, and congressional politics had important impacts in limiting what the "central decision makers" could do. Foreign policy figures to become all the more politicized in the post–Cold War era.

"Intermestic issues" refers to those matters of international relations which, by their very nature, closely involve the domestic economy of a nation. In the United States, such issues as international trade, oil imports, immigration, and transnational pollution (acid rain, etc.) are "intermestic," for they all combine American foreign relations with the state of the economic health of the nation. They are issues that have been growing in importance for years, as the oil crisis of the 1970s demonstrated, and will be even more important in the future. . . . In many ways, trade is the classic intermestic issue: it is about the American economy as it interacts with the rest of the world. . . .

Richard Nixon had long been an advocate of freer international trade [i.e., minimal tariff and other barriers imposed by governments against foreign goods], but at the same time was sensitive to political pressures which moderated that view. In his 1968 campaign for the presidency, he had reaffirmed his commitment to free trade . . . but cited textiles as a "special case" to be given special treatment. The textile industry, concentrated in the South, had been hardest hit by Japanese competition, and Nixon sought to win Southern votes by promising that aforementioned special treatment. . . . The result of this combined pledge of free trade and help for textiles was the Trade Act of 1970, sent to Congress on November 18 of that year. . . . In general, it sought to enhance free trade by renewing the lapsed tariff-cutting authority of the 1962 Trade Expansion Act, modify and expand presidential control over trade barriers and retaliation to barriers, and protect domestic industry. . . .

The bill was soon caught up in a whirl of protectionist trade proposals submitted to the 91st Congress. Responding to a poor balance-of-trade and pressure from domestic interests, over three hundred members of the House had introduced some sort of import quota legislation. The Ways and Means Committee had before it fifty-nine bills related to steel imports, forty-seven to textiles, forty to dairy imports, twenty-four to footwear. . . . Of great importance was the fact that among this crowd was Wilbur Mills, chairman of the committee and long an advocate of free trade. At the Administration's request, he introduced a textile-import quota bill. . . .

The Mills bill was part of an overall strategy for dealing with the complex problem of trade, by dealing with an issue closely related to the Nixon trade proposal. That issue was an Administration effort to negotiate a voluntary agreement with Japan to reduce textile exports by that country. . . . Honoring his campaign pledge, and interested in the 1970 congressional elections, Nixon sought an agreement with the Japanese in order to aid the domestic textile industry through Japanese restraint. . . . Nevertheless, despite extensive secret and public discussions, meetings between President Nixon and Japanese prime minister Eisaku Sato, and Mills' proposal, no agreement was ever reached. . . .

Meanwhile, in the Senate, trouble was mounting for the President. Aware that time was running out for the 91st Congress, the Finance Committee began working on the trade bill in October. . . . Unfortunately for the President, the committee was chaired by Senator Russell Long, who favored protection of American industry because he felt that the United States was not being treated fairly by its trading partners. Under Long's influence, the committee voted on October 13 to attach the trade bill to the Social Security Amendments Act of 1970. . . .

On November 20, the Finance Committee reported the combined trade and Social Security bill to the Senate. Not only was it caught up in the controversy over free trade and protection, but over welfare and provisions in the Social Security bill as well. . . . At the urging of Senator Long, the Senate deleted the trade provisions of the combined bill and thus killed what remained of the Trade Act of 1970.

In the 1970 case [unlike an earlier trade policy episode in 1962], the force of domestic politics worked [against passage of trade legislation]. . . .

Throughout the 1960s, there was growing [protectionist] sentiment in the United States. . . . In this environment, even traditionally pro–free trade labor unions shifted to a protectionist stance. The AFL-CIO called for important quotas to protect American jobs, and the resulting labor-management coalition favoring protection was keenly felt in Congress. This general labor-management coalition was especially pronounced in certain areas and industries, such as the textile industry in the South and the shoe industry in Massachusetts, Pennsylvania, and New York. The result was strong pressure on Congress to do something about imports.

[1] Stephen D. Krasner, "Policy Making in a Weak State," in Stephen D. Krasner, *Defending the National Interest: Raw Materials, Investments, and U.S. Foreign Policy* (Princeton, N.J.: Princeton University Press, 1978), pp. 55–90.

[2] Aaron Wildavsky, "The Two Presidencies," *Trans-Action* (December 1966), pp. 7–14.

Source: Excerpted from Ryan J. Barilleaux, "The President, 'Intermestic' Issues, and the Risks of Political Leadership," *Presidential Studies Quarterly,* 15 (Fall 1985), pp. 754–767 (footnotes are omitted). Permission granted by the Center for the Study of the Presidency, publisher of *Presidential Studies Quarterly.*

of the external environment, rather than pursuing the national interest broadly defined.[18] Given these trends, it is likely to become that much harder in the future to conceptualize states as unitary, rational actors in world politics.

Note, for example, the number of actors that have been involved in developing U.S. policy with regard to protection of the ozone layer, which shields the planet from ultraviolet radiation:

At the end of what Ambassador Richard Benedick calls 'the interagency minuet' in preparation for the Vienna Convention for the Protection of the Ozone Layer, the final U.S. position 'was drafted by the State Department and was formally cleared by the Departments of Commerce and Energy, the Council on Environmental Quality, EPA [Environmental Protection Agency], NASA, NOAA [National Oceanographic and Atmospheric Administration], OMB [Office of Management and Budget], USTR [U.S. Trade Representative], and the Domestic Policy Council (representing all other interested agencies).' In addition to this formidable alphabet soup, White House units, like the Office of Science and Technology Policy . . . and the Council of Economic Advisors also got into the act.

In the United States in recent years, increasing involvement of Congress—and with it nongovernmental organizations (NGOs) and the broader public—has introduced a new range of interests that must ultimately be reflected in the national position. Similar developments seem to be occurring in other democratic countries.[19]

In the next section we examine the dynamics of foreign policy decision making, noting how nonrational (or at least quasi-rational) factors can intrude throughout the foreign policy process, even in the most threatening situations, when one might expect and hope that the greatest rationality would prevail.[20]

Nonrational Factors in Foreign Policy

Nonrational (or quasi-rational) factors can operate at various stages in the foreign policy process. This process includes (1) definition of the situation, (2) consideration of goals and means, and (3) the implementation and evaluation stages.

DEFINITION OF THE SITUATION

The need for a foreign policy decision does not exist until somebody identifies a problem "out there" that seems to require a response. We noted in the previous chapter that there can often be a gap between the "objective" environment ("reality") and the "psychological" environment ("image" of reality) of an individual. If the gap is wide, it can seriously distort the character of a problem and cause nonrational decision making from the start, because the definition of the situation—for example, whether some event constitutes a crisis—tends to structure the entire decision process, including *who* becomes involved in the decision and the time frame within which officials assume a decision must be reached.

A decision maker's failure to grasp the facts of a situation can have less to do with the quantity or quality of information received than with the manner in which the information is digested. To understand this point, one needs to understand the nature of *images*. All of us have a collection of images of the world, which constitutes a belief system or filter, through which we interpret the myriad events we are exposed to from one day to the next. Images help us construct reality, but they can also blind us to reality or severely bias our assessment of a given occurrence. In particular, there is a common tendency to filter out any stimuli—incoming bits of information—that do not square with our image of the world and, hence, threaten to upset our established mindset. Psychologists speak of *selective attention*, seeing only what we want to see or are habitually inclined to see, as well as *rationalization*, dismissing as unimportant "flukes" any happenings that cannot escape attention but do not conform to our image of things.[21]

Foreign policymakers are as susceptible to distorting reality as are any other decision makers. Robert Jervis has suggested that they have a natural tendency to misperceive their environment to some extent, particularly to view many states as more hostile than they really are and to assume not only that the *other* side is more "ruthless" and "devious" than their own state but also that it is cognizant of this.[22] Associated with such misperception is the tendency of a country's leadership to admonish the other side for what are thought to be aggressive designs and deceitful tactics without realizing that their own behavior may perhaps be a precise mirror image of their opponent's. It has been said that much of the Cold War and especially the nuclear arms race between the United States and the Soviet Union can be explained in terms of mutual distrust based on misperceptions of each other's intentions.[23]

Considerable research has been done in recent years in the area of **threat perception.** In a pioneering article, J. David Singer hypothesized that one nation's actions depends on the former's estimates of the latter's *capability* to do harm and the *intent* to do it.[24] When an adversary suddenly doubles its military spending or mobilizes several divisions of troops, decision makers find themselves of necessity speculating about the underlying intentions behind such behavior, in particular whether it seems to portend an imminent military attack or simply represents a bolstering of national defense. Given the great difficulty in determining an adversary's intentions, a country's foreign policymakers often engage in "worst-case analysis," i.e., assume the *worst* of the adversary and worry not about intentions but only about capabilities (what the latter *can* do). This is a standard tenet emphasized by the military establishment in most countries, based on the assumption that it is easier to estimate an enemy's capabilities than its intentions. However, even capabilities can be grossly misjudged, as in the case of the mythical "missile gap" that was reported to exist between the United States and the Soviet Union in the late fifties based on a top-level U.S. study; there was a gap, but contrary to the study, the United States was in the lead rather than the Soviet Union.

Although it might seem rational to be prepared for any contingency, however improbable, worst-case analysis can produce unwarranted fears that may lead to a conflict neither side wants. It should be added that the lenses through which leaders view the world are not always shaded dark and given to exaggerated perceptions of threat but can at times be rose-tinted and given to "wishful thinking" that can cause leaders to overlook a threat that truly exists. One of the most frequently cited examples of this is the Pearl Harbor attack, when American officials—operating on the assumption that the Japanese would not and could not launch an aerial raid on the U.S. naval base—ignored a stream of information that signaled an impending attack, including the actual radar detection of an approaching squadron of planes.[25] Other nations have suffered from such wishful thinking, including Israel in 1973 and the Netherlands in 1939–1940, when warned of probable enemy attacks.[26]

Because images color reality for foreign policymakers and shape their perceptions of situations, it is important to understand how images themselves are shaped. Some images are based on a nation's *historical experiences.* As such, they may be widely shared among the members of a country's foreign policy establishment and even by its populace as a whole. For example, we noted earlier that the "Munich" experience had a profound impact on an entire generation of Americans after World War II. The problem with historically based images is that they can be misapplied to contemporary circumstances. The failure of the Western democracies to resist aggression in Austria, Ethiopia, Manchuria, and, finally, Czechoslovakia in the 1930s was the first thought that popped into President Truman's mind as he flew from Independence, Missouri, to Washington to handle the fast-breaking events at the start of the Korean War in 1950.[27] Conceivably, the Korean situation could have been interpreted as a civil war or as a confined regional conflict; but Truman, like most of his contemporaries, viewed it in larger terms as part of a global challenge that had to be confronted. A decade later the same Munich analogy was applied again by American leaders to events in Vietnam, a country that was depicted as a "domino"—if it were allowed to fall, the result would be the collapse of all other "dominoes" in Southeast Asia. In the case of both Korea and Vietnam, scholars have argued that a historically based image, wrongly applied, caused a fundamental misreading of the situation and contributed to imprudent U.S. foreign policy decisions. In the words of Ernest May, "history overpowered calculation."[28]

Kenneth Boulding has noted that a nation's image of itself and of others is shaped not only by *specific* historical events such as Munich (which may affect only the generation that lived through them) but even more so by *cumulative* historical experiences as retold in family gatherings or in the civics textbooks to which all children are exposed in school.[29] Some peoples have experienced conflict between each other so often in the past that there develops an ingrained animosity that affects their perceptions of each other. Rivalries that may have been founded on real conflicts of interest, such as border disagreements, can be sustained through the years by less tangible factors. The traditional Franco-German and Russo-Chinese rivalries, for example, have been much discussed.[30] Culture and ideology can also form the basis for worldviews held by a country's leadership and citizenry that are resistant to change and greatly impact its foreign policy. Ideas, such as "free trade" and "sovereignty," when they are internalized by the foreign policy establishment and become habits of mind, can be far more powerful in driving foreign policy than the pure calculation of national interests.[31]

We have noted that some images are widely shared by the members of a country's foreign policy establishment and by its people. However, some images are held much less widely and may be peculiar to only a few individuals, based on their particular past experiences as well as present circumstances. Regarding *personal past experiences,* we have mentioned Kennedy's humiliating meeting with Khrushchev in Vienna, which affected the two leaders' views of each other. The Vienna encounter may have contributed, along with Kennedy's rather restrained policies during the Berlin Wall and Bay of Pigs episodes in 1961, to Khrushchev's expectation that Kennedy would not contest the installation of nuclear missiles in Cuba in October 1962. The Vienna experience also may have contributed in part to Kennedy's perception of Soviet missile deployments as a crisis situation involving a high threat to U.S. security. Some other U.S. officials, such as Robert McNamara, defined the situation in much less menacing terms and did not feel it justified going to the brink of war.[32] It has been argued that Kennedy *wanted* to believe that U.S.-Soviet relations could be improved and that Khrushchev would not dare risk a confrontation by deploying missiles ninety miles away from the United States. Given this image of reality, Kennedy initially ignored early intelligence warnings suggesting otherwise—even ordering the cessation of U-2 reconnaissance flights over the western half of Cuba that might have produced conclusive proof of missile deployment earlier than October—and became all the more outraged when later discovery of the missiles ultimately shattered his image.[33]

The *personal present circumstances* of decision makers also may shape their image of the world and, hence, their perception of a situation. It has been pointed out, for example, that where one *sits* in the foreign policy bureaucracy at a given moment may well determine where one *stands* on some issue and, in particular, what "face" of the issue one sees.[34] Even within a country's military bureaucracy, as suggested earlier, disagreements occur between different branches of the armed services: "Every rival group within the American system—the bomber pilots, the fighter jockeys, the missilemen, and the carrier admirals—[during the Cold War produced] its own interpretation of Soviet behavior to justify its claim for more money."[35] Although this might be an overly cynical view of the American military, there is little question that bureaucratic "blinders" exist, which can subconsciously bias one's definition of a problem.

Although all decision makers approach situations with certain built-in predispositions grounded in their image of reality, some individuals have more *open* images than others, i.e., they are more receptive to information that contradicts their image and are more amenable to revising that image. A classic study of U.S. Secretary of State John Foster Dulles revealed that his image of the world, which was not only based on Munich but reinforced by his strict anti-communist, Presbyterian upbringing, was particularly *closed;* more than most of his contemporaries, Dulles was inflexible in his negative view of the Soviet Union during the 1950s and refused to interpret any Soviet action in a positive light, even when the Soviets planned to reduce their armed forces by 1 million.[36] Ronald Reagan, as ideologically driven as Dulles in his anti-communism, nonetheless came to adjust his view of the Soviet Union during his second term in office when Gorbachev's peaceful overtures on Afghanistan and other matters rendered the President's "evil empire" image untenable. The degree to which a decision maker is open to new information can depend on the situation itself. Some scholars have hypothesized that in crisis situations, for example, decisions makers may feel a need to be as open-minded as possible to get the most accurate picture of reality, but because of conditions of stress and urgency, there may be a tendency to fall back on established, stereotypical images of the enemy.[37]

Until now, we have been speaking primarily in terms of *individual* decision making. It might be argued that the problems we have cited that are associated with individual images are exaggerated, because foreign policy decisions are rarely if ever the product of a single individual but normally result at least indirectly from the input of *groups* and *organizations* involved in the decision process. Can we not assume that "reality testing" will occur and a reasonably accurate definition of a situation will emerge from the competing images likely to be found among many different individuals in either a group or organizational setting?

Although *groups* might be expected to produce better decisions than individuals acting alone, two (or more) heads may not necessarily be better than one. Irving Janis, who has studied small-group dynamics, has noted that under certain circumstances groups can breed their own sort of irrationality and cause individuals to act less rationally than they might if they were alone. In particular, he has described a phenomenon called **groupthink,** whereby pressures for group conformity may lead individual members to suppress any personal doubts they may have about the emerging group consensus regarding the definition of the situation or some other aspect of a foreign policy decision.[38] For example, in the case of the surprise attack on Pearl Harbor, Janis argues that the failure to anticipate the Japanese raid despite several prior intelligence clues was at least partly due to the clubby atmosphere that prevailed among the American admirals in Hawaii, causing any surfacing of individual reservations about the vulnerability of the naval base to be drowned out by a sense of collective invincibility. Janis and others have pointed out that crisis situations, in particular, are dominated by small-group decision making, with the size of the group tending to shrink as the gravity of the situation increases.[39]

One might expect individual or group errors to be minimized by the existence of fairly large *organizations* within the foreign policy bureaucracy of most countries, on which decision makers rely for information in defining a situation. There are certain "standard operating procedures" whereby problems are brought to the attention of various levels of the foreign policy establishment. Such procedures, designed for efficiency, may appear cut-and-dried. However, when several events break simultaneously and compete for attention, communications systems can become so overloaded that some important problems are placed on the "back burner" or are responded to in an inflexible manner. In addition, when many different people handle information as it is circulated up and down the bureaucracy and is condensed at various points, the possibility always exists that some key information will be lost or refined beyond recognition along the way.

There is a special problem of subordinates passing along only that information that they think their superiors will want to hear. Patrick McGarvey, a former employee of the U.S. Defense Intelligence Agency (DIA), has written that during the Vietnam War the intelligence reports emanating from DIA field personnel tended to conform to the needs of the Joint Chiefs of Staff; when the generals wanted to show success after the Tet Offensive of 1968, the reports inflated enemy body counts, and later when the generals needed to justify their request for an additional 200,000 men, the reports projected gloomier estimates.[40] One way around this problem is to create multiple sources and channels of information in the hope that "good" information will drive out "bad" information. U.S. leaders, for example, rely not only on the Defense Intelligence Agency but the Central Intelligence Agency (CIA) and a variety of other information-gathering agencies. Still, the dynamics of organizational behavior can further complicate the problems associated with individual and group decision making and contribute to inaccurate definitions of the situation.

CONSIDERATION OF GOALS AND MEANS

Biased views of the world can foster irrationality not only in defining a situation but also in subsequent stages of the decision process, including the consideration of goals and means relevant to the situation. To the extent that decision makers seriously attempt to formulate concrete foreign policy goals, they may at times confuse *national* interests with *personal* interests or goals. The statement by John Kennedy on discovering the Soviet deployment of missiles in Cuba ("He [Khrushchev] can't do that to *me!*")[41] suggests that it was not only security but prestige at stake in 1962—in particular, Kennedy's own personal prestige and credibility, and not necessarily that of the nation.

Likewise, Lyndon Johnson's escalation of the Vietnam War in a search for "peace with honor" might have been guided more by his own desire to salvage some respect for his presidency after the loss of thousands of American lives than by a need to defend national honor and vindicate the nation's suffering. Admittedly, there can be a fine line between a nation's reputation or credibility being at stake and that of an individual leader, but it is a line that can mean the difference between rationality and nonrationality when it leads to foreign policy decisions based on *machismo.*

We noted earlier that foreign policymakers take into account to some extent the possible domestic political repercussions of their decisions. For leaders in democratic countries, in particular, the goal of reelection may well blur their foreign policy judgments; arms control proposals that might be entirely rational in the context of international politics might represent political suicide in the context of domestic politics, if accepted by a leader in a country in which the electorate is in favor of tougher policies against an adversary. One would expect leaders in crisis situations, more than in other situations, to subordinate domestic political considerations in particular and personal goals in general to the "national interest," although it may be impossible to untangle all these concerns. Even in as explosive a situation as the Cuban missile crisis, there was at least one instance in which domestic political concerns were aired, as one member of ExCom (the Executive Committee of the National Security Council) passed a note to another suggesting "the very real possibility that if we allow Cuba to complete installation . . . of missile bases, the next House of Representatives [after the upcoming November congressional elections] is likely to have a Republican majority."[42] Most evidence shows that domestic politics played only a marginal role in the blockade decision, but even the possibility that midterm congressional elections could have remotely affected such a momentous decision should give one pause for reflection.

In addition to self-interests, *group* or *organizational* goals can become the overriding preoccupation of officials. Janis's study of groupthink indicates that the maintenance of group cohesion and consensus may become an end in itself and subtly dominate all other considerations. He suggests that this was one factor that operated in the deliberations of the "Tuesday lunch group" that advised Lyndon Johnson on bombing and other decisions during the Vietnam War without ever rethinking the basic Vietnam policy.

Many studies, including Graham Allison's, have pointed to the tendency of bureaucrats to articulate foreign policy goals that happen to coincide with the organizational mission of their particular unit. Bureaucratic units at times may feel as threatened by their own possible extinction as by the extinction of the nation, although one is reminded of the remark by a former U.S. Secretary of State that "the nearest thing to immortality on Earth is a government bureau."[43] When President Carter was attempting to reduce the Washington bureaucracy, his acting budget director was quoted as saying: "Only two federal programs have ever been flatly abolished—Uncle Sam no longer makes rum in the Virgin Islands and no longer breeds horses for the U.S. cavalry."[44] Interestingly, the horse cavalry unit within the U.S. Defense Department managed to justify its existence well into the atomic era, with the unit not being disbanded until 1951 and the last army mule retired in 1956. Edward Katzenbach has noted that the U.S. horse cavalry was not alone in its survival instincts and that similar units managed to persist for a long time as part of the armed forces of several European countries as well.[45]

In a bureaucratic society such as Russia as well, decisions that to some outsiders might appear to be carefully aimed at national security concerns may in fact be more a function of the vagaries of **bureaucratic politics.** For example, one writer observed during the Cold War that "new Soviet missiles seem to be born as quadruplets. In the 1960s they deployed the SS-7-8-9-11 missiles; the 1970s generation are the SS-16-17-18 and 19 missiles. In the 1980s they . . . deployed another generation of four missiles. Why always in fours? U.S. experts say that the organization that designs Soviet missiles has four separate design bureaus, and that each is allowed to design a new generation."[46] Hence, foreign leaders who brooded about Soviet strategic intentions underlying such missiles may have missed part of the rationale behind them. It is interesting to speculate on whether this pattern will continue in the future, even in a vastly changed international climate. Both the Russian and American defense establishments have been resistant to any significant retrenchment and restructuring of their armed forces, although the recent systemic developments are necessarily prompting considerable rethinking.

We noted earlier that decision makers rarely come close to compiling an exhaustive list of possibilities when searching for alternative means of achieving a given goal. In many instances, particularly in crisis situations, time constraints seriously limit the number of alternatives that can be discussed. In addition, the same images that can distort the definition of the situation can restrict the menu of alternatives considered, foreclosing certain options in the minds of decision makers. Leaders may even believe there is "no choice" but to act in a certain fashion.[47] There is a tendency for one nation's leaders to assume that leaders in other states have a greater range of choices and more decision latitude.[48]

In the final selection of alternatives, the tendency is to engage in "satisficing" rather than "maximizing" behavior, i.e., to choose what seems to be the first satisfactory solution to the problem, which is not necessarily the best alternative.[49] Especially in *organizational* decision making, there is a tendency to make *low-risk* decisions that are calculated to avoid "rocking the boat," the concern being not so much upsetting the ship of state but upsetting existing organizational routines. On the latter point, Joseph de Rivera has hypothesized that "while an individual official might be willing to take great risks, the process of consultation and group discussion will produce a more moderate, conservative policy."[50] Although a low-risk mentality, based on a concern about "damage limitation," may be a sound approach to foreign policy decision making in general, it may prove harmful if a particular situation or problem calls for more drastic, innovative measures.

Occasionally decision makers engage in the opposite kind of behavior, taking *high-risk* decisions that represent a gigantic "roll of the dice." In contrast to de Rivera, Janis argues that *groups* under certain conditions may be more prone than individuals to act on the basis of passion and emotion rather than reason. He cites the German philosopher Friedrich Nietzsche, who observed that "madness is the exception in individuals but the rule in groups."[51] High-risk decisions made without careful consideration of the possible consequences clearly have the potential for more disastrous outcomes than low-risk decisions, although both may contain some element of nonrationality. Scholars have pointed out that crisis situations, almost by definition, involve some degree of heightened commitment to "risk taking" by national leaders.[52]

IMPLEMENTATION AND EVALUATION

Bureaucracies have standard operating procedures not only for channeling information but also for ensuring that decisions taken toward the top will be implemented routinely by those below. Although much implementation occurs routinely, some does not. Especially with "macro" decisions, decision making at the top usually produces only the broad outlines of policy, so that much is left to the discretion of middle-level and low-level bureaucrats involved in the execution of policy. Hence, decisions may be misinterpreted by those responsible for implementation. The implementation of decisions may also be consciously delayed or even totally ignored at times by parts of the bureaucracy that have been ordered to take some action with which they disagree, particularly when it entails a major change in established organizational practices.[53]

The President of the United States has sometimes been referred to as the "single most powerful person in the world," owing to the black code box that always travels with him that can enable him to order a nuclear strike at any moment. However, the president may frequently have great difficulty getting his orders obeyed within his own bureaucracy. The frustrations experienced by Harry Truman were reflected in his much-quoted statement on handing the presidency over to General Eisenhower in 1952: "He'll sit here and he'll say, 'Do this! Do that!' And nothing will happen. Poor Ike—it won't be a bit like the Army."[54]

Even in a crisis situation, when one would hope that the utmost rationality would prevail throughout the decision process, there may be a gap at the end between the making of a decision and its implementation. The Cuban missile crisis case is rich with examples of presidential decisions that were either ignored or almost ignored. When Khruschev offered to remove Soviet missiles from Cuba in exchange for the removal of U.S. Jupiter missiles from Turkey, Kennedy became livid, because he discovered only at that moment that the obsolete American missiles were still there despite his order for their withdrawal, issued twice in previous months. When an American U-2 plane accidentally strayed into Soviet air space at the height of the crisis, threatening a serious provocation, Kennedy could only remark about the unauthorized act that "there is always some so-and-so who doesn't get the word."[55] Another incident involved Secretary of Defense McNamara, who paid a visit to the office of Admiral Anderson, the Chief of Naval Operations, to ensure personally that the blockade decision reached by ExCom would be implemented by the Navy exactly as the President had intended, i.e., with armed force to be used only as a last resort. McNamara asked Anderson what the Navy would do if a Soviet ship's captain refused to permit an inspection of his cargo, at which point the admiral waved a copy of the *Manual of Naval Regulations* and shouted "It's all in there." McNamara responded: "I don't give a damn what John Paul Jones would have done. I want to know what you are going to do, now." The meeting ended with the admiral admonishing the Secretary of Defense: "Now, Mr. Secretary, if you and your deputy will go back to your offices, the Navy will run the blockade."[56] A particularly glaring lapse in presidential control over operational military activities during the crisis—one that was unknown even to ExCom members until 1987, when 25th anniversary retrospectives brought together participants in the event—was the decision of the commanding general of the Strategic Air Command to place American forces on full-scale nuclear alert by using open channels of communication easily accessible to Soviet intelligence rather than using coded messages.[57]

We cite these examples not to suggest that bureaucratic "snafus" are inevitable, only that they can happen and can conceivably have dire, unintended consequences. When a mistake does occur, at whatever point in the decision process, one would hope that corrective actions would be taken to avoid similar mistakes in the future. References are commonly made to the "lessons" of Munich or Vietnam or some other experience, as if foreign policymakers regularly sit down and systematically review the consequences of their decisions.[58] Program evaluation, whereby one assesses the impact of a foreign aid program or some other policy decision, is supposedly an important activity in which bureaucracies engage to determine if goals are being achieved.

However, given the dynamics of individual, group, and organizational decision making, it is questionable how often serious evaluation occurs and how much learning results. Postmortems on the anatomy of decisions may be carefully performed after a catastrophic event such as a major war, but on other occasions evaluation may be a cursory exercise. More thought normally goes into the making of a decision than into the reexamination of one, because foreign policymakers (like most of us) feel too busy to dwell at any length on the past. Careful reflection by statesmen may often have to wait until they write their memoirs, long after their foreign policy decision-making days are over and at a time when their reconstruction of events may be biased by their desire to preserve their place in history in the best possible light.

Even when evaluation does occur, some lessons are misapplied, as in the case of the Munich analogy. Other lessons are never learned, as reflected in the use of strategic bombing of North Vietnamese villages by the United States during the Vietnam War in an effort to lower the enemy's will and ability to resist, despite the findings of U.S. Strategic Bombing Surveys after World War II that showed similar tactics had failed to have much impact on Nazi Germany.[59] As noted at the outset of this book, many elements of "conventional wisdom" manage to persist among leaders even though history has proved such assumptions to be of dubious validity.

To conduct policy evaluation, goals must be sufficiently articulated so that clear-cut criteria can be employed whereby one can determine success or failure. In some cases, however, foreign policy goals can be so sketchy to begin with that it may be impossible to assess performance accurately when it comes time for evaluation. In other cases, where concrete goals have been identified and ample criteria exist to judge the impact of a policy, decision makers are more apt to exaggerate success than admit failure, as with the unwillingness of U.S. officials during the Vietnam War to recognize all the indicators showing that the war was a losing proposition.

We have been discussing evaluation in the context of rationality. However, there is another context in which it can be treated. When one measures success or failure in terms of such criteria as the square miles of territory gained or lost, the number of enemy soldiers or one's own soldiers killed, or the number of friendly dictators one is able or unable to keep in power, one is engaging in the kinds of judgments that move decision making from the realm of rationality into another realm—the realm of *ethics*.

Ethics and Foreign Policy

It is frequently said, primarily by those harboring realist notions of world politics, that "morality has no place in foreign policymaking." It is not always clear whether such statements mean morality *does not* play any role in foreign policy decisions, or *should not* play any role in foreign policy decisions. Let us briefly examine, then, two distinct issues. One is an empirical question. To what extent, if any, do ethical considerations (as opposed to cold, hard calculation of self-interest) influence foreign policy decisions? The second is a normative question. To what extent, if any, should ethical considerations be allowed to enter the foreign policy decision calculus?

In addressing the first question, ethical principles have regularly been sacrificed to self-interests in the affairs of states, as we stated earlier, notably in the case of the United States, which has consciously cultivated a "do-gooder" image in the world. Still, does this mean morality never affects the foreign policy decisions of the United States or any other country? Only an extreme cynic would answer that morality is totally irrelevant. Indeed, one can cite many examples in the American case and other cases in which foreign policymakers freely took action that on balance contributed nothing to national interests and may have even entailed considerable national sacrifice. For example, in 1979, the United States admitted roughly 15,000 Indo-Chinese refugees a month, imposing a substantial economic burden on many local American communities responsible for relocating the "boat people." The skeptic might argue that a large, wealthy country such as the United States could afford to absorb a few thousand refugees and that it did so out of a desire to turn world opinion against the communist regimes of Southeast Asia and out of pangs of conscience for contributing to the refugees' plight, which stemmed from the Vietnam War; the skeptic also might note the tendency of the United States to accept refugees fleeing from left-wing dictatorships more readily than those fleeing from right-wing persecution. However, the fact remains that the rescue of the boat people was in many respects a generous gesture that did not have to be made.

Likewise, the ultimate decision by the United States and NATO allies to send troops into the former Yugoslavia in the name of "humanitarian intervention" could be viewed as a belated effort to salvage respect and prestige, but it nonetheless entailed considerable national sacrifice and risks, aimed at stopping the carnage in what was Europe's worst fighting since World War II. If one is prepared to read ulterior motives into every foreign policy action, then admittedly one is not likely to find too many cases of genuine altruism. Earthquake and other international disaster relief efforts will be dismissed as world public relations gimmicks; the keeping of commitments and promises will be dismissed as expedients necessary to maintain one's credibility; and so forth.

Although moral pronouncements often can cloak self-serving decisions, there is evidence that even in crisis situations—when one would most expect practical considerations to override all else—ethical concerns may be seriously weighed in the decision-making process. Irving Janis discusses the explicit treatment of moral issues by the members of ExCom during as volatile a situation as the Cuban missile crisis:

> During the Cuban missile crisis, members of the Executive Committee explicitly voiced their concerns about the morality of the policy alternatives they were considering, thus forestalling deceitful, clandestine actions. . . . For example, on the second day of the crisis, George Ball vigorously objected to the air-strike option, arguing that a surprise attack would violate the best traditions of the United States and would harm the moral standing of the nation, whether or not the attack proved to be militarily successful. To the surprise of several members of the group, Robert Kennedy continued the argument, calling attention to the large toll of innocent human lives that would result. Urging a decent regard for humanity, the Attorney General pointed out that a surprise air attack would undermine the United States' position at home and abroad by sacrificing America's humanitarian heritage and ideals. He emphasized this moral stance by stating that he was against acting as the Japanese had in 1941 by resorting to a "Pearl Harbor in reverse."[60]

As this commentary suggests, there sometimes may be a fine line between morality and self-interest, with the two not necessarily being incompatible. In Robert Kennedy's mind, the thought of launching a surprise attack on Cuba appeared both immoral and against America's long-term interests, with the former concern seemingly weighing at least as heavily as the latter. Similarly, the end of colonialism can be traced not only to its increased costliness and diminished payoffs for colonial powers but also to new normative ideas that took hold after World War II.[61] Some observers have noted also that decision makers generally feel a need to take only those actions that can be publicly justified in some fashion, so that some options will be rejected if they are considered so immoral and indefensible as to defy justification.[62]

Clearly, then, foreign policy decision makers to some extent include ethical considerations in their deliberations, although we do not want to exaggerate their role. The question remains, however, whether ethics *should* be included

SIDELIGHT

THE ETHICS OF SPYING IN THE POST–COLD WAR ERA

Clandestine intelligence gathering in international affairs—spying—has long been recognized as both necessary and legitimate for national security purposes. During the Cold War, intelligence agencies such as the American CIA and NSA (National Security Agency), the Soviet KGB, and the British MI5 used both high-tech electronic and satellite reconnaisance devices ("TECHMINT") as well as James Bond–type secret agents ("HUMINT") to acquire valuable information about their adversaries' intentions and capabilities. The NSA was so shrouded in secrecy that some said the acronym stood for "No Such Agency." Far more controversial—and more open to moral question—than the intelligence-gathering function performed by the CIA and KGB was the so-called "covert action" function, i.e., the use of assassination and other "dirty tricks" to intervene actively in the internal affairs of foreign countries. For example, based on reports in several publications, including Victor Marchetti and John Marks, *The CIA and the Cult of Intelligence,* CIA agents reputedly made repeated assassination attempts against Fidel Castro of Cuba in the 1960s; the methods they employed included the use of exploding seashells, a poisoned fountain pen, a diving suit treated with tuberculosis bacteria (to be given to him as a gift), and reliance on Mafia operatives.

In the post–Cold War era, intelligence agencies are searching for new missions to perform and, as seen below, have found "economic spying" to be a growth industry. Ethical questions continue to surround such activities, especially when allies spy on each other.

Imagine you are in the White House, drawing up a list of hot spots abroad where the nation's intelligence agencies should be nosing around. A few things to watch are obvious: Serbian troop movements, the Iraqi and North Korean nuclear programs, and China's military maneuvers off Taiwan's coast.

But does it make sense for the Central Intelligence Agency to leap on the rumors . . . that a major Japanese bank might be about to go under? If it happened, such a collapse could set off a cash crisis that could circle the globe in minutes, requiring the Federal Reserve to pump billions of dollars into the system to prevent what the Treasury Department delicately calls "a contagion effect."

in such deliberations. Some students of international politics go so far as to argue that the normal canons of morality observed between individuals—honesty, trustworthiness, and the like—simply do not apply between nations and that any statesman who attempts to behave morally when acting in behalf of the nation is a fool.

With the Japanese Government unlikely to volunteer much information, learning the truth could require waging a surveillance campaign against Japan—America's most important political friend in the Pacific—with the same ferocity as is customary against a military opponent . . . With so many in Washington repeating the mantra that economic security and national security are now synonymous, is such spying to be expected?

The question of how far to go to secure American economic interests is especially sensitive in Washington these days, after revelations that the CIA listened in on the conversations of Japanese negotiators [and Toyota and Nissan auto executives] during heated automobile talks last spring—one example of what has quietly become routine practice. Japanese officials (who are among the world's premier practitioners of economic espionage) feigned shock and demanded explanations.

There is nothing new about spying on allies: Just ask the Israelis. Nor is assessing the economies of friends and enemies a new CIA task: Its analysts spent four decades tracking the Soviet Union's industrial capability and the better part of last year peeling back the layers of Mexico's financial balancing acts. Still, the elevation of commercial interests to what Secretary of State Christopher calls "the very top of our foreign policy agenda" has deepened the agency's clandestine economic intelligence-gathering. . . .

In just a few years, what had been a trickle of economic intelligence about Japan, Germany, France, Britain and others has turned into a torrent. Every day the Treasury, the U.S. Trade Representative's Office, and the Commerce Department receive raw and digested intelligence on everything from France's position on letting more Hollywood movies into the European Union to the blandishments that foreign governments offer Indonesia's ministers for a slice of the boom in power generation. The intelligence agencies, eager to prove that their $28 billion budget is as vital to American security as it was in the days of counting Soviet missiles, are more than happy to oblige. . . .

If the economic stakes are high enough, it may make perfect sense to turn the nation's satellites on Japanese bankers. The problem is how to explain it to the Japanese when it all becomes embarrassingly public, as this sort of thing inevitably does. The State Department is still working on that one, and no one expects it to have a convincing answer any time soon.

Source: David E. Sanger, "When Spies Look Out for the Almighty Buck," *New York Times*, October 22, 1995. Copyright © 1995 by the New York Times Company. Reprinted by permission.

It is true that any statesman who seeks to act ethically in world affairs faces great difficulties. The first problem involves the issue of "moral relativism." One cannot assume that actions taken on moral grounds will be appreciated by others as such, especially in a system with such sharp ideological and cultural differences as the international system. One of the factors that complicated Jimmy

Carter's well-intentioned human rights policy was the fact that the values that Americans seemingly wished to promote ("political rights" such as freedom of speech and press) were not as important to people in some societies as certain other values ("economic rights" such as the right to full employment); in the case of cultures that had no tradition of democratic government or individual liberty, the United States found itself in the position of attempting to impose its value system on other people, an ethically questionable posture. Although it may be true that there are many competing notions of morality in the world, the moral relativism argument can be carried only so far. There are, after all, at least a few norms that are universally or widely held (e.g., the prohibition against murder).

Another weakness in the Carter human rights policy points to the second problem surrounding ethical considerations in international relations: the assumption that one country alone by its example can move others to act morally if they are not so inclined. Carter discovered that trying to save the world by oneself may lead only to martyrdom. When the Carter administration initially withheld nuclear technology and other economic items from certain authoritarian regimes in Latin America and elsewhere, making such benefits contingent on liberalization of their political systems, those regimes were able to turn to France, West Germany, and other countries for whom the opportunity to do business overrode any moral objections about the customers. Given this example and other similar examples, such as the case of the Carter administration's initial attempt to exercise unilateral restraint in arms sales abroad only to find other countries plugging the gap, it is commonly argued that "if we don't sell it to them, somebody else will, so why should we be the ones to make the sacrifice?" Such arguments are frequently heard today in the post–Cold War era, as many countries see the promotion of arms exports as critical to their economies.

In other words, this is the familiar "two wrongs make a right" or "everybody does it" problem. Similar arguments have been used to justify the practice of corporate bribery of foreign government officials to obtain lucrative contracts, the logic being that international business is conducted according to a different code of rules than that considered acceptable within national economies. Such arguments are not without cogency, although there is a certain fatalism about them that tends to produce self-fulfilling prophecies.

The third problem is the "ends justify the means" syndrome, i.e., the temptation to excuse the most heinous deeds if they are done in the pursuit of what are thought to be noble causes. Given the ends that may be at stake in international politics, such as national survival, there is a special temptation for leaders to adopt an "anything goes" attitude. Dropping atomic bombs, supporting ruthless dictators, and assassinating foreign agents have all been done in the name of such things as national defense and the preservation of liberty. Whereas Robert Kennedy felt that a surprise air strike against Cuba in 1962 would have been morally repugnant, Dean Acheson and some other members of ExCom considered it absolutely essential for U.S. security. The atomic bombs that were dropped on Hiroshima and Nagasaki in 1945 were thought to be the only measures capable of convincing the Japanese to surrender unconditionally and, hence, shortening the war and limiting further Allied casualties.[63] Actually, the A-bomb decision did not pose as deep and unprecedented an ethical dilemma for American leaders as sometimes depicted, because decisions made earlier in the war to bomb Dresden and Hamburg as well as Tokyo with conventional weapons had already contributed to more civilian casualties than were to be produced at Hiroshima and Nagasaki.[64] More recently, the Reagan administration invoked national security arguments to justify its secret mining of Nicaraguan harbors aimed at harassing Nicaragua's Marxist government, an action that seemed hardly in character for a country that the President had proclaimed was a "beacon to the world" as an exemplar of civilized and enlightened conduct. Although the ends might occasionally justify the means, relying on this axiom too much may leave a nation physically intact but ethically bankrupt; particularly in a democracy, excessive reliance on secrecy and violence in foreign policy can undermine the very societal values one is presumably seeking to protect. (See the Sidelight on pages 246–247 for a discussion of "dirty tricks" played in international relations.)

Related to all these problems is the criticism many realists make that moral considerations may contribute to irrational foreign policy decisions based on either naive sentimentality or reckless messianism. In this sense, then, morality may be yet another source of nonrationality at times. One can only conclude that the issues associated with ethics in international affairs are indeed delicate, although not necessarily so insurmountable that one must dismiss ethics as a component of foreign policy decision making.

Conclusion (One Last Thought on Rationality)

It is safe to say that one would generally prefer rational to nonrational behavior on the part of foreign policymakers.[65] However, one cannot assume that a decision rationally made will necessarily be a "good" one even if a leader follows the rational actor decision process almost perfectly. Passing judgment on the soundness of some foreign policy decision must ultimately await the response of *other* states. As Janis and others have pointed out, although the ExCom decision-making process during the Cuban missile crisis was in many ways the model of rationality, the resultant blockade decision could have produced a nuclear holocaust *if the Soviets had decided to react differently than they did.* In Secretary of State Rusk's own words at the time: "We're eyeball to eyeball, and I think the other fellow just blinked."[66]

The simple fact is that the outcome of a given situation depends on the decisions made by at least *two* sides. It depends on *your* decision as well as *their* decision and the interaction between the two. Hence, we turn in the next chapter to an examination of the dynamics of international *interactions* as we observe the "game" of international politics.

SUMMARY

1. Although the foreign policymaking process differs from country to country, leaders in all countries can experience similar psychological pressures and other pressures in their deliberations.

2. Foreign policy is seldom a single overall plan, but rather a series of hundreds of decisions that fall into several categories; one classification scheme includes macro-decisions, micro-decisions, and crisis decisions.

3. Macro-decisions are general decisions that involve such determinations as the level of defense spending or foreign aid. They normally occur in a setting in which the need for a decision has been anticipated, there is a relatively lengthy time frame, and a large variety of actors can be involved in the decision process.

4. Micro-decisions normally involve concerns that are relatively narrow in scope, carry a low threat, and are handled at the lower levels of the bureaucracy. Taken together, however, they can often add up to major foreign policy developments.

5. Crisis decisions are normally characterized by a sense of high threat (including the possibility of military hostilities), a finite time frame, and involvement of officials at the highest levels.

6. Foreign policy is commonly viewed as the work of a unitary, rational actor—"the United States," "Japan," etc. In this view, which is grounded in the realist paradigm, foreign policy decision making is assumed to be a rational process in which government officials—responding to stimuli from the international environment—carefully define the situation, specify goals, consider all possible alternative means of achieving these goals, select the final alternative, implement the decision, and evaluate the consequences for the nation as a whole.

7. An alternative, and in some respects more accurate, view of foreign policymaking treats the foreign policy establishment as a pluralistic collection of individuals, groups, and organizations who may or may not act rationally and who respond to domestic stimuli and not only to external stimuli.

8. This latter view recognizes that nonrational or quasi-rational factors can operate at all stages of the decision process. For example, the definition of a situation may well be distorted by individual policymakers' images of reality, leading them to misperceive their environment. Such distortion can produce either exaggerated threat perception and paranoia, or wishful thinking—which may cause overreaction or underreaction to an adversary's actions.

9. Some images are held by a nation's people as a whole, based on a nation's historical experiences (e.g., historical Franco-German frictions); other images are developed by specific individuals, based on their personal experiences (e.g., Kennedy's negative view of Khrushchev stemming from their Vienna meeting).

10. The problems associated with individual images are often compounded in group and organizational decision making. Group pressures ("groupthink") can cause in-

dividuals to act less rationally than usual. Bureaucratic organizations tend to develop biased images of the world that are consistent with organizational (and not necessarily national) interests.

11. Nonrational factors not only can bias the definition of a situation but also can foreclose certain foreign policy options, lead to excessively low-risk or high-risk decisions, and prevent proper implementation and evaluation of decisions.

12. Although ethical principles have regularly been sacrificed to self-interests in international affairs, morality nonetheless frequently enters into foreign policy decisions. There are, however, many difficulties associated with introducing morality into foreign policy. One is the problem of moral relativism, particularly in the presence of sharp ideological and cultural differences among peoples. Another problem is whether one country alone can move others to act morally if they are not so inclined. Still another problem is the temptation to justify questionable means if they are in the pursuit of noble ends. Finally, morality may at times be yet another source of irrationality if it leads to decisions based on naive sentimentality or overly zealous crusading.

SUGGESTIONS FOR FURTHER READING AND STUDY

An excellent overview of the literature on foreign policy analysis is Valerie M. Hudson, "Foreign Policy Analysis Yesterday, Today, and Tomorrow," *Mershon International Studies Review,* 39 (October 1995), pp. 209–238. For general discussion of the concepts of rationality and nonrationality as applied to the international relations field, see Sidney Verba, "Assumptions of Rationality and Non-Rationality in Models of the International System," in Klaus Knorr and Sidney Verba, eds., *The International System: Theoretical Essays* (Princeton: Princeton University Press, 1961), pp. 93–117. In addition to the writings of Graham Allison cited in the notes for this chapter, many other works have challenged the "rational actor" premises associated with the traditional analysis of foreign policy. Among those scholars who have examined the general role of images and psychological factors as possible sources of nonrationality are Kenneth Boulding, *The Image* (Ann Arbor: University of Michigan Press, 1956); Martha L. Cottam, *Foreign Policy Decision Making: The Influence of Cognition* (Boulder, Colo.: Westview Press, 1986); and Robert Jervis, *Perception and Misperception in International Politics* (Princeton, N.J.: Princeton University Press, 1976). Also see Jon Hurwitz et al., "Foreign Policy Belief Systems in Comparative Perspective: The United States and Costa Rica," *International Studies Quarterly,* 37 (September 1993), pp. 245–270.

A lively scholarly debate has been going on between the "rationalist" and "reflectivist" schools, the former stressing the importance of the objective, raw calculation of interests as the driving force behind foreign policy decisions, and the latter stressing the importance of subjective ideas, norms, and ideological constructs. Different views are presented in Judith Goldstein and Robert O. Keohane, *Ideas and Foreign Policy: Beliefs, Institutions and Political Change* (Ithaca, N.Y.: Cornell University Press, 1993); Ngaire Woods, "Economic Ideas and International Relations," *International Studies Quarterly,* 39 (June 1995), pp. 161–180; Robert O. Keohane, "International Institutions: Two Approaches," in *International Institutions and State Power* (Boulder, Colo.: Westview Press, 1989), pp. 158–179; Alexander Wendt, "The Agent-Structure Problem in International Relations Theory," *International Organization*, 41 (Summer 1987), pp. 335–370; and Roxanne Lynn Doty, "Foreign Policy as Social Construction: A Post-Positivist Analysis of U.S. Counterinsurgency Policy in the Philippines," *International Studies Quarterly*, 37 (September 1993), pp. 297–320.

A writing that attempts to "lay the foundation for a Realist theory of state action which bridges domestic and international politics" is Michael Mastanduno, David A. Lake, and G. John Ikenberry, "Toward a Realist Theory of State Action," *International Studies Quarterly*, 33 (December 1989), pp. 457–474. Also, see Wendy L. Hansen and Kee Ok Park, "Nation-State and Pluralistic Decision Making in Trade Policy: The Case of the International Trade Administration," *International Studies Quarterly*, 39 (June 1995), pp. 181–211; Judith Goldstein and Stefanie Lenway, "Interests or Institutions: An Inquiry into Congressional-ITC Relations," *International Studies Quarterly*, 33 (September 1989), pp. 303–327; and E. Ray, "Changing Patterns of Protectionism: The Fall in Tariffs and the Rise in Non-Tariff Barriers," *Northwestern Journal of International Law and Business*, 8 (1987), pp. 285–327.

There are several volumes that contain a series of brief but insightful case studies of specific foreign policy decisions along with an analytical framework. These include Morton H. Halperin and Arnold Kanter, eds., *Readings in American Foreign Policy: A Bureaucratic Perspective* (Boston: Little, Brown, 1973), focusing primarily on the dynamics of *organizational* decision making; Irving L. Janis, *Groupthink*, 2nd ed. (Boston: Houghton Mifflin, 1982), focusing primarily on the dynamics of *group* decision making; and Lawrence S. Falkowski, *Presidents, Secretaries of State, and Crises in U.S. Foreign Relations: A Model and Predictive Analysis* (Boulder, Colo.: Westview Press, 1978), ch. 5, focusing on the behavior of *individual* decision makers, particularly in crisis situations. An excellent work that looks at individuals, small groups, and organizations together as three "interrelated subsystems of the policymaking system" and contains numerous examples of "impediments to information processing" in foreign policy is Alexander L. George, *Presidential Decisionmaking in Foreign Policy* (Boulder, Colo.: Westview Press, 1980); also see Margaret G. Hermann and Charles F. Hermann, "Who Makes Foreign Policy Decisions and How: An Empirical Inquiry," *International Studies Quarterly*, 33 (December 1989), pp. 361–387. For lengthier, in-depth case studies of various foreign policy decisions, see the works cited in the notes, including Allison (on the Cuban missile crisis), Paige (on Korea), and Wohlstetter (on Pearl Harbor). Although all of these volumes deal only with U.S. foreign policy, the general conclusions drawn by authors about the dynamics of foreign policymaking are intended to apply to other countries as well.

On the role of ethics in international relations, see Arnold Wolfer's essay "Statesmanship and Moral Choice" in *Discord and Collaboration* (Baltimore: Johns Hopkins University Press, 1962), pp. 47–65; Stanley Hoffman, *Duties Beyond Borders: On the Limits and Possibilities of Ethical International Politics* (Syracuse, N.Y.: Syracuse University Press, 1981); Joseph S. Nye, *Nuclear Ethics* (New York: Free Press, 1986); and Rachael M. McCleary, ed., *Ethics and International Affairs* (Boulder, Colo.: Westview Press, 1991).

Playing the Game of International Relations: Diplomacy Before Force

International relations has been compared to ballroom dancing. One cannot do it alone. To quote a former American president, "It takes at least two to tango" in international relations.

Although the similarity between ballroom dancing and affairs of state may begin and end with the above observation, a more applicable metaphor can be cited, again with some caution. As suggested in an earlier chapter, international relations has often been depicted as a *game* (or series of games) in which nation-states compete for various stakes. National governments play the "game of nations" not for the sheer joy of competition but because they hope to achieve certain payoffs from it in regard to foreign policy goals or, in some cases, domestic political gains. How successful a given player is depends essentially on the amount of **influence** that can be exerted on the other player(s) in terms of shaping the latter's behavior in a desired fashion. This chapter examines the way countries *normally* play the game and seek to influence each other.

To many spectators, especially those who rely primarily on front page newspaper headlines as the basis for their observations, the game of international relations seems to involve an inordinate amount of violence. However, although there is usually a war going on somewhere in the world at any given time, the problem of interstate violence is not as common as it might appear if one considers the hundreds of interstate transactions that occur day to day that are largely free of hostilities. This is depicted in Figure 7.1, which gives a frequency count of the level of hostility displayed in the interactions of states between 1950 and 1986. Of the 16,322 recorded observations among pairs of states, or "dyads," 15,830 (97%) were classified as peaceful.[1] Another careful estimate is that out of 250 serious confrontations involving major powers between 1815 and the mid-twentieth century, fewer than 30 (12 percent) resulted in actual war.[2] Much of international relations is conflictual, but *most* conflict is *nonviolent* in form. Just as resorting to fisticuffs or gunplay is not the norm in poker or chess, resorting to armed force—as a means of influencing the outcome of the game—is not the norm in international politics.

It is especially true in the contemporary nuclear age that national governments, rather than relying on the use of armed force, generally attempt to exercise influence and to achieve desired results through what is commonly called **diplomacy.** The term "diplomacy" has taken on a variety of meanings in the international relations literature. In its traditional sense, diplomacy refers to the formal practices and methods whereby states conduct their foreign relations, including the exchange of ambassadors, the dispatch of messages among official representatives, and the participation in face-to-face negotiations; the traditional study of diplomacy focuses on such concerns as the legal status of ambassadors, the functions performed by embassies, and the qualities needed to be a successful negotiator.

In recent years scholars have broadened the concept of diplomacy to mean the general process whereby states seek to communicate, to influence each

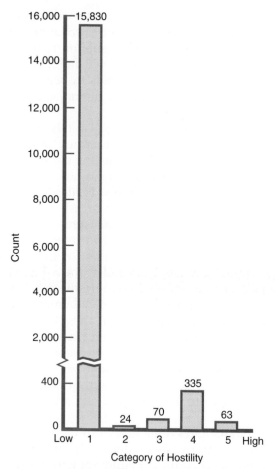

Figure 7.1
HOSTILITY LEVELS AMONG PAIRS OF STATES, 1950–1986
Source: Patrick James, Eric Solberg, and Murray Wolfson, "An Identified Systemic
Test of the Democracy-Peace Nexus," paper presented at the annual meeting of the
Peace Science Society (International), Columbus, Ohio, October 1995, p. 9. Repro-
duced by permission of the authors.

other, and to resolve conflicts through *bargaining*—either formal or informal—short of the use of armed force. Some scholars have stretched the concept of diplomacy even further, suggesting that force itself, when applied in a
very limited and selective way to make a point, can represent a kind of diplomacy—the "diplomacy of violence." Clearly, diplomacy and force can go on
simultaneously, as when the message is "we will bomb you until you cooperate, and then we will stop." Such messages were attempted in Vietnam, where

Washington's peace overtures were sometimes punctuated by bombing runs. In the Bosnian war of the 1990s, NATO forces also launched bombing raids on Serb forces, in an effort to bring added pressure on them to come to the bargaining table and reach an agreement. Some see diplomacy and violence as antithetical, arguing that it confuses the signals in negotiations. Nevertheless, others see the occasional need to reinforce diplomatic appeals with force in certain circumstances.

We will discuss the use of armed force separately in the next chapter; although there admittedly can be a fine line between the use of diplomacy and the use of force as bargaining vehicles, that line constitutes one of the most critical distinctions in all of international relations, because crossing it tends to raise the stakes in the game considerably. Leaders generally resort to force only when diplomacy fails or appears likely to fail, although at times force is used before diplomacy has been entirely exhausted.

Diplomatic methods may appear slow and tedious, certainly less direct than the use of force. Diplomats are famous for their oblique and mildly worded language. Diplomacy has been called the art of allowing parties in conflict to save face and to search for solutions they can agree on rather than reject, even if this often results in watered-down compromise.[3] In this way, losers as well as winners may stay in the game for the long run and forge a more constructive basis for future agreements. It is also important to remember that diplomacy is not a magic formula or an automatic key to harmony. Diplomats can succeed only when backed by the full extent of their government's power, influence, and authority. They can help in dealmaking only if the parties to a dispute see the mutual benefit of an agreement.

As practiced by nation-states, diplomacy can be open or secret, bilateral or multilateral, formally or informally conducted. It can take place around green-topped tables in imposing government buildings with bottles of mineral water and note pads, across great distances by teletype or "hotline," or in secluded retreats. (See the Sidelight on pages 258–259 for the merits of conducting diplomacy in secluded settings.) It can occur at the highest official level ("summitry"), or much lower, among junior officials or special envoys, and can even involve private emissaries (as when President Carter dispatched heavyweight boxing champion Muhammad Ali to seek peace agreements in Africa). Diplomacy can include the making of promises (the "nice guy" or "carrot" approach) as well as threats (the "tough guy" or "stick" approach), designed either to induce or extort concessions from the other side—making opponents an offer they won't, or can't, refuse. It can go on between friends over issues on which they are not far apart, or between enemies whose positions seem intractable. And it can be supported by economic, military, or any other resources employed to influence competitors through means other than outright physical coercion. The various strategies and instruments that can be used to win (or not lose) the game, as well as their relative effectiveness, are discussed in this chapter.

The Changing Nature of Diplomacy

British diplomat Sir Harold Nicolson, in his classic work, *Diplomacy*, cites a conventional definition of diplomacy: "Diplomacy is the management of international relations by negotiation; the method by which these relations are adjusted and managed by ambassadors and envoys. . . ."[4] Although much of today's diplomacy still involves the art of negotiation as practiced by ambassadors and envoys, the nature of diplomacy has changed somewhat over the years as conditions in the international system have changed. We will examine a number of ways in which diplomacy in the contemporary era is somewhat different from years past. We will focus on (1) the role of the embassy and the ambassador, (2) the role of public (as opposed to secret) diplomacy, (3) the role of multilateral (as opposed to bilateral) diplomacy, and (4) the role of tacit (as opposed to explicit or formal) diplomacy.

THE ROLE OF THE EMBASSY AND THE AMBASSADOR

Today's **ambassadors** can conceivably trace their roots as far back as prehistoric times, when even the members of primitive societies no doubt occasionally felt the need to deal with mutual concerns through emissaries of some sort. The earliest ambassadors did not come by their roles through any specialized training, although some were more skilled than others. As Nicolson notes in regard to diplomacy during the Middle Ages: "Louis XI sent his barber on a mission to Maria of Burgundy, Florence sent a chemist . . . to Naples, and Dr. de Puebla, who for twenty years represented Spain in London, was so filthy and unkempt that Henry VII expressed the hope that his successor might be a man more fitted for human society."[5] As the nation-state system developed, states gradually established professional, career foreign services from whose ranks ambassadors and lower-level envoys, presumably more presentable and knowledgeable than the amateurs of the past, were recruited. In some countries, such as the United States, nonprofessionals can still be found in ambassadorial posts—for example, Walter Annenberg, the publisher of *TV Guide*, was appointed by President Nixon as U.S. Ambassador to the Court of St. James's in London, and John Gavin, a movie star of Hispanic heritage, was appointed as U.S. Ambassador to Mexico by President Reagan. Although the emphasis remains on the development of a professional diplomatic corps, ambassadorial posts frequently are offered to persons thought to have special ties to the host country or as a reward to long-time political supporters.

Although the practice of dealing with foreign societies through official emissaries is an ancient one, the **embassy** as an institution—i.e., the establishment of *permanent* missions on foreign soil—is of more recent vintage. The concept of a permanent mission to represent a country's interests abroad was first employed by the Italian city-states during the fifteenth century and was later adopted by England and other nation-states that recognized the growing importance of institutionalized diplomacy in managing relations between sovereign entities. In 1815, at the Congress of Vienna after the Napoleonic

SIDELIGHT

"WALK-IN-THE-WOODS" DIPLOMACY

Diplomacy is often associated with stuffed shirts and stuffy protocol. However, there is at times another face to diplomacy, as Christopher Wren's piece below, entitled "How to Set a Peace Table," depicts.

When Syrians and Israelis sat down last week to try to make peace, they did without the traditional trappings of a diplomatic discourse—a formidable table separating the sides, name plates, microphones and an opening photo-op.

Instead, their American hosts seated them cheek-by-jowl in a cozy room around a circular mahogany table, with only a centerpiece of white tulips dividing them, while a wood fire glowed in the hearth. Outside, cows grazed on a snow-streaked pasture and a few white-tailed deer scampered from a copse of bare trees in the frosty Maryland countryside.

Versailles this was not. Purposely so.

Never mind that River House, a secluded retreat at the Wye Conference Centers, was hired from the Aspen Institute, that negotiators slept in luxury bedrooms with telephone voice mail, and that the cows belonged to the University of Maryland's agricultural program. The bucolic ambiance, like the deliberate informality, was intended to break down the kind of barriers of mistrust and distance between negotiators that can wreck deal-making even after two Governments have decided they want a deal.

Such studied mood-making is a technique popular these days with Americans as they try to broker deals in intractable conflicts. It includes encouraging first-name informality, walks in the woods and bans on both neckties and reporters.

On the simplest level, this makes common sense. It's hard to dislike your adversary when he asks you to pass the butter.

The Norwegian Foreign Minister Johan Jorgen Holst, who died early last year, proved the value of this approach in 1993, throwing in hearty home-cooked meals when he invited Israelis and the Palestine Liberation Organization for a succession of secret talks at farmhouses, hotels and his own home. These talks produced the agreement for mutual recognition between Israel and the P.L.O., laying the ground for Palestinian self-rule.

"If the results are positive, it's a little difficult to argue with them," said Casimir Yost, director of Georgetown University's Institute for the Study of Diplomacy. "I do think that when negotiators can get people into the room and away from telephones and the press, and can work through issues in a systematic sort of way, that can at least enhance prospects for success."

The strategy was not invented in Washington. When World War I ended, some details of the peace were thrashed out in quiet Swiss or Italian hotels with alpine vistas. "In those days, diplomats never took their ties off," a Government historian recalled, "but to the extent they could relax, that's where they went." The Versailles peace conference was a full-dress affair, of course, but even there some key decisions were worked out in private.

A more recent precedent for the Syrian-Israel talks, which continue this week, was the marathon negotiation at Camp David in September 1978 that paved the way for peace between Egypt and Israel. For more than two weeks, President Anwar el-Sadat of Egypt and Prime Minister Menachem Begin of Israel paced and argued in the sylvan seclusion of the Presidential retreat in the Catoctin mountains.

Then there was Dayton, Ohio, where the leaders of Serbia, Bosnia and Croatia initialed their peace accord in November. The Clinton Administration ruled out the Wye conference site then because it didn't want the visitors commuting into Washington to pitch their respective positions on television. So it opted for the protective custody of Wright-Patterson Air Force Base near Dayton, where Serbia's President, Slobodan Milosevic, protested that he had been "locked up like a monk" (he became a regular at the officers' club).

The attempt to choreograph the right atmospherics can backfire, as happened in 1989, when the Bush Administration chose sunny Malta to talk arms reduction with Mikhail Gorbachev. The two leaders were to have visited each other aboard their warships anchored offshore. But an unanticipated storm kicked up seas so rough that American officials donned medicated seasickness patches. Mr. Gorbachev declined to join Mr. Bush aboard his pitching American cruiser, the Belknap, preferring a Russian ocean liner moored dockside.

President Clinton's press secretary, Michael D. McCurry, contends that this President "is better at 'in-your-moccasins' diplomacy." Like the crafty matchmaker of "Hello Dolly," the Administration tries to make its clients feel at home while they size one another up. When President Milosevic balked at one last-minute detail last month, his American interlocutors poured him another stiff whisky and the deal got done. At the Syrian-Israeli talks last week smoking was allowed in deference to Syria's chain-smoking Ambassador, Walid al Moualem. The Syrians rejected an American proposal to don sweatsuits, the Israel newspaper Yediot Ahronot reported, but they did remove their neckties.

Wars, the first attempt was made to reach agreement among states on a standard set of rules regarding the appointment of ambassadors and the operation of embassies. This was especially designed to avoid quarrels between states over ambassadorial rank and privileges, such as that which had occurred in London in 1661, when "the coach of the Spanish ambassador tried to push in front of that of the French ambassador, a battle occurred with loss of life among the footmen, . . . diplomatic relations were severed between Paris and Madrid and a very real danger of war arose."[6]

From the start, embassies were found by national governments to be useful institutions for performing a variety of functions, including the continuous collection and transmission of information back to the home country concerning conditions in the host country; the maintenance of a regular line of communication between the home government and the host government; the cultivation of friendly relations with the host government through ongoing social contacts provided by rubbing elbows at embassy balls and other gatherings; the extension of home government protection to one's citizens traveling through host countries; the expansion of commercial interests; and—most notably—expeditious on-the-spot negotiation of issues of concern to home and host governments. Over time, many more routine functions were added, such as processing international travel requests (visas) and registering births and deaths of one's citizens living in the host state.

In the nineteenth and early twentieth centuries, embassies tended to be small, sometimes staffed only by an ambassador and a handful of aides. Ambassadors were expected to be generalists, adept at handling a variety of functions. Today, although ambassadors and other diplomatic personnel are still often generalist in aptitude, large embassy staffs include specialists such as information officers (responsible for disseminating "public relations" propaganda), consular officials (responsible for providing legal assistance as well as handling travel requests to and from the host country), commercial attachés (responsible for promoting economic interests in the host country), military attachés or economic development specialists (responsible for dealing with host country military and economic requests), and intelligence officers (sometimes posing as one of the above officials, responsible for monitoring and reporting on local political developments). The increased bureaucratization of embassies has reflected the growing volume and complexity of international transactions. It should be added that many poorer countries simply lack the money and personnel needed to maintain the kind of modern embassies described.

It is perhaps ironic today that as the diplomatic service in many countries has become more professionalized, it has also in some respects come to play a lesser role in negotiation, its main historic function. The advanced communications and travel technology of the modern age have made leaders less reliant on their ambassador on the scene as their chief representative in dealing with a foreign government. In the days of carrier pigeons and sailing vessels, a country's ambassador might have had to deal with a host government without benefit of instructions from home for several months. The installation of telephone, teletype, and satellite hook-ups between home office and embassy has lessened the discretion with which ambassadors abroad can make decisions and the need for them to do so, although resourceful ambassadors can still have considerable policy impact in certain situations.

In an era of supersonic jets, fax machines, and hotlines, many leaders bypass embassy personnel altogether, preferring either to send high-level government ministers on "shuttle diplomacy" missions (such as Henry Kissinger's excursions in the Middle East in 1974) or to play the role of diplomat themselves by directly engaging in communications and negotiations with their counterparts in other countries (as in the case of Nixon and Chou En-lai at Beijing in 1972, Carter, Begin, and Sadat at Camp David in 1978, and Bush and Gorbachev on a ship in the middle of the Mediterranean in 1989). President Bush, during his first year in office, undertook such personal diplomacy in approximately 135 face-to-face meetings with world leaders as well as 190 phone calls, including only the third on record between an American president and his Soviet counterpart; the pace of such exchanges, on average a phone call every other day, was quickened by the changing European scene.[7] In 1991, at the height of the Iraq-Kuwait crisis, there was a much-publicized ninety-minute phone conversation between Bush and Gorbachev aimed at ironing out details of a U.N.-sponsored cease-fire.

Meetings between heads of state have been labeled **summitry.** Summit diplomacy is not completely new—even the monarchs of Europe during the classical era would occasionally meet to exchange pleasantries and discuss mutual concerns. However, summitry has become much more common in the contemporary era. As a form of diplomatic activity, summitry has been both applauded and criticized. Meetings among heads of state can help leaders develop greater understanding of each other and can expedite the negotiation process by cutting through bureaucratic "red tape." However, as U.S. diplomat George Ball commented, such meetings are rarely capable of producing the kind of major diplomatic results that one is led to expect from all the hoopla normally accompanying them:

> What really happens at even the most serious . . . summit conference where there are significant issues to be discussed? Though little serious conversation takes place at the banquet table, the time consumed in eating and drinking is appalling. In the Far East it is not polite to discuss business over food, and in many countries in the Middle East no conversation at all takes place during meals. Wherever the meeting occurs, toasts are normally set speeches. When Communists are present, toasts may be useful for making diplomatic hints—particularly if the toasts are afterward handed out to the press—but by and large the time consumed in communal feeding is time wasted. Nor is anything serious likely to be said over the brandy, for, in spite of the diplomatic mystique with which tradition has surrounded this postprandial ritual, the heads

of state are usually too tired to make sensible conversation, which they would probably not be able to remember with precision the next day anyway. . . .

Thus, in trying to measure the period permitted for a substantive exchange of views during ten hours of top-level propinquity, one should deduct at least four hours for eating and drinking, another hour or two for small talk . . . then divide the remainder by two and one half for the translation. What is left is about two or three hours in which positions are stated and ideas exchanged.[8]

Interestingly, Ball's impatience at time "wasted" reflects something of a Western cultural bias, although he notes the importance of cultural differences in diplomacy; in the East, for example, though no formal business may be discussed at dinner, the opportunity often is taken to size up the guests and to determine their degree of authority and credibility.

Critics are correct to point out that chief executives seldom are experts in international affairs, often lacking the kind of familiarity with diplomatic procedures and foreign cultures that trained diplomats are able to bring to the negotiating table. Although elaborate presummit briefings can help heads of state to some extent, Ball and others nonetheless have lamented the trend toward the theatrics and photo-ops (photographic opportunities) of summitry as a substitute for quiet, behind-the-scenes discussions.

PUBLIC VERSUS SECRET DIPLOMACY

The increase in summitry, with all its "media event" characteristics, reflects another trend in diplomacy, namely the increased role of *public* as opposed to *secret* channels. Although much diplomacy still is conducted secretly, democracies especially have been under increased pressures to open the process and widely publicize the resulting decisions.

It is not clear whether open diplomatic practices produce better international agreements. At least since the time of Woodrow Wilson, it has been argued that "open covenants openly arrived at" would remove much of the suspicion and paranoia that pervade international relations. In other words, many argue that secrecy in the negotiating process is necessarily bad, in terms of not only frustrating the public's "right to know" but also adding to the sense of insecurity and distrust experienced by all nations in the international system. However, many students of diplomacy argue just the opposite, that conducting diplomacy "in a fishbowl" under the glare of television cameras tends to promote "atmospherics"—either empty gestures of friendship or outbursts of rhetoric and the adoption of rigid positions for political gain either at home or abroad—rather than the kind of serious discussion of issues and compromises so essential to effective negotiations. Particularly in the case of highly sensitive and delicate negotiations, even if the final outcome ought ultimately be publicized, there might be legitimate reasons for keeping the diplomatic process itself insulated from public scrutiny while it is going on, as Israel and the PLO did in the early days of their talks by accepting Norway's offer of quiet, remote conference facilities.[9]

MULTILATERAL VERSUS BILATERAL DIPLOMACY

The time-honored practice of pairs of countries exchanging ambassadors and maintaining permanent diplomatic missions on each other's soil reflects the traditional emphasis that states have placed on **bilateral** (two-country) **diplomacy.** It was not until the late nineteenth century that **multilateral diplomacy** (the meeting together of several countries) became a common mode of diplo-

AN EXAMPLE OF MULTILATERAL (OR, SOME MIGHT SAY, "MINILATERAL") DIPLO-MACY: LEADERS OF THE MAJOR INDUSTRIALIZED DEMOCRACIES—THE GROUP OF SEVEN—MEETING AT THEIR ANNUAL ECONOMIC SUMMIT IN PARIS IN 1989, IN FRONT OF THE LOUVRE. FROM LEFT TO RIGHT: ITALY, GERMANY, UNITED STATES, FRANCE, UNITED KINGDOM, CANADA, AND JAPAN.

macy; before that time, multilateral diplomacy was limited mostly either to special meetings called at moments of crisis when war threatened or peace conferences after major wars, such as the Congress of Vienna in 1815, in which winners and losers gathered to determine the division of the spoils and to settle other matters. Even at the turn of the twentieth century, multilateral diplomacy had still not become a highly developed phenomenon.

However, multilateral diplomacy has become increasingly prevalent, owing to a number of factors: (1) the existence of many problems (not only arms control but economic and environmental concerns and other matters related to the growth of interdependence) that spill over several national boundaries and do not lend themselves to purely bilateral solutions; (2) the proliferation of intergovernmental organizations at the global and regional levels, such as the United Nations and the European Union, which provide ongoing institutional settings for the conduct of multilateral diplomacy; and (3) as noted earlier, the existence of many less developed countries that have come to rely on the UN and other multilateral forums for the bulk of their official diplomatic contacts. Although traditional bilateral relations continue to play an extremely prominent role in contemporary diplomacy, several studies have found that "international organizations are by far the most common method of diplomatic contact for most nations—much more so than traditional bilateral exchanges."[10]

Multilateral diplomacy occurs not only through institutions such as the UN but also through *ad hoc* conferences, such as the series of global conferences held during the 1990s on nuclear proliferation, population, ecology, and human rights. Summit meetings themselves can be both bilateral and multilateral in form, such as the gathering of well over one hundred heads of state at the "Earth Summit" that addressed environmental and development concerns in Rio de Janeiro in 1992. Related to trends in public diplomacy, the Rio meeting also included over 9,000 journalists, as well as some 25,000 representatives of nongovernmental organizations (NGOs) lobbying on behalf of environmental groups, indigenous peoples, women, scientific bodies, business associations, and other interested parties. Multilateral institutions and conferences are viewed as playing a constructive role in international relations by involving many relevant participants at once in collectively helping to define accepted international norms; but such large open forums—with so many diverse parties represented and with an emphasis on speech-making, voting procedures, and "statements of principle" as outcomes—also can complicate problem solving, paper over differences, and provide little enforcement of the final resolutions. As we note in Chapter 10, some today suggest that countries should rely less on broad, global forums such as the UN and engage instead in "minilateral" diplomacy that brings together a few "like-minded" actors (e.g., the annual economic summits of the Group of Seven major industrialized democracies).

One other form of multilateral diplomacy has attracted special attention in the post–Cold War era. The use of "third parties" in the conflict resolution process has long been a part of diplomatic history, one vivid example being President Theodore Roosevelt's Nobel Prize–winning mediation of the treaty ending the Russo-Japanese War in 1905. **Mediation** is a specialized process in which a neutral third party undertakes to facilitate discussions between disputants to help them arrive at a settlement themselves. The term sometimes is mistakenly used when a major power participates in a dispute settlement process and the disputants attempt to extract promises from the latter as a quid pro quo for acquiescing to an agreement. This form of diplomatic intervention is best termed "brokering" an agreement. Mediation requires more subtle efforts to produce constructive alternatives for the parties to consider, and suggest paths out of an impasse, without interjecting oneself into the final accord.[11]

TACIT VERSUS FORMAL DIPLOMACY

Although in popular usage "diplomacy" and "negotiation" often are considered synonymous terms, one should keep in mind that **negotiation**—i.e., *formal*, direct communication through face-to-face meetings, cables, or third-party intermediaries—is only one mode of diplomacy.[12] In addition to negotiation, governments often engage in **tacit diplomacy**, i.e., *informal*, indirect communication through words (e.g., press conference statements) and actions (e.g., placing troops on alert) designed to signal intentions or the importance one attaches to some issue. Of course, in practice states tend to combine the two forms, using tacit diplomacy for "posturing" purposes either before or during a formal negotiating session to reinforce the messages they wish to convey. Apart from its use in conjunction with formal negotiations, tacit diplomacy is often employed by itself simply to influence another government's future behavior, particularly when seeking to dissuade the other side from taking some undesired action. For example, Washington has staged numerous military exercises and resupply demonstrations in Europe and Korea to convince "friend and foe alike" that the defense of these areas is feasible, that the United States is committed to guaranteeing the security of its allies, and that any attempted aggression would not succeed.

Tacit diplomacy is not a modern invention. It has always been a part of statecraft along with more formal diplomacy. However, the speed of modern communications technology has enabled leaders to exploit the signaling possibilities of tacit diplomacy much more effectively than in the past. Tacit diplomacy allows communication between governments that for ideological or other reasons do not have official diplomatic relations or whose relations are so strained that they do not wish to be seen formally talking to each other. Such diplomacy, then, can be a useful surrogate for formal diplomacy in managing conflicts.

One problem with tacit diplomacy, however, is that although actions such as troop mobilizations might speak louder than words at a negotiation table, they can also be more easily misinterpreted. Because such signals are frequently designed for multiple audiences, including the listening public or political opponents at home, they can lose impact and clarity. A government can seldom be certain that signaling at long range conveys the desired message unambiguously to the desired target, especially given the large amount of "noise"—random, unrelated events—that can drown out signals in the international arena.

OTHER CHANGES

In previous chapters we focused on foreign policy behavior and suggested that as interdependence increases and the foreign policy agendas of states expand, domestic political forces tend to play a greater role in foreign policy decision-making processes, making it harder to view states as unitary actors. "Complex interdependence" increasingly is complicating the process of diplomacy as well.

Robert Putnam has argued that when national leaders get together, "the politics of many international negotiations can usefully be conceived as a two-level game [one pitched at the international level and the other at the domestic level]." He states that "each national political leader appears at both game boards. Across the international table sit his foreign counterparts, and at his elbows sit diplomats and other international advisors. Around the domestic table behind him sit party and parliamentary figures, spokespersons for domestic agencies, representatives of key interest groups, and the leader's own political advisors."[13] Putnam quotes Robert Strauss, the chief U.S. official at the Tokyo Round trade negotiations in the 1970s, as saying that "during my tenure as Special Trade Representative, I spent as much time negotiating with domestic constituents (both industry and labor) and members of the U.S. Congress as I did negotiating with our foreign trading partners."[14] Similarly, former U.S. Secretary of Labor John Dunlop is said to have commented that "bilateral negotiations usually require three agreements—one across the table and one on each side of the table."[15] Maria Cowles has shown that in some cases, such as the negotiations that currently go on in the European Union—where multinational corporations and NGOs lobby EU officials directly and compete with national governments in determining what decisions are reached in Brussels on trade policy and other matters—we need to go beyond treating diplomacy as a "two-level" game; to understand fully the nature of the diplomatic process here, she suggests we view it as a "three-level" game in which not only subnational and state actors are involved but also transnational actors.[16]

The point here is that, although diplomacy can still be construed in traditional terms as the art of statecraft, or "bargaining" among states—as treated below—practioners of this art must be ever sensitive to the different audiences to whom they are playing.[17]

The Concept of Bargaining

Regardless of whether diplomacy is conducted openly or secretly, multilaterally or bilaterally, tacitly or formally, by ambassadors or by heads of state, the essence of the process remains **bargaining.** Bargaining can be thought of as a means of settling differences over priorities between contestants through an exchange of proposals for mutually acceptable solutions. It has been referred to as "the search for common ground."[18] There must be conflict over priorities for bargaining to take place, for if there were total agreement there would be nothing to bargain about. Nevertheless, a given conflict can be mild as well as severe. In some cases the differences among disputants might be virtually incompatible and irreconcilable, whereas in other cases it might be possible for all sides to benefit in some way from the bargaining process.

Bargaining should be a familiar concept, because the same basic process is at work when nations bargain as when friends decide what movie to see on a Saturday night, or when opponents decide on the ground rules for a soccer match. Even people who are not quite sure how they feel about each other bargain to resolve disputes, which can range from child custody battles in a divorce case to arguments between two drivers over a parking space. The elements of both rational and nonrational decision making that were introduced in the last chapter can enter the bargaining process.[19]

A simple example close to home will illustrate the main aspects of bargaining. Suppose a woman is in an automobile showroom seeking to purchase a new car. She has her eye especially on the little red sports car in the corner. The prospective buyer can communicate to the salesperson directly or indirectly what she is willing to settle for in terms of price, delivery date, and other issues. The salesperson in turn tries to assess the buyer's degree of interest in and resources committed to purchasing the car. As they bargain, the woman can either say she will not pay more than x dollars for the car, or she can get up and head for the door when the dealer quotes what she believes is too high a price. In either case, the buyer tries to communicate something about her own terms and about the unacceptability of the dealer's offer. The salesperson might counter with a reference to the boss who won't allow a deal below a certain level. The "game" might boil down to a contest over how many steps toward the door the buyer takes before the dealer gives in (or appears to give in). The "endgame" might include more offers and counteroffers to raise the perceived benefits of agreement for "rational" (benefit-maximizing, cost-minimizing) players—a "free undercoat," a set of "high-performance tires," "2.9% financing," a "deluxe stereo system."

Good bargainers, either in an automobile showroom or in the international arena, have a clear idea of their priorities. Negotiators presumably have certain minimum and maximum limits regarding how far they are willing to go to reach agreement. In fact, in certain diplomatic bargaining situations, such as the Panama Canal Treaty negotiations during the mid-1970s, the United States government even has hired a consulting firm to help the negotiating team rank desired outcomes in priority order.[20] The bargaining contest consists of each side trying to strike a final agreement as *far* from their own *minimum* and as *close* to their *maximum* demands as possible.

Depending on the intensity of their desires regarding possible outcomes, the bargainers have three basic strategies to employ: (1) contending aggressively (confrontation); (2) yielding or giving in (accommodation); and (3) problem solving so that they jointly gain.[21] The structure of the situation and the relative power of the parties may have a great deal to do with which strategy is employed. In situations of great power imbalance, it may be possible aggressively to dictate a solution to the weaker party (as the UN coalition essentially did to Iraq after the 1991 Gulf War). If one party is relatively disinterested in the outcome or quite interested in improving relations with the other party, it might yield voluntarily and go on to some other issue (as British Prime Minister Neville Chamberlain did in dealing with Hitler over the partition of Czechoslovakia in 1938). Finally, if each party values the mutual relationship and sees prospects for joint gains, or if there has been a long stalemate that cannot be resolved by force, the parties might mutually compromise over an issue (as the Israelis and PLO recently agreeing in principle to autonomy for the occupied territories). The auto showroom essentially is structured to bring out the problem-solving approach, by linking buyer and seller in a long-term service relationship.

In essence, the bargaining process consists of pulling and pushing an opponent toward more or less acceptable positions along a kind of "bargaining curve" as indicated in Figure 7.2. Here parties A and B contend along the bargaining line of points representing maximum benefits or payoffs achievable for the parties. Party A wishes the final agreement to be toward its maximum demand, which might represent a loss for B; and B presumably wants the same thing in reverse. In "problem-solving" situations, negotiators will move toward a settlement in the bargaining zone (quadrant) where both A's and B's values ("utilities") are above zero, i.e., above the minimum. The box on page 270 provides an interesting way of looking at the bargaining process. We should add that the bargaining process can occur over several "rounds," including "prenegotiation" and "negotiation" phases, as the players search for general principles to agree to at first and then work toward pinning down the details.[22]

A good example of the problem-solving approach, which tends not to produce a clear victory or defeat for either side, is the set of bargains reached during the Cold War between East and West over the Berlin Wall. Some saw the construction of the Berlin Wall in 1961 as a tacit understanding between East and West that the status quo would be allowed to prevail in Germany. The Soviets could thus back down from their prior threats to oust Western forces from Berlin if the West did not recognize East Germany; the East Germans

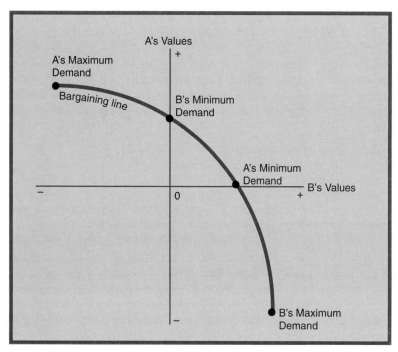

Figure 7.2
THE BARGAINING GAME: MAXIMUM AND MINIMUM DEMANDS
Source: Adapted from Glenn H. Snyder and Paul Diesing, *Conflict Among Nations: Bargaining, Decision Making, and System Structure in International Crisis* (Princeton, N.J.: Copyright © 1977 by Princeton University Press), p. 69. Reprinted-reproduced by permission of Princeton University Press.

could stem the tide of skilled personnel escaping to West Berlin; and the West could restabilize the situation and retain access to the city.[23] Eventually, when greater mutual trust had been established and when its declining internal and international position forced Moscow to relinquish control over Eastern Europe, this status quo gave way to acceptance of a reunited Germany through negotiations among German, Soviet, and NATO leaders. In a sense, East and West had moved beyond "coexistence" toward "dialogue."

Although the construction of an ugly wall through a city cannot be termed an optimal solution, the Berlin case illustrates how agreements can be based on pragmatic, "prominent solutions." **Prominent solutions** are alternatives that are so self-evidently better than others, even if not optimal, that all parties would tend to settle on them even without clear signals to that effect. As an example, suppose a group of ten students were deposited one morning in

STAGES OF THE BARGAINING PROCESS

In the following passage, Oscar Nudler stresses the necessity, particularly in cases of severe conflict, to reconcile the parties' different worldviews and change the basic way they *frame* their dispute as bargaining unfolds. This is critical if they are ever to get beyond confrontation to problem solving.

Stage 1: Primitive Conflict

At this stage, each party represents the other in utterly negative terms: mistaken, unjust, immoral, inferior, and so on. True dialogue is impossible since lack of mutual confidence prevails. Depending on the context, different types of occasional or systematic violence are exerted. There may even be a refusal to admit the other's right to exist . . .

Stage 2: Coexistence

At this stage, each party accepts the other's right to exist, though lack of mutual understanding still predominates. Coexistence results more often than not from resignation to the fact that the physical and/or moral strength shown by the opponent makes aggression highly risky and possibly self-defeating. However, in a more advanced phase of this stage, more positive reasons for coexistence may emerge such as an awareness of the potential benefits of dialogue.

Stage 3: Dialogue

At this stage, each party is prepared to enter a true dialogue with the other, frequently with the help of a third, facilitating party . . . , "true dialogue" means that each party, though still sticking to his/her own preferred metaphor (or preferred way of building worlds and frames), develops at the same time a capacity adequately to represent the other party's metaphor, and eventually learn from it. Mutual deterrence and mistrust are gradually replaced by dialogue based on an understanding of the other's needs and ways of representing them.

Stage 4: Restructuring

This is the highest phase in conflict resolution. Both parties now cooperate in building a new frame [of reference] transcending their original frames and the conflict between them. This does not imply the end of all possible conflicts but only of the old, primitive form of the conflict. New forms of conflict may emerge and new cycles of conflict resolution then occur.

Source: Oscar Nudler, "On Conflicts and Metaphors: Toward An Extended Rationality," in John Burton ed., *Conflict: Human Needs Theory* (New York: St. Martin's Press, copyright © 8/90), pp. 197–198. Reprinted with permission of St. Martin's Press, Inc.

different parts of Manhattan in New York City and were told to find each other before the end of the day; it is likely that, without communicating, they would each show up at a prominent place and time that they calculated would have the greatest probability of attracting the others. Past surveys have shown that one such prominent solution would be Grand Central Station at noon.[24] Similarly, many observers watching Israeli-PLO negotiations in the 1990s envision that a Palestinian state in the West Bank and Gaza areas occupied by Israel in 1967 will likely eventuate as a prominent solution to this long conflict.

The Dynamics of International Bargaining

THE MANIPULATION OF CARROTS AND STICKS

As the auto showroom example suggested, bargainers can attempt to influence each other's behavior through the conscious manipulation of "carrots" and "sticks." In international relations in particular, states make considerable use of both carrot and stick approaches when they rely on four types of bargaining tactics: threats, punishments, promises, and rewards. Two of these tactics (**threats** and **punishments**) represent the stick approach, the former involving some hypothetical action and the latter a real action. The other two tactics (**promises** and **rewards**), which represent the carrot approach, also involve hypothetical and real action. Although those who view international politics as being violent and anarchical tend to place greater faith in the stick approach than in the carrot approach, as exemplified by Theodore Roosevelt's famous admonition to "walk softly but carry a big stick," there is no clear evidence that one approach is inherently more effective than the other as a bargaining strategy. Both can be effective, depending on the context in which they are used.

For example, in 1962, President Kennedy *threatened* Premier Khrushchev with war if the missiles in Cuba were not removed, but at the same time *promised* not to invade the island in the future if the Soviets would give in on the missiles. As this example illustrates, states often use threats and promises together, especially when one side wants to provide the other side a face-saving way out of a confrontation.

As states bargain, they often discover that it is more difficult to *compel* than to *deter* certain behavior on the part of another state. In the case of **compellence,** one seeks to persuade the other side to do something it does not wish to do, either to undertake or continue some desired behavior, or to stop some undesired behavior (e.g., the United States attempting to influence South Africa in the 1980s to grant independence to its colony Namibia, then called South-West Africa). In the case of **deterrence,** one seeks to discourage the other side from doing something it might wish to do (e.g., the United States attempting to discourage the Soviets from launching a nuclear strike against intercontinental missiles based in the United States). In other words, with compellence the successful exercise of influence requires one to make something happen; with deterrence, success consists of nothing happening.[25] It is often difficult to know whether a state has been deterred, especially in the case of military deterrence. That depends on whether the state had intended to attack in the first place and on whether it decided not to for fear of retaliation or because of other reasons, such as snafus in its own military operations or the vagaries of weather conditions. We will discuss military deterrence at greater length later in the chapter.

It is not enough simply to make timely promises or threats. For promises or threats to work, they must also be sufficiently (1) *credible* and (2) *potent*, as perceived by the *other* side. Regarding the element of **credibility**, state A can intend fully to honor a promise or to carry out a threat; however, both are meaningless and unlikely to influence state B's behavior unless B believes that A has the capability and willingness to follow through with its promise or threat. By the same token, leaders can be bluffing in their promises or threats; all that counts is that the target state is convinced. As Henry Kissinger noted, "A bluff taken seriously is more useful than a serious threat [or promise] interpreted as a bluff."[26] Of course, a state might ultimately be called on to carry out a threat or promise, and it must be prepared to do so if it values its future credibility.

Regarding the element of **potency**, for state A to influence state B to adjust its behavior in a desired direction (see Fig. 7.2), a promise or threat by A not only must be believable but it also must be sufficiently weighty in the eyes of B's leaders—either too attractive to pass up (in the case of a promise) or too potentially harmful to absorb (in the case of a threat). In other words, the carrot must be juicy enough for the target state to want to bite, and the stick must be menacing enough for the target state not to want to test it; the target state might well believe that the other state will execute a given promise or threat, but it might not *care* about the consequences, at least not enough to warrant rethinking its behavior.

Promises and threats that are credible but lack potency are likely to fail in the bargaining process. For example, if we recall Henry Kissinger's flirtations with Moscow in the early 1970s, during the period of relaxed tensions known as détente, Soviet leaders were quite convinced of American willingness to provide agricultural and technological benefits to the Soviet Union in exchange for their cooperation in keeping regional conflicts in Africa and elsewhere under control, especially because he demonstrated his sincerity by rewarding them in advance before any changes in Soviet behavior had occurred. The failure to influence Soviet behavior as fully as Kissinger had hoped was not attributable to lack of U.S. credibility but rather at least partially to the fact that the incentives Washington was offering were not of sufficient weight to induce the Soviets to give up their geopolitical goals. Food and technology might have been important to the Soviets, but they were not so desperate for U.S. exports that they were willing to pass up opportunities to enhance their own influence in Africa and Asia in return. Perhaps if the Soviet Union had been more dependent on U.S. trade, American threats to withhold exports, or promises to expand them, would have been more potent. However, as we will see later in the chapter when we focus on the use of economic instruments, one should be careful not to overestimate the leverage provided by such ties.

Promises and threats that might be potent but lack credibility are just as likely to fail as those that are credible but lack potency. The need to communicate in a credible fashion is especially important in an era in which misperception and miscalculation can lead to nuclear holocaust. A great deal has been written about how governments can enhance the credibility of their threats as well as their promises, but there are pitfalls in overemphasizing credibility; some critics have noted that during the Cold War the U.S. government became obsessed with the credibility of its pledges to defend allies, and intervened in places such as Vietnam to reinforce such credibility (even though South Vietnam was never formally an ally). One frequently stated guideline for increasing credibility is that "the more specific a promise or threat is, and the more authoritative its source, the greater the credibility of the intentions it expresses."[27] Thus, leaders desiring a particular concession from a foreign state stand a better chance of achieving it if it is spelled out clearly along with the specific consequences that will follow compliance or noncompliance.

Thomas Schelling, who has written many important works dealing with the dynamics of international bargaining, has suggested a number of other ways in which states can increase the credibility of their threats and promises.[28] To Schelling, the "art of commitment" is central to success in the bargaining process. He stresses the importance of reinforcing declarations of intent with the kinds of tacit bargaining actions noted earlier, such as using budgetary allocations, troop mobilizations, and demonstrations of sealift capabilities to buttress threats, or sending a noted diplomat abroad to lend seriousness and authority to one's promises. One strategy that Schelling suggests as being particularly effective in making threats believable is the "burn all your bridges behind you" approach, i.e., creating a situation in which you convince the other side that if they take a particular action that you wish to deter, you will have *no choice* but to carry out the threat you have posed. For example, one reason for stationing thousands of American troops in Western Europe during the Cold War was to act as a "tripwire," to convince Moscow that any military aggression on its part against America's NATO allies would automatically trigger U.S. involvement—with some American soldiers inevitably getting killed by enemy troops—and make it nearly impossible for Washington to renege on its commitment to defend Western Europe. Although sizable American troop reductions occurred in the 1990s, many have questioned whether the tripwire function is still needed as thousands of American soldiers remain in Western Europe in the post–Cold War era.

In an effort to enhance its credibility, a government can try to cultivate a certain image or reputation abroad. A reputation for being "reliable" can be especially helpful in making one's promises believable, whereas a reputation for being "erratic" or "reckless," which some would argue characterizes leaders such as Libya's Muammar Qaddafi, can be helpful in making one's threats believable. A reputation for recklessness can backfire, however, as Qaddafi discovered when foreign leaders began shying away from agreements with him and when U.S. forces attacked his residence in 1986. Other states, such as Algeria and Tunisia, have at times cultivated an image of "reliable go-between" in offering help to those wishing to negotiate with states such as Libya.

GAME THEORY

A large body of **game theory** literature exists that provides useful insights into the nature of international bargaining and the way in which cooperation can occur amid conflict.[29] Two basic types of games are common to discussions of international bargaining, one emphasizing the potential for confrontation and the other the potential for cooperation. The **zero-sum game** is structured so that what one party wins, the other party automatically loses; conflict, in other words, is total. An international example would be a territorial dispute in which two states claim the same parcel of land but obviously cannot both exercise sovereignty over it at once. However, through creative diplomacy it might be possible to turn such a zero-sum game into a **variable-sum game** in which both parties can simultaneously win something, even though one might

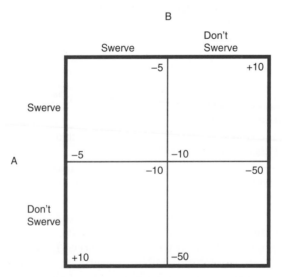

Figure 7.3
THE GAME OF CHICKEN
Payoffs to player A are shown in the lower lefthand corner of each cell, and payoffs to player B are shown in the upper righthand corner of each cell.

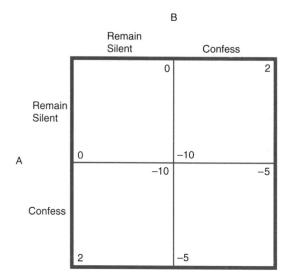

Figure 7.4
THE PRISONERS' DILEMMA GAME
Payoffs to player A are shown in the lower lefthand corner of each cell, and payoffs
to player B are shown in the upper righthand corner of each cell.

benefit more than the other. If the disputants determined that they could share
the land, or if the party occupying the land satisfactorily compensated the
other party, the game would feature a "positive sum" ("win-win") outcome.

Most situations in international relations resemble variable-sum games.
Figures 7.3 and 7.4 illustrate two mixed-motive games frequently cited as especially relevant to the study of international relations. Such games often
have prominent solutions based on the gains or losses expected (with a general
rule of thumb being to maximize gains and minimize losses—the so-called
"minimax" rule).

The first example is the game of "chicken," in which opponents drive toward each other on a single-lane highway, with the first one to swerve considered the loser, or chicken. Each player is faced with essentially two options
(swerve or don't swerve), with neither player knowing which option the other
will choose and neither one alone able to control the outcome of the game.
The hypothetical values (payoffs) gained or lost by each player as a result of
swerving or not swerving are represented by the numbers appearing in each
cell of the matrix in Figure 7.3. It should be evident that on the basis of projected gains and losses, each party would be better off "cooperating," i.e.,
swerving to avoid the risk of total and mutual destruction in a collision. However, the temptation remains to try and win through a confrontative—don't
swerve—strategy. The choice of the tempting but risky option might depend
on how "risk acceptant" or daring the players are. This game often is used to
illustrate problems of threat and counterthreat, or deterrence in international

conflict, particularly relating to the danger of nuclear war (as with the sailing of Soviet ships toward the U.S. naval blockade of Cuba during the 1962 missile crisis).

Figure 7.4 illustrates another simple but somewhat different two-person game, the "prisoners' dilemma." Here it is assumed that two suspects found together are arrested for a crime and are interrogated separately. Each prisoner is told that he will receive the maximum sentence if he remains silent while the other prisoner confesses. However, he will get probation or go free if he confesses and implicates his partner while the partner remains silent. If both parties confess, they will each receive intermediate sentences; if both remain silent they will receive the minimum sentence. Given the hypothetical payoff values listed in Figure 7.4, the two prisoners—assuming they are both rational players adopting a "minimax" strategy—would probably confess jointly, each thereby receiving moderately long prison terms (e.g., five years) when they could have done much better by jointly remaining silent. Thus, this game finishes with the players failing to reach the points on the bargaining line of optimal solutions in Figure 7.2, at which both A and B are relatively satisfied. Though each could do better by cooperating through joint silence, their problem, or "dilemma," is that neither can trust the other to keep quiet, since there is much to gain by pinning the crime on the partner—a strategy known as "defecting." The game is structured so that each prisoner is worried about the possible maximum loss (ten years) through the other's defection. The element of trust or enforced compliance is missing, and would be missing even if the two players were allowed to communicate with each other without a binding guarantee. This situation has been compared to international arms races, in which both sides would be better off with reduced defense expenditures and an arms control agreement, but neither trusts that the other will refrain from taking significant advantage of such an agreement.

Although governments often seem to be locked into conflict, as in the case of arms control negotiations, it is possible to develop cooperative strategies over time through trial and error so that the parties can share in winnings rather than losses. Fortunately, in international relations, games are seldom one-shot affairs. Often they consist of moves and countermoves, offers and probes, and negotiations across time. States may back down on some issues but stand firm on others, and in the sequence of moves it may be possible to reach a mutually agreeable outcome. The Berlin crisis of 1958–1962, involving the construction of the Berlin Wall, can be viewed as such a sequence. There were confrontational elements typical of chicken games, with the United States and the Soviet Union facing possible humiliation in a backdown, and also facing possible mutual destruction in a war over Berlin and its access routes. There were also elements of common interest and distrust typical of the prisoners' dilemma.

One complication in many such crises is misperception about what game the opponent is playing. U.S. leaders thought the Soviets were playing chicken with a Berlin ultimatum in 1958. Soviet leaders assumed that there was plenty of room for compromise and joint face-saving formulas. The West stood firm on the initial Soviet ultimatum, but ultimately yielded on the building of the wall in 1961. The Soviets backed away from their threat of a separate peace treaty with East Germany. Gradually the Americans made clear their minimum demands: self-determination and economic survival for West Berliners; continued presence of Western troops in Berlin; freedom of access to Berlin. While Washington signaled intentions to fight for these demands, other related issues were treated as lower priorities, leaving room for a settlement.[30]

Another complication is that, although game theory generally presumes that states act as unitary, rational actors, we have noted that diplomacy is often a "two-level game" played with not only one's adversary in mind but also various domestic constituencies. Still, if players can communicate to each other their intention to reward cooperative play, to resist or penalize conflictual play, and to seek mutual benefits, then solutions for difficult interstate disputes can be engineered. It has even been argued that there are "best" ways to play chicken or the prisoners' dilemma that help avert collisions or mutual losses. Frequently such strategies involve signals that cooperation will be rewarded with cooperation while conflictual play will be met with equally conflictual responses. Generally the object is to prevent miscalculations by opponents, minimize ambiguity and maximize predictability of behavior, prevent escalation of hostilities to higher levels, and remove emotional or ideological factors as much as possible from the bargaining process.[31]

The Instruments of International Bargaining

MILITARY RESOURCES AS BARGAINING TOOLS

Until now, we have discussed the dynamics of international bargaining in general. Let us now focus on specific instruments of bargaining, looking first at military resources and then at economic resources. With the Vietnam and Afghanistan war experiences as examples, and with the rise of technological and economic competition among major powers in the contemporary international system, some analysts have concluded that military force has lost much of its central importance in international relations. Contrary arguments are heard from those pointing to the continued use of military power for purposes of deterrence, compellence, posturing, as well as territorial defense.[32]

Military resources enable a state to bargain through both explicit and implicit threats and promises as well as punishments and rewards. Regarding the use of military instruments as *carrots*, during the Cold War both the United States and the Soviet Union wooed less developed countries (LDCs) with offers of sophisticated military equipment, hoping to win friends by catering to their security needs or to their desire for weapons as status symbols. However, some LDCs also had carrots available for bargaining purposes, particularly if their location was strategically attractive to a major power seeking to establish a military base in a given area.[33] In the post–Cold War era, the bargaining position of LDCs has eroded somewhat as the end of bipolar competition between Washington and Moscow has reduced LDC leverage, although the United States continues to attach importance to maintaining certain foreign bases.

Regarding the use of military instruments as *sticks,* many would argue that successful diplomacy depends mainly on the number of guns backing it up. This is illustrated by Stalin's reply when asked how much attention he paid to the Vatican's views: "How many divisions does the Pope have?" However, as we have already suggested, the relationship between military power and diplomatic effectiveness is far more complicated than this. For one thing, in disputes between some countries (e.g., the United States and Canada) the threat of armed force is largely irrelevant to the bargaining process, because of the implausibility of one side actually employing such weapons against the other no matter what the substance of the dispute. Even in disputes between enemies, in which military threats are more plausible, their relevance and ultimate usefulness depend on a variety of factors and not only on which side has overall military superiority.

Military resources are particularly relevant to deterrence strategies and the tacit bargaining that goes with them. Although deterrence refers to any attempt by one party to prevent another party from taking some undesired action, the term is most commonly and importantly associated with preventing military attack by making the potential costs of such action exceed the potential benefits in the eyes of the would-be aggressor. Billions of dollars have been spent yearly in the name of such deterrence, and billions of lives rest on deterrence calculations. If deterrence fails—if the opponent strikes—the game changes from diplomacy to war, from deterrence to defense.

Theoretically, deterrent threats are more likely to work against weaker states than against opponents that are equally powerful or superior in military capabilities. Hence, the logic of the well-worn axiom invoked by leaders to justify increased military spending: to maintain the peace (i.e., to prevent aggression), prepare for war. However, several empirical studies have shown that arming to the teeth provides no assurance that one can deter an attack on oneself or on one's allies, and that other factors can be more crucial to successful deterrence than simply superior military strength. In fact, the saber rattling often associated with arming to the teeth can make the other side increasingly paranoid and provoke the very act one wishes to deter by causing the other side to engage in a preemptive strike. For deterrence to work, a prospective attacker must be convinced that the defender actually will stand firm in resisting the attack, and that the costs of attacking will be greater than the value of the goals at stake.[34]

It is generally easier to deter an adversary from attacking one's *own* home-land than to deter it from attacking *another* state, if only because the commit-ment to retaliate in the first case is invariably stronger. However, certain steps can be taken to deter attacks on allies or other countries, such as the "burn all your bridges behind you" ploy used by the United States to enhance the credi-bility of its deterrent doctrine in Western Europe during the post–World War II period. Strong, visible economic and military ties to a threatened state as well as short-term advantages in the balance of forces, rather than heavy-handed bullying, are evidently among the best ways to "extend" deterrence. In a study of seventeen cases of deterrence involving protection of a third party, the at-tacker held back most frequently when there was both economic interdepen-dence and military cooperation between the prospective defender and the threatened state. Formal pronouncements of defense commitments (alliances) were not nearly as effective in deterring aggression.[35]

Another study of deterrence has shown that wishful thinking frequently makes attackers go ahead despite deterrent threats. Leaders who are pressed to-ward aggressive foreign policies by severe domestic or international problems often redefine reality to suit their needs and miscalculate risks as low and ben-efits of attack as high. This has been true throughout the twentieth century in crises from Fashoda (in North Africa) to Korea to Kuwait. "To the extent that leaders perceive the need to act, they become insensitive to the interests and commitments of others that stand in the way of success of their policy."[36]

ECONOMIC RESOURCES AS BARGAINING TOOLS

As military bargaining has become more problematic and dangerous in the nu-clear age, there has been increased attention paid to economic levers of influ-ence.[37] Embargoes, boycotts, multinational investment, frozen assets in banks, and strings attached to foreign aid packages all capture the headlines these days; and all can be used in formal or tacit bargaining.

Under certain conditions, economic levers can be quite effective, especially with states highly dependent on the influencer in an unequal relationship. In colonial days, a foreign power's economic penetration of another society gen-erally was accompanied by its formal incorporation into that power's empire. Today, economic penetration can produce similar domination in more subtle form (sometimes referred to as **neocolonialism**), although penetrated states frequently can counter with leverage of their own. In 1995, for example, the value of the Mexican peso fell precipitously because of financial overcommit-ments, endangering the viability of the North American Free Trade Agree-ment (NAFTA) that Mexico had just entered into with the United States and Canada. Mexico asked Washington for loan guarantees to shore up the Mexi-can currency, and the Clinton administration—to gain the approval of the U.S. Congress—in turn required Mexico to sign over its future oil income to American banks in case of default of payments. Despite some problems, the Mexican government ultimately was able to repay the loans in a timely fashion. Among the economic *carrots* that states attempt to use to induce cooperative behavior from other states are foreign aid grants and credits as well as foreign investment funds and "most favored nation" trading status; economic *sticks* include the withdrawal of the latter benefits as well as **embargoes** (refusing to export needed goods to another state), **boycotts** (refusing to import goods from another state), and expropriation or freezing of a foreign state's assets. Economic resources also can enable a state to purchase what political or military pressure will not provide, as when the United States subsidized South Korean and Thai participation in the Vietnam and Laos wars during the 1960s. Economic means have been used both to strengthen friendly governments (by pumping money into their national economies to relieve domestic political pressures) and to weaken unfriendly ones (by damaging their economies or underwriting subversive activities).[38]

It has been argued that although preponderant military power remains in only a few hands, the ability to influence events around the world has expanded to a variety of relative military weaklings that possess economic prowess, such as Japan, Saudi Arabia, and Germany (notwithstanding the fact that both Germany and Japan have considerable military establishments). Japan has been using foreign aid to China, South Africa, and other countries as a means of gaining influence and smoothing Japanese entry into those markets.

However, it bears repeating that diplomatic influence depends on having appropriate resources for the situation at hand. In the case of economic threats, their effectiveness depends on whether they are relevant to the issue in dispute and whether the country threatened has a sufficient degree of vulnerability to economic penalties. Klaus Knorr has noted that for country A to have "coercive" economic power over country B, the following conditions must exist:

> (1) A must have a high degree of control over the supply of something B values. . . . (2) B's need for this supply must be intensive, and (3) . . . B's cost of compliance must be less than the costs of doing without the supply.[39]

In other words, country B not only must be **sensitive** to the threat posed by country A (i.e., it must have reason to be concerned about the potential damage that might be caused by A's actions) but also must be **vulnerable** (i.e., it must be unable to make policy adjustments to overcome the damage without suffering prohibitive costs in the process).[40] A fourth requirement seems in order as well, namely, that the cost to country A of carrying out the economic sanctions must be lower than the potential benefits, or else country A is not likely to carry them through.

Historical analysis has shown that these conditions rarely prevail and that "one government is almost never able to persuade another to alter its foreign policy significantly by the use of economic sanctions alone."[41] A study of eighteen attempts at economic sanctions between 1933 and 1967 found that only three could be viewed as even partial successes.[42] Another study has shown that of twenty-two cases of trade sanctions by one state against another, trade restrictions succeeded in achieving foreign policy goals in only four cases, with three more resulting in compromise settlements; thus, trade sanctions appeared to "work" to some degree about one-third of the time.[43] The availability of alternate trade sources proved to be a major reason for the fifteen outright failures in the latter study. For example, when the United States tried to punish Cuba during the Cold War by boycotting its sugar and embargoing its oil shipments from Western companies, the Cubans were able to turn to the Soviet Union as a market for their sugar and as a source of oil; even after the collapse of the Soviet Union and the loss of this trade option, Castro managed to keep the Cuban economy afloat by attempting to open Cuba to foreign tourism and investment.[44] At the same time, recent UN trade sanctions aimed at punishing Iraqi aggression against Kuwait and Serb atrocities against Muslims have had at least modest impacts on behavior, as Saddam Hussein opened Iraq's borders to UN nuclear weapons inspectors and the Serb leadership was pressured to come to the bargaining table.

The example of South Africa illustrates the many complications surrounding the use of economic sanctions. For years South Africa weathered relatively half-hearted attempts at international restrictions on its exports and imports, aimed at pressuring the white minority regime in Pretoria both to relinquish colonial rule over Nambia and to end its apartheid system of racial discrimination against South African blacks. Although the United Nations General Assembly called for strict sanctions, many countries retained continued interests in the trade of gold, diamonds, platinum, and other prized goods from South Africa. Western powers also expressed concern that sanctions directed at South Africa would harm the economies of black African states dependent on ties to South Africa. The South African government became adept at transshipping goods from one country to another and buying through intermediary agents.

The type and timing of international economic sanctions have much to do with their effectiveness. Where trade embargoes do not work, it is possible that quieter sanctions such as reducing capital flows—either foreign private investment and loans or foreign aid—can succeed. When the South African financial system began to suffer in the 1980s from denial of international lending and bank credits, much of the business community began to pressure the government about the need to reform South African racial policies. Combined with military setbacks in nearby Angola, these pressures finally bore fruit. The Pretoria government shocked many of its hardline supporters by repealing certain offensive race laws, releasing political prisoners, beginning a dialogue with the African National Congress and its previously jailed leader, Nelson Mandela, and ultimately allowing the "all party" elections that brought

Mandela and the ANC to power in a majority-rule government.[45]

Economic threats or punishments involving foreign aid or investment tend to be most effective when the government under pressure is highly dependent on the country applying the pressure and lacks strong domestic support, as in the case of the Manley government in Jamaica during the 1970s. Prime Minister Manley had moved to nationalize American corporate properties in Jamaica. Loans by United States–dominated international financial institutions then were denied the Jamaican government, resulting in a decline in Jamaica's foreign currency holdings and driving up the cost of goods to the point where the Manley government was defeated by a pro–United States faction in a 1980 election. Similar economic pressures have contributed to the downfall of regimes in Chile, Nicaragua, and elsewhere in Latin America.[46] Yet such measures failed to topple the government of Panamanian dictator Manuel Noriega in the late 1980s and left the Bush administration with only military levers ultimately to bring him down.

As we will see in later chapters, it is increasingly necessary for states to forge agreements to coordinate the world's economic transactions. Economic confrontation and coercion not only are often ineffective as a form of international bargaining, but also tend to undermine the international economic order by producing disruptive effects on employment, prices, and human welfare in general. Yet, sometimes oppressed populations—such as South Africa's black majority—favor foreign sanctions against their own state to gain political rights even if it means added economic hardships. If policymakers are not careful, confusion about ends and means can make a mockery of economic bargaining efforts. In addition to intervening militarily, Washington was called on to spend billions in the 1990s to help rebuild the Panamanian and Haitian economies after the fall of dictatorial regimes, both of which had previously been propped up with U.S. aid and security ties and had subsequently been subject to failed U.S. economic sanctions. Unless sanctions are appropriate, are consistently pursued, and can be enforced effectively, their diplomatic value is questionable.

The Good Diplomat and Good Diplomacy: Rules to Follow in Negotiations

A number of writers have recommended various "rules" that statesmen ought to follow to be good diplomats and to conduct successful diplomacy, particularly regarding formal negotiations (as opposed to tacit bargaining). Many of these rules are related to the ingredients of successful bargaining discussed earlier. We first look at the personal characteristics thought to be essential to serving as a model diplomat, and then at what is required for model diplomacy.

The diplomat: precision without tact

RULES FOR GOOD DIPLOMATS

For those who believe the key to diplomatic negotiations is deception, then the chief "virtue" a good diplomat presumably should have is the ability to lie with a straight face. Indeed, diplomacy has often been defined as "the ability to say and do the nastiest thing in the nicest way"; another famous definition describes a diplomat as "an honest man sent abroad to lie for his country."[47] This rather seedy view of diplomats was captured in a statement by a Polish representative assigned to Moscow during the 1940s, who commented on a Soviet diplomat by the name of Andre Vyshinsky: "In a way, Vyshinsky was the perfect diplomat. He was capable of telling an obvious untruth to your face; you knew it was a lie and he knew that you knew it was a lie, but he stubbornly adhered to it. No other diplomat was able to do this with such nonchalance."[48]

Given the importance of the credibility factor that we noted earlier, however, deceitfulness is hardly very useful as a diplomatic quality. Although any good bargainer might well wish to conceal certain information, and there can be some occasions when duplicity is necessary, there usually is good reason for a diplomat, on balance, to be honest and truthful when conducting negoti-ations—if only to retain future credibility and effectiveness. Of the five quali-ties that Harold Nicolson lists as essential to being an ideal diplomat, the first is truthfulness. The others include precision, in terms of clarity of expression; calmness; modesty, because vanity makes a diplomat more likely to alienate the other side with arrogant behavior or to succumb to its flattery; and loyalty to one's own government, a quality that can sometimes be lost, especially in cases in which a diplomat has spent so much time abroad in a particular post that he or she unconsciously develops an affinity for the local culture and peo-ple, which can affect one's judgment concerning the interests one is represent-ing.[49] Additional traits that have been mentioned over the centuries as essen-tial qualities in a diplomat are presented in the Sidelight on page 285.

RULES FOR GOOD DIPLOMACY

In a sense, a good diplomat must be both persistent and patient. This is the case especially in complicated, drawn-out multilateral diplomacy when the contrasting interests and priorities of many states must be reconciled to reach an agreement, such as the negotiations over the Law of the Sea (discussed in Chapter 15) and the Nuclear Non-Proliferation Treaty (discussed in Chapter 11). Lead negotiators here must be adept at building coalitions of states and using key states to bring along their friends and allies as, for example, the United States prevailed on France to do with its former African colonies dur-ing the Non-Proliferation Treaty (NPT) renewal debate in 1995. Among the complications in this type of diplomacy is the need to "look the other way" when those key states do something objectionable on some issues. At the same time that France helped the United States obtain broad support for re-newal of the NPT that was due to expire in 1995, France angered many states by conducting underwater nuclear weapons tests in the South Pacific. The United States and other states interested in extending the NPT had to be re-strained in their condemnation of France despite opposition to the tests.[50] Diplomats must keep their "eye on the prize"—the ultimate agreement they wish to produce.

In terms of tactics to use in greasing the diplomatic process along, de Cal-lieres, writing in the eighteenth century, urged envoys to "exploit the flush of wine."[51] At the beginning of this chapter we included a Sidelight suggesting how creating an air of informality can also help. Among the rules that diplo-mats ought to observe in the negotiating process, according to Roger Fisher and other serious scholars who have written on bargaining, are the following:[52]

1. *Determine whether the other side is serious about negotiating.* Just because a particular country shows up at the negotiating table does not necessarily mean

SIDELIGHT

AN HISTORICAL CHECKLIST FOR THE MODEL DIPLOMAT

In 1546, at a time when diplomats could be a pretty disreputable lot, the Dutch writer Erasmus advised diplomatic envoys on proper etiquette:

When you spit, turn your back so that you do not dirty anyone else.

Do not spit on the table. Do not blow your nose in the tablecloth; it is to wipe your greasy fingers on.

Do not blow your nose with the same fingers with which you reach into the common dish.

Do not dip half-eaten morsels in the common sauce a second time.

Vomiting is no disgrace provided one does not dirty others.

By 1716, diplomatic service had developed to the point where de Callieres laid down a more professional-sounding series of diplomatic requirements, also with emphasis on self-restraint, discretion, and discipline:

Do not act arrogantly.

Do not show contempt.

Do not immediately resort to threats.

Do not give in to fits of rage.

Do not show off or flaunt yourself.

Above all, the good negotiator must have sufficient control over himself to resist the longing to speak before he has really thought what he shall say.

A man who is naturally violent and easily carried away is ill fitted for the conduct of negotiations.

And finally, he must remember that if once he permits his own personal or outrageous feelings to guide his conduct in negotiation, he is on the sure and straight road to disaster.

Source: The quotes are from F. de Callieres, *On the Manner of Negotiating With Princes.* A. F. Whyte, trans. (Notre Dame, Ind.: University of Notre Dame Press, 1963). Reprinted by permission; and D. Erasmus, *Goede Manuslycke Seden* (Antwerp: Van Waesberghe, 1546. Reprinted in *Het Boeckje van Erasmus Aengaende de Beleeftheidt*. University of Amsterdam, 1969).

it is earnestly interested in reaching an agreement through diplomacy. It might merely be using the negotiations as a vehicle for gaining publicity for its cause and promoting propaganda, or for gathering further information about its opponent's intentions and capabilities. The success of bargaining often depends not so much on the skills of negotiators as on the parties' political interests in a settlement. However, even an "exchange of views" without real negotiation can be helpful in itself if it contributes to greater understanding.

2. *Do not dismiss what might appear to be purely cosmetic or symbolic procedural concerns expressed by the other side.* Sometimes the sticking point in negotiations can occur at the very start, based on such procedural concerns as the shape of the table or the identity of the parties who will be permitted to sit at the table. The United States haggled with the North Vietnamese for several months in Paris over the shape of the negotiating table and who should represent Vietnam. While the raising of procedural issues often reflects a desire to obstruct negotiations, it can also point up the real crux of the problem in a dispute between countries. Imaginative seating arrangements can often be the start of constructive negotiations.

3. Related to points 1 and 2, *show some empathy and understanding toward the other side's position.* As the nineteenth-century French diplomat Talleyrand is reported to have remarked, "For every hour you negotiate, put yourself in your opponent's position for ten minutes." This does not mean caving in to their demands, only understanding what they can reasonably be expected to accept in negotiations. There is a tendency to be self-righteous in defense of one's position and to admonish the other side for "aggressive" behavior or some other misdeed, on the assumption that feelings of guilt can be inflicted on an opponent. However, chances are the other side feels equally self-righteous, so that by exchanging accusations and insults the two sides will likely be merely talking past each other. As Fisher notes, "How they [other parties] feel about the choice we will be asking them to make is just as important to us as how we feel about it."[53]

4. *Offer proposals that are concrete enough for the other side to think about and respond to.* As we noted earlier, the specificity of promises (and threats) can increase their credibility and effectiveness in the negotiating process. In Fisher's words, give the other side a "yesable proposition."

5. *If a comprehensive settlement of all aspects of a dispute is not possible, slice up the problem into narrower, more manageable issues to be negotiated separately.* For example, among the separate issues at stake in the 1978 Camp David accords that President Carter helped to facilitate between Egypt and Israel were: stages of Israeli withdrawal from occupied territory, mutual recognition of each other's sovereignty and normalization of relations, settlement of boundary disputes, the future of the Palestinians, and the future of Jerusalem.[54] Some items were deferred to a later date. Partial settlements based on "salami" tactics (slicing up the package of issues) can endure—as the Camp David agreements did despite the assassination of Egypt's Anwar Sadat by Muslim fundamentalists three years after he had concluded the peace treaty—but they also can leave lingering problems and irritations.

6. *Do not humiliate the other side.* Make it as easy as possible for the other side to accept your terms. As long as you get what you want, you might as well let

the other side *look* good by providing face-saving concessions. You should not gloat over diplomatic triumphs but instead make them appear to be equitable compromises. Even if one side is practically in a position to dictate the terms, a humiliating outcome is likely to leave feelings of bitterness and pressures for revenge in the future, as the punitive Versailles Peace Treaty did after World War I, contributing heavily to German revanchism in the interwar period.

Conclusion

Although this chapter has dealt with diplomacy as something in which national *governments* engage, a variety of actors can become involved in the international bargaining game. Indeed, the game board seems to have expanded, with "terrorist" or "national liberation" groups (depending on one's perspective) seizing hostages and negotiating with foreign governments, as well as other types of *nonstate* actors getting into the act. Still, students of international relations remain most interested in the game as it is played by nation-state leaders and official representatives.

Miles Copeland, a former CIA agent, has tried to detail the "game of nations" by focusing on the cat-and-mouse maneuvers of the U.S. and Egyptian governments in the 1950s and 1960s. As Secretary of State Dulles and President Nasser attempted to make use of each other, they employed a variety of tactics—carrots and sticks—some of which involved official diplomatic channels and others more seamy "cloak and dagger" operations. The two sides were trying to convince each other to cooperate in pursuing important goals, or at least not to impede the pursuit of such goals. A feel for the game can be derived by examining the chapter subtitles in Copeland's book, which is essentially as relevant today as it was when it was written:

> The first prerequisite for winning a game is to know that you're in one.
> If you can't change the board, change the players . . . but settle for a true player, not a pawn.
> That is to say, the new player you bring into the game will have his *own* objectives and policies . . . and his first objective will be to stay in the game—any way he can.
> His second objetive will be to strengthen his position by *constructive* means.
> The stategy of the weak player is to play off the strong players against one another . . .
> . . . and if a single weak player can do this to good effect, a "union" of weak players can do it to better effect.
> If you're going to have a union, you've got to make life intolerable for the scabs . . .

. . . and run the risk of pushing their powerful opponents too far . . .
. . . and push upward, beyond what you can afford, the costs of maintaining
the facade required of an international power . . .
. . . and the gameboard may change on you, making your role irrelevant . . .
. . . and you are likely to come to a Sad End.[55]

In some ways the game analogy applied to world politics is a very useful one, but in some ways it is also unfortunate. The stakes of international politics are all too real and much weightier than World Series and Super Bowls. Human lives, and in fact the fate of the entire planet, are at stake. The language of American sports pastimes has come to reflect international politics lingo; however, throwing "long bombs" and mounting "blitzes" on Monday Night Football should not be confused with the horrors, broken bodies, and bereaved families caused by the real thing. Armies, too, play war games, complete with mock battles and fictitious deaths. Hopefully, military officers and civilian leaders also can distinguish between games and reality.

The world Copeland cites is the world of the realist power broker, but he notes the ultimate futility of the single-minded pursuit of such power. The difference between the "game of nations" and other sorts of games is nicely pointed out in a passage in the Copeland book, where the author quotes Egyptian Vice-President Zakaria Mohieddin speaking before the Egyptian War College in 1962; the following remarks provide a fitting transition to the next chapter:

> The Game of Nations . . . differs from other games—poker, . . . commerce—in several important respects. First, each player has his own aims, different from those of the others, which constitute "winning"; second, every player is forced by his own domestic circumstances to make moves in the Game which have nothing to do with winning and which, indeed, might impair chances of winning; third, in the Game of Nations there are no winners, only losers. The objective of each player is not so much to win as to avoid loss.
>
> The common objective of players in the Game of Nations is merely to keep the Game going. The alternative to the Game is war.[56]

SUMMARY

1. In the game of international relations, national governments attempt to exercise influence through diplomacy—the general process whereby states seek to commnicate, to influence each other, and to resolve conflicts through bargaining. The threatened use of force, and at times even the actual use of force, can be a part of such bargaining.

2. The nature of diplomacy has changed somewhat over the years. In an era of advanced communications and travel technology that has facilitated direct contact between heads of state, the role of the ambassador as a country's representative abroad has diminished somewhat today. Also, there has been a trend toward greater public and multilateral diplomacy, even though much diplomacy remains secret and bilateral in nature. In addition to formal negotiation, countries increasingly make use of more informal, tacit forms of communication. Finally, diplomacy is complicated more than ever by the growing need for officials to play to multiple audiences, not only foreign governments but also domestic constituencies.

3. The essence of diplomacy is bargaining, a process by which each side tries to strike a final agreement as far from its own minimum demands and as close to its maximum demands as possible. Depending on the situation, a party might choose confrontational, accommodative, or problem-solving approaches and strategies. Bargaining parties rely heavily on four types of tactics: threats and punishments (the stick approach) and promises and rewards (the carrot approach). The timing of all these approaches is crucial, as is their credibility and their potency.

4. International bargaining can be described and analyzed in terms of two types of games: zero-sum games, in which one party wins and one party loses; and variable-sum, or mixed-motive, games, in which both parties can simultaneously win something. Most situations in international relations resemble mixed-motive games of some sort. Over time and depending on perceived payoffs, parties can learn to play more cooperatively and with greater mutual payoff.

5. States use both military and economic resources as instruments of international bargaining, to either compel or deter certain behavior on the part of other states. Military resources enable a state to bargain through both threats and promises as well as punishments and rewards. However, the relationship between military power and diplomatic effectiveness is complicated by many factors, including the tenacity with which either side holds on to its goals as well as images and perceptions held by both sides. There is no assurance that arming to the teeth will deter an adversary's attack.

6. As problems with the use of military instruments have increased, more attention has been paid to economic tactics in bargaining. Economic means such as embargoes or foreign aid can be used to strengthen friendly governments and weaken unfriendly ones, but the effectiveness of economic carrots or sticks depends on their timing, their relevance to the issue in dispute, and the degree of a country's vulnerability to various forms of economic pressure.

7. Patience, discretion, and empathy are among the traits of effective diplomats. Rules that successful diplomats generally observe in the negotiating process include the following: (1) Determine whether the other side is serious about negotiating. (2) Do not simply dismiss apparently cosmetic or symbolic procedural concerns expressed by the other side. (3) Show understanding toward the other side's position. (4) Offer proposals concrete enough for the other side to think about and respond. (5) Divide the problem into narrower, more manageable issues to be negotiated separately if a comprehensive settlement is not yet possible. (6) Be aware of other complicating conflicts or problems in which the various negotiating sides are also involved. (7) Keep one's own priorities straight. (8) Do not humiliate the other side.

SUGGESTIONS FOR FURTHER READING AND STUDY

For additional pointers on diplomacy, especially the delicate art of negotiation, see Hans Binnendijk, ed., *National Negotiating Styles* (Washington, D.C.: Center for the Study of Foreign Affairs, Foreign Service Institute, 1987); Janice Gross Stein, *Getting to the Table: The Processes of International Prenegotiation* (Baltimore: Johns Hopkins University Press, 1989); Alfred D. Wilhelm, *The Chinese at the Negotiating Table: Style and Characteristics,* microform (Washington, D.C.: National Defense University Press, 1994); Lavinia Hall, ed., *Negotiating Strategies for Mutual Gain: The Basic Seminar of the Harvard Program on Negotiation* (Newbury Park, Calif.: Sage, 1993); I. William Zartman, *International Multilateral Negotiation: Approaches to the Management of Complexity* (San Francisco: Jossey-Bass, 1994); Jacob Bercovitch, *Resolving International Conflicts: The Theory and Practice of Mediation* (Boulder, Colo.: Lynne Rienner, 1995); Raymond F. Smith, *Negotiating with the Soviets* (Bloomington, In.: Indiana University Press, 1989); and Edwin H. Fedder, "Negotiating Among Nations: A Review Article," *Background,* 9 (February 1966), pp. 339–350. An especially good discussion of tacit diplomacy and "the art of diplomatic signaling" can be found in Raymond Cohen, *Theatre of Power* (New York: Longman, 1987); also see Yoel Cohen, *Media Diplomacy: The Foreign Office in the Mass Communications Age* (London: Frank Cass, 1986). On the relationship between force and diplomacy, see Gordon A. Craig and Alexander George, *Force and Statecraft: Diplomatic Problems of Our Time,* 3rd ed. (New York: Oxford University Press, 1995). For firsthand accounts of personal diplomatic experiences, see memoirs such as Dean G. Acheson, *Present at the Creation* (New York: W. W. Norton, 1969); Nikita S. Khrushchev, *Khrushchev Remembers,* S. Talbot, ed. and trans. (Boston: Little, Brown, 1970); and Henry A. Kissinger, *The White House Years* (Boston: Little, Brown, 1979).

Approaches to conflict and dispute resolution are presented in Roger Fisher, *Beyond Machiavelli: Tools for Coping with Conflict* (Cambridge, Mass.: Harvard University Press, 1994); Muhammad Rabi, *Conflict Resolution and Ethnicity* (Westport, Conn.: Praeger, 1994); I. William Zartman, *Elusive Peace: Negotiating an End to Civil Wars* (Washington, D.C.: Brookings Institution, 1995); Arthur R. Day and Michael W. Doyle, eds., *Escalation and Intervention: Multilateral Security and its Alternatives* (Boulder, Colo.: Westview Press, 1986), Reinhard Rose, ed., *GATT and Conflict Management: A Transatlantic Strategy for a Stronger Regime* (Boulder, Colo.: Westview Press, 1990); Louis Kriesberg, *International Conflict Resolution: The U.S.-USSR and Middle East Cases* (New Haven, Conn.: Yale University Press, 1992); *Intractable Conflicts and their Transformations* (Syracuse, N.Y.: Syracuse University Press, 1989); Raimo Vayrynen, *New Directions in Conflict Theory: Conflict Resolution and Conflict Transformation* (London: Sage, 1991); Tom Woodhouse, *Peacemaking in a Troubled World* (New York: Berg/St. Martin's, 1991); I. William Zartman, ed., *Resolving Regional Conflicts: International Perspectives* (Newbury Park, Calif.: Sage, 1991); Mark Perry, *A Fire in Zion: The Israeli-Palestinian Search for Peace* (New York: Morrow, 1994); and *Resolving Conflict in the Post–Cold War Third World: The Role of Superpowers* (Washington, D.C.: U.S. Institute of Peace, 1991).

For futher insights into the dynamics of bargaining and game theory in various international situations, see Bromley Kniveton, *The Psychology of Bargaining* (Aldershot,

Hants, England: Avebury, 1989); L. N. Rangarajan, *The Limitation of Conflict: A Theory of Bargaining and Negotiation* (London: Croom Helm, 1985); Shibley Telhami, *Power and Leadership in International Bargaining: The Path to the Camp David Accords* (New York: Columbia University Press, 1990); and Joshua S. Goldstein and John R. Freeman, *Three-Way Street: Strategic Reciprocity in World Politics* (Chicago: University of Chicago Press, 1990). On deterrence, see Alexander L. George and Richard Smoke, *Deterrence in American Foreign Policy* (New York: Columbia University Press, 1974); and Patrick M. Morgan, *Deterrence: A Conceptual Analysis* (Beverly Hills, Calif.: Sage, 1977). On the use of economic sanctions, see Miroslav Nincic and Peter Wallensteen, *Dilemmas of Economic Coercion: Sanctions in World Politics* (New York: Praeger, 1983); David Cortright and George Lopez, eds., *Economic Sanctions* (Boulder, Colo.: Westview Press, 1995); and Gary C. Hufbauer and Jeffrey J. Schott, *Economic Sanctions Reconsidered: History and Current Policy* (Washington, D.C.: Institute for International Economics, 1985). Multidisciplinary discussions of bargaining and game theory also can be found in issues of the *Journal of Conflict Resolution* and *Conflict Management and Peace Science.*

Breakdown in the Game:
The Resort to Armed Force

When diplomacy breaks down or seems to promise little, governments today, as in the past, may resort to the use of armed force in international relations. As noted in the previous chapter, violent conflict constitutes only a relatively small fraction of the totality of international interactions. Nevertheless, violence occurs often enough that many observers consider it to be not a breakdown or an aberration but rather a normal part of world politics.

Indeed, what we would recognize as warfare has been known in human society at least since 7500 B.C. (at the battle of Jericho in the Middle East), with evidence pointing to separate origins in at least three regions: ancient Mesopotamia (now Iraq), China, and Mesoamerica (the Mexican–Central American coast).[1] One observer has noted that between 3600 B.C. and the 1980s, there were "only 292 years of peace,"[2] and another remarked that during the 1945–1978 period, "there were not more than twenty-six days . . . in which there was no war [of some kind] somewhere in the world."[3] At that time, in the late 1970s, on an "average" day, about twelve wars were being fought.[4] Yet intriguingly, in the years since, war frequency seems to have diminished, to the point that in 1993, not a single war *between* states was underway, although thirty-four serious armed conflicts *within* states were ongoing.[5] This leaves open the question of how "normal" war is as a global phenomenon, and what form it is likely to take at any given time.

Historical trends may offer some encouragement to those seeking a more peaceful world, especially in regard to large-scale fighting. Certainly one can take heart from the fact that the Cold War gave way to the post–Cold War era essentially without a shot being fired. Many, especially in Europe, have been tempted by this remarkably peaceful systemic transition to conclude that war, at least among major industrialized societies, may have lost its "usefulness" entirely today because economic and technological competition seems a safer and more productive mode of pursuing national interests. Others have speculated that war, like slavery, may be an old human institution whose time has finally gone, because of not only cost but also normative progress.[6] Such thinking was reflected by a poster on the wall of a German university in 1989, amid the swirl of changes occurring in East-West relations and elsewhere in the contemporary international system, advertising a seminar discussion on "Security in the Post-Military Era." This optimism was rudely jarred, however, by the 1990 Iraqi invasion of Kuwait and the American-led retaliation, which some called the first "post–Cold War crisis."

Before we conclude that the end of war is imminent as societies mature, we should examine the body of research on the nature of war, including its causes, so that we can better judge when violent conflict in its various forms is likely to erupt. In this chapter, we discuss the reasons leaders cross the line between diplomacy and force, the ways in which force is used, and the costs and benefits associated with the resort to arms.

As a starting point, let us consider the following quotations, which illustrate two different, though not necessarily mutually exclusive, ways of viewing the use of force in world affairs:

> War is an instrument of policy. . . . The conduct of war . . . is policy itself which takes up the sword in place of the pen. . . .[7]
>
> The quest for international security involves the unconditional surrender by every nation, in a certain measure, of its liberty of action. . . . The ill success . . . of all the efforts . . . to reach this goal leaves us no room to doubt that strong psychological factors are at work, which paralyze these efforts.[8]

According to the first statement, uttered by the famous nineteenth-century Prussian strategist, Karl von Clausewitz, war is merely the "continuation of policy by other means." When the diplomacy of the conference table fails to achieve desired goals, force can be used to seize objectives or to apply sufficient pressure to kindle an adversary's interest in negotiation or bring on capitulation. Bargaining, then, does not necessarily cease when the pen is traded for the sword (or cannon or grenade); leaders still try to convince other leaders to make concessions and adopt acceptable terms of settlement. For example, Iran maintained its embassy and diplomatic relations with Iraq through most of their war in the 1980s.[9]

Those adopting Clausewitz's realist view of war assume that cost-benefit, or "rational" calculations, similar to those discussed in Chapter 7, underlie war-making decisions, and that war is a *deliberate,* conscious policy designed to achieve political goals. One influential version of this argument posits that individual leaders calculate the "expected utility" of making war before undertaking military action. Such expected utilities consist of the values or priorities the leadership attaches to outcomes that might stem from a war, as well as the leaders' willingness to take risks, and estimates of various key probabilities—such as the probability of winning an armed struggle against one or more opponents and the probability of receiving help or encountering opposition from other states in the system. The greater the expected utility of going to war as opposed to remaining at peace, the greater the chance that marching orders will be given.

The chief recent proponent of this view that war is usually a calculated decision is American political scientist Bruce Bueno de Mesquita, who offers as evidence the fact that of fifty-eight interstate wars identified between 1815 and 1974, the attacking nation won forty-two, considerably more than one would expect by chance alone. Looked at a bit differently, "only about 10 percent of the wars fought since the defeat of Napoleon at Waterloo have been quickly and decisively lost by the nation that attacked first."[10] Logically, however, the fact that an attacker wins does not necessarily mean that its attack was carefully planned and timed. Indeed, Bueno de Mesquita might well have divided his study into phases, because it appears that although initiators won most wars between 1815 and 1910, they lost three-fifths of those fought between 1910 and 1965.[11] Yet, although Bueno de Mesquita might acknowledge that war initiators may end up losing, he would probably maintain that, like Japan in World War II, they nevertheless calculate the prospect of at least short-term success in the war effort.

The goals leaders pursue through warfare can be relatively simple and limited, such as the acquisition of a slice of territory, or complex, as in trying to remake an enemy country's entire political system or alter fundamentally the world balance of power. It can be argued that wars based on limited objectives and confined to geographically narrow limits are easier to resolve or win than wars involving complex goals, many regions, or numerous participants.[12] The unanticipated expansion of wars—to include more participants, third parties defending allies, and new issues—may be one reason for initiators' poorer showing in the twentieth century, because wars tended to become more complex and larger during the century.

Bueno de Mesquita and others, in analyzing individual leaders' war decisions, have concluded that the goal of survival in office plays a large role along with the goal of building the state's overall power: ". . . if the policies chosen by leaders are selected because leaders believe they will enhance their position, then the conflicts we see in history do not represent a random sample of all possible conflicts, but rather are a biased sample of wars that were selected by the leader of the initiator because he or she had the expectation of a favorable outcome that would enhance their position."[13] Interestingly, *both* sides in war often have such expectations of success, indicating that misperception and flawed estimations are a major threat to international peace, because both sides obviously cannot be right simultaneously about their expectation of victory. It has been argued that the key mistake leading war initiators to defeat is failure to predict correctly whether their target is likely to receive third-party defense assistance and protection.[14]

Bueno de Mesquita also cautions us not to evaluate the "rationality" of war decisions by the saneness or soundness of leaders' goals, or to expect that emotions will play no part in decision making. Rather, rationality depends on leaders clearly ordering priorities, whether or not those priorities make sense to others, and deliberately weighing costs and benefits in pursuing them through various strategies. Adolf Hitler carried out a systematic plan to conquer Western Europe, and, therefore, technically was rational, although his ultimate goals—world domination and selective genocide—were diabolical and demented. Evidently, though, emotional instabilities and misperceptions, such as those displayed by Hitler, materially distort leaders' estimates of success probabilities, and hence often lead to failure in warfare.[15] Hitler, after all, overextended his forces in attacking the Soviet Union and declaring war on the United States in 1941, hardly rational policy for one intent on building a "1,000-Year Reich" (the so-called Third Reich or German Empire).

Such emotional factors that complicate the rational use of force as a bargaining vehicle are suggested by the second quotation above, from a letter by Albert Einstein in a famous exchange in the 1930s with Sigmund Freud. When emotions become involved in international violence, as Freud argued they inevitably do, reasoned calculations can give way to unlimited and unreasonable applications of force. Freud attributed war to largely unconscious processes of the human mind and speculated that humans have both a life and death wish or instinct, the latter leading them toward world destruction, and the former allowing some hope that culture might be shaped to control destructive impulses.[16] One does not have to go as far as positing such ingrained human instincts, however, to agree that leaders can become caught up with motives of revenge, self-glorification, jealousy, or dominance in warfare, and—despite cunning and calculation—can go beyond the bounds of reason in pursuing violence.

Those adopting the second viewpoint, then, assume war to be mainly the result of visceral responses to the environment based on either (1) a human instinct for violence[17] or (2) complex emotions of fear, frustration, and anger of the type discussed in Chapter 6.[18] Whole nations are sometimes categorized, perhaps inaccurately, as frustrated, vengeful, or warlike in mood by those investigating psychologically rooted causes for international violence.[19] Ambitious leaders might seek to generate, play on, or respond to such moods. Even small-scale conflict over relatively limited territorial goals can, therefore, escalate beyond expectations as emotions creep in and produce hardened hatreds.

No *single* perspective, neither that of Clausewitz nor that of Einstein and Freud, can fully account for the occurrence of international violence. Just as those who see war as a rational bargaining exercise must contend with the often irrational nature of violence, those who see it as the product of deep, dark psychological or biological drives must contend with the fact that not all people fight all of the time; some nations may be warlike at one moment in history and peaceful at other times, and others may be peaceful nearly all the time.[20] Therefore, certain conditions must set the stage for, and ultimately trigger, the decision—calculated or emotional—to go to war. War has been compared to a disease process that, like cancer, seems to occur in multiple forms and have multiple causes.[21] Only by understanding these can we hope to offer possible antidotes to international violence.

Trends in the Use of Armed Force

Traditionally, those who have studied the use of armed force in world politics have been interested primarily in interstate **war,** which is generally thought of as sustained armed combat between the organized military forces of at least two countries. However, war is only one form of hostilities between nation-states. Other forms include isolated or sporadic fighting such as border skirmishes, raids, interventions, and other armed clashes that represent "force without war."[22] Some trends relating to one aspect of force without war, military interventions, were discussed in Chapter 4.

Distinctions between war and other forms of international violence used to be clearer, because wars in the past were definable in *legal* terms and had fairly clear beginnings and endings. A war usually was said to begin when one state issued a formal declaration of war against another state (as in World War II); it normally ended with a formal treaty of peace between the warring parties. Today, however, states tend not to issue declarations of war when they begin fighting, perhaps partly because armed aggression is illegal under the United Nations Charter. One reads instead of "police actions," or "anti-insurgency" or "anti-terrorist" activity, or just plain "self-defense." Fighting sometimes simply fizzles out, or is snuffed out by third-party intervention; the combatants form cease-fire agreements merely to suspend hostilities; these can be broken easily, or they might hold for years before any actual peace treaty is signed (as it finally was between Israel and both Egypt and Jordan after decades of intermittent warfare).

In the midst of confusing labels, it is best to identify various categories of international violence according to the type and extent of fighting that goes on rather than according to whether leaders actually admit to being at war. Although the sustained nature of war tends to make for greater loss of life, all forms of international violence potentially can produce large numbers of casualties. Below we examine in more detail the use of armed force in three categories: (1) international war, (2) force without war, and (3) civil war or internal strife.

INTERNATIONAL WAR

Defending high U.S. defense spending in an era of tight federal budgets in 1995, columnist George Will criticized the sense of optimism, noted at the outset of this chapter, that lasting peace was at hand and large military establishments might not be needed in the future. Will cited Yale historian Donald Kagan, who wrote: "Over the past two centuries the only thing more common than predictions about the end of war has been war itself . . . ; statistically, war has been more common than peace, and extended periods of peace have been rare in a world divided into multiple states."[23] Put another way by a political scientist serving as Assistant Secretary of Defense in 1995, "Through much of history, war has been the norm rather than the exception in relations among nations. For example, there have been wars among the great powers for 60 percent of the years since 1500."[24]

Although the world seldom has been without war somewhere, one needs to put the phenomenon in proper perspective. Using a relatively standard statistical definition of war as the onset of sustained military hostilities between at least one recognized state and another state or foreign armed force culminating in at least 1,000 battle deaths, we find that there were approximately 118 international wars between 1816 and 1980. War incidence during that time generally *declined,* although the trend was a modest one.[25] However, even as the number of international wars initiated has diminished over the years, the *severity* of wars, as measured by casualties, has mounted with the introduction of new weapons throughout the twentieth century. Although some wars in prior centuries killed proportionately large numbers of people, at least twice as many soldiers died in twentieth-century wars (over 22 million) as in *all* the wars from 1500 to 1899 combined (an estimated 11.2 million).[26]

If one takes into account the enormous proliferation of new nation-states since the end of World War II, which has tripled the number of potential candidates for interstate war participation, then a more impressive case can be made that the post–World War II period up to the present has been relatively free of international wars compared with previous eras of world politics. (See Fig. 8.1 for historical trends). Roughly 10 percent of the states in the world since 1965 have been involved in international wars, most waged by lesser military powers (though many with the arms and support of major powers).[27] Although some modern wars (e.g., the Iran-Iraq war of the 1980s) have dragged

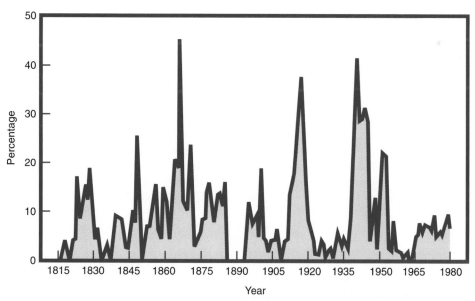

Figure 8.1
PERCENTAGE OF SOVEREIGN STATES ENGAGED IN INTERNATIONAL WARS, 1815–1980
Source: Harold K. Jacobson, *Networks of Interdependence,* 2nd ed. (New York: Knopf, 1984), p. 191. Reproduced with permission of The McGraw-Hill Companies.

on inconclusively for up to a decade or more, generally there have been fewer of the very long wars (lasting thirty years or more) that marked prior centuries. Periods of relative peace may be getting longer as periods of warfare become more condensed.[28]

One distinct trend is a long-term historical decline in the frequency of *great power* war. One study found that wars among major powers in the nineteenth and twentieth centuries were underway only about one-sixth of the time, compared with an estimated 80 percent of the time in the sixteenth to eighteenth centuries.[29] Indeed, perhaps the most striking feature of the Cold War era was the paucity of war involvement by major powers, and in particular, the absence of war *between major powers themselves* (unless one counts the Korean conflict, in which the United States and China fought against each other). Although the United States and Soviet Union faced off in a number of serious crises, such as those concerning Cuba and Berlin—and shot at each other's forces on occasion—they did not directly engage in sustained fighting. The Soviets even proved willing to sustain casualties among their military advisors, inflicted by U.S. air strikes, in war zones such as Vietnam. Some attributed this restraint to the overall effect of nuclear deterrence, whereas others merely noted that no issue in the third world was deemed worthy of world war between Moscow and Washington. As noted in Chapter 3, the absence of great power war in the half century since 1945—the longest such period on record—has been called "the long peace."[30]

Again, optimism about such restraint must be tempered. After all, the other long peace of recent memory—the forty-three-year peace after the end of the Franco-Prussian War in 1871—was followed by one of history's most destructive wars in 1914. It appears likely that international wars will continue to be confined to lesser powers in regions of the developing world rather than waged by major actors engaged in "great power conflicts over the global balance of power."[31] However, recent fighting in the former Yugoslav and Soviet areas renews prospects of larger European warfare, whereas recent tensions between China and Taiwan are fraught with possibilities for escalation beyond the Asian region; thus there remains the potential for major power confrontation, as between the United States and Russia or China.

FORCE WITHOUT WAR

Although the frequency of international war has declined over time, notably among major powers, the distinction between war and peace becomes blurred when one takes into account the amount of **force without war** since 1945. For example, one study examined more than 200 different incidents during the Cold War in which the United States used armed force in some fashion short of war, and a related study identified 190 such incidents in the case of the Soviet Union.[32] In addition to twenty-eight interventions, another study tallied twenty-eight border conflicts and rivalries and twelve blockades, clashes, and crises involving violence during the same period in various regions of the globe.[33]

Abundant cases of force without war can be found in the post–Cold War system. Note, for example, the border clashes between Peru and Ecuador in 1995 (over a boundary dispute dating back more than fifty years),[34] the sporadic exchange of fire between India and Pakistan along the Kashmir cease-fire lines, the skirmishes in the Aegean Sea between Greek and Turkish naval and air forces, episodic fighting between former Soviet republics such as Georgia, Armenia, and Azerbaijan, and China's 1996 conduct of missile "tests" in waters within thirty miles of Taiwan's major ports (aimed at intimidating Taiwan into refraining from declaring its independence from the mainland).

As the Chinese case especially shows, in many instances force has been used more as a political instrument than as a raw military instrument. When force is applied to inflict pain or to persuade an adversary to cease or refrain from some undesired behavior, it represents a kind of "coercive diplomacy," or "diplomacy of violence."[35] For example, over the years the Israeli strategy of harsh reprisals against Arab states hosting Palestinian raiders often has been aimed not so much at physically injuring those countries or destroying their military capabilities as at psychologically convincing their leaders of the intolerable costs of continuing to harbor or support the Palestinians. It often happens, however, that people in pain can become more angry and determined to retaliate and fight on, as demonstrated by Palestinian counter-retaliations. In addition to using force to *influence* an adversary, countries also can use force to *seize* what they want from an adversary. For example, when Israel sent fighter aircraft to destroy Iraq's nuclear reactor in 1981, Israel was not seeking to influence Iraqi decisions about nuclear weapons production but rather to eliminate altogether Iraq's nuclear weapons capability, at least for a time.

It has been argued by some that, along with demonstrative threats to use force (such as troop mobilizations), acts of low-level violence (such as the American bombing of Libya in 1986)[36] have become *surrogates for war* in the nuclear age.[37] Strategists today speak of the "controlled" use of military force in "low-intensity" conflict situations or **limited wars.** The question remains, however, whether such conflicts can remain under control and be kept from exploding into larger conflagrations. The tension between Greece and the former Yugoslav republic of Macedonia in the 1990s—Greece refused to recognize the republic's use of the name "Macedonia" because of the Greeks' historical ties to the area—showed the danger of spillover. In this case, the complications potentially leading to conflict escalation included possible Serbian claims on the territory; the presence nearby of Greece's traditional foe, Turkey; Turkey's opposition to Serb attacks on Muslims in Bosnia; Russia's traditional support of the Serbs; joint Turkey-Greece membership in NATO; NATO's importance for Western security; and Russia's suspicions of NATO. It was determined that the deployment of a NATO peacekeeping force in Macedonia would be helpful as a preemptive measure in calming the situation.

CIVIL WAR

One cannot meaningfully discuss violence in contemporary world politics without discussing **civil wars.** Civil (internal) wars clearly are not a new or recent phenomenon; as long as there have been nation-states, there have been conflicts *within* states that have led to fighting between organized rival armies of the same country. Some of these episodes have produced a greater death toll than conflicts *between* states (e.g., the T'ai P'ing rebellion in China between 1850 and 1864, which is estimated to have cost as many as 30 million lives).[38]

Although civil strife is not a new phenomenon, it has been an especially visible feature of world affairs since 1945, and it has come increasingly to preoccupy the international community in the post–Cold War period. The decolonialization process after World War II produced new states often having highly unstable political and social systems and prone to internal unrest. Civil wars also have taken place in long established states, in Latin America and elsewhere. An estimated twenty-eight civil wars began in the 1980s, with six more continuing from the 1970s during that decade; the late 1980s and 1990s witnessed settlements in some cases (such as Nicaragua and Mozambique), but also new instances of civil strife (as in several former Soviet republics). Nearly all of the roughly forty states involved in major armed conflicts (with at least 1,000 deaths) during the 1990s were engaged in civil wars.[39]

As one writer states, "today's typical war is civil, started by rebels who want to change their country's constitution, alter the balance of power between races, or secede."[40]

> Current conflicts are generally struggles for the control of a state, the secession of a region, or the autonomy of a particular identity group. Most of the victims are civilians, and most of those are women and children. The typical armed conflict does not result from a state's ambitions for regional or global dominance, but from its failure to foster or maintain a society that can provide adequately for its own citizens, either for their political and social rights or for their basic physical needs.[41]

A case in point is the Kampuchea civil war of the 1980s and 1990s. It started with the massive destruction inflicted by government forces of the Khmer Rouge regime on Kampuchea's peasants and professional classes during the late 1970s—a time and place known as the "killing fields"—and led to internecine warfare between competing factions assisted by external powers (the government in Phnom Penh backed by the Vietnamese and the opposi-

KAMPUCHEA'S KILLING FIELDS: 1–2 MILLION WERE LEFT DEAD.

tion backed by the Chinese and to an extent the United States) until a United Nations–sponsored truce restored a measure of order in 1994.

As suggested by the Kampuchea case, of special consequence for international politics has been the increasing tendency over time for civil wars to become *internationalized* (to involve foreign military forces). According to one study, the "percent of civil wars internationalized" rose from 18 percent in the 1919–1939 period to 27 percent in the 1946–1965 period to 36 percent in the 1966–1977 period.[42] During the Cold War, much of the internationalization was driven by the East-West geopolitical competition, with military interventions by third parties seeking to bolster one side or the other in places such as Vietnam, Ethiopia, El Salvador, Afghanistan, and Yemen. The Soviet Union and proxy states often assisted in "wars of national liberation," in which revolutionary groups trying to overthrow colonial rule (for example, in Angola and Mozambique) resorted to **guerrilla warfare** tactics to overcome the stronger conventional military forces of the established authorities, which in turn were trained by the United States or its regional allies in **counterinsurgency** tactics to resist the guerrillas. In contrast, as we noted in Chapter 4, interventionism in the post–Cold War era has tended to be multilateral in character, often approved by regional or global organizations seeking to play a peacekeeping role (e.g., in the Yugoslav civil war). "Failed states"—in which the central government has been replaced by almost total anarchy—pose a special problem for the international community today. In Liberia during the 1990s, as a multinational African force led by Nigeria tried to restore order, the rival Liberian warlords—presiding over marauding bands of youthful soldiers—controlled various parcels of territory and shared different floors of the executive office building in the capital city of Monrovia.

Ethnopolitical conflicts in particular, involving matters of racial, cultural, or religious group identity, have captured recent newspaper headlines.[43] We saw how ethnic tensions in Bosnia and other parts of Yugoslavia, long repressed during the period of Marxist rule, boiled over in the 1990s. Floods of Hutu refugees fled Rwanda in 1994, where Tutsi rebels succeeded in winning control from a Hutu-dominated government they blamed for the slaughter of thousands of Tutsis; tribal warfare threatened to spill across the border into

HUTU REFUGEES FLEEING RWANDA DURING THE 1994 CIVIL WAR.

Burundi and Zaire. Numerous other examples of ethnic-based civil violence can be cited, many of which have become internationalized as refugees flee to neighboring countries to seek sanctuary or claim land, as foreign states send arms or supplies to favored ethnic factions or to governments resisting them, and as multilateral efforts are mounted to bring an end to the conflict.[44]

One can also find long periods of relative calm among ethnic groups in such locales as Bosnia and Rwanda. It appears that the triggering of ethnic violence depends on particular catalysts, such as economic hardship and ruthless political leadership, which inflame peoples' fears and passions.[45] What appears to be ethnically based fighting may actually reflect deeper motives related to territory, wealth, power, and political control. Although "longstanding ethnic tensions can be important, most ['ethnic' conflicts] are really conflicts over other issues that have broken down along ethnic lines, in which people have turned from a state that could or would not meet their needs to the community that they trust to pursue their interests."[46]

In the mid-1990s, it was estimated that nineteen of thirty-four major ongoing armed domestic conflicts were over territory, as opposed to governmental control issues. Only in Africa and Latin America was control of governments more of an issue than control of territory in domestic fighting.[47] This trend would appear to reflect ethnic groups' distrust both of each other and of the state to meet their needs; thus, the goal is to abandon the political system and create one's own state through secession. Unless reversed, this trend figures to be worrisome for governmental leaders in many parts of the world, because there are thousands of different ethnic groups, with relatively few of the 185 nation-states being culturally homogeneous.[48]

HAS THE WORLD BECOME MORE PEACEFUL OR MORE WARLIKE?

If one puts together all of these trends in the use of armed forced in world politics, there is reason to be both hopeful and concerned about the future level of violence on this planet. There has been no war of global magnitude for well over a generation, and international war itself has diminished from a level of about a dozen wars underway in the late 1970s to virtually none in the mid-1990s. As seen in Figure 8.2, international disputes involving either the threat, display, or actual use of force, including wars and force without war, generally have been no higher on average recently than they were in the nineteenth century, allowing for the greater number of independent states today.[49]

However, the human propensity for political violence remains very much in evidence, as demonstrated by the estimated half million to one million people killed in the Rwandan fighting of 1994–1996. All told, over 18 million people have died in civil and international warfare, including force short of war, since 1945, with the carnage continuing into the post–Cold War era. Because

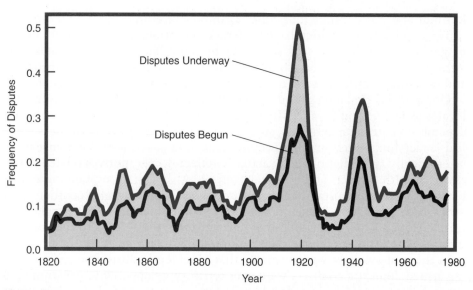

Figure 8.2
FREQUENCY OF MILITARIZED DISPUTES, 1816–1976
These are five-year moving averages of disputes begun and already underway in any given year in the international system, normalized by the number of independent states in the system. Included are threats to use force, troop alerts, mobilizations, shows of force, blockades, invasions, clashes, and wars.
Source: Charles S. Gochman and Zeev Maoz, "Militarized Interstate Disputes, 1816–1976: Procedures, Patterns, and Insights," *Journal of Conflict Resolution,* 28 (December © 1984), pp. 585–616. Reprinted by permission of Sage Publications, Inc.

of the outbreak of domestic fighting and civil wars, civilians have come to represent nearly 90 percent of all war casualties, and the number of refugees fleeing warfare has mushroomed tenfold, from about 2.5 million in the mid-1970s to more than 23 million in 1995.[50] In the mid-1990s, Africa remained the "most warring region on the planet," with fourteen major armed conflicts. Despite the end of the Cold War, the level of total global military spending remains at approximately $750 billion, only modestly reduced from the high-water mark of the 1980s.[51]

Moreover, various countries—whether in the name of deterrence or defense—are *preparing* for ever more sophisticated, exotic forms of warfare, including thermonuclear, chemical, and biological war. This, of course, does not even take into account the other, *nonstate* sources of political violence in the international system, such as international terrorism. We discuss later in the book what steps the international community is taking to regulate international violence. First, though, we must look more carefully at the causes of international violence and war in particular.

The Causes of War: Theories and Evidence

A POTPOURRI OF THEORIES

The search for causes of war and peace has gone on for centuries and has included historical, philosophical, and scientific approaches.[52] Among the more interesting perspectives are those found in anthropological studies of human warfare as it has evolved over the past one million years. It seems that human history has been replete with organized violence, although the exact patterns have varied in different periods and regions. "Primitive" tribal or clan warfare tended to be ritualized, with blood revenge, religious duty, occult beliefs, individual prestige, social responsibility, and the capture of possessions—including women and children—impelling the warriors. Although relatively few deaths seemed to result, massacres were not unknown, and the effect of war often was to relieve population pressure on food and resources.[53] Some of these same basic motivations, in different form, may be present in "modern" warfare. As societies became agriculturally based and settled in fixed locations by the fourth century B.C., large-scale territorial conquest and empire building became feasible as well; the scale of modern warfare and the preparations for it expanded considerably.[54]

As with the determinants of foreign policy behavior in general, outlined in Chapter 5, it is helpful to focus on *individual, nation-state,* and *international system* levels of analysis in examining theories about the causes of war. The classic treatment of war using this framework is Kenneth Waltz's *Man, the State and War,* which referred to the three levels as offering three different "images" or sets of explanations of war.[55] The most complex explanatory theories attempt to link factors across all three levels. Some researchers have argued persuasively that satisfactory explanations can only be derived by examining leaders' perceived "opportunity" and "willingness" to indulge in warfare, which depend on factors operating at each of the three levels;[56] a war decision depends not only on whether the environment presents leaders with opportunities to achieve gains through warfare but also on leaders' perceptions and how willing they are to respond to those opportunities.

When we speak of *individual-level* causes, we are referring to a host of psychological and social-psychological factors related to the use of force. We already have mentioned that aggressive instincts common to all humans have been proposed as a cause of war, but aside from the widespread occurrence of human fighting, there is little evidence to support the instinct theory.[57] Some scholars argue that certain "personality types" (as opposed to human beings in general) are especially prone to violence and that when such individuals are found in leadership positions in nation-states, the possibilities of their states becoming involved in war increase.[58] Other scholars contend that inherent personality traits of individual leaders are less important than the nature of the decision-making and communications processes that often result in widespread misperceptions of policies and signals.[59] Still others argue that war, like other forms of violence, is often the product of anger, frustration, fear, the desire for dominance or survival, and other basic drives or emotions.[60]

Of central concern at the individual level of analysis are the factors that make the use of force acceptable or desirable. Acts that in other circumstances would be classified as murder become legal when carried out in the name of and at the behest of the state. There are factors at work in the roles individuals play as citizens or government officials that seem to allow this transference from unacceptable to acceptable violence. Nationalistic beliefs among a country's population and leaders' sense of responsibility for the security of that population can be used to justify the use of force.

Just as national attributes at the *nation-state* level can affect foreign policy behavior in general, they can influence the resort to violence in particular. Bueno de Mesquita and Lalman fault classical realist theories, which view states as driven by the pursuit of power and national interests in the international arena, for paying too little attention to domestic political factors—particularly the desire of incumbents to survive in political office—as determinants of war decisions.[61] They link individual leaders' motivations to remain in office with the pressures they encounter inside democratic governments to help explain the phenomenon we referred to in Chapter 5 as "democratic peace," i.e., the tendency of democracies not to fight *each other*. Leaders of democratic states facing each other in an international dispute supposedly will each rationally calculate that the other will have to pay a relatively heavy political price to go to war against a fellow democracy, and so, not having to fear a surprise attack, they will each be rather restrained in the tactics they employ to settle the dispute.[62]

Another proponent of the "democratic peace" thesis also relies on domestic processes, this time focused on economic interest groups, linked to international free trade and the development of democracies: "I propose a causal chain: trade within as well as between nations promotes prosperity. Prosperity promotes democracy. There is almost no risk of war among democracies."[63]

Although democratic political systems seem unlikely to fight each other very frequently,[64] other hypotheses about the effects of domestic political system characteristics do not seem to have been verified. For example, the notion that internal governmental instability prompts leaders to identify foreign scapegoats and adopt belligerent foreign policies has not been supported generally, though it may be true in specific cases. Such instabilities, of course, may tempt foreign leaders to attack or intervene to take advantage of internal problems.[65] Cultural explanations, too (for example, that the Germans or others are militaristic in character) generally have failed to be substantiated by researchers. However, one recent study has isolated the potential importance of cultural similarity, in the form of either ethnic similarity or religious dissimilarity, between pairs of warring states.[66]

A number of studies have verified that there is a correlation between national strength and hostile tendencies, with countries having sizable military and economic establishments being historically somewhat more inclined to engage in violent conflict than other states, perhaps because they become involved in more foreign crisis situations and transactions generally.[67] Clearly, though, states of all shapes and sizes have been known to participate in war (especially in recent times).

Finally, it also has been suggested that war cycles may exist and correspond to "national moods," i.e., there may be initial enthusiasm for war, followed by exhaustion and then disillusionment, followed perhaps in a twenty-year interval by renewed willingness to engage in warfare (coinciding with the rise to power of a new generation of leaders untouched by the memory of war).[68] At most, though, such mood swings only make war more or less possible; they do not account for the actual decisions to undertake fighting.

Recent research indicates that, to the extent war cycles of the type alluded to exist, they are related not only to individual and national level causes, but also to factors operating at the *international system* level. Many systems theorists have come to explain large-scale wars as struggles for dominance, or "hegemony," in the system—for control of economic resources, territory, and the power to make rules.[69] George Modelski has argued that recurrent "global wars" are attributable to periodic changes in the international system, whereby dominant states, such as Britain, might decline in power, because of internal economic or political problems, leading to increased competition among rising powers such as Germany or Japan. Global wars generally have ended with the establishment of a new international leadership structure, which itself then begins to degenerate over time, much as people have argued that American hegemony has declined since the immediate aftermath of World War II.[70] In other words, what might appear to be war cycles are really reactions to the "deconcentration" and "reconcentration" of power aimed at domination or regulation of the international system.

At the level of the international system, many theorists focus on power relationships as a cause of war, with a favorite explanation being that a balance of power (military parity) tends to deter aggression.[71] However, others argue just the opposite, that war is more likely between equals than unequals, because between unequals "the weaker *dare* not fight and the stronger *need* not."[72] The empirical evidence is inconclusive; as we noted, wars can occur between equals as well as unequals, although the grosser the inequality the less likely it appears that war will occur or will be of long duration.[73] It is sometimes suggested that wars result from *changes* in power relationships, and that war is more likely in a period of "power transition," when one state—particularly one dissatisfied with the status quo—is gaining on another and seeks to be accorded enhanced status.[74]

Scholars also have looked for causes of war in such aspects of the international system as the number and type of alliances, the number of major powers or power centers and their flexibility, the proportion or concentration of total world power held by the latter, and the number of unresolved disputes in the system.[75] It has been hypothesized that a multipolar world of flexible alignments tends to be more peaceful than a bipolar world of rigid alliances; others, however, have argued the contrary.[76] Patrick James has summarized the some-times contradictory research on system effects on war as follows:

> In the nineteenth century, war proneness was greater in bipolar systems; in the twentieth century, it has been greater in multipolar systems. Concentration of capabilities was similarly linked to war. In the nineteenth century, preponderance in concentration was associated with war; in the twentieth century, systems with parity in capabilities seemed more war-prone . . . [though] the likelihood of war [may peak] at a moderate level of concentration. . . . Alliance formation is positively associated with war in the twentieth century, and negatively associated with war in the nineteenth. Finally research on polarization, or the rigidity of alliances, has produced the most strongly confirmed results of all. War appears to be associated with increasing systemic tightness, although one study . . . suggests . . . the likelihood of war being minimized at a moderate level of polarization.[77]

Explaining the seeming contradiction that inequality and equality in the structure of the international system can, at varying times, both deter and fail to deter war, Most and Starr argue that the key is, once again, in the opportunity for war that is afforded individual pairs of states (or "dyads") by the overall system structure, and the individual decision maker's willingness to seize that opportunity. Presuming that it is easier for stronger powers to attack weaker ones than vice versa, and counting the number of balanced and unbalanced pairs of states in various historical and imagined ("simulated") international systems with different combinations of major and minor powers, Most and Starr determine that unbalanced pairs rise and fall in frequency depending on the overall size of the system of states. Therefore, it is less the overall structural power balance of the system than the number of pairs with the opportunity to fight that determines war probability.[78]

One additional key systemic factor, alluded to in Chapter 5, is the number of borders countries share and their geographic proximity to each other. Distant countries seldom fight, partly because they lack the power to reach each other militarily. John Vasquez is among those scholars who argue that the key recurring motive for wars is contention over borders, as countries basically fight for territory as a means to security (and occasionally wealth).[79] Territorial imperatives also trigger domestic fighting in many cases, as for example, when ethnic groups seek to dominate a particular area of a country and resort to "ethnic cleansing" of rival groups.

The causes of war are difficult to pinpoint because the phenomenon defies single-factor explanation. Although at times we may wish to account for the overall *amount* of war underway in the international system, at other times we may want to explain the outbreak of a *specific* war.[80] Some causes might apply to large global wars and others to more limited, regional wars. One way to obtain a better grip on causation is to distinguish *long-range*, underlying causes of war ("background conditions") from the more *immediate* causes (which might be termed "triggers").[81] Background causes can be likened to the combustible conditions—what could be called *permissive* factors—that make a fire possible, and immediate causes correspond to the spark that sets off the flames. Both background and immediate causes must be explored to fully comprehend the "story" of moves and countermoves leading to any particular war.[82] (See the box below.)

"THE STEPS TO WAR"

Wars normally do not just happen out of the blue with no warning. Usually there is a process of escalation of tensions that gives early indication that a warlike situation is developing, for those interested in reading the barometer and conceivably taking steps to avoid armed confrontation. That process is outlined in the following excerpt, based on generalizations derived from research studies:

> As a situation develops that might portend the use of force, leaders and various policy influencers become concerned primarily with security goals and/or the use of force to gain stakes that they have been unable to attain up to this point. In order to test their rival and to demonstrate resolve, leaders rely on threats and coercive tactics, which involves them in crises (or serious disputes). Leaders respond to a crisis and to security issues that are perceived as posing a long-term threat by attempting to increase their military power through alliances and/or a military build-up. In a tense environment, military build-ups lead to arms races, and alliance-making may result in a polarization (of blocs), both of which increase insecurity. . . . Eventually a dispute arises that escalates to war. Disputes or crises are most likely to escalate if there is an ongoing arms race, and if (1) they are triggered by physical threats to vital issues; (2) they are the second or third crisis with the same rival (. . . tactics becoming more coercive and hostile in each succeeding crisis); (3) a hostile interaction spiral emerges during the crisis; and (4) hard-liners dominate the leadership of at least one side.

Thus, although rational decision-making theorists see war as a product of calculated choice, to understand why some situations and crises end up in combat and others do not, a more complete picture of the context leading up to the occasion for decision is necessary, complete with the action-reaction sequences, such as arms races and prior crises, and misperceptions that add to tension levels.

Source: John A. Vasquez, "The Steps to War: Toward a Scientific Explanation of Correlates of War Findings," *World Politics,* 40 (October 1987), p. 117. Reprinted by permission of the Johns Hopkins University Press.

BACKGROUND CONDITIONS

Among the background conditions that set the stage for war are (1) leaders and citizens who are highly nationalistic or dedicated to social group identity and obedient to political authority; (2) military-industrial complexes; and (3) arms races. We have chosen to discuss these partly because they are subject to change and human control and, therefore, offer hope of controlling the onset of warfare. Also, these three factors each operate at different levels of analysis: obedience to authority is an individual characteristic; military-industrial complexes are nation-state characteristics; and arms races occur in the international system.

Examining *obedience to authority,* Dr. Stanley Milgram conducted a series of dramatic experiments in the 1960s at Yale University using a sample of American male adults aged twenty to fifty years who represented diverse occupations. The experiments showed that the subjects were willing to administer painful and potentially fatal electric shocks to selected victims in a supposed training session at the command of individuals posing as authority figures. The victims pretended to receive shocks when unsuspecting subjects were asked by the authority to turn a dial on a control panel to successively higher voltage levels. Milgram noted that:

> War too moves forward on the triad of an authority which commands a person to destroy the enemy, and perhaps all organized hostility may be viewed as a theme and variation on the three elements of authority, executant, and victim.[83]

Milgram went on to investigate the limits of obedience as he tried to make the victims increasingly human and real to those called on to shock them:

> What is the limit of such obedience? At many points we attempted to establish a boundary. Cries from the victim were inserted: not good enough. The victim claimed heart trouble; subjects still shocked him on command. The victim pleaded to be let free, and his answers no longer registered on the signal box; subjects continued to shock him. . . . The final effort . . . was the Touch-Proximity condition. But the very first subject in this condition subdued the victim on command, and proceeded to the highest shock level.[84]

As the subjects became less remote from the victims they were shocking, the average shock they were willing to administer declined; yet 25 percent of the subjects still administered the maximum shock (450 volts), even to victims they had touched. There may be a cause for some optimism in that 70 percent of the subjects were willing to defy the authority when they were put in touch contact with the victim, i.e., ordered to force the victim's hand onto the shockplate; yet 30 percent went ahead with shocks even then. Analogously, it has been argued that soldiers find it easier to bomb anonymous victims from the air than to engage people in face-to-face combat.

The Milgram experiments do not indicate that sadism was rampant in New Haven, Connecticut, but rather that society seems to produce authority-obedience relations in which people may lose their sense of independent judgment. This loss may or may not transfer directly to the battlefield; studies of American infantry in World War II have shown that only an average of 15 to 25 percent of soldiers actually fired their weapons at the enemy.[85] Apparently, commanders' orders to fire are not always obeyed. Nevertheless, government orders continue to carry considerable authority in all countries, and government interpretations of threats to the nation carry considerable weight. The willingness of a people to go to war and to kill others for their country depends in part on that authority.

Citizen obedience to national authorities, especially in long-established states, stems largely from a strong national identity. Such identity, as well as group identity in civil wars, is based on socialization processes in each society channeled through families and educational and cultural institutions. As we have noted, nationalism has been a powerful force in human affairs. It has been called humanity's most fanatical religion and has caused some to define a nation as "the largest group for which one would be willing to die." While identifying as a nation, the group also identifies outsiders as "foreign," in a "we-they" dichotomy. Nationalism was a major factor in both twentieth century world wars—in World War I as large empires broke up, and in World War II as German leaders indulged in hatred and subjugation of foreigners and racial or ethnic minorities, and Soviet, British, American, Chinese, and Japanese leaders called on citizens to defend their homelands.

Although some would contend that **military-industrial complexes** also are a necessary condition for war, the evidence is less conclusive.[86] At the very least, such complexes would seem to be background factors contributing to war-making *potential* and to high armament levels that might not necessarily be warranted by security needs. When President Eisenhower left office in 1961, the former general commented about the growth of a permanent arms industry and vastly increased peacetime military force in the United States:

> This conjunction of an immense military establishment and a large arms industry is new in the American experience. The total influence—economic, political, and even spiritual—is felt in every city, every statehouse, every office of the federal government. We recognize the imperative need for this development. Yet we must not fail to comprehend its grave implications. Our toil, resources, and livelihood are all involved; so is the very structure of our society.
>
> In the councils of government, we must guard against the acquisition of unwarranted influence, whether sought or unsought, by the military-industrial complex. The potential for the disastrous rise of misplaced power exists and will persist.[87]

President Eisenhower appeared troubled by the effects that a powerful alliance between arms manufacturers and defense bureaucrats might have on

American democracy. This was not a new concern in American thinking; after World War I, those interested in laying blame for the costly U.S. involvement tended to single out captains of industry and their linkages to military brass in pursuit of bigger munitions profits. Leftist thinkers, in the tradition of Marx and Lenin, likewise have contended that capitalist societies such as the United States naturally come to develop a military-industrial complex geared toward war because, in addition to the imperialistic impulses of such societies, maintenance of jobs and prosperity comes to depend on large standing armies and arms industries. The point is often made, for example, that it was World War II that brought the United States out of the Great Depression of the 1930s and fueled the post-1945 prosperity. Indeed, the defense sector has been one of the largest spending "engines" that the government can apply to the economy.

However, many scholars have questioned this line of analysis, arguing that even though a military-industrial complex might exist in the United States and other Western countries, and heavily influences decisions about defense spending, it does not necessarily have power over foreign policy in general. Furthermore, both Soviet Russia and Communist China have had massive military-industrial interests and establishments.[88] It is also questionable whether most elements of the business community in America and elsewhere are necessarily hawkish in their foreign policy attitudes, and whether they tend to benefit financially more from war than from peace (which brings stability and favorable international trade markets). The lively debate about the extent and effects of the American military-industrial complex is illustrated in the box on pages 315–316. To the extent that there is a connection between such complexes and war, it is generally a case not so much of individuals directly conspiring to create a hostile international climate, but rather of institutionalized pressures for arms spending that *indirectly* move a nation toward a war footing. The elevation of military priorities in a society, part of the process of *militarization,* can move that society toward accepting the necessity of war and toward support of increased armaments production.

Thus, the kind of complexes about which Eisenhower warned bear some relation to the excessive obedience problem noted by Milgram. They also relate to **arms races,** which at the system level represent a third important harbinger of war. Arms races are at least partly an action-reaction process between states and seem to depend on governments' mutual threat perception as well as the contestants' capacity and desire to pay the costs of armament. Each country increases its armaments in response to the opponent's arms, according to their mutual distrust and hostility, and in line with domestic spending priorities; the race might escalate slowly or rapidly, become frozen at a point of mutual security, or even deescalate. Many scholars have hypothesized that when an arms race gets out of control, there is a tendency for it to culminate in war—or at least a preemptive military attack on arms facilities—as a result of increasing tension and insecurity.[89]

Not all wars are preceded by arms races, and not all such races result in wars. In one study of eighty-four wars ending between 1820 and 1928, only ten

THE DEBATE ABOUT THE U.S. MILITARY-INDUSTRIAL COMPLEX

Pros

A military-industrial complex exists and it is dangerous for peace:

1. There is a revolving door through which an elite group rotates between positions in the Department of Defense (DOD) and in corporate board rooms, with generals and admirals retiring to work for defense firms and corporate executives taking leaves of absence to serve as Pentagon managers. More than 3,000 retired high-ranking military officers went on to work for major U.S. defense contracting corporations in the 1980s.

2. The American armed services tailor their weapons orders at least partially to the needs of favored contractors; orders frequently are placed to keep important production lines operating. Close to 70 percent of every federal dollar allotted to research and development in the 1980s, and 60 percent in the 1990s, went into military R&D. A new line of exotic and expensive military hardware already is being planned for the twenty-first century despite the lack of a defined major power "enemy" of the United States.

3. The main sectors of the American economy have come to depend on the built-in obsolescence and costly technology typical of military production. DOD annually receives the largest single allotment of discretionary funds in the entire federal government budget. Over the course of the Cold War, an estimated $4 trillion was spent on U.S. nuclear preparations alone.

4. America's largest industrial firms tend to be defense contractors with overseas interests. More than 30,000 U.S. companies were engaged in military production during the 1980s. Such corporations have interests in arms sales abroad, which can lead to or escalate wars.

5. American states with numerous defense industries and military installations have enjoyed disproportionate representation on House and Senate Armed Services Committees in the U.S. Congress. There is a tendency for local citizenry and their representatives from such districts to develop hawkish attitudes on national defense to justify and legitimize the continuation of government funding. Of 3,041 U.S. counties, only nine received less than $1,000 in Defense Department funds in 1984. In 1995, Congress tried to force the President to accept approximately $7 billion *more* in arms expenditures than DOD had even requested.

Cons

The military-industrial complex is not a monolith and it does not endanger peace:

1. Most large American corporations derive only a small percentage of their business and profits from defense production, and with post–Cold War government spending cutbacks, that percentage has been declining. Even major defense contractors tend to have diversified interests and have increasingly produced "dual-use" products suitable for civilian or military applications. Former military officers can serve important watchdog functions in defense plants to increase efficiency.

2. American military expenditures have not consistently increased over time, especially as a percentage of federal spending and the gross national product. These expenditures began to decline in real terms after 1985.

3. Other powerful interest group complexes, such as agriculture and health care, compete with the military complex for government influence and R&D spending.

4. Wars disrupt business operations and can contribute to inflation. During the Vietnam War, the U.S. stock market went up, not down, in response to reports of peace initiatives. Arms transfers to some warring parties can help to put a stop to fighting by reestablishing balances of power and assisting in self-defense.

5. Although individual representatives and senators might be affected by defense interests in their constituencies, their votes on defense issues in Congress have not closely correlated to the number or impact of military facilities in congressional districts. Indeed such facilities have been sharply reduced in budget-cutting exercises in the 1990s.

Sources: Most of these and other arguments are presented cogently in Steven Rosen, ed., *Testing the Theory of the Military-Industrial Complex* (Lexington, Mass.: Lexington Books, 1973), especially pp. 23–25. See also Seymour Melman, *Pentagon Capitalism: The Political Economy of War* (New York: McGraw-Hill, 1970); Bruce Russett, *What Price Vigilance?* (New Haven: Yale University Press, 1970); *The Defense Monitor,* 15 and 22 (Washington, D.C.: Center for Defense Information, 1986 and 1993); Bob Adams, "Revolving Door: Contractors Hire Away Watchdogs," *St. Louis Post-Dispatch,* December 17, 1985, pp. 1–7; Lloyd J. Dumas, *The Overburdened Economy: Uncovering the Causes of Chronic Unemployment, Inflation, and National Decline* (Berkeley: University of California Press, 1986); Dumas, *Making the Peace Possible: The Promise of Economic Conversion* (Oxford: Pergamon Press, 1989); Frederic S. Pearson and Michael Brzoska, *Arms and Warfare: Escalation, Deescalation, Negotiation* (Columbia, S.C.: University of South Carolina Press, 1994); and Jonathan S. Landay, "Study Reveals US Has Spent $4 Trillion on Nukes Since '45," *Christian Science Monitor,* July 12, 1995, p. 3.

were preceded by arms races thought to have been a cause, although several of the other seventy-four were preceded by races of one sort or another.[90] However, several studies have shown the background importance of such races in creating an atmosphere for war. International disputes since 1816 that were accompanied by arms races were much more likely to result in war than those without such races.[91] Another study of thirteen arms races since 1840 concluded that wars resulted in five of the cases; thus arms races could not be said to be a sufficient condition of war. In attempting to explain these findings, the author pointed to (1) the duration of the race, with shorter ones leading to war; and (2) the nature of the race, with competition over numbers of weapons rather than technology evidently more likely to end in war.[92] Causation is difficult to demonstrate in such circumstances, because the contestants could have seen war coming first and then armed themselves; arms races might be more a symptom than a cause of tension. Although military preparation sometimes can lead to war, failure to arm quickly enough, as in the case of European allies opposing Hitler, also can hasten war's onset.[93]

Many different background conditions are likely to operate in the unfolding story of any given war. Briefly taking World War I as an example, one could identify colonial competition between England and Germany and other states, nationalism, arms races, geographical peculiarities, and the formation of two hostile alliances as important background causes when August 1914 dawned. Germany was surrounded by Russia on the east and France on the west, with Russia and France in close alliance. Austria, Germany's ally, meanwhile felt threatened by Russian support of Slavic nationalism in Serbia and other parts of the Austro-Hungarian Empire. The delicate house of cards was balanced precariously, waiting for an ill wind to blow it down.

IMMEDIATE CAUSES

In speaking of immediate causes of war, we refer to the triggers, the ill winds, that directly set off the fighting. Often these triggers relate to sudden crises and overburdened diplomacy. For example, the assassination of the Austrian archduke in July 1914, in Sarajevo (what is now Bosnia), created a crisis situation that set off a chain reaction of troop mobilizations leading to World War I. Austrian leaders blamed the killing on Serbian-trained Slavic nationalists seeking to destroy the Austrian empire. To seize the opportunity in a vain attempt to crush such nationalism, Austria issued an ultimatum to Serbia. Germany gave a blank check of support to the Austrian ultimatum, failing to push strongly for diplomatic restraint on the part of its ally. Russia backed its Slavic Serbian allies. The great European powers, in two basic alliance structures, began to square off. Leaders tended to react to the tension by employing existing inflexible military plans. Germany, worried about Russian mobilization and a two-front war, prepared to attack and eliminate France. Russia, limited by a ponderous mobilization system, reacted on both the Austrian and German fronts. France, worried by German preparations, mobilized and attempted to involve England. The failure to negotiate the disputes sent Europe and the rest of the world headlong over the brink.[94]

Thus, the ineffectiveness of crisis decision making and diplomacy has much to do with the outbreak of war. As noted in Chapter 6, crises are high-threat situations in which decision makers tend to be under severe stress and are highly susceptible to misperception. Misperception of diplomatic messages and signals, and an exaggerated sense of time pressure, greatly accelerated the slide toward war in 1914. Leaders under stress can react violently to sudden changes in either their domestic or international environments.[95] In particular, if a government fears imminent attack by a neighboring state, it is more likely to launch a preemptive attack.

Changes in the environment not only can increase threat perception, but also can produce a sense of *deprivation* and *frustration* if decision makers are blocked from realizing crucial needs, a factor that has been linked to human aggression in a number of studies.[96] Crises seem especially likely to result in the use of armed force when a state is faced with sudden loss of control over a region or territory where it is accustomed to exercising influence; witness the dispatch of Soviet troops to Afghanistan in 1979 and of U.S. troops to Lebanon in 1958 and Vietnam in 1965.[97] However, although frustrations can produce aggressive behavior, they do not invariably do so.[98] Countries that at a given time have been growing industrially but lag behind world leaders in standard of living, access to resources, and international status frequently have resorted to war to push for an increased share of these benefits.[99] Yet such war triggers often have been defused through diplomacy.

The Outcomes and Consequences of War

WHO WINS?

The side with the largest armies does not invariably win all wars, as Vietnam and other cases obviously demonstrate. Bueno de Mesquita found that the side with the most "power" on paper (measured by military and economic resources combined) did prevail in 75 percent of all of the interstate wars he studied between 1815 and 1974.[100] The bulk of historical evidence indicates that wars are most likely to be won not so much by states with only raw military capabilities as by those states able effectively to mobilize their populations in a united fashion and extract sufficient revenue and economic resources from their societies to support the war effort.[101]

HISTORICAL CONSEQUENCES OF WAR

Regardless of whether one wins or loses, war can involve enormous human, political, and economic costs for the participants. As weapons have become more powerful, we have seen that war has produced increased carnage in the twentieth century. For example, counting military and civilian casualties, approximately 60 million people died in World War II; altogether, the death toll represented 3 percent of the world's population at that time. Most European countries from Germany eastward lost approximately 10 percent of their populations. Death tolls frequently have been as high or higher for war winners as for losers (a result found in 45 percent of all wars).[102]

Aside from the human costs, wars can have profound effects on the international power structure, sustaining or overturning the prevailing hierarchy. In World War II, Germany and Japan entered the war as major world powers and came out as also-rans, with the emergence of the United States and the Soviet Union as superpowers after 1945. Yet, there are those who argue that the effects of war on national power and influence are exaggerated, because both Germany and Japan gradually regained their international influence and have emerged as leading industrial powers. It is argued that power, like water, finds its own level; if a country has the population and technological skills and resources, it will eventually bounce back from war approximately to the point where it was heading before the war.[103] It is well to remember, though, that four massive empires crumbled in World War I and never fully recovered.

Political leaders often are among the "casualties" of war, because states participating in wars frequently experience changes in government soon after the conflict has ended. Ninety-one percent of the losers in World Wars I and II had nonconstitutional changes of government within three years after the war, whereas 20 percent of the winners underwent such changes. Aggregate data for wars between 1815 and 1965 show that 36 percent of the losers and 18 percent of the winners experienced such changes.[104] This means that war is a high-risk proposition for governments; there is nearly a 40 percent probability that they will not be around long if they lose, and a 20 percent risk even if they win. Monumental revolutions throughout history, including those in America and France in the eighteenth century and in Russia and China in the twentieth century, developed during or after international wars. Warfare can so weaken governments and embitter populations that old regimes are thrown out. Even national heroes such as Winston Churchill and Charles de Gaulle were quickly voted out of office after World War II, although both made subsequent comebacks.

Other domestic consequences of war—those often associated with the ouster of wartime governments—can include changed social values and the disruption of entire economies. World War I generally is regarded as the origin of the "lost generation" and the "roaring twenties," in which Victorian mores finally were discarded in a "live for now" era.[105] Although World War II coincided with the end of the Great Depression, it does not appear that war generally is good for economies. Although war often has served as a short-term stimulant in reducing unemployment, it also has tended to be accompanied by high inflation in the cost of goods as well as by higher taxes.[106] As President Johnson found during the Vietnam War, it is difficult to wage a "war on poverty" at home at the same time that one is expending billions of dollars to fight a war abroad.[107]

POTENTIAL CONSEQUENCES OF WAR TODAY

As costly as war has been in the past, it has clearly reached unprecedented levels of potential destructiveness today. Not only have the new twentieth century weapons greatly increased war's damage potential, they also have shortened the time needed to reach that potential. In the past, leaders at least had considerable time to reevaluate their decisions to use force, even if they did not always take advantage of the opportunity. Now there are fewer second chances to disengage from poor decisions. President Kennedy seemed acutely aware of these dangers when he sought to control escalation during the Cuban missile crisis and referred to the mistakes of World War I and II in doing so. A sign outside the U.S. State Department room where ExCom made its decisions during the crisis reminded the participants that "in the nuclear age, superpowers make war like porcupines make love—carefully."[108]

SURVIVORS OF THE ATOMIC BOMB AT HIROSHIMA, 1945.

It is tempting to attribute the fact that major powers have not fought each other directly since 1945 to the fear of nuclear destruction. If this is so, these weapons have made an important, if ironic, contribution to peace. However, in the past even highly destructive weaponry has not dissuaded leaders bent on conquest from launching war if they calculated it to be worth the risk. In 1860, Alfred Nobel predicted that his invention of dynamite would inspire a "golden" era of peace; similar arguments have been made about artillery, smokeless powder, machine guns, and other deadly technologies. Hence, it may take the emergence of new norms against violence, and not merely the existence of weapons of mass destruction, to render major war passé.[109]

The suspicion persists that many military and civilian leaders see nuclear weapons as irrelevant to war-making and assume that conventional wars involving nuclear powers can be fought with little regard to nuclear escalation. We cannot know for sure whether such conventional war could be contained below nuclear thresholds. There is ample reason to think not, especially if one side clearly began to lose. For the past several decades, the editors of *The Bulletin of the Atomic Scientists* have kept a "nuclear clock," set to the number of minutes before midnight thought to represent the danger of major-power nuclear war. With the end of the Cold War, they turned the hands back from about four minutes to midnight to about a quarter to. No longer are U.S. and Russian missiles said to be directly targeted on each other's cities; nuclear testing has been curtailed, and many nuclear bombs (missile warheads) have been dismantled on each side according to arms control agreements discussed in Chapter 11. Yet thousands of nuclear weapons remain in the arsenals of the current "nuclear club," while concerns mount as smaller states come within reach of gaining access to nuclear technology. Even today's "small-scale" *tactical* nuclear weapons have several times the explosive power of the 20 kiloton bombs (each equivalent to approximately 20,000 tons of TNT) that leveled the Japanese cities of Hiroshima and Nagasaki in 1945.

Even if aimed exclusively at military targets, nuclear bombs would do massive collateral damage to nearby cities, and—depending on the wind—entire continents could be blanketed with deadly radiation. The debris from several such blasts also could blot out sunlight for long periods, bringing on what some have termed "nuclear winter." As has been commonly said, "The survivors might envy the dead."

The Causes of Peace: Approaches to World Order

In Chapter 7 we explored diplomatic alternatives to war. Diplomacy also is a way out of wars, once negotiations on peace settlements begin. The remarkable fact is, however, that many disputants never seek an end to war through the mutual search for a diplomatic solution.[110] William Zartman, based on his analysis of both interstate and internal wars, notes:

> Internal conflicts . . . are the most difficult of conflicts to negotiate. Only a quarter to a third of modern civil wars (including anticolonial wars) have found their way to negotiation, whereas more than half of modern interstate wars have done so. About two-thirds of the internal conflicts have ended in the surrender or elimination of one of the parties involved; fewer than a quarter of the international conflicts have so ended. Yet in internal conflicts more than in interstate wars, defeat of the rebellion often merely drives the cause underground, to emerge at a later time.[111]

Zartman goes on to list factors conducive to peace negotiations, factors that can apply to interstate as well as intrastate fighting; these include presence of "a mutually hurting stalemate," "valid spokespersons" for each side, and a "formula for a way out."[112]

Once parties negotiate, win, or lose a war, the question of the next war, or preserving peace, arises. Wartime experiences can affect the probability of another war occurring. A war can foment desires for revenge or breed a distaste for further hostilities. At least in the immediate aftermath of most major wars, leaders and the citizens they represent seem especially disillusioned and gun-shy. Occasionally this can be a problem (for example, when a state fails to resist a new aggressor), but restraint and war-weariness also can cause serious consideration of peaceful diplomatic options. Although the concept of appeasement was seemingly forever besmirched by British Prime Minister Neville Chamberlain's accession to Hitler's demands regarding Czechoslovakia at the Munich conference on the eve of World War II, there was a poignancy and a certain logic to Chamberlain's recollections of World War I that might apply to other situations and other times:

> When I think of four terrible years and I think of the 7,000,000 young men who were cut off in their prime, the 13,000,000 who were maimed and mutilated, the misery and the suffering of the mothers and fathers, the sons and daughters, and the relatives and friends of those who were killed and wounded, then I am bound to say again what I have said before . . .—in war, whichever side may call itself victor, there are no winners, but all are losers. It is these thoughts which have made me feel that it was my prime duty to strain every nerve to avoid repetition of the Great War in Europe.[113]

Given the causes of war that we have discussed in this chapter, the question remains: What can be done to address such causes and to increase the prospects of avoiding war? Just as a plethora of contending theories have been advanced regarding the causes of war, so also has there been a long-standing debate over the "causes of peace," as well as over the definitions of just what "peace" is.[114] In the following discussion, we identify some of the main *approaches to world order* proposed by scholars and policymakers.

BALANCE OF POWER, CONCERT OF POWERS, AND HEGEMONY

We have noted that from the very beginnings of the nation-state system, emerging out of the seventeenth century Peace of Westphalia, the *balance of power* at the system level has been viewed as at least a crude mechanism for maintaining order and stability in a world lacking central regulation of the use of force. That is, there has been a widely held assumption that as long as states individually or in alliance do not allow adversaries to gain military superiority, peace will be maintained.

We also have noted, however, that the balance of power often has failed to deter aggression and that states equal in power or even weaker than their adversaries have initiated war at times. Because of the failure of "balance of power politics" to prevent war in the Napoleonic era, the major European powers tried to adopt a somewhat different approach to world order at the **Congress of Vienna** in 1815, after the Napoleonic Wars. They established the **Concert of Europe,** a system of "great power" consultation whereby the powers would take responsibility together for keeping the peace by convening multilateral conferences to resolve problems any time a dispute threatened to erupt into war.[115] The Concert met more than thirty times in the nineteenth century, although with decreasing effectiveness as the consensus against French revolutionary ideas deteriorated. The Concert finally collapsed with the formation of rival alliances on the eve of World War I. The *concert of powers* approach to world order was to be revived in modified form later by the founders of the League of Nations and the United Nations, both of which were premised in part on the willingness of the major powers to recognize their mutual interests in resolving their disputes nonviolently and in enforcing the peace against any would-be aggressors.

Was it, as many contend, the Concert of Europe that made the nineteenth century a relatively peaceful era (at least in terms of the absence of systemwide war despite numerous lesser wars), or was it, as others argue, the presence of *one* key power (the "first among equals")—Great Britain—that through its military and economic dominance was able to maintain whatever international order there was (the so-called Pax Britannica)? According to the **theory of hegemonic stability,** throughout history large-scale wars involving major powers have tended to produce among the victors a dominant power (a *hegemon*, or leader) capable of maintaining a degree of order over the international system as a whole. Just as some point to the Pax Britannica after the Napoleonic wars, it has been suggested that World War II was followed by a period of American leadership over the international political and economic order known as "Pax Americana," which some have argued ended with the U.S. defeat in Vietnam.[116] The theory posits that a hegemon is able to maintain stability through a combination of coercion (i.e., threatening to use armed force against any state violating system norms or rules established by the hegemon) and positive inducements (i.e., conferring economic and other benefits on states that cooperate in preserving order). Hegemony as a source of order, however, tends to break down eventually, as the hegemonic power inevitably declines because of the draining costs of maintaining large armed forces and extensive economic commitments; other powers rise to challenge the hegemon, leading ultimately to a new cycle of warfare and postwar reconstruction of world order.[117] In other words, war cycles are the flip side of peace cycles.

Although this theory may offer useful insights into historical patterns of war and peace, it would seem of questionable relevance to the problem of world order in the nuclear age. Assuming that any large-scale global war in the future would involve nuclear weapons or other weapons of mass destruction, it is highly unlikely that any "victor" would emerge from the fray with enough resources intact to play a hegemonic role. Future hegemons would have to emerge through means short of all-out war.[118] If world order is to be maintained in the contemporary age, it may well depend not so much on one single state holding a preponderance of power, or on a balance or concert of powers, but rather on more positive efforts at international cooperation such as those mentioned in the following sections.

ARMS CONTROL AND DISARMAMENT

We have noted that arms races often can lead to war, with adversaries at times driven to match or exceed each other in armaments to protect their respective national security, thereby creating spiraling tensions and insecurity (the so-called security dilemma), perhaps eventuating in a preemptive attack. *Arms control*, i.e., agreement on the quantity or quality of allowable arms, is one way to break the action-reaction sequences that characterize arms races and lead to conflict escalation. We will discuss various arms control efforts at some length in Chapter 11.

The logic of arms control as an approach to world order is that it can reduce the danger of war not only by removing some of the instruments of war, but more importantly, by opening up lines of communication, developing confidence-building attitudes, and reducing mutual insecurity through the very process of forging and verifying arms agreements. One example often cited in support of this logic is the Rush-Bagot Agreement of 1817, the oldest and perhaps the most successful arms control pact in history, by which the United States and Britain agreed to demilitarize the American-Canadian border and the Great Lakes, thereby paving the way for long-term peaceful relations among these countries.

Curbs on arms races also require controlling or retooling those parts of the military-industrial complexes that generate new arms in various countries.[119] One must remember, of course, that weapons are more symptoms than causes of international conflict. For the most part, in Hans Morgenthau's words,

"Men do not fight because they have arms. They have arms because they deem it necessary to fight."[120] As in the Great Lakes example of U.S.-British arms control, it is necessary to settle the *political* disputes underlying arms races. If somehow the security dilemma that states regularly experience were to be resolved, it might be possible to go beyond arms control to *disarmament*, i.e., the complete elimination of weapons from national arsenals. However, disarmament remains a distant prospect given the nature of the nation-state system.

INTERNATIONAL ORGANIZATION, PEACEFUL SETTLEMENT, AND COLLECTIVE SECURITY

Some have argued that the only way to overcome the security dilemma in a system of sovereign states is to develop *international organization* machinery that includes both an elaborate set of *peaceful settlement* procedures and *collective security* mechanisms. The emphasis is thereby put on states' *common* interests, especially in finding ways out of "chicken" confrontations or "prisoners' dilemmas" (see Chapter 7). Peaceful settlement refers to the formal techniques used to resolve conflicts short of armed force, including diplomatic procedures such as impartial third-party mediation and conciliation (of the type used in labor-management disputes) as well as legal procedures such as arbitration and adjudication. Adjudication, whereby the parties to a dispute agree to submit it to an international tribunal and to accept the body's decision as binding based on international law, is clearly among the most ambitious forms of peaceful settlement. Collective security refers to the agreement by states to use force or other sanctions collectively, through a single international organization, to punish an aggressor if peaceful settlement procedures fail.

Inis Claude has said that the growth of international organization, particularly in the twentieth century, is "fundamentally, even though not exclusively, a reaction to the problem of war."[121] Both the League of Nations after World War I and the United Nations after World War II represent attempts to go beyond the balance of power and other power politics approaches to world order and to conduct international affairs on a higher, more civilized plane. Founders of the League and UN, although relying to some extent on the "concert of great powers" notion, sought to introduce a new level of institutionalization into world politics and to make the concepts of peaceful settlement and collective security the institutional cornerstones. We discuss the extent to which these approaches to world order have had any success in Chapters 9 and 10.

International organizations such as the UN, along with regional organizations, hold some promise as vehicles for dealing with such causes of war as frustration or deprivation, not only because they provide ready machinery for engaging states in peaceful bargaining processes that can resolve specific grievances and defuse crisis situations, but also because they provide multilateral forums for addressing a much broader range of economic and social concerns that often underlie the resort to violence. It is impossible to eliminate all national frustrations and pressures to seek more resources or territory, such as the "lateral pressures" mentioned earlier; leaders cannot and should not be granted everything they want. Nonetheless, through creative bilateral or multilateral diplomacy, it can be possible to discover "prominent solutions" to problems that can satisfy conflicting parties and obviate the resort to armed force.[122]

If war cannot be avoided and violence erupts, the problem shifts from war prevention to war termination. Decisions to make peace in these cases are part of, in fact the culmination of, war stories. In any given war, the participants, through factors ranging from exhaustion to the pressures brought to bear by allies, arms donors, or other outside powers, may decide to move toward settlement or at least suspension of hostilities. As in all bargaining situations (see Chapter 7), the path to agreement depends on how close the parties come to achieving the goals for which they went to war, whether these goals still seem feasible, and the cost of achieving them compared with the benefits of peace. Many of the same techniques and mechanisms available to forestall a war also can be used to terminate one if the parties are ready for peace. For example, in the case of Morocco's decade-long desert war with Polisario guerrillas for control of the former Spanish Saharan territory and its rich phosphate deposits, the building of a 1,400-mile sand wall complete with radar and gun emplacements (through American military assistance) allowed Moroccans to consolidate their territorial holdings, whereas pressures by Algeria, Polisario's primary source of weapons and sanctuary, helped pave the way for UN-mediated talks in the early 1990s. Morocco had largely prevailed in military strategy and firepower, but had failed to achieve political success, because more than seventy nations around the world had recognized Polisario as the rightful Saharan rulers. A peace settlement and UN-supervised plebiscite for the local population offered both sides a way out of the impasse.[123] Constructive approaches to war termination can include, in addition to plebiscites, such possibilities as demilitarized zones, neutralization of disputed territory, and population exchanges.[124] Of course, as we noted above in citing Zartman's findings, many conflicts end only when one side ultimately imposes its will on the other.

Perhaps in time national leaders and publics will come to change their perceptions of other peoples as enemies and of war as a legitimate means of pursuing goals through organized killing. Increasing the accuracy and breadth of news coverage available to people throughout the world, including on-the-spot reporting of acts of aggression—a feat technically if not altogether politically feasible in the age of the satellite dish and other technology—and making foreigners seem more human also might help restrain unconditional obedience to authority and, thereby, warfare.

Conclusion

War is a type of conflictual social relationship. Earlier in the book, we noted that such conflicts often resemble a social system in which the parties take turns in mimicking each other's behavior—reacting in kind to each other's arms buildups, for example—and engage in strange dances of violence that can last for years. Yet, periods of war and recurrent violence frequently have been broken, and long and stable periods of peace have developed among adversaries. Researchers even speak of **security communities,** groups of states among which war is no longer a serious option for pursuing goals or resolving differences.[125] The United States and Great Britain, the United States and Canada, and—perhaps most remarkably, considering their record of recurrent warfare in the past 150 years—France and Germany can be labeled virtual security communities today. They may have their disagreements and tensions on a variety of policy issues, but they see far more advantage in settling them peacefully than through war.

This transition from warlike social systems to systems of "stable peace" is a key mystery for human survival. Peace theorists have argued that the successful transition has basically to do with reducing stresses and strains on international relationships and building trust.[126] If habits of cooperation in solving economic and other problems can be learned by states, it is conceivable that a much wider, perhaps even global security community could develop among them. The search for community evidenced by the creation of the United Nations and other international organizations would seem to offer some hope in this regard. Future progress may lie in the further development and strengthening of such institutions, a subject to which we now turn in Part III.

SUMMARY

1. When diplomacy in international relations breaks down, governments frequently resort to the use of armed force. War is sometimes viewed as simply another form of diplomacy—a deliberate, conscious policy designed to achieve political goals. At other times war is seen as the result of unplanned responses to the environment based on complex emotions of fear, frustration, and anger. Despite evidence of cost-benefit planning, no single perspective provides a complete understanding of war; wars occur in multiple forms and have multiple causes.

2. Violence in world politics can be divided into three categories based on the type and the extent of the fighting: international war; force without war; and civil war.

3. International war—sustained military hostilities between at least two states—has become less frequent but more deadly over time. Since 1945, there has been no war between the major powers. War between democratic states also is very rare. Most wars have come to involve less developed countries, and in the 1990s, interstate war itself has practically vanished in most regions.

4. There have been many cases of force without war. To some extent, the controlled use of military force in the form of displays, skirmishes, and interventions has become a surrogate for war in the nuclear age.

5. Civil wars within states have become more frequent and severe since 1945, as well as more internationalized. Ethnopolitical violence has been especially prevalent in the post–Cold War era. The persistent occurrence of force without war and of civil war raises the prospect of wider wars developing in the future.

6. The causes of war can be found at the individual, nation-state, and international system levels, with the interplay of factors from all three levels combining to give us the richest explanation of war-making decisions.

7. It is necessary to distinguish between the background conditions leading to war and the more immediate causes. Among the former are leaders and citizens who are highly obedient to political authority, military-industrial complexes, and arms races.

8. The immediate causes of war, or triggers, often relate to sudden crises and overburdened diplomacy. Crises—high-threat situations in which decision makers tend to be under severe stress and are highly susceptible to misperception—seem especially to result in violence when a state is faced with sudden loss of control over a region where it is accustomed to exercising influence.

9. War involves enormous human, political, and economic costs for both winners and losers. Today it has reached new, unprecedented levels of potential destructiveness. It is questionable whether conventional war between states armed with nuclear weapons would be contained below nuclear thresholds, and whether nuclear war itself, once initiated, could be kept limited.

10. A number of approaches to ending wars and reducing their occurrence have been proposed. In addition to theories of balance of power, concert of powers, and hegemonic stability (all of which emphasize traditional power politics), theories have been developed around the concepts of arms control and disarmament, peaceful settlement, and collective security (which emphasize states' collective interests).

SUGGESTIONS FOR FURTHER READING AND STUDY

Good general works on both the "causes of war" and the "causes of peace" are Seyom Brown, *The Causes and Prevention of War*, 2nd ed. (New York: St. Martin's, 1994); Martin Patchen, *Resolving Disputes Between Nations: Coercion or Conciliation?* (Durham, N.C.: Duke University Press, 1988); and John J. Weltman, *World Politics and the Evolution of War* (Baltimore: Johns Hopkins University Press, 1995). See also Hugh Miall, *The Peacemakers: Peaceful Settlement of Disputes Since 1945* (New York: St. Martin's Press, 1992); and Jay Rothman, *From Confrontation to Cooperation: Resolving Ethnic and Regional Conflict* (Newbury Park, Calif.: Sage, 1992). Ted Gurr and

Barbara Harff, *Ethnic Conflict in World Politics* (Boulder, Colo.: Westview Press, 1994) focuses on the phenomenon of ethnopolitical conflict, as does Donald M. Snow, *Uncivil Wars: International Security and the New Pattern of Internal War* (Boulder, Colo.: Lynne Rienner, 1996). On the future of war in the post–Cold War era, see Richard K. Betts, ed., *Conflict After the Cold War* (New York: Macmillan, 1994), especially the articles in the section entitled "Does War Have A Future?"

Scientific approaches: J. David Singer et al., *Explaining War: Selected Papers From the Correlates of War Project* (Beverly Hills: Sage, 1979); Singer and Paul Diehl, eds., *Measuring the Correlates of War* (Ann Arbor: University of Michigan Press, 1990); Charles S. Gochman and Alan Ned Sabrosky, eds., *Prisoners of War? Nation States in the Modern Era* (Lexington, Mass.: Lexington Books, 1990); K. J. Holsti, *Peace and War: Armed Conflicts and International Order, 1648–1989* (Cambridge, Eng.: Cambridge University Press, 1991); William R. Thompson, *On Global War: Historical-Structural Approaches to World Politics* (Columbia, S.C.: University of South Carolina Press, 1988); Manus I. Midlarsky, *The Onset of World War* (Boston: Unwin Hyman, 1988); Bruce M. Russett, *Grasping the Democratic Peace* (Princeton, N.J.: Princeton University Press, 1993); and John A. Vasquez, *The War Puzzle* (Cambridge, Eng.: Cambridge University Press, 1993).

Political approaches: Charles Reynolds, *The Politics of War: A Study of the Rationality of Violence in Inter-State Relations* (Sussex, Eng.: Harvester-Wheatsheaf, 1989); Robert J. Art and Kenneth N. Waltz, *The Use of Force: Military Power and International Politics* (Lanham: University Press of America, 1993); Philip E. Tetlock et al., eds., *Behavior, Society, and Nuclear War*, 3 vols. (New York: Oxford University Press, 1989, 1991, 1993); Louis Kriesberg and Stuart J. Thorson, eds., *Timing the Deescalation of International Conflicts* (Syracuse, N.Y.: Syracuse University Press, 1991); Muhammad Rabi, *Conflict Resolution and Ethnicity* (Westport, Conn.: Praeger, 1994); T. V. Paul, *Asymmetric Conflicts: War Initiation by Weaker Powers* (New York: Cambridge University Press, 1994); and Alexander L. George, *Forceful Persuasion: Coercive Diplomacy as an Alternative to War* (Washington, D.C.: United States Institute of Peace Press, 1991).

Economic approaches: Richard J. Barnet, *Roots of War* (Baltimore: Penguin, 1972); Edward D. Mansfield, *Power, Trade, and War* (Princeton, N.J.: Princeton University Press, 1994); Mark R. Brawley, *Liberal Leadership: Great Powers and Their Challengers in Peace and War* (Ithaca, N.Y.: Cornell University Press, 1993); and John A. Agnew and Stuart Corbridge, *Mastering Space: Hegemony, Territory, and International Political Economy* (London: Routledge, 1995).

Historical approaches: Robert I. Rotberg and Theodore K. Rabb, eds., *The Origin and Prevention of Major Wars* (Cambridge, Eng.: Cambridge University Press, 1988); Robert L. O'Connell, *Of Arms and Men: A History of War, Weapons, and Aggression* (New York: Oxford University Press, 1989). See also issues of the journals *Peace and Change* and *Current History* and diplomatic histories of particular wars, such as Barbara Tuchman's *The Guns of August* (New York: Macmillan, 1988), depicting the events of World War I.

Literary approaches (novels): Stephen Crane, *The Red Badge of Courage;* Ernest Hemingway, *A Farewell to Arms;* Erich Maria Remarque, *All Quiet on the Western Front;* Normal Mailer, *The Naked and the Dead;* James Jones, *From Here to Eternity;* Gunter Grass, *Cat and Mouse;* Joseph Heller, *Catch-22;* Leo Tolstoy, *War and Peace;* and Marge Piercy, *Gone to Soldiers.*

Philosophical approaches: Douglas P. Lackey, *The Ethics of War and Peace* (Englewood Cliffs, N.J.: Prentice-Hall, 1989); Jean Bethke Elshtain, *Just War Theory* (New York: New York University Press, 1992); James Turner Johnson, *Can Modern War Be Just?* (New Haven, Conn.: Yale University press, 1984).

Peace research approaches: Thomas Keefe and Ron E. Roberts, *Realizing Peace: An Introduction to Peace Studies* (Ames, Iowa: Iowa State University Press, 1991); Samuel S. Kim, *The Quest for a Just World Order* (Boulder, Colo.: Westview Press, 1984); Raimo Vayrynen, ed., *New Directions in Conflict Theory: Conflict Resolution and Conflict Transformation* (London: Sage, 1991); Tom Woodhouse, *Peacemaking in a Troubled World* (New York: Berg/St. Martin's Press, 1991); *Resolving Conflict in the Post–Cold War Third World* (Washington, D.C.: United States Institute of Peace, 1991); David Dewitt, David Haglund, and John Kirton, *Building a New Global Order: Emerging Trends in International Security* (Toronto: Oxford University Press, 1993); Jeremy Brecher, John Brown Childs, and Jill Cutler, *Global Visions: Beyond the New World Order* (Boston: South End Press, 1993); Gareth J. Evans, *Cooperating for Peace: The Global Agenda for the 1990s and Beyond* (St. Leonards, Australia: Allen and Unwin, 1993); and Richard Smoke with Willis Harman, *Paths to Peace, Exploring the Feasibility of Sustainable Peace* (Boulder, Colo.: Westview Press, 1987).

PART III

International Institutions

In relations between nations, the progress of civilization may be seen as movement from force to diplomacy, from diplomacy to law.
LOUIS HENKIN, *How Nations Behave*

No one can observe the international political system without being aware of the fact that order does exist and that this order is related in important ways to . . . a body of law and to a process of law-government.
MORTON A. KAPLAN AND NICHOLAS DeB. KATZENBACH,
The Strategy of World Order: International Law

We should recognize the United Nations for what it is—an admittedly imperfect but indispensable instrument of nations in working for a peaceful evolution towards a more just and secure world order. The dynamic forces at work in this stage of human history have made world organization necessary. DAG HAMMARSKJOLD, UN SECRETARY-GENERAL,
in his Annual Report, August 22, 1957

Amid the din of conflict that surrounds international relations, there does exist some degree of order. In fact, many kinds of transactions across national boundaries, such as mail and travel flows, tend to occur in such a routine, cooperative fashion that they generally go unnoticed by the average citizen. The orderly nature of many international interactions is largely a function of the mutual interests that states share in having at least some modicum of stability in their day-to-day affairs. To this end, states have created a body of international law designed to help regulate relations between countries, as well as a network of intergovernmental organizations designed to facilitate conflict management along with collaboration in economic and social problem solving at the regional and global level. The development of these institutions, "primitive" as they might be, is a manifestation of humanity's continual quest for order in a fragmented system of sovereign nation-states lacking any central authority.

Institutional links among national governments have been increasing in today's interdependent world, with the growth of the United Nations system being the most visible symbol of the international organization phenomenon. Just as governments have been developing greater organized ties across national boundaries, so have private individuals and groups such as multinational corporations, whose contacts and interests transcend national frontiers. In fact, there are many more nongovernmental international organizations than intergovernmental ones. There is some question whether the existing body of international legal rules and intergovernmental organizations are adequate to cope with the burgeoning volume of transnational activities and the new agenda of international issues—economics, the environment, food and population, and other concerns—noted in our earlier discussion of the general setting of contemporary international relations.

Opinions about the effectiveness of international law and organization in a decentralized political system have traditionally ranged from extremely harsh cynicism to extremely naive idealism, and observers today still tend to view international institutions in these terms. Where cynics see international law and international organizations as simply additional instruments that dominant powers in world politics seek to use to maintain the status quo, idealists see these as representing noble experiments in world order possibly leading eventually to world government. In Part III we examine the role that *international institutions* play in contemporary world politics, focusing on international law (Chapter 9) and a variety of international organizations (Chapter 10). We will attempt to refrain from the excesses of both pessimism and optimism that have characterized so much discussion on this subject over the years.

9

International Law: Myth or Reality?

On November 4, 1979, fifty-two Americans in the U.S. Embassy in Tehran were seized by a group of Iranian militants. The hostages were to be used to extract certain concessions from the U.S. government, an endeavor that had the blessing of the new regime in Iran headed by Ayatollah Khomeini. It was not until January 20, 1981, after 444 days in captivity, that the American diplomatic personnel were finally released by the Iranian government. Though a somewhat distant memory now, this event preoccupied the nation for over a year and raised some interesting questions about the role of international law in international affairs.

To many, the Iranian hostage episode seemed a vivid illustration of the lawless character of international relations. However, rather than reflecting the nonexistence or impotence of international law, the episode in some respects illustrated its general reliability, In particular, what made the incident such a *cause célèbre* was precisely the fact that it involved a virtually unprecedented violation of one of the most sacred rules of international conduct, namely, the immunity of diplomats from host government seizure and punishment. The actions of the Iranian government represented such a departure from the routinely honored canons of state practice that observers at the time feverishly searched through history books to discover the last time such a violation had occurred. There was a certain irony involved, too, because it was in Persia—in the land that is today called Iran—that the principle of **diplomatic immunity** first evolved a thousand years ago.[1]

Still, long after the hostages were returned, questions remained as to what kind of legal system would allow such a violation to go unpunished. There was renewed debate over whether international law has any relevance to the major issues of international politics, or whether it could even be said to exist at all. The believer in international law might ask a number of questions: Why, if international law were irrelevant, would the U.S. State Department Legal Advisor's Office maintain a staff of more than sixty international lawyers, and why would multinational corporations employ hundreds more? Why would a Canadian secretary of state remark that "in my office and in my department, we are, first of all, students of international law"?[2] The skeptic might respond that much of international law is a charade in which states pick and choose to obey those rules that happen to coincide with their interests at a given moment; even if international law is grudgingly acknowledged to exist, it is considered to be feeble in those situations "that really matter." Cynics might note, for example, that the United States, which was so quick to invoke international law in the Iranian hostage case, chose to ignore it in 1986, when Washington refused to acknowledge that its mining of Nicaraguan harbors violated the rule against aggression despite widespread condemnation by international legal experts.

In this chapter we examine the case for and against international law, investigating the manner in which international law operates and the degree to which it has an impact on international affairs. In our introduction to Part III,

THE RETURN OF U.S. EMBASSY PERSONNEL AFTER 444 DAYS IN CAPTIVITY IN IRAN, 1981.

we quoted Louis Henkin's eloquent statement that "in relations between nations, the progress of civilization may be seen as movement from force to diplomacy, from diplomacy to law." We leave it to the reader to judge how much progress has been made.

Is International Law Really Law?

A basic question that arises here is whether **international law,** as a body of rules governing relations between states, is really "law." To answer this question, we first need to define what law is. Law can be defined as a set of rules or expectations that govern the relations between the members of a society, that have an obligational basis, and whose violation is punishable through the application of sanctions by society.[3] It is the obligational character of law that distinguishes it from morality, religion, social mores, or mere protocol. The definition implies that three fundamental conditions must be present if law can be said to exist in a society: (1) a process for developing an identifiable, legally binding set of rules that prescribe certain patterns of behavior among societal members (i.e., a lawmaking process); (2) a process for punishing illegal behavior when it occurs (i.e., a law-enforcement process); and (3) a process for determining whether a particular rule has been violated in a particular instance (i.e., a law-adjudication process).

The reader will recognize these three conditions as the basic characteristics normally associated with domestic law within national societies. Certainly, such conditions exist in the United States or China or any other nation-state. Although some national legal systems might be considerably more effective than others—for example, in achieving compliance with the law—all have the basic elements noted above, as manifested by legislatures, police agencies, and courts. Even so-called failed states have these basic structures in place, at least on paper.

What about *international* law? How does it compare with law in *national* political systems (commonly called **municipal law**)? The most obvious difference is that the central governmental institutions that are associated with law within nation-states simply do not exist, or operate only very weakly, in relations between nation-states. There is no world government, no supreme law-giver, no squad of traffic cops riding herd over international affairs, and no court with compulsory jurisdiction. However, if one is willing to overlook the lack of strong central authoritative institutions in the international system—in other words, to abandon the stereotype of law as "a centralized constraint system backed by threat of coercive sanctions"[4]—then it would leave open the possibility of accepting international law as law. At least international law could conceivably fit our definition of law cited above, if not a stricter or more traditional definition. One must be prepared to demonstrate, however, how law can operate in a decentralized political system such as the international system. Let us examine each aspect of the international legal system separately, looking at how international law is made, enforced, and adjudicated, in the absence of a global government.

The Making of International Law: Where Does the Law Come From?

If one is a legal advisor in the foreign ministry of a country involved in an international dispute over maritime boundaries, or a judge on a country's highest court hearing a case involving some international dimension, there is no single body of world statutes that can be consulted to discover what the relevant law is. However, there is an identifiable set of rules accepted by states as legally binding, derived from the *sources* of international law specified in Article 38 of the International Court of Justice Statute that is attached to the United Nations Charter. The officially recognized sources of international law include (1) custom, (2) treaties or conventions, (3) general principles of law recognized by civilized nations, (4) judicial decisions of national and international tribunals, and (5) the writings of legal scholars. Because custom and treaties are by far the most important sources of international law, we confine our discussion here to them.

CUSTOMARY LAW

Customary rules of international law are those practices that have been widely accepted as binding by states over time as evidenced by repeated usage. In the early life of the international system, custom was an especially important source of international law. Hugo Grotius, a seventeenth-century Dutch writer often cited as the "father of international law" for his classic treatise *On the Law of War and Peace,* noted even in his day the development of certain common practices whose routine observance by governments led to their acceptance as required behavior in relations among states. One such custom was the practice of diplomatic immunity granted by a host government to a foreign government's ambassadors. Another was the designation of a three mile limit within which coastal states were assumed to exercise sovereignty over territorial waters adjacent to their land; the three mile limit was based on the effective range of cannon fired from shoreline fortifications. Numerous other rules developed.

Nowhere were any of these rules specifically written down, but they were nonetheless understood to constitute rules of prescribed conduct. Given the decentralized nature of the international system, a customary rule technically became binding only on those states that, through their compliance over time, indicated their willingness to be bound by the rule in question. For example, the Scandinavian countries long insisted on maintaining a four-mile territorial sea, whereas practically all other states observed the three mile limit. However, once a state demonstrated its acceptance of a customary rule by repeated observance, it was expected to continue to be bound by it; customary law was not something that could be arbitrarily adopted and rejected from one moment to the next.[5]

Today, many customary rules continue to form part of the body of international law. Customary rules of law are to be distinguished from rules of etiquette, known as *comity;* in the case of customary rules, an established pattern of conduct (e.g., diplomatic immunity) is based on a sense of legal obligation (*opinio iuris*) and invites legal penalties if breached, whereas in the case of comity, it is merely a matter of courtesy (e.g., two ships saluting each other's flag while passing at sea). Admittedly, when states engage in certain standard practices toward each other, it is not always clear whether they do so out of a sense of legal obligation or simply out of politeness. Moreover, given the unwritten nature of customary law, there is great potential for ambiguity and misinterpretation of the rules. For these reasons, there has been a distinct trend in recent years to *codify* customary law, i.e., to embody customary rules in more precise, written documents to which states can explicitly give or withhold consent.

TREATIES

Written agreements between societies can be found from the beginnings of human history—"archeologists have discovered a treaty between the city-states of Umma and Lagosh written in the Sumerian language on a stone monument and concluded about 3100 B.C."[6]—and have grown in importance as the modern nation-state system has evolved. **Treaties** or **conventions** are formal written agreements between states, which create legal obligations for the governments that are parties to them. As with customary law, treaties are binding only on those states that consent to be bound by them. A state normally indicates its consent by a two-step process in which its authorized representative *signs* the treaty and its legislature or other constitutionally empowered body *ratifies* the agreement. For example, President Carter in 1977 signed a landmark human rights treaty, the International Covenant on Civil and Political Rights, but failed to win the approval of the U.S. Senate; the treaty was not ratified by the Senate until 1992, when it finally became binding on the United States. Once a state becomes a party to a treaty, it is expected that its government will honor the fundamental principle associated with treaties—***pacta sunt servanda,*** which specifies that treaties are to be obeyed.

Many treaties are simply bilateral in nature—agreements between two states seeking, for example, to establish trade relations or an alliance, or regarding the use of each other's air space or the extradition of criminals from each other's territory. Other treaties are multilateral and can involve such subjects as international commerce, patent and copyright regulations, regulation of mail and other communications, use of the oceans for fishing and exploration, treatment of prisoners of war, and development and deployment of various kinds of weapons. Although the past century has witnessed much more multilateralism than previous eras, an overwhelming majority of treaties in force are bilateral.[7] Multilateral agreements, though, are the ones of greatest relevance to international law, especially those multilateral treaties that deal with issues of broad importance and seek to involve as many members of the international community as possible, such as the UN Charter.

As we have noted, there have been increased efforts to use treaties to codify traditional, customary rules of international law. For example, the Vienna Convention on Diplomatic Relations of 1961, ratified by almost every country, reiterated the rule of law requiring that the immunity and inviolability of embassies and diplomats be respected. Among the provisions of the treaty are the following: diplomatic agents and members of their families cannot be arrested and prosecuted by the host government for any crimes committed, even a blatant act of murder or a hit-and-run accident; diplomatic agents are immune not only from host state criminal jurisdiction but also from civil jurisdiction, which means that they cannot be prosecuted for damaging someone's property or passing bad checks. In New York City alone, where diplomats abound at UN headquarters, it is estimated that 250,000 parking tickets worth $5 million have gone unpaid as diplomats continue to triple park, block major thoroughfares, and generally go about their business blissfully free from the restrictions that apply to most motorists. However, what might seem to be a grossly unfair system of rules to the New York City cab driver or the person on the street is necessitated by the desire of national governments to ensure that their diplomats are not harassed in any fashion by the host country to which they are assigned. If a diplomat were to abuse such diplomatic immunity, by becoming a mass murderer or a notorious hotrodder and check bouncer, the remedy would be for the host state to request a waiver of immunity from the diplomat's government or to declare the diplomat *persona non grata* and expel that individual from the country.

Although some treaties simply transcribe customary law into written form, keeping the traditional rules intact, other treaties are designed to revise the customary law. For example, the 1982 UN Convention on the Law of the Sea, a 200-page document negotiated by more than 150 countries, incorporated some elements of the traditional law of the sea—such as the right of "innocent passage" enjoyed by all ships in the territorial waters of coastal states, the right of "hot pursuit" by coastal state vessels against foreign ships violating the laws of the coastal state, and absolute freedom of navigation of all ships on the high seas outside any state's boundaries—but also modified some existing rules, such as extending the width of the territorial seas from three to twelve miles.

In some instances, treaties have been used to develop rules in new areas of concern for which no law has existed or been necessary before. For example, the Outer Space Treaty of 1967, ratified by almost 100 states, requires the signatories to refrain from deploying weapons of mass destruction in outer space and to consider the moon and other celestial bodies *terra nullius*—territory belonging to no one—and beyond any state's sovereign control. As a party to the treaty, had the United States attempted to declare the moon its sovereign territory when it was the first to land there in 1969, the government would have been acting illegally in violation of the 1967 agreement.

It is evident that even in the absence of a world legislature, machinery exists to create written rules that are considered legally binding, with bilateral treaties drafted by the foreign ministries of individual countries and multilateral treaties drafted by the UN International Law Commission or bodies such as the Law of the Sea Conference. There are literally thousands of treaties in effect around the world, and the number is growing not only as a function of the proliferation of states but, more importantly, as the increased volume and complexity of international interactions lead governments to seek more formalized arrangements in regulating intercourse between states. One estimate is that more than 40,000 international agreements have been concluded in the twentieth century, most of them since 1945.[8] The growth of treaties in modern times is reflected in the fact that in 1892 the official compendium of treaties entered into by the United Kingdom numbered only 190 pages, whereas by 1960 it exceeded 2,500 pages.[9] For the international system as a whole, "treaties concluded between 1648 and 1919 fill 226 thick books, between 1920 and 1946 some 205 more volumes, and between 1946 and 1978, 1,115 more tomes."[10]

There is even a treaty on treaties—the Vienna Convention on the Law of Treaties of 1969—which codifies the customary rule of *pacta sunt servanda.* This convention also stipulates the circumstances whereby a state unilaterally can *legally terminate* its involvement in some treaty. A state can back out of a treaty commitment, for example, if the agreement has an "escape hatch" provision (say, a requirement to provide at least six months' advance notification of intent to withdraw). This was the case with the U.S. decision to terminate its mutual defense agreement with Taiwan in 1979 in an effort to cultivate better relations with the Beijing government on the Chinese mainland. A state can also legally terminate its treaty obligations if it can demonstrate that it had been coerced into signing the treaty originally, that the treaty was founded on fraudulent grounds or signed by an unauthorized national representative, or that present conditions are so radically different from those existing at the outset of the treaty as to render it impossible for that party to continue honoring the terms of the pact (the last condition is known as **rebus sic stantibus**). Despite the availability of these loopholes, states tend to use them only sparingly.

Admittedly, the making of international law occurs in a quite different fashion from lawmaking in national political systems. One criticism of international law is that the formulation of rules occurs in such a disjointed manner without any centralized machinery that there remains considerable disagreement over exactly what the rules are at a given moment. However, legal ambiguities—in terms of vaguely worded statutes, unclear judicial precedents, and conflicting interpretations of the law—are not unknown in municipal systems. Indeed, one frequently finds in the United States that legislators are uncertain of the meaning of the U.S. Constitution, bureaucrats are uncertain about the intent of Congressional acts they must implement, and Supreme Court justices reach 5–4 split opinions on the prevailing requirements of the law. The problems associated with discovering the content of the law in the international system are not of a completely different character from those found in municipal systems, only somewhat more pronounced and more serious.[11]

A further criticism of international law has to do with its essentially voluntary nature. Individuals in the United States and other municipal legal systems do not have the prerogative of deciding whether to agree to be bound by some rule of law, or whether to terminate their acceptance of some rule. The consent basis of law is generally unheard of in such systems, including democracies; once a rule of law is promulgated, everyone in the society is expected to abide by it regardless of whether everyone approves of it. However, the effectiveness of a legal system may consist not so much in how many members of the society have an obligation to obey the law as how many actually *do* obey the law. We next examine the extent to which international law is obeyed and enforced.

The Breaking of International Law: How Is the Law Enforced?

The most common indictment of international law is not the absence or ambiguity of the rules but the lack of enforcement—the complaint that international law is broken regularly with impunity because of the lack of a central policing agent. United Nations peacekeeping forces are perhaps the closest thing to an international police body, but they are organized sporadically as temporary responses to certain crisis situations and are designed to maintain peace, not necessarily to enforce law. At least twice in its history, the United Nations helped to organize a military force to punish aggression, in the case of North Korea in 1950 and Iraq in 1991, but those were exceptional.

Sanctions against violators of international law exist, but they are primarily based on the principle of *self-help*; if one state harms another state (e.g., seizes its financial assets) it is usually left to the aggrieved state to take action to punish the offender through **reprisals** or retaliation of some kind (e.g., reciprocal seizure of the offender's assets held by the aggrieved state's banks). Although self-help also operates to some extent in municipal legal systems—for example, defending oneself against assault or reclaiming stolen property or making a citizen's arrest—it tends not to be the norm in those systems.

However, what is most striking about the international legal system is not how often the law is broken but how often it is *obeyed*, despite the lack of "traffic cops" to provide a central coercive threat of punishment against would-be offenders. To be sure, there are frequent violations of international law, most notably those serious breaches that are reported on front pages of newspapers, such as the seizure of the U.S. Embassy in Iran, the genocidal acts committed in the Bosnian and Rwandan civil wars in the 1990s, and various acts of violent aggression. Although people tend to notice these conspicuous failures of international law, they neglect to notice the ordinary workings of international law in the everyday life of the international system. The fact is that, if one takes into account the myriad treaties and customary rules of international law that exist today, it can be said that most states obey most of the rules most of the time.[12] In other words, international law gets "enforced" in its own way.

To understand why this is so, we need to consider the basic reasons why people obey laws in any society. The first is the already mentioned threat of punishment for illegal behavior (the *coercive* motive). A second is the mutual interests that individuals have in seeing that laws are obeyed (the *utilitarian* motive). A third is the internalization of the rules by the members of the society, i.e., habits of compliance; people obey the law because that is what they have come to accept as the right thing to do (the *identitive* motive). All of these elements can operate to produce obedience to the law. Think for a moment why most people bother to obey a stop sign at an intersection. One reason is the coercive element—the possibility that a police officer might stop you if you do not stop yourself. Another is the utilitarian motive—the possibility that another car might accidentally hit your vehicle if you pass through the intersection without stopping. As powerful as these motives are, the main driving force behind the inclination to stop at a stop sign is probably the simple habitual nature of the act and the fact that it has been inculcated as part of the "code of the road." (Even if one were driving through the middle of Death Valley in California, where no police cars or other vehicles were in evidence for miles, there would be a tendency to stop if somehow one were to encounter a red stop sign sticking out of the desert sand!)

The point here is that law and order can function to some extent even in the absence of police; indeed, any society that relies primarily on coercive threats as the basis for order is one that is terribly fragile. Although habits of compliance—the most solid basis for law—are not very well developed in the international legal system, the mutual interests of states in having a set of rules that prescribe as well as proscribe patterns of behavior provide a foundation for the international legal order. States are willing to tolerate certain constraints on their own behavior because it is widely recognized that international commerce, travel, and other forms of international activity would be exceedingly precarious otherwise.

It is curious that critics argue that international law is virtually nonexistent because it is frequently broken. If one were to apply the same test of effectiveness to municipal law that is generally demanded of international law—i.e., 100 percent conformity to and enforcement of the law, or close to it—then one would have to conclude that there is no law anywhere in the world, not only between nation-states but also within them. One writer com-

Grin and Bear It by Lichty and Wagner © 1981 Field Enterprises, Inc. Courtesy of Field Newspaper Syndicate.

"You see a car come by here traveling within the speed limit?"

Law enforcement in municipal law

ments on the degree of which laws are broken and offenders go unpunished in the American legal system:

> In one study of criminal behavior by adults, people were asked which of forty-nine offenses other than traffic violations they had committed without being caught. Ninety-nine percent of the people admitted they had committed one or more offenses for which they might have received jail or prison sentences had they been caught. Among the males, 26 percent admitted auto theft, 17 percent burglary, and 13 percent grand larceny. Some 64 percent of the males and 29 percent of the females admitted to committing at least one felony for which they had not been caught.
>
> The fact is that only about a third of all serious crimes (murder, forcible rape, robbery, aggravated assault, burglary, larceny over $50, and auto theft)

are ever even reported to the police by the victims. Of all serious crimes reported, in only 19 percent of cases is a suspect ever arrested, although the figure can go as high as 78 percent for murder. Only about half of all suspects arrested are ever convicted. And only a quarter of those convicted actually ever "do time" for their crime.[13]

If one adds the number of people who exceed the speed limit on America's highways, then the effectiveness of law enforcement in the United States becomes much more dubious. (It is true that one can find total obedience to speeding regulations in parts of Europe, such as on the German Autobahn—but only because there are *no* limits to how fast cars can go on some highways!) More seriously, many national legal systems experience not only methodical violations of speeding laws but also civil violence against the state itself. The international order is not alone, then, in experiencing lawlessness. We do not mean to minimize the problem of law enforcement in international law, only to suggest that unfair and unrealistic standards are sometimes applied in evaluating the effectiveness of international law.

The Adjudicating of International Law: Who Are the Judges?

In municipal legal systems, courts are used to determine whether a particular law has been violated in a particular instance when one party accuses another party of an infraction. In the international system, judicial institutions also exist, such as the **International Court of Justice** (commonly referred to as the **World Court**), which can be used when one state accuses another of violating the law. However, such international institutions are extremely weak insofar as disputants tend to judge for themselves whether an infraction has occurred, or at least tend to reserve for themselves the decision of whether to go to court. Whereas in municipal systems one disputant can normally compel the other party to appear in court, international tribunals such as the World Court generally lack any compulsory jurisdiction. As in the *United States Diplomatic and Consular Staff in Tehran* case, which the United States brought before the World Court in 1979, one party—in this instance, Iran—can simply refuse to acknowledge the jurisdiction of the Court and to participate in the judicial proceedings. The United States itself refused to accept the jurisdiction of the Court in the 1986 case in which Nicaragua filed suit criticizing the United States for mining Nicaraguan harbors and carrying on illegal intervention.

The World Court consists of fifteen judges whose term of office is nine years. Elected by the UN membership, the judges are generally drawn from every major legal system in the world, with certain countries such as the United States each assured of one seat at all times; if the Court happens to be hearing a case involving a state that does not have a seat on the Court, that state may appoint one of its own nationals as an *ad hoc* judge for that particular case—despite the fact that judges on the Court are supposed to be impartial international jurists and not representatives of their national governments. Only states are eligible to appear as litigants before the Court, based on the traditional view that only states are "international legal persons" having rights and obligations under international law. If private individuals have a grievance against their own government, they are expected to resolve the matter in their own state's courts; if they have a grievance against a foreign government, they must ordinarily use that country's courts or persuade their own government to take the case before the World Court.

The World Court sits in The Hague, Netherlands. Some wags might note that all the Court seems to do for the most part is, indeed, sit. Despite the fact that more than 180 states are parties to the ICJ Statute that established the Court, the Court has received fewer than sixty contentious cases since its creation in 1946; in roughly one-third of these, it has not even been able to render a judgment. In fact, the caseload of the Court has been declining over time, with twenty-nine cases submitted during the 1950s, only six during the 1960s, seven during the 1970s, and five in the 1980s.[14] There has been a modest revival of late, however, with one observer noting that "we are seeing something new. Canada and the United States led the way by using the [special] Chambers procedure of the Court—a panel of judges from the Court plus one each from the opposing states—in the *Gulf of Maine* case. Mali and Burkina Faso (formerly Upper Volta) followed suit. Then came El Salvador and Honduras, in a case concerning the Land Island and Maritime Frontier dispute. More recently, the United States and Italy agreed to submit an investment dispute to the ICJ Chambers in a case concerning *Electronic Sicula*. . . . Not exactly a thundering herd, but a sign of something new leading perhaps to the more frequent and effective use of the Court."[15]

The lack of business, again, has been largely due to the lack of compulsory jurisdiction. As of 1996, only fifty-seven states—less than one-third of the international system—had signed the **Optional Clause** of the ICJ Statute, agreeing to give the Court compulsory jurisdiction in certain kinds of disputes. Moreover, even states that have signed have attached so many reservations to their acceptance of the Court's jurisdiction as to render the clause meaningless. The United States, for example, before it formally withdrew its declaration of acceptance in 1986 over the Nicaraguan incident, had agreed to give the Court compulsory jurisdiction except for those "disputes . . . which are essentially within the domestic jurisdiction of the United States *as determined by the United States of America*" (the so-called Connally Amendment).[16]

Where the Court has made a judgment in a case, that judgment has been deemed binding on both the winner and loser. The fundamental problem is that, in disputes involving vital interests, states have been unwilling to entrust a third party with ultimate decision-making competence; and in disputes over more trivial matters, states have not felt the need to use the Court because it is far simpler and cheaper to settle "out of court." In fairness to the Court, it might be said that the great bulk of disputes that arise in domestic law are also settled out of court through a process of bargaining not unlike that found in the international system. At times, the very act of one state bringing suit against another state before the Court has put pressure on the parties to reach a settlement on their own, such as Nauru's 1989 ICJ filing against Australia asking it to pay for the rehabilitation of one-third of the island damaged by phosphate mining during the colonial era, which resulted in Australia paying $75 million in restitution in 1993 to avoid further litigation. Still, even the most charitable apologist for the Court would have to conclude that it has been an extremely ineffective, largely ignored international institution despite its representing the "highest legal aspiration of civilized man."[17]

Fortunately for the international legal system, the World Court is not the only adjudication vehicle. A variety of other courts exist, including several at the regional level, such as the European Court of Justice. More importantly, *national* courts play a key role in the application of international law in those instances in which international issues arise in domestic suits. The constitutions or basic laws of most countries stipulate that treaties and other elements of international law are considered to be the supreme law of the land, at least co-equal with the highest national law, and are to be given due respect in the deliberations of national courts; in this sense, national judges are agents of not only municipal law but also international law. It is true that if a conflict exists between some rule of municipal law (say, an act of Parliament in the British system) and a rule of international law (say, a treaty entered into by the United Kingdom), national judges are inclined to favor municipal law. However, these problems do not arise as often as one might think and are not always resolved in favor of the national law. In the United States, for instance, when there is a conflict between an act of Congress and a treaty entered into by the United States, the one that was enacted later takes precedence; treaties take precedence over any state or local statutes in the United States, regardless of the timing element.

It is sometimes difficult to separate international law from municipal law. An often overlooked function that international law performs is the *allocation of legal competences*. International law provides the members of the international community with guidelines that help define their rights and obligations vis-à-vis each other, in particular who has what *jurisdiction* to deal with a legal matter in a given situation somewhere in the world.[18] For example, if a Frenchman kills a Pole on a cruise ship owned by a Canadian flying the Panamanian flag in U.S. territorial waters, whose courts have jurisdiction to try the crime? Any state involved in the incident? No state? The flag state? The state on whose territory the incident occurred? The shipowner's state, the victim's state, or the defendant's state? The answers to these questions are found in the box on pages 347–348, where we discuss how jurisdictional problems are sorted out in the international system. Although most situations in

DETERMINING JURISDICTION IN THE WORLD

What happens if a Frenchman kills a Pole on a ship owned by a Canadian flying the Panamanian flag in U.S. territorial waters?

"Jurisdiction" refers to the competence of a state to prosecute certain acts of individuals in its courts. The subject of jurisdiction is sufficiently complicated to fill hundreds of pages in most international law casebooks. We will try here to summarize briefly the basic aspects of the problem.

One must first understand that any given country is composed of a multitude of individual persons, most of whom are citizens, or *nationals,* of that state. However, also traveling or residing within each state are *aliens,* persons who are nationals of another state or may even be stateless (if their citizenship has been lost for some reason). In general, a "national" refers to a person owing permanent allegiance to a particular state, and it is a status acquired either through birth or through naturalization. Regarding birth, some countries, such as the continental European states, stress the *jus sanguinis* principle, whereby a child automatically acquires the nationality of the parents regardless of where the child is born. Other states, such as the United States, use not only the *jus sanguinis* principle but also the *jus soli* principle, whereby any child (with a few minor exceptions) who is born on their soil is eligible for citizenship regardless of the nationality of the parents. Hence, a child born to Belgian parents in the United States would be eligible for both American and Belgian citizenship. The conflicts inherent in dual, and sometimes multiple, citizenship are usually resolved through residency requirements imposed by most states. Nationality can also be gained through naturalization, the process whereby a foreigner attains citizenship after complying with the application procedures stipulated by the state.

Jurisdiction can be claimed by states on five possible grounds:

1. The *territorial* principle, whereby a state may exercise jurisdiction over the acts of anyone—nationals or aliens (except for certain classes of aliens such as foreign diplomats)—committed within its territorial borders (e.g., U.S. courts trying an Englishman for a theft committed in New York City);

2. The *nationality* principle, whereby a state may exercise jurisdiction over any acts perpetrated by its own nationals, no matter where they are committed in the world (e.g., U.S. courts trying an American for a murder committed in Egypt);

3. The *protective* principle, whereby a state may exercise jurisdiction over the acts of any persons—nationals or aliens (with a few exceptions)—

committed anywhere in the world, if such acts threaten a state's national security (e.g., U.S. courts trying a Hungarian for counterfeiting U.S. currency in Mexico);

4. The *universality* principle, whereby a state may exercise jurisdiction over the acts of any persons—nationals or aliens (with a few exceptions)—committed anywhere in the world, if such acts constitute crimes against the community of nations (e.g., U.S. courts trying a Belgian for engaging in an act of piracy on the high seas by seizing a French fishing vessel, or trying a Palestinian for skyjacking a Jordanian jetliner);

5. The *passive personality* principle, whereby a state may exercise jurisdiction over any person who has injured one of its nationals, no matter where in the world the act was committed (e.g., U.S. courts trying a Syrian for killing an American in Lebanon).

The first two principles are the most commonly invoked and accepted bases of jurisdiction, with the territorial principle being most adhered to by states in the Anglo-Saxon legal tradition, and the nationality principle most recognized by states in the continental European tradition. The other three principles, only occasionally invoked, are exceptions to the general notion that states should not seek to prosecute in their national courts those acts committed by aliens abroad. It is clearly possible for more than one state to have legitimate grounds on which to claim jurisdiction over some act, as in the case of a person shooting across a national frontier and killing a person on the other side. As a practical matter, one state—namely, the one that has the offender in custody—is usually in a position to determine whether to exercise jurisdiction itself or to *extradite* that person to another state seeking jurisdiction.

In the hypothetical case cited at the beginning of this box, it is conceivable that France could invoke the nationality principle, Poland the passive personality principle, and the United States or Panama the territorial principle. As a general rule, if the "good order" of the port of the coastal state (here, the United States) were not disturbed by the incident—if a wild shooting spree did not ensue—then the coastal state ordinarily would be willing to defer to the authority of the flag state (Panama), which in turn could decide to hand over the perpetrator to his government (France) for trial. In any event, it is not likely that the Frenchman would go scot-free.

international relations involve a much less tangled set of jurisdictional possibilities than the case mentioned here, numerous incidents occur daily that require some determination of jurisdiction. The international system has been able to handle such jurisdictional concerns relatively smoothly, although the problems become more acute as transnational activities increase.

Adjudication, then, like lawmaking and law enforcement, tends to occur in a more convoluted fashion in the international system than in national systems. In many ways, although international law is most criticized for the ineffectiveness of its law-enforcement and lawmaking institutions, it is the adjudication area that is probably the weakest link in the international legal system. Still, an adjudication process does exist, as we have suggested.

Special Problems in Contemporary International Law

In the international system, as in national societies, law is essentially based on politics. That is, the legal rules developed by a society—although they might have some utilitarian value for all members—tend to reflect especially the interests of those members of society who have the most resources with which to influence the rule-making process. Although the law in some societies might be based on a wider, more just set of values and interests than in other societies, underlying political realities nonetheless invariably shape the law.[19] Much of the current body of international law, for example, evolved from the international politics of the nineteenth and early twentieth centuries, when Western states dominated the international system. The traditional rules that were created to promote freedom of the seas, protection of foreign investment, and many other international activities tended to reflect the needs and interests of these powers.

However, when political realities change along with technological conditions and other factors, pressures mount to *alter* the law so that it better reflects the new environment. The contemporary international system can be thought of as a society in ferment, with nuclear weapons, economic interdependence and the growth of multinational corporations, and revolutionary advances in travel and other kinds of technology threatening to render many of the existing rules obsolete. An equally important impetus for change in the legal order is provided by the shifting power equation in world politics, as traditional powers find it difficult to impose their will on former colonies clamoring for a rewriting of the rules more compatible with their interests. In some problem areas, such as environmental pollution and uses of outer space, a body of international law is only beginning to evolve.

Hence, many efforts are now underway to revise and expand international law. Although the recent depolarization of the East-West and North-South conflicts should make it more possible to reach consensus on international legal principles, there are still differences of opinion between developed and less developed countries, as well as differences between various cultural traditions ("the West vs. the rest," as noted in Chapter 3), which complicate such efforts.[20] We will discuss the politics of global problem solving and "regime formation" in Part IV. Before finishing our discussion of international law, we want to call attention briefly to three specific problems in contemporary international law: (1) the laws of war, (2) the treatment of aliens, and (3) human rights.

LAWS OF WAR

Although the bulk of international law consists of the "laws of peace," there also exist the "laws of war." Some of these laws pertain to the *conduct* of war, i.e., the kinds of behavior that are legally permissible by governments once a war is underway, regardless of how it started. Other rules pertain to the *commencement* of war, i.e., the circumstances under which it is legal for a state to resort to the use of armed force against another state. If the latter rules were totally effective, there would be little need for the former.

There is a long history of states attempting to regulate the conduct of war through agreed-on rules regarding the rights and obligations of *neutrals* (e.g., exempting ships of neutral countries from seizure unless they carried contraband goods destined for one of the warring countries) as well as the *belligerents* themselves (e.g., according humane treatment to captured soldiers). Some of the attempts to inject a dose of civility into warfare have seemed paradoxical and almost comical, such as the prohibition (embodied in The Hague Conventions of 1907) against the use of "dum-dum" expanding bullets and the use of "deceit" in the form of misrepresenting a flag of truce or wearing Red Cross uniforms as a disguise—especially at a time when poisonous gas and other atrocities were legally permissible. However absurd as they might appear and as erratic as their observance has been, the laws governing the conduct of war have at least succeeded in limiting the savage nature of war to some extent, notably through such instruments as the 1929 and 1949 Geneva Conventions on the treatment of prisoners of war (POWs). The Sidelight on pages 352–353 focuses on one current effort to "humanize" war.

There also have been attempts throughout history to regulate the very outbreak of war, although in the eighteenth and nineteenth centuries legal efforts were devoted more to making war a more civilized affair than actually banning or restricting its occurrence. Not until the twentieth century, with the **League of Nations Covenant** and the **Kellogg-Briand Pact** drawn after the ravages of World War I, were efforts made explicitly to *outlaw* war. The latter treaty, ratified by almost every nation, provided that "the settlement of all disputes . . . of whatever nature . . . shall never be sought except by pacific means."[21] World War II, of course, demonstrated the hollowness of such pious denunciations of violence. In the **United Nations Charter** of 1945, an attempt was made to specify more clearly the proscription against the use of armed force in international relations and to provide stronger enforcement machinery. Under the UN Charter, all members are obligated to "refrain . . . from the threat or use of force against the territorial integrity or political independence of any state." This language has been generally interpreted to mean that not

only war but *any first use of armed force* by one state against another state—
no matter how limited—is *illegal* today. Force may be legally used only under
three conditions: (1) in self-defense by an individual state or alliance of states
against the armed attack of another state, (2) in the service of the UN as part
of a "collective security" or "peacekeeping" operation, or (3) in the service of a
regional peacekeeping organization. In short, armed *aggression* is illegal today,
which might be why states no longer have "war departments" but "defense
departments."

"Aggression" and "self-defense" naturally are often in the eyes of the be-
holder, with some states at times going so far as to claim the legal right of ini-
tiating the use of force in *anticipatory* or *preemptive* self-defense; Israel relied
on such a justification in 1967, when its troops crossed the border and attacked
Egyptian forces thought to be massing for an impending invasion of Israel, and
in 1981, when its planes destroyed an Iraqi nuclear reactor thought to be a
threat to Israeli security.[22] There is a long "just war" tradition in international
relations that provides some support for the Israeli position, although the UN
Charter sought to curtail the circumstances under which states could "justly"
resort to violence.[23] Although we noted in the previous chapter that the resort
to armed force continues to be a feature of contemporary international relations, at least one respected observer contends that "the norm against the unilateral national use of force has survived. Indeed, . . . the norm has been largely
observed . . . and the kinds of international wars which it sought to prevent
[wars between states] have been infrequent."[24] One reason Iraq's attempted annexation of Kuwait in 1990 sparked such universal condemnation was the fact
it was the first time since World War II that one state had been so bold as to try
to eliminate completely another member of the international community
through the use of armed force. The rub here, however, is that the nonaggression norm has been much less effective in cases that are not as blatant, including many involving what we earlier called "force without war."

Moreover, the rules governing the outbreak of hostilities have been especially inadequate to deal with the most common form of planetary violence
today—internal wars and mixed internal/external conflicts (internal wars involving outside intervention). In the case of mixed conflicts, it is not clearly
one state engaged in armed attack on another state but rather a government
seeking foreign support to quell a rebellion or a rebel group seeking foreign
support to overthrow a government. There is no question that a foreign army's
inviting itself into a domestic conflict ordinarily would constitute aggression
and would be a violation of the UN Charter, but what if it is invited in by a
government on the brink of collapse? A government has a legal right to invite
foreign military assistance only if it can rightly claim to exercise effective
control and authority (i.e., sovereignty) over its own population, a condition
that is often disputable during a civil war.

Internal wars and military interventionism pose special problems today for
the implementation of POW conventions and other rules governing the con-

SIDELIGHT

MAKING WARFARE MORE HUMANE: THE EFFORT TO DE-MINE THE WORLD

U.S. Senator Patrick Leahy, who is helping to lead a crusade to ban all land mines from use in warfare, has called these inexpensive but deadly devices "the Saturday night special of civil wars." Cambodia (Kampuchea), the locale of a brutal civil war in the 1980s and 1990s, has been called "a nation of amputees." The article below depicts the current effort in the United States and worldwide to produce an international agreement that would totally eliminate these weapons from being employed in civil or interstate conflicts. Depending on whether one views this issue through the idealist paradigm or the realist paradigm, one might well reach very different conclusions as to the proposal's feasibility. Where does the reader stand?

For years, warring parties have seeded their battlefields with land mines— cheap, camouflaged explosives designed to kill and maim people. Six million land mines have been planted across Bosnia in the past four years. Now these land mines are one of the greatest dangers facing U.S. soldiers there.

On the day that an American soldier is injured or killed by a land mine in Bosnia, he or she will be one of 70 people worldwide victimized by land mines that day, one of 26,000 that year. As soldiers, they will be a minority. Ninety percent of land mine victims are civilians. . . .

Land mine victims are found in almost every area of the world. There are 350 types of land mines, produced by 56 countries, including the United States. The State Department estimates that there are now more than 100 million land mines sown globally, with the highest concentration in Cambodia, Afghanistan, Angola, Kuwait, Mozambique, Somalia, and Bosnia.

duct of warfare because those rules have generally been developed over the years to apply to conventional armed struggle between states.[25] In guerrilla warfare, armies do not normally confront each other across well-defined fronts, and soldiers do not even always wear uniforms. Customary distinctions between civilians and combatants are blurred, as are distinctions between neutrals and belligerents. A national government experiencing rebellion is understandably reluctant to extend to rebels the same status normally reserved for enemy soldiers, preferring to dismiss them as "rioters" or "gangsters" rather than legitimizing them as "freedom fighters." The result is that the rights and obligations traditionally associated with the conduct of warfare have become muddled and often ignored. During the Vietnam War, for exam-

Land mines can be purchased for as little as $3 apiece. The cost of clearing them ranges up to $1,000 apiece. . . . UN de-mining experts are able to clear only a few yards a day. Although 100,000 mines worldwide were removed last year, between 2 million and 5 million more were laid. Land mines can be scattered from the air at a rate of 2,000 a minute.

Uncleared mines leave whole sections of countries unsuitable for settlement, agriculture, or economic development. The mines lay dormant until triggered by returning refugees, farmers, children, peacekeeping forces or tourists. Two Americans on their honeymoon last June were touring the Sinai Desert, an area fought over during the 1948–67 conflict between Egypt and Israel. . . . The newlyweds were killed when their vehicle hit a mine. . . .

The International Campaign to Ban Land Mines, launched in 1992 by veterans, human rights, medical and development organizations, calls for a complete ban on the production, stockpiling, sale, transfer or export of antipersonnel mines. Nineteen countries are on record calling for an immediate ban. . . .

Though the U.S. government is not yet willing to subscribe to a complete ban on land mines, Congress did enact a moratorium in 1992 on U.S. export of mines. The moratorium was extended in 1993 for several more years. . . .

Though some military analysts want to continue using land mines, many combat veterans wish they never existed. A third of the American casualties in Vietnam were estimated to have been caused by mines, many of those American-made. . . .

A ban on land mines . . . will be too late for our troops en route to Bosnia. And too late for the men, women and children they join there. But what a gift it would be for the next generation.

Source: Virginia Nesmith, "Land Mines Are A Lingering Killer," *St. Louis Post-Dispatch,* December 31, 1995. Adapted by permission of author Virginia Nesmith.

ple, there was disagreement over whether Communist Viet Cong troops captured by U.S. and South Vietnamese forces ought to have been treated as prisoners of war entitled to protection under the 1949 Geneva Conventions, or as common criminals to be prosecuted for murder, insurrection, and treason against the South Vietnamese government. Similar problems surrounding the application of the laws of war pervaded the Yugoslav conflict of the 1990s.

We noted in Chapter 4 that foreign involvement in civil conflicts in the post–Cold War era has frequently taken the form of "humanitarian intervention," i.e., a unilateral or, more commonly, a collective, multilateral response by the international community triggered by the following kinds of situations: "genocide, 'ethnic cleansing,' . . . and similar atrocities entailing loss of life on a mass scale (Yugoslavia, Iraq, Liberia); interference with the delivery of humanitarian relief to endangered civilian populations (Yugoslavia, Iraq, Somalia); . . . collapse of civil order, entailing substantial loss of life and precluding the possibility of identifying any authority capable of granting or withholding consent to international involvement (Liberia, Somalia); [and] irregular interruption of democratic governance (Haiti)."[26] Although humanitarian intervention is viewed by idealists as an important new concept in international relations, realists have noted that it seems to contradict Article 2, section 7 of the UN Charter, which states that "nothing contained in the Charter shall authorize the UN to intervene in matters which are essentially within the domestic jurisdiction of any state." Questions have been raised about whether recent UN-authorized interventions in Iraq to protect the Kurds and in Haiti to unseat a dictatorial government there set troublesome precedents for outside interference in the domestic affairs of sovereign states generally.[27] Some states, such as Russia in its brutal suppression of civil strife in Chechnya in 1995–1996, may be able to resist humanitarian intervention more readily than others.

Even in those armed conflicts that are purely interstate in nature, the absence of formal declarations of war today can make it difficult to determine whether the rules governing the conduct of war are in effect at a given moment. Then, too, the technology of modern warfare—strategic bombing, submarine-launched missiles, napalm, herbicides and defoliants, and the like—has tended to make many of the classic rules practically inoperable, such as the standard proscription against indiscriminate attacks on civilians on land and sea, although governments can still design military strategies to minimize civilian casualties if they are so inclined. Efforts have been made to adapt the laws of war to these new realities, such as the two Geneva Protocols of 1977; but the evolution of international law in this area remains problematical.[28]

TREATMENT OF ALIENS

The distinction between **nationals** and **aliens** was discussed earlier in the context of jurisdiction (see the box on pages 347–348). With the increased volume of transnational business-related and tourist travel in the world, countries are generally finding more aliens visiting or residing within their borders. The basic maxim that has always applied to foreigners is "when in Rome, do as the Romans do." That is, foreigners are expected to obey host country laws and (with the exception of foreign diplomatic personnel) can be prosecuted by the latter's courts for committing crimes of murder or theft, or engaging in any other activities proscribed by the state. However, international law has traditionally stipulated that, in certain respects, aliens are entitled to special treatment different from the manner in which the host government deals with its own nationals. In particular, just because a host government might be a dictatorship that denies its citizens any semblance of due process of law and the right to a fair trial, this does not mean that an alien accused of committing a crime in that country must necessarily settle for the same level of justice reserved for nationals of that state. Governments can invoke a legal right to have their citizens accorded a *minimum international standard of justice* by any host state in which their citizens happen to be while abroad, no matter what the standard of justice is in the host country. If the minimum standard is not observed, injured parties can request their own government to seek redress from the host state.

These are not mere academic issues and they can critically affect individual lives—for example, if you are an American accused and convicted of theft in Saudi Arabia, where the penalty meted out to Saudis in such cases can be the amputation of a hand; or, as two Australians found out in a celebrated 1986 case, if you are caught possessing a cache of hard drugs in Malaysia, where the automatic penalty is death by hanging. In Singapore, where chewing gum is illegal in a highly regimented society, an American was "caned" (punished with a whipping) in 1994 for prankishly spray-painting automobiles. Many governments, notably in the developing world, have voiced opposition to the customary notion of a minimum *international* standard, viewing it as an artifact of the old colonial era when the United States and other Western states tended to dictate legal norms. Instead, several states today claim their only obligation to foreigners is to ensure that the latter obtain equal treatment with their own citizens in accordance with the established *national* standard. Even for those states that accept the idea of an international standard, differences obviously arise as to what constitutes a "minimum" degree of justice. Hence, this is another area in which international law is in flux.

Controversy over the treatment of aliens has been especially heated on the subject of **expropriation,** i.e., government seizure of foreign-owned property or assets. It is not surprising that this should be a controversial issue today, at a time when private overseas investment has reached enormous levels; the foreign assets of American-owned companies alone are currently valued at over $1 trillion. The customary rule of international law is that any state has the right to expropriate alien-owned property, but only for "public purposes, if no discrimination is made between aliens and nationals, and if prompt, adequate and effective payment" is provided by the government as compensation.[29] Here, too, many less developed countries have challenged the established rule as an infringement on their sovereignty left over from the colonial era, and they have argued their only obligation is to give "appropriate" compensation based on their national standards. Other LDCs still acknowledge the customary rule but often disagree with Western states over what constitutes "adequate and effective" compensation, as in the case of several Middle East states that have nationalized foreign oil company facilities in recent years. Attempts at replacing the customary law with multilateral treaties that embody more widely accepted codes of conduct have encountered great difficulty, causing states such as the United States to resort instead to a series of bilateral conventions with individual countries.[30] The post–Cold War era may well see expropriation issues becoming more muted, as even Marxist states seek increased foreign investment and try to avoid offending potential sources of capital.

HUMAN RIGHTS

Since World War II, an ongoing effort has been made to require national governments to observe the minimum international standard of justice not only with regard to aliens within their borders but also with regard to their very own *citizens*, on the assumption that there are certain "rights one has simply because one is a human being."[31] In other words, there has been a movement to extend **human rights** protection under international law to *all* individuals on the globe, regardless of whether they are aliens or nationals. For example, at the **Nuremberg Trials** after World War II, leaders of Nazi Germany were charged with having committed, along with other crimes, crimes against humanity. In particular, German officials were accused and then convicted of having violated the rights of the indigenous Jewish population in Germany by engaging in genocide against it; as a result, several German leaders were sentenced to life imprisonment or execution. The Nuremberg precedent suggested, therefore, that *individuals* have rights (and, indeed, obligations) under international law.

Critics of the Nuremberg Trials have argued that they did not reflect the evolution of international law but simply amounted to "victors' justice," i.e., the winners of a war arbitrarily asserting the existence of certain rules that were used as a pretext to punish the political and military leaders of a vanquished state. These critics point out that the United States, which supported such strong penalties against German leaders at Nuremberg, resisted any calls for international tribunals to hold American officials accountable for atrocities allegedly committed during World War II (and later in Vietnam). Although the United States was not guilty of atrocities on the scale of the Germans, Washington was perhaps guilty of a certain amount of hypocrisy in refusing to permit any scrutiny of its own behavior by an international body. These issues surfaced again in the 1990s, when the United States and other countries called on the United Nations to organize war crimes tribunals to address alleged acts of genocide committed in Bosnia and Rwanda, the first such tribunals to be created since Nuremberg; the tribunals posed a dilemma insofar as efforts by the international community to arrest and prosecute selected combatants risked breeding a new round of hostilities.

Still, granted the uneven application of the Nuremberg principles, the significance of Nuremberg nonetheless was that it clearly challenged the traditional notion that only *states*—not individuals—were subjects of international law. Nuremberg was followed by the Universal Declaration of Human Rights, a resolution adopted by the UN General Assembly in 1948. The Declaration, which was a moral pronouncement rather than a legally binding document, urged national governments to promote a variety of human rights, both civil and political (e.g., the right to a fair trial, protection from cruel and inhumane punishment, freedom of expression and religion) as well as economic and social (e.g., the right to an adequate standard of living, the right to work). Since that time, a number of treaties have been drafted that attempt to articulate human rights more clearly and that are binding on those states choosing to ratify them. Included among these are five conventions dealing with genocide, racial discrimination, discrimination against women, political and civil rights, and economic and social rights. The latter two conventions, along with the Universal Declaration, are often referred to as the "International Bill of Human Rights."

To date, only about half of the states in the world have ratified these conventions, and many that are parties have interpreted the requirements loosely. A fundamental problem is that national governments tend to resist accepting international legal obligations in this area, because the entire concept of "human rights" is viewed as undermining their sovereign authority within their borders. Even the United States, generally an outspoken supporter of human rights over the years, did not ratify the Convention on Genocide until 1988, forty years after it was drafted, and did not ratify the Covenant on Civil and Political Rights (drafted in 1966) until 1992, because certain language in these treaties—notably the prohibition against capital punishment—ran counter to U.S. domestic policy and municipal law; in acceding to these treaties, the U.S. attached various "reservations" permitting it to be excused from some provisions. The United States is still not a party to the Covenant on Economic and Social Rights, because it is viewed by many members of the U.S. Senate as promoting excessive governmental regulation, for example, by guaranteeing paid leave for women before and after childbirth. Despite the drive for "universal" agreement on human rights protection, the greatest progress in this area has occurred at the *regional* level, in Western Europe, where the West Europeans have created institutions such as the European Court of Human Rights, in which individual citizens can bring grievances against their own government before a supranational tribunal.

Some observers have argued that, with the demise of the Soviet bloc, there is an opportunity to forge a global consensus on human rights built around Western, liberal-democratic principles. The following statement is representative of this viewpoint:

> For the first time [since the Concert of Europe immediately following the Napoleonic Wars, when conservative political views prevailed among the major actors] . . . , the world is united in its view on what constitutes legitimate rule. This, in itself, is a momentous political development. Liberal democracy is the unchallenged standard of legitimacy almost everywhere on earth. . . . Francis Fukyama [who wrote an article in 1989 proclaiming

SIDELIGHT

THE DRIVE FOR NONHUMAN RIGHTS

The following news item appeared some time ago under the headline "UN Espouses Animals' Lib," alerting the public that a new dimension had been added to the crusade for a more humane world. Nonhuman rights seemingly were being taken more seriously by some than human rights, although it remained to be seen how they would be enforced.

Man's feathered and four-legged friends have won a Universal Declaration of the Rights of Animals, and they have got the United Nations on their side.

Adopted Sunday at a ceremonial meeting of the UN Educational, Scientific, and Cultural Organization, the Animal Charter opens with the words: "All animals are born with an equal claim on life and the same rights to existence."

The ceremony, attended by statesmen, artists, and Nobel prizewinners, included a display of 2.1 million signatures collected around the world in defense of animal rights.

The charter . . . spells out what animal lovers are pushing governments the world over to embody in legislation. Basically, it says that it is wrong to abandon one's dog in the street when one goes on vacation; it is unfeeling

the "end of history"] has observed that 'as mankind approaches the end of the millennium, the twin crises of authoritarianism and socialist central planning have left only one competitor standing in the ring as an ideology of potentially universal validity: liberal democracy, the doctrine of individualism and popular sovereignty.'[32]

Others, however, question this. Recalling our earlier point about the "clash of civilizations," it has been said that

efforts to promote human rights in Asia must . . . reckon with the altered distribution of power in the post–Cold War world. . . . Western leverage over East and Southeast Asia has been greatly reduced. . . . There is far less scope for . . . sanctions to force compliance with human rights. . . . For the first time since the Universal Declaration [on Human Rights] was adopted in 1948, countries not steeped in the Judeo-Christian and natural law traditions are in the first rank. That unprecedented situation will define the new international politics of human rights. It will also multiply the occasions to gas stray cats; it is hideous to keep pigs or cattle locked inside container trucks, sweating or freezing, while customs officials settle disputes; it is cruel to raise chickens or rabbits in shoebox-sized cages, drop live lobsters in boiling water or force-feed geese to fatten their livers for foie gras.

Singled out for special condemnation are scientists, the entertainment world and hunters on the grand scale.

"Animal experimentation involving physical or psychological suffering is incompatible with the rights of animals," the charter says. "No animal shall be exploited for the amusement of man. Exhibitions and spectacles involving animals are incompatible with their dignity."

"Scenes of violence involving animals shall be banned from cinema and television, except for humane education."

"Any act involving mass killing of wild animals is genocide, that is, a crime against the species."

Signing of the charter by the 142 member states of UNESCO does not mean that blue-capped UN troops will now be rushed to the defense of persecuted pooches. The organizers hope that it will help animal lovers pressing for animal rights legislation.

It should be added that one group calling itself the Animal Liberation Front went so far in 1990 as to claim responsibility for fire-bombings of several British department stores in protest against the fur trade.

Source: "UN Espouses Animals' Lib," *St. Louis Post-Dispatch* (October 16, 1978), p. 10A. Used by permission of the Associated Press.

for conflict. . . . The self-congratulatory, simplistic, and sanctimonious tone of much Western commentary at the end of the Cold War and the current triumphalism of Western values grate on East and Southeast Asians.[33]

In addition to cultural differences between the Orient and the West, there are several political systems in the Middle East and elsewhere that have a strong theocratic bent and have difficulty elevating secular legal precepts above religious law, especially over matters such as the status of women and privacy rights. There is also a continued disagreement surrounding the concept of economic and social rights, with many governments in the South insisting that the traditional Western emphasis on civil liberties and free markets neglects the rights of economically disadvantaged groups and societies. All of these divergent viewpoints were expressed at the 1993 UN World Conference on Human Rights in Vienna, as well as the 1995 UN World Conference on Women in Beijing, where national delegations debated everything from "the right to development" to "the rights of women and of the girl-child" to "the rights of the disabled," with both meetings producing declarations embodying a fragile, uneasily patched together consensus.

There remains a gap between the rhetoric used by governments in support of human rights and their actual observance of human rights. Respect for even basic rights, such as free speech, is still very weak in many countries, although the recent democratization movements in Eastern Europe and elsewhere have improved the overall picture considerably. According to one often-cited source that annually reports statistics on human rights trends, the "world stands at the high water mark of freedom in history," with almost 70 percent of the world's people living in countries that are rated as either "free" (25 percent) or "partly free" (44 percent).[34] Yet not only does that leave one-third of humanity living in "not free" countries—where arrest and imprisonment for "political" crimes occur regularly, along with torture and death squads—but even in many democracies "human rights violations occur everyday."[35] In highly repressive societies, data on such abuses are difficult to obtain because of government secrecy and distortion, but various NGOs have managed to improve the monitoring of governmental human rights records worldwide; these groups include Amnesty International, the International Commission of Jurists, and Freedom House. The UN Human Rights Commission also has expanded its role in recent years in investigating complaints brought against Chile, Israel, South Africa, Cuba, Iran, and other states, and has attempted to use "mobilization of shame" as a tactic for promoting compliance with international conventions and norms.[36] Even though enforcement machinery remains weak, such widespread attention, tied to increased concern about image-building in many capitals, has given human rights issues more importance on the global agenda than many realists might have predicted.[37]

The human rights movement persists in the quest for enhanced individual dignity and is part of a larger movement today to bring other kinds of *nonstate* actors directly under the purview of international law.[38] Related to the globalist paradigm, not only human beings but also international organizations and corporations, as they proliferate, are grudgingly being accorded some degree of status as "international legal persons" alongside nation-states. (In fact, as the Sidelight in this section indicates, even animals are now being recognized as deserving of protection under international law.) Hence, in this area too, international law is evolving in new directions in response to the changing international environment.

Conclusion

We have noted that international law is a product of international politics. But we have also noted how international politics, in turn, is partly affected by international law, in the sense that international law helps to shape the behavior of states and other actors in regard to diplomatic protection, commercial transactions, and other matters. Even in the Iranian hostage crisis, international law—if nothing else—served as the primary medium of communication and bargaining between the United States and Iran, because the conflict was largely played out through the exchange of legal broadsides. The importance of international law can be seen in the debates that are taking place today in the assembly halls of various world bodies, mostly over the question of what rules are going to govern the conduct of international relations; the importance attached to international law can also be seen, less visibly perhaps, in the haggling over the fine print of legal parchments that occurs in the backroom corridors. In the next chapter, we examine the forums in which many future discussions of international law are likely to be held, as we focus on the role of international organizations as actors in world politics.

SUMMARY

1. Three fundamental conditions must be present for law to exist in a society: a law-making process, a law-enforcement process, and a law-adjudication process. Despite the lack of a world legislature, a world police force, or other strong central authoritative institutions, international law meets these criteria—although it functions differently from law found in national societies.

2. The officially recognized sources of international law include custom, treaties, general principles of law recognized by civilized nations, judicial decisions of national and international tribunals, and the writings of legal scholars, with the first two being by far the most important.

3. Customary rules and treaties are binding only on those states that consent to them. Given the ambiguity often surrounding customary rules, there has been an increasing trend in recent years to codify them in written treaty form. Treaties are formal written agreements creating legal obligations for the governments that sign and ratify them, and may be bilateral or multilateral. Of special importance are the many multilateral treaties that have been concluded that regulate international interactions in broad areas of concern, such as the law of the sea.

4. The most common criticism of international law is the apparent lack of enforcement, i.e., that rules are violated regularly with no "traffic cop" available to punish offenders. However, the fact is that most states obey most of the rules most of the time, primarily because of their mutual interests in having some degree of order in international relations and their fear of sanctions that individual states might apply in retaliation against lawbreakers.

5. Institutions for adjudicating international law exist but are extremely weak, because disputants cannot ordinarily be compelled to appear in court. The World Court has been an ineffective, largely ignored institution, with little or no compul-

sory jurisdiction over states. However, national and regional courts have been more successful in applying international law.

6. When political realities change, along with technological conditions and other factors, pressures mount to alter the law so that it better reflects the new environment. Much of the current body of international law evolved from the nineteenth century, when Western states dominated the international system and created rules designed to promote freedom of the seas, protection of foreign investment, and other interests. Today, many traditional rules are being rendered obsolete by technological change, are being challenged by developing countries as artifacts of the colonial era, or are being questioned by states with differing cultural perspectives. Hence, contemporary international law is under great strain.

7. There are three problem areas that exemplify how international law is in flux: the laws of war, the treatment of aliens, and human rights.

8. States have long tried to regulate the conduct of war and have even made some attempts explicitly to outlaw war altogether. Today, armed aggression is illegal. However, rules governing conventional warfare are inadequate in dealing with more common forms of international violence, such as force without war, internal wars, and military interventionism.

9. Traditionally, a host state has been obligated under international law to accord foreigners within its borders a "minimum international standard of justice," even if it treats its own citizens according to different standards. However, many developing countries question whether foreigners are entitled to special treatment. An especially controversial subject has been the expropriation of foreign-owned property.

10. Since World War II there has been an ongoing effort to extend human rights protection to all individuals, forcing states to observe a minimum international standard of justice with regard not only to aliens within their borders but also to their own citizens. National governments tend to resist accepting international legal obligations in this area, however, because the entire concept of human rights is viewed as undermining their sovereign authority within their borders.

SUGGESTIONS FOR FURTHER READING AND STUDY

Excellent introductory texts presenting an overview of the rules of international law include very concise treatments by Michael Akehurst in *A Modern Introduction to International Law*, 6th ed. (London: Allen and Unwin, 1987) and Ray August in *Public International Law* (Englewood Cliffs, N.J.: Prentice-Hall, 1995), and a more in-depth treatment by Gerhard von Glahn in *Law Among Nations*, 6th ed. (New York: Macmillan, 1992). Two good readers that explore various contemporary problems in international law are *International Law: A Contemporary Perspective* (Boulder, Colo.: Westview Press, 1985), ed. by Richard Falk et al.; and *International Law Anthology* (New York: Anderson Publishing Co., 1994), ed. by Anthony D'Amato. Also see Robert Bledsoe and Boleslaw Boczek, *The International Law Dictionary* (Santa Barbara, Calif.: ABC-Clio, 1987); and Thomas Buergenthal and Harold G. Maier, *Public International Law In A Nutshell*, 2nd ed. (St. Paul: West Publishing, 1990).

Among the works that deal generally with the relationship between international law and international politics, see William D. Coplin, "International Law and Assumptions About the State System," *World Politics,* 17 (July 1965), pp. 615–634; Louis Henkin, *How Nations Behave,* 2nd ed. (New York: Columbia University Press, 1979); Karl W. Deutsch and Stanley Hoffmann, eds., *The Relevance of International Law* (Garden City, N.J.: Doubleday, 1971), especially pp. 177–202; Francis Boyle, *World Politics and International Law* (Durham, N.C.: Duke University Press, 1985); Christopher C. Joyner, "The Reality and Relevance of International Law, in Charles W. Kegley and Eugene R. Wittkopf, eds., *The Global Agenda,* 3rd ed. (New York: McGraw-Hill, 1992), pp. 202–215; and Abram Chayes and Antonia Chayes, "On Compliance," *International Organization,* 47 (Spring 1993), pp. 175–205.

Several case studies exploring the operation of international law in various historical situations are available, including Abram Chayes, *The Cuban Missile Crisis* (New York: Oxford University Press, 1974); W. Michael Reisman and Andrew R. Willard, eds., *International Incidents* (Princeton, N.J.: Princeton University Press, 1988); and several discussed in the Henkin book mentioned above. Discussions of specific international legal cases and issues also can be found in numerous articles appearing in the *American Journal of International Law.*

On how the post–Cold War era is posing challenges to the traditional laws of war, including the notion of "humanitarian intervention," see Anthony Clark Arend and Robert J. Beck, *International Law and the Use of Force* (London: Routledge, 1993); on the application of the "just war" concept, see Robert F. Turner, "What's Wrong with Killing Saddam Hussein?," *Washington Post National Weekly Edition,* October 15–21, 1990, p. 24. On human rights, see Jack Donnelly, *International Human Rights* (Boulder, Colo.: Westview Press, 1993); Thomas G. Weiss, David P. Forsythe, and Roger A, Coate, *The United Nations and Changing World Politics* (Boulder, Colo.: Westview Press, 1994), Part Two; Tom J. Farer and Felice Gaer, "The UN and Human Rights: At the End of the Beginning," in Adam Roberts and Benedict Kingsbury, eds., *United Nations, Divided World,* 2nd ed. (Oxford: Clarendon Press, 1993), pp. 240–296; and David P. Forsythe, "The UN and Human Rights at Fifty: An Incremental but Incomplete Revolution," *Global Governance,* 1 (September/December 1995), pp. 297–318.

International Organizations: Links between Governments and between Peoples

Item: Of the top hundred economic units in the world, roughly half are corporations, not countries.[1]
Item: By 1997, there were more than 300 IGOs and more than 10,000 NGOs in the world, compared with less than 200 nation-states.[2]
Item: The European Union (formerly called the European Community) maintains diplomatic missions in more than 100 countries, and more than 150 countries have established diplomatic missions in Brussels, the Union's headquarters.[3]

The increased status that lawyers and statesmen have recently accorded nonstate actors in the international *legal* system has coincided with the increased attention that scholars have given those actors as distinctive elements in the international *political* system. Echoing some general observations we offered in Part I, one writer notes that "the state-centered view of world affairs, the interstate model which still enjoys so much popularity in the study of international relations, has now become too simplistic," mainly because "nation-states are not the only actors on the world scene. [In addition to subnational and other actors] some NGOs probably have more power and influence in their respective fields than some of the smaller nation-states. The same applies to several IGOs and undoubtedly to many multinational business enterprises which have more employees and a larger production output than most countries."[4] In this chapter, we will look at "IGOs" and "NGOs"— in common parlance, *international organizations*—and attempt to show how they fit into the overall equation of world politics.

Clearly, international organizations have proliferated greatly in recent times, as was documented in our historical treatment of the development of the international system. There is also no question that several international organizations have made valuable contributions to global problem solving. For example, it is an international organization that has been responsible for virtually eradicating smallpox, once one of humanity's most prevalent scourges; another international organization has made it possible for airplanes to fly readily from one country to another despite the potential language barriers between airport control tower personnel and pilots seeking landing permission; and still another international organization permits over 8 billion pieces of mail to flow across national boundaries each year with a minimum of disruption.

However, the significance of international organizations as actors in world politics is still much debated, particularly whether they can be considered as having a life of their own rather than merely being collections of nation-state delegations. As with international law, viewpoints range from the realist perspective that treats international organizations as mere extensions of nation-states or as peripheral to the major power struggles of world politics, to the idealist perspective that envisions international organizations as largely autonomous agents—the possible precursors of a *supranational* government presiding over a world without borders. More and more articles are appearing in the scholarly literature having to do with the growth of "international civil society" (private, transnational networks) and the need for improved "global governance."[5] Although the growth of international organizations may be seen as an *integrative* force in human affairs, pulling against the somewhat anarchic, *disintegrative* tendencies of the centuries-old Westphalian state system, it is open to question how effective such institutions have been in forging world order and whether they can ever expect to displace national sovereignty and national loyalties. Harold Jacobson frames the question nicely when he notes that the idealist perspective

> is vividly, if simplistically, portrayed in the tapestries hung in the *Palais des Nations* in Geneva [the headquarters of the League of Nations in the period between the two world wars, and the frequent site of international conferences today]. They picture international organizations as a stage in the process of humanity combining into ever larger and more stable units for the purpose of governance—first the family, then the tribe, then the city-state, and then the nation—a process which presumably would eventually culminate in the entire world being combined in one political unit. Few if any serious observers would be willing to accept this view so baldly stated as a comprehensive explanation and forecast except in the broadest historical sense and for the most remote future. . . . [However, if] international organizations are not way stations on the route toward the creation of ever larger territorial sovereignties, what then are they?[6]

To understand the role of international organizations in contemporary world affairs, and to evaluate the varying claims, we first need to identify the many different types of international organizations that exist today and to describe their major distinguishing characteristics. Not all international organizations look alike, and not all have equal impacts on world politics.

A Typology of International Organizations: IGOs and NGOs

Although the term **international organization** is often equated with the United Nations, it refers to a much larger phenomenon. The United Nations is only one among hundreds of international organizations that come in many different shapes and sizes. In fact, if one defines international organization in the broadest possible sense—i.e., as any group of individuals from at least two different countries that has a formal institutional apparatus that facilitates regular interactions between members across national boundaries—there are literally thousands of such entities in the world. We can classify international organizations according to at least three basic criteria: (1) membership, (2) geographical scope, and (3) functional scope. We will see how the role of international organizations in world politics varies with organizational characteristics.

MEMBERSHIP

The most fundamental basis for categorizing international organizations is in terms of their *membership* characteristics. Some international organizations, labeled **intergovernmental organizations (IGOs),** have *national governments* as members and are created through treaties between states. Other international organizations, labeled **nongovernmental organizations (NGOs),** are generally composed of *private* individuals or groups. Included in the IGO category are such bodies as the United Nations, the World Bank, and the North Atlantic Treaty Organization. Altogether, over 300 IGOs currently exist in the world. Included in the NGO category are such organizations as the International Red Cross, the Baptist World Alliance, the International Confederation of Midwives, and the International Planned Parenthood Association. The *Yearbook of International Organizations,* the most comprehensive and authoritative source of information on international organizations, counts over 10,000 NGOs in the world, more than thirty times the number of IGOs. Not included in the *Yearbook* are multinational corporations and transnational revolutionary groups, which are special variants of nongovernmental organizations.[7] See Tables 10.1 and 10.2 for listings of just a few of the IGOs and NGOs in the world.

Several organizations do not fall neatly into the intergovernmental or nongovernmental categories. For example, the International Labor Organization (ILO), an IGO, is composed predominantly of governments but also provides for labor union and employer group representation as well; similarly, the International Telecommunications Satellite Organization (INTELSAT), through which over half of the world's transoceanic telecommunication services are furnished, is an IGO in which business enterprises are members along with governments. Conversely, the International Criminal Police Organization (INTERPOL), an association of official police agencies from more than 100 countries organized to facilitate worldwide cooperation in fighting crime, is technically considered an NGO even though its members are governmental bodies. Distinctions can be further complicated by the fact that in many countries today, communist and noncommunist alike, the line between the "public" or "governmental" sector and the "private" or "nongovernmental" sector can be quite blurred. The European Broadcasting Union and the International Air Transport Association are considered NGOs even though most of the members are state-owned radio and television companies in the first case and state-owned airlines in the second case. As we will see, some NGOs and their constituent units are less subject to governmental control than others. Given the difficulty at times in ascertaining the governmental or nongovernmental

Table 10.1

INTERNATIONAL INTERGOVERNMENTAL ORGANIZATIONS: A SAMPLER

Organization	*Headquarters*
African Groundnut Council	Lagos, Nigeria
Arab Postal Union	Cairo, Egypt
Association of Southeast Asian Nations	Djakarta, Indonesia
European Union	Brussels, Belgium
Food and Agricultural Organization	Rome, Italy
Inter-American Tropical Tuna Commission	La Jolla, Calif.
International Bank for Reconstruction and Development (World Bank)	Washington, D.C.
International Labor Organization	Geneva, Switzerland
International Red Locust Control Organization for Central and Southern Africa	Mbala, Zambia
International Telecommunications Satellite Organization	Washington, D.C.
Latin American Economic System	Caracas, Venezuela
North Atlantic Treaty Organization	Brussels, Belgium
Organization of African Unity	Addis Ababa, Ethiopa
Organization of American States	Washington, D.C.
Organization of Petroleum Exporting Countries	Vienna, Austria
Union of Banana Exporting Countries	Panama City, Panama
UN Educational, Scientific, and Cultural Organization	Paris, France
United Nations	New York, N.Y.
World Health Organization	Geneva, Switzerland

Source: Yearbook of International Organizations, 32nd ed. (Brussels: Union of International Associations, 1995).

character of an organization's membership, the ultimate criterion relied on is whether it came into being through a formal intergovernmental agreement; if it was created by a treaty, it is an IGO.

GEOGRAPHICAL SCOPE

As Tables 10.1 and 10.2 suggest, another important dimension on which international organizations differ is *geographical scope.* Although there is a common tendency to think of IGOs in *global* terms, along the lines of the United Nations, only roughly one-quarter of all IGOs can be considered truly global, drawing their members from every region in the world. The vast majority of IGOs are primarily *regional* in scope, and in some cases subregional or even bilateral. Regionalism, then, has been a more powerful force than globalism in the development of intergovernmental organizations,[8] which is perhaps not surprising given the tendency for states to have more intense ties at the regional level than the global level, as well as the generally greater ease and

Table 10.2

INTERNATIONAL NONGOVERNMENTAL ORGANIZATIONS: A SAMPLER

Organization	*Headquarters*
Afro-Asian Peoples' Solidarity Organization	Cairo, Egypt
Amnesty International	London, England
Arab Lawyers Union	Cairo, Egypt
European Broadcasting Union	Geneva, Switzerland
International Air Transport Association	Geneva, Switzerland
International Alliance of Women	London, England
International Chamber of Commerce	Paris, France
International Committee of the Red Cross	Geneva, Switzerland
International Confederation of Accordionists	Surrey, England
International Confederation of Free Trade Unions	Brussels, Belgium
International Council of Scientific Unions	Paris, France
International Criminal Police Organization	Paris, France
International Federation of Air Line Pilots Associations	London, England
International Olympic Committee	Lausanne, Switzerland
International Political Science Association	Brussels, Belgium
International Union Against the Venereal Diseases and the Treponematoses	London, England
Nordic Association of Advertising Agencies	Oslo, Norway
Salvation Army	London, England
World Council of Churches	New York, N.Y.
World Federation of Master Tailors	Paris, France
World Federation of United Nations Associations	New York, N.Y.

Source: Yearbook of International Organizations, 32nd ed. (Brussels: Union of International Associations, 1995).

lesser expense of regional organizational participation. Such intergovernmental organizations as military alliances and customs unions in particular are found at the regional rather than the global level.

Not all regions are equally represented in the IGO network. Africa, Asia, and Latin America tend to be underrepresented. As noted earlier (in Table 4.2), sixteen of the twenty states that belong to the greatest number of IGOs are found in either Western Europe or North America (along with Australia and Japan); the Europeans, in particular, occupy the top ten spots, led by Denmark.[9] The Western European nations' dominance in IGO membership is owed not only to their heavy participation in global IGOs but, more importantly, to the proliferation of regional IGOs in that part of the world since the 1950s related to the formation of the European Community. Although less developed countries belong to many IGOs and rely on them for diplomatic contacts, the countries with the smallest number of IGO memberships overall tend to be found in Africa and Asia, this being a function primarily of their relatively young age and financial limitations. These countries are gradually becoming more fully involved in the IGO network and are accounting for an increasing share of IGO memberships.

A similar pattern can be seen in the NGO network. Only about one-fourth of the web of 10,000 NGOs are global. Even more than the IGO network, the NGO network draws its members overwhelmingly from Western, developed countries. Fuller participation in the NGO network by developing countries is inhibited by economic factors, although they are gradually being drawn into the web of NGO relationships. Indeed the fastest rates of growth in national participation in NGOs have been occurring lately in Africa and Asia.[10] In the past, developed communist countries have been inhibited from greater NGO participation by political factors, namely, governmental restrictions, the East-West rivalry, and the ideological problems entailed by the involvement of the citizens of such countries in "private" associations. However, with the decline of orthodox Marxism and the opening up of East bloc societies, the latter are now seeking to become more active in NGOs as well as IGOs. Reflecting the dominant position of established Western capitalist democracies in the worldwide network of international organizations, the countries that are headquarters for the most global IGOs and NGOs are the United Kingdom, France, the United States, and Switzerland.[11]

As with the IGO-NGO distinction, the global-regional distinction is not always clear-cut. Many international organizations, although not global in scope, do draw their members from more than one region. For example, the Organization of Petroleum Exporting Countries (OPEC) includes members from almost every region of the world, excluding only North America and Europe (even though its operational headquarters are in Vienna); the North Atlantic Treaty Organization (NATO) stretches from Canada and the United States to Turkey. As the OPEC example illustrates, membership in many international organizations may be limited not so much by geographical criteria as by political or economic criteria. The main point here, however, is that many international organizations are conceived as "limited membership" institutions, whereas others are open to any and all countries; only the latter truly approximate "universal" organizations.

FUNCTIONAL SCOPE

Referring again to Tables 10.1 and 10.2, one can discern that international organizations are established to serve a great variety of purposes, some of which seem rather trivial and others more significant. In terms of *functional scope,* some international organizations are general, *multipurpose* organizations, and others are characterized by specific, *limited purposes.* In the case of both IGOs and NGOs, however, limited-purpose organizations far outnumber multipurpose ones.

Among IGOs, a few institutions such as the United Nations, the Organization of American States (OAS), and the Organization of African Unity (OAU) have mandates to deal with a broad range of political, economic, and social concerns of members. Most IGOs have more narrow, specialized functions, either military (e.g., NATO), economic (e.g., the World Bank), social and cultural (e.g., the United Nations Educational, Scientific, and Cultural Organization), or technical (e.g., the World Health Organization). Economic organizations constitute the largest single category, accounting for more than half of all IGOs.[12] NGOs tend by nature to be single-purpose organizations even more than IGOs, given the fact that nongovernmental organizations ordinarily serve a clientele that shares specialized interests, either economic, religious, social, cultural, educational, or professional. The largest numbers of NGOs are found in the areas of commerce and industry as well as health and medicine.[13]

Trying to classify international organizations according to function can also be complicated. For example, NATO has increasingly become involved in a host of economic, scientific, and technological activities even though it was conceived solely as a military alliance and retains that role as its overriding mission. The World Bank has become involved increasingly in environmental concerns through its funding of development projects in the third world, so that calling it a limited-purpose economic organization hardly does it justice. As with the other key dimensions of international organizations, fitting particular institutions into particular pigeonholes on the functional dimension is less important than knowing what the various pigeonholes look like. Figure 10.1 visually summarizes the classification scheme we have presented and includes examples in each category.

The Causes and Effects of International Organization

International organizations require expenditures of money and effort to create and maintain. They exist not for their own sake but presumably because they serve certain purposes, as noted in our discussion of functional scope. Although IGOs and NGOs each have a distinct logic, the common thread running through both types of organizations is the presence of a set of concerns that transcend national frontiers. If IGOs are a bridge between governments, NGOs are a bridge between peoples. Generally speaking, IGOs are considered more important actors on the world stage than NGOs, because IGOs tend to be of more direct interest to national governments. Admittedly, NGOs such as the International Confederation of Accordionists and the World Federation of Master Tailors are not likely to alter the course of world affairs. However, certain nongovernmental organizations, such as the Roman Catholic Church,

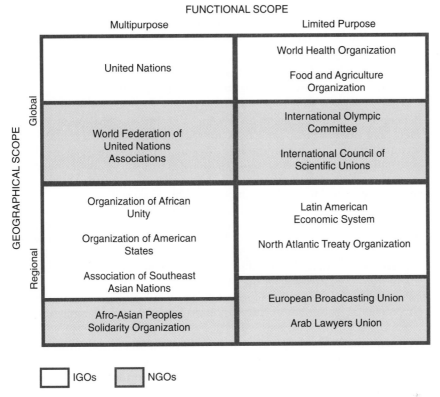

FUNCTIONAL SCOPE

	Multipurpose	Limited Purpose
Global	United Nations	World Health Organization Food and Agriculture Organization
	World Federation of United Nations Associations	International Olympic Committee International Council of Scientific Unions
Regional	Organization of African Unity Organization of American States Association of Southeast Asian Nations	Latin American Economic System North Atlantic Treaty Organization
	Afro-Asian Peoples Solidarity Organization	European Broadcasting Union Arab Lawyers Union

GEOGRAPHICAL SCOPE

☐ IGOs   ▨ NGOs

Figure 10.1
THE BASIC TYPES OF INTERNATIONAL ORGANIZATIONS (IGOs AND NGOs)

multinational corporations such as Exxon or General Motors, and revolutionary groups such as the Islamic Jihad can have significant impact insofar as they are often in a position to act independently of national governments in shaping major events in the international arena.

THE LOGIC OF NGOs

Transnational relations, interactions between private individuals and groups across national boundaries, have existed since the very beginnings of the nation-state system; consider the early wanderings of explorers, missionaries, spice merchants, and slave traders to distant corners of the earth. Nevertheless, it was not until the improved communications and transportation technology that accompanied industrialization in the nineteenth century that large numbers of people were able to interact more readily across national boundaries. Industrialization also created specialized economic and commercial groups for whom national frontiers were somewhat artificial and irrelevant barriers; not only business executives but also labor union activists, scientists, artists, members of fraternal societies, and professionals of various stripes were added to the ranks of transnational actors. James Field describes the emergence of the "new tribe" of transnational actors:

> Among the humanitarians there developed an international peace movement and international campaigns for the abolition of . . . slavery, for women's rights, and for temperance. Working class groups supported the international labor movement, international socialism. . . . From the managers there came a network of private [agreements] . . . trusts, cartels, and the like—designed to regulate competition abroad as well as at home.
>
> In much of this activity, of course, private and public sectors found themselves intertwined; governments would intermeddle, and private groups would seek governmental aid. Among the actors, governments were . . . the most visible, and the easiest to watch and describe. But while the apparatus of the state continued to grow throughout the period, and particularly from the latter part of the nineteenth century, its role . . . was less one of initiating policy than of responding to conditions produced by nongovernmental factors whose influence transcended national boundaries.[14]

As transnational interactions—travel, mail exchanges, and other flows—expanded during the nineteenth and twentieth centuries, these ties increasingly became *institutionalized* in the form of nongovernmental organizations designed to provide more durable bonds between transnational actors. The number of NGOs grew from only five in 1850 to 330 by 1914, 730 by 1939, 2,300 by 1970, to the present level of over 10,000.[15] As one would expect, NGO growth has been minimal during major wars and has tended to spurt dramatically after wars, notably after World War II. In many cases, governments themselves have encouraged the creation of NGOs, especially those involving cultural exchanges. The same forces that have contributed to NGO growth in the past—technological developments, industrialization, and urbanization—are likely to continue to operate in the future, even though national governments may well respond by placing increasing restrictions on the transnational activity of their citizenry if threatened by loss of control of some aspect of national policy.

If the reasons that nongovernmental organizations exist are fairly simple and obvious to analyze, assessing the effects of such institutions is more difficult. NGOs are hypothesized to have a number of impacts on world politics. Perhaps the most indirect and subtle impact—and potentially the deepest—has been suggested by Robert Angell in a major empirical study of "transnational participation."[16] Examining hundreds of transnational interactions, Angell concluded that sustained exposure to other peoples and cultures through NGO involvement tends to produce a more cosmopolitan, less nationalistic outlook in participants. If the latter are business executives or other elites having access to high-level foreign policymakers at home, they can promote more accommodative foreign policies and greater understanding among governments themselves; in other words, "international socialization" experienced by private individuals is gradually transferable to national governments.

However, many scholars consider the connection between NGO participation and foreign policy behavior a weak one, arguing that the flow of influence in the foreign policy process is more complicated than the preceding paragraph might suggest and that persons who become *too* cosmopolitan in their world view may well lose access to and political effectiveness with their governmental leaders. There is some question, also, about the extent to which business executives and other types of transnational actors are capable of truly shedding their national identity and thinking in larger terms; the fact is that several NGOs are dominated by the citizens, if not the government, of one country. Related to this point, even Angell acknowledges that certain kinds of transnational organizations (e.g., multinational corporations or religious movements) can foster resentment and tension rather than empathy and harmony among different peoples. Familiarity, in other words, can breed contempt, although on balance Angell finds that transnational relations represent "peace on the march."

A second NGO impact is based on the special consultative status that many NGOs have been granted in regional and global IGOs, enabling them to have input into the latter's decision making. Hundreds of NGOs are permitted direct involvement in the activities of several UN agencies, sharing information and advancing proposals as part of a web of governmental, intergovernmental, and nongovernmental efforts aimed at global problem solving. For example, many transnational scientific bodies (sometimes called "epistemic communities") have played an important role in getting environmental issues on the global agenda and in providing technical expertise at such conferences as the 1992 UN Conference on the Environment and Development (the "Earth Summit") held in Rio de Janeiro. One such NGO is the International Council of Scientific Unions (ICSU), whose members include the main scientific academies and national research councils in the physical sciences in more than sixty countries; as one writer notes, "its committees on oceanic research, antarctic research, space research, water research, and science and technology in developing countries all deal with politically significant and sensitive subject areas."[17] Likewise, Amnesty International, which we noted in the previous chapter is an NGO active in the human rights field, has been so extensively relied on for accurate monitoring of human rights violations that some view it as "almost an arm of the UN."[18] The consultative status of NGOs usually allows them to exercise only limited influence over the actual decisions reached by IGOs, although their lobbying efforts can be extremely effective in certain cases. Most notable in this regard are the many transnational agricultural, labor, and manufacturing interest groups that have been organized to promote the concerns of their members in dealing with governmental and intergovernmental officials in the European Union. It should be added that many NGOs do not enjoy a privileged consultative status in IGOs but nonetheless are active in trying to shape outcomes in the international arena, such as numerous feminist groups that showed up at the 1995 UN World Conference on Women in Beijing as well as at the Earth Summit in Rio. (See the Sidelight on "NGOs and the Growth of International Civil Society," on pages 376–377.)

A third impact that NGOs have on world politics is more direct and sizable and has nothing to do with socialization or consultation processes. This impact, alluded to earlier, is the role of some NGOs as distinct, autonomous actors that compete with and threaten the sovereignty of national governments in areas of great international significance. In some cases, the part played by NGOs in the international political system can be quite visible—for example,

SIDELIGHT

NGOs AND THE GROWTH OF INTERNATIONAL CIVIL SOCIETY

While the 1995 UN-sponsored World Conference on Women was being held in Beijing, some 30,000 delegates from various feminist organizations worldwide gathered at a separate NGO forum in Huairou, a remote suburb of the Chinese capital city, to articulate their own demands. At the Earth Summit in Rio in 1992, a similar number of "unofficial" NGO representatives met in their own "Global Forum" to address environmental concerns. The following article discusses yet another such event, an NGO gathering during the 1995 UN World Summit for Social Development held in Copenhagen, Denmark. Although many observers would question the importance of these happenings, others see them as part of a larger phenomenon, namely the emergence of a nascent "international civil society."

It started in Rio de Janeiro, with the 1992 Earth Summit. Now no big United Nations conference takes place without it. It is called the NGO Forum, a gathering of private organizations on the edges of the main event. . . .

This week, as delegates to the World Summit for Social Development were bickering over phrases on touchy issues like debt cancellation and whether a statement on workers' rights would be offensive to national sovereignty, the NGO Forum was generating more headlines, news conferences and controversy as it busied itself lobbying and sometimes attacking the establishment.

The Alternative Declaration of Principles, the NGO Forum's plan for the role of the Palestine Liberation Organization in affecting relations be-tween Israel and other Middle Eastern states, of the multinational oil compa-nies in influencing world energy politics, and of the International Olympic Committee in sidestepping the U.S.-Soviet confrontation over Afghanistan and the 1980 Moscow Olympic Games. In other instances, NGOs might have a lower profile but nonetheless significant implications for world politics—for example, the role of the International Federation of Airline Pilots Associa-tions in pressing governments to adopt stronger air safety and anti-skyjacking measures, or the role played by a handful of agribusiness corporations in deter-mining the world distribution of food and possibly the success or failure of government-imposed grain embargoes. Although, more often than not, gov-ernments might "win confrontations" with transnational actors—govern-ments could nationalize foreign corporate assets, and so forth—"more relevant

fighting poverty and rectifying social wrongs, was finished well before the Social Summit's formal document. . . .

With each United Nations conference, the forum grows to encompass a wider spectrum of groups and causes. When the subject is as broad as social development, there seems to be no limit.

Along Main Street of the Global Village, which sprung up in a hanger-sized hall on the former Danish navy base where the forum was meeting, women's organizations from Africa set up shop selling handicrafts near Eu-ropean advocates for greater AIDS awareness. A Danish neocommunist dis-tributed leaflets in front of a Pakistani self-help project's stall. Two rows of little blond children from a local school dressed in exotic foreign costumes tried gamely to sing about humankind above the din of a thousand voices.

Strollers could buy a tiny symbolic plant to help raise money for refugees returning to farms thousands of miles away, hear from Zapatista rebels about their plight in southern Mexico, encounter people's health col-lectives and listen to Swami Agnivesh, standing beside a heavy chain, talk-ing about slave labor in India. . . .

In a few years representatives of some of these private organizations have become members of official delegations or sought-after consultants on issues politicians do not follow with such zeal.

[UN] Secretary General Boutrous-Ghali said . . . this week that the im-portance of the private organizations as partners of the United Nations was growing.

Source: Barbara Crosette, "Once A Sideshow, Private Organizations Star At U.N. Meet-ings," *New York Times*, March 12, 1995. Copyright © 1995 by The New York Times Co. Reprinted by permission.

than 'who wins' direct confrontations are the new kinds of bargains, coalitions, and alliances being formed between transnational actors and between these actors and segments of governments and [intergovernmental] organizations."[19]

The multinational corporation, in particular, is seen by some observers as an alternative form of human organization to the nation-state, pursuing its own objectives apart from those of any national government and—for better or for worse—undermining (or at least confusing) traditional notions of national interest, citizenship, and patriotism. (Note, for example, the curious role of Toyota, the Japanese car manufacturer, as the leading corporate financial sponsor of the 1980 U.S. Olympic Team's training.) We will reserve judgment on the implications of the multinational corporation until Chapter 13, when we focus on its role in the international economy. Multinational corporations, like other NGOs, can have both positive and negative impacts in terms of world order.

THE LOGIC OF IGOs

IGO growth has always lagged behind NGO growth, no doubt because of the simple fact that people have outnumbered governments as potential candidates for forming international organizations and, also, that IGOs have tended to entail a somewhat greater investment of resources. As with NGOs, IGO growth historically has been least pronounced during major wars and most pronounced after major wars, when states normally seek to resurrect some semblance of world order. The network of IGOs has expanded from fewer than ten in 1870 to almost 50 in 1914, to some 100 by 1945, to more than 200 by 1970, to more than 300 today.[20]

We noted in Chapter 2 that IGOs were partly a response to the expansion of interstate commerce and the need for new structures to assist national governments in promoting orderly economic relations in an emergent world capitalist economy. Craig Murphy has argued that the growth of IGOs ("public international unions") in the nineteenth century coincided with the gradual growth of the welfare state and modern industrial society, with nation-states experiencing mounting pressures to produce a better standard of living for their citizenry and recognizing that material well-being could only be maximized through enhanced international cooperation. Murphy adds that other forces also contributed to IGO growth, notably scientific and intellectual elites seeking to improve the human condition through social engineering that took advantage of new technologies spanning national boundaries.[21] Inis Claude (cited in Chapter 8) has attributed the accelerated growth of IGOs in the twentieth century, particularly the creation of organizations such as the UN, to more profound causes:

> The organizing movement of the twentieth century can be interpreted as a reaction to the increasingly terrible consequences of armed conflict. As war has become more devastating, the need to prevent it has grown more obvious and urgent, and the sense of moral obligation to strive for its prevention has become more compelling.[22]

The substantial growth of IGOs after World War II reflects the impetus of the UN in spawning several other global organizations as part of the UN system, although IGO growth has had even more momentum at the regional level.

States today form intergovernmental organizations for the same practical reasons that have always provided the fundamental rationale behind IGOs, i.e., problems exist that either cannot be handled unilaterally within the capabilities of a single state or can be dealt with more efficiently through collaboration with others. International institutions help to reduce uncertainty, provide information, and lessen transaction costs.[23] Some problems may involve only two states and, hence, may call for merely a two-member IGO (e.g., the St. Lawrence Seaway Authority established by the United States and Canada), whereas other problems may be defined as requiring regional or global approaches. In a given problem area, the first impulse of governments is not to create an organization but to try to deal with the situation simply through treaties or informal *ad hoc* arrangements, which are less costly. However, if a problem is viewed as an ongoing one, more elaborate collaborative machinery may be found necessary and an intergovernmental organization may be born that permits a "pooling of sovereignty."

It should be stressed that although IGOs are generally conceived to be instruments of *cooperation*, they also inevitably involve *conflict* and, indeed, can be thought of as forums for managing interstate disagreements as well as mutual problem solving. In fact, member states vie for control of IGOs as they attempt to use international organizations partly as tools for legitimizing various national policies.

As Claude and Murphy suggest, problems that give rise to IGOs can be of the **high politics** or **low politics** variety. "High politics" refers to those issues involving the most crucial and the most controversial interests of states (especially military-security issues); "low politics" refers to those issues that are relatively narrow, technical, and noncontroversial (for example, setting international mail rates, sharing weather forecasting data or cancer research findings, or managing river basins). Although the distinction between "high politics" and "low politics" is a useful one, several issue-areas fall somewhere in-between (e.g., regulation of international news information and satellite broadcasting services, reduction of tariff barriers, or dissemination of peaceful nuclear technology). Moreover, even in seemingly low politics areas, issues can become highly politicized, such as the furor raised by the United States over what it believed was growing Marxist influence in the International

Labor Organization's activities in the field of worker-management relations, leading to a two-year American withdrawal from the ILO in 1977. The United States, along with Britain, also withdrew from the UN Educational, Scientific, and Cultural Organization (UNESCO) in the 1980s, complaining about not only excessive Marxist influence in the organization's top leadership but also financial mismanagement. In the contemporary era in particular, as military-security, economic, and other issues are becoming more and more intertwined, the high politics–low politics distinction is becoming increasingly blurred.

The typical IGO has at least a plenary assembly or conference in which all member governments discuss and vote on policies, along with a secretariat or bureau that is responsible for implementing decisions and running the organization's administrative apparatus. However, IGOs differ considerably in the amount of decision-making power that states vest in the organization. A few IGOs approach a **supranational** decision-making model; i.e., the organization is empowered to make decisions that are binding on the entire membership, requiring all member states to abide by the collective will no matter whether they are on the winning or losing side of a roll call vote. Far more IGOs, though, are at the opposite extreme, empowered by member states merely to offer recommendations or resolutions of an advisory nature that each individual national government is free to accept or disregard as it sees fit. Other IGOs fall somewhere in-between, respecting the sovereignty of individual members in most organizational matters but evidencing a degree of supranationalism in certain areas.

States have generally been more willing to cooperate and entrust decision-making competence in organizations having narrow, well-defined goals rather than in organizations having broader, more open-ended missions. The first IGOs—the Central Commission for the Navigation of the Rhine created in 1815, the European Commission for the Control of the Danube created in 1856, and the International Telegraph Union and Universal Postal Union created a few years later—all were designed to deal with rather specific, technical matters. The ITU and UPU exist to this day as part of the UN system, along with many other limited purpose organizations, which together constitute the Specialized Agencies of the United Nations. These organizations collect and disseminate information, administer programs, and help to develop rules governing relations between states. Several specific purpose organizations do approximate the supranational model in some respects. In the case of UPU and some other organizations, governments have even allowed officials in IGO bureaucracies ("technocrats") to exercise considerable discretion in making and implementing policies on behalf of the entire membership. These IGOs can be said to have a direct impact in several fields of international activity, including health, transportation, education, social welfare, and communications.

The past century has also witnessed the development of multipurpose IGOs designed to deal with a broad range of political concerns, including the "big" questions of war and peace. In addition to the United Nations at the global level, such institutions as the Organization of American States, the Organization of African Unity, the Arab League, and the Association of Southeast Asian Nations have been conceived as "regional security organizations" designed to facilitate general cooperation and peaceful settlement of disputes among their members (and in some cases, even eventual political unification). Although these general purpose IGOs potentially could have far greater impact than the specific purpose IGOs, governments have been much less willing to entrust these organizations with any degree of supranational decision-making competence, given the more volatile nature of the issues that can arise in such forums. Nevertheless, these regional organizations have often played a useful role in preventing or resolving violent conflict between states, as in the case of the "football war" between El Salvador and Honduras in 1969, when the OAS instituted a cease-fire to stop hostilities related to a football match riot and reports of Honduran atrocities against Salvadorans. In some cases, regional organizations have even played a role in trying to help end civil wars, such as the efforts made by the Community of West African States (a subset of OAU) during the 1990s to stop the brutal internecine fighting in Liberia. One scholar, examining nineteen cases of OAS, OAU, and Arab League involvement in regional conflicts, found that these organizations, overall, "helped to abate conflicts among members in more than half of the cases" and "helped to provide a permanent settlement in a third of the cases."[24] We will discuss the UN role in the peacekeeping field later in the chapter.

The **functionalist school** of international relations scholars hypothesizes that as states collaborate and surrender some measure of sovereignty to IGOs in low politics issue-areas, their governments will learn *habits* of cooperation that will slowly induce further collaboration and surrender of sovereignty in high politics areas, all leading ultimately to a possible supranational community (i.e., a regional or world government.)[25] In other words, willingness to entrust IGOs with power to make decisions regarding, say, locust control may be the beginning of a process that could eventually "spill over" into the realm of arms control. Some functionalist theorists (called **neofunctionalists**) emphasize that certain sectors of intergovernmental cooperation are more likely candidates for **spillover** than others because they create not only a desire but a need for ever more ambitious cooperation across issue-areas. (An example might be a group of countries discovering that the benefits they have derived from sharing a common fishing ground cannot be sustained without additional collaboration in environmental policymaking pertaining to ocean pollution.)[26]

A number of scholars have criticized functionalist theory, however, noting that some collaborative experiences can be painful and counterproductive, that politics can never be completely removed from even the most seemingly apolitical, technical set of issues, and—most importantly—that there are obvious limits to the extent to which national governments can be expected to relinquish political power to a higher authority in areas that bear on their very survival. Although intergovernmental cooperation in one field might well breed cooperation in other fields, the available evidence indicates that the "spillover" process does not lead inexorably to supranationalism.[27] Still, even if there is little evidence to support functionalist expectations about supranationalism, there is evidence to support the more modest functionalist view that "entanglement in a web of IGOs would tend to make states less bellicose"; the latter proposition is at least somewhat supported by a study that found that the growth of IGOs, particularly since World War II, has coincided with a relative decline in the number of interstate wars.[28]

In general, IGOs thus play a role both as *arenas* for interstate conflict and cooperation and as *actors* in their own right that affect state behavior and outcomes in world politics. In the remainder of this chapter, we will focus on two specific IGOs, the United Nations at the global level and the European Union at the regional level. These institutions are clearly among the most important intergovernmental organizations in the world today, and have a variety of impacts on world affairs.

Global Intergovernmental Organizations: The United Nations and the UN System

After each of the two catastrophic wars in the twentieth century, the participants came together at a peace conference, vowed "never again," and proceeded to create a global organization whose primary mission was to preserve the peace. The **League of Nations,** founded at the 1919 Paris Peace Conference after World War I, set the precedent of a large assembly of nations meeting in regular annual session. Like the League, the creation of the **United Nations** after World War II was accompanied by great fanfare and a sense of euphoria. U.S. President Harry Truman opened the San Francisco Conference in 1945 (shortly after V-E Day in Europe) with the prediction that the delegates were about to create "machinery which will make future peace not only possible, but certain."[29] Former U.S. Secretary of State Cordell Hull declared: "There will no longer be need for spheres of influence, for alliances, balances of power, or any other of the special arrangements through which, in the unhappy past, the nations strove to safeguard their security or to promote their interests."[30] Yet another delegate proclaimed that "the UN Charter has grown from the prayers and prophecies of Isaiah and Micah."[31]

Inevitably, idealism competed with realism in shaping the UN, no less than the League. As one would expect, the war *winners* were the chief architects of these organizations. In creating a peace organization, the winners were also creating an organization designed to promote their own interests in maintaining the postwar status quo as much as possible. The UN, like the League, was founded on the concept of **collective security,** which envisioned the weight of the entire international community—through the mobilization of the military forces of all the members of a global organization—being thrown against any state intent on committing aggression and upsetting the existing order. Like the founders of the League, the founders of the UN expected that collective security would be implemented primarily through the leadership of a handful of important states. This concept thus resembled in some ways the "concert of great powers" approach to world order borrowed from the nineteenth-century Concert of Europe.

In the case of the United Nations, the "Big Five"—the United States, the Soviet Union, the United Kingdom, France, and China—assigned themselves a special role in 1945 as the "world's policemen" under the new UN Charter. The initial hope was that great-power unity would enable the United Nations to function more successfully than its predecessor, which had been hampered by the absence of several major countries (including the United States) from its membership roster. Although most of the major powers in 1945 were represented in the United Nations, assumptions about great-power cooperation quickly faded as the Cold War between the U.S.-led Western bloc and the Soviet-led Eastern bloc began before the ink had dried on the UN Charter. From the start, the United Nations became a microcosm of world politics, with developments within the institution tending to mirror battles and other happenings occurring outside its walls. We briefly trace the evolution of the United Nations below, in terms of both its structure and activities.

STRUCTURE AND ACTIVITIES

Figure 10.2 is an organization chart of the United Nations and its affiliated agencies that together constitute the "UN system." As the chart indicates, there is a bewildering array of councils, commissions, committees, and assorted other bodies, which can be confusing not only for the casual observer but also for policymakers seeking to understand the workings of the United Nations. As the chart shows, also, the UN is involved in a host of concerns in addition to war and peace.

Under the UN Charter, the **Security Council** was given primary responsibility in the area of peace and security. Chapter VII of the Charter provided that, should **peaceful settlement** procedures (such as mediation and adjudication) under Chapter VI fail, the Council would be empowered to adopt military and economic sanctions on behalf of the UN membership against any nations engaging in actions that constituted a "threat to the peace." Such sanctions were to be the basis for the collective security role of the United Nations, a role that at least on paper was buttressed by far more elaborate ma-

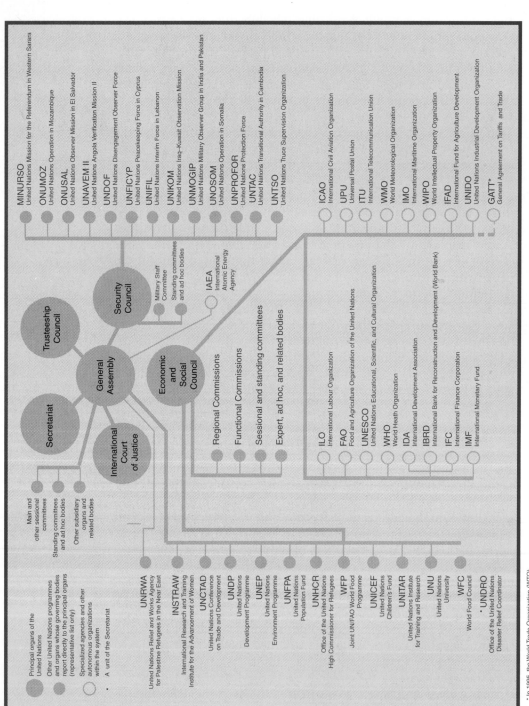

Figure 10.2
THE UNITED NATIONS SYSTEM

Source: Robert E. Riggs and Jack C. Plano, *The United Nations: International Organizations and World Politics*, 2nd ed. (Belmont, Calif.: Copyright © Wadsworth Publishing, 1994), p. 24.

* In 1995, the World Trade Organization (WTO) was created as a successor organization to GATT.

Principal organs of the United Nations

Other United Nations programmes and organs whose governing bodies report directly to the principal organs (representative list only)

Specialized agencies and other autonomous organizations within the system

A unit of the Secretariat

General Assembly

Trusteeship Council

Security Council

Secretariat

International Court of Justice

Economic and Social Council

Military Staff Committee

Standing committees and ad hoc bodies

IAEA
International Atomic Energy Agency

Regional Commissions

Functional Commissions

Sessional and standing committees

Expert, ad hoc, and related bodies

Main and other sessional committees

Standing committees and ad hoc bodies

Other subsidiary organs and related bodies

MINURSO
United Nations Mission for the Referendum in Western Sarara

ONUMOZ
United Nations Operation in Mozambique

ONUSAL
United Nations Observer Mission in El Salvador

UNAVEM II
United Nations Angola Verification Mission II

UNDOF
United Nations Disengagement Observer Force

UNFICYP
United Nations Peacekeeping Force in Cyprus

UNIFIL
United Nations Interim Force in Lebanon

UNIKOM
United Nations Iraq–Kuwait Observation Mission

UNMOGIP
United Nations Military Observer Group in India and Pakistan

UNOSOM
United Nations Operation in Somalia

UNPROFOR
United Nations Protection Force

UNTAC
United Nations Transitional Authority in Cambodia

UNTSO
United Nations Truce Supervision Organization

ICAO
International Civil Aviation Organization

UPU
Universal Postal Union

ITU
International Telecommunication Union

WMO
World Meteorological Organization

IMO
International Maritime Organization

WIPO
World Intellectual Property Organization

IFAD
International Fund for Agriculture Development

UNIDO
United Nations Industrial Development Organization

GATT*
General Agreement on Tariffs and Trade

ILO
International Labour Organization

FAO
Food and Agriculture Organization of the United Nations

UNESCO
United Nations Educational, Scientific, and Cultural Organization

WHO
World Health Organization

IDA
International Development Association

IBRD
International Bank for Reconstruction and Development (World Bank)

IFC
International Finance Corporation

IMF
International Monetary Fund

UNRWA
United Nations Relief and Works Agency for Palestine Refugees in the Near East

INSTRAW
International Research and Training Institute for the Advancement of Women

UNCTAD
United Nations Conference on Trade and Development

UNDP
United Nations Development Programme

UNEP
United Nations Environment Programme

UNFPA
United Nations Population Fund

UNHCR
Office of the United Nations High Commissioner for Refugees

WFP
Joint UN/FAO World Food Programme

UNICEF
United Nations Children's Fund

UNITAR
United Nations Institute for Training and Research

UNU
United Nations University

WFC
World Food Council

* UNDRO
Office of the United Nations Disaster Relief Coordinator

chinery than had ever been considered by the League. The powers granted the Security Council in this area were far greater than the powers given any other UN organ, because the Council could theoretically take decisions under Chapter VII that would be *binding* on *all* UN members. However, only on rare occasions have the collective security provisions of Chapter VII actually been used to organize a UN military force against an aggressor. A standing UN army, with contingents drawn from the armed forces of member states and ready to be deployed quickly as needed, was originally provided for in Chapter VII but has never materialized.

Since 1945, the Security Council has been expanded from eleven members to its present membership of fifteen. This includes the Big Five, who were accorded permanent seats under the UN Charter, along with ten other states serving two-year terms on a rotating basis. (The Chinese seat held by Taiwan was assumed by the People's Republic of China in 1971.) Although many objections have been raised recently about the composition of the Security Council—for example, whether countries such as Japan or Germany are not at least as deserving of permanent seats as the United Kingdom and France, or whether any states should even be accorded special status as permanent members—the present arrangements are difficult to alter for one simple reason: the Charter gives each of the Big Five the power to *veto* any decision taken in regard to collective security operations, Charter amendments, or other substantive matters requiring Security Council approval.

In other words, the Security Council cannot take decisions, binding or otherwise, unless the permanent members are in unanimous agreement (along with at least four other votes needed for passage of a Council resolution). Hence, the veto power gives each permanent member the ability to block a move to oust it from the Security Council. More importantly, the veto enables any permanent member to paralyze Council efforts to enforce the collective security provisions of Chapter VII or to take any other actions that might be objectionable to one of the Big Five. Although the veto rule has been widely criticized, it was inserted in the UN Charter not only to protect the interests of the major powers but also to preserve the organization, ensuring that no key national actor would feel threatened by the organization and be impelled to walk out.

The United States and the Soviet Union each used its veto power frequently during the Cold War. The Soviet Union cast more than 100 vetoes between 1945 and 1970, and the United States did not use the veto at all until 1970. However, between 1970 and 1990, the United States cast more than fifty vetoes, compared with fewer than thirty by the Soviet Union. The main explanation for this shift is that as the postwar era progressed the temporary seats on the Security Council, once dominated by pro-Western states, became increasingly occupied by nonaligned third world states often in disagreement with Washington and voting with Moscow for passage of resolutions that were seen as inimical to American interests, thereby triggering the American veto.[32] In the 1990s, in the post–Cold War era, there has been virtually no resort to the veto, as the Big Five generally have been able to cooperate in supporting resolutions authorizing UN involvement in numerous troublespots from Bosnia to Kampuchea, along the lines of the "concert of great powers" approach to world order originally intended by the UN founders.

Commenting on the reenergizing of the Security Council, one recent work notes:

> Since the late 1980s and the demise of the Cold War the Security Council's power and prestige have once again grown. Between 1987 and 1993 the number of official meetings rose from 49 to more than 171, and the number of annual resolutions passed increased from 13 to 93. Over time the Security Council has conducted an increasing amount of its work in informal, private consultations and reached more decisions by consensus than by formal voting. . . . Since 1987 the permanent members have themselves engaged in informal consultations as a group, a practice that enhanced their close cooperation in the Persian Gulf conflict and other crises. Also since 1987 the Security Council has taken action on more armed conflicts, made more decisions under Chapter VII of the Charter, and spent more on peacekeeping than at any previous time. These trends reflect the absence of Cold War hostility. . . . Only one veto has been cast since 1991.[33]

It should be noted that the "clubby" nature of recent Security Council proceedings has added to concerns about the composition of the Council on the part of other states and has furthered calls for institutional reform. However, Big Five unanimity may be difficult to sustain in the future, given growing frictions between the United States and Russia and China. Also, as discussed below, recent UN efforts in the peace and security field have included a number of failures, leading some critics to question the UN's effectiveness in conflict management and resolution; in particular, the Council has been accused of passing too many resolutions, creating dozens of UN missions without adequate funding and oversight.

The **General Assembly** is the main deliberative body in which the entire UN membership is represented and which is authorized by the Charter to deal with a broad range of political, economic, and social issues. Resolutions passed by the General Assembly are *nonbinding* on the members; they are only *recommendations* carrying no legal or other obligations. The General Assembly's main power is therefore merely the power to discuss. However, Assembly resolutions, whether pertaining to a redistribution of the world's wealth from North to South or some other issue, at the very least have symbolic significance and create additional pressures for changes in the international system.

The General Assembly has been the primary forum in which smaller, less developed states have been able to articulate and promote their positions on a wide variety of concerns. The Assembly originally had only fifty-one mem-

OPENING OF THE 50TH UNITED NATIONS GENERAL ASSEMBLY IN 1995.

bers in 1945, with an overwhelming majority being pro-Western; with the exception of the Latin American states, which were heavily infuenced by the United States, the only less developed countries in the world body initially were a handful of countries from North and South Asia. American influence in the General Assembly declined as the decolonialization process brought dozens of newly independent states into the UN. By 1980, there were more than 150 members of the General Assembly, with more than 100 of these being less developed countries—often at loggerheads with the United States. Citing evidence of the erosion of U.S. influence in the General Assembly, one scholar notes that the United States found itself on the winning side of General Assembly roll call votes 74 percent of the time between 1946 and 1950, a figure that steadily declined to 35 percent by the mid-1970s and 12 percent by the end of the 1980s.[34]

When the United States was in a position to dominate the General Assembly with its allies in the early postwar period, few Americans spoke of a "tyranny of the majority." Clearly such criticism from the United States since the 1970s has been hypocritical, although it is perhaps understandable given the fact that the United States is the single biggest financial supporter of the United Nations, obliged to pay 25 percent of the annual UN budget (compared with less than 1 percent for most member states). The United States has fared better in the General Assembly of late, partly because most decisions taken by the GA in the 1990s have been by consensus; if one counts all the consensus decisions plus those recorded votes in which the United States joined the majority, then the overall majority agreement score for the United States in the 1990s has approached 80 percent. Furthermore, the United States has had less reason to be hostile to the General Assembly since the latter's visibility and potential to harm American interests has receded somewhat in the post–Cold War era with the revival of the Security Council as the center of UN decision making.

The ranks of the third world in the United Nations have been swelled in recent years by the addition of such mini-states as the Marshall Islands and Palau (having populations of well under 100,000 on their admission in 1991 and 1995, respectively). The 1990s also have seen many other states enter the UN, including some tiny Western European countries (Monaco, Liechtenstein, and San Marino) as well as almost twenty states created out of the breakup of the Soviet Union and Yugoslavia. As of 1997, the total membership stood at 185. The admission of so many new members, especially of the mini-state variety, has caused renewed controversy about General Assembly voting procedures. As the UN Charter stipulates, voting in the General Assembly is based on majority rule (a two-thirds majority required for "important" questions), with *each state having one vote.* Hence, a country such as Seychelles with under 75,000 people possesses the same voting power in the General Assembly as the People's Republic of China with over 1 billion people. The "one state–one vote" principle is based on the sacred notion of sovereign *equality* among nations. Critics have argued, however, that the voting formula reflects neither power realities nor democratic principles of representation ("one person–one vote") nor fairness in terms of who pays the organization's bills. The absurdity lies in the fact that a two-thirds majority coalition can be formed in the General Assembly by 124 states representing less than 10 percent of the world's total population and an even smaller percentage of UN budget contributions. Although various weighted voting schemes based on population or other criteria have been proposed, they are politically controversial and unlikely to replace the current formula in the near future. However, led by the United States, pressures have been increasing to force the General Assembly to be more responsive to the concerns of the major financial supporters, who have threatened to withhold funds if the UN does not change certain practices and programs. Indeed, as of 1997, the United States was over $1 billion in arrears of paying its assessed UN dues.[35]

The **Economic and Social Council (ECOSOC)** is a fifty-four-member UN organ charged with offering recommendations, issuing reports, organizing conferences, and coordinating the activities of various UN agencies in the economic and social field. In performing these tasks, ECOSOC works closely with the General Assembly. Much of its work is carried out through five regional economic commissions (for Europe, the Pacific, Latin America, Africa, and Western Asia) and six functional commissions (including, for example, commissions on population, the status of women, and narcotic drugs).

The **Trusteeship Council,** presently consisting of the five permanent members of the Security Council, has decreased in importance over the years, largely being a victim of its own success in fulfilling the Charter's intention that it preside over the dismantling of colonial empires. Almost all colonial possessions administered as "trust territories" by the British, French, Dutch, and others after 1945 have achieved independence, so that there is little work left for the Council to do.

The **Secretariat** is the administrative arm of the United Nations. It is headed by a **Secretary-General** whom the Charter designates as "the chief administrative officer of the Organization." The United Nations has had seven Secretaries-General to date: Trygve Lie of Norway (1946–1952), Dag Hammarskjold of Sweden (1953–1961), U Thant of Burma (1961–1971), Kurt Waldheim of Austria (1972–1982), Javier Pérez de Cuéllar of Peru, (1982–1992), Boutros Boutros-Ghali of Egypt (1992–1997), and Kofi Annan of Ghana (appointed in 1997). Before his death in an airplane crash while on a UN mission to the Congo, Hammarskjold had elevated the Secretary-General post to one of considerable importance, going beyond mere administrative duties and using Article 99 of the UN Charter as justification for taking political initiatives involving the United Nations in peacekeeping operations. (Article 99 states that "the Secretary-General may bring to the attention of the Security Council any matter that in his opinion may threaten the maintenance of peace and security.") However, Hammarskjold's successors have adopted a much lower profile and have largely confined themselves to a caretaker role in running the day-to-day administrative apparatus of the organization, except for occasionally engaging in "good offices" and other forms of third-party mediation of disputes. Boutros Boutros-Ghali was an exception, attempting to use his office in the 1990s as a bully pulpit for expanding the UN's role in the post–Cold War order but meeting with some resentment over his perceived flamboyance and arrogance.

For any candidate aspiring to be Secretary-General or for an incumbent seeking to retain the job, there are considerable pressures to avoid controversy, owing to the selection process. The Secretary-General is selected through nomination by the Security Council, and then election by a majority of the General Assembly for a five-year term subject to possible renewal. Hence, the candidate must be someone who is innocuous enough to be acceptable to all five permanent Council members as well as the bulk of the Assembly membership. It was Hammarskjold's penchant for controversy that angered the Soviets and caused them ultimately to demand his replacement with a "troika" arrangement (three-person executive body), a proposal that was withdrawn after his death. More recently, U.S. disenchantment with Boutros-Ghali led to his replacement by Kofi Annan.

The "international civil service" that the Secretary-General heads consists of some 10,000 staff members—economists, agronomists, planners, and various managerial personnel—drawn from practically every country, with approximately 5,000 members working at UN headquarters in New York City and the remainder scattered among UN offices in Geneva, Nairobi, and elsewhere around the world.[36] Although the UN Charter stresses that staff appointments are to be made on the basis of "efficiency, competence, and integrity," it also adds that "due regard shall be paid to the importance of recruiting the staff on as wide a geographical basis as possible." These two criteria are not incompatible, but they reflect a built-in contradiction that characterizes the UN Secretariat—it is expected to be an independent body of technocrats whose primary responsibility is to serve impartially the interests and needs of the *UN* organization as a whole, yet who remain citizens of particular countries subject to potential pressures from their *national* governments. Pressures are particularly felt by those UN civil servants, roughly one-third of the upper Secretariat, who are on "fixed term" appointments with the United Nations, i.e., are on temporary loan from their government for one- or two-year periods and must then return to their home governments. However, even countries that allow their citizens to become career civil servants in the United Nations usually screen applicants to ensure that persons recruited to the Secretariat are loyal to the home country. Hence, in performing UN bookkeeping and other services, in staffing the hundreds of field operations mounted by the United Nations, and in facilitating the 5,000 meetings held annually under UN sponsorship, the Secretariat acts as an international civil service, yet is not completely free of the nationalism found in other UN organs.[37]

One cannot discuss the United Nations, especially its technical activities, without also noting the global **Specialized Agencies** that are affiliated with it. There are more than a dozen Specialized Agencies, each essentially a separate IGO having its own membership, budget, secretariat, and decision-making machinery apart from the United Nations but also intimately linked to ECOSOC and other UN organs. For example, the aforementioned Universal Postal Union is headquartered in Berne, Switzerland, and includes as members several states that are not members of the United Nations, such as the Vatican and Switzerland itself. We will describe these agencies very briefly here, discussing many of them more fully in subsequent chapters.

The **International Labor Organization (ILO),** a holdover from the League of Nations, was created to monitor working conditions worldwide and to promote cooperation in improving the general standard of living of the world's workers through the drafting of an international labor code and other activities. The **Food and Agriculture Organization (FAO)** has engaged in research, technical assistance, and financial support aimed at improving agricultural production and addressing the food needs of less developed countries; among its accomplishments, FAO has played a leading role in bringing the "green revolution" to countries in South Asia and elsewhere, alleviating food shortages through the dissemination of "miracle" high-yield varieties of rice, wheat, and corn. The **World Health Organization (WHO)** has made substantial progress in controlling communicable diseases, including the virtual elimination of smallpox and a dramatic reduction in malaria, in addition to promoting health education and public health services in less developed countries.

The **Universal Postal Union (UPU),** in accordance with its constitutional mandate to treat the world as "a single postal territory," facilitates the flow of mail across national boundaries through fixing weight limits and maximum postage rates and developing procedures to expedite mail delivery. The **International Telecommunication Union (ITU)** similarly helps to manage the flow of telegraph, telephone, radio, and television communications across the globe; indeed, ITU (profiled in the box on pages 392–393) even deals with communications *above* the globe. The **United Nations Educational, Scientific, and Cultural Organization (UNESCO)** has undertaken a variety of activities designed to improve literacy rates in less developed countries, promote scientific and cultural exchanges, and facilitate the dissemination of information by drafting universal copyright conventions and related rules. UNESCO has also been involved in the past in drafting a set of controversial guidelines governing regulation of the mass media, attempting to forge an agreement between developed and developing countries regarding the degree of government control over press freedom and the international flow of news information.

The **International Civil Aviation Organization (ICAO)** has been responsible for drafting a number of conventions establishing uniform practices and standards with regard to pilot licensing, aircraft specifications, air traffic control, and anti-skyjacking measures, all of which have contributed immeasurably to international air safety. The **International Maritime Organization (IMO)** has performed a similar function in regard to the oceans, helping to manage international traffic on the two-thirds of the earth's surface that is covered with water. The **World Meteorological Organization (WMO)** engages in the collection and exchange of global weather forecasting data through its World Weather Watch program and monitors conditions relating to the global environment and climatic change.

Among the most important of the Specialized Agencies are several economic institutions. The **International Monetary Fund (IMF)** plays an important role in promoting international monetary cooperation, including stabilizing exchange rates of dollars and other national currencies and providing foreign exchange funds for needy states so that the maximum amount of world trade can occur. The **International Bank for Reconstruction and Development (IBRD)**, commonly called the **World Bank,** annually provides billions of dollars in loans to the governments of less developed countries to finance the building of bridges, dams and roads, and other developmental needs. The

PROFILE OF A UN SPECIALIZED AGENCY: THE INTERNATIONAL TELECOMMUNICATION UNION

The International Telecommunication Union (ITU) is in a sense the oldest intergovernmental organization to become a part of the UN system, with its roots going back to 1865, when twenty states created the International Telegraph Union and established a headquarters bureau in Berne, Switzerland, which was to operate through World War II. At the same time, the ITU is an organization that finds itself today involved in the most modernistic of concerns, regulating not only international telephone and telegraph traffic but also space satellite broadcasting and transborder flows of computerized data.

The ITU has more than 180 members and is headquarterd in Geneva, Switzerland, where it has a General Secretariat run by its own Secretary-General. The supreme body of the ITU is the Plenipotentiary Conference, which meets every five to seven years to set general policy and draft possible revisions in the International Telecommunication Convention. Each state has one vote in the decision-making process, with efforts made to arrive at decisions through consensus as much as possible. Administrative conferences are convened periodically in two telecommunications areas, one dealing with telephone and telegraph communications and the other with radio and other forms of wireless transmission. A smaller Administrative Council consisting of thirty-six members meets more frequently, at least once a year, to oversee implementation of decisions reached by the larger bodies. In addition, there is an International Frequency Registration Board (IFRB) responsible for maintaining a record of all radio frequencies or wavelengths that have been allocated to countries for various uses.

One must realize that commercial radio stations, coast guard shortwave operators, ham radio enthusiasts, space satellite transmitters, microwave oven cooks, and a host of other users share the same seemingly endless but actually limited range of radio frequencies. ITU reserves specific segments of the "radio frequency spectrum" for specific categories of users and requires member states to notify the IFRB of any new frequency assignments made to individual stations. With the proliferation of space satellites put into orbit by developed countries and broadcasting stations established by less developed countries, the spectrum is becoming overcrowded and interference is increasing among users. Less developed countries are concerned that by the time they develop their own space statellites, there will not be any "slots" left for them in the geostationary orbit, a band roughly 23,000 miles above the equator—a preferred band for economic and other reasons—where satellites are fixed relative to the earth's surface. It is in ITU conferences where bargaining occurs over the allocation of frequency bands among countries.

The highly technical nature of telecommunications can lead one to overlook the high political stakes potentially involved in ITU deliberations. Space satellite technology has become so advanced that there is the possibility that one country's broadcasting stations will be able to beam television programs (not only "Sesame Street" but more propagandistic material) directly into the home receiving sets of people in other countries, further increasing the permeability of national boundaries and threatening the sovereignty of national governments. Through "remote sensing" technology, it is already possible for satellites belonging to the United States and other nations to gather detailed information about any country's soil conditions and food production capabilities, the location of raw materials, and other features of the landscape. Although such data can be extremely helpful to less developed countries in anticipating crop shortages and discovering natural resources, those countries are concerned that developed states may not fully share the information and that the eyes in the sky may represent an unwarranted "invasion of privacy." The less developed states have had to rely for years on four Western news agencies—AP, UPI, Reuters, and Agence France-Presse—for the bulk of international news stories, transmitted to third world press rooms via satellite. The ITU was a central forum in which the battle over the so-called New World Information Order was waged during the 1980s.

World Bank group also includes the International Development Association (IDA), often referred to as the "soft loan window" because it channels capital specifically to governments of the very poorest countries at much lower interest rates, along with the International Finance Corporation (IFC), which provides loans to individuals and companies in the *private* sector of less developed countries. The IMF and World Bank were created after World War II as key elements in the postwar international economic order (often referred to as the "Bretton Woods system," named after the site of the 1944 conference at which UN economic institutions were first planned). Another important institution established in the immediate postwar period was the **General Agreement on Tariffs and Trade (GATT).** Designed to facilitate the reduction of international trade barriers, GATT created a new organization in 1995, the **World Trade Organization (WTO),** to assist in moving the world toward free trade in the twenty-first century.

There are many other parts to the UN system, but space does not allow us to even mention them. The system is a maze-like network of organizations with overlapping concerns and complicated linkages. In the case of both the United Nations and its Specialized Agencies, the organizations ultimately work only as effectively as the member governments will permit. Sometimes the level of effectiveness can be quite high, as with those Specialized Agencies whose officials are given considerable discretion to act within their limited sphere of responsibility. Other times, talking far exceeds acting (although as Winston Churchill once said, "jaw-jaw" is better than "war-war").[38] To put the United Nations into proper perspective, let us do a quick "cost-benefit" analysis.

AN APPRAISAL: THE UN BALANCE SHEET

It is common to base one's judgment of the United Nations solely on its record in the area of war and peace. Although there have been some successes, the failures and disappointments have undoubtedly been far greater in number. On the only occasion before 1990 in which the Security Council took collective security action in the form of military sanctions under Chapter VII, during the Korean War, a UN expedition against North Korea was made possible only because the Soviet Union happened to be boycotting the Council (in protest against the occupation of the Chinese seat by Taiwan rather than the People's Republic of China).

However, there have been other occasions when, faced with the paralysis of the Security Council because of the veto, the General Assembly or the Secretary-General has taken action in the peace and security area. At times, such involvement has merely taken the form of mediation and other peaceful settlement efforts under Chapter VI of the Charter, such as U Thant's intervention in the 1962 West Irian conflict between the Netherlands and Indonesia. In other instances, stronger and more visible action has been taken, such as the sending of a peacekeeping force of 6,000 soldiers (UNEF) to the Middle East during the Suez crisis of 1956, and the force of 20,000 (ONUC) dispatched to the Belgian Congo in 1960. In the Suez case, the General Assembly acted on the basis of the "Uniting for Peace Resolution," which authorizes Assembly involvement in war and peace questions if the Security Council is paralyzed, whereas in the Belgian Congo case it was essentially Secretary-General Hammarskjold who took the initiative. Strictly speaking, both incidents were **peacekeeping** operations, neither of the "peaceful settlement" variety intended in Chapter VI nor of the "collective security" variety envisioned in Chapter VII; often labeled "Chapter VI and 1/2" actions, they went far beyond a mediating role yet fell short of collective security, because they were sent to provide a neutral military presence rather than punish an aggressor and could be ordered out at any time the host countries desired (as happened when Egypt ordered UNEF's withdrawal in 1967).

The Security Council itself has authorized similar peacekeeping forces over the years, including UNFICYP (in existence since 1964) to help quiet the civil war between Turkish and Greek Cypriots on Cyprus, UNEF-II sent to police the Egyptian-Israeli border after their 1973 war, and UNIFIL sent to help manage the Lebanon civil war in 1978.[39]

During the Cold War, the Security Council was most likely to take constructive action in those situations, such as the Middle East war of 1973, where the Big Five, particularly the United States and the Soviet Union, shared a mutual desire to see a de-escalation of a conflict in which they were not directly involved but into which they could be drawn. Through **preventive diplomacy,** the UN helped to keep local conflicts from escalating into larger conflagrations directly involving major powers. Although one should not exaggerate the UN's successes during the Cold War—given its conspicuous absence from Vietnam and other troublespots—one should not minimize them either. One scholar examined 123 disputes submitted to the UN for settlement between 1945 and 1981 and concluded that the organization helped to resolve or at least manage ("ameliorate") conflict, through reducing hostilities, in 51 percent of the cases.[40] The same author in a subsequent study found that the early 1980s marked a low point in the life of the UN, with the "lowest share" of "all disputes involving military operations and fighting" being referred to that body "in the history of the organization."[41]

However, as we noted earlier, the United Nations experienced a substantial revival in the war-peace field in the late 1980s with the end of the Cold War, being called on to mediate the withdrawal of Soviet troops from Afghanistan and the removal of Cuban and South African forces from Angola and Namibia, to arrange an armistice between Iran and Iraq in their decade-long war, to provide neutral observers to monitor elections ending the Nicaraguan civil war, and to facilitate an end to Vietnamese occupation of Kampuchea.[42] In addition to these generally successful efforts, the UN found itself in 1990 at the center of a major international conflict after Iraq's invasion of Kuwait and its attempted annexation of that country. Although no UN army as such was formed under Chapter VII of the Charter, the Security Council did authorize (1) mandatory economic sanctions as a collective security measure against Iraq in punishment for its aggression, obligating the entire UN membership to participate in a worldwide trade embargo against Baghdad,[43] and (2) the use of armed force by any individual states coming to the defense of Kuwait and attempting to enforce the embargo, thereby legitimizing the presence of a multinational force the United States had mobilized in the Persian Gulf (including over 400,000 American troops as well as contingents from some Arab states). A number of countries, including Britain, France, Japan, and the Soviet Union, provided either military, economic, or diplomatic support. The Iraqi conflict was viewed at the time as a test of the extent to which "great power" leadership and partnership through the UN could provide a cornerstone of a new world order in the post–Cold War era.

The Gulf War operation in many respects was a model of collective security, as the Iraqi invasion was repelled and Kuwait's sovereignty restored. On the heels of the Gulf War success, many other new missions were added, mostly entailing peacekeeping rather than collective security, although in some cases the distinctions became blurred. More UN peacekeeping missions were authorized in the five years after the end of the Cold War than in the entire previous forty-five-year history of the organization. By 1997, the UN had over 60,000 blue-helmeted and blue-bereted soldiers as well as numerous unarmed observers drawn from more than 60 countries serving in various hotspots around the world. Although there have been some recent successes (e.g., the role of the UN in arranging a ceasefire and conducting democratic elections in Kampuchea), the failures have been more conspicuous (e.g., the inability to end savage tribal warfare in Somalia and Rwanda, as well as the ineptness demonstrated by UNPROFOR in the Yugoslav civil war discussed in Chapter 3).

The UN's recent problems can be attributed to a variety of factors. First, the Charter envisioned that the UN would deal mainly with traditional interstate wars, but most conflicts the UN has been asked to manage in the post–Cold War era have been of an intrastate variety. Second, in many of these conflicts,

A UN PEACEKEEPER FROM KENYA HOLDS A CROATIAN CHILD IN A SERBIAN VILLAGE, ON COVER OF *THE BULLETIN OF THE ATOMIC SCIENTISTS*.

the UN has been put in the position of having to create the conditions necessary for democratic elections in societies that have never experienced democracy and that in some cases have been bordering on total anarchy. Third, in some cases, well-intentioned humanitarian intervention by the UN has led to UN peacekeeping forces becoming embroiled in a messy civil conflict and engaging in "peace enforcement" actions against one faction branded as an aggressor for its interference with delivery of relief supplies and other mission objectives (actions that some have suggested fall under "Chapter 6 and 3/4"). Fourth, as noted in Chapter 9, the UN has had to contend with charges by some member states that its interventions have violated state sovereignty protected under Article 2 (7) of the Chapter.[44] Fifth, the UN has suffered from the basic absence of a careful organizational structure tying the military chain of command in the field to the political leadership of the Council and, most importantly, an insufficient amount of financial resources and will on the part of the UN membership, leaving the organization seriously overextended.

In his 1992 *Agenda for Peace* proposal, Boutros Boutros-Ghali suggested ways to improve the UN capabilities in the peace and security area. He urged that the international community think in terms of a number of conflict management roles the UN might play, arranged along a continuum of situations. One is peace maintenance; where disputes have not yet erupted in actual fighting, the UN might help by maintaining a computerized early warning system and dispatching diplomats to defuse a crisis or sending troops at the request of the disputants for purposes of "preventive deployment." A second is peacemaking; where hostilities have already been initiated, the UN might prevent any further escalation by mounting quick efforts at mediation. A third is peacekeeping; once peacemaking has worked and a ceasefire has been instituted, the UN might need to send in peacekeeping units to police and sustain the ceasefire. A fourth is peace-building; the UN could help foster conditions for a long-term, durable peace through providing such assistance as infrastructure repair, refugee repatriation, de-mining minefields, and in general promoting postwar reconstruction. A fifth is collective security and peace enforcement; where there has been an act of aggression in violation of the UN Charter, the UN must have the capability to respond with either economic or military sanctions (with some commentators suggesting the creation of a small standing UN rapid deployment force of some 60,000 soldiers).[45] To date, there has been little attempt to implement these ideas. The creation of a UN standing army has aroused special concerns on the part of conservatives in the United States wary of world government and reluctant to place American soldiers under a foreign commander.

The United Nations has played a more subtle and less controversial peacekeeping role as a forum in which countries can vent hostilities verbally rather than physically; unfortunately, there is no way of knowing how many outbreaks of violence the United Nations has averted in this fashion. It is difficult to assess, also, how much the United Nations has contributed to war prevention through its efforts at addressing various economic and social ills that often underlie the resort to violence. Although the United Nations is usually judged according to its record in the war-peace area, its work in other fields is no less important. Indeed, over the years the UN has spent a far greater percentage of its budget (at times as much as 80 percent) and an even greater share of its energies on economic and social problem solving rather than peacekeeping per se.

If the *benefits* produced by the United Nations are modest, the *costs* associated with it are even more modest. Its regular annual operating budget is roughly $1 billion (smaller than the annual budget of the New York City police department). If one adds the $3 billion currently being spent annually on peacekeeping, UN expenses still barely exceed the cost of running the New York City police and fire departments. Considering the fact that the world's governments today spend almost $1 trillion a year on weapons of war, the amount spent on the United Nations should seem a bargain. Even if one adds the several billion dollars in voluntary contributions to organizations such as the United Nations International Children's Emergency Fund (UNICEF) and in assessments to the Specialized Agencies, it would seem that, on balance, the United Nations earns its keep. Although many Americans complain about the financial burden the United States has assumed as the chief benefactor of the United Nations, it is estimated that it costs the American taxpayer an average of only $2.50 a year (roughly the price of renting a home video). For the other 5 billion constituents of the United Nations, what has been called "the best hope for mankind" comes even more cheaply.

The future of the United Nations remains uncertain. The recent flurry of UN activity in the peacekeeping field and the possible role of the organization as a linchpin for great power cooperation in a new world order has occasioned considerable optimism among some globalist thinkers. Conversely, the UN's lackluster performance of late has buttressed the case made by its critics. There is also a serious budget crisis the UN must overcome in the short term, caused by dues withholdings on the part of the United States and other states.[46] In the long term, there are deeper concerns relating to broad structural changes in the international system and their implications for global institution building. In particular, even supporters of multilateralism have expressed doubts about the practicality of relying on formal global forums for bargaining and problem solving on economic and other matters given the enormous size and diversity of the contemporary international system, including so many mini-states.[47] An intriguing puzzle in the current era is that "the need for coordinated problem-solving on a global scale—in matters of security, economics, and ecology—is arguably greater than ever before [due to technology-driven interdependence], at the same time that . . . 'central guidance' mechanisms seem less feasible [in some respects] than in previous historical periods."[48] Although there was some shift during the 1980s toward greater use of smaller, "minilateral" diplomatic bodies on the part of the

United States and other states, the 1990s have witnessed renewed efforts to explore global solutions to problems through global institutions. This experimentation with both global and subglobal approaches will no doubt continue.

Regional Intergovernmental Organizations: The European Union

For those who consider the growth of international organization to be a key to world order, international institution-building efforts at the regional level are sometimes seen as at least modest stepping-stones toward the development of a larger, global community. Nowhere has regional institution building been more fully attempted than in Western Europe, where a regional entity has been established complete with its own flag and anthem. What is today called the **European Union** (the **EU,** also at times referred to as the European Community, which had been the name commonly used for the entire enterprise before 1993) is really three IGOs in one: the European Coal and Steel Community (ECSC), the European Atomic Energy Community (EURATOM), and the European Economic Community (EEC or Common Market).[49] This "union" today consists of fifteen member states—France, Germany, the United Kingdom, Italy, the Netherlands, Belgium, Luxembourg, Denmark, Ireland, Greece, Spain, Portugal, Austria, Sweden, and Finland—that together constitute the third largest demographic unit in the world, its population of over 360 million exceeded only by China and India. The key question surrounding the European Union, however, is the extent to which it can be considered a *single* unit or actor. As we note later, in some respects it comes close to being a unified, supranational entity, whereas in many other respects it seems little more than a fragile collection of sovereign states.

The dream of a "United States of Europe" can be found as far back as Dante in the fourteenth century. In the more recent past, Charles de Gaulle and Winston Churchill mused about the possibilities of a union between France and Britain when the latter proposed a merger before the Nazi occupation of France during World War II.[50] However, it was not until the 1950s that the idea of a European Community was seriously pursued. At first, only six states on the continent (the "inner six," which included France, West Germany, Italy, and the Benelux countries) joined together to form the ECSC in 1952, designed to promote cooperation in coal and steel production and commerce. The same six states signed the Treaty of Rome in 1957, establishing the Common Market and EURATOM, thereby pledging cooperation in all economic sectors as well as atomic energy research and development. The Community expanded to nine in 1973, with the addition of the United Kingdom, Denmark, and Ireland, then to ten with the admission of Greece in 1981, and to twelve with the entrance of Portugal and Spain in 1986 (with Spanish television trumpeting the event with the words "Good evening, citizens of Europe"). German unification brought the former East Germany into the Community in 1990, and Austria, Sweden, and Finland were added in 1995. Several other states in Western Europe, such as Norway and Switzerland, have considered joining the EU but have not yet entered; a number of former East bloc states, such as Hungary and Poland, as well as Mediterranean rim states, such as Turkey, have applied for membership but have not yet been admitted because of failure to meet EU economic, human rights, or other criteria.

Although the two men considered to be the "fathers" of the European Community—Jean Monnet and Robert Schuman, both of France—envisioned eventual *political* unification among the members, most national leaders in the Community have from the start viewed the undertaking in more narrow terms, as a vehicle for joint problem solving mainly in the *economic* sphere. A primary rationale behind the Community was the desire to follow the economic model of the United States, where the absence of trade and related barriers between the constituent units made for a single, large economic market that facilitated economies of scale and generally promoted economic efficiency and prosperity; the hope was that goods and services, labor, and capital would flow as freely between, say, Belgium and France as they did between New York and New Jersey. Although economic integration was not as ambitious a goal as political unification, it nonetheless represented an impressive effort at cooperation that was virtually unprecedented on a continent whose members had fought two major wars in the twentieth century.

The plan was to proceed in several stages: (1) a **free trade area,** in which all tariff barriers were to be eliminated between the member states themselves (so that, for example, French agricultural products could be exported to Belgium without French farmers having to pay an entry duty or tax); (2) a **customs union,** whereby all member states would impose a common external tariff on goods exported to the Community from nonmember states (so that, for example, the French and Belgians would charge the same duty on Japanese automobiles entering their countries); (3) a **common market,** in which not only goods and services but also workers and investment funds would be able to move freely across national boundaries (so that, for example, an Italian construction worker could seek employment in Germany without worrying about a work permit or other obstacles); and (4) an **economic and monetary union,** in which all member states would harmonize their economic policies and introduce a single European currency (in place of French francs, German marks, and so forth).

To facilitate this process, several institutions were created, with the ECSC, EEC, and EURATOM initially each having its own separate decision-making apparatus. By the 1970s, a single set of institutions had been established to serve the Community as a whole. The 1993 Treaty on European Union, discussed later, further consolidated decision-making structures as the European Community evolved into the "European Union." The European Council, consisting of the heads of state of the fifteen member countries, meets a few times a year to set broad policy. Brussels, the "capital" of the European Union, is where the Council of Ministers and the European Commission meet. The Council of Ministers, composed of members of the national cabinet from each state (usually the foreign ministers but sometimes agriculture or transportation ministers or other cabinet officials, depending on the issues to be discussed at monthly meetings), is the most powerful decision-making body in the Union other than the European Council. On paper, the Council of Ministers seems to operate in an almost supranational fashion, with each state allocated weighted votes based on population (so that France, Germany, Italy, and the United Kingdom have more voting strength than any of the other states) and with most decisions to be determined by majority rule rather than unanimity. In practice, however, decisions are normally reached only through general agreement based on consensus among the entire membership. In other words, although a coalition of states could technically impose binding decisions on the other members, there is the practical recognition that engaging in such domineering behavior could jeopardize the continued existence of the whole collective enterprise.

The Council of Ministers, on instructions from their home governments, decides the major economic and related policies of the Union. It is the European Commission that is expected to implement these policies. Although the individuals who sit on the Council of Ministers explicitly represent the interests of their particular governments, the twenty individuals who serve on the Commission theoretically represent the interests of the Union as a whole. Though nominated by their governments for renewable five-year terms (two from each of the five biggest states and one from each of the other states), these "Eurocrats" along with their 18,000-member staff have tended to display considerable independence of judgment over the years and have generally sought to expand the power of the Union institutions as much as possible. One of the Commission's main roles is not only to implement Council decisions but to take the initiative in identifying Union problems and proposing policies for consideration by the member states.

The Union political process involves not only interaction between the Council of Ministers and the Commission but also consultation with a variety of other bodies, including the European Parliament and the Economic and Social Committee. The Parliament, situated in Strasbourg, France, is essentially a "watchdog" designed to oversee the functioning of the Commission and other Union institutions and has little legislative power as such. The members of the Parliament were appointed from the individual legislatures of each country until 1979, when citizens were allowed to vote directly for their representatives in the European Parliament (with seats allocated to countries according to population). An interesting feature of the European Parliament is that the political parties are organized across national lines, with Socialists from Italy sitting with Socialists from France and other states, with Christian

Democrats sitting together, and so forth. Although direct election and transnational party organization give the appearance of supranationalism, it must be emphasized that the Parliament is only a consultative body. Concerned about the power wielded in the Union by nonelected officials (the members of the Council of Ministers and the Commission), some critics have complained about a "democratic deficit" problem and have sought to expand the authority of the Parliament but have not made much progress.

The Economic and Social Committee is composed of representatives from various groups involving agricultural, manufacturing, transportation, and business interests, with both worker and employer groups organized transnationally to lobby in support of or in opposition to various Union proposals that affect them. As important decisions are increasingly being taken in Brussels that affect people throughout the Union (e.g., in 1992 the Commission enacted a ban on cigarette advertising on television in all member states), many multinational corporations, consumer and environmental advocacy associations, and other political actors are focusing their pressure group activities there and are bypassing national capitals.[51]

The Union political process, then, is a complicated one that involves governmental, intergovernmental, and nongovernmental actors. In addition to the political institutions we have mentioned, there is also a European Court of Justice that sits in Luxembourg and adjudicates disputes related to the Treaty of Rome, the Treaty of European Union, and other agreements. The Court has handled hundreds of cases, ranging from hiring and firing grievances filed by Union civil servants to governmental requests for judicial interpretations of treaty provisions pertaining to social security for migrant workers. Unlike most international tribunals, the Court allows individual citizens to bring suit against their own government, as happened in a 1976 case brought by a Sabena airlines stewardess in which the Court ruled that the state-owned Belgian airline had violated Treaty of Rome provisions regarding sex discrimination in pay practices.[52]

Despite an impressive institutional infrastructure, the European Union has only partially fulfilled its initial goal of economic integration and remains a long way from realizing the larger aspiration of political unification harbored by some of its founders. Although the Union has progressed to the point where it is essentially a single free trade area and customs union, problems still abound in trying to realize a true common market and to coordinate economic policies. The Union has succeeded in forging a common agricultural policy (CAP) with respect to government involvement in the agricultural sector, has facilitated the free movement of people by instituting accident insurance coverage for all motorists throughout the Union and by eliminating work permit requirements along national lines, and has developed a uniform set of safety standards for autos and many other products sold in the Union. Economic barriers still persist, however: French brewers were, until 1987, prevented from selling beer in the German market because their product did not meet "beer purity" standards specified by the Germans; French wine-growers, in turn, have conducted "wine wars" against the cheaper Italian wines that have threatened to flood the French market; the Italian government has insisted that all pasta products sold in Italy must be made (as all Italian pasta is) from durum (hard) wheat; and doctors, lawyers, and other members of the professional labor force wanting to relocate across national boundaries are inhibited by language and educational training differences (there are eleven official languages spoken in the Union) that prevent professionals from meeting licensing requirements.

These and other problems gradually are being overcome as the Union continues to move forward toward the goal of total economic integration. Special impetus was provided by the "Europe 1992 Project," a plan that had set January 1, 1993, as the target date for implementing a set of directives issued by the European Commission to eliminate various technical, physical, and fiscal nontariff barriers to the free flow of people, goods, and services within the European Community. The "Europe 1992 Project" culminated in the adoption of the **Treaty on European Union** (the so-called **Maastricht Treaty**) in November 1993, designed to take the integration effort to the next level by putting some finishing touches on the common internal market and establishing a single currency and monetary system.

The common currency remains a major stumbling block, because Britain and a few other EU members view it as a direct challenge to national sovereignty. In 1996, led by the French and Germans, Brussels announced that the new European currency would be called the Euro and would be put into circulation for bank use by 1999 and for the general public by 2002. Immediately questions arose as to which countries' national symbols would appear on the Euro, with the British insisting that the Queen's image be retained on their coinage and paper and giving little indication of a willingness to become a party to the monetary union. (See the Sidelight on pages 404–405.) The British and others also refused to join the Schengen group—nine EU members (France, Germany, Belgium, the Netherlands, Luxembourg, Portugal, Spain, Italy, and Greece) that have committed themselves to a total dismantling of all border controls between their countries, meaning the cessation of *all* passport and customs checks. This has been an extremely difficult issue, given the sensitivity national governments have toward insuring secure borders and regulating the movement of would-be terrorists, drug traffickers, and illegal aliens and refugees. Even among the Schengen members, there has been some delay in implementing the plan because of concern about liberal drug policies in the Netherlands (where soft drugs such as marijuana are readily available for purchase in coffee shops) and lax enforcement of immigration restrictions on the part of some members; the fear is that the end of border controls could mean that drug traffickers and terrorists might be free to roam around the continent. Britain has also been one of the major holdouts against the imposition of an EU-wide "Social Charter" that would guarantee all workers throughout

SIDELIGHT

PROBLEMS OF GOVERNANCE IN THE EUROPEAN UNION: THE SEARCH FOR A COMMON CURRENCY

We will focus on international economics in Chapter 13. Suffice it to say, fluctuations in the exchange rate between different currencies in a free trade area can play havoc with the conduct of business. As one observer has put it, commenting on the problems posed by multiple currencies used in the European Union, "We can't durably have a situation in which trade is as free as in the U.S., but where the Texas dollar suddenly devalues massively against the New York dollar. That's approximately what we have in Europe today." ("Monetary Chaos Precedes Europe's Single Market," *Wall Street Journal*, July 28, 1995, p. A6.) The article below looks at the problems involved in moving toward a single currency in Western Europe; the article was written before the decision taken by the EU to name the common currency the "Euro."

Will Rembrandt adorn the franken? In a small office here [in Frankfurt, Germany], central bankers, historians, artists and even a psychologist are laboring over the vexing task of how to set up a single currency for Europe.

It is three years since European leaders agreed to forge a unified economy and create one currency, and it is probably seven more years before the currency enters circulation. Many hurdles have to be cleared away, and they are not just economic. For example, what should the currency be named? What places or faces should be on the bills? How large should they be?

Few Dutch would want to see the Reichstag on a European bill. Germans would dislike the Eiffel Tower. And the British would harrumph at any currency without a portrait of the Queen.

These are not easy issues for a Continent that cannot agree on a single phone or mail system. In fact, Europe has myriad rules for things as mundane as importing bananas.

Europeans thought they had settled at least part of this in 1992, when the Maastricht Treaty decreed that the currency's name should be the inelegant ECU, short for European Currency Unit. . . . But German bankers and politicians balked because Germans cannot easily pronounce the word. Germans would say "ein ECU," and to Chancellor Helmut Kohl that sounds like "eine Kuh," or cow, hardly the image for a new-age Europe. . . .

Instead, Germany has proposed "franken." The French like that because it is similar to their franc. . . . But the British, who fear that a single currency would lead to the supremeacy of Germany, deride the franken as a Frankenstein.

If the politicians cannot figure all this out, perhaps Madame Bourdon can. This former pornographic star in France is miles ahead of the technocrats, having run a Europe-wide contest to come up with a design for the currency. The results of voting on 10 different styles will be announced this fall. Among the images put to a vote are ones of Caesar, Michelangelo's David, a green leaf, Europa and a bull, and a grand piano. . . .

But Ms. Bourdon's project will probably not greatly influence the look of the currency. In the end there will be a political compromise.

"European symbols are not easy to find," said [one leading economist]. "What is really European, without raising nationalistic objections? Even the birds are not exactly the same from one country to another."

Many countries are lobbying to put a "national symbol" on the bills they issue. The bills would reassure local voters but would circulate throughout Europe. For Germany, a symbol might be the Brandenburg Gate or the Reichstag; for France, the Arc de Triomphe. The European Monetary Institute [in charge of the project] has resigned itself to the idea, partly because the British will not have it any other way. Even if all of Europe decides to put Voltaire on a bill, the British insist that the Queen be there too. . . .

Then there is the issue of the currency's size. The French franc is much larger than the German mark. How would automated teller machines be refitted? Germany is already lobbying for its dimensions. . . .

Even if all these symbolic matters can be cleared up, there is plenty of foot-dragging over the merits and timing of unity.

The earliest anybody expects a single currency to start to take shape is 1999, when several countries, including Germany, Austria, and Belgium, expect to meet the complex series of economic criteria necessary for monetary union. . . .

Experts believe that the savings from a common currency could exceed $50 billion a year. Travelers would also benefit by not having to bother with currency exchange and the hefty fees that go with it.

For corporations, it would eliminate many currency losses, the costs of hedging against fluctuations in the markets, price discrepancies from country to country and excessive accounting measures.

The leading motivation for a single currency is not economic, however, but political: a single currency is seen as a big step toward a unified Europe and a deterrent to conflict within Europe. . . .

In Britain, however, the skeptics see a single currency as a prelude to the reemergence of an imperial Germany. They say Britain would lose its independence to set interest rates and currency values to a new central bank dominated by the Germans. . . . "This is about such fundamental questions as who governs Britain . . ." [says a British member of Parliament].

the Union the same minimal set of welfare, unemployment, work safety, and other benefits; the British have viewed these regulations as representing excessive interference in the operation of the economy and as antithetical to the concept of a continental free market on which the European Community was founded. Among the more difficult problems the EU continues to face is the need to reconcile the demands of those member governments that tend ideologically to be highly "statist" and those that are more "laissez-faire"–oriented. Hence, although beer battles and wine wars and other such conflicts show signs of being resolved, there is an ongoing struggle to forge further cooperation and unity among Union members.

It is important to keep in mind that, under the Treaty of Rome that created the European Community, the decision-making competence of Community institutions generally has extended only to economically related matters, with the Community having no authority to deal with defense issues. Rather than presiding over a single community and deciding the great issues of European security and political affairs as envisioned by Monnet, Community officials for the past four decades have mostly found themselves sitting in "mirrored halls on centuries-old chairs to argue . . . over the price of a leg of lamb."[53] The diverse group of national governments has experienced great difficulty in arriving at a common set of foreign policies. Attempts to coordinate foreign policy through a process called "European Political Cooperation" (EPC) have at times produced some degree of unity, as happened during the 1973 Israeli-Arab war, but more often than not have resulted in disarray, as in the case of the Yugoslav civil war in the 1990s.

The 1993 Maastricht Treaty goes beyond the Treaty of Rome in calling on the membership to forge a "Common Foreign and Security Policy [CFSP] including the eventual framing of a common defence policy, which might in time lead to a common defence [i.e., a single European Army]." There is evidence that the member countries "are acting as a unit" in the United Nations and that "the European Union is being viewed increasingly as a distinct actor to be negotiated with not only over economic issues but also over international environmental, narcotics, and other issues."[54] For example, the European Commission has taken the lead in coordinating Western assistance to the economies of Poland and Hungary and other former East bloc states.[55]

The question remains whether the substantial progress made thus far toward *economic integration* will lead to *political integration,* and whether that progress is even sustainable without further development of the Union's political institutions. The tensions surrounding this issue were evident in the disagreements over the wording of the Maastricht Treaty, especially the use of the "F word":

> Much time and effort was expended haggling over how the Treaty should describe the European Union. . . . Most states wanted the word "federal" included, and would have settled for a phrase which appeared in drafts

where the Treaty was described as marking "a new stage in the process leading gradually to a Union with a federal goal." The UK government, however, was completely unwilling to see "the F word" appear in any form at all and in the political trading which occurred at the Maastricht summit this point was conceded to the United Kingdom and the reference to federalism was replaced by "This Treaty marks a new stage in the process of creating an ever closer union among the peoples of Europe. . . . To most Continental Europeans the phrase "ever closer union" sounds more centralist than the word "federal," but the UK delegation was satisfied."[56]

The likely prospect for the foreseeable future is that the Community will continue muddling along in what has become a kind of halfway-house between a collection of sovereign states and a supranational entity. New challenges may complicate the community-building process in the future. The applications already submitted by more than a dozen European states seeking to join the Union, including eight former East bloc states as well as the likes of Turkey, Cyprus, and Malta, raise questions about the optimal size of the Union; how large and diverse can it become and still remain viable in terms of the ability to reach mutually agreeable decisions? This has become known in Europe as the "widening versus deepening" dilemma; i.e., the more states that are added, the harder it will be to develop a closer sense of community and build more intensely integrated, supranational institutions among the membership.[57] Further complicating the picture is the trend toward greater regional autonomy *within* some EU states, notably Belgium, Spain and Italy (e.g., the parliaments of Flanders, Wallonia, and the Brussels region were permitted to ratify the Maastricht Treaty separately from the Belgian parliament); as we have noted, integrative and disintegrative forces are often to be found alongside each other in contemporary world politics. Another future concern is whether the movement toward a single internal market in Europe will add to external tensions with the United States, Japan, and other nonmember states seeking access to that market or whether it can be achieved in a manner that averts trade wars. Finally, it is unclear what role the European Union will play in a new European regional security system in the post–Cold War era.

Coinciding with the euphoric predictions of a United States of Europe that accompanied the initial signing of the Treaty of Rome, a whole literature sprouted in the 1950s and 1960s dealing with **integration theory** and examining the conditions under which political units tend to merge together and transfer loyalty to a larger community.[58] At that time, when Western Europe seemed on the brink of a political integration, theorists pondered whether the European experience could serve as a model for regional integration in other parts of the world such as Latin America and Africa, where a Latin American Free Trade Association, Central American Common Market, and Arab Common Market were in the process of being born. Today, the European experiment itself is at a crossroads, with most Western Europeans retaining primary loyalty to their individual nation-states but also wedded to the vision of a European Union.[59]

Conclusion

Despite the justifiable attention that world politics scholars have given transnational and supranational phenomena recently, the experiences of the European Union and the United Nations offer a lesson in the staying power of *nationalism* in the contemporary world. In Part IV we will delineate further the relationship between nation-states and nonstate actors, as we examine the congeries of forces involved in the politics of global problem solving in specific issue-areas (arms control, management of the international economy, and other areas). One type of nonstate actor (NGO) we will take a closer look at is the multinational corporation. Although multinational corporations (MNCs) have not erased the boundary lines that separate countries, they have managed to transcend those lines in a manner that is reshaping relations between people across the world in significant ways. More than most institutions, the MNC reflects the tension that exists today between the impulses of nationalism and the impulses of internationalism. In the international economy, as in other parts of the international system, humanity's search for order through global institution-building continues against centrifugal pressures pulling in the opposite direction. We will see where all this is leading in Part IV, as we discuss efforts to create *regimes* in areas where chaos threatens to reign.

SUMMARY

1. International organizations can be classified according to three criteria: membership, geographical scope, and functional scope. Those that have national governments as members and are created through treaties between states are called intergovernmental organizations; those that are composed generally of private individuals or groups are called nongovernmental organizations. There are over 300 IGOs in the world today, compared with more than 10,000 NGOs—which indicates that the bridges between peoples far outnumber the bridges between governments.

2. Although there is a common tendency to think of international organizations as global organizations (like the United Nations), the vast majority are regional or subregional in scope. Western developed countries belong to the most IGOs and NGOs.

3. Some international organizations are general, multipurpose organizations, though far more have specific, limited purposes. More than half of all IGOs are economic; most NGOs are in commerce and industry or health and medicine.

4. As transnational relations expanded during the nineteenth and twentieth centuries, and merchants, scientists, and other groups found that they shared interests that

transcended national boundaries, these ties became institutionalized in the form of NGOs. The effects of NGOs are disputed. Their members tend to develop a more cosmopolitan outlook, but the impact of this on relations between governments is uncertain. NGOs sometimes have considerable consultative input into IGO decision making. They can also have a significant impact in their role as autonomous actors who compete with national governments in the international arena.

5. As has been the case with NGOs, IGO growth has been dramatic since World War II. IGOs are instruments for managing interstate disagreements and problems. Problems may involve the most crucial and controversial interstate issues (high politics) or more narrow and technical matters (low politics), with states more willing to cooperate and give decision-making power to IGOs in low politics than high politics issue-areas. Functionalists hypothesize that cooperation in low politics areas will spill over into high politics areas and eventually lead to development of supranational institutions, although little if any supranationalism yet exists.

6. The United Nations is a global IGO created in 1945 as the successor of the League of Nations. The major UN organs are the Security Council (including the "Big Five" who have veto power); the General Assembly (the plenary body, with developing countries having a majority of votes); the Economic and Social Council; the Secretariat (headed by the Secretary-General); and the Specialized Agencies (more than a dozen IGOs affiliated with the United Nations).

7. The United Nations is usually judged on its performance in the war-peace area, but much of its budget over the years has been spent on economic and social problem solving. Although the United Nations has often been ineffective in the war-peace area, it has organized several peacekeeping forces, has mediated disputes, and has served as a surrogate for violence by providing a forum in which states can vent their hostilities verbally. The post–Cold War era has especially seen a revival of the UN role in peacekeeping and collective security, with mixed results as the organization has become seriously overextended.

8. The European Union (formerly called the European Community) is a regional IGO that consists of fifteen states participating in a major regional integration effort. Started in the 1950s, the Community was designed to create among member countries a single economic market (like that in the United States) that would promote economic efficiency and prosperity. Decision making in the Union occurs through an elaborate set of institutions that make policies binding on all members. Although the Union has made considerable progress toward economic integration— moving from a free trade area to a common market—it has made less progress toward the political integration envisioned by some of its founders.

SUGGESTIONS FOR FURTHER READING AND STUDY

A good general introduction to the concept of international organization, including realist, idealist, Marxist, and other views of the phenomenon, is offered by Clive Archer in *International Organizations* (London: George Allen and Unwin, 1983). Werner J. Feld and Robert S. Jordan, *International Organizations: A Comparative Approach*, 3rd ed. (New York: Praeger, 1994), furnishes a comparative analysis of IGOs and NGOs.

An excellent historical overview of the NGO phenomenon is provided by Kjell Skjels-baek in "The Growth of International Nongovernmental Organization in the Twenti-eth Century," in Robert O. Keohane and Joseph S. Nye, Jr., eds., *Transnational Relations and World Politics* (Cambridge, Mass.: Harvard University Press, 1971), pp. 70–92. The latter source contains several case studies focusing on the role of NGOs and transnational actors in a variety of issue-areas in world politics. A more recent work that serves the same purpose is Thomas G. Weiss and Leon Gordenker, eds., *NGOs, the UN, and Global Governance* (Boulder, Colo.: Lynne Rienner, 1996).

For a discussion of global IGOs, a basic text is A. Leroy Bennett, *International Organizations,* 6th ed. (Englewood Cliffs, N.J.: Prentice-Hall, 1995). A good overview of the IGO phenomenon is furnished by Harold K. Jacobson, *Networks of Interdependence,* 2nd ed. (New York: Knopf, 1984). An edited volume treating various aspects of international organization is Paul F. Diehl, ed., *The Politics of Global Governance: International Organizations in An Interdependent World* (Boulder, Colo.: Lynne Rienner, 1996). On the European Union as a case study of a regional IGO, see Neill Nugent, *The Government and Politics of the European Union,* 3rd ed. (Durham, N.C.: Duke University Press, 1994); Desmond Dinan, *An Ever Closer Union?* (Boulder, Colo.: Lynn Rienner, 1994); and Anne Daltrop, *Politics and the European Community,* 2nd ed. (London: Longman, 1987).

A somewhat dated but nonetheless classic work treating the history, problems, and prospects of the United Nations is Inis Claude's *Swords Into Plowshares,* 4th ed. (New York: Random House, 1984). Also, see Robert E. Riggs and Jack C. Plano, *The United Nations: International Organization and World Politics,* 2nd ed. (Belmont, Calif.: Wadsworth, 1994). On the UN's role in the post–Cold War era, see Karen A. Mingst and Margaret P. Karns, *The United Nations in the Post–Cold War Era* (Boulder, Colo.: Westview Press, 1995); and Thomas G. Weiss, David P. Forsythe, and Roger A. Coate, *The United Nations and Changing World Politics* (Boulder, Colo.: Westview Press, 1994). Among the spate of articles coinciding with the 50th anniversary of the UN, see Paul Kennedy and Bruce Russett, "Reforming the United Nations," *Foreign Affairs,* 74 (September/October 1995), pp. 56–71; and—from a more "realist" perspective—Abba Eban, "The UN Idea Revisited," in the same volume, pp. 39–55. The *UN Chronicle* is a periodical that provides summary descriptions of UN activities and developments, as do the annual volumes of *Issues Before the UN General Assembly.*

International Organization is an important journal that contains scholarly articles dealing with a wide range of international organizations and transnational activities at the regional and global levels, with an emphasis on analyzing their roles in world politics. Included are many studies on integration.

PART IV

The Global Condition: The Politics of Global Problem Solving

The traditional agenda of international affairs—the balance among major powers, the security of nations—no longer defines our perils or our possibilities. HENRY A. KISSINGER, U.S. SECRETARY OF STATE, IN A 1975 SPEECH

We have been more or less brought up to believe that the bonds of community, responsibility, and obligation run only to the [national] frontiers. Should we extend our vision to include all the people of our planet? BARBARA WARD, *The Lopsided World*

Usually we speak of violence only when it has reached an extreme. But it is also violence when children are dying of malnutrition, when there is no freedom of unions, where there is not enough housing, not enough health care. ADOLFO PÉREZ ESQUIVÉL, ARGENTINA, 1984

All the preceding quotations have one common thread: the recognition that the contemporary world is beset with numerous problems that are global in scope and require global responses. Human problem solving can occur at several levels—local, national, and international. At the international level, although bilateral and regional approaches might be sufficient to deal with some problems, they necessarily can offer only partial solutions to others, such as nuclear weapons proliferation and climatic disturbances. The existence of problems that are truly global in scale poses unparalleled dangers of international conflict but, perhaps also, unparalleled opportunities for international cooperation.

The notion that all problems must be solvable is in some sense a Western and even a particularly American bias. Nevertheless, governments representing various world cultures, including, for example, India and China, have campaigned for solutions to such pressing concerns as international violence, poverty, overpopulation, and scarcity of resources. Many of the efforts being undertaken today to deal with the new agenda of global issues take the form of *regime-making.* **Regimes** can be thought of as "recognized patterns of practices around which expectations converge," which "may or may not be accompanied by explicit organizational arrangements."[1] In other words, regimes constitute widely accepted rules, procedures and institutions, or "governing arrangements,"[2] which allow the international community to function and cope with some set of concerns in the absence of a world government. The drafting of treaties and international agreements, the cultivation of shared norms and values, and the creation of international organizational machinery all are part of regime-building, of "governance without government."[3] Regimes represent an alternative to each country pursuing strictly its own unilateral foreign policies. In considering global efforts at regime-building, one should bear in mind our initial definition of international politics—the process of deciding who gets what, when, and how in the world. As in national politics, some actors are in a better position than others to shape regimes and, in the process, either to facilitate or frustrate problem solving.

In Part IV, we examine the politics of global problem solving, focusing on three sets of issues: the *control of violence,* particularly nuclear and conventional arms races as well as terrorism and unorthodox violence (Chapters 11 and 12); the *promotion of economic well-being,* including both coordination of the global economy and the economic development of impoverished societies (Chapters 13 and 14); and the *management of renewable and nonrenewable resources,* including environmental concerns (Chapter 15). In each chapter, we will (1) define the *nature and magnitude* of the problem; (2) identify the congeries of state and nonstate *actors* whose interests and demands are relevant to the *politics* surrounding the problem; and (3) describe the recent *outcomes* of the political process, including any *regimes* that might have been produced by the international community in response to the problem.

11

The Control of Violence: Arms Races and Arms Control in the Nuclear Age

In Chapter 8, we considered the possibility that the world may be entering a phase in which the use of military force is deemphasized. We found that the evidence does not yet warrant such a conclusion, although there have been positive signs with the continuation of the "long peace" among major actors, reduction in some regional tensions, and the dip in the frequency of international (as opposed to domestic) war. These trends have been reflected in declining defense budgets (in real terms, adjusted for inflation) in many countries, including the United States (see Fig. 11.1).

With the major powers moderating their military spending, it appears that the annual global arms budget, which reached $1 trillion in 1987, may have peaked and is on a downward path.[1] Likewise, international sales of arms peaked in 1984 and again in 1987 at approximately $70 billion annually (expressed in 1993 dollars), and fell by approximately 70 percent through the mid-1990s (though the rate of decline tended to slow as the decade progressed). As seen in Figure 11.2, this trend held for sales to both developed and developing states, mainly because of economic difficulties in many arms-purchasing countries, but also because of the temporary eclipse of Russia as a

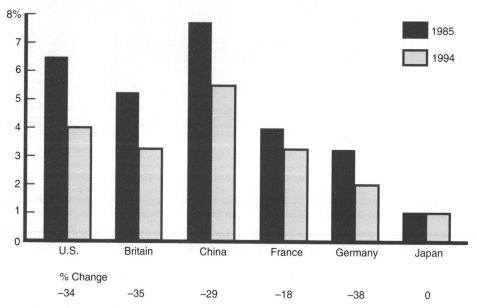

Figure 11.1

THE DOWNSIZING OF MILITARY ARSENALS: DEFENSE SPENDING AS PERCENT-AGE OF GROSS DOMESTIC PRODUCT AND PERCENTAGE CHANGE FROM 1985 TO 1994

Based on data from International Institute of Strategic Studies, *The Military Balance, 1995/96* (London: Oxford University Press, 1995), pp. 264–266.

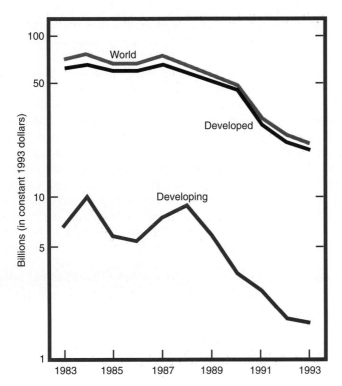

Figure 11.2
WORLD ARMS EXPORTS, 1983–1993
Source: U.S. Arms Control and Disarmament Agency, *World Military Expenditures and Arms Transfers, 1993–94* (Washington, D.C.: 1995), p. 14.

major source of arms and the decline of Iraq as a major arms importing state after its defeat in the Gulf War.[2]

One must be cautious in interpreting these trends. They conceivably could be reversed, as major powers push arms sales for commercial purposes and as customers seek to further modernize their forces. Some countries, such as China, Iran, India, and Pakistan, continue to spend significant resources on new weapons and armed forces, at least partly for enhanced regional influence.[3]

In a 1996 report, the U.S. Defense Department warned of the continued spread of weapons of mass destruction, including "everything from a chemical weapons plant under construction in Libya to biological toxins made by Iraq." Defense Secretary William Perry added that no matter how economically backward a country might be, "it can still have the capability to build [nuclear] reactors and to generate plutonium," as in the case of North Korea.[4] Although the nuclear weapon development programs of the major powers had been considerably downsized by the mid-1990s, this still left the world with more than 30,000 nuclear warheads, some 1,100 tons of deadly plutonium, and over 1,700 tons of highly enriched uranium. Even the agreements to dismantle large numbers of U.S. and Soviet weapons left daunting challenges of recycling, storage, and waste disposal.[5]

Secretary Perry argued that the best way to address these threats was through intergovernmental cooperation, "as in pacts concluded with the former Soviet Union; improvised agreements to stop nations from acquiring weapons-grade plutonium, as in North Korea [where the government had agreed to halt nuclear weapons development in return for advanced nuclear power reactors shipped under U.S. auspices]; collective sanctions like those imposed on Iraq; and effective export controls to stop allies from selling weapons technology to potential enemies."[6] Thus, disarmament issues continue to spark much debate, with discussions occurring in both multilateral forums, such as UN special sessions and meetings among high technology–exporting states, and bilateral settings, such as those between Washington and Moscow. Among the assumptions underlying these talks is the argument that if the tools of violence can somehow be controlled, the violence itself might be controlled.

Although violence is obviously not a new phenomenon, humanity's capacity to do violence clearly has reached new heights. In addition to the weapons of mass destruction discussed above, antiship guided missiles, TV- or radar-guided "smart bombs," napalm, antitank missile batteries with "night vision" capabilities, "stealth" (radar-evading) fighters and bombers, and assorted other advanced weapons, along with the development of the electronically controlled battlefield, have made it possible to kill more people and destroy more targets with fewer personnel than before. The capacity for violence is ever more closely tied to technological capacity; controlling global violence, therefore, relates to the way states define their *security, technological,* and *economic* interests. This can be seen in this chapter as we focus on international arms races and arms control, which will be among the most critical dimensions of the larger problem of controlling global violence in the twenty-first century.

The Nature and Magnitude of the Problem

By *arms races,* we generally mean competitive armament by two or more states seeking security and protection against each other. However, as noted in Chapter 8, one country's rate of armament is not always related to another's or to specific threats by other states. Governments have many additional reasons for arming: to preserve defense industries and jobs; to become dominant regional powers; to gain prestige; to reach the top ranks of technology; to suppress domestic opponents and unrest. Therefore, one country can race along with its own armaments quite apart from actions taken by enemy states; despite the downfall of the Soviet Union, and without a clearly defined enemy, the U.S. military still announced plans in the mid-1990s for the next generation of costly and sophisticated weaponry, including devices that would allow fighter pilots to control their aircraft by eye movements.[7] Countries engaged in competitive races often confront the "security dilemma," in that the more they arm in the quest for security, the more their adversaries are likely to arm and the *less* secure each side may feel.

States can obtain arms either by manufacturing them or by acquiring them from another country through gift, capture, or purchase. Both methods have the same potential result: weapons *proliferation*, i.e., the spread of weapons among more and more states. Countries manufacture arms by using either their own engineers' designs or, through licenses, the designs of engineers in other countries. As such weapon "systems" as jet fighter planes—complete with their associated armament (e.g., air-to-air or air-to-ground missiles)—become more sophisticated and expensive, the weapons business becomes more complex as well. Few countries can design and build an entire aircraft, for example, including air-frame, engines, and advanced electronics. Sometimes a small country, such as Israel, can design or manufacture part or most of the weapon system, but must rely on imported components to complete the job, hence limiting its options in producing or selling such equipment. Even larger countries, such as those in Western Europe, often collaborate in the "co-production" of expensive weapon systems, so as to pool their resources and expertise in manufacturing, buying, and selling the product. Arms-purchasing states often seek to "offset" the cost of their purchases by insisting that the seller agree to buy other products in return or farm out some of the production to the purchaser's own munitions plants.[8]

It is difficult to keep track of the worldwide distribution of weapons, partly because governments generally keep exact armament levels secret and partly because it is hard to track indirect and clandestine arms shipments (e.g., during the Yugoslav conflict in the 1990s, arms traffickers posing as Bolivian government officials ordered Chinese-made weapons, which were then diverted to Croatia, Serbia, and Bosnia in an effort to circumvent the UN arms embargo).

Recently, renewing a practice first instituted by the League of Nations, the UN has published a yearly register of conventional arms imported and exported. Although there has been a relatively high level of cooperation among member states in reporting their arms shipments, thereby opening up the possibility of achieving more accurate "threat assessments" and greater "transparency" in verifying compliance with arms control agreements, ambiguities and secrets remain.[9] It is often hard to determine what technologies are "weapon-related." For example, should computers or pickup trucks, which may be converted to launching or transporting missiles, be reported and restricted? Some have tried to distinguish between offensive and defensive arms, the former used to attack targets and the latter to defend against incoming weapons. Most such distinctions break down, however, especially when "multirole" weapons, such as jet fighter-bombers, or "dual-use" equipment, such as helicopters (which have both civilian and military application), are considered. These uncertainties, along with the insistence that states have a "sovereign right to arm," plague efforts to control weapon proliferation.

Both **nuclear** and **conventional arms** proliferation are causes for concern today. The current world stockpile of nuclear weapons, even with the sizable cuts in American and Russian arsenals, has an explosive yield equivalent to 650,000 Hiroshima-sized bombs, enough "to destroy civilization as we know it several times over."[10] This threat is magnified by the availability of various delivery systems, ranging from aircraft to missiles and naval craft. By 1990, at least 52 less developed states had acquired supersonic aircraft, 71 had tactical missiles, 107 possessed armored fighting vehicles, and 81 had modern warships.[11] Depending on how small and portable nuclear weapons become, they could conceivably be delivered by such means, or by individual terrorists entering a city in a rental truck. Hence, nuclear weapons proliferation is related to conventional weapons proliferation. Chemical and biological weapons are also a major source of concern. Moreover, research continues on exotic weapons of the future, including laser and particle beam, antisatellite, and antimissile devices, some envisioned for deployment in outer space.

ECONOMIC ASPECTS OF THE PROBLEM

As we noted in Chapter 8, arms races may or may not result in war. However, the potential physical destruction that expanding arsenals can cause is only one cost associated with arms races. Developed and less developed countries alike have invested huge sums of money in their military establishments. Economists have long debated whether military spending retards other sectors of the economy; in other words, could each dollar spent on defense be more productively invested in other pursuits, such as health, education, or transportation, all of which are arguably important to a country's "security"? Those answering "not necessarily" point to the stimulus of defense spending in producing jobs and technological spin-offs that benefit other sectors (e.g., the development of miniaturized electronics and optics). One analyst, studying less developed countries, has found a positive relationship between military spending and economic growth.[12] A study of the American economy found relatively little trade-off between defense spending and social welfare between 1947 and 1980, although specific social programs suffered under the heavy defense build-up of the Reagan years.[13]

Those on the other side of the debate who doubt the benefits of military spending describe a variety of socioeconomic "opportunity costs," such as the essentially nonconsumable and inflationary nature of much military spending (for instance in producing overpriced and quickly obsolete weapons), the prospect of greater job creation through civilian spending, and the diversion of limited research and development funds from the civilian sector.[14] In regard to the developing world, many are critical of the role of military spending in aggravating the debt burden of LDCs and contributing generally to a wasteful allocation of scarce resources. Most empirical analyses have found that military expenditures by developing states generally produce more negative than positive effects, particularly reducing national savings and capital accumulation.[15]

If military spending is a drag on developing economies, though, this drag has lessened in recent years. Defense spending as a percentage of gross national product has declined for both developed and developing countries; between 1983 and 1993, the average for developed countries dropped from 5.5 percent to 3.4 percent, whereas the average for LDCs dropped from 6.1 percent to 3.1 percent. Many countries that in the 1980s had invested rather heavily in their military establishments (over 8 percent of GNP), including such impoverished states as Egypt, Guyana, Ethiopia, Mongolia, and Nicaragua, retrenched in the 1990s with the settlement of various disputes. But other poor states, such as Tunisia, Sudan, and Mozambique, as well as conflict-ridden Middle Eastern states such as Israel, Syria, Jordan, Kuwait, and Saudi Arabia, continued at a high level of military expenditure.[16] In these patterns, one can see the impact of conflict on armament.

The bulk of world military spending is still concentrated among a few countries. Just seven states—the United States, Russia, China, France, Japan, Germany, and the United Kingdom—account for over 75 percent of all military expenditures.[17] "Generally as countries grow wealthier over time, their available budget funds increase, and military expenditures and mobilization rise accordingly. . . ."[18] Most countries, as they develop, not only spend more on weapons but also seek to develop some capacity to produce weapons themselves rather than relying entirely on foreign sources. Keith Krause has noted that "with few exceptions (such as Mexico), the attractiveness of an arms industry as a symbol of national power is such that few states with the capacity to maintain one will forgo it."[19] In other words, high levels of military preparation and spending appear to go along not only with high levels of threat perception and foreign policy ambition, but also with industrial and manufacturing capability.

Despite the slowing trend in global arms expenditures, the world still was spending approximately $1 million per minute on weapons and military forces in the 1990s. During the Gulf War, each electronically sophisticated cruise missile among the hundreds fired by U.S. forces against Iraq cost $1 million per copy, and even so-called "dumb bombs" cost $1,000 each. One B-2 Stealth bomber by 1996 was priced at $1 billion, making the plane almost too expensive to use and risk losing.

The world's priorities clearly are open to serious question when so many resources are allocated to instruments of destruction. The total annual military expenditure by all countries in recent years roughly has equaled the entire annual income and the total debt level of the poorest half of humanity. Funding of worldwide medical research has amounted to less than 25 percent of the support given to military research and development. The world's governments spend approximately 80 times more per soldier than per child in schools.[20] Although it cannot be presumed that cutting military programs will automatically result in higher social spending, some of the potential trade-offs can be seen in Table 11.1, which illustrates how the savings achieved by various reductions in military spending might be channeled into vital social services in a country such as the United States.

ARMS TRANSFERS

Many states, of course, do not have indigenous arms industries and, hence, must rely entirely on imports, i.e., **arms transfers** from foreign suppliers. Arms transfers include both sales and gifts (military aid grants) of weapon systems, support services such as base construction and troop training, spare parts, and designs. Generally when analysts track arms transfers, they are monitoring transfers of conventional arms from one government to another or from a government to a faction or foreign nongovernmental actor of some sort. Arms transfers, where they help foster military parity and mutual deterrence in a region, can play a constructive role in promoting peace, but they can just as easily cause heightened security anxieties and destabilization.

Over time the emphasis has shifted from arms transfers in the form of military aid to transfers in the form of military sales. With the oil price hikes of the 1970s, the sale of sophisticated weaponry to Middle Eastern OPEC members in particular reached staggering proportions; at one point Iran under the Shah had a larger tank arsenal than Britain, as well as the largest helicopter fleet in the world. A "trickle down" effect also began, as wealthier states

Table 11.1
THE SOCIAL COSTS OF MILITARY SPENDING

Civilian Programs (in $ millions)		Military Programs (in $ millions)	
Drug-abuse Prevention	$2,000	F-22 Stealth fighters	$2,200
National Park Service	$1,200	One Seawolf attack submarine	$1,526
Child Immunizations	$844	F/A/Hornet fighters	$845
Corporation for Public		Four Trident II missiles	$348
Broadcasting	$306	164 Tomahawk cruise missiles	$168
National Endowment for the Arts	$172		

Source: Randall Forsberg, "Force Without Reason," *Boston Review,* 20, no. 3 (Summer 1995), p. 8, citing data from U.S. federal budget, FY 1996, and Council for a Livable World Education Fund, 1995.

bought new weapons and handed down their older models to poorer states, creating an international used weapons network.[21] Another recent trend has been away from the transfer of entire finished systems toward sales of weapon components that recipient states can assemble at home, and that often involve the type of "offset" manufacturing, co-production, and trade agreements discussed earlier. As fewer expensive, complete weapon systems can be sold, manufacturers have turned to producing component parts to upgrade existing weapons and to combine into new ones. Thus, the arms market of the future might resemble the global auto market, with subassemblies produced in various countries by multinational firms and consortia of firms to pool resources, enlarge markets, and cut labor costs.

Less developed countries as a group, led by the Middle East and East Asia, accounted for nearly 80 percent of all arms imports between 1983 and 1993, although the dollar value of arms imports fell across all regions as the decade progressed and the Cold War ended.[22] Over time, the Middle East and East Asia have increased their share of global arms imports relative to Latin America and Africa. In the 1990s, Saudi Arabia remained the world's largest single importer by a wide margin, with over half of the entire Middle Eastern total. Europe is now the second largest importing region after the Middle East. A combination of disposable income and perceived military threat or opportunity tends to underlie the arms acquisition patterns of the top importing states.[23]

Figure 11.3 shows the leading arms exporters in the world and their share of the global arms market. Developed states account for roughly 92 percent of total arms exports, led by the United States, which itself had captured almost half of the world market by 1993. By the late 1990s, U.S. dominance had grown even greater, to well over 50 percent.[24] As U.S. defense spending in the 1990s declined from Cold War levels, foreign customers were looked to increasingly to sustain American defense industries; in 1995, for the first time in history, American companies produced more fighter jets for export than for the U.S. armed forces. Still, overall global arms exports declined sharply in the 1990s from their 1980s levels.[25] This created something of a "buyer's market," with fewer ready customers.

Some arms supplying states, such as the United States and the United Kingdom, traditionally have imposed relatively strict limits on the type of arms that can be exported, hoping to control the spread of advanced technologies or weapons of mass destruction. Washington also has attempted to set limits on the use of its equipment; such restrictions have not always been enforced, as when Israel used American-supplied weapons to attack Arab forces in Lebanon during the 1980s. The United States also has tried restrictions on conventional weapon supplies to states thought to be developing nuclear weapons, such as Pakistan, hoping to convince them to abandon such projects. Other arms suppliers, such as China, have been less restrictive and, when criticized by Washington, have accused the United States of hypocrisy

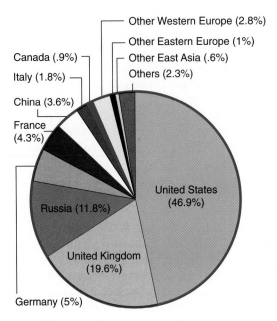

Figure 11.3
WORLD ARMS EXPORT SHARES
Source: Data are for 1993 and are from U.S. Arms Control and Disarmament Agency, *World Military Expenditures and Arms Transfers, 1993–94* (Washington, D.C.: 1995), p. 15.

as the largest "arms merchant" in the world. Although it is extremely difficult to impose one's will simply by regulating the supply of arms, properly timed embargoes have sometimes succeeded in bringing wars to a halt and have been one factor influencing arms negotiations.

In addition to formal transfers between governments, we have noted that weapons can be shipped clandestinely by or to private traders. Weapons also can be captured by victorious armies or raiders breaking into armories when governmental authority in a territory breaks down (as in parts of the former Soviet Union), can be reexported from one country to another, can be supplied to guerrilla groups, or can be copied by unauthorized users.[26] It is likely that the most advanced arms will remain under relatively effective government control, but the spread of increasingly destructive conventional weapon technologies and potent secondhand or redesigned equipment is becoming a growing international concern. The problem is further complicated by the availability of dual-use equipment, which can be converted to weapons, as when long hollow tubes, thought to be useful for perfecting "super gun" long range artillery, were discovered during shipment from Britain to Iraq at the end of the Iran-Iraq War; indeed, several Western arms makers, as well as the USSR, were criticized for contributing to Iraq's bellicosity in the 1980s and 1990s by selling key components that enabled Iraq to extend the range of its Soviet-supplied SCUD missiles. Failure to evaluate carefully the potential effects of arms transfers can result in security nightmares for the supplying state, as when British forces were nearly blown out of the water during the Falklands fighting in the South Atlantic in 1982 by weapons previously supplied to Argentina by Britain and its NATO allies, France and the United States.

NUCLEAR WEAPONS PROLIFERATION

Nowhere is concern about arms greater than in the area of **nuclear proliferation.** Table 11.2 compares the strategic nuclear arsenals of the five states commonly referred to as the "nuclear club." (**Strategic weapons** are nuclear weapons of global range, as opposed to tactical or intermediate-range nuclear weapons, with a range up to 3,500 miles.) Both the United States and Russia have reduced their arsenals significantly from the Cold War era, but still have enormous destructive capabilities, as do Britain, France, and China. Nuclear arms races would be terrifying enough if these five states were the only entrants. However, India (which set off a "peaceful nuclear explosion" in 1984), Pakistan (which is presumed to possess the technical skill and components to assemble several nuclear weapons), and Israel (which is thought to have at least 100 nuclear bombs but has not yet conducted any outward tests) are all considered de facto members of the "club," with Iran and a few other states

Table 11.2
STRATEGIC NUCLEAR ARSENALS

Country	Total Deployed Warheads	On Land–Based Missiles	On Sub–Based Missiles	On Bombers
Russia*	10,100	6,078	2.560	1,410
United States	8,500	2,090	2,880	3,528
France	482	18	384	80
China	284	110	24	150
Britain	234		134	100

The United States, Russia, and China also have tactical (short-range) nuclear arsenals.
*Includes states of the former Soviet Union.
Source: From *Newsweek,* John Barry, July 24, 1995, p. 36. © 1995, Newsweek, Inc. All rights reserved. Reprinted by permission.

suspected of having active nuclear weapon programs as well. Figure 11.4 provides a worldwide overview of the nuclear proliferation problem.

The ominous threat of regional nuclear arms races is evident in the following description:

> At a closed door seminar at the Institute of Defense Studies in New Delhi, it was the naval officer's turn to speak. With a diffident air, he proposed a crash investment of five billion dollars that would give India a small but effective force of submarine-launched ballistic missiles . . .
>
> Eight hundred miles away in Bombay, where the Arabian sea laps against the boundary fence of the Bhabha atomic research centre, a scientist also reacts to Pakistan's growing nuclear capability. 'We need funds to develop small nuclear warheads to take out major targets in Pakistan without also harming India,' he said. 'Imagine dropping a three megaton bomb on Lahore. The blast and radioactivity would wash right back on us.'[27]

India and Pakistan have pioneered what has been termed "non-weaponized deterrence," i.e., developing the reputation for possessing nuclear arms without actually deploying them. This allows these states to avoid potential negative repercussions if they "go nuclear," such as trade and military sanctions, while at the same time holding each other off with the implied threat that they already have gone nuclear. Thus India also can maintain its traditional moral stance against the use of force and at the same time demand that the rest of the world must first reduce their nuclear forces before India will give up the right to acquire them.[28] Indian nationalists, however, have pressured the government to drop any pretense and formally achieve nuclear weapon status.

Although most major powers have agreed not to provide nuclear weapons technology to non-nuclear states, China, for one, has been willing to sell late model missiles to its long-time client, Pakistan, mainly for commercial benefits, and perhaps to balance off India's capabilities and keep New Delhi preoccupied to its west. The nuclear proliferation problem is complicated by the challenge of distinguishing between "peaceful" and "nonpeaceful" nuclear technology. Peaceful nuclear technology includes such devices as PNEs (peaceful nuclear explosives), which can be used in construction or mining operations to level mountains or dig holes and tunnels, along with nuclear power generating reactors, which can provide an alternate energy source. Both developed and less developed states have sought such technology despite the obvious fallout dangers. India used "peaceful" materials supplied by the United States and a reactor supplied by Canada in its 1974 blast. In addition to the members of the nuclear club, at least sixteen other states had, by the 1980s, built or purchased nuclear reactors capable of producing weapons-grade fuels.[29] In 1981, Israel staged a "preventive strike" against such a "research reactor" provided by France to Iraq, although the Iraqi nuclear weapons development program continued into the 1990s.

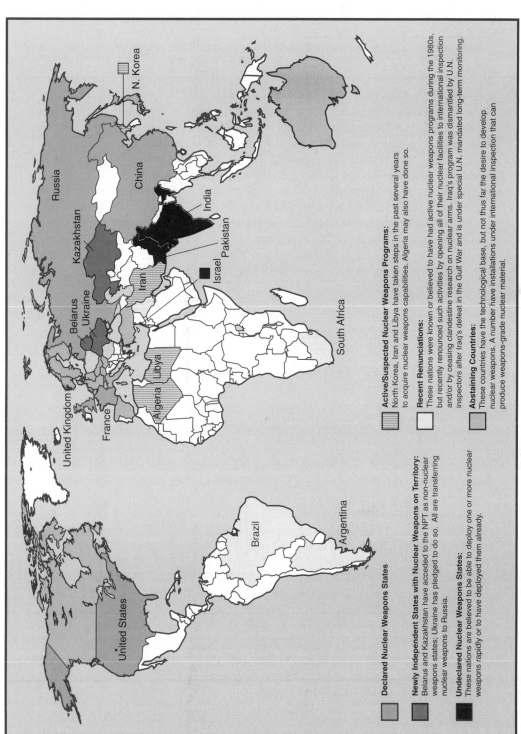

Figure 11.4
THE NUCLEAR PROLIFERATION MAP
Source: Ronald J. Bee, "Nuclear Proliferation: Can It Be Capped?," *Great Decisions 1995* (New York: Foreign Policy Association, 1995), p. 17.

The following legend appears within the map figure:

Declared Nuclear Weapons States

Newly Independent States with Nuclear Weapons on Territory:
Belarus and Kazakhstan have acceded to the NPT as non-nuclear weapons states; Ukraine has pledged to do so. All are transferring nuclear weapons to Russia.

Undeclared Nuclear Weapons States:
These nations are believed to be able to deploy one or more nuclear weapons rapidly or to have deployed them already.

Active/Suspected Nuclear Weapons Programs:
North Korea, Iran and Libya have taken steps in the past several years to acquire nuclear weapons capabilities. Algeria may also have done so.

Recent Renunciations:
These nations were known or believed to have had active nuclear weapons programs during the 1980s, but recently renounced such activities by opening all of their nuclear facilities to international inspection and/or by ceasing clandestine research on nuclear arms. Iraq's program was dismantled by U.N. inspectors after Iraq's defeat in the Gulf War and is under special U.N. mandated long-term monitoring.

Abstaining Countries:
These countries have the technological base, but not thus far the desire to develop nuclear weapons. A number have installations under international inspection that can produce weapons-grade nuclear material.

Although nuclear weapons might deter aggression by one state against another, the laws of probability suggest that the more fingers on nuclear triggers, the more likelihood a bomb will go off. Perhaps a local commander with tactical nuclear forces feels surrounded by hostile forces and launches the first shot, or perhaps a local crisis escalates into a series of cross-border nuclear attacks. Once that happens, it is not known whether a nuclear war could be kept from spreading and involving other states in other regions.

A special concern has arisen over the security of nuclear weapon installations and nuclear secrets in the former Soviet Union. After the 1991 breakup of the USSR, Russia inherited the bulk of the weapons, but three other former republics (Ukraine, Kazakhstan, and Belarus) were left with nuclear weapons on their soil as well. Although these states have agreed to transfer their nuclear arsenals to Moscow in return for various economic benefits, all of the weaponry is not yet fully accounted for. Moreover, economic problems in the former Soviet Union have tempted poorly paid or unemployed nuclear scientists and weapons technicians to "peddle their wares" to states or groups with cash to pay. Much of the post–Cold War aid program to the former Soviet Union was designed to provide employment for nuclear engineers, to improve governmental abilities to account for and control access to nuclear weapons, and to convince Moscow not to sell advanced technologies to states such as Iran. The Sidelight on page 427 suggests the seriousness of the problem.

CHEMICAL AND BIOLOGICAL WEAPONS PROLIFERATION

Although nuclear proliferation has received the lion's share of the world's headlines, **chemical** and **biological weapons** are potentially just as deadly. States lacking the ability to develop nuclear weapons might resort instead to chemical or biological arms to threaten mass destruction and thus deter enemies, including neighbors with nuclear capabilities. There has been speculation that Syria and Egypt have researched such means of deterring Israel, for example. Chemical gas agents and germ warfare have been around since the early twentieth century. Gas was used in World War I; the British, Americans, and Germans lugged gas canisters around the battle sites of World War II but never used them for fear of opening the door to retaliation. Biological weapons capable of producing anthrax or cholera epidemics also were available in smaller quantities. Mustard gas was used in the 1980s by Iraq in its war with Iran and its civil war against the Kurds.

By the mid-1990s, a U.S. government study confirmed only four countries—Iran, Iraq, Russia, and the United States—known to possess chemical weapons, whereas an additional twenty-one were classified as either "probable" or "suspected." The bacteriological weapon states were fewer in number, with Russia the only confirmed case (the United States having disposed of its arsenal earlier), whereas ten others were said to be probable or suspected pos-

SIDELIGHT

**FALLOUT FROM THE BREAKUP OF THE SOVIET UNION:
WHO IS MINDING THE NUCLEAR STORE?**

While security for the U.S. nuclear program depends on high-tech gadgetry backed by armed guards, Russia has depended on control of people. "They had watchers watching watchers, backed by very strict control on movements," said one Energy Department official. Will hard times fray the watchers' loyalty? . . . A Princeton physicist noticed big new dachas going up inside the barbed-wire perimeter of Chelyabinsk-70, a closed city for Russian nuclear scientists. When he asked who owned the houses, his Russian companion cut him a glance and replied, "the night people—the black marketers." [A] [f]ormer Los Alamos weapons designer Stephen Younger recalls how the director of the weapons lab at another closed city, Arzamas-16, called him aside to beg for emergency financial aid, adding that his scientists were going hungry. "You are driving us into the hands of the Chinese," the man said.

How much [nuclear material] may already have leaked? The CIA lists 31 cases of thefts or seizures, most allegedly involving low-grade Russian materials found by German police. . . . But many of the cases resulted from "sting" operations, part of a pre-emptive strategy initiated by Western intelligence agencies since 1992. Some Russians charge that the operation has actually created a market. Still, some cases are chilling. In Prague . . . police found almost six pounds of highly enriched uranium in the back seat of a Saab; also in the car were a Czech nuclear scientist and two colleagues from Belarus and Ukraine. "We're starting to see significant quantities of significant material," says a White House source. Adds a Pentagon official, "if just one bomb's worth gets out, people are going to wake up real fast."

Source: John Barry, "Future Shock," *Newsweek*, July 24, 1995, p. 36. © 1995, Newsweek, Inc. All rights reserved. Reprinted by permission.

sessors.[30] Such weapons have been increasingly refined over the years. Chemical arms tend to be stored in "binary" components, which are inert until being mixed together when ready for use. Paralysis, respiratory failure, and death can occur within a few minutes or hours by not more than .4 milligrams of certain nerve gases.

Research in nerve and toxic gases and microorganisms is related to civilian chemical and biological programs, and therefore is very difficult to police. Poisonous gases such as hydrogen cyanide and phosgene are useful in manufacturing dyestuffs and other consumer chemicals. Nerve gases are closely related chemically to certain pesticides. It is relatively simple to convert from civilian to military production; one such chemical plant in Libya was a point of contention between the United States and Libyan governments in the 1990s.

With the widespread use of nuclear fuels as well as chemical and biological products, concern persists that weapons of mass destruction produced from these substances will be obtained not only by governments but also by private individuals, criminals, and terrorist organizations. Weapons-grade materials produced as by-products of industrial nuclear power generation, such as plutonium 239, have become plentiful. Instructions for making nuclear weapons are also now widely available. Several years ago, a Princeton University undergraduate designed a crude atomic bomb for about $2,000. Nuclear wastes and bombs generally are packaged in sizes too large to be picked up and carried off by thieves, but smaller versions theoretically could be obtained by well-organized groups that might be able to hold whole populations at ransom. These dangers make the control of international violence, particularly arms races, an ever more pressing concern.

The Politics of Arms Control

In the words of one arms analyst, "disarmament, deficits, dollars, development, and debt all interrelate with politics, personalities, passion, and policy to produce a complex set of causes and effects" of military spending.[31] To understand why the control of international violence has proved exceedingly difficult, one must consider the variety of actors whose interests and demands affect global problem solving in this area. In this section we discuss the politics of controlling arms races, examining the negotiating positions taken by different states as well as the role of nonstate actors in shaping outcomes.

ACTORS AND ISSUES

Those wishing to stop arms races have advocated arms control or disarmament, two separate but related approaches to peace mentioned in Chapter 8. **Disarmament,** entailing the actual elimination of weapons, is generally a more ambitious undertaking than **arms control,** which can include not only reducing armaments but also more modest measures—"freezing" arsenals at existing levels or placing "ceilings" on future weapons stockpiles, as well as limiting the development, deployment, or use of certain weapons. Arms control and disarmament talks have occurred in several settings, including such multilateral forums as the Geneva-based Conference on Disarmament, special sessions of the UN General Assembly, and informal meetings of the "Nuclear Suppliers Group" of advanced nuclear technology powers, as well as bilateral forums such as the Strategic Arms Reduction Talks (START) between the United States and the Soviet Union during the 1980s and 1990s.

Governments' views on conventional or nuclear arms control depend substantially on their definitions of national interests. For example, less developed states have been prone to criticize major powers for carrying on costly arms races. But, as noted previously, these critics also insist on their own right to receive or manufacture arms, and generally resist efforts by Washington and others to impose limits on military sales or on the spread of advanced weapons technology. Nevertheless, certain LDCs, such as Costa Rica and Gambia, deliberately have limited the size and budgets of their armed forces and have renounced the acquisition and use of certain types of weapons. In fact, as seen below, nearly all LDCs have explicitly agreed not to pursue any nuclear weapons programs. However, their willingness to accept such restraints has been contingent on promises by the major nuclear states to supply them with the benefits of peaceful nuclear technology and to pursue meaningful nuclear arms reduction negotiations. Some developed states that possess the technology to develop nuclear weapons, such as Germany and Japan, also have forsworn such armament, but might nevertheless feel compelled to rethink their positions in the future.

The dilemma for states seeking to maximize their security but to avert arms races is well expressed in the following passage on nuclear proliferation:

> To arrest the spread of nuclear weapons would be to perpetuate an international status quo in which some societies are denied political and strategic assets that other societies, certainly no more deserving, are entitled to have. Yet to condone nuclear proliferation in the interest of reducing the inegalitarian nature of the international system would be to abdicate responsibility for minimizing the risk of nuclear conflict.[32]

The politics of limiting conventional or nuclear weapons proliferation is fraught with cross-pressures. During the Carter administration, for example, the American government initiated a series of talks with the Soviets on limiting the spread of conventional arms (so-called CATT, or Conventional Arms Transfer Talks). During the course of the ultimately unsuccessful negotiations, it became clear that Washington and Moscow each intended these limits only for regions in which the other was the major weapons supplier. The talks broke off with each side proposing negotiating positions that would hamper the opponent's policies while leaving itself relatively free to pursue business as usual.[33] Even with the end of the Cold War, it is still relatively difficult for arms suppliers and recipients to agree on a formula for apportioning the flow of arms and meeting regional security needs.[34] Nonetheless, efforts to restrain lethal weapons shipments continue, as in ongoing U.S.-Russian consultations as well as the 1987 agreement among Washington and other Western capitals to limit certain types of missile exports.[35]

The weapons trade continues because both major and minor powers have deep political and economic interests in it. As noted, in addition to commercial interests, major powers distribute weapons to favored clients and allies to gain political influence over recipients, to balance off hostile forces in key regions or states (in some cases seeking stalemated endings of local wars), to keep friendly regimes in power, to buy good will and concessions such as the right to use military bases in foreign countries, and to lessen foreign states' desire for nuclear weapons. Minor powers seek weapons for security, access to technology, economic trade-offs, prestige, and influence.[36]

Proliferation continues even though there is no evidence that the benefits listed above are reliably obtained through arms transfers. For example, arms sales to the Shah of Iran did not prevent his downfall and the loss of U.S. influence in Iran; U.S. sales to Pakistan, sometimes allowed and sometimes embargoed, evidently have not appreciably slowed that country's nuclear weapons program; rather than stabilizing a region by balancing powers, arms transfers frequently have been used by both sides in regional wars; trade benefits are marginal when arms make up only 3 to 5 percent of the total exports of major Western arms producers such as the United States, the United Kingdom, and France; and the security dilemma of weapons acquisition, mentioned earlier, calls into question the security rationale itself.[37] However, rather than questioning the benefits of arms transfers, governments normally operate on the assumption that they offer at least some influence over foreign states and crises (as in Washington's felt need to beef up the Bosnian government against Bosnian Serb rebels in the mid-1990s),[38] and some payoff for influential interest groups at home.

One cannot understand the international politics of arms control without also taking into account the domestic political forces that impact on the arms spending decisions of states. Earlier in the book, we mentioned the existence of military-industrial complexes. Among the actors who constitute such complexes are scientists working on weapons research, politicians seeking military contracts and other income-generating defense activities for their local constituencies, military and civilian officials in defense bureaucracies who draw up arms shopping lists, and munitions manufacturers and financiers. Although such actors often have conflicting views among themselves,[39] all tend to have a stake in maintaining large defense expenditures.

Although national governments have been the primary buyers and sellers of arms, much of the equipment is manufactured and marketed by private companies, selling either to their own or to foreign governments. In certain countries, the government itself directly owns and operates weapons research, development, and production facilities. However, because of budgetary limitations, increasingly government facilities have been privatized; private defense contractors often compete, especially where the home and export markets are large enough to support multiple manufacturers. Governments also have subsidized or encouraged the consolidation of defense manufacturers so that they

SIDELIGHT

THE ARMS BAZAAR

Sleek fighter jets made in the USA glimmer on a desert tarmac while American top-gun pilots hover like car salesmen. Courting oil-rich sheiks and princes, the pilots enthrall the royalty with war stories from Desert Storm. This is the Dubai Air Show, where the glitter of marketing meets the drab-green reality of war. It is a six-day extravaganza that is the Third World's largest showcase of the latest high-tech weaponry.

"These things can fight, we found that out," Gulf War hero Eric Dodson boasts to a group of Emirates' royalty viewing the merchandise. With $5 billion to spend, they are in the market for 80 jet fighters.

An Emirates air force commander among the entourage seems in awe of the decorated American pilot. As Dodson swaggers out to the F-16 Fighting Falcon, he waves the commander up into the cockpit. Flanked by marketing experts from the manufacturer, Lockheed Martin, the two men climb into the jet and get down to business, going over the weapons-delivery systems. When the royal entourage leaves, a Lockheed Martin technical representative sprays the cockpit with a can of Glade air freshener and spit-shines the windshield. And the sales team waits for the next customer among scores of countries—from Jordan to Indonesia. . . .

In huge air-conditioned auditoriums, prospective buyers saunter by pavilions marked US Defense Department and US Department of Commerce as if they were storefronts at a shopping mall. The US Army booth has an enticing video presentation with a hard-rock beat and a voice straight out of FM radio promoting McDonnell Douglas Apache attack helicopters: "Anytime, anywhere, any weather . . . death awaits in the dark." As the announcer speaks, tanks on the ground burst into flames. . . .

The Italian flying team . . . presented a baroque splendor. . . . There were 10 jets streaking in intricate formations, leaving a green-white-red trail of exhaust that lingered like an enormous Italian flag unfurled in the sky. The pilots—with their fashionable jumpsuits, dark sunglasses, and slicked back hair—were the playboys of the airshow . . . signing autographs for spectators. . . .

At night there were parties. Under the glow of a full moon at the Hilton Beach Club, 1,500 people from the roughly 400 companies and foreign delegations registered at the air show gathered for a banquet.

Lobbyists and marketing specialists for every American contractor huddled with sheiks and princes. They gorged on pepper steaks and filet mignon flown in from Texas, and shrimp and lamb sizzling on mesquite grills. There were five bars stocked with single-malt scotch and Sam Adams ale. And a 12-piece jazz ensemble from Atlanta serenaded the arms dealers and their customers as the deals were cut into the night.

Source: Charles M. Sennott, "Armed for Profit: The Selling of US Weapons," *The Boston Globe,* February 11, 1996, pp. B2–B3. Reprinted courtesy of *The Boston Globe.*

can compete with those of other countries. Governmental arms purchases frequently are balanced among defense contractors to keep valued production lines in operation and design teams employed in case they are needed in wartime. In short, high-technology weapons are designed, produced, and merchandised with close industry-government cooperation, and growing cross-national links (such as between American and Japanese aerospace firms).

Today's weapons marketing and promotion resembles that of cars or toys, with giant exhibitions complete with attractive models trying to convince buyers of the merits of their wares. The "Madison Avenue" approach to arms peddling is vividly captured in the Sidelight in this section, which contains an account of the Dubai Air Show in the United Arab Emirates, typical of the arms exhibits and fairs held annually in various parts of the world. In the weapons business, shadowy middlemen often are hired, and at times use bribery, to ease the way for sales to certain countries where they have government connections. Intermediaries also can help conceal the identity of arms buyers and sellers, thereby avoiding political embarrassment or "end use" violation charges. The complicated arms traffic flow, including covert and third-party connections, is one reason why arms embargoes are so difficult to enforce.[40]

With so many elements contributing to arms races, it is a wonder that any arms control occurs at all. However, many actors furnish support for arms control efforts—including domestic interest groups, such as antinuclear protestors in Europe, Japan, the South Pacific, and North America, and NGOs, such as Greenpeace, which apply public pressure on governments; officials in the United Nations and other IGOs that facilitate arms control talks; and certain national government agencies that are specifically charged with responsibility for arms control (such as the U.S. Arms Control and Disarmament Agency). In one post–Cold War initiative, antinuclear groups, the World Health Organization, and representatives of sixteen nonnuclear states collaborated in an effort to have the International Court of Justice issue an advisory opinion declaring nuclear weapons inhumane and their possession illegal, although the final judgment reached by the Court was an ambiguous split decision.[41]

NUCLEAR DETERRENCE AND ARMS CONTROL

One complication in arms control negotiations is the need to preserve "stability" in the nuclear arms race, i.e., to maintain the so-called balance of terror, which in theory at least deters the use of nuclear weapons. **Nuclear deterrence** is a specific form of military dissuasion, of the type discussed in Chapter 7, and a separate logic and language grew up around it during the Cold War. In the case of nuclear deterrence, the government of a nuclear-armed nation threatens to use such weapons if an adversary initiates a nuclear or perhaps even a conventional strike against it or its allies. As applied to allies, this is a variation of deterrence called "extended deterrence." For example, during the 1950s, Secretary of State Dulles threatened **massive retaliation** with America's largest nuclear weapons if the Soviet Union committed even the smallest conventional aggression in Western Europe or elsewhere. Even after the Soviets developed **inter-continental ballistic missiles (ICBMs)** capable of hitting the continental United States in the 1960s, thereby eliminating any credibility the massive retaliation doctrine might have had, Washington (under its "flexible response" doctrine) continued to hold out the possibility of responding with nuclear weapons if Warsaw Pact countries, generally ahead of the West in quantities of conventional weapons such as tanks, launched any kind of attack on NATO countries.[42]

Although nuclear weapons are in a sense designed precisely *not* to be used—i.e., to be so frightening that opponents will refrain from war—the fact remains that weapons are always designed not only for deterrent purposes but for combat uses. This paradox complicates deterrence. Indeed, part of the growth of antinuclear sentiment in the 1980s was the realization that the threatened use of nuclear weapons to defend a region like Western Europe against aggression actually risked destroying the region itself in a "limited nuclear war."

Nuclear deterrence has meant, above all, each side convincing the other that a first strike by one side on the other's homeland would be suicidal—causing the attacked state to retaliate with a devastating second strike on the aggressor. For such deterrent threats to be effective, the would-be aggressor must be convinced that the other side (1) would still have a second-strike capability left after absorbing the first blow, (2) would be willing to unleash the second strike, and (3) would be able to inflict "unacceptable damage" on the aggressor. Former U.S. Defense Secretary Robert McNamara maintained persuasively in the 1960s that *both* the United States and the Soviet Union should possess **mutual assured destruction (MAD)** capability, and that both should place their missiles in impenetrable silos or on undetectable submarines so that no first strike could disable them and prevent retaliation. The result presumably would be stable deterrence and peace.

Since the 1960s, American strategic posture has been that any disruption to stable deterrence should be avoided. Even such protective measures as building fallout shelters in U.S. cities have been discouraged. It is argued that shelters or **anti-ballistic missile (ABM)** defenses might signal to the opponent that one has the intention and capability of surviving a nuclear war, and therefore might be tempted to start one; this in turn could make one's adversary more trigger-happy and might cause them to contemplate a preemptive strike themselves. However, beginning with the Reagan administration and its proposed "Strategic Defense Initiative" (dubbed "Star Wars" by some), and continuing throughout the 1990s, advocates of ballistic missile defenses reasserted their demands for extensive measures to protect against attacks, particularly by smaller nuclear powers.

Technological advances have made it increasingly possible to destroy land-based missiles and even to detect submarines carrying **submarine-launched ballistic missiles (SLBMs).** At the same time, technological advances in radars, lasers, and other electronic systems tempt leaders to invest in missile defense projects. The cost, technical feasibility, and reliability of such defenses, as well as their effect on stable deterrence, have been hotly debated.

Aside from technology, the problem for nuclear strategy and arms control negotiations is whether one should rely on the logic of deterrence, or whether one should abandon MAD and move to a different form of security. It is still not certain whether the peace among major powers since 1945 has been attributable to the balance of terror or to other factors. The reader already has seen that the logic and "mind games" of deterrence can become extremely convoluted: "What do we think the opponent would think we think we could get away with if we took this action?" It has been clear since China attacked American forces in Korea in 1950, thereby facing possible retaliation by the world's preeminent nuclear power, that if a political goal is important enough to a government, it might even risk nuclear devastation to achieve it. Although leaders would be likely to hesitate before bringing on the incineration of their own societies, no one knows to what extent or for how long they would hesitate. One further complication for the coming decades is the uncertainty of "non-weaponized deterrence," such as that practiced by India and Pakistan. The meaning of concepts such as threat, security, risk, and stability in other non-Western cultures is relatively unexplored.[43]

Responses to Arms Race Problems: Arms Control Regimes

As noted in Chapters 9 and 10, the UN Charter essentially outlaws the use of armed force by states except in self-defense, provides alternative mechanisms whereby states can resolve their differences peaceably (through such vehicles as the World Court), and establishes enforcement procedures for applying sanctions against states should aggression occur (through the Security Council). The UN Charter, along with the machinery established by it, is a central component of a global regime for controlling violence. Regional organizations play a role as well. Related to this regime are a number of treaties and institutions dealing specifically with arms control.

As with the UN Charter itself, the arms control regime is imperfect. Not all states have ratified relevant agreements; even among those states that have, compliance can be erratic (as in the case of reporting accurate data for the UN arms register). Verification of whether agreements are being honored is often difficult. Many issues are not covered by agreements. Treaties expire and must be renewed. Nevertheless, global cooperation is emerging to lessen the worst effects of arms races.

One observer has maintained that "it seems that the agreements already concluded . . . are designed not to halt or reverse the arms race but rather to institutionalize it and regulate it."[44] However, this statement somewhat understates the degree of arms control that has occurred since World War II, especially since the late 1980s, when the United States and the Soviet Union committed themselves to the actual elimination of certain categories of existing nuclear weapons. The box on pages 436–438 lists major multilateral arms control agreements in effect in recent years. As one can see, numerous restrictions have been imposed on the testing, production, stockpiling, transfer, deployment, and use of various kinds of weapons.

The arms control regime can be divided into those agreements dealing with weapons of mass destruction, particularly nuclear weapons, and those concerning conventional armaments. The former category includes partial test bans, bans on the placement of nuclear weapons in certain locations and regions, prohibitions on the transfer of nuclear weapons from nuclear to non-nuclear states, and limitations on the size and nature of nuclear arsenals. Agreements on conventional weapons mainly include obligations by major powers to consult on the distribution of certain technologies and efforts to increase transparency in weapons transfers through data reporting.

A key element of the arms control regime is the **Nuclear Non-Proliferation Treaty (NPT) of 1970.** Nuclear states that are parties to the NPT are pledged not to transfer nuclear weapons to nuclear have-nots, while the latter are pledged not to acquire such weapons. Although the treaty has been ratified by almost all UN members, there remain a few holdouts, notably Pakistan, India, and Israel. A remarkable accomplishment was the agreement, in 1995 (as the NPT was about to expire), to renew the NPT in perpetuity. The nuclear powers had to overcome objections by many states that argued that the United States and other members of the nuclear club had not done enough to reduce their own nuclear arsenals and to adopt a comprehensive ban on any future nuclear testing. Negotiations are underway to replace the **Partial Test Ban Treaty of 1963,** which prohibited atmospheric testing of nuclear weapons but permitted underground testing, with a comprehensive test ban that would prevent further weapon developments and buildups; after having overcome the reluctance of France and China, the negotiators concluded a draft treaty in 1996 without the approval of India, which insisted that the nuclear states set a timetable for complete nuclear disarmament.[45]

Several regional nuclear weapon–free zone (NWFZ) agreements supplement the NPT in limiting the spread of weapons. Under these agreements, member states in the region agree not to develop nuclear weapons, and states outside the region agree not to introduce them into the region. By the late 1990s, at least five such zones had been established or were being negotiated. In Latin America, Argentina and Brazil, the chief nuclear candidates, renounced their nuclear aspirations and joined the Treaty of Tlatelolco in 1994. In the South Pacific, the Treaty of Rarotonga has created an NWFZ, although France has in-

FORMAL ARMS CONTROL AGREEMENTS
(STATUS AS OF 1995)

Antarctic Treaty   Declares the Antarctic an area to be used exclusively for peaceful purposes. Prohibits military bases, fortifications, maneuvers, and weapons testing there, as well as nuclear explosions and waste material storage, subject to possible future agreement. The question of territorial sovereignty in Antarctica has not definitely been resolved, although the contracting parties meet together periodically to discuss outstanding issues. Signed: 1959; entered into force: 1961; number of parties: 42.

Partial Test Ban Treaty   Prohibits nuclear weapons tests or any nuclear explosions in the atmosphere, outer space, and under water. It has helped curb radioactive pollution caused by nuclear fallout. But testing underground has continued, making it possible for parties to the treaty to develop new generations of nuclear warheads. May be replaced soon by a comprehensive test ban agreement that has been signed by many states but is not yet in force. Signed and entered into force: 1963; number of parties: 124.

Outer Space Treaty   Prohibits the emplacement in orbit around the earth of any objects carrying nuclear weapons or any kinds of weapons of mass destruction, the installation of such weapons on celestial bodies, or the stationing of them in outer space in any other manner. The establishment of military bases, installations, and fortifications, the testing of any type of weapons, and the conduct of military maneuvers on celestial bodies are also forbidden. Outer space has remained open, however, for the passage of ballistic missiles carrying nuclear weapons, and for the deployment of weapons not capable of mass destruction. Signed and entered into force: 1967; number of parties: 94.

Treaty of Tlatelolco   Prohibits nuclear weapons in Latin America. It thus established the first internationally recognized nuclear-weapon–free zone in a populated region of the world. Also, extraregional nuclear powers that are signatories undertake not to use or threaten to use nuclear weapons against the zonal states. Signed: 1967; entered into force: 1968; number of parties: 29 regional, 6 extraregional.

Treaty on the Non-Proliferation of Nuclear Weapons (NPT)   Prohibits the transfer of nuclear weapons by nuclear states and the acquisition of such weapons by non–nuclear weapon states. The latter are subject to IAEA safeguards to prevent diversion of nuclear energy from peaceful uses to nuclear explosive devices. The parties undertake to make the benefits of peaceful nuclear technology available to non-nuclear weapon states adhering to the treaty. Signed: 1968; entered into force: 1970, extended indefinitely under a 1995 agreement; number of parties: 179.

Sea-Bed Treaty   Prohibits emplacement on the sea-bed and the ocean floor and in the subsoil thereof beyond a twelve-mile zone of any nuclear weapon or other weapon of mass destruction, as well as structures or facilities for storing, testing, or using such weapons. However, the treaty presents no obstacle to a nuclear arms race in the whole of the marine environment. Signed: 1971; entered into force: 1972; number of parties: 92.

Biological Weapons Convention   Prohibits biological means of warfare, including development, production, and stockpiling of bacteriologic and toxin weapons, and calls for destruction of existing arsenals. Signed: 1972; entered into force: 1975; number of parties: 133.

Environmental Modification Convention   Bans military or other hostile use of techniques to produce "widespread," "long-lasting," or "severe" changes in weather patterns, ocean currents, the ozone layer, or ecological balance. Signed: 1977; entered into force: 1978; number of parties: 63.

Inhumane Weapons Convention   Bans the use of fragmentation bombs in the human body; bans the use against civilians of mines, booby traps, and incendiaries. Signed: 1981; entered into force: 1983; number of parties: 41.

Rarotonga Treaty   Bars the possession, testing, and use of nuclear weapons or dumping of nuclear waste in the South Pacific. Establishes a consultative committee to determine whether special inspections should be carried out. Spurred by continued French nuclear testing in the region. Signed and entered into force: 1986; number of parties: 11 regional, 5 extraregional.

Confidence-Building and Security-Building Measures and Disarmament in Europe Agreement   Requires prior notification and mandatory on-site inspection of conventional military exercises in Europe. Signed and entered into force: 1986; number of parties: 29.

Missile Technology Control Regime (MTCR)   Restricts and requires consultation on the export of ballistic missiles and related production facilities. Signed and entered into force: 1987; number of parties: 25.

Conventional Armed Forces in Europe Agreement   Limits five categories of weapons in Europe and reduces levels of forces. Signed: 1990; entered into force: 1992: number of parties: 30.

Confidence and Security-Building Measures Agreement   Provides for exchanges of detailed information on weapons, forces, and military exercises. Signed and entered into force: 1990; number of parties: 53.

Chemical Weapons Convention (CWC)   Builds on the 1925 Geneva Protocol that had prohibited the first use of chemical weapons but had permitted manufacture and stockpiling. Requires that all stockpiles of chemical weapons be destroyed within ten years. Establishes the Organization for the Prohibition of Chemical Weapons, to oversee implementation of the agreement and conduct inspections. Signed: 1993; entered into force 1997; number of parties: 147.

UN Register of Conventional Arms   Requires states to submit data on seven categories of major weapons exported or imported during the previous year. Signed: 1991; entered into force: 1993; number of parties: 80.

Sources: Based on Ruth L. Sivard, *World Military and Social Expenditures, 1989* (Washington, D.C.: World Priorities, 1989), p. 40; *SIPRI Yearbook 1995* (Oxford: Oxford University Press, 1995); and William Lewis and Stuart Johnson, eds., *Weapons of Mass Destruction: New Perspectives on Counter-Proliferation* (Washington, D.C.: National Defense University Press, 1995).

sisted on conducting nuclear tests in the area. In Southeast Asia, negotiations were entering their final stage in the late 1990s, whereas in the Middle East Israel has demanded the end of the threat of war with its neighbors before signing a pact. In South Asia, discussions have involved a "nuclear safe zone," which would allow Indian and Pakistani possession of weapons and would require formal admission of such possession. In Africa, although South Africa shut down its nuclear program in 1993, no regional pact has yet materialized. In addition to regional NWFZs, there are also current bans on the placement of nuclear weapons in orbit around the earth, on the moon, on the ocean floor, and in Antarctica. Thus, "when the membership of NPT is added to states participating in an NWFZ or considering joining an NWFZ, no nation is left untouched by nonproliferation efforts."[46]

Controversy surrounding nuclear arms control in the past has centered on the bilateral **Strategic Arms Limitation (SALT)** and **Strategic Arms Reduction (START) agreements** between the United States and the Soviet Union/Russia. The SALT I and SALT II agreements (1972 and 1977) set ceilings on the number of offensive nuclear launch vehicles (missiles and bombers) and "multiple independently targeted reentry vehicles" (MIRV warheads placed on missiles and bombers) each side could possess.[47] Whereas the SALT agreements permitted the two sides to add to their arsenals (up to the designated ceilings), the subsequent START negotiations, begun during the Reagan administration, called for actual *reductions* in launchers and MIRVs. (START followed an important breakthrough in 1988, with the signing of the Intermediate-Range Nuclear Forces Treaty that called for the United States and the Soviet Union to eliminate worldwide an entire class of missile systems with a range of 300 to 3,400 miles.) The START I accord, which entered into force through mutual ratification in 1994, obligates each side to get down to 6,000 strategic nuclear warheads over seven years. START II encountered difficulties in ratification on both sides. It set even lower warhead levels of no more than 3,000 to 3,500 on each side, and aimed to eliminate all land-based ICBMs carrying MIRVs.[48] As American and Russian arsenals proceeded downward, concern about the relative size of Chinese and European nuclear armaments made it difficult to devise further agreements without the participation of these states.

IN 1996, THE DEFENSE MINISTERS OF RUSSIA, UKRAINE, AND THE UNITED STATES PLANT SUNFLOWER SEEDS ON THE SITE OF A FORMER SOVIET MISSILE SILO AT A UKRAINE MILITARY BASE.

Control of nuclear weapons is incomplete without limits on potential warfare in outer space. The **Outer Space Treaty of 1967,** banning the placement of weapons of mass destruction in orbit around the earth or on celestial bodies, leaves certain gaps into which "hunter-killer" satellites, particle and laser beam generators, and partial orbit weapons could sail. Satellites have become vitally important as communications and intelligence links in monitoring enemy capabilities and verifying arms control agreements. If the aforementioned devices were used to disable an opponent's satellites, that side would become effectively blinded; threats of such an attack could provoke some sort of preemptive strike and heighten the chances of war. In 1981 at the UN, the Soviet Union proposed a treaty banning antisatellite (ASAT) weapons, but there was no favorable American response. A joint ASAT moratorium was unofficially observed, however, by both sides.[49]

The **Geneva Protocol of 1925** prohibits the first use of lethal biological and chemical weapons by the signatories against each other. Ratified by more than

100 states, the Protocol has been widely honored, although there have been recent troubling violations in the Middle East. The **Biological Weapons Convention of 1972,** also signed by more than one hundred states, goes further than the Geneva Protocol in outlawing germ warfare, insofar as it forbids not only the use of biological weapons but even their production and stockpiling. Hence, countries that are party to the agreement, such as the United States, have been obliged to destroy any biological arsenals in their possession. In this sense, the 1972 Convention is a measure not only of arms control but of actual disarmament. In an effort to extend the same blanket ban to chemical weapons, more than 140 countries have signed the **Chemical Weapons Convention of 1993,** calling for all parties to refrain from developing these weapons and requiring those parties already in possession of such weapons to dispose of them within a decade; the agreement entered into force in 1997, but still faces several implementation hurdles.[50]

Certain agreements in the arms control regime are less verifiable than others. The Biological Weapons Convention, for example, has no inspection machinery. Although the Chemical Weapons Convention has created the Organization for the Prohibition of Chemical Weapons to conduct on-site inspections and monitor compliance, a country suspected of violating the agreement must be given several days' notice before the inspectors enter one's borders, enough time perhaps for the government to hide violations; in addition, there are restrictions on access to factories producing herbicides, paints, and other consumer products that could have chemical weapons applications. By contrast, information on compliance is easier to obtain in the case of Antarctic demilitarization agreements, because all expeditions to the area must be reported and can be photographed. Notification of activities in outer space generally also is sent to the UN Secretary-General, although the exact nature of satellite missions often is withheld. The SALT I agreement became feasible after the perfection of satellite photography in the 1960s, which aided detection of cheating; even numbers of SLBMs could be estimated by counting ships going in and out of ports.

The **International Atomic Energy Agency (IAEA)** is responsible for monitoring the use of nuclear fuels and disposal of wastes consistent with the requirements of the NPT and NWFZ agreements. NPT signatories receiving nuclear fuels from other governments for power generation or research must return weapons-grade wastes (such as plutonium) to the donor country for disposal and must not use such fuels to manufacture weapons. The IAEA can inspect the civilian nuclear plants and warehouses of NPT signatories to detect any attempted diversion of fuels to weapons, and has placed photographic, TV, and other monitors in such plants for continuous surveillance. However, the ability of Iraq and North Korea—both NPT members—to develop nascent nuclear weapons programs that went undetected until the 1990s shows how treaty ratification does not assure compliance and how a determined government can circumvent the safeguards.[51]

Despite progress, verification remains a difficult feature of arms control. A special challenge in the future will be to monitor hard-to-detect high-tech weapons such as concealable cruise missiles and radar-evading "Stealth" planes and ships.[52] How can one be sure a party is not violating its treaty commitments? There is no totally reliable approach. Effective verification often depends on a combination of methods. Important violations have been detected both by supersophisticated techniques and by old-fashioned spies, inadvertent leaks of information in publications or conversations, and by careful analysis of aerial photography and technical data. It is important to bear in mind, as well, the importance governments frequently attach to making agreements work and to gaining a reputation for trustworthiness.

With all of its flaws, the arms control regime has produced some major benefits for humanity. For example, the Partial Test Ban Treaty of 1963 clearly improved the global environment by reducing atmospheric radiation and contamination of the food chain. It is important to remember that, before 1963, thermonuclear blasts equivalent to the destructive 1986 Chernobyl nuclear reactor fire in the Ukraine occurred routinely in the atmosphere several times a year. Then too, President Kennedy predicted in 1963 that within a decade as many as 25 states would be declared nuclear powers unless a non-proliferation agreement were signed. Given the fact that since the establishment of the NPT regime in 1970 not a single country (as of 1997) had been added to the official nuclear club, and several candidates had renounced their nuclear aspirations, the regime must be judged a success even if some holdouts remain.[53]

Conclusion

Peaceful solutions to the world's pressing conflicts are necessary if arms races are to be contained. The year 1990 marked the beginning of the Third UN Disarmament Decade, ushered in by the UN Disarmament Conference in Kyoto, Japan, which brought together political and technical experts to discuss various options for arms reductions. The decade of the 1990s actually saw some significant reductions, but also left leaders facing new arms control challenges. At an earlier UN Special Session in 1982, the General Assembly unanimously expressed its "profound preoccupation over the danger of war, in particular nuclear war, the prevention of which remains the most acute and urgent task of the present day." These sentiments were echoed by the Independent Commission for Disarmament and Security Issues (the Palme Commission), whose 1983 report, *Common Security*, linked military concerns to other concerns: "A doctrine of common security must replace the present expedient of deterrence through armaments. International peace must rest on a commitment to joint survival rather than a threat of mutual destruction. . . . The economic and social costs of military competition constitute strong reasons for countries to seek disarmament." Such conferences and commissions, even when they fail to produce substantive results, symbolize humanity's continued quest to fulfill the biblical prophesy that nations "shall beat their swords into plowshares, and their spears into pruning hooks . . . and neither shall they learn war anymore" (Isaiah 2:4).

Unfortunately, despite the arms control regime, weapons are likely to remain plentifully available in the coming years. One recurring nightmarish concern is that lethal weapons of mass destruction could end up in the possession of nonstate actors such as terrorist organizations. Arms control and antiterrorism regimes, then, seem intricately linked. As one nuclear strategist put it, referring to the danger of nuclear terrorism, "the best way to keep weapons and weapons-material out of the hands of nongovernmental entities is to keep them out of the hands of national governments."[54] In the next chapter we look at another dimension of the problem of controlling global violence as we consider the morally and politically complicated issues related to unorthodox forms of international violence.

SUMMARY

1. Improved technologies have vastly increased the ability of humans to do violence to each other in the international arena. Security as well as nonsecurity (economic and technological) concerns are involved in arms races. Arms can be used both to stabilize and destabilize crises situations.

2. Global military spending declined considerably between the late 1980s and 1990s, though still leaving considerable stocks of nuclear and conventional arms. Even if such weapons are never used, their enormous cost potentially diverts funds from more constructive social purposes. Developing countries, no less than developed countries, continue to insist on their right to arm; many LDCs rely on arms transfers from abroad. The Middle East and Asia have been the main arms-importing regions, with the United States the leading arms exporter.

3. Five states are members of the "nuclear club," with several others considered either unofficial members or in the process of developing nuclear weapons capabilities. Although American and Russian arsenals—which are roughly equal—dwarf those of other states, nuclear capability of any size represents tremendous damage potential.

4. Along with nuclear weapons, chemical and biological arms are considered weapons of mass destruction. Both are potentially as deadly as nuclear weapons and extremely difficult to police. The Biological Weapons Convention of 1972 and the Chemical Weapons Convention of 1993 are attempts to develop regimes in these areas.

5. Progress has been achieved in nuclear arms control, with significant reductions in U.S. and Russian arsenals, renunciation of nuclear ambitions by South Africa, Brazil, Argentina, and some other previously aspiring states, creation of nuclear weapon–free zones, renewal of the NPT, and movement toward a comprehensive test ban. However, matters are complicated by concerns about nuclear deterrence, by the feared breakdown in control over the movement of nuclear materials (especially in the former Soviet Union), and by a debate about the benefits of relying on a balance of terror as opposed to greater efforts to do away with or defend against nuclear weapons.

6. Given the mutual distrust among nation-states, arms control—i.e., reductions or restrictions in armaments—remains a more realistic solution to arms race problems than is complete disarmament. Agreements extend mainly to areas where actors have common interests or to issues of low-level concern. However, arms control remains difficult, given the state and nonstate actors who see benefits in weapons procurement, and given the problem of verification.

SUGGESTIONS FOR FURTHER READING AND STUDY

There are three major research groups that attempt to keep track of international arms levels. They use different definitions and measurements, however, and their estimates must be used carefully: (1) the Stockholm International Peace Research Institute (SIPRI), which publishes *Yearbooks* and specialized studies; (2) the International Institute for Strategic Studies (London), which annually publishes *World Military Balance*; (3) the U.S. Arms Control and Disarmament Agency (ACDA), which issues annual reports in *World Military Expenditures and Arms Transfers*. In addition, in recent years the Congressional Research Service of the Library of Congress has published global arms transfer data, and the UN Arms Register is an important new source of data on conventional armament. The U.S. Institute of Peace, the Arms Control Association (Washington), and the Council for Arms Control (London) publish series of topical studies. On the relative merits of different data sources, see Michael Brzoska, "Arms Transfer Data Sources," *Journal of Conflict Resolution*, 26 (March 1982), pp. 39–75.

For general studies of global armament, including the link between security and economic concerns, see Keith Krause, *Arms and the State: Patterns of Military Production and Trade* (Cambridge, UK: Cambridge University Press, 1992); Frederic S. Pearson, *The Global Spread of Arms: Political Economy of International Security* (Boulder, Colo.: Westview Press, 1994); Michael T. Klare and Daniel C. Thomas, *World Security: Trends and Challenges at Century's End*, 2nd ed. (New York: St. Martin's Press, 1994); Stuart A. Bremer and Barry B. Hughes, *Disarmament and Development: A Design for the Future?* (Englewood Cliffs, N.J.: Prentice-Hall, 1990); Nils Petter Gleditsch, Adne Cappelen, and Olav Bjerkholt, *The Wages of Peace: Disarmament in A Small Industrialized Economy* (London: Sage/International Peace Research Institute, Oslo, 1994); and Bonn International Center for Conversion, *Conversion Survey 1996: Global Disarmament, Demilitarization, and Demobilization* (Oxford, Eng.: Oxford University Press, 1996).

On the dangers of nuclear arms races, see Michael D. Wallace, Brian L. Crissey, and Linn I. Sinnott, "Accidental Nuclear War: A Risk Assessment," *Journal of Peace Research*, 23 (1986), pp. 9–27; Robert McNamara, *Blundering into Disaster: Surviving the First Century of the Nuclear Age* (New York: Pantheon, 1986); and various issues of the *Bulletin of the Atomic Scientists*.

Good discussions of nuclear, chemical, and biological weapons proliferation and control can be found in issues of *The Nonproliferation Review* (published by the Center for Nonproliferation Studies at the Monterey Institute of International Studies), and *Disarmament: A Periodic Review by the United Nations*. See also Morris McCain, *Understanding Arms Control* (New York: W. W. Norton, 1989); Jozef Goldblat, *Arms Con-*

trol: A Guide to Negotiations and Agreements (London: Sage/International Peace Research Institute, Oslo, 1994); Randall Forsberg, William Driscoll, Gregory Webb, and Jonathan Dean, *Nonproliferation Primer: Preventing the Spread of Nuclear, Chemical, and Biological Weapons* (Cambridge, Mass.: The MIT Press, 1995); Joseph Rotblat, Jack Steinberger, and Bhalchandra Udgaonkar, *A Nuclear-Weapon-Free World: Desirable? Feasible?* (Boulder, Colo.: Westview Press, 1993); J. B. Poole and R. Guthrie, eds., *Verification 1996: Arms Control, Peacekeeping, and the Environment* (Boulder, Colo.: Westview Press, 1996); Bruce D. Larkin, *Nuclear Designs: Great Britain, France, and China in the Global Governance of Nuclear Arms* (New Brunswick, N.J.: Transaction Books, 1996); and *Basic Papers* of the British-American Security Information Council, Washington, D.C.

Conventional arms proliferation and control are discussed in *Conventional Arms Transfer Restraint in the 1990s* (Washington, D.C.: Center for Defense Information, November 1994); Jeffrey Boutwell, Michael T. Klare, and Laura W. Reed, *Lethal Commerce: The Global Trade in Small Arms and Light Weapons* (Cambridge: American Academy of Arts and Sciences, 1995); and Robert E. Harkavy, "The Changing International System and the Arms Trade," *Annals of the American Academy of Political and Social Science* (September 1994), pp. 11–28. The characteristics of weapons and weapon-related programs are often described in the periodicals *Aviation Week and Space Technology; Jane's Defense Weekly; The Defense Monitor* (Center for Defense Information, Washington, D.C.); and *Defense News.*

The Control of Violence: Confronting Terrorism and Unorthodox Violence

On February 26, 1993, a bomb-laden van blew up in the parking garage under New York City's giant World Trade Center. The massive explosion created a 900-square-meter crater in the garage, and filled the 110th floor of the north tower with smoke. The blast, fire, and smoke caused six deaths and 1,000 injuries. This attack, subsequently attributed to Middle Eastern Islamic extremists, was perhaps the most spectacular of 431 reported international terrorist attacks that year. After declining by 25 percent in 1994, the world terrorism total advanced again to 440 in 1995; the most shocking incident that year probably was the March 20 nerve gas attack in the Tokyo subway system by Japanese Aum Shinrikyo cult members, killing twelve and injuring 5,500 people, including several foreigners, in the first major use of chemical weapons by terrorists.[1] The World Trade Center bombing (along with thwarted plans to destroy as well the Holland and Lincoln tunnels and the United Nations building in New York City) and the Tokyo gas attack highlight the challenge of terrorism both to analysts seeking explanations and to policymakers seeking remedies.

As indicated in Figure 12.1, although there has been a modest overall decline in international terrorism (i.e., terrorism involving the citizens or the

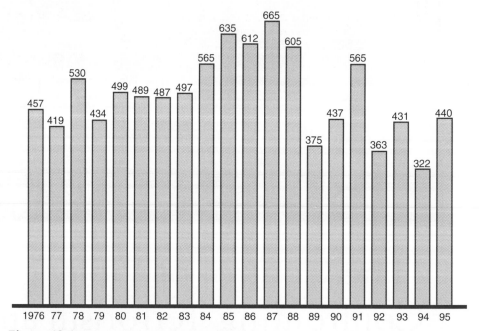

Figure 12.1
INTERNATIONAL TERRORIST INCIDENTS, 1976–1995
Source: U.S. Department of State, *Patterns of Global Terrorism, 1995* (Washington, D.C.: Office of Counterterrorism, U.S. Department of State, April 1996), p. 71.

territory of more than one country) since the mid-1980s, the incidence of such acts remains high.[2] For example, in 1995 there were almost 100 attacks on U.S. interests around the world. The detonated explosion of a gasoline tanker truck outside an American military housing compound in Dharan, Saudi Arabia, in June 1996, killing nineteen service personnel and leaving a thirty-five-foot crater, was a rude reminder of the vulnerability of U.S. outposts given widespread American commitments around the world.

As front-page headlines frequently remind us, terrorism continues to be a prominent global concern. However, there is considerable disagreement over what constitutes terrorism and what are the proper responses for combatting the problem. In this chapter, we seek to go beyond the headlines and explore the phenomenon in greater depth.[3] Our framework of analysis includes discussion of definitional questions, trends in international terrorism, and the dilemmas of combatting this form of political violence.

We are mainly interested here in terrorism as it occurs across national boundaries. However, there is also the matter of "state terrorism" that some governments practice against their own citizens and that may or may not spill over borders, as well as violence perpetrated by groups within a society against the civil order. Indeed, domestic terrorism, such as the recent Kurdish Workers' Party attacks on Turkish governmental targets and the 1995 bombing of the Oklahoma City federal building in the United States, seems to be on the rise relative to international terrorism, just as we saw in Chapter 8 that civil wars have tended to displace interstate wars. There are growing efforts by the international community to address both the external and internal dimensions of terrorism, and the problem of controlling "unorthodox violence" in general. These efforts relate to another global concern, the promotion of human rights, a subject we discussed in Chapter 9 and that we touch on here also.

The Nature and Magnitude of the Problem

DEFINITIONAL QUESTIONS

Among scholars, lawyers, and policymakers, there is no general agreement on a clear definition of **terrorism;** indeed, one study notes that the term had at least 109 different definitions between 1936 and 1981, and many others have appeared since.[4] This is partly because the term itself is so highly charged emotionally that it has become an epithet hurled by opponents at each other.[5] Not everyone would concur that all the incidents noted above necessarily were the acts of terrorists. It has been said that one person's "terrorist" is another person's "freedom fighter." According to this logic, the American revolutionaries participating in the Boston Tea Party could have been considered terrorists, at least in the eyes of the British authorities they were trying to

overthrow. Likewise, Yassir Arafat and his followers in the Palestine Liberation Organization (PLO), fighting against Israeli occupation of what they consider their homeland, contend that it has been hypocritical for Israeli leaders
such as Menachem Begin and Yitzhak Shamir to denounce the PLO as "mur-
dering terrorists"; Begin and Shamir themselves had engaged in violent acts as
leaders of the Israeli pre-independence underground movements (the Irgun and
Stern Gang) that struggled against the British and the Arabs in the late 1940s.[6]

However, if one accepts the view that "one person's terrorist is another's
national liberation hero" and that the distinction is completely arbitrary and
dependent on which side of the fence one sits on, then any act of violence can
be excused and legitimized so long as someone invents a justification. Aside
from being a recipe for chaos and anarchy, this type of logic ignores the principle that not all acts of violence are equally acceptable and condonable. At a
minimum, certain acts, such as the infamous shooting and pushing of wheel-
chair-bound Leon Klinghoffer, a Jewish-American passenger on the *Achille
Lauro* oceanliner, into the sea during a 1985 Palestinian hijacking, seem so
barbaric and insensitive to universal standards of civilized behavior that one
can reasonably label such acts "terrorist" in nature.[7]

Terrorism can be usefully defined from both legal and political perspectives. Either way, the definition ought to help draw critical distinctions between justifiable "insurgency" and terrorism and should capture the profound
anxiety and dread that the act of terrorism is designed to bring about in the
target. One writer defines terrorism as follows:

> the threat, practice or promotion of force for political objectives by organi-
> zations or a person(s) whose actions are designed to influence the political
> attitudes or policy dispositions of a third party, provided that the threat,
> practice or promotion of force is directed against: (1) non-combatants; (2)
> military personnel in non-combatant or peacekeeping roles; (3) combat-
> ants, if the aforementioned violates juridical principles of proportionality,
> military necessity and discrimination; or (4) regimes which have not com-
> mitted egregious violations of the human rights regime that approach
> Nuremberg category crimes. Moreover, the act itself elicits a set of images
> that serve to denigrate the target population while strengthening the indi-
> vidual or group simultaneously.[8]

A simpler definition considers terrorism "the use of violence for purposes
of political extortion, coercion, and publicity for a political cause."[9] This definition suggests that terrorism entails a combination of at least three elements:
First, terrorism ordinarily involves the threatened or actual use of *unconventional violence*—violence that is spectacular, violates accepted social mores,
and is designed to *shock* so as to gain publicity and instill fear. Terrorists generally observe no "rules" of combat whatsoever (such as the rules of the
Geneva Convention governing treatment of POWs); there are virtually no limits to the degree or type of violence they are prepared to use.[10] In addition to

bombings and hijackings, their tactics can include kidnappings, assassinations, and even injections of deadly substances. (In 1978, a Bulgarian journalist was stabbed in a London subway with an umbrella treated with a deadly toxin derivative of castor beans.) Such acts need not even be costly: would-be terrorists need only the price of a phone call, because they can *threaten* any of the above acts and, if believed, achieve the desired effect.

Terrorism is characterized, secondly, not only by unconventional violence but also by violence that is *politically* motivated. The political context of terrorism distinguishes it from mere criminal behavior such as armed robbery or gangland slayings, which may be every bit as bizarre or spectacular but which are driven primarily by nonpolitical (private rather than public) motives. One would not ordinarily call the Mafia, for example, a terrorist organization—even though it is heavily involved in international drug trafficking and other criminal activities, at times in league with terrorist groups—precisely because its existence and activities are not motivated by any recognizable political goals.[11] The distinction becomes somewhat blurred, though, in the case of the assassinations of government officials, such as those carried out by Colombia's Cali cartel, because the latter has been basically a Mafia-like criminal conspiracy to extort money through the drug trade and paralyze law enforcement through terror, in the process threatening the political viability of an entire nation-state. This type of quasi-political, criminally related terrorism, which also has been seen in parts of Italy and other countries, has been labeled "narco-terrorism" and has drawn a widespread international response. Incidents such as the *Achille Lauro* affair and others noted at the outset of this chapter, however, are more clearly motivated by political goals, ranging from the creation of a national homeland to the elimination of foreign cultural influence in a region to the total political and economic transformation of society. One can debate whether these goals are legitimate, and whether "political" offenses committed in pursuit of these goals should be punished in the same manner as "criminal" offenses, but in any case the inherently political nature of terrorism must be understood.

A third key distinguishing characteristic of terrorism, following from the first two, is the almost incidental nature of the *targets* against whom violence is committed. That is, the immediate targets of terrorism—whether persons or property, civilian or military—usually bear only an indirect relation to the larger aims impelling the terrorist, but represent considerable shock potential. Sometimes the targets are carefully chosen individuals—well-known business leaders, government officials, or diplomats, such as the oil ministers at a 1975 OPEC meeting in Vienna who were held hostage by the notorious international terrorist named "Carlos the Jackal"; at other times the targets are faceless, nondescript masses—ordinary men, women, and children, as in the random slaughter that has occurred in airports, department stores, and other public places. In any case, the victims generally are chosen for their symbolic value and are merely pawns used in violence that is staged with the intent of reaching a much wider audience and pressuring for desired concessions.[12]

One might add a fourth ingredient of terrorism, having to do with the nature of the *perpetrators* of such violence. It can be argued, with some qualifications, that organized terrorism is an activity engaged in essentially by *non-state* actors; i.e., it is mainly the tactic of "outgroups" denied legitimate status and of the politically weak and frustrated (e.g., the *Hizballah* Islamic faction in Lebanon or the Irish Republican Army in Northern Ireland), who see terror as the best tool for contesting the sizable armies and police forces of the governments of nation-states, or as the best means of discrediting rival groups that may have foresworn violence.[13]

One wonders what motivates or possesses dedicated young members of a terrorist organization to strap hundreds of pounds of explosives to their body, cross a crowded street, and detonate themselves on or near a packed bus, as happened in Israeli cities in the run-up to national elections in 1996. Is this the act of a crazed zealot or a self-styled calculating "soldier"? Is terrorist violence rational or irrational by the standards we mentioned in Chapter 8? Certainly the Jerusalem bus bombers aimed to upset the momentum of the Israeli-Arab peace process by creating such terror that the Israeli public would vote against leaders thought to be too accommodative, and by provoking such harsh Israeli reprisals that Arabs would lose hope for the process as well. The young Israeli extremist who assassinated Prime Minister Rabin in late 1995 probably had similar intentions.[14] Given organized indoctrination, and the frustrations of continued perceived injustices, young terrorists can be convinced both of the tactical advantages of their acts and of their ultimate place as heroes or martyrs in heaven. Thus, terrorist acts generally are well planned and aimed at achieving specific outcomes, even at high personal costs; the costs may well go beyond what "normal" people would pay.[15]

It is true, of course, that governments frequently use violence and armed force, either internally as part of the "police" function or externally as part of the "defense" or "security" function. Although certain excessive forms of violence used by authorities are sometimes referred to as "state terrorism"—in particular, the systematic torture and repression a government inflicts on dissidents within its own society, or assassinations and "dirty tricks" committed by secret state agencies abroad—the terrorism label normally does not apply to actions taken by official government bodies.[16] For example, although some have called the dropping of the atomic bomb on Hiroshima in 1945 an act of terrorism—because it represents to them seemingly indiscriminate violence against innocent civilians—this is more accurately designated an act of interstate warfare. It should be added that many governments do at least indirectly support and sponsor terrorist groups. Syria, Iran, and Libya have been accused of harboring terrorists, looking the other way at their exploits or at times encouraging them to act, in support of government objectives in the anti-Israeli and anti-Western struggles of the Middle East.[17]

TRENDS IN INTERNATIONAL TERRORISM

Terrorism is not a new phenomenon. The term itself can be traced to the Reign of Terror during the French Revolution in the eighteenth century. It was a terrorist's bullet that set off World War I with the assassination of Austria's Archduke Franz Ferdinand. A classic historical example of prolonged terrorism is the struggle of the Irish Republican Army (IRA) to pressure Britain to grant independence to Ireland, beginning with the Easter Rebellion of 1916, continuing through the establishment of the Irish Republic (Eire), and extending into contemporary times in Northern Ireland.

Although terrorism is not new, it is a more serious concern today in several respects. Modern industrial society seems especially vulnerable to spectacular displays of violence, given such inviting targets as jumbo jets, nuclear power stations, and computer networks. The existence of modern communications technology enables terrorists to receive instant publicity through the world's mass media and can contribute to an epidemic effect worldwide. This same technology enables terrorists to operate on a global scale. Today's hijackers, bombers, and other terrorists often have strong international ties that permit them to coordinate their efforts in various regions.

The U.S. State Department has estimated that a total of almost 6,000 international terrorist incidents occurred during the 1980s, and more than 2,500 between 1990 and 1995.[18] We noted earlier in the chapter, as reflected in Figure 12.1, a slight decline over time in the annual levels of terrorism. There has been a movement away from hijackings and kidnappings toward greater reliance on bombings and other types of assault. Ironically, despite the frequency of terrorist attacks, most such attacks have resulted in relatively few casualties. There were approximately 4,000 terrorist-related deaths and 11,000 injuries altogether during the 1980s, averaging less than one death and two injuries per incident.[19] Terrorism is politically effective not so much because of mass killings, but because of the psychological effect of not knowing where and when the killing will take place, and because of the attackers' capability of choosing prominent and highly valued targets.

A regional breakdown of terrorist acts shows the most incidents occurring in the Middle East and Western Europe. In the mid-1990s, for example, Western Europe experienced the most terrorism, with 272 incidents in 1995, only eleven of which resulted in one or more deaths. However, mass killing in Europe, by snipers and paramilitary forces, was all too evident during the 1990s in the ethnic carnage of the Bosnian war. After Europe, terrorism was greatest in the Middle East and Latin America. The spectacular Rabin assassination, a continued series of Palestinian suicide bombings in Israel, and attacks on U.S. forces garnered the main headlines, but Algerian and Egyptian Islamic militants also continued a campaign against what they perceived as political repression in their countries with attacks on tourists and government installations.[20]

As the World Trade Center incident showed, terrorism has risen in North America, though the region continues to be relatively free of such attacks. North America has been the scene of a low-profile series of threats and attacks, such as the expulsion of a Libyan embassy official in what was alleged to be an assassination plot against anti-Qaddafi activists in the United States in 1995, Salvadoran right-wing agents terrorizing antigovernment Salvadoran activists in California in 1987, and the seizure of five dissident Sikhs by Canadian authorities in an alleged plan to bomb an Air India jet en route from New York to New Delhi in 1986. More frequently than incidents on U.S. soil, American citizens and property abroad have been targeted, with the largest share of anti-American attacks taking place in Latin America, Asia, and Western Europe. "Between 1976–86, for example, American officials or installations abroad were attacked by 'terrorists,' on the average, once every seventeen days."[21] Among the other "most victimized nationalities" in recent years have been the British, French, Israelis, Iraqis, and Libyans.[22]

One reason that terrorism has been such a popular pursuit over the years is that it has often produced precisely those results sought by terrorists, at least in terms of attracting vast international attention to themselves and their causes. For example, the bombing and other acts of violence carried out by various Palestinian nationalist groups in the past, although technically not always successful in achieving political objectives, clearly helped make "Palestinian" a household word throughout the world. In addition to attracting attention, terrorism also frequently has paid off in concrete terms. Terrorists generally have been remarkably successful in achieving their immediate goals relative to the costs incurred. One study of sixty-three major kidnappings and barricade operations between 1968 and 1974 produced the following statistics: terrorists had an 87 percent success rate in seizing hostages; there was a 79 percent probability of all members of the terrorist team involved in an operation escaping punishment or death, a 40 percent chance that at least some of their demands would be met, a 29 percent chance of full compliance with their demands, and an almost 100 percent probability of obtaining major publicity. Another study showed that terrorists suffered casualties in only 14 percent of all incidents.[23]

Conversely, many of these statistics reflect only short-term success for terrorists. Larger causes and ultimate political goals are rarely realized through terrorist methods. As one student of terrorism has put it: "Terrorism has indeed resulted in political change, but it has had a lasting effect only in fairly rare circumstances when political mass movements used terrorist tactics in the framework of a wider strategy. There is no known case in modern history

THE CENTRAL SHOPPING DISTRICT IN MANCHESTER, ENGLAND, WHERE AN IRISH REPUBLICAN ARMY TRUCK BOMB EXPLODED IN JUNE 1996, WOUNDING MORE THAN 200 PEOPLE.

of a small terrorist group seizing political power; society usually tolerates terrorism only so long as it is no more than a nuisance."[24] In the words of a bystander who was sitting in a cafe during the 1996 truck bombing of a central shopping district in Manchester, England, "It doesn't work. We are not scared. It makes people more determined not to give in to them."[25]

Although some groups, in their rise to political respectability and influence, have renounced the use of terrorism (such as the PLO and some factions of the IRA in the mid-1990s), there is reason for continued concern. Although there has been much rejoicing over the rise of "pro-democracy" movements around the globe and over the loosening of one-party rule and centrally controlled economies, in the process the long-suppressed aspirations of ethnic minorities and other groups within these societies have again risen to the surface, holding out the prospect of increased communal violence and resort to terror by those seeking to advance secessionist and other causes. Rapid social and economic change has often been associated with violence.[26] The prospect of counterterror by state authorities seeking to maintain order likewise looms large. There has been increased terrorist activity, for example, in Africa, where ethnic divisions, economic deprivation, and security problems along with relatively weak governments nourish such activity, including rampaging local militia and paramilitary groups with members as young as 10 years of age.

The Politics of Combatting Terrorism

Terrorism, then, continues to pose a serious threat because of the disruptive violence and fear it generates within and across national boundaries. Efforts to combat the problem have come up against a variety of competing interests represented by nonstate as well as nation-state actors. In this section, we look further into the motivations and demands involved in terrorism, and the politics surrounding the attempt to forge a global counterterrorist consensus.

THE DILEMMAS OF COMBATTING TERRORISM

On May 9, 1978, Italian police found the crumpled, bullet-ridden body of former Italian Prime Minister Aldo Moro in the trunk of a car, after weeks of desperate searching for his kidnappers, who had identified themselves as the Red Brigades, a group intent on overhauling all of Italy's societal institutions. The Italian government, composed of some of Moro's closest friends and former colleagues, had refused to deal with the terrorists or consider their demands and had ignored Moro's poignant letters pleading for assistance. Aldo Moro, one of the most noted of history's terrorist victims, was "tried and convicted" by a "People's Court" and executed by its order. (Moro's kidnappers were themselves sentenced to life imprisonment by an Italian court in 1983.)[27]

The Moro case illustrates the perplexing dilemmas that can be experienced in the attempt to control terrorism. The Italian government was roundly criticized by some for inflexibly refusing to negotiate for the life of a statesman. Yet, the leaders reasoned that any negotiations under such duress would encourage future kidnappings and put national leaders as well as ordinary citizens at further risk. The horrifying impact of the Moro murder hardened the Italian authorities, so that when the same Red Brigades group four years later expanded their operations into the international arena and kidnapped American NATO General James Dozier, the Italian government's refusal to negotiate, along with a well-coordinated manhunt, resulted in the freeing of the hostage and the deaths of the terrorists. It also resulted in the decline of the Red Brigades, as most of the leaders either were imprisoned or fled the country; an organization that had numbered in the hundreds had been reduced to a mere handful.

Although the Italian authorities' success in combatting the Red Brigades suggests the virtues of adopting a hard-line strategy toward terrorists, the dilemmas have not been eliminated. Other groups, both indigenous to Italy and of external origin, came to fill whatever void was left by the demise of the Red Brigades.[28] Hard-line strategies may or may not discourage or deter terrorism in specific cases. It is also not clear that negotiations generally encourage terrorists to be any bolder than they otherwise would be. However, ill-conceived negotiations may lead to fiascos, such as the Iran-Contra affair during the Reagan administration, which was a hostage negotiation (for U.S. intelligence officials and journalists held by Islamic militants in Lebanon) gone wrong (with misguided efforts to sell arms to Iran in return for influence on the terrorists, and a plan to use the revenue from the arms for illegal aid to right-wing "contra" rebels in Nicaragua).

Terrorism is difficult to combat as a political tactic for a variety of reasons. Many terrorist groups are tightly organized by cells, so that the members do not know the identity of members of other cells or those in command, and therefore cannot expose them under interrogation or torture.[29] Elaborate routines are developed to separate advanced teams of planners from those actually entrusted with the execution of terrorist actions, with only the top leadership knowing the various elements of the organization. Many countries prepare specially trained counterterrorist squads, and private security firms also are employed to train business executives and public officials in methods to avoid terrorist attack. Many of the directions given to potential victims—such as varying their schedules and routes to and from work—can become as complex as the plans used by terrorist cells themselves. These efforts seem worthwhile, yet if the fight against terrorism is carried beyond certain limits, basic human and civil rights can be abridged and endangered. Governments must balance the costs of terrorism against the costs of the political repression necessary to stop it. Does the population want constant searches in public places and private homes, with troops lining the streets? Can a democracy survive using such means? Troublesome as these domestic political issues are, the international politics of combatting terrorism pose still further difficulties, as we will see in the following discussion.

"FREEMASONRY"[30] OF TERRORISTS: ACTORS, TARGETS, AND LINKAGES

Who are the most important actors involved in terrorism, and what are their goals, targets, and interrelationships? We have noted that organized terrorism is mainly the tactic of "outgroups," such as the Red Brigades, seeking to upset the established order in some fashion. Distinctions among terrorist groups can be made according to their goals, which include (1) creation of new states (e.g., Bosnian Serbs in the former Yugoslavia, Basques in

Spain, Kurds in Iraq and Iran, Chechens in the former Soviet Union, and at one time during the 1970s, the Front de Liberation de Quebec in Canada); (2) destruction of existing states (e.g., Hamas and various factions of the Popular Front for the Liberation of Palestine); (3) liberation of territory from the control of others (e.g., historically, the Armed Forces for National Liberation of Puerto Rico, and the Irish Republican Army); (4) subversion of regimes (e.g., Marxist groups such as the Philippine New People's Army, M-19 and other guerrillas in Colombia, and Shining Path in Peru); (5) elimination of foreign cultural influence from a region (e.g., Islamic Jihad); and (6) complete transformation of the world political and economic order (e.g., Red Brigades, Red Army Faction, which succeeded the Badermeinhoff Gang in Germany during the 1980s, United Red Army in Japan, and Action Direct in France).[31]

Terrorist organizations often experience internal dissension among their membership over goals and strategies, so that splinter factions, such as those within the Palestinian movement, can develop and produce a further proliferation of groups. Because of frustrations over unfulfilled political expectations, the Palestinian movement has splintered into groups more or less willing to indulge in terrorism and more or less committed to secular precepts (such as the PLO) or religious precepts (such as Hamas). One recent empirical study of Middle East terrorism examined the behavior patterns and targeting practices of various types of terrorist groups. Among the variables thought to affect targetting, for example, were political ideology, group size, group age, location, and type of terrorist action. Results suggested a systematic relationship between certain of these variables and choice of targets, with the overwhelming number of targets being civilians rather than government installations. Among Islamic or Arab groups, highly ideological or theocratic terrorists more frequently targeted government targets (installations or officials), whereas newer or splinter groups, and those committed more to concrete goals such as acquisition of territory, tended to aim at civilian targets. Jewish extremist groups, by contrast, tended to attack civilian targets but with less intensity, producing, on average, fewer deaths and less property damage, because usually they were operating in "friendly" territory.[32]

Figure 12.2, based on the latter study, lists the main Middle Eastern groups that have practiced terrorism since 1968. The figure shows the relative frequency of attacks by different groups. The fact that, despite terrorists' interest in notoriety, responsibility for most acts goes unclaimed further hampers efforts to control or limit terrorism.

Clearly, the politics of controlling international terrorism is complicated by the fact that the world's governments are not universally opposed to terrorism, or at least do not all define it in the same way. In UN General Assembly sessions and in other forums where controls on international terrorism have been discussed, states have often taken conflicting positions. In the early 1970s, the United States introduced a draft convention on terrorism requiring the extradition or prompt trial of hijackers and kid-nappers, especially in cases in which hostages were government officials. Generally, the United States and other industrialized states favored the principle that terrorists are criminals and that the world community shares a responsibility to apprehend them and bring them to trial. In con-trast, less developed states, while deploring the deaths of innocent vic-tims, tended to argue that terrorism is often the only available weapon of the oppressed, and that before it can be outlawed, measures should be adopted to rectify the political and economic injustices perpetrated partic-ularly by industrialized states and their allies. The latter argument, for ex-ample, was invoked to condone PLO violence against Israel and to justify support for rebel groups in Southern Africa. Latin American countries and other developing countries were also concerned about the traditional right of states to offer asylum to "political prisoners" on the run and seeking po-litical sanctuary.

The ultimate fate of the American draft convention and of similar measures to deal with unorthodox violence is discussed later in our examination of in-ternational responses to the problem. It has often taken nonstate actors to move the international community toward some acceptance of controls on terrorism. One cannot fully describe the politics of controlling skyjacking, for example, without noting the role of an IGO such as the International Civil Aviation Organization (ICAO) in helping to draft anti-skyjacking conventions, as well as the role of the NGO such as the International Federation of Air Line Pilots Associations (IFALPA) in pressuring governments to adopt stronger air safety measures and to refuse asylum to skyjackers. It was IFALPA—in essence, a transnational labor union—that threatened not to fly into countries harboring skyjackers, after a particularly brutal murder of a Lufthansa Airlines pilot during a 1977 skyjacking. The IFALPA action, combined with pressure from the United States and other governments, resulted in a token but nonetheless unprecedented UN General Assembly resolution condemning aerial hijacking.

Responses to Terrorism: Anti-Terrorism Regimes

It is possible for countries individually to develop improved capabilities for combatting terrorism. Counterterrorist techniques might include launching preemptive strikes against terrorist bases before terrorists can act; launching retaliatory strikes against such bases after terrorist incidents, both for punish-ment and deterrent purposes; improving intelligence-gathering methods so as to penetrate and subvert terrorist groups; fortifying and protecting likely ter-rorist targets such as embassies and airports; and creating elite rescue and counterterrorist units capable of intervening in hostage-taking and other crisis

Name of Group

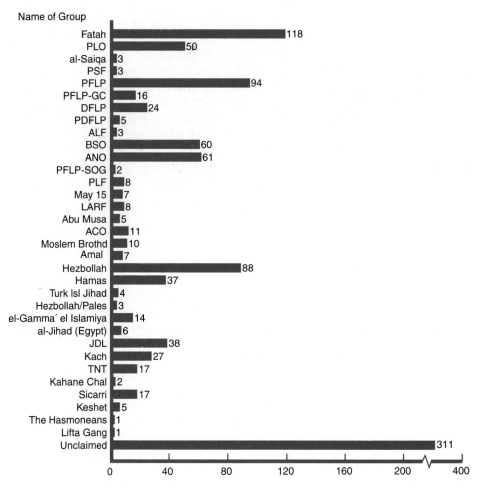

Group	Value
Fatah	118
PLO	50
al-Saiqa	3
PSF	3
PFLP	94
PFLP-GC	16
DFLP	24
PDFLP	5
ALF	3
BSO	60
ANO	61
PFLP-SOG	2
PLF	8
May 15	7
LARF	8
Abu Musa	5
ACO	11
Moslem Brothd	10
Amal	7
Hezbollah	88
Hamas	37
Turk Isl Jihad	4
Hezbollah/Pales	3
el-Gamma´ el Islamiya	14
al-Jihad (Egypt)	6
JDL	38
Kach	27
TNT	17
Kahane Chal	2
Sicarri	17
Keshet	5
The Hasmoneans	1
Lifta Gang	1
Unclaimed	311

0   40   80   120   160   200   400

Arab/Islamic Militant Groups
- Fatah 1959
- Palestine Liberation Organization (PLO) 1964
- al-Saiqa 1966
- Popular Struggle Front (PSF) 1967
- Popular Front for the Liberation of Palestine (PFLP) 1967
- PFLP General Command (PFLP-GC) 1968
  (PLFP splinter group)
- Democratic Front for the Liberation of Palestine
  DFLP) 1969 (PFLP splinter group a.k.a. PDFLP)
- Arab Liberation Front (ALF) 1969
- Black September Organization (BSO)
  1971–1974 (i.e., Fatah)
- Abu Nidal Organization (ANO) @ 1973
  (PLO/Fatah splinter group)
- PFLP-SOG. PFLP-Special Operations @ 1974
  PLFP splinter group)
- Palestine Liberation Front (PLF) 1976
  (A PFLP-GC splinter group)
- Arab Organization of 15 May 1979
- Lebanese Armed Revolutionary Faction (LARF) 1979
- Abu Musa Faction 1983 (Fatah splinter group)
- Arab Communist Organization* (ACO)

- Moslem Brotherhood (1928 Egypt, 1946 Palestine)
- Amal @ 1975 (Splinter groups: Islamic Amal 1982;
  Youth of ´Ali @ 1975–76)
- Hezbollah 1983
- Hamas @ 1987
- Turkish Islamic Jihad late 1980s
- Hezbollah/Palestine @ 1991
- el-Gamma´ el Islamiya*
- Al-Jihad (Egypt)*

Jewish Militant Groups
- The Jewish Defense League (JDL) 1968
- Kach (JDL splinter group) 1971
- Terror Against Terror (TNT) @ 1980
- Kahane Chal (Kach splinter group) @ 1990
- the Sicarri*
- Keshet*
- The Hasmoneans*
- Lifta Gang

situations. (See the Sidelight on "SWAT Teams and Nuclear Terrorists" on pages 460–461.) The success of such measures depends very much on circumstances, as those hunting for hostages in places like Iran and Lebanon have discovered; terrorist bases seldom can be isolated from the surrounding countryside, and attacking them in foreign countries can have serious political consequences.

Because of the international character of much contemporary terrorism, unilateral efforts by governments to combat the problem are not as likely to succeed as concerted efforts of governments acting together. As with the arms control regime, steps to control international terrorism have involved mainly the drafting of treaties.[33] National and international judicial institutions have also come into play because terrorism cannot be stopped without the arrest, trial, extradition, or jailing of the perpetrators. Under international law, a state traditionally has been free to choose whether to return fugitives sought by other states, to prosecute those individuals in its own courts, or to set them free. Only if a state has an extradition treaty with another state does it incur obligations to surrender fugitives, although even these treaties normally do not require the return of those accused of "political" crimes. However, the concept of global responsibility for preventing certain wanton acts of terror and for apprehending terrorists has been slowly gaining acceptance in recent years. Even bitter rivals such as the United States and Cuba have agreed on the need to control hijackings and assassinations, to protect diplomats, and to extradite or refuse asylum to terrorists.

Increased global concern about terrorism was particularly evident after the slaughter of Israeli athletes by Palestinian commandos at the 1972 Olympic Games in Munich. This led to efforts to prevent both kidnappings and assassinations, especially of so-called internationally protected persons (diplomats and other national representatives). The UN General Assembly passed a resolution on the status of such persons in 1973, and a UN Convention on the Pre-

Figure 12.2
THE RELATIVE FREQUENCY OF MIDDLE EAST TERRORIST ATTACKS BY TERRORIST GROUP, 1968–1993
An underlying problem for analysis is that comparatively little information is available about many of the terrorist proto-groups/groups marked here with an asterisk. Information about terrorist groups and group-types can be found in the source for this figure, Richard J. Chasdi, *The Dynamics of Middle East Terrorism, 1968–1993: A Functional Typology of Terrorist Group Types,* Ph.D. Dissertation, Purdue University, 1995, Figs. 6.3, 6.4, and 6.8. In addition to works cited there, the following additional sources were used by Chasdi to obtain data on terrorist group splitting: As'ad AbuKahalil, "Lebanon," in Frank Tachau, ed., *Political Parties of the Middle East and North Africa* (Westport, Conn.: Greenwood Press, 1994); and Michael R. Fischbach, "The Palestinians," in Tachau.

SIDELIGHT

SWAT TEAMS AND NUCLEAR TERRORISTS

It might be hard to picture at this juncture in American history, but there are times, even now, when working for the government can be exciting. Consider a secret Department of Energy training exercise—code name: Mirage Gold—that was staged in New Orleans in October 1994. Hundreds of normally lab-bound nuclear scientists fanned out through the French Quarter carrying briefcases with hidden radiation detectors, while rental vans packed with high-tech electronics roamed the streets and planes fitted with spy cameras swooped overhead. After three days, they found what they were hunting for: a simulated nuclear weapon hidden on a nearby naval base.

There is more to these games than merely giving government employees the chance to play James Bond. The point is to test the preparedness of a secretive task force organized to combat the possibility—eventuality, some would say—of nuclear terrorism in the U.S. Welcome to Fail Safe, the post–cold war edition.

Until now, and hopefully for a long time to come, the spectacle of the U.S. government being blackmailed by nuclear terrorists has been the province of books, movies (including a . . . John Travolta film) and . . . attention-getting commercials by attention-needing presidential candidate[s]. . . . Of course, the appeal of nuclear weapons to terrorists is obvious: if destabilizing society or drawing attention to one's cause is the goal, a mushroom cloud outranks truck bombs and sarin [gas] attacks. . . .

vention and Punishment of Crimes Against Internationally Protected Persons Including Diplomatic Agents was opened for ratification in the same year. A UN Committee on International Terrorism also was established. Eventually, after many years of debate—particularly on terrorism's role in national liberation struggles—an International Convention Against the Taking of Hostages was drafted in 1979; during the 1980s, more than forty countries, including the United States, signed it. The convention provides that states shall prosecute or extradite all hostage-takers, though rights of national liberation movements are recognized.[34]

Three other conventions, developed by the International Civil Aviation Organization, specifically address crimes relating to air travel. The **Tokyo Convention of 1963** obligates signatory states to effect the safe release of hijacked aircraft, passengers, and crews entering their borders. The **Hague Convention of 1970** goes further in requiring states to extradite or prosecute hijackers in their custody. The **Montreal Convention of 1971** broadens the Hague provisions to include not only skyjackers but anyone committing any acts of sabo-

NEST [Nuclear Emergency Search Team] was formed in 1975 after an extortionist threatened to blow up Boston with a nuclear device unless he was paid $200,000. Since then, NEST has evaluated 110 threats, and mobilized itself to deal with about 30 of them; like the Boston incident, all have been hoaxes. Yet NEST is more than a high-tech SWAT team. At the remote Pajarito site in the Los Alamos Nuclear Weapons Laboratory complex in New Mexico, 17 scientists are using technology found on the shelves of Radio Shack and the type of nuclear fuel sold on the black market to construct homemade bombs. To dismantle a makeshift device, scientists first must know the various ways in which it might be constructed; so far, the team has assembled more than a dozen. . . .

In various game-playing scenarios, NEST has imagined itself presenting the President of the U.S. with the worst choices of his life, choices he may have only minutes to make. In one apparently plausible scenario, there is a 10% chance that if NEST tries to defuse a bomb it will accidentally detonate with its full 10-kiloton yield, which would vaporize a mere 10,000 citizens. It will be cold comfort for survivors to know that the government has a special emergency room for just this eventuality at the Methodist Medical Center in Oak Ridge, Tennessee.

Some nuclear scientists like John Nuckolls, associate director at the DOE's Livermore lab, believe that America's nuclear preparedness team will eventually have to join others overseas in an international NEST force. "The destruction of any city in the world by nuclear terrorists would threaten all cities and nations," he insists. If so, we are all potential hostages.

Source: Douglas Waller, "Counterterrorism: Nuclear Ninjas, A New Kind of Swat Team Hurts Atomic Terrorists," *Time*, 147, no. 2 (January 8, 1996), pp. 38–40. © 1996 TIME Inc. Reprinted by permission.

tage against airports or aircraft on the ground, with ICAO empowered to suspend air travel to states that fail to comply. These conventions have been only "the first stage in the development of an international regime for the control of aircraft hijacking."[35] Additional multilateral agreements have outlawed the hijacking of naval vessels, the theft of nuclear material, the use of the mails for delivery of explosives and other dangerous substances, and the illicit traffic in narcotic drugs. Loopholes in their coverage, and the fact that many states have not yet ratified these conventions, undermine the effectiveness of international law in this area. However, a growing number of governments are becoming parties to these agreements, if only for fear of the potential consequences of nonsigning, particularly regarding the threat of nuclear terrorism.[36]

Some regional IGOs have gone even further to outlaw certain types of terror tactics. For example, in 1976 the Council of Europe (composed of most Western European states) decided that political causes would be no excuse for leniency in punishing or extraditing terrorists committing offenses involving various lethal devices, although several European states did not ratify the agreement and some that did stated reservations qualifying the extent of their obligations.[37]

In addition to legal responses, states have shared technological innovations aimed at countering terrorism. Electronic search devices have been installed in airports and other public buildings, and warnings of inadequate safety and surveillance at specific airports are now posted around the world. The movements of terrorists are tracked through international police agencies such as INTERPOL, and information from national computer data banks is exchanged between states.[38] Of course, none of these measures guarantee success against terrorism. Italian police ignored Turkish warnings about the terrorist who eventually shot Pope John Paul II in 1981, and other warnings were ignored in a little-known but shattering 1977 incident described as follows:

> So complex is our modern world and so close the margins for error that terrorist disruptions can produce unforeseen tragedies. The explosion of a time bomb in the airport flower shop on Gran Canaria in Mach 1977 by a little-known terrorist group seeking independence for the Canary Islands from Spain was responsible for the diversion of air traffic to the airport at Santa Cruz de Tenerife. Two jumbo jetliners that had been redirected to Tenerife collided, producing the worst civil aviation disaster in history.[39]

One modest but hopeful sign of growing global recognition of the need to curb unorthodox violence appeared two months after the *Achille Lauro* affair. On December 9, 1985, the UN General Assembly for the first time, by unanimous approval, passed a resolution containing a blanket condemnation of all terrorism. The resolution "unequivocally [condemned] all acts . . . of terrorism whenever and by whomever committed" and "deeply [deplored] the loss of human lives which results from such acts of terrorism." It also called upon all states to "refrain from organizing, instigating, assisting, or participating in terrorist acts in other states, or acquiescing in activities within their territory directed towards the commission of such acts." The resolution even managed to include a single if vague agreement on the definition of terrorism, as acts "that endanger or take innocent human lives, jeopardize fundamental freedoms, and seriously impair the dignity of human beings." The problem has remained one of getting universal agreement in the application of these general principles to specific cases.[40]

There is reason to consider the global anti-terrorism effort at least a partial success. The number of skyjackings and their success rate has been vastly reduced over the past two decades, with the most recent episodes mainly involving individuals wishing to flee from one state to another rather than seeking to extract political concessions. Notwithstanding several high-profile terrorist acts in the 1990s, there has been a general overall decline in the total number of reported terrorist incidents since the mid-1980s. It is hard to know if this trend can be attributed to the strengthening of global regimes against terrorism, to a shift in terrorist tactics, or to other factors, and whether it might be reversed in the future.[41]

Conclusion

A variety of approaches can be used to combat terrorism, ranging from unilateral national policies to global regime-building, from highly visible displays of force to more quiet behind-the-scenes diplomacy and intelligence work, and from actions directed at government sponsors of terrorism to actions directed at terrorist groups themselves. Counterterrorist tactics in many cases, however, fail to come to grips with the root causes of the problem, and therefore provide only momentary relief.

We have noted that groups employing terrorist tactics are driven by a variety of motivations. Although some groups are almost wholly nihilistic, calling for sweeping changes that amount to the total destruction of society, others are animated by more limited and even persuasive concerns, although their methods may be highly objectionable. If humanity hopes to achieve the goal of maintaining *peace* and reducing "physical violence" in the world—whether in the form of terrorism or more traditional warfare—it is unlikely to succeed without also addressing concerns about *justice* and what has been called "structural violence," that is, hunger, poor health care, and other forms of economic deprivation that can kill and maim just as surely as guns and that so often underlie the resort to violence. Hence, in the next two chapters we turn to international economic concerns, focusing first on the functioning of the global economy as a whole and then on the economic development of less developed societies.

SUMMARY

1. There is considerable disagreement over which groups and which actions can be considered "terrorist" in nature, with the argument frequently heard that "one person's terrorist is another's national liberation hero."

2. However, terrorism conceptually tends to be characterized by at least three common ingredients: (1) it involves the threatened or actual use of unconventional violence designed to shock so as to gain publicity and instill fear; (2) it is politically motivated; and (3) the immediate target or victims, whether persons or property, usually bear only an indirect relation to the larger aims impelling such violence. One might add a fourth characteristic: the tendency for the perpetrators to be non-state actors, i.e., "outgroups" denied legitimate status and seeking to upset the established order in some fashion.

3. Some governments themselves participate at least indirectly in terrorism either through clandestine agencies or by funneling arms and other forms of support to terrorist groups. Anti-terrorist tactics adopted by governments also can come to resemble the terrorist methods they are meant to quell, and can pose moral problems about whether to negotiate with terrorists and about the civil rights of citizens.

4. Although terrorism is not a new phenomenon, it has become a more serious concern in the contemporary era because of the increased vulnerability of modern society, the existence of communications and travel technologies that permit terrorists to operate on a global scale, and expanded ties among terrorist groups across national boundaries.

5. The frequency of terrorist acts has diminished during the 1990s as compared with the 1980s, when there were on average over 500 incidents reported annually, although the number of incidents remains high. Western Europe, the Middle East, and Latin America have been the main locales for terrorist attacks, with American property and citizens being primary targets along with Europeans, Arabs, and Israelis. There has been a movement away from hijacking and kidnappings toward greater reliance on bombings and other types of assault. Terrorist acts generally result in relatively few casualties, despite the horrific nature of the phenomenon.

6. Selection of targets and methods can vary among terrorist groups, with factors such as group ideology, size, age, and location affecting the pattern of their behavior.

7. Terrorists generally have been successful in achieving their immediate goals relative to the costs incurred, even if their larger aspirations—which can range from creation of an independent homeland, to the elimination of foreign cultural influence from a region, to the transformation of the world political and economic order—are rarely fulfilled. Current political and socioeconomic upheavals in various parts of the world may add to terrorism problems.

8. Efforts to combat terrorism are complicated by the fact that governments often have conflicting views about terrorism, with some, particularly in the developing world, arguing that it is a legitimate weapon of the oppressed. However, the concept of global responsibility for combatting terrorism has been slowly gaining acceptance. There are now numerous treaties dealing with skyjacking and other aspects of terrorism. Other multilateral cooperation involves the sharing of police resources and surveillance technologies. There is also widespread interest among governments in limiting the potential for nuclear and mass destruction by terrorists.

SUGGESTIONS FOR FURTHER READING AND STUDY

Several research groups carefully monitor trends in international terrorism. Two in particular that prepare often-cited annual reports are the U.S. State Departrment's Office Of Counter-Terrorism (in its *Patterns of Global Terrorism* series) and the Rand Corporation's Program on Political Violence (in its *Chronologies of International Terrorism* and *Trends in International Terrorism* series). See also David E. Long, *The Anatomy of Terrorism* (New York: The Free Press, 1990); Edward R. Mickolus, *International Terrorism in the 1980s: A Chronology of Events* (Ames, Iowa: Iowa State University Press, 1989); Per Baltzer Overgaard, "The Scale of Terrorist Attacks as a Signal of Resources,"

Journal of Conflict Resolution, 38 (December 1994), pp. 452–478; and the periodicals *Terrorism: An International Journal* and *Journal of Terrorism and Political Violence.*

Good conceptual treatments of terrorism can be found in the following works: Leonard B. Weinberg and Paul B. Davis, *Introduction to Political Terrorism* (New York: McGraw-Hill, 1989); Donna M. Schlagheck, *International Terrorism: An Introduction to the Concepts and Actors* (Lexington, Mass.: Lexington, 1988); Todd Sandler, John T. Tschirhart, and Jon Cauley, "A Theoretical Analysis of Transnational Terrorism," *American Political Science Review*, 77 (March 1983), pp. 36–54; Michael Stohl, ed., *The Politics of Terrorism*, 3rd ed. (New York: Marcel Dekker, 1988); Robert O. Slater and Michael Stohl, eds., *Current Perspectives on International Terrorism* (Basingstoke, N.H.: Macmillan, 1988); Michael Aaronson, "Terrorism or Freedom Fighting? A Minefield of International Relations," *International Relations*, 8 (November 1986), pp. 611–634; Leonard Weinberg, "Turning to Terror: The Conditions Under Which Political Parties Turn to Terrorist Activities," *Comparative Politics*, 23 (December 1991), pp. 423–438; Paul Wilkinson, *Terrorism and The Liberal State*, 2nd ed. (London: Macmillan, 1986); and David A. Charters, ed., *The Deadly Sin of Terrorism: Its Effect on Democracy and Civil Liberty in Six Countries* (Westport, Conn.: Greenwood Press, 1994).

Among studies of anti-terrorism approaches, note Brunos Frey, "Fighting Political Terrorism by Refusing Recognition," *Journal of Public Policy*, 7 (April/June 1987), pp. 179–188; Nehemia Friedland, "Fighting Political Terrorism by Refusing Recognition: A Critique of Frey's Proposal," *Journal of Public Policy*, 9 (April/June 1898), pp. 207–216; Robert A. Friedland, ed., *Terrorism*, 2 vols., Series 1, Vol. 6 (Dobbs Ferry, N.Y.: Oceana Publications, 1992); Henry H. Han, *Terrorism and Political Violence: Limits and Possibilities of Legal Control*, Series 2, Vol. 1 (Dobbs Ferry, N.Y.: Oceana Publications, 1992); and Burleigh Taylor Wilkins, *Terrorism and Collective Responsibility: Points of Conflict* (London: Routledge, 1992).

On other aspects of terrorism, see David Rapaport, ed., *Inside Terrorist Organizations* (New York: Columbia University Press, 1988); Gabriel Weimann and Conrad Winn, *The Theater of Terror: Mass Media and International Terrorism* (White Plains, N.Y.: Longman, 1994); Francis P. Hyland, *Armenian Terrorism: The Past, the Present, the Prospects* (Boulder, Colo.: Westview Press, 1991); David Pion-Berlin, "Of Victims and Executioners: Argentine State Terror, 1975–1979," *International Studies Quarterly*, 35 (March 1991), pp. 63–86; Robert P. Clark, *The Basque Insurgents* (Madison, University of Wisconsin Press, 1984); J. Bowyer Bell, *The Secret Army: A History of the IRA, 1916–1970* (Cambridge, Mass.: MIT Press, 1974); Helena Cobban, *The Palestinian Liberation Organization: People, Power, and Politics* (New York: Cambridge University Press, 1984); Jacobo Timerman, *Prisoner Without a Name, Cell Without a Number* (New York: Knopf, 1981); Brian M. Jenkins, "Will Terrorists Go Nuclear?," *Orbis*, 29 (Fall 1985), pp. 507–515; Lawrence Freedman, et al., *Terrorism and International Order* (London: Routledge and Kegan Paul, 1986); and Ted Robert Gurr, ed., *Violence in America*, 2 vols. (Newbury, Calif.: Sage, 1989.)

CHAPTER 13

The Promotion of Prosperity: Keeping the World Economy Running

All countries today find themselves part of a larger global economy that has become sufficiently interdependent to move some observers to speak of the world as a "global shopping mall."[1] Along these lines, the U.S. State Department in recent years has supplemented U.S. Commerce Department reports on Gross National Product with its own periodic reports on the "Planetary Product"—the sum of the GNPs of all nation-states—which had exceeded $30 trillion by 1995.[2]

The existence of a *world* economy is manifested in many different ways. We have already commented on the intricate international ties that characterize the global arms trade. More visibly, Americans traveling abroad will find McDonald's hamburgers sold in Singapore, Kent cigarettes in Rumania, Pepsi in Russia, and Coca-Cola in China (the latter product is reputedly served 600 million times daily in 163 countries).[3] Japanese travelers will find Toyotas peddled in Germany, Nikon cameras in Brazil, and Minolta copiers in the United States. French tourists will find Michelin tires, French designer clothes, cosmetics, and wines sold not only throughout the European Union but throughout the world. Other nationalities can likewise find their "native" products advertised on billboards in various corners of the globe, although the financing, production, and distribution of goods and services around the world are becoming so internationalized that it is difficult to determine the national identity of many products. We noted at the beginning of this book the creation of the "world car," the Ford Escort, with shock absorbers made in Spain, steering gears in Britain, rear brakes in Brazil, door lifts in Mexico, wiring in Taiwan, and assorted other parts from other countries, all assembled in the United States and sold in showrooms in America and abroad.

Escorts are not the only "American" products that are in reality manufactured largely *outside* the United States for import into the United States and other markets. Most Singer sewing machines, Kodak cameras, and even the baseballs used in the "all-American" game of major league baseball are produced overseas. Moreover, many items that are "made in U.S.A." and are commonly assumed to be "as American as apple pie"—such as Alka-Seltzer, Nestlé chocolate bars, Foster Grant sunglasses, Pepsodent toothpaste, and Girl Scout cookies—are produced by companies owned by foreign interests.

Clearly, the international economy is characterized by a complicated web of relationships that cut across national boundaries and touch every part of the globe. However, recalling our earlier discussion of interdependence, it is important to keep in mind that the flow of international trade and other economic activities is uneven. Some countries, such as those in Western Europe, have especially strong regional ties, and others have intense bilateral ties. Not all countries are equally involved in the international economy and not all share equally in the planetary product. Moreover, national borders continue to pose major barriers inhibiting economic transactions. For example, American pharmaceutical companies seeking to export products such as Tylenol to Japan not only must meet safety standards set by the U.S. Food and Drug Administration but also must pass the additional scrutiny of Japanese health officials, who often insist the drug be tested on Japanese subjects before being sold in the Japanese market; the U.S. government itself has placed various restrictions on autos and other Japanese imports. Attempts to reduce these impediments and to integrate the international economy through global institutions in the UN system have met with only partial success.

In this chapter we want to convey a sense of the overall structure and dynamics of the international economy. We will examine the problems associated with the coordination of the international economy, the politics of economic problem solving, and the various regime-building efforts that have been undertaken. Comparing regime-building in the economic sphere with that in the peace and security (control of violence) area, one observer comments: "Conflict and cooperation are, of course, comingled in both [economic and security] issues, but . . . economic issues are characterized far more by elaborate networks of rules, norms, and institutions."[4] Still, people disagree not only over how much coordination of the international economy is necessary, but also what purposes coordination should serve—for example, greater overall economic growth and efficiency, or also economic justice (a more equitable distribution of wealth). There is also disagreement over what role international institutions should play in the process. An entire field of inquiry with long historical roots has developed around these questions, called **international political economy,** which is the study of the interplay between economics and politics in world affairs. Before examining the problems, politics, and regimes found in specific sectors of the international economy, we first should review a number of widely different, conflicting perspectives on the nature of international economic relations as a whole.

The Nature and Magnitude of the Problem: Alternative Views

It is commonly observed that the first three decades after World War II generally were characterized by steady economic growth and rising employment and living standards worldwide. These trends began to be reversed in the early 1970s, after the OPEC-induced oil price shocks and other developments resulted in growing economic problems for developed and less developed countries alike. Whereas in the 1960s Western developed states had grown economically at an average rate of roughly 5 percent a year, this rate of growth declined to 3.2 percent in the 1970s, fell below 3 percent in the 1980s, and slid below 2 percent in the early 1990s. Despite some improvement as the 1990s progressed, GNP growth remained sluggish compared with the early postwar period; joblessness remained high, particularly in Western Europe, where by 1995 the EU-wide unemployment rate had reached almost 12 percent. Economic problems were far worse in the former Soviet bloc, with Russia's economy actually shrinking by 10 percent annually during the 1990s and many Eastern European states experiencing declining outputs of goods and services as well, although some states such as Poland and the Czech Republic were beginning to rebound. The economic growth rates of the less developed countries decreased on average from over 5 percent in the 1960s and 1970s to under 4 percent in the 1980s, with most of this growth concentrated in only a few relatively advanced LDCs while the rest of the third world suffered through a dismal decade. The 1990s have seen rapid GNP growth in some parts of the developing world (notably in East Asia, led by China's double-digit increases), but continued problems elsewhere (notably in Africa, where economies in some countries were shrinking by as much as 20 percent).[5]

Taken as a whole, a world economy that had expanded robustly at a rate of about 5 percent annually in the 1950s and 1960s contracted to 3 percent growth during the 1980s and had sunk to 1.1 percent in the early 1990s before showing signs of recovery later in the decade. Coincident with this trend was some instability in the growth of world trade. Total world exports had expanded rapidly since World War II and had reached $2 trillion by 1980, but then leveled off and even declined in the 1980s before accelerating again in the 1990s, exceeding $4 trillion by 1995. International trade flows have been dramatically overshadowed since the mid-1980s by the explosive growth in international financial flows (loans and investments), with the world's chief financial markets now turning over hundreds of billions of dollars daily. The picture that emerges from an analysis of statistical trends, then, is a dynamic but highly volatile global economy in which benefits are distributed unevenly within and between nation-states. Adding to this uncertainty is growing worker anxiety and insecurity in the United States and elsewhere over the "downsizing" of companies seeking to become more efficient for purposes of "global competitiveness," the related dislocation of jobs as companies shift production from one country to another in search of optimum profits, and the stagnation of real wages earned by middle classes.[6]

There are three major schools of opinion on what can and should be done by the international community to revive the world economy and to keep it running smoothly. Each of these intellectual traditions offers its own set of explanations of the workings of the international economy, and its own prescriptions.

THE LIBERAL INTERNATIONALIST SCHOOL

This school of thought developed in reaction to the so-called **mercantilist school** of international economics, which predominated in the seventeenth and eighteenth centuries. The main tenets of mercantilism were the following: the pursuit of *national* power and wealth were the primary ends of foreign policy, with power dependent on wealth and vice versa; to maximize national interests, a state's international economic transactions had to be subject to strict *governmental control*, including restrictions on exports and imports, foreign investment, and other economic activity; and, given the presumed absence of any harmony of interests among states, economic decision making had to be based on *unilateral* policies rather than collective problem solving through consultation and participation in international institutions.[7]

In contrast, the **liberal internationalist school,** first championed by Britain in the nineteenth century and later by the United States after World War II, holds that even though national governments can be expected to pursue foreign economic policies designed primarily to serve the national interests of their own individual societies, there are benefits to be derived from *cooperation* with other states. In the process of interstate competition over the distribution of the world's wealth, states are likely to share certain mutual interests in collaborating to open up trade and investment opportunities for each other so as to maximize the special economic advantages of each country. Some countries have low labor costs, others high technology, still others raw materials, and so forth. Ultimately, consumers in all nations can expect to benefit from an international economy that is based on the most efficient allocation and use of resources among countries. To this end, liberals argue that governments should reduce tariffs and other barriers to international economic activity, allowing goods and services to flow as freely as possible across national boundaries.

Given their emphasis on the importance of market forces and open borders in international economic relations, classic liberal thinkers in the tradition of Adam Smith (discussed below) go so far as to envision international economic cooperation and interdependence eventually leading to a global capitalist economy knowing no boundaries whatsoever and driven by multinational corporations rather than national governments:

> This vision of the future has been portrayed most dramatically by Norman Macrae, . . . who foresees a world of spreading affluence energized perhaps by "small transnational companies run in West Africa by London telecommuters who live in Honolulu." New computer-based . . . information systems will facilitate the rapid diffusion of skills, technologies and industries to lesser-developed countries. . . . More and more of the old manufacturing industries will move to the underdeveloped world. The entire West and Japan will be a service-oriented island in a labor-intensive global archipelago. Thus, whereas the telephone and jet aircraft facilitated the internationalization of production in the Northern Hemisphere, the contemporary revolution in communications and transportation will encompass the whole globe.[8]

From the perspective of the liberal internationalist school, the role of international institutions such as the International Monetary Fund and the World Bank should be to maintain as much order and stability as possible in economic relations between states while helping to facilitate international economic activity and expand the planetary product.[9] This view of the international economy is one that is widely held in developed capitalist societies today.

THE MARXIST SCHOOL

The Marxist school includes a variety of viewpoints. According to **dependencia** theorists, the international economy, rather than consisting of over 180 national economic units competing on roughly equal terms, instead consists of two sets of states pitted against each other in a pattern of interstate competition that clearly favors one group at the expense of the other.[10] In particular, *dependencia* theorists argue that the world economy is divided into an exploitive Northern tier of developed states ("the core") and a dependent Southern tier of less developed states ("the periphery"). This relationship, which can be traced back to the colonial era, is supposedly perpetuated by an international division of labor whereby the North concentrates on producing and exporting more lucrative, high-priced technology and manufactured products while the South concentrates on producing and exporting relatively low-priced raw materials, agricultural commodities, and unfinished goods. Even where more manufacturing is transferred to the South, it is on terms dictated by the North, which retains technological dominance. The result of this unequal exchange, the *dependencia* school contends, is massive poverty in the South and massive wealth in the North. *Dependencia* ideas, originally formulated in the context of U.S.–Latin American relations, peaked in popularity in the 1970s, but still retain currency among many intellectuals throughout the developing world.

Marxists who adopt a **world system** approach, like *dependencia* thinkers, conceive of the world economy in terms of core and peripheral areas. However, they view international economic relations not so much as a contest between rich and poor states but as a contest between rich and poor classes in a world society.[11] In other words, rather than viewing international economic relations as interactions between states controlled by national governments, the world system school tends to focus attention on interactions between *nonstate* actors, namely, economic elites and non-elites that often transcend national frontiers. This school argues that the international economy is shaped not by national interests but by the interests of economic elites in various countries, particularly in developed capitalist societies, who compete with each other in accumulating wealth. National governments are generally assumed to be the instruments of economic elites, although conflicts can arise between political and economic leadership circles. Instead of national political capitals (such as Washington and Ottawa) being the key loci of economic decision making in the world, it is the financial capitals (such as New York and Toronto) that are thought to be the major power centers; in places such as

London, Paris, and Tokyo, the political and economic capitals happen to be in the same location. These three cities are in fact among a dozen "global cities"—the "command and control centers" of the world economy that are the headquarters sites of the world's largest multinational corporations and banks.[12] Strictly speaking, this network of global cities, and not the North as a whole, is the core of the international economy, although these cities are generally found in the Northern Hemisphere. The surrounding towns, villages, and urban areas of the world constitute the semiperiphery and periphery, with wealth "trickling down" to the masses more and more slowly the farther one lives from the global cities.

Hence, world system theorists share a degree of commonality with the liberal internationalists in that they also see national boundaries as increasingly irrelevant in an expanding world capitalist economy, although rather than welcoming these trends they are highly critical of them. According to this analytical perspective, multinational corporations and intergovernmental organizations are simply the latest institutional responses of modern economic elites to a changing world, just as economic elites in an earlier era developed the nation-state as the chief mode of human organization. Marxists generally call for the empowerment of the world's masses and contend that the role of international institutions should not be to help order and manage international economic relations in ways that promote the operation of market forces but rather to change those relations in a manner that redistributes wealth more evenly between the core and the periphery.

THE NEOMERCANTILIST (REALIST) SCHOOL

The **neomercantilist school** holds that liberals and Marxists both neglect the real driving force behind the workings of the international economy; i.e., rather than the management of international economic relations being about the promotion of global prosperity, efficiency, or justice, it is about the pursuit of national self-interest and power that characterizes all international relations. According to this school, "realist" assumptions about the mercantilist tendencies of all states are still valid even in the contemporary international system.[13] Indeed, it is argued that "welfare state nationalism"— the twentieth-century phenomenon of publics looking to their national government as the provider of not only security but also general well-being—if anything has enhanced the role of the state relative to the market in shaping economic outcomes.

Neomercantilists note that, although pressures on national governments to satisfy the growing demands of their citizens may lead them to seek to coordinate trade and other policies through intergovernmental organizations or to promote the growth of multinational corporations, there are limits to the extent to which they are prepared to surrender sovereignty or to compromise vital state interests. Leaders of states seek to insure that international economic activity produces not only *absolute* gains for their state (in the form of increased tax revenues, jobs, defense capabilities, and other valued goals) but also *superior* gains *relative* to other states. As Robert Gilpin comments, "nations continually try to change the rules or regimes governing international economic relations in order to benefit themselves disproportionately with respect to other economic powers. . . . Therefore, a liberal international economy cannot develop unless it is supported by the dominant economic states whose own interests are consistent with its preservation [such as the United States after World War II]. Whereas liberals stress the mutual benefits of international commerce, nationalists [mercantilists or neomercantilists] regard these relations as basically conflictual."[14]

THE ANALYSIS OF INTERNATIONAL ECONOMIC RELATIONS

It should be clear from the previous discussion that there are many different ways in which one can think about the international economy and analyze current problems.[15] Whereas neomercantilists as well as Marxists rightly remind us of the conflictual nature of international economic transactions, neither school can account fully for the many cooperative linkages that have developed across national boundaries among governmental and nongovernmental actors enmeshed in economic interdependence. At the same time, some liberal internationalist thinkers can be accused of overlooking the continued importance of the state in organizing economic life and of power relationships in driving the international economy.

During the Cold War, much of international economic analysis revolved around how the first, second, and third worlds fit into the world economy. The first world (the developed capitalist democracies), led by the United States, dominated the international economy; a common enemy in the Soviet Union provided strong incentives for these states to cooperate around a liberal internationalist ideology. The **Organization for Economic Cooperation and Development (OECD)**, consisting of the developed states of North America, Western Europe, Oceania, and Japan, served as an umbrella organization for first world collaboration and consultation on economic issues; within OECD, the **Group of Seven** (the United States, Japan, Britain, France, Germany, Italy, and Canada) emerged as a core "directorate." The second world (the developed communist states) chose to remain relatively aloof from the Western-dominated international economy, and the third world found itself marginalized in terms of lacking the necessary economic resources to be a key player. As we noted in Chapter 3, the situation in the post–Cold War era is more complex. The OECD industrialized democracies remain the major engine behind the world economy, although the removal of the Soviet threat and the erosion of U.S. hegemony have contributed to added friction among these actors, whereas the for-

THE WORLD'S LARGEST MCDONALDS IN CHINA: IS IT LIBERAL INTERNA-TIONALISM, MERCANTILISM, OR MARXIST THEORY THAT BEST EXPLAINS THE WORKINGS OF THE WORLD ECONOMY?

mer second and third worlds along with everyone else are becoming more integrated into the world economy through a process of "globalization."

Globalization refers to the internationalization of production, finance, and exchange, as alluded to by Norman Macrae on page 471 and illustrated by the anecdotal examples cited at the outset of this chapter. To the extent that the globalization phenomenon grows, it threatens to undermine "the capacity of the individual . . . state to control its own economic future. At the very least, there appears to be a diminution of state autonomy, and a disjuncture between the notion of a sovereign state directing its own future and the dynamics of the contemporary world economy."[16] Later in the chapter, special attention is devoted to multinational corporations and how they relate to national governments, both their own "home" government (of the country in which they are headquartered) as well as "host" governments (of countries in which they do business). We will address the question of whether multinational corporations are merely extensions of the nation-state or autonomous actors that compete with governments in running the world economy. One can see that the historic tension between the state and the market as the organizing principle of international economics remains very much a part of contemporary international relations.[17]

In the discussion that follows, we will draw on insights from the various schools of thought as we focus on specific sectors of the international economy. One can conceptualize the international economy as consisting of three distinct but interrelated components (the "three c's")[18]: (1) the commerce sector, (2) the currency sector, and (3) the capital sector. Within each of these sectors, we will examine the issues at stake as they impinge on both developed and developing countries. Within each of the three sectors, we will also examine the relevant international institutions that have been established to help manage the global economy.

The Commerce Sector: Problems, Politics, and Regimes

When most people think about the international economy, they usually think first of international **commerce,** or trade—imports and exports of oil, autos, coffee, oranges, television sets, computers, zinc, and countless other commodities and products that flow across national boundaries. There are many reasons why countries engage in international trade. In many cases, certain goods, such as petroleum or coffee, are simply unavailable at home and are impossible to produce domestically given climatic or other physical features of the country; even if a state does have indigenous supplies, they might not be sufficient to meet the demands of the population. In the case of such items as computers and nuclear reactors, countries may lack the technological capabilities to produce these goods within their borders. In still other cases, with shoes and textiles, for example, countries might well be able to supply all their own needs through domestic sources but choose to obtain these from foreign producers because the latter are more cheaply priced for consumers. Just as countries **import** goods for various reasons, they also **export** them for various reasons, one of which is simply to pay for their imports. Countries also seek to expand exports because foreign markets offer additional opportunities for the growth of their domestic industries, including increased jobs at home. All of these motives for participating in international trade are economic in nature and are in addition to the political motives noted earlier when we discussed the use of economic tools as bargaining instruments, for example, to develop friendlier ties with countries having strategic value.

The classical liberal internationalist school emphasizes the virtues of **free trade,** i.e., encouraging as much international trade as possible by removing "artificial" government-imposed tariff and nontariff barriers between states and instead relying on the "natural" forces of supply and demand. It was Adam Smith, a Scottish economist and author of *The Wealth of Nations*, published in 1776, who became identified as the "father of free trade," arguing that the same capitalist *laissez-faire* economic principles and rules of commerce that were being introduced *within* the emerging industrialized countries of Western Europe should also apply *between* them; a minimum of government regulation in national and international economics, he argued, would enable all countries to make the best use of their resources and to prosper. Another eighteenth-century economist, David Ricardo, buttressed Smith's arguments with his *theory of comparative advantage*, positing that countries should specialize in producing those goods that they can produce most efficiently and trade these for other needed goods from other countries. Both Smith and Ricardo were reacting against the mercantilist policies that governments had traditionally used to control economic activity and that fostered economic nationalism rather than an open international economy.

Although we have noted many good reasons for engaging in international trade, there are also many reasons why countries historically have frequently sought to limit their international commercial involvement. Free trade brings numerous benefits, but also possible costs. If countries are attempting to develop "infant industries" at home that are not yet competitive with more established and more efficient foreign producers, free trade can result in a flood of cheaper imports that outsell the domestic line and prevent the new domestic industries from growing. In many instances, domestic opposition to free trade comes not from infant industries but from workers and managers in older industries that have failed to adapt to changing conditions and have become inefficient compared with their counterparts abroad; at least in the short run, free trade can damage these local industries severely and cause massive plant shutdowns and layoffs. Then, too, in specializing in certain economic areas (say, computers) and relying on foreign industries for other needed goods (say, shipbuilding or auto parts), countries risk becoming excessively dependent on external sources of supplies that might be cut off during wartime or in crisis situations. Pressures for restricting imports can also arise when a country finds itself with a negative **balance of trade**—the value of its imports exceeding the value of its exports—which signals that the nation might be living beyond its means. Even exports, which one would expect governments normally to promote as much as possible, might be curtailed if the effect of selling certain goods (for example, tons of wheat) on the world market is to create shortages of that good along with higher prices at home. For all these reasons, in addition to political inspired boycotts and embargoes, national governments often opt for restricting trade rather than expanding it.

There are a variety of ways governments attempt to protect domestic producers from foreign competition, all of which have the effect of constraining international trade. The most blatant approach is simply to prohibit certain foreign goods from entering one's territory or to impose a **quota** regarding the maximum volume of allowable imports (tons of steel, numbers of cars, etc.). A more common instrument is a **tariff,** or import tax, which is imposed on foreign products entering a country and which has the effect of raising the selling price of those goods relative to domestically produced goods, thereby making the latter more attractive to consumers. Governments also often rely on more subtle techniques to inhibit imports, such as requiring all products sold in one's market to meet certain safety standards or technical specifications as to labeling or size or some other product feature—regulations designed not so much to protect the domestic public from defective foreign merchandise as to add further obstacles for foreign producers, who must spend extra money retooling their production lines or coping with bureaucratic red tape to comply with the local standards. We earlier cited the example of Japanese regulations relating to Tylenol and other pharmaceuticals, which from Tokyo's perspective may constitute legitimate precautions to protect the health of its citizenry, but from Washington's perspective represents protectionism. Although these tariff and nontariff barriers are usually instituted by states acting individually, they can also be instituted by groups of states acting collectively against outsiders through regional customs unions or common markets, such as the European Union.

As appealing as protectionism might seem to a country experiencing domestic economic problems, it is a two-edged sword. Not only does it tend to reward inefficient domestic industries at the expense of consumers who would otherwise benefit from lower-priced foreign imports, it also invites retaliation from targeted countries and, hence, damages one's own export-oriented sectors. Therefore, governments are often faced with difficult choices as to what sectors might have to be sacrificed if the national economy as a whole is to benefit. Most economists agree that the high degree of protectionism that was practiced after World I, in contrast to the relatively free trade of the nineteenth century, contributed significantly to the contraction of business activity and increased worldwide unemployment leading to the Great Depression in the 1930s. This is precisely why after World War II major efforts were made to lower trade barriers so that the "beggar thy neighbor" mistakes of the interwar period would not be repeated.

World trade did, indeed, increase more than twentyfold between 1945 and 1995. However, not all countries shared equally in this growth. The major traders have been the twenty-five Western developed capitalist states belonging to OECD, accounting for roughly 70 percent of all exports worldwide in recent years—selling mostly to each other. The United States, with imports and exports together exceeding $1 trillion in 1995, is the single most active trading country in the world (West Germany had surpassed the United States briefly in the 1980s as the chief exporter). The European Union as a whole, however, with over $800 billion in "intra-EU" trade alone, accounts for over one-third of total world trade.[19]

The developed communist states participated relatively little in the international commerce sector during the Cold War. They were responsible for less than 5 percent of world trade annually, interacting mostly with each other rather than with the capitalist developed states or third world states. During the 1980s, for example, roughly 30 percent of Soviet trade was with the West, 10 percent with developing countries, and the largest share with fellow East bloc members.[20] The marginal role played by the Soviet Union and the Eastern European states in the international trade sector was explained partly by the fact that these states attempted to pursue a policy of **autarky** (economic self-sufficiency) within the "Communist Commonwealth," seeking to insulate themselves from Western trade winds that could upset their planned economies and create unwanted dependencies. With the end of the Cold War and the movement of the former East bloc countries from "command economies" to "market economies," they are now seeking a much fuller involvement in the international economy as a whole. As discussed in Chapter 10, the Eastern Europeans have expressed interest particularly in expanding their economic ties with Western Europe and the European Union.[21] Russia likewise has contemplated pursuing stronger links with Western Europe, although some Russian nationalists warn of excessive Western influence. Several former Soviet republics, such as Belarus, appear destined to link their economies quite firmly to Moscow.

Although the Western developed capitalist states trade mostly with each other, they have come to rely on less developed countries as an important source of imports as well as markets for their exports. In the 1990s, almost one-third of the exports of OECD states have gone to less developed countries.[22] The exports supplied by the West are mostly industrial products and technology, including tractors and farm equipment, refrigerators, computers, and machine tools that have to be imported by developing countries for them to meet their economic modernization needs; some developed countries, such as the United States, also sell wheat and other agricultural commodities to developing countries, along with weapons. To help pay for these costly imports, the less developed countries export various goods to the developed capitalist states. These are mostly primary products, either agricultural commodities such as bananas, sugar, or coffee, or raw materials such as petroleum, copper, or chromium.[23] Altogether, approximately 70 percent of the exports of less developed countries go to developed countries, with the less developed countries engaging in relatively little commerce between themselves, mainly because (except for the OPEC nations and a few others) they lack sufficient purchasing power to generate a significant trade volume.[24]

However, the structure of world trade has been undergoing some changes in terms of not only East-West relations but also North-South relations. Led by a few "newly industrializing countries" (NICs), such as Brazil, Mexico, South Korea, Taiwan, and Singapore (the latter called the "Asian tigers"), the developing countries have begun to take advantage of cheap labor and other assets and to shift the composition of their exports away from primary commodities to labor-intensive consumer goods (shoes, textiles, toys) and semifinished or finished manufacturers.[25] One observer notes that

> the world's largest plastics firm is now Taiwanese (Formosa Plastics), the largest petrochemical complex is in Jubail, Saudi Arabia, and the largest selling import car in Canada is Korea's Pony, made by the Hyundai Corporation. Brazil is being used by Volkswagen and others as an export base for autos. Mexico is being used by Ford as an engine manufacturing base for its North American auto operations. . . .[26]

Coincident with the growth of manufacturing in the South has been the increasing role of the "service" sector in Northern economies. Where once manufacturing dominated developed state economies, service industries (banking, insurance, telecommunications, transportation, and so forth) now constitute over 60 percent of the GNP of industrialized countries.[27] Still, one must put these trends into proper perspective. Only a few LDCs thus far have benefited significantly from this shift toward industrialization in the South, with the Asian tigers, along with China, responsible for two-thirds of all LDC manufactured exports.[28] A list of the top ten U.S. trade partners in the late 1990s is instructive about current world trade patterns; the top two partners, as they have been for decades, are developed states (Canada and Japan), but over half the list consists of LDCs (all in Asia, except for neighboring Mexico).[29]

As *dependencia* theorists point out, the pattern of trade relations between North and South still tends to favor the former, for a variety of reasons. First, the technologically sophisticated finished products sold by the North tend to carry a higher price tag than the primary and unfinished or processed goods sold by the South, even though many Northern products could not be made without the raw materials and other inputs from the South. Second, many less developed countries are still excessively dependent on certain items, such as bananas or tin, for the bulk of their export earnings and, hence, are extremely vulnerable to world recession and other conditions that can cause price fluctuations and economic uncertainty. Third, even developing countries, such as the NICs, that have diversified their economies have encountered tariff barriers thrown up by developed states seeking to protect domestic producers from a flood of cheap footwear, china dolls, and other manufacturers, just as cane sugar growers and other agricultural producers in the South have frequently encountered quotas, excise taxes, and other barriers in the North. Although the developing world as a whole has accounted for a growing percentage of total world exports in the last two decades, the growth in LDC exports has been contributed mostly by just a few countries, the OPEC states along with the NICs.

Despite adverse terms of trade, less developed countries find themselves so reliant on international trade that it is difficult to extricate themselves from the present web of relationships. As a group, less developed countries depend on international trade for 40 percent of their combined gross domestic products (GDPs). Developed countries as a group are somewhat less dependent, with international trade accounting for 30 percent of their combined GDPs. However, some individual developed states, notably in Western Europe, are heavily dependent on international commerce. If a country's **trade dependence** is defined as the sum of its imports and exports as a percentage of its GDP, this figure has reached at least 60 percent in Germany, Belgium, the Netherlands, and some other European Union countries. In contrast are Japan, 20 percent, and the United States, 22 percent.[30]

In the U.S. case, even though it is the world's largest single trading nation in terms of the absolute dollar volume of its imports and exports, its domestic economy is so huge that international trade accounts for relatively little of its overall $6 trillion GNP. Still, the dependence of the United States on foreign *imports* of oil and other key raw materials used in industry cannot be minimized; the United States depends on imports to meet over half of its consumption needs in a dozen categories.[31] Less commonly recognized is the growing *export* dependence of the United States, with sales abroad accounting for more than one-fourth of all cash receipts in the U.S. agricultural sector, one of every eight jobs in manufacturing, and a growing percentage of profits in the service sector. Indeed, trade has become so important to many localities that mayors and governors are becoming U.S. "trade ambassadors" alongside federal officials, as subnational political units increasingly see themselves as competitors in a world economy. Forty-one of the fifty states in the United States had overseas trade offices in 1995, compared with only nineteen in 1976.[32]

Recognizing the benefits of international trade, governments have attempted to cooperate through various intergovernmental organizations established after World War II to deal with trade problems. Initial attempts to create an International Trade Organization as a United Nations agency alongside the World Bank and the International Monetary Fund failed. In its place, the General Agreement on Tariffs and Trade (GATT) was created in 1947 to serve as a global forum for multilateral negotiations aimed at reducing tariff and nontariff barriers. Although GATT membership was open to all states, many communist states and less developed states were reluctant to participate during the Cold War, viewing the organization as an instrument of the capitalist developed countries. Nonetheless, for nearly fifty years, GATT remained the major international trade forum, with its membership responsible for more than four-fifths of all world trade. In the words of one official, "GATT . . . provided a rule of law for world trade" and represented "an attempt to banish into history the jungle of restrictions and bilateral dealings that strangled world trade in the 1930s like jungle weed."[33]

A series of GATT negotiations were conducted over the years, including the so-called Kennedy Round in the 1960s and the Tokyo Round in the 1970s, which succeeded in substantial tariff reductions, particularly on industrial goods, where tariffs were cut by an average of 35 percent from their 1945 level. However, by 1985, it was clear that if the liberal trade regime was to be strengthened further, there was a need not only to involve more states but also to address protectionist practices in areas where GATT rules were weak or nonexistent, such as agriculture, textiles, tropical products, and services. Begun in Punta del Este, Uruguay, in 1986, while the Cold War was still being waged, the Uruguay Round was to engage more than one hundred countries in a decade-long diplomatic effort that ultimately proved to be "the first big test of economic cooperation in the post–Cold War era."[34] The final product was the Marrakesh Agreement, a 22,000-page treaty containing a delicate set of bargains that expanded GATT rules into new areas and established a new successor body to GATT, the World Trade Organization (WTO), which came into existence in 1995. The World Trade Organization had 131 members as of 1997, with most former East bloc countries having joined and with Russia and China having applied for membership but not yet granted admission.

The main principles adopted by WTO, carried over from GATT, are the following: First, where governments feel a need to protect domestic industries, protection should be accomplished primarily through tariffs rather than quotas and other nontariff barriers. Second, governments should work gradually toward reduction of the general level of tariffs through multilateral negotiations based on the **most favored nation principle,** i.e., when one member state lowers tariffs on certain kinds of imports from another member state, all member states are entitled to the same favorable treatment with regard to their goods. Third, any trade disputes that arise among members should be settled through established procedures of the organization. The WTO strengthened dispute settlement procedures considerably beyond those provided by GATT, although there remain many controversial issues surrounding the role of the WTO in regulating world trade (see the box on pages 484–485).

Although much progress has been made in relaxing trade barriers since 1945, further progress has been stalled by a revival of protectionist sentiment in many countries experiencing domestic problems in recent years. Even the United States, the champion of free trade after World War II, has retrenched somewhat from that role. American vacillation can be traced to 1971, when the United States experienced its first negative trade balance in almost eighty years. The U.S. trade deficit exceeded $100 billion annually throughout most of the 1980s and 1990s. The U.S. government has come under increasing pressure from American management and labor unions in slumping industries such as textiles, electronics, automobiles, steel, and shoes to get Japan and other countries to accept Voluntary Export Restraints (VERs) and Orderly Marketing Arrangements (OMAs) limiting imports into the United States. A particular complaint by American producers is that Japanese companies are able to "dump" television sets and other goods on the American market at prices lower than their U.S. competition (and even lower than the same products sell for in Japan) because their production costs are partially offset by subsidies from the Japanese government. Although the U.S. government also has indulged in subsidizing certain exports (for example, weapons)—a practice that goes against the spirit of free trade—Japan has been notorious for blocking foreign access to the Japanese market through a variety of subtle nontariff barriers, including administrative regulations such as import licenses, technical requirements regarding product size and markings, assorted taxes and fees that are tacked on to the cost of imported items, and a business culture that gives preference to domestic suppliers.[35] In 1995, United States-Japanese relations reached a low point when, in response to Japan's failure to satisfy Washington's demands to open up its market to U.S. auto parts, the United States threatened to impose a 100 percent tariff on all high-priced Japanese cars (above $30,000), a clear violation of WTO rules; the two sides were able to paper over their differences, but the incident reflected continuing trade disagreements.

The European Union also remains protectionist in several areas, notably agriculture. Even with the trade liberalization measures produced by the Uruguay Round, EU farmers still are shielded somewhat from American and other foreign competition by government subsidies as well as continued tariff walls. In the industrial sector, EU members engage in trade restrictions as well. For example, before the conclusion of the Marrakesh Agreement, Italy allowed an upper limit of only 5,000 Japanese cars to be imported annually into the country, while Britain, France, and Spain had similar "understandings" with Japan that only a fixed percentage of their domestic markets would be open to Japanese auto imports (11 percent in Britain, 3 percent in France, and 1 percent in Spain). Attempting to adjust to new WTO rules, the EU recently negotiated a voluntary restraint agreement with Japan allowing Japanese car imports a steadily increasing market share, reaching a ceiling of 15 percent of the European auto market by 1999, after which all restrictions might be lifted. EU members and other developed states have also become increasingly wary of developing countries, fearful of a flood of cheap imports capturing Northern markets and undercutting Northern producers, and hence have especially targeted VERs and OMAs at the LDCs.[36]

As for less developed countries, they generally have supported lower trade barriers in those areas where they can compete best with foreign producers—in labor-intensive industrial goods and textiles as well as raw materials and agricultural commodities—while insisting on their prerogatives to protect other, more vulnerable domestic industries and service sectors. Rather than relying on GATT for trade negotiations, the less developed countries have preferred using the **United Nations Conference on Trade and Development (UNCTAD)**, a UN General Assembly organ established in 1964 to supplement GATT as a world trade forum but largely ignored by the developed states. We

THE WORLD TRADE ORGANIZATION: A THREAT TO NATIONAL SOVEREIGNTY OR A FORUM FOR COMMON GROWTH?

The preamble to the Marrakesh Agreement that established the World Trade Organization (WTO) in 1995 embodies the liberal internationalist school's view of global commerce. Trade relations are aimed at "raising standards of living, ensuring full employment . . . , and expanding the production of and trade in goods and services, while allowing for the optimal use of the world's resources in accordance with the objective of sustainable development, seeking both to protect and preserve the environment . . . consistent with their respective needs and concerns at different levels of development." WTO members agree to enter into "reciprocal and mutually advantageous arrangements directed to the substantial reduction of tariffs and other barriers to trade and to the elimination of discriminatory treatment in international trade relations."

These words rested on a fragile consensus that had been forged among developed and developing countries during the Uruguay Round. During the negotiations, the United States, enjoying a competitive advantage in most service industries, had met resistance from less developed countries in its efforts to promote liberalization in telecommunications, advertising, and other service sectors and to strengthen intellectual property rights in the form of patents and copyrights that prevent international pirating of software, CDs, and other products. The United States itself had resisted efforts by LDCs to reduce protectionism in the area of textiles. European Union farmers, led by the French, had resisted efforts by the United States, Australia, Canada, and major grain-exporting states to liberalize trade in agriculture. In the end, a number of compromises on these and other contentious issues were worked out that permitted an agreement to be reached.

The Marrakesh Agreement set up a special dispute-resolution process at WTO headquarters in Geneva to handle trade disputes. If any WTO member brings a complaint against another state charging it with violating WTO rules, a panel of independent trade experts is expected to investigate the complaint and can order the imposition of sanctions against the offending party should the latter be found guilty of a violation. Previously, under GATT procedures, no enforcement action could be taken in a dispute unless there was a consensus among the entire GATT membership, meaning that each state effectively had a veto power and could ignore the judgment of investigators.

The greater enforcement power possessed by the WTO has raised concerns about infringement of state sovereignty. In the United States, in particular, an unusual coalition has spoken out against the WTO, consisting of liberal environmentalists, consumer advocates, and labor union supporters such as Ralph Nader and leaders of the Sierra Club and Greenpeace, as well as conservatives such as Pat Buchanan, Ross Perot, and Jesse Helms—all of whom fear that the WTO could challenge certain U.S. government policies and laws as promoting unfair trade practices in violation of treaty obligations. For example, a panel in Geneva has upheld Mexico's complaint that the U.S. Marine Mammal Protection Act was a violation of free trade; the legislation had been passed by Congress to prohibit the import of tuna caught with nets that killed dolphins. A WTO panel has also ruled that a section of the U.S. Clean Air Act discriminates against foreign oil refiners by banning certain kinds of gasoline imports thought to increase pollution. There are concerns that bans on asbestos imports, on import of shrimp caught with nets that slaughter sea turtles, on imports made with prison labor, and other such federal or state legislation might be called into question. Buchanan expressed the fears of many with his statement that "WTO means putting America's trade under foreign bureaucrats who will meet in secret to demand changes in U.S. laws. . . . WTO tramples all over American sovereignty."[1] In less polemical language, attorneys general from forty-two states wrote President Clinton in 1994 expressing concern over the possibility that the WTO agreement might even undermine states' rights (for example, California's practice of banning imports of certain fruits thought to carry diseases).[2]

It is uncertain how far the WTO will go in attempting to exercise its enforcement powers. Ultimately, the future viability of the organization will depend on the continued support of major actors such as the United States, so that there are limits to the extent to which WTO officials are likely to take actions that alienate key members. Because the United States has one of the most open, laissez-faire economies in the world, and because the American market is highly prized abroad, it figures to have less to fear than other states from a trade regime that seeks to reduce government restrictions on the flow of goods and services. No doubt efforts will be made by the international community to reconcile the demands of environmental protection with the demands of free trade,[3] although this tension will continue to pose problems, as will the tension between liberal internationalist and mercantilist impulses generally.

[1]Quoted in Robert Dodge, "Grappling with GATT," *Dallas Morning News,* August 8, 1994; cited in Bruce E. Moon, *Dilemmas of International Trade* (Boulder, Colo: Westview Press, 1996), p. 91.
[2]Ibid.
[3]Works that treat this problem include C. Ford Runge, *Freer Trade, Protected Environment* (New York: Council on Foreign Relations, 1994); Daniel C. Esty, *Greening the GATT* (Washington, D.C.: Institute for International Economics, 1994); and David Vogel, *Trading Up* (Cambridge, Mass.: Harvard University Press, 1995).

Free trade, or managed trade?

discuss LDC concerns in greater detail in the next chapter when we focus on economic development.

An added challenge to the liberal internationalist vision of an open world economy is being posed by the possible fragmentation of that economy into regional trading zones, including an American-led North American bloc, an EU-led European bloc, and a Japanese-led Asian bloc.[37] The U.S.-Canada trade agreement of 1989 created a "free trade zone . . . stretching from the Arctic Circle to the Rio Grande,"[38] whereas the 1993 NAFTA agreement extended the area to Mexico, with some observers envisioning the eventual inclusion of the entire Western Hemisphere; the European Union was exploring a special trading relationship with a collection of other European states, which might establish a "giant and virtually borderless . . . market extending from Finland to Spain"[39]; and Japan has helped to launch the Asia Pacific Economic Cooperation organization, bringing together the economies of the "Pacific Rim."[40] The question was whether these groupings would become inward-oriented rivals closed off to each other, evolving in a manner incompatible with the operation of WTO global free trade principles, or whether such a confrontation could be avoided.

The major trading powers continue to make efforts to promote a liberal trade system worldwide and to mitigate West-West conflict among OECD members through discussions in WTO as well as at the smaller annual economic summits of the Group of Seven. The G-7 summits have become increasingly visible meetings in which the major industrialized democracies have discussed a variety of concerns, not only their own economic affairs but also ways to integrate the developing world along with the former East bloc states into the global economy. Clearly, even though most states today "talk" free trade, the specter of economic nationalism and trade wars persists. At the same time that trade liberalization is being pursued in some areas, neomercantilism seems on the rise in other areas. These conflicting tendencies are also at work in sectors of the international economic system other than trade.

The Currency Sector: Problems, Politics, and Regimes

The international economy is generally not a barter economy, in which people exchange one set of goods (say, apples) for another (say, oranges). It is rather an economy in which people exchange goods and services for *money*. Some barter exists, but such arrangements are relatively rare.

What complicates transactions in the international economy is that not all countries have the same **currency** to use as a medium of exchange. The United States has as its major monetary unit the dollar, and the Japanese have the yen, the Germans the mark, the British the pound, the Indians the rupee, the Russians the ruble, the Brazilians the cruzeiro, and so forth. When a government or any of its citizens buys something from another state (oil, cars, or whatever), the seller ordinarily will accept payment only in the seller's national currency or in a currency whose value is fairly stable relative to other national currencies. Otherwise, the sellers may find they have been paid in money that has become worthless or greatly depreciated in value. Hence, most international economic transactions are based on a few select, widely accepted "international" (or "hard") currencies, such as the dollar or mark, as well as gold. In other words, many countries find that their national currencies are usable only within their own borders and perhaps in a few other nations.

Because each national monetary system has its own logic, national currencies differ in terms of the value attached to each monetary unit. Put simply, one U.S. dollar, for example, does not equal one Italian lira; one U.S. dollar equals roughly 1,500 Italian lira, so that one would much rather have a million dollars than a million lira. The rate at which one country's currency can be purchased with another country's currency is called the **exchange rate.** The exchange rate is the mechanism through which different national currencies are reconciled for trading and other purposes. The exchange rate determines what people in a given country must pay for foreign goods. Hence, it would take one U.S. dollar to purchase an item that is priced at 1,500 lira in Italy.

It needs to be added that the exchange rates can fluctuate from year to year, and, indeed, from day to day.[41] Exchange rates are determined either by agreement between governments or, more commonly, by market forces of supply and demand. Although the value of such international currencies as the dollar and mark is subject to change, wild fluctuations that could erode confidence in these currencies among traders have generally been prevented through joint action by governments. Intergovernmental monetary management in recent years has been complicated by the growing globalization of private financial markets. One commentator notes that "in 1973 a typical day's world trading in foreign-exchange amounted to $15 billion; by 1983 the figure had risen to $60 billion; by 1992 it had reached $900 billion."[42] By 1996, it was observed that "currency traders keep $1.3 trillion sloshing around the planet every 24 hours."[43] These markets are largely beyond the control of national governments, because the sheer scale of the funds involved "far exceeds what any government, or even governments acting in concert, can put against [them]. Foreign exchange trading in the world's financial centers exceeds a trillion dollars a day, a multiple of fifty times, or more, of the daily amount of world trade, and greater than the total stock of foreign exchange reserves held by all governments."[44]

Because international currencies such as the dollar are readily *convertible* into other currencies and are therefore readily usable in international economic transactions, countries seek to accumulate sizable reserves of these hard currencies for foreign exchange. Some countries are able to accumulate more reserves than others. When states import goods, they ordinarily spend hard currency. When they export, they earn hard currency. If the value of a country's imports exceeds the value of its exports, this negative trade balance can exhaust all of its foreign exchange holdings, so that theoretically it cannot engage in further international economic transactions. However, it is important to understand that international trade is only one type of international economic transaction whereby hard currency can be obtained or lost. Foreign aid and foreign investment, which are discussed later in this chapter, also involve hard currency transfers, as do international tourism and many other kinds of activities. Hence, a country can try to compensate for an adverse trade balance by accumulating hard currency in other areas.

Because it is difficult to participate in the international economy without adequate reserves of foreign exchange monies, national governments carefully monitor their state's overall record of foreign expenditures and earnings. A state's **balance of payments** is a financial statement of its economic transactions with the rest of the world that takes into account both outflows and inflows of money. If a state is spending more in other countries than it is receiving from other countries, then the state is running a *deficit;* conversely, if it is receiving from other countries more than it is spending abroad, it is running a *surplus.* National governments much prefer surpluses to deficits, just as any household bookkeeper would.

The balance of payments can be thought of as an accounting ledger, with certain types of activities producing an inflow of funds and appearing as entries on the *credit* side, and other kinds of activities producing an outflow of

Credits	Debits
Trade exports from Country X to other countries	Trade imports from Country X to other countries
Foreign investments by other countries in Country X	Foreign investments by other Country X in other countries
Profits returned (repatriated) to Country X from its investments in other countries	Profits returned (repatriated) to other countries from their investments in Country X
Foreign aid received by Country X from other countries	Foreign aid sent by Country X to other countries
Military expenditures by other countries to support overseas bases in Country X	Military expenditures by Country X to support its overseas bases in other countries
Money spent by foreign tourists visiting Country X	Money spent by Country X visiting other countries

Figure 13.1
THE BALANCE OF PAYMENTS LEDGER (FOR COUNTRY X)

funds and appearing on the *debit* side. Figure 13.1 shows the main ways in which countries accumulate credits and debits in their yearly balance of payments computations.

A country experiencing a balance of payments deficit can unilaterally pursue several possible policies in an effort to lessen the deficit. One strategy is to try to *reduce* the *outflow* of funds, through either raising tariffs and other barriers to imports, cutting back foreign aid (if one is a foreign aid donor), increasing restrictions on the amount of foreign investment abroad by one's citizens, reducing overseas military commitments (if one has bases overseas), or limiting foreign travel by one's citizens. However, each of these strategies involves potential costs. Raising trade barriers invites retaliation from foreign governments; reducing foreign aid donations and overseas military bases could pose political and security problems; restricting foreign investment risks alienating not only one's own corporate and banking community but also other governments dependent on such funds, and additionally might even be counterproductive in the long run in terms of reducing the flow of investment income returning as profits to the investing country; restricting foreign travel likewise can alienate tourists and the countries to which they travel.

Another strategy for reducing a deficit is to try to *promote* a greater *inflow* of funds, through government subsidies or improved labor productivity measures that support export expansion, tax benefits and other inducements to attract more foreign investment funds, and development of one's own tourist industry aimed at the international globetrotter. Some of the approaches can also present problems; in particular, the encouragement of foreign investment in one's economy might produce economic benefits but political costs if foreign penetration of the national economy leads to foreign domination.

One special technique available to a government attempting to grapple with a balance of payments deficit is currency **devaluation.** A government deliberately can decide to lower the value of its currency relative to other currencies, thereby increasing the buying power of foreigners seeking to purchase its goods and services while at the same time decreasing the buying power of its own people abroad (without markedly affecting its internal economy). In other words, when a country devalues its currency, this tends to enhance its ability to export goods and to attract foreign tourists while making it more expensive and difficult for its own citizenry to buy imported products and to travel abroad. Although devaluation might seem a very useful "quick fix" for a deficit problem, it is usually viewed only as a last resort, because it upsets foreigners who happen to be holding large quantities of the devalued currency and undermines confidence in the currency; in addition to its international repercussions, devaluation can harm the domestic economy, possibly leading to higher prices and inflation if one has no choice but to import certain items such as oil from abroad. There are clearly no easy solutions to a balance of payments problem, although a deficit can be erased through a careful blend of policies, assuming private currency speculators and other nonstate actors do not render governmental efforts futile.

If many countries are simultaneously experiencing balance of payments problems, a serious global problem can result, for two reasons. First, major shortages of hard currency resulting from deficits mean that countries lack the ability to finance their imports and other international economic activities, so that overall world trade is likely to dry up, producing in its wake decreased worldwide production and increased worldwide unemployment. The inadequacy of international currency reserves to keep the international economy going is known as a "liquidity" problem. Second, if several governments attempt to solve their deficit problems by resorting to currency devaluation, this can spur other governments to devalue their own currencies in a counterattack to regain a competitive edge in the international economy. The resulting instability in exchange rates can shake the very foundations of the international economic order.

It was precisely in anticipation of these kinds of monetary problems that the United States after World War II took the lead in establishing the so-called Bretton Woods system as the basis for global management of international monetary affairs. First discussed in 1944 at a wartime conference in Bretton Woods, New Hampshire, this system—which tied together concerns in the commerce, currency, and capital sectors—featured the creation of the International Monetary Fund (IMF) as a key Specialized Agency of the United Nations designed to (1) provide a central fund of hard currency reserves that could be made available to countries with periodic deficits to ease liquidity problems, and (2) provide a central forum for negotiating adjustments in currency values to prevent disruptive fluctuations in exchange rates.

Between 1945 and 1971, the system operated essentially on the basis of "fixed" foreign exchange rates, with most currencies valued in relation to the U.S. dollar as well as to gold. The central role of the American dollar was owed simply to the economic primacy of the United States after World War II. The value of the dollar itself was fixed at $35 per ounce of gold, which meant that any foreigners holding dollars could redeem them for a set guaranteed amount of gold if they wished. This "gold and dollar standard," founded on the assumption that "the dollar was as good as gold," worked fairly well as long as the United States had sufficient gold reserves in Fort Knox to make good on any claims made by foreigners seeking to exchange their dollar holdings for gold. However, when foreign dollar holdings had reached the point where they exceeded U.S. gold reserves in 1960, after chronic American balance of payments deficits arising from extensive overseas commitments, confidence in the dollar began to wane. U.S. deficits continued throughout the 1960s, fueled largely by the huge American expenditures in Vietnam. The U.S. balance of payments deficit had soared to a record $9.5 billion by 1971, aggravated by the first *trade* deficit the United States had experienced since 1893. With foreigners concerned that the United States might be forced to devalue the dollar to cope with its rising balance of payments deficit, pressures mounted to turn dollars in for gold and other "harder" currencies such as the German mark. Finally, the Nixon administration took the drastic step of terminating the sale of gold at $35 an ounce and allowing the price of gold to be determined by market forces, which were eventually to raise the price drastically, at one point to over $800 an ounce. With this decision, the Bretton Woods monetary regime crumbled.

Since 1971, the international monetary system has operated on the basis of "floating" exchange rates, with the relationships between different currencies determined mostly by what values they have on the open market. Some degree of intergovernmental coordination remains, however, with implicit agreement among IMF members to keep currency fluctuations within reasonable limits. At another level, coordination efforts also occur within the Group of Seven, as well as within the European Union, where (in Chapter 10) we noted there are ongoing efforts to establish a common currency—the "Euro"—and monetary union.

The IMF has more than 180 members, its ranks having swelled in the 1990s with the addition of the Russian Federation, the former Soviet republics, and former communist East bloc states after the end of the Cold War. Admission of the East bloc states (Poland, Hungary, and Rumania had already joined in the 1980s) was an important step that signaled their desire to become more involved in the global economy. IMF membership qualified these states for financial assistance in the form of credits and loans to help their transition from command to market economies. The OECD states, led by the United States and Japan, dominate decision making in the organization, having two-thirds of the votes due to a system of weighted voting based on each state's financial contributions to the central fund of currency reserves.

Just as the developed capitalist states dominate IMF decision making with regard to exchange rate concerns, they likewise dominate IMF efforts to deal with liquidity problems. The way IMF has attempted to deal with liquidity problems is for member governments to deposit assigned shares of gold and currency in a central fund, which then entitles them to borrow from the fund at times when they are short on foreign exchange holdings. In recent years, the IMF has multiplied its reserves through the creation of Special Drawing Rights (SDRs), or "paper gold," an international currency that represents a combination of several hard currencies that adds to the assets available to the international community. Because less developed countries, in particular, regularly experience shortages of hard cash, they often have to prevail on the IMF to make its currency reserves available. To receive assistance, LDC governments have had to agree to adopt often painful "structural adjustment" policies calling for draconian cuts in their public expenditures and services, drawing the ire of Marxist critics who advocate a big welfare state.

In the international currency sector, as in the international commerce sector, one can see a tension between pressures for unilateral policymaking and the felt need for multilateral cooperation. There are obvious limits to the willingness of states to integrate the international economy in this area, for example, to create a single common currency worldwide in place of individual national currencies. Regional efforts have proved difficult enough, as in the European Union, where divergent monetary policies have held up the implementation of a Euro-currency; domestic politics have played an important role, exemplified by the French government's struggle during the 1990s to cut its domestic budget enough to meet stringent EU standards for controlling deficits, causing major labor strikes by public sector employees in the process. Yet, amid great diversity and divisiveness, there does exist some degree of central management in the international monetary system.[45]

The Capital Sector: Problems, Politics, and Regimes

The **capital** sector of the international economy refers to the flow of resources across national boundaries that are invested in a country's economy and contribute to economic development and growth. Capital is to an economy what blood is to the human body. Virtually all countries partially rely on external infusion of capital to nurture their economy rather than relying solely on their own capital formation, although some countries are more dependent than others on outside stimulants. Two general types of capital flows warrant discussion here: (1) foreign aid and (2) foreign investment.

Foreign aid is a transfer of resources between countries, given on generous "concessionary" terms, to assist in economic development and meeting humanitarian needs. Usually these transfers occur between governments, either bilaterally (from one government to another) or multilaterally (from an IGO to a government), but they can also involve NGOs and private actors. Aid can take several forms: grants, in the form of money or food or other resources that are donated as gifts (e.g., disaster relief provided to countries experiencing earthquakes or other catastrophes); loans, which must be repaid but carry little or no interest charges (ordinarily used by the recipient country to finance the building of dams, roads, and other economic infrastructure); export credits, which enable the recipient to purchase the donor country's exports; technical assistance, which helps meet the needs of a country in agriculture, engineering, or other fields where skilled personnel might be in short supply (e.g., U.S. Peace Corps volunteers or the United Nations Development Program); and military assistance, either giving a country weapons or selling it weapons at below market value, as well as providing military training.

Foreign investment can likewise take a variety of forms: an investor can buy foreign stocks and bonds; banks in one country can make loans to businesses or to the government of another country; corporations can build manufacturing or sales facilities abroad, and contract with foreign governments to develop and manage various concerns, such as mining operations. Much foreign investment is of a *portfolio* nature, where investors merely seek a return on their financial contribution but do not seek to exercise any controlling interest in the overseas operations that use the capital. Somewhat less prevalent, but far more controversial, is *direct* foreign investment, where finance capital is used by a firm (say, Ford Motors) to create new overseas enterprises or to buy up existing overseas enterprises as subsidiaries of the parent company, which exercises control over pricing, production levels, and other economic decisions of the foreign operations.

Before discussing foreign investment, we first will examine the flow of foreign aid in the contemporary international economy. Since World War II, the *donor* countries, giving aid directly or channeling it through multilateral institutions, have been mostly developed capitalist states, while the *recipient* countries have tended to be less developed states (although the Marshall Plan, the first large-scale aid program in the postwar era, was targeted at the developed states of war-ravaged Western Europe). By 1995, the total volume of foreign aid given annually by the Western industrialized democracies in OECD had reached $60 billion, although this amounted only to .34 percent of their combined GNPs. The United States has been the single biggest national donor, contributing over $10 billion annually in recent years but ranking at the bottom of aid donors in terms of effort relative to ability to pay (.20 percent of its GNP). Japan since the late 1980s has challenged the United States as the chief donor, increasing its foreign aid flows substantially, although still contributing only .32 percent of its GNP (compared with, say, Norway's 1.1 percent allocation). During the Cold War, the bloc of developed communist states, led by the Soviet Union, contributed sizable amounts of foreign aid; however, in the post–Cold War era, with their economies undergoing painful transformations, these countries are now more likely to be on the receiving rather than the giving end of foreign aid. Although third world countries generally have not been in a position to serve as aid donors, a few have managed to contribute foreign aid in recent years. In particular, during the 1970s the OPEC countries as a whole accounted for over 20 percent of all aid given, although their share of foreign aid donations dropped along with their actual aid expenditures in the 1980s as declining oil revenues took their toll.[46]

As we have noted, the recipients of foreign aid not surprisingly are almost exclusively less developed countries. The bulk of foreign aid is dispensed to these countries through bilateral means, such as the U.S. Agency for International Development (AID), allowing the donor government to exercise total discretion as to which governments should receive the assistance and under what terms. As one would expect, the political aims of the donor state play at least as much a role in determining aid relationships as the economic needs of the recipients. Although foreign aid is commonly viewed as a form of charity, one should keep in mind that most aid is in the form of loans rather than outright gifts and hence must be paid back, usually with interest. In addition, much aid is "tied," i.e., the donor attaches strings that require the recipient to use the aid funds to purchase donor products even if those goods can be obtained from other countries more cheaply. Moreover, a large quantity of aid is military in nature, given to countries of strategic value to the donor and not usable for economic development purposes. For example, during the 1980s, two-thirds of all U.S. aid was "security assistance" rather than "development assistance." Only one-fourth of all American aid went to low-income LDCs.[47] Even in the post–Cold War era, only 23 percent of the total aid disbursements from OECD countries have been targeted at the poorest, "least developed countries."[48]

Between 1946 and 1987, the United States gave the bulk of its foreign aid to pro-Western or strategically placed states, with the major recipients being Israel and Egypt (each $13.8 billion), India ($11 billion), Pakistan ($6.7 billion), South Korea ($6.1 billion), Turkey ($4.3 billion), and Indonesia ($3.5 billion).[49] With the Cold War over, one might have expected foreign aid patterns to change in the 1990s. Although roughly half of the U.S. foreign aid budget in the 1990s was still targeted at two Cold War clients (Egypt and Israel), the United States, along with fellow OECD members, shifted some aid allocations to Russia and the Eastern European countries, aimed at supporting these countries in their efforts to establish private-market economies. This has caused the developing world to complain that scarce development capital is being diverted from the South to the North.[50]

Although most aid is given bilaterally, multilateral institutions at the regional and global level also play a significant and increasing role. Even though individual foreign aid donors lose some degree of control over the purse strings when channeling aid through multilateral institutions, certain countries are still able to dominate foreign aid decisions in many of these institutions. In the case of the World Bank, the chief global institution in the capital sector of the international economy, the developed capitalist states generally and the United States in particular have tended to dominate. Headquartered in Washington, D.C., the World Bank consists of more than 170 members, including former East bloc states that finally joined in the 1990s. Decision making in the Bank is based on weighted voting. Member governments are assigned voting power according to the size of their capital contribution to the Bank. G-7 states account for almost half of the total shares in the Bank, with the United States being the largest single contributor.

The World Bank obtains its funds mainly through soliciting government subscriptions and issuing interest-bearing bonds and notes that are purchased by governments as well as investors in the private sector. These funds are then supposed to be loaned to needy governments on relatively generous terms, particularly by the International Development Association, the "soft loan window" of the Bank, which is capable of offering fifty-year repayment periods at low interest rates. In recent years, the Bank has experimented with giving funds directly to local village associations and nongovernmental organizations in third world countries rather than funneling it through their national governments, hoping the monies might be used more efficiently. In 1995, the Bank lent a total of $17 billion in supporting 134 projects. Although the World Bank has played an indispensable role in providing capital to less developed countries, many problems have arisen, not the least of which is the servicing of the more than $1 trillion debt that the third world has accumulated over the years.

Because foreign aid frequently has failed to produce the political and economic results intended by the donor, many donor countries have suffered "donor fatigue" and have scaled down their foreign assistance programs. Given the limited supply of foreign aid, many less developed countries began in the 1970s and 1980s to turn increasingly to private commercial bank lenders as sources of capital, although the poorest LCDs had to continue to rely on "official development assistance." By the 1980s, the growing "privatization" of international financial flows had led to half of all third world debt being owed to private Western banks. This trend continued in the 1990s.[51] We discuss the "debt crisis" in the next chapter when we examine the problems associated with economic development.

Many less developed countries have also increasingly sought *direct* foreign private investment, particularly to promote industrial capabilities. As with foreign aid, the major *providers* of investment capital are the OECD developed capitalist states, accounting for 95 percent of all direct investment. However, unlike foreign aid, the developed capitalist states are also the main *targets* of foreign investment, because they tend to offer a more favorable investment climate than politically unstable developing states. Roughly two-thirds of the direct foreign investment by OECD states is in other OECD states, mostly in the manufacturing, sales, and services areas.[52] As one writer comments, "North America, Japan, and Europe dominate as originators and as destinations of most international investments."[53] Even the few less developed countries with the means to engage in overseas investment have channeled most of their investment funds into developed capitalist states rather than into fellow third world states. As for former East bloc states, recent economic liberalization reforms in those societies are opening up new investment opportunities: "Western companies have already begun to invest in the old East bloc. . . . At some point investment is likely to flow in the other direction. Perhaps early in the 21st century, or sooner, a Czech company will make *Fortune's* top 100."[54]

Although the bulk of finance capital flows from developed states to other developed states, substantial foreign investments have occurred in certain sectors of developing country economies. Traditionally, the primary or extractive sector of less developed countries—mineral mining, oil drilling, and agriculture—has attracted major direct investment from the likes of Alcoa (in the Caribbean), Exxon (in the Middle East), and United Fruit Company (in Central and South America). More recently, the lure of cheap labor has attracted increased direct investment in manufacturing by companies such as Ford, General Electric, and Nike in a number of third world countries. According to the *UN Human Development Report*, "one of the most remarkable developments of the past decade has been the acceleration in private investment flows to developing countries. . . . Between 1970 and 1992, these flows [including both portfolio and direct foreign investment] increased from $5 billion to $102 billion [with over half being direct investment]."[55] Similarly, the World Bank's *World Development Report* observes that there was "an explosion of international flows of long-term capital to developing countries in the 1990s."[56]

However, related to our earlier discussion of trends in global trade, the growing role of the developing world in the capital sector is limited to a relatively few countries concentrated in Asia and Latin America. For example, "in 1994 a record $80 billion of FDI [foreign direct investment] went to the 'developing countries.' One third was committed to China alone; another third was split between just four countries—Malaysia, Thailand, Argentina and Mexico. A further quarter was split among another 15 countries. In other words, some 20 countries in Asia and Latin America took 90 percent of FDI flows. The other 130 states were left to scramble for the residual 10 percent."[57]

For less developed countries, direct foreign investment poses a serious dilemma, bringing in much needed capital but adding to the foreign penetration of economies that are already heavily dependent on outsiders. The growing involvement of foreign interests in national economies has also been a source of concern for developed states, many of which are themselves highly penetrated. To understand these concerns, it is necessary to examine the nature of the *multinational corporation* and its relationship to the nation-state.

THE MULTINATIONAL CORPORATION

The **multinational corporation (MNC),** also referred to as transnational corporation (TNC), has become a key agent for the globalization of the international economy, with its tentacles connecting national economies in every corner of the planet. One finds many different definitions as to what makes a company "multinational." One study defines a multinational corporation as any company that appears on the *"Fortune* 500" list of top industrial firms and has manufacturing subsidiaries in six or more foreign countries.[58] However, this is a very narrow definition insofar as it includes only the largest MNCs and only those engaged in industrial activity. Another, far broader definition considers MNCs to be "corporations which have their home in one country but operate and live under the laws and customs of other countries as well."[59] Still another definition of MNC is a "cluster of corporations of diverse nationality joined together by ties of common ownership and responsive to a common management strategy."[60] Whatever definition one uses, the key feature of an MNC is that it has branch operations abroad that are connected with and subordinate to a headquarters office in another country.[61]

MNCs are not exactly new actors on the world scene. The British East India Company and other trading companies chartered by the British, Dutch, and other governments in the seventeenth century were the ancestors of present-day MNCs, and the big oil companies were already beginning to stake out claims to the Middle East oil fields in the nineteenth century. International Nickel and other mining companies had established extractive operations overseas by the turn of the century; Singer Sewing Machines already had an overseas factory in Scotland in 1878; Ford Motors had an assembly plant in Europe in 1911; and Woolworth, General Electric, and Otis Elevator were among other U.S. companies establishing foreign subsidiaries before World War I. Indeed, as early as 1902, F. A. MacKensie's *The American Invaders* was warning Europeans about increasing U.S. penetration of European economies, much as J. J. Servan-Schreiber's *The American Challenge* was to do sixty years later.[62]

Although the beginnings of multinational operations can be traced far back, the MNC phenomenon did not really take off until after World War II, when a number of factors spurred spectacular growth in direct foreign investment. First, rather than trying to break through tariff and other trade barriers to export their goods to foreign markets, many companies found it easier to gain access simply by building separate production facilities inside those countries,

Table 13.1

RANKING OF COUNTRIES AND CORPORATIONS ACCORDING TO SIZE OF ANNUAL PRODUCT

Countries are ranked according to gross national product. Corporations (headquarters in parentheses) are ranked according to total sales. Although not exactly comparable, they are sufficiently close to illustrate size relationships. Only industrial companies are included here.

Rank	Economic Entity	U.S. Dollars (Billions)	Rank	Economic Entity	U.S. Dollars (Billions)
1	United States	6,387.69	26	Turkey	126.33
2	Japan	3,926.67	27	Thailand	120.24
3	Germany	1,903.01	28	South Africa	118.06
4	France	1,289.24	29	Norway	113.53
5	Italy	1,134.98	30	Saudi Arabia	111.10
6	United Kingdom	1,042.70	31	**Exxon**	101.46
7	China (PRC)	581.11	32	Ukraine	99.68
8	Canada	574.88	33	Finland	96.22
9	Spain	533.99	34	**Royal Dutch/Shell** (Neth./UK)	94.88
10	Brazil	471.98			
11	Russian Federation	348.41	35	Iran	90.00
12	South Korea	338.06	36	**Toyota Motor** (Japan)	88.12
13	Mexico	324.96	37	Poland	87.32
14	Netherlands	316.40	38	Portugal	77.75
15	Australia	309.97	39	Greece	76.70
16	India	262.81	40	Israel	72.66
17	Switzerland	254.01	41	**Matsushita Electric Industrial** (Japan)	69.95
18	Argentina	244.01			
19	Sweden	216.29	42	**General Electric** (US)	64.69
20	Belgium	213.44	43	**Daimler-Benz** (Germany)	64.17
21	Austria	183.53	44	**IBM** (US)	64.05
22	**General Motors** (US)	154.95	45	Malaysia	60.06
23	Denmark	137.61	46	**Mobil** (US)	59.62
24	Indonesia	136.99	47	Venezuela	58.92
25	**Ford Motor** (US)	128.44	48	**Nissan Motor** (Japan)	58.73

especially if they could save transportation and other costs that would make their goods more competitive. Second, many countries offered cheap labor, special tax treatment, lax pollution laws, and other advantages to foreign firms willing to invest in their economies, prompting many firms to build overseas plants from which they could serve not only their foreign markets but their home markets as well. Third, the new technology, including advances in the speed of communications and travel, the containerization of cargo, and the development of computers capable of storing large amounts of data, all made it possible for MNCs to expand their operations. Fourth, the economic primacy of the United States and the special status of the dollar after World War II enabled U.S.-based corporations, in particular, to expand their overseas investments rapidly, with direct foreign investment by Ameri-

Table 13.1 (Continued)

Rank	Economic Entity	U.S. Dollars (Billions)	Rank	Economic Entity	U.S. Dollars (Billions)
49	Singapore	55.37	75	**Mitsubishi Motors** (Japan)	34.37
50	Philippines	54.61	76	Hungary	34.26
51	**Philip Morris** (US)	53.78	77	Kuwait	34.12
52	Pakistan	53.25	78	Peru	34.03
53	**Chrysler** (US)	52.22	79	**Texaco** (US)	33.77
54	**Siemens** (Germany)	51.05	80	**Philips Electronics** (Neth.)	33.52
55	**British Petroleum** (UK)	50.74	81	Nigeria	32.99
56	Colombia	50.12	82	**Fujitsu** (Japan)	32.80
57	**Volkswagen** (Germany)	49.34	83	**Mitsubishi Electric** (Japan)	32.73
58	**Toshiba** (Japan)	48.23	84	**ENI** (Italy)	32.57
59	**Unilever** (UK/Neth.)	45.45	85	**Renault** (France)	32.19
60	Ireland	44.91	86	**Chevron** (US)	31.06
61	New Zealand	44.67	87	**Hoechst** (Germany)	30.60
62	Algeria	44.35	88	**Proctor & Gamble** (US)	30.30
63	Chile	42.45	89	**Peugeot** (France)	30.11
64	**Nestle** (Switz.)	41.63	90	Belarus	29.29
65	**Fiat** (Italy)	40.85	91	**Nippon Steel** (Japan)	29.00
66	**Sony** (Japan)	40.10	92	**Mitsubishi Heavy Industries** (Japan)	28.68
67	**Honda Motor** (Japan)	39.93			
68	**Elf Aquitaine** (France)	39.46	93	**Pemex** (Mexico)	28.19
69	United Arab Emirates	38.72	94	Czech Republic	28.19
70	**NEC** (Japan)	37.95	95	Morocco	27.65
71	Egypt	36.68	96	**Amoco** (US)	26.95
72	**Daewoo** (South Korea)	35.71	97	**BASF** (Germany)	26.93
73	Iraq	35.00	98	**Bayer** (Germany)	26.77
74	**E.I. DuPont De Nemours** (US)	34.97	99	Kazakhstan	26.50
			100	**BMW** (Germany)	25.97

Source: GNP data are from *World Bank Atlas* (Washington, D.C.: World Bank, 1995), pp. 18–19, supplemented by *The World Factbook 1995* (Washington, D.C.: Central Intelligence Agency, 1995); sales data are from *Fortune,*

can companies alone increasing tenfold between 1950 and 1970; between 1971 and 1990, the book value of the stock of American overseas investments increased from $82.8 billion to over $345 billion.[63] The "bottom line" explanation for the growth of MNCs is that, purely and simply, foreign investment has been found increasingly profitable by corporations; by the 1980s, for example, nearly half of the "*Fortune* 500" corporations depended on their international operations for over 40 percent of their profits.[64] Of course, the MNC phenomenon could not have mushroomed as it has without general acceptance of liberal internationalist principles by governments in support of the idea of an open world economy.

Today there are over 35,000 MNCs in the world, controlling over 150,000 subsidiaries.[65] Their cumulative FDI is some $2 trillion, one-third of which is controlled by the 100 largest corporations.[66] The United States continues to be the most prominent headquarters country, being the base of operations for 151 of the 500 largest industrial and service companies in 1995, trailed by Japan (149); G-7 countries as a whole were headquarters for 435 of the companies listed in the *Fortune* 500.[67] MNCs headquartered in Western Europe and Japan have been proliferating, challenging American dominance.[68] MNCs have grown to the point where their resources now exceed those of many nation-states. As indicated in Table 13.1, if the annual product of nation-states and MNCs are compared, almost half of the top one hundred economic units in the world are corporations. General Motors is "bigger" than Nigeria and Norway, not to mention Vanuatu.[69] It is estimated that just 500 corporations control 70 percent of world trade, almost half of which is intrafirm (from one subsidiary to another),[70] whereas the 300 largest transnational firms control roughly a quarter of the world's productive assets.[71] On other measures of comparison between states and MNCs, Exxon has three times as many employees stationed overseas as the U.S. State Department; and IBM has a bigger research and development budget than most national governments in the world.

As impressive as the MNC appears in statistical comparisons with nation-state, the statistics only hint at the potential power and impact of MNCs in the world. As two writers note, "In the process of developing a new world, the managers of firms like GM, IBM, . . . Volkswagen . . . and a few hundred others are making daily business decisions which have more impact than those of most sovereign governments on where people live; what work, if any, they will do; what they will eat, drink, and wear; what sorts of knowledge schools and universities will encourage, and what kind of society their children will inherit."[72] MNCs have been labeled "invisible empires"[73] and "the new sovereigns,"[74] referring to the desire and ability of MNCs to escape the constraints of national boundaries. One scholar has characterized the emerging relationship between MNCs and national governments as "sovereignty at bay," meaning that the power and authority of national governments is being at least challenged.[75]

The latter observations all tend to buttress the arguments of those who view the international economy from a world system (and, to some extent, a liberal internationalist) perspective, which emphasizes the role of nonstate actors in shaping the international economy. However, there are many others who argue that the major decisions affecting international relations, economic or otherwise, continue to be made in official governmental circles rather than in corporate board rooms, and that MNCs have only limited autonomy vis-à-vis governments.[76] In assessing the impact of the MNC, two kinds of relationships need to be examined: (1) MNC–host government relations and (2) MNC–home government relations.

MNC–Host Government Relations. By **host government,** we are referring to the government of a country in which a foreign-based MNC operates subsidiaries. For various reasons, foreign MNCs and host governments tend to have a "love-hate" relationship. In less developed countries especially, MNCs are often credited with creating jobs, introducing modern technology, and generally helping the host country's balance of payments by bringing in fresh capital and helping to develop export industries through their subsidiaries. However, third world critics of MNCs argue that they ultimately take more out of a country than they contribute, using a variety of devices to evade host government taxes, squeezing out smaller local firms, drawing away the most talented indigenous human resources (creating a "brain drain"), engaging in advertising that creates local demand for expensive Western consumer goods, and reaping enormous profits that are repatriated to the home country rather than reinvested in the host country.

In the view of *dependencia* theorists, in particular, MNCs are not only exploitive of less developed countries but are often so enmeshed in the economy of a host country that they are able to dominate its political life as well. Although the "one-company country" (e.g., Liberia under the half-century control of Firestone Rubber) is rarely if ever found today, many foreign MNCs control huge sectors of host country economies in the developing world. For example, one writer notes that "foreign affiliates control 32 percent of production, 32 percent of exports, and 23 percent of the employment of Brazil's manufacturing sector. In Singapore foreign affiliates control 63 percent of production, 90 percent of exports, and 55 percent of employment in manufacturing."[77] Another writer finds that "MNCs sponsored 75–80 percent of radio and newspaper ads in Swahili and English in Kenya and were responsible for 45 percent of all advertising placed."[78]

Given their pervasive presence in third world economies, foreign MNCs have often been in a position to exert considerable influence over host government domestic and foreign policy. However, as developing countries have become increasingly sensitive about foreign penetration, in some cases they have become more assertive in their dealings with MNCs, using the threat of expropriation and other sanctions to bring MNCs under greater control. The most obvious case of host governments exercising power against MNCs has been the successful efforts of OPEC countries to gain ownership of (i.e., at least 51 percent controlling interest in) the oil production facilities operated by oil companies within their borders. Although many developing countries have tried to follow the OPEC example, few have had the degree of leverage enjoyed by the oil producers, so that "get tough" policies against MNCs have frequently resulted in their closing up shop in the host country and transferring their movable assets elsewhere to a more hospitable business environment, even if they have had to absorb some losses in the process. In the 1990s, with third world countries looking to attract increased foreign investment and with MNCs looking for new investment opportunities, MNC-LDC relations have been marked more by mutual accommodation than antagonism.[79]

Sensitivity to foreign economic penetration is not confined to less developed economies. As suggested in Servan-Schreiber's *The American Challenge*, many developed countries in Western Europe and elsewhere have expressed concern over growing foreign MNC involvement in their economies. Although the governments of these countries have usually been in a position to exercise greater control over MNC activity than their counterparts in the third world, they have often found MNC subsidiaries within their borders resistant to their authority (e.g., the German government has had difficulty in getting subsidiaries of U.S. firms to abide by the German national policy of facilitating worker representation on corporate boards of directors).

Perhaps nowhere is there a better example of foreign penetration of a developed economy than in Canada, where U.S. companies alone in recent years have owned or controlled over 90 percent of Canada's theaters, 55 percent of its manufacturing sector,[80] and 70 percent of its oil and gas industry,[81] figures which help account for the fact that Canada remains America's single biggest trade partner in combined U.S. exports and imports. American dominance in the area of culture is seen in the fact that "only 3 to 5 percent of all theatrical screen time in Canada goes to Canadian films; 96 percent of profits from films shown in Canada go out of the country, 95 percent to the U.S.; 95 percent of English-language TV drama is non-Canadian; Canadian-owned publishers have only 20 percent of the book market; 77 percent of the magazines sold here are foreign; 85 percent of record and tape sales are non-Canadian."[82] The Canadian government has been under increasing domestic political pressure to lessen foreign control, at the same time that under NAFTA Washington is pressuring Ottawa to open up its economy even more in return for easier Canadian access to the U.S. market.

Even in the United States, where the domestic economy is so large that foreign penetration accounts for only a small fraction of total economic activity, there has been growing concern over increased direct investment by foreign interests engaged in the "buying of America"[83]—the slices of "Americana" include Beverly Hills estates and hotels (by Arab interests), Rockefeller Center in New York City (by the Japanese), Holiday Inn and Travelodge (by the British). In fact, by the mid-1980s, the United States—long the predominant home (headquarters) country of MNCs—had become the predominant host country as well, attracting more direct investment than any other single state (over 40 percent of the world's direct investment).[84] In 1994, for example, the $46 billion in FDI outflows sent overseas by American MNCs was matched by $49 billion in FDI inflows from foreign-based MNCs.[85] One author notes:

> Overseas investors can now claim ownership to over one-half of the U.S. cement, tire, and consumer-electronics industries, 40 percent of the nation's gold-mining capacity and heavy-truck production, one-third of the chemical industry, 30 percent of copper mining, 20 percent of the U.S. domestic banking market, and a rapidly expanding percentage of the machine-tool, book publishing, automotive parts and record companies. . . .

Approximately 13 percent of the jobs in Delaware and 6 percent in South Carolina are supplied by foreign companies, and the Japanese alone provide 5 percent of all civilian employment in Alaska. Foreigners own over one-half of the commercial property in downtown Los Angeles, about 40 percent in Houston, one-third in Minneapolis, and 20 percent in Denver. Two-thirds of the major hotels in Hawaii are Japanese-owned, as are 70 percent of the private golf courses. The Japanese own 6 of the 12 largest banks in California, and account for about one-quarter of the deposits and more than 30 percent of the business loans in America's most populous state.[86]

In some cases, foreign investment in the United States has been perceived by Americans as economically healthy and has been encouraged (e.g., the offer of a $300 million loan and financial incentive package by the state of Alabama to Mercedes Benz, which led to the German automaker building a new plant in the state, employing hundreds of workers). In other cases, foreign investment has been viewed as potentially risky in terms of national security and has been severely restricted (e.g., the U.S. government's restriction on foreign investment in the communications and air transport sectors of the American economy). Special concerns have been raised about the growth of Japanese banks in the United States and the increasing financial power exercised by the Japanese in the American economy. In the agricultural sector, although foreigners own less than 1 percent of the 1 billion acres of private farmland in the United States, compared with much more sizable holdings by United Brands and other U.S.-based agribusiness MNCs in Latin America and elsewhere, many states in the American farm belt have become so alarmed at the prospect of foreign takeovers that they have passed legislation that bans or severely restricts foreign ownership of farmland.

In the case of both less developed and developed countries, one can see that host governments are extremely ambivalent about foreign MNCs within their borders. Most empirical studies have found generally positive impacts produced by MNCs in developed states, whereas their impacts in developing states are more varied, beneficial in some cases and harmful in others.[87] Although foreign firms can provide important benefits to host countries, they also can produce invidious effects, such as the 1984 disaster in Bhopal, India, where a chemical leak from a Union Carbide plant caused the deaths of over 2,000 people and injuries to 50,000 others. Such incidents have renewed calls in the United Nations and elsewhere for the establishment of a uniform code of conduct that would spell out MNC responsibilities and obligations toward host states in which they operate, as part of a general MNC regime. There is a special concern that subsidiaries controlled from abroad will become "Trojan horses," serving the interests of the home country in which the parent country is headquartered rather than the host country.[88] This leads us to consider the nature of MNC–home government relations.

MNC–Home Government Relations. If MNCs often pose problems for host governments, what about MNC relations with their **home government?** It is curious that although MNCs are commonly portrayed by *dependencia* theorists and other observers as agents of home government "imperialism" and "neo-colonialism," the evidence is mixed as to whether MNCs fully act in the interest and under the control of their home state. As they do with host governments, MNCs tend to have a "love-hate" relationship with home governments as well.

It is true that MNCs typically have special bonds with the nation-state in which they are headquartered, insofar as their ownership and top management tend to consist predominantly if not exclusively of nationals of the home country.[89] In a few cases such as Unilever, the giant British-Dutch conglomerate that makes Pepsodent and Close-Up toothpaste and numerous other products, there is joint control by two countries. However, such internationalization of ownership and management is rare. The typical case is Nestlé, the Swiss-based MNC, which has almost 100,000 stockholders drawn from many different countries but which is required to have 51 percent of the voting stock held by Swiss citizens. Ties between Japanese MNCs and the Japanese government are so close that Japan is often referred to as "Japan, Inc." One observer notes that as of the mid-1990s, "it was almost impossible to find any transnational corporation which has relocated its corporate headquarters to a completely different country."[90] In terms of ownership and management, then, MNCs are closely associated with their home country.

In other ways, too, notwithstanding all the talk of globalization, MNCs appear to be rooted in their home state. "Only 18 companies in *Fortune's* Global 500 maintain the majority of their assets abroad, and only 19 maintain at least half of their workers abroad. . . . Even the icons . . . of corporate globalization—from Coca-Cola through Ford and McDonald's . . . [are heavily home state–oriented]. Coca-Cola has no foreign shareholdings, more than half its assets are in America, and over 40 percent of its sales are at home. Ford, which is famous for trying to produce the 'global' car, still has 80 percent of its assets in America. As for McDonald's—the corporate embodiment of global spread—two-thirds of sales and over half its assets are still in America."[91]

It is also true that MNCs have often been used as instruments of home state foreign policy. Attempts by the U.S. government to use foreign subsidiaries of American MNCs to serve U.S. foreign policy ends are well documented. For example, the U.S. government used its control over IBM to prevent IBM's French subsidiary from selling computers to the French government for France's nuclear program during the 1960s, and also from exporting high technology from France to the Soviet Union and other East bloc countries. In banning such exports to the East bloc, the United States was attempting to extend U.S. law—the Trading with the Enemy Act—to operate within French borders and to shape French foreign economic policy. In the early 1970s, the U.S. Central Intelligence Agency and International Telephone and Telegraph followed a parallel course in helping to create economic chaos in Chile designed to undermine the Allende government, although it was not clear whether ITT was serving as an instrument of the U.S. government or whether the U.S. government was simply responding to the threat posed to ITT and other American MNCs in Chile.[92] In 1997, the U.S. government ordered Wal-Mart (headquartered in Arkansas) to ban the import of Cuban pajamas by its Canadian subsidiary, as part of an anti-Castro campaign waged under the Helms-Burton Amendment passed by the U.S. Congress. The sense of partnership between the U.S. government and U.S. MNCs over the years is captured in Raymond Vernon's observation that in support of American business abroad, Washington "has landed Marines in half a dozen Caribbean countries, threatened to cut off aid to several dozen others from Peru to Sri Lanka, and at some point put other forms of pressure on almost every [other government]."[93]

However, tensions can arise between MNCs and their home government, in the U.S. case as well as other cases, with MNCs at times engaging in activities that are seemingly at odds with home state interests and beyond home government control. Home government attempts to adopt "tight money" policies to dampen high domestic inflation in the price of goods are often frustrated by the ability of MNCs to borrow money readily through their overseas channels. Home government problems in reducing domestic unemployment

NAFTA and globalization: The Smith-Corona typewriter company moves its North American operations to Mexico.

are often aggravated by "runaway shops," whereby MNCs relocate their factories from the home country to another country in which the labor force can be hired at cheaper wages (e.g., American workers fear that NAFTA will cause a loss of jobs, because the average hourly compensation for workers in manufacturing in the United States is $14.83, compared with $1.85 in Mexico.)[94] See the Sidelight on "Profile of a Multinational Corporation: The Nike Company" on pages 506–507, for a focused look at this phenomenon. Even in regard to foreign policy concerns, MNC and home government policies are not always

SIDELIGHT

PROFILE OF A MULTINATIONAL CORPORATION: THE NIKE COMPANY

Labor union members in the United States and other developed countries commonly express concern over globalization of the international economy producing a "race to the bottom" as MNCs use the threat of relocating to low-wage developing countries as leverage to resist worker demands at home, resulting in downward pressure on wages worldwide. During the 1996 U.S. presidential primary election campaign, Republican hopeful Pat Buchanan commented: "What's good for General Motors is not good for America if General Motors has become a transnational corporation that sees its future in low-wage countries and in abandoning its American factories." (*New York Times*, December 31, 1995, p. 10). MNC spokespersons, and liberal internationalists generally, would counter that the rising tide of a global economy will ultimately "lift all boats," providing desperately needed employment in the LCDs and creating new jobs in next-generation industries in developed economies. Although evidence can be found to support the arguments on both sides, the following excerpt does raise troubling questions. The excerpt provides a glimpse into the workings of one MNC, the Nike Company, and also into the workings of an increasingly "globalized" international economy. (We should add, that as of this writing, Nike was considering moving its shoe production operations out of Indonesia and some other Asian countries to Vietnam, where wages were even lower.)

Nike is the number-one maker of sports shoes in the world. Founded in 1964 by Philip Knight, a former University of Oregon accounting student and running enthusiast, the company sells $2 billion worth of basketball, track, and running shoes a year. . . . Its headquarters in Beaverton, Oregon, is made up of a series of low buildings each named for a sports superstar like Michael Jordan . . . and others whose promotional efforts were critical in propelling Nike to the top. From this complex, surrounded by $1 million worth of Japanese cherry trees, Nike presides over a global network of pro-

"in synch." By the early 1980s, Pittsburgh-based Gulf Oil had invested over $500 million in Angolan facilities and maintained a cordial working relationship with the Marxist Angolan government, at a time when 15,000 Cuban troops were helping that government ward off a pro-Western faction seeking power with the support of the Reagan administration. A Philippine subsidiary of Exxon refused to sell oil to the U.S. Navy at Subic Bay during the Arab oil embargo of 1973. At the beginning of World War II, the U.S. State Department had difficulty getting U.S. oil and chemical companies to terminate their close ties with German companies operating in Latin America.[95] And in the 1990s,

duction facilities around the world, only a few of which Nike owns. As Neal Lauridsen, vice-president for Asia, puts it, "We don't know the first thing about manufacturing. We are marketeers and designers."

Virtually 100 percent of Nike's shoe assembly is in Asia. In the last five years the company has closed down twenty production sites in South Korea and Taiwan as wages have risen and opened up thirty-five new ones in China, Indonesia, and Thailand, where wages are rock bottom. The company has a global payroll of over 8,000, virtually all in management, sales, promotion, and advertising. The actual production is in the hands of about 75,000 Asian contractors.

Along with Reebok and some other large global distributors of high-price running and tennis shoes, Nike purchases a significant share of the sporting shoes it distributes around the world from contractors in Indonesia. Four of the plants are owned by South Korean companies that formerly made the shoes in Korea, and two are local Indonesian enterprises. Nikes made in Indonesia cost $5.60 to produce, and sell on the average in North America and Europe for $73 and as much as $135. The Indonesian girls who sew them can earn as little as fifteen cents an hour. . . . Overtime is often mandatory, and after an eleven-hour day that begins at 7:30 A.M. the girls return to the company barracks at 9:15 P.M. to collapse into bed, having earned as much as $2.00 if they are lucky.

A research institute in Bandung . . . complained that Nike was profiting from the exploitation of Indonesian workers. "Exploitation?" John Woodman, Nike's general manager in Indonesia, responded to an American journalist. "Yes, they are low wages. But we've come in here and given jobs to thousands of people who wouldn't be working otherwise." The statement is undoubtedly true. But it neatly skirts the fundamental human-rights issue raised by these production arrangements that are now spreading across the world.

Source: Reprinted with permission from Richard J. Barnet and John Cavanagh, *Global Dreams: Imperial Corporations and the New World Order* (New York: Simon and Schuster, 1994), pp. 325–326. Copyright © 1994 by Richard J. Barnet and John Cavanagh.

a German arms manufacturer was discovered to be engaging in secret shipments of technology to Iran in violation of government policy and understandings Bonn had reached with its NATO allies.

Acknowledging the ambivalent nature of MNC–home government relations, Raymond Vernon has added that as these relations evolve, the identity of MNCs "is likely to become more and more ambiguous in national terms. Commingling human and material resources of many nations, formulating problems and solutions on lines uninhibited by national boundaries, multinational enterprises may not be as easy to classify in terms of national association."[96] "Alliances" are being forged between MNCs based in different countries, exemplified by recent joint ventures undertaken by Daimler-Benz (Germany) and Mitsubishi (Japan), Siemens (Germany) and IBM (U.S.), Volvo (Sweden) and Renault (France), British Airways (UK) and American Airlines (U.S.), and Lufthansa (Germany) and United Airlines (U.S.).[97] "Companies that a few years ago were nationalized United Kingdom public utilities— British Gas, British Telecom, British Airways—are now global companies with increasingly tenuous connections with Britain."[98]

Charles Kindleberger has suggested that the divorce is already final: "The international corporation has no country to which it owes more loyalty than any other, nor any country where it feels completely at home."[99] Robert Reich, the U.S. Secretary of Labor in the Clinton administration, has written of "the stateless corporation": "As almost every factor of production—money, technology, factories, and equipment—moves effortlessly across borders, the very idea of an American economy is becoming meaningless, as are the notions of an American corporation, American capital, American products, and American technology."[100] Another writer argues that "the allegiance of the world's largest corporations is purely to their bottom lines."[101] One of the strongest expressions of MNC detachment from its national roots, at least in terms of aspirations, came from the chairman of a major MNC, the Dow Chemical Company:

> I have long dreamed of buying an island owned by no nation, and of establishing the World Headquarters of the Dow company on the truly neutral ground of such an island, beholden to no nation or society. If we were located on such neutral ground, we could then fully operate in the United States as U.S. citizens, in Japan as Japanese citizens, and in Brazil as Brazilians rather than being governed in prime by the laws of the United States.[102]

The detachment of the MNC from the nation-state is still just that—a dream. Most MNCs are still firmly anchored to the home country. As for those MNCs that forget their national roots, home governments still have the authority ultimately to restore control over them, given the vast regulative role that modern societies have assigned to government. In fact, pressured by domestic labor unions damaged by runaway shops, the U.S. government and the governments of other developed countries have considered imposing further restrictions on the level and type of foreign investment their MNCs can engage in overseas. Then, too—to paraphrase Stalin's famous remark about the limits of power possessed by the Pope—General Motors and other MNCs have no (army) divisions. In short, national governments would still appear to be in charge of the "global shopping mall," even if their custodianship is becoming ever more complicated. As one scholar notes, "the clash between the integrating forces of the world economy and the centrifugal forces of the sovereign state has become one of the critical issues of contemporary international relations."[103]

Conclusion

Although governments are still running the world economy, that economy sputtered through much of the 1980s and 1990s as many countries experienced recession and serious economic problems. Nowhere are the problems greater than in the developing world. As we have noted, the liberal international economic order that was fashioned under American leadership after World War II, commonly referred to as "the Bretton Woods system," can be credited with expanding the planetary product and providing a degree of management over trade, monetary, and aid relations through institutions such as GATT, the IMF, and the World Bank. However, as we have also noted, this system and the regimes associated with it have come under increasing strain, particularly as governments have attempted to cope with the globalization process. Although many in the developed states believe the system can be made to work, others in the developing states have called for a "new international economic order" or at least an overhauling of the existing order, a subject to be taken up in the next chapter.

SUMMARY

1. There are three predominant schools of thought on the international economy. The liberal internationalist school, which developed in reaction to mercantilist thought that predominated in the seventeenth and eighteenth centuries and which is popular in developed capitalist countries today, argues that goods and services should flow as freely as possible across national boundaries. In this way, consumers in all nations can benefit from the cheapest prices based on the most efficient allocation of resources among countries. The role of international institutions is to provide multilateral vehicles for intergovernmental coordination of international economic relations, helping to maintain stability while expanding the planetary product.

2. The Marxist school includes both *dependencia* and the world system theorists. *Dependencia* theorists argue that the world is divided into two sets of states—the developed, exploitive Northern states and the less developed, dependent Southern states—and that international institutions should act to redistribute wealth more evenly between the two sides. The world system theorists also posit an exploitive relationship, but view international economic relations as a struggle between the rich and poor classes in world society; i.e., they focus on the role of nonstate actors in the form of economic elites found inside and across national boundaries.

3. The neomercantilist school essentially adopts a "realist" view, arguing that the management of international economic relations is not about the promotion of global prosperity, efficiency, or justice, but rather the pursuit of national self-interest and power that characterizes all international relations. Hence, the degree of cooperation that is possible through international institutions is inherently limited.

4. The international economy has three interrelated components: the commerce sector, the currency sector, and the capital sector. The current "globalization" process, driven by liberal internationalist principles, is characterized by growing internationalization of production, finance, and exchange that is threatening to undermine the sovereignty and autonomy of national governments. Globalization is competing with neomercantilist pressures.

5. In the commerce sector, free trade carries both benefits and costs. It increases the availability of goods, often at favorable prices, as well as opportunities for growth of certain local industries. However, it can also damage a country's "infant" industries or older, inefficient industries unable to compete with foreign producers, and thus lead to higher unemployment at home and excessive dependence on external sources of supply. To constrain international trade, countries can use quotas and tariffs as well as more subtle protectionist measures.

6. The major participants in world trade since World War II have been the developed capitalist states belonging to OECD, headed by the largest industrialized democracies constituting the Group of Seven. During the Cold War, the communist states traded mostly with each other, but are now seeking greater involvement in the international economy as they move toward market-oriented systems. The developed countries rely on the less developed countries as sources of raw material imports as well as markets for their exports of technology and manufactured goods, with the terms of trade tending to favor the developed states. Some LDCs, notable the NICs in Asia and Latin America, have made significant progress in developing an export-oriented manufacturing sector. Despite postwar efforts at relaxing trade barriers through organizations such as GATT and WTO, many protectionist practices continue.

7. Most international economic transactions are based on a few "hard" currencies belonging to key developed capitalist states. Because of the importance of maintaining adequate supplies of hard currencies, countries carefully monitor their balance of payments, attempting to correct deficits by adjusting the outflow or inflow of funds (in such areas as tourism, foreign investment, and trade). If many countries

experience balance of payments problems at once, a serious global problem can result if there is not enough "liquidity" to finance international economic activity and if countries resort to currency devaluation as a solution.

8. The international monetary system now operates on the basis of floating exchange rates. Intergovernmental coordination occurs primarily through the IMF, which provides a central fund of hard currency reserves as well as a forum for controlling disruptive currency fluctuations. The IMF now has over 180 member states, including the former East bloc states, which remained outside the organization during the Cold War.

9. The capital sector consists of foreign aid and investment. Foreign aid, either bilateral or multilateral, can be in the form of grants, loans, export credits, technical assistance, or military assistance. Donor countries are mostly the OECD states. The chief multilateral source of aid, the World Bank, is dominated by the developed capitalist states, primarily the United States.

10. Unlike foreign aid, foreign investment (either portfolio or direct) has been targeted at both developed and less developed countries, with the bulk of it occurring in the former. An important development in the 1990s has been the increased flow of foreign direct investment to LDCs, although this has been concentrated in only a few NICs in Asia and Latin America.

11. An important vehicle for foreign investment has been the multinational corporation. The enormous assets controlled by MNCs make them influential both in their home states where they are headquartered and in the host countries where they operate subsidiaries.

12. Although MNCs bring capital, jobs, and technology to developing countries, critics argue that they take even more out than they contribute; they also exert considerable influence over host government domestic and foreign policy. Developing as well as developed countries have become increasingly sensitive about foreign penetration of their economies.

13. Tension can also arise between MNCs and their home government, with MNCs at times acting seemingly at odds with home state interests. Nevertheless, MNCs tend to be closely associated with their home countries and often have been used as instruments of foreign policy by their home governments. Globalization of the international economy is likely to add to MNC–home government tensions in the future.

SUGGESTIONS FOR FURTHER READING AND STUDY

For an excellent introductory overview of the international economy, especially the relationship between international economics and international politics, see David H. Blake and Robert S. Walters, *The Politics of Global Economic Relations,* 4th ed. (Englewood Cliffs, N.J.: Prentice-Hall, 1992); Joan E. Spero and Jeffrey A. Hart, *The Politics of International Economic Relations,* 5th ed. (New York: St. Martin's Press, 1997); and Thomas D. Lairson and David Skidmore, *International Political Economy: The Struggle for Power and Wealth* (New York: Harcourt Brace, 1993). Two good readers on international political economy are Jeffrey A. Frieden and David A. Lake, eds., *Interna-*

tional Political Economy, 3rd ed. (New York: St. Martin's Press, 1995) and David N. Balaam and Michael Veseth, eds., *Readings in International Political Economy* (Englewood Cliffs, N.J.: Prentice-Hall, 1996).

Writings that focus on the international trade sector, particularly relations between developed capitalist states (North-North trade), include Bruce Moon, *Dilemmas of International Trade* (Boulder, Colo.: Westview Press, 1996); the series of articles on "global competitiveness" found in *Foreign Affairs* in the March/April, May/June, and July/August 1994 issues; and Michael E. Porter, *The Competitive Advantage of Nations* (New York: Free Press, 1990). On North-South trade relations, see Robert L. Rothstein, *Global Bargaining: UNCTAD and the Quest for a New International Economic Order* (Princeton, N.J.: Princeton University Press, 1979); David Yoffie, *Power and Protectionism: Strategies of the Newly Industrializing Countries* (New York: Columbia University Press, 1983); and John W. Sewell et al., *Growth, Exports, and Jobs in a Changing World Economy: Agenda 1988* (New York: Transaction Books, 1988). Also see L. Haus, *Globalizing the GATT* (Washington, D.C.: Brookings Institution, 1992); Peter F. Cowhey and Jonathan D. Aronson, "A New Trade Order," *Foreign Affairs,* 72, no. 1 (1993), pp. 183–195; and Peter E. Drucker, "Trade Lessons from the World Economy," *Foreign Affairs,* 73 (January/February 1994), pp. 99–108.

Works that focus on the international currency sector include Joanne Gowa, *Closing the Gold Window: Domestic Politics and the End of Bretton Woods* (Ithaca, N.Y.: Cornell University Press, 1983); Howard M. Wachtel, *The Money Mandarins: The Making of a Supranational Economic Order* (New York: Pantheon, 1986); and Anthony Sampson, *The Money Lenders* (New York: Penguin, 1981).

On foreign aid, see Sarah J. Tisch and Michael B. Wallace, *Dilemmas of Development Assistance: The What, Why, and Who of Foreign Aid* (Boulder, Colo.: Westview Press, 1994); Richard Feinberg, "The Changing Relationship Between the World Bank and the International Monetary Fund," *International Organization,* 42 (Summer 1988), pp. 545–560; and Richard Feinberg and Valerina Kallab, eds., *Between Two Worlds: The World Bank's Next Decade* (New Brunswick, N.J.: Transaction Books, 1986). For a variety of viewpoints on MNCs, foreign investment, and the globalization phenomenon, see Peter Dicken, *Global Shift: The Internationalization of Economic Activity,* 2nd ed. (New York: Guilford Press, 1992); Richard Barnet and John Cavanaugh, *Global Dreams: Imperial Corporations and the New World Order* (New York: Simon and Schuster, 1994); Peter F. Cowhey and Jonathan D. Aronson, *Managing the World Economy: The Consequences of Corporate Alliances* (New York: Council on Foreign Relations, 1993); Joseph Greenwald and Kenneth Flamm, *The Global Factory* (Washington, D.C.: Brookings Institution, 1985); Theodore H. Moran, *Multinational Corporations: The Political Economy of Foreign Direct Investment* (Lexington, Mass.: Lexington Books, 1985); and Thomas Biersteker, *Multinationals, the State and Control of the Nigerian Economy* (Princeton, N.J.: Princeton University Press, 1987).

For data on international economic activity, the following sources are especially helpful: *Direction of Trade,* published by the International Monetary Fund; *World Development Report,* published by the World Bank; *Survey of Current Business,* U.S. Department of Commerce; *Handbook of Economic Statistics,* U.S. Central Intelligence Agency; the various reports of the Organization for Economic Cooperation and Development (OECD); and *Fortune* magazine.

CHAPTER 14

Economic Development:
Bridging the Rich-Poor Gap

*"*Three turquoise laser beams, indicating the tripod for development—poverty, unemployment and social exclusion—were to converge every evening high up in the Copenhagen sky as a pinnacle of the tasks the World Summit for Social Development was to tackle" in March 1995. "The beams were there but their convergence was hardly seen in the overcast sky . . . It was perhaps symbolic of the summit itself. Millions of words were spoken there . . . but there was no action. It was called the Summit of Hope."[1]

This global gathering (discussed earlier in a Chapter 10 sidelight) brought together 180 national leaders (including an unprecedented 117 heads of state), more than 2,780 NGO representatives, and 2,800 media reporters. It was one of a series of high-level gatherings on social themes convened under UN auspices in the 1990s, beginning with the 1990 World Summit for Children and continuing through the UN Conference on Environment and Development (1992), the World Conference on Human Rights (1993), the Global Conference on the Sustainable Development of Small Island Developing States (1994), the Third UN Population Conference (1994), the Fourth World Conference on Women (1995), the Second UN Conference on Human Settlements (Habitat II) and the World Food Summit in 1996, and the planned 10th World Conference on Smoking and Health scheduled for 1997 and a People's Summit scheduled for 1998. Some have interpreted this series as a "UN road show," a sort of diplomatic World's Fair. One reporter described the scene at the Copenhagen conference as follows:

> They turned on the lights at the Tivoli Gardens last week and it wasn't even spring. Copenhagen wanted the 20,000 attending the first World Summit for Social Development to get a glimpse of its most famous park, even if that meant bundling up against the cold. Tivoli's 100,000 twinkling colored lights added the right carnival atmosphere to the traveling United Nations global road show—fresh from appearances in Cairo, Vienna, and Rio. . . . The basic work product is the same: incremental agreements, offering something more than platitudes but something less than action. But amid the pomp and comedy of the traveling show something happens that is rare at the home office: national leaders get involved, if briefly, with the gritty details of economic, environmental and personal misery.[2]

There had been some hope that the end of the Cold War would permit the world to focus on pressing global socioeconomic problems. However, not surprisingly, poverty-related issues have not made their way to the top of the global agenda any more than they have been given the highest priority on national, domestic agendas. The UN-sponsored conferences serve as attention-getting exercises in multilateral diplomacy, focusing on concerns that might otherwise be ignored. Even though they tend to produce far more words than actions,[3] they nonetheless represent an attempt to raise global consciousness and to convey a sense of urgency. The inclusion of NGOs seems also to mark a democratic and participatory turn in such diplomacy, with grassroots national and transnational interest groups bringing pressure on heads of state just by their presence and articulated demands.

The problems these meetings are meant to address stem in large part from the uneven level of global economic development that we have described in Chapters 3 and 13, and the unfinished business of the North-South conflict that had been waged alongside the East-West conflict during the Cold War.[4] The rich-poor gap between the world's nation-states remains starkly clear. Some previously underdeveloped states have made great economic strides, becoming "newly industrializing countries" (NICs) or, in some cases, what are referred to as "big emerging markets" (BEMs); others, however, have been left far behind, never having experienced the industrial revolution even as the world's leading economic powers have moved into the "post-industrial era." In addition to the rich-poor gap *between* states, there is also a large rich-poor gap *within* states, which is another dimension of the problem of world poverty. Within both developed and less developed states, one finds huge differences in wealth among the citizenry, although the disparities tend to be particularly pronounced in less developed countries.

By the time of the Copenhagen conference, global bargaining had gone beyond the long-standing debates of the 1970s and 1980s over international trade, foreign aid, and capital transfers and had come to include as well a consideration of domestic social policies regarding children, women, the unemployed, and other "disadvantaged" groups, although many countries understandably were resistant to such intrusion into their internal affairs. One of the outcomes at Copenhagen was the so-called "20:20 principle," a nonbinding declaration that urged donor governments to earmark 20 percent of their foreign aid for projects on education, health, and other human services, while asking other states, including aid recipients, to target 20 percent of their budgets for such projects.[5] In this chapter, we first will review a variety of economic and social dilemmas facing large numbers of people, with special reference to the developing world, and will then examine the politics of bridging the rich-poor gap between North and South.

The Nature and Magnitude of the Problem

Before examining efforts to address the global problems of poverty and underdevelopment, it would be well to consider both the definition of development and the nature of the world's rich-poor gap. When first conceived in the 1950s and 1960s, the concept of **economic development** often was equated with undergoing the industrial revolution and becoming more like the "advanced" economies of the West. A notion of "modernization" and constant progress was built into such definitions, with a period of "take-off" leading to industrially based consumer economies involved actively in international trade.[6] In the early post–World War II period, third world leaders often undertook massive industrial and infrastructure projects, such as building large steel mills and international airports, investing huge sums of scarce capital without necessarily first thinking through the feasibility of such schemes.

Since that time, the obstacles to development have become clearer, along with some of the adverse social and environmental consequences of rapidly expanding industrial economies. In 1980, the Brandt Commission, chaired by former West German Chancellor Willy Brandt, stated that development primarily had to do with "improvements in income distribution and employment," as well as "greater human dignity and justice," and that traditional notions of development were not always supportive of these goals.[7] New concepts such as "sustainable development" have come into vogue, meaning that countries should produce and consume goods in ways that are sensitive to maintaining the quality of the natural environment.[8] Hence, development can be taken to mean the improvement of techniques of production and distribution of goods and services, with less waste of resources or energy. In this sense, all countries are still developing, but some have much further to go than others. It also has been argued that one must distinguish between socioeconomic underdevelopment (the failure to produce an adequate standard of living and quality of life) and what might be called "political underdevelopment" (the failure to establish viable, stable governmental institutions that serve to enhance opportunities for socioeconomic development.)[9] Development, then, entails the establishment of conditions that enable the average man or woman, on the street or on the farm, to engage in productive work and attain a decent standard of living, and for children to be secure and rise to this same status.

As noted in Chapter 13, the global economy as a whole has grown substantially since World War II, expanding from $4 trillion in output in 1950 to $30 trillion by 1995. It grew $4 trillion alone in the decade from 1985 to 1995, more than from the beginning of recorded time to 1950.[10] However, this growth has been very uneven, resulting in a widening rich-poor gap, as seen in Figure 14.1. The UN Development Program (UNDP) has warned:

> During the past five decades, world income increased sevenfold (in real GDP) and income per person more than tripled (in per capita GDP). But this gain has been spread very unequally—nationally and internationally—and the inequality is increasing. . . . One fifth of humankind, mostly in the industrialized countries . . . has well over four-fifths of global income and other developmental opportunities. . . . Such disparities entail consequences for other aspects of human security. They encourage overconsumption and overproduction in the North, and they perpetuate the poverty-environment link in the South. Inevitably, they breed resentment and encourage migration from poor countries to rich.[11]

The 1980s and 1990s saw many LDCs, notably in sub-Saharan Africa and South Asia, slide backward and become poorer not just relative to the North

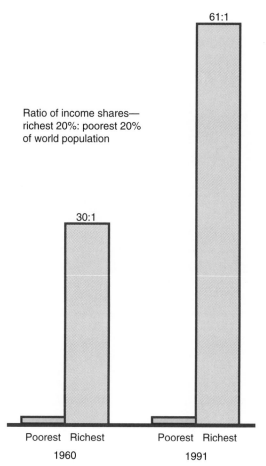

Ratio of income shares—
richest 20%: poorest 20%
of world population

Figure 14.1
THE WIDENING GAP BETWEEN THE RICH AND THE POOR
Source: United Nations Development Program, *Human Development Report, 1994*
(New York: Oxford University Press, 1994), p. 35.

but relative to their own previous experience because of population growth, reduced government expenditures, and adverse trade and other economic trends. The number of people living on less than $1 per day increased from an estimated 1.2 billion in 1987 to 1.3 billion in 1993.[12] However, as we have noted, other LDCs, notably in East Asia, fared much better. One writer observes that in some cases

countries industrializing now are doing so much faster than in the past, simply because they can draw on the experience and technology of those

A CHILD PLAYING IN THE LIBERIAN CAPITAL OF MONROVIA AS THE GUNS QUIETED AFTER ANOTHER OUTBURST OF CIVIL WAR LEFT THE CITY AND COUNTRY IN RUINS DURING THE 1990s.

who went first. Economic growth in East Asia, for instance, has averaged some 8 percent annually in recent years. And from 1991 to 1995, the Chinese economy expanded by a staggering 57 percent, raising the income per person of 1.2 billion people by more than half.[13]

Hence, there is now something of a "South-South" gap. As shown in Table 14.1, East Asia represents a far greater success story than sub-Saharan Africa, South Asia, the Middle East and North Africa, and Latin America and the Caribbean. The UN Development Program has created a "Human Development Index" (HDI), whereby all countries are ranked annually according to their overall level of development based on a composite measure of national

Table 14.1

POVERTY IN THE DEVELOPING WORLD, 1985–2000

Region	Percentage of Population Below the Poverty Line			Number of Poor (Millions)		
	1985	*1990*	*2000*	*1985*	*1990*	*2000*
All developing countries	30.5	29.7	24.1	1,051	1,133	1,107
South Asia	51.8	49.0	36.9	532	562	511
East Asia	13.2	11.3	4.2	182	169	73
Sub-Saharan Africa	47.6	47.8	49.7	184	216	304
Middle East and North Africa	30.6	33.1	30.6	60	73	89
Latin America and the Caribbean	22.4	25.5	24.9	87	108	126

Note: The poverty line used here—$370 annual income per capita in 1985 purchasing power parity dollars—is based on estimates of poverty lines from a number of countries with low average incomes. In 1990 prices, the poverty line would be approximately $420 annual income per capita. The estimates for 1985 have been updated from those in *World Development Report 1990* to incorporate new data and to ensure comparability across years.
Source. Found in and adapted from *World Development Report 1992* (New York: Oxford University Press, 1992), p. 30.

life expectancy, educational attainment, and income. Sub-Saharan states such as Mali, Chad, Niger, and Guinea, along with war-torn Afghanistan in Asia, have tended to be grouped at the bottom of the HDI annual rankings, whereas some NICs, such as Singapore, South Korea, and Chile, now register scores comparable to several European nations and above those of Russia.[14]

An estimated 1.3 billion people—about one-fifth of humanity—live in abject poverty.[15] Looked at another way, it is estimated that the top 20 percent of the world's population receives about 83 percent of the world's income, while the poorest fifth of humanity receives about 1.4 percent (in dollar terms, this amounts to $22,808 annually for the former and $163 a year for the latter).[16] More than half of sub-Saharan Africans, nearly half of Southeast Asians, approximately a third of South Asians, and almost 20 percent of Latin Americans and Caribbeans still lack safe drinking water, and about one-third of humanity remains without electricity, and one-quarter lack basic health care.[17]

Domestic income gaps tend not to be as great as the international inequalities but still are quite substantial.[18] The UNDP has sought to document not only the rich-poor gap between countries but also the rich-poor gap within them; its annual report of HDI rankings includes an analysis of intrastate differences in life expectancy, educational levels, and income levels disaggregated among males and females,[19] as well as ethnic groups, regions, and social classes (e.g., showing differences between blacks and whites in the United States, and between various geographical areas in Mexico).

Economists have hypothesized that inequalities are greatest in the early stages of economic development, and even out later as more income is available for more people, assuming expanding societies adopt "growth with equity" policies.[20] The largest income gap within a country reported in the mid-1990s was in the African state of Botswana, where the richest 20 percent of the population received over 47 times more income than the poorest 20 percent; Brazil was the second most inegalitarian society, with a ratio of 32:1, closely followed by Guatemala and Panama.[21] According to one study, Mexico's twenty-four billionaires in 1994 (up from just one in 1987) accounted for $44.1 billion in collective wealth—making these two dozen individuals richer than the bottom 33 million.[22] Latin America is the region with the world's largest income gaps, followed by Africa.[23]

Depending on how one looks at the developing world, one can see the glass as either half-empty or half-filled. Development problems remain daunting. As one observer notes, "Almost one-third of the Earth's 2.8 billion workers are either jobless or underemployed, and many of those who are employed work for very low wages with little prospect for advancement."[24] Another projects that in the first twenty years of the twenty-first century some 38 million people will be looking for work in less developed countries each year, adding to the 700 million already unemployed or underemployed.[25]

At the same time, among the signs of improvement over the past two or three decades has been a remarkable increase in the average human life expectancy, which now stands at 65 years of age, an increase of nearly twenty years since 1950, representing the greatest improvement in human history. Notwithstanding grinding poverty in much of the South, the average life expectancy there (63 years) is not as far behind the North (74 years) as some might think. Even amidst squalor, there have been immunization programs and other steps taken that have had the effect of increasing longevity. In both India and China, in particular, investments in simple public health services have raised the life expectancy to 59 and 70 years, respectively.[26]

Although most analysts expect that the South will continue to lag behind the North, some see a relatively rosy long-term economic forecast for many LDCs: "The structure of the world economy is undergoing steady and very considerable change" among "the most important elements of [which] is the growing economic role of the South."[27] Hopes reside in both decreasing population growth rates in many regions as well as increasing technology transfers and job creation through investment in the South.[28] Related to gains in life expectancy, it is noted that "average consumption per capita in developing countries has increased by 70 percent in real terms . . . and primary school enrollment rates have reached 89 percent. If these gains were evenly spread, much of the world's poverty would be eliminated."[29]

The challenge, then, is to understand and apply the economic development models that allow some less developed states to grow rapidly and distribute income more equitably, while others falter and end up heavily in debt. At the same time, of course, history has shown that development rates cannot be assumed to go on in a "linear" growth mode without interruption. When states start from relatively low levels, as China did, it is statistically easier to show high annual growth percentages; it is much more difficult to sustain these rates without political, social, or environmental disruptions over very long periods.[30] The trick will be somehow to feed, clothe, shelter, and employ between 6 and 15 billion people in the twenty-first century on a planet of limited resources administered by governments that cannot now manage acceptable living standards for millions of its inhabitants.

In this chapter, we focus on three specific dimensions of the economic development puzzle: *food, population,* and *the transfer of capital and technology.* Keep in mind as we review these concerns that they strongly affect each other, and that they are keys to improvements in the Human Development Index. Capital is needed to improve a country's food production and distribution network, as well as the education system that qualifies its population for work; food supply has to meet the population's nutritional requirements; poorly fed people get sick more often, becoming less productive and dying prematurely; lack of production contributes to poverty; poor people cannot afford food, and so on. Essentially we are describing a cycle of underdevelopment that must be broken for constructive change to occur.

FOOD

Most Northerners have seen photos of starving African and Asian children with distended bellies and listless stares. Televised starvation in distant lands seems almost unreal at times, and viewers are tempted to "tune out." Yet starvation is very real, as in the African famines of the 1980s, with the deaths of an estimated 5 million children in 1984 alone.[31] In addition to millions who die of starvation and related health problems, it is estimated that at least 700 million people suffer from malnourishment.[32] The global hunger problem is difficult to comprehend partly because it comes and goes—with wars, droughts, political turmoil—and affects some regions more severely than others.

Since World War II, total world food production generally has kept pace with population growth. However, by the mid-1990s some troubling trends had begun to emerge, as grain reserve stocks were depleted to their lowest level on record, an estimated forty-nine days of consumption. Food distribution continued to be highly uneven, with industrialized countries, having less than a fourth of the global population, consuming 60 percent of the world's food supplies. Troubling signs also included a steep, demand-driven rise in grain prices, which could even be seen in pasta and cereal prices on U.S. grocery shelves.[33] China, for example, shifted in 1995 from a net grain exporter of 8 million tons to a net grain importer of 16 million tons, ranking second on this score only to Japan.[34] The fluctuating food picture seems related to a variety of factors, including poor weather conditions, regional conflicts and population dislocations, land degradation, economic slowdowns that hinder funding for agricultural improvements, and continued population and urbanization growth in some regions.[35]

Africa is the one region where per capita food production has consistently declined. "As recently as 1970, Africa was essentially self-sufficient in food. [By the mid-1980s], however, some 140 million Africans—out of a total of 531 million—were fed with grain from abroad."[36] The African soil structure, under the stress of population doubling over the last 25 years, now is among the most fragile in the world.

> Although many African small farmers have devised ingenious ways to preserve their land while intensifying cultivation, overuse has taken its toll. Where poverty has limited the use of new technologies and fertilizer, the cultivation of marginal areas and shortened fallow periods have degraded soils. . . . Rwanda provides an extreme example of demographic cause and effect. During the 1980s, exceptionally high population density and consequent overcultivation transformed one of Africa's best agricultural performers into one of its worst. The country's 4.7% annual growth in agricultural output from the late 1960s to the early 1980s fell to about 1% a year between 1982 and 1991— resulting in a drop of nearly 20 percent per capita by the early 1990s.[37]

However, a major part of the world food problem has less to do with production than distribution; i.e., the lack of purchasing power by many people in Africa and elsewhere means that plentifully available food often never gets to those in need. Indeed, some have argued that Africa's per capita food production has been underestimated by foreign observers, and that the region's food problems are far less due to absolute shortages than to governmental policies that fail to supply the food to the masses. Either food is diverted to a relative few who hoard or sell it, or the masses lack the income to afford food purchases. "Nowhere does an absolute shortage of food explain chronic hunger."[38] Commenting on the irony of starvation amidst plenty during the 1980s, one study noted that "food held in the silos and cold stores of America, Europe, and Japan could meet the food needs of Africa five times over."[39]

Given the expected growth in world population and urbanization, there may well be a long-term food problem brewing beyond Africa, especially if one considers the economic and environmental costs of opening up new farmland or trying to make more productive use of existing acreage. In Latin America, where distribution problems are compounded by land-holding patterns (the poorest 70 percent of the people owning less than 3 percent of the land), much of the land also is owned by foreign interests, more concerned about producing farm products for export than about meeting local food needs. Although beef production in Guatemala and Costa Rica doubled between the 1960s and 1980s, for example, per capita beef consumption in those countries declined as more than half of the beef was exported, primarily to the United States for fast-food chains.[40] Even among native farmers, land often is used to grow "cash crops," such as cotton, coffee, or even opium poppies and coca leaves for the drug trade, to support farmers' debts rather than for food crops. However, some economists argue that cash or export crops help the rural population by increasing their incomes and increasing employment so they can afford to operate farms and also purchase food on the market.[41]

Only 15 percent of the planet's land area is suitable for agriculture; half of it already is under cultivation, and in a number of places suffers from increasing soil erosion, desertification, deforestation, and urban sprawl.[42] The world's oceans, another source of food supply, also have suffered from overfishing in recent years, with the global catch of tuna, cod, and other species in decline after dramatic growth with the introduction of new fishing technologies between 1950 and 1970.

Despite such disturbing trends, there is some cause for optimism, notably in such success stories as India's shift from being the world's largest food aid recipient in the 1960s to running an annual agricultural trade surplus of over $1 billion in the 1980s; it has been over thirty years since India's last recorded famine. Still, India and Indonesia together account for well over a third of the world's hungry.[43] There is concern that India, China, and other states showing agricultural improvements may be nearing a plateau in their production capabilities.[44]

A long-term solution to the global food problem could lie in making as many Southern states as possible more self-sufficient in food production. Self-reliance in some instances requires introduction of new farming methods and high-yielding seeds developed since World War II, and requires inputs of capital for farm loans and extension programs for technical assistance.[45] This so-called **green revolution** is based on the heavy application of petroleum-based chemical fertilizers and on extensive irrigation.[46] These in turn depend on expensive foreign imports and are hampered by natural conditions—including water scarcities—as well as price hikes and cuts in spending for agricultural assistance and research.[47] There is need not only to supplement the green revolution with more egalitarian land reform and better use of the rural labor supply and traditional farming techniques, but also for more disposable income for poorer farmers and consumers alike.

POPULATION

At least since the time of Thomas Malthus, an eighteenth-century English clergyman and economist, who became famous for his prediction that the world's population would inevitably outstrip its food supply and cause massive famine, the problems of food and population have been seen as intimately linked. The close connection between population growth and food availability is seen in predictions that developing countries will gain an average of 86 million people each year until the year 2050, more than doubling demand for food in these lands by 2025.[48] Scientists have tried to assess the maximum number of people the earth conceivably could feed. The answer, according to one study, is in the range of 10 to 11 billion—roughly double the current world population—although this "would require some changes in food habits, as well as greatly improving the efficiency of traditional agriculture."[49] Of course one does not live by bread alone. The growth of the world's population today raises many concerns that go far beyond food problems.

Not only is world population growing, but the growth over the centuries has been accelerating. It took roughly 2 million years—until 1830—for the earth's population to reach 1 billion; it took only 100 years for the total to grow by another billion, and just 50 years for that number to double again. The recent "doubling time" has been reduced to less than 40 years. In the 1990s, the equivalent of a city the size of Los Angeles (10 million people) was being added to the planet every month, raising policy concerns ranging from housing demand to family planning.

Population growth has been most dramatic in the South, where introduction of advanced medical care since World War II has lowered death rates while birth rates have remained relatively high. Whereas many developed states of the North have become virtually "ZPG" (zero population growth) countries, many less developed states, particularly in Africa, are experiencing population growth of more than 2 to 3 percent annually. The South is expected to account for over 90 percent of global population growth over the next two decades.

Population problems are aggravated by the fact that the age distribution in LDCs is increasingly weighted toward the young, with 45 percent or more of the citizenry typically under the age of fifteen. In addition to being of prime childbearing age, these young people are restless for job opportunities and are moving from the countryside to cities in search of a better life—sometimes ending up instead in armed militias or on the streets. Hence, a "population bomb" is ticking away. More than half the human race now lives in cities.[50] By the early twenty-first century, it is projected that there will be some fifty cities in the developing world having populations of over 5 million, including twenty "megacities," each exceeding 10 million. (See the growth of such cities in Figure 14.2.) The largest of these urban areas, whether Mexico City or Sao Paulo, or some other megacity such as Tokyo in the North, is expected to have a population rivaling that of Canada.

Aside from causing overcrowding, such population growth places tremendous strains on a nation's economy. Even with Mexico's remarkable 6 percent average annual economic growth rate between 1940 and 1980, roughly 20 percent of the total Mexican workforce has been driven to seek employment, often illegally, in the United States in recent years.[51] It has been estimated that

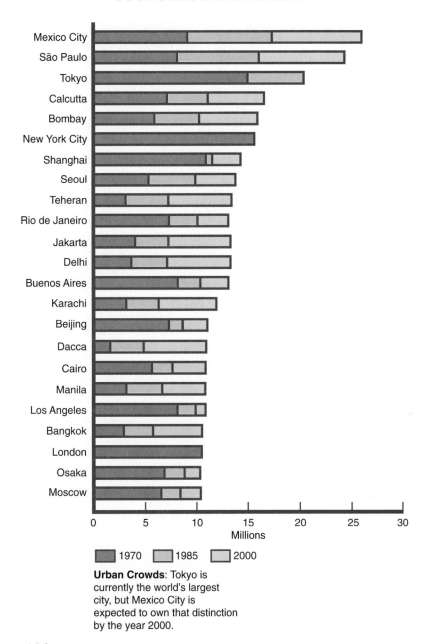

1970 1985 2000

Urban Crowds: Tokyo is currently the world's largest city, but Mexico City is expected to own that distinction by the year 2000.

Figure 14.2
CITIES WITH OVER 10 MILLION PEOPLE BY 2000
Source: © Christian Science Monitor, February 21, 1991, p. 12.

despite having curbed its population growth (down from 3.2 annual growth in 1970 to 1.8 percent by 1995), Mexico nevertheless must create nearly 1 million jobs a year, build millions of new houses, thousands of new schools, and scores of roads while trying to protect its already fragile environment, keep its peso a stable currency, and combat illegal immigration to the United States.[52]

Despite the problems that seem to be associated with population growth, people and governments do not fully agree on its implications or remedies. The North in the past has urged the South simply to control its numbers; the South in turn has argued that its mass of humanity would not be such a problem if more wealth were available to distribute among its people. Social scientists have indeed found evidence, as seen in European growth rates, that the population growth rate almost invariably declines when people in a society improve their income. Large families are no longer necessary when parents have sufficient income, because fewer children are needed to work, to provide old-age security, and to serve as status symbols. The problem, of course, is that of the chicken and the egg—how to produce improved economic conditions when such progress is hampered by the very population growth it could curb.

Some believe the population problem has been exaggerated. In the words of the famed French medical relief organization, Medicins Sans Frontieres:

> The rhetoric commonly used . . . is more often inspired by unrealistic anxieties than by careful analysis. Galloping birth rates are described in apocalyptic terms alongside famines, war and devastation. Yet apart from a few notable exceptions, densely populated countries produce more than they consume, while penury and malnutrition haunt a number of thinly populated countries. The equation "more population = more hunger and poverty = more immigration" owes less in fact to lucid observation than to a Malthusian obsession slapped on to carefully selected situations. Playing on fear, confusing images of famished hordes, destroyed forests and dried lakes, the . . . Malthusian rhetoric does a lot to blur understanding.[53]

As with food production trends, population news is not all bad. More than thirty countries now are ZPG countries, including most of Europe as well as Japan. The annual world population growth rate has fallen from 2 percent in 1970 to below 1.6 percent in 1997. One of the key factors responsible for these lowered population growth rates has been marked improvement in women's literacy and employment opportunities in many parts of the world, where females are no longer viewed as mere childbearers.[54] All this has contributed to a remarkable drop in the average size of households from six children in the early 1960s to 3.8 children in the 1990s.[55]

Even states with strict religious traditions that tend to discriminate against women and frown on population control have adopted social policies encouraging smaller families. For example, in the Islamic Republic of Iran, which faces both land and water scarcities, public subsidies for housing, health care, and insurance have been limited to three children per family.[56] The result has been an increase in the percentage of couples in LDCs using some form of contraception to over 50 percent (from just 10 percent in the 1960s). East Asia in general is the greatest success story in curbing population growth, though in China, where over 70 percent of all couples practice contraception, coercive measures have been adopted that limit people's liberty to choose the size of their families. As one analyst puts it, "governments will have to carefully balance the reproductive rights of the current generation with the survival rights of the next generation."[57] Thailand (in Southeast Asia) and Bangladesh (in South Asia) are commonly cited for dramatic progress in reducing family size, the former going from seven children per family in the early 1970s to two in the 1990s, and the latter decreasing from seven to 5.5 over the same period (with Bangladesh's progress especially noteworthy because it was achieved in the absence of any real economic progress).[58] Major population control strides also have been made in Latin American, particularly Chile, Costa Rica, Columbia, Mexico, Argentina, and Venezuela. However, though suffering mass deaths in wars and epidemics, African population growth has doubled in the last three decades and is expected to triple again during the next three before stabilizing.[59]

We have noted that death rates have been lowered throughout much of the South through medical advances, notably in eliminating smallpox, reducing the incidence of cholera, malaria, and measles, and perfecting cheap, simple rehydration kits composed of salt solutions to treat infants suffering from potentially fatal diarrhea. Nevertheless, serious problems remain as growing populations put added burdens on already inadequate health care systems.[60]

Continued public health policy dilemmas are highlighted by the treatment of the AIDS epidemic:

> Dispatches from the Eighth International Conference on AIDS held in Amsterdam [in 1992] . . . were troubling. The conference was previously scheduled to be held in Boston, Mass., but organizers, primarily the World Health Organization (WHO), moved the conference to protest the U.S. government policy of denying entrance to visitors and immigrants who have the human immuno-deficiency virus (HIV) that causes AIDS. . . . The World Health Organization has estimated that some 30 million to 40 million people could be infected with the disease by the year 2000. . . .[61]

Although there has been much progress in improving health care worldwide, the AIDS epidemic and other health issues still pose staggering challenges.

THE TRANSFER OF CAPITAL AND TECHNOLOGY

In reviewing development problems, it is clear that societies must have funds at their disposal to invest in job-creating industries, food production, and population services such as health and education. Yet capital tends to be scarce in

Southern countries, especially when people cannot afford to pass savings along to banks or to the government for reinvestment in the economy.

Many LDCs have run up huge debts to foreign banks and governments, a trend that despite remedial efforts continues to rise. By 1995, LDCs owed some $2 trillion.[62] "Developing countries spend more each year servicing their debt than they do on the military. . . . Debt servicing takes more than four times as much from their budgets as health care, and almost twice as much as education. . . . Most Third World debt is not likely to be paid back anytime soon. The countries that owe it are not earning enough money to repay it. Instead, they make occasional payments of the interest that has come due, rather than paying off the principal. Taken as a whole, the Third World owes an amount equal to about half its yearly income."[63] Aggravating the problem is the "donor fatigue" phenomenon noted in the previous chapter, i.e., the growing reluctance of developed states to continue foreign aid transfers (including grants and loans given on generous concessionary terms), leaving many states unable to maintain health and sanitation programs.[64]

The tendency of LDCs, including many NICs, to accumulate heavy international debt burdens is traceable to their own mismanagement, to high interest rates and generally worsening economic conditions, and to questionable bank lending practices back in the 1980s. The "debt crisis" became acute at that time, as it appeared that the largest third world debtor nations might default on their loans primarily owed to Western commercial banks, hence threatening the solvency of the international banking system. As a U.S. treasury official reportedly put it, the crisis began in 1982 when the Mexican finance minister "showed up on our doorstep and turned his pockets inside out."[65] By 1990, the acute crisis for banks had eased somewhat through internationally coordinated approaches to debt rescheduling and repayment.

As noted in our earlier discussion of the international economy, the developing world claims that existing international relationships benefit the North more than the South. In all, the world's "poorest people have access to barely .2 percent of all commercial bank lending, 1.3 percent of all investment, and 1 percent of all trade."[66] In the trade sector, although an increasing number of LDCs have diversified into manufactured exports (e.g., Brazil, which had relied on coffee for over half of its export earnings in the 1960s, reduced such reliance to only 9 percent in the 1980s), sixty-four Southern countries continued to depend excessively on income from the export of a single primary product or commodity in the 1990s, which made them vulnerable to the vagaries of global supply and demand for these products.[67] Those that do export manufactured products often are left with the assembly of low-cost goods (such as shoes and clothes), at relatively low labor rates that in the worst cases, as in Haiti, barely afford a living wage.

Some states have successfully weaned themselves from commodity dependence, and have emerged as more developed economies, though with lingering problems, which can include shortage of certain types of skilled employees

MALAYSIA'S PETRONAS TOWERS IN KUALA LUMPUR, COMPLETED IN 1996, RISE 1,462 FEET IN THE AIR, SURPASSING AMERICAN SKYSCRAPERS AS THE WORLD'S TALLEST BUILDINGS.

and severe disparities between elites doing business with foreign firms and the ordinary workers or unemployed. One writer describes Malaysia:

> In little more than a decade, Malaysia has transformed itself from a commodity-based economy—dependent on palm oil, rubber and tin—into one of the new growth engines of Southeast Asia. Foreign investment has been pouring in, the Government has been spending huge amounts on a host of construction projects, and home-grown conglomerates have become a force not only here but also throughout the region. Yet the 9 percent pace of growth, the rush of capital spending, and the swell of national stature are

taking their toll. . . . Inflation is on the rise and imports are increasingly outstripping exports. A few foreign companies have already relocated some of their operations to cheaper markets. . . . In short, Malaysia seems to be at a turning point, one that sooner or later faces every developing country that tries to move ahead in a hurry.[68]

Multinational corporations have been viewed by many LDCs not only as key potential sources of capital, through foreign investment, but also as a major source of modern technology. Southern governments, like their Northern counterparts, have come to identify high technology as the economic hope of the future, and have been alarmed at the technological gap between themselves and more developed states, gap that exists in part because technological innovations spurred by research and development (R&D) funds still originate almost exclusively in the North. Technology transfers to the South have occurred mainly through the sale of patents and licenses held by Northern MNCs, and by work farmed out to Southern firms (as in Bangalore, India's computer software companies). Furthermore, a **"brain drain,"** or in Indian terminology, "body shopping," occurs when talented Southern personnel, sent abroad to study in Northern universities or to fill jobs in technologically advanced fields, fail to return to their home country.

The communications and information sector is one technological area that, despite rapid changes, remains especially troublesome for the South and is considered crucial to success in today's global economy. Figure 14.3 shows the worldwide access to the latest in telecommunications and the Internet. The preponderance of access still resides in the North, with a few leading Southern states wired in prominently as well. It is noteworthy that only in central Africa and remote parts of Asia do we find a total lack of access to the "information highway." Yet, as a country such as Vietnam (with an annual per capita income of $200) gears up to attract international investment and trade—seeking to emulate successful export-oriented neighbors such as Malaysia and Singapore—it confronts the harsh reality of having only one phone for every 150 people.[69] Even in an emerging economic power such as Brazil, half the homes lack a telephone. One study notes that "in 1990, Bangladesh, China, Egypt, India, Indonesia, and Nigeria together had fewer telephone connections than Canada, which has only 27 million people."[70]

The "communication gap" also entails a lack of modern news gathering and dissemination capabilities in the South, which means that much of humanity must depend on Northern news sources such as CNN or the Reuters News Agency, located thousands of miles away in Atlanta or London. Although news reaches them, for many the choice of relevant topics and the slant of the coverage may seem quite foreign. A near Northern monopoly on satellite technology also means that LDCs' access to vital information, even about such concerns as their own natural resources, weather, and arable land, may depend on the North.

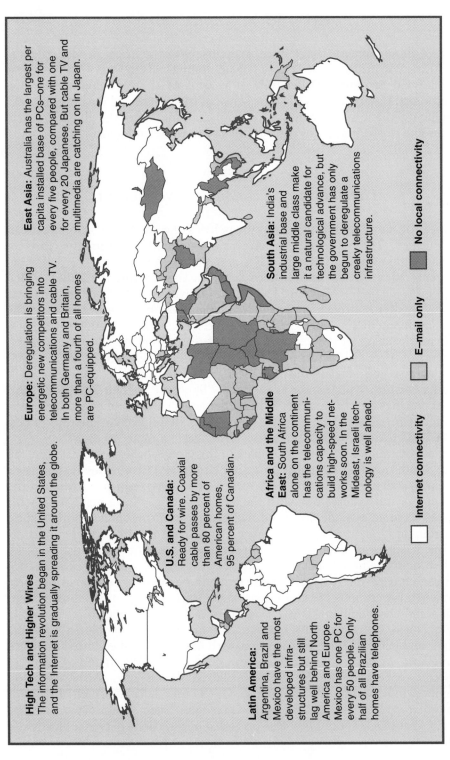

High Tech and Higher Wires
The information revolution began in the United States, and the Internet is gradually spreading it around the globe.

U.S. and Canada: Ready for wire. Coaxial cable passes by more than 80 percent of American homes, 95 percent of Canadian.

Latin America: Argentina, Brazil and Mexico have the most developed infrastructures but still lag well behind North America and Europe. Mexico has one PC for every 50 people. Only half of all Brazilian homes have telephones.

Europe: Deregulation is bringing energetic new competitors into telecommunications and cable TV. In both Germany and Britain, more than a fourth of all homes are PC-equipped.

Africa and the Middle East: South Africa alone on the continent has the telecommunications capacity to build high-speed networks soon. In the Mideast, Israeli technology is well ahead.

East Asia: Australia has the largest per capita installed base of PCs—one for every five people, compared with one for every 20 Japanese. But cable TV and multimedia are catching on in Japan.

South Asia: India's industrial base and large middle class make it a natural candidate for technological advance, but the government has only begun to deregulate a creaky telecommunications infrastructure.

☐ Internet connectivity   ☐ E-mail only   ■ No local connectivity

Source: Larry Landweber and the Internet Society, International Data Corp., IDC/Link

Figure 14.3
THE DISSEMINATION OF COMMUNICATION TECHNOLOGY ACROSS THE GLOBE
Source: Newsweek, February 27, 1995, p. 39. Newsweek-Blumrich. © 1995, Newsweek, Inc. All rights reserved. Reprinted by permission.

All of these concerns have been tied closely to the larger debate over the best strategy to bridge the rich-poor gap, including calls in the 1970s for a **New International Economic Order (NIEO)** as well as alternate approaches suggested since. Having conveyed some sense of the nature and magnitude of developmental dilemmas, we now turn to an examination of the global political process and the formation of regimes related to these problems.

The Politics of Economic Development

A variety of actors with interests in the politics of economic development can be identified. These include nation-states and their governments, interest groups within nations, and both IGOs and NGOs. In the 1970s the policy debate centered on the set of Southern demands constituting the NIEO, which called for trade preferences for LDCs, debt forgiveness, increased multilateral aid, and greater Southern control over global economic institutions. At the 1981 development summit at Cancun, Mexico, and at other such gatherings, NIEO as a package of proposals was largely rejected by the North. However, elements of it are still debated, as seen in the remainder of this chapter. Even if the tactics and slogans have changed, and even though more LDCs are building Western-type market economies, "by virtue of their situation, third world countries are still making familiar demands for debt relief, development capital, technical assistance, access to markets, stabilized commodity prices, food aid and the wherewithal to satisfy other basic human needs."[71]

Among nation-states, two main bargaining groups have participated in the North-South debate. One is the so-called **Group of 77** countries representing the South, actually numbering well over one hundred countries. Although the sheer size of this group along with the South-South gap have made it difficult at times to forge a single Southern negotiating position on economic issues, the Group of 77 generally has displayed a high level of solidarity in emphasizing the need for a new set of international economic relationships.[72] (A smaller supplementary body of leading Southern states, the so-called G-15, has risen on occasion to speak for the group in negotiating sessions.) The second bargaining group is the aforementioned Organization for Economic Cooperation and Development (OECD), with its G-7 core membership, representing the North. Consisting of the advanced industrial states of North America, Europe, and Japan, OECD was an outgrowth of efforts by the United States to help rebuild Western European economies after World War II and to promote economic cooperation among the industrialized democracies. Although many differences exist within this group also, OECD members have consulted with each other closely and have largely agreed on basic economic principles, namely, that LDCs should rely less on global negotiations between North and

South aimed at broad changes in international economic relations and more on self-help and internal reforms aimed at promoting free enterprise.

Of course there are other subgroupings on both sides, with organizations such OPEC and the Group of 24 in the IMF representing some Southern states, and organizations such as the EU or the Club of Paris (on questions of debt) sometimes speaking for segments of the North. With the Eastern bloc's breakup, a number of former members, including Russia, entered development negotiations in the 1990s seeking investment, aid, and trade opportunities as well as OECD membership.[73]

One can see that IGOs serve partly as vehicles for articulating the interests of different sets of *states*. IGOs, through their secretariats, also seek to articulate and promote *organizational* interests of their own, such as bigger budgets and expanded powers. In addition to the World Bank and the IMF, many other IGOs in the UN system are involved in economic development concerns and have a stake in development politics. A partial listing would include the Food and Agriculture Organization (FAO), World Health Organization (WHO), Education, Scientific and Cultural Organization (UNESCO), and International Labor Organization (ILO). The UN General Assembly itself has been a central forum for much of the debate. Within the United Nations, the Economic and Social Council (ECOSOC) and its regional economic commissions, the UN Conference on Trade and Development (UNCTAD), the UN Industrial Development Organization (UNIDO), the UN Development Program (UNDP), and the UN Childrens' Fund (UNICEF) are among the many agencies active in the economic development area. To this list of global IGOs can be added regional development banks and other regional organizations. Finally, among nonstate actors, one cannot overlook the role played by private banks, multinational corporations, and other nongovernmental entities in affecting economic relations between North and South.

The North has criticized a number of UN agencies for their supposed anti-Western bias and for organizational inefficiency. Proposals for cutting organizational budgets, as well as Washington's refusals to pay assessments in some cases, have been meant to increase pressure on IGO secretariats to change direction. The South, in turn, has objected to staffing cuts in many of these bureaucracies in the social and economic sphere. The South also has tended to criticize regional development banks, such as those in Latin America, along with the IMF for attempting to impose ideologically based economic policies favored by rich industrial powers.

Among the more far-reaching proposals advanced by the South over the years have been calls for a comprehensive World Development Authority, to be run by a board elected by the LDC-dominated UN General Assembly and empowered to regulate short- and long-term credit, expand trade opportunities, and supervise global efforts to address development problems involving population, food, and related issues. Included in such an Authority would be an International Central Bank, a Development Fund, and a World Food Authority.[74] Indeed, the World Trade Organization grew out of this set of proposals, although the North continues to dominate in the WTO and other trade forums.

The North-South confrontation has been compared to the confrontation between management and labor during negotiations for a new contract. Southern governments mostly have operated within the general framework of the existing rules and institutions while working for change. There have been relatively few "strikes" on the part of poorer states (i.e., boycotts of the industrialized North, repudiation of debt obligations, or refusals to honor patent rights and pay royalties).[75] On occasion, though, Southern governments have taken actions against the established order (e.g., expropriation of MNC property without compensation). Although the entire fabric of rules governing international economic relations has been on the brink of unraveling in recent years, Northern and Southern governments alike at least have continued both bilateral and multilateral negotiations to prevent regime collapse; national central banks are in constant touch with each other, trying to shore up shaky currencies, for example, while the Board of the IMF debates overall regime rules, such as the amount of reserve currencies IMF will hold and the terms by which members will have access to them.[76]

With this backdrop, let us focus in greater detail on the politics and regimes found in the specific issue-areas of food, population, and capital and technology transfer. We have noted that many developmental problems stem from conditions and inequalities within states, so that solutions reside in part with policies that states themselves adopt. However, internationally coordinated efforts also have been adopted. It has been easiest to develop widely accepted norms and rules in those instances in which both North and South have stood to benefit jointly. It has been easier, for example, to generate consensus behind the rescheduling of Southern debt repayment than behind the creation of a new international aid agency. The former benefits both Northern and Southern economic interests by preventing debt default and protecting bank and governmental investments. In contrast, a new international aid agency might lessen Northern control of development funds.[77] The task for regime formation, here as elsewhere, is one of discovering mutual interests.

Food: Politics and Regimes

In global food politics, the debate centers on the fact that food supplies are unevenly distributed, with certain Northern countries and certain regions accounting for the bulk of production, consuming disproportionate amounts, and controlling distribution. Most of the food exported commercially in the 1980s went to relatively large or wealthy countries, including Russia, Japan, and oil-rich Middle Eastern states. Although a quarter of sub-Saharan Africa's population relied on imported grain in the mid-1980s, that region's imports generally accounted for less than 10 percent of the global grain trade in the decade.[78] Southerners were quick to point out that more grain was being consumed by livestock in the United States and the Soviet Union than by the human inhabitants of less developed countries.[79]

The 1974 UN-sponsored **World Food Conference** in Rome made a series of recommendations for improving the world food situation that were endorsed by the UN General Assembly in 1975, at a time of high grain prices and dangerously low reserve food supplies. The recommendations included (1) increased agricultural development funds; (2) a global early-warning system to share information about projected weather patterns, harvests, and other factors that would make it possible to anticipate and deal with imminent food shortages; (3) an internationally coordinated system of nationally held grain reserves; (4) an annual world food aid target of 10 million tons; and (5) more international institutions, such as a World Food Council, devoted to finding solutions.

Some of these proposals have been implemented. Global satellite surveillance of cropland and weather patterns has become relatively routine under the Global Information and Early Warning System (GIEWS) administered by the UN. Although the international grain reserve is not under a common administrative center, data are gathered and reported regularly on available supplies. The World Food Council was created in 1975, consisting of representatives (agricultural ministers) from thirty-six countries along with a secretariat staff reporting to ECOSOC, and was charged with monitoring and coordinating all aspects of the UN food security system. An International Fund for Agricultural Development (IFAD) also was launched in 1977 as a vehicle to help the poorest of the rural poor in developing states to improve food production. IFAD supplemented the agricultural project funding provided by the World Bank and the UN Development Program.

Agricultural assistance and shipments of food surpluses generally mounted during the 1980s, reaching values of over $1 billion per year under the U.S. Public Law 480 "Food for Peace" program. However, budget cuts during the 1990s have meant less subsidized farm produce in the North, and therefore less available surplus food for foreign assistance. Doubts about sustained food "handouts" as a viable economic development policy also have restricted some of the humanitarian assistance. Much of the food supply to chronically undernourished populations in South Asia and Africa has come to be handled through NGOs such as Oxfam and CARE, as Northern-controlled IGOs have increasingly been contributing to these and other grassroots organizations with the expectation that aid will get to the needy in LDCs more reliably than through often corrupt government channels.[80]

Agricultural development also is spurred by the work of the UN's Consultative Group on International Agricultural Research. As testimony to the urgency of potential food shortfalls in the twenty-first century, CGIAR collaborated with the World Bank to hold a 1995 meeting of experts in Switzerland to identify new agricultural technologies. CGIAR operates a network of research centers in various Southern regions, ranging from the International Rice Research Institute in the Philippines and the International Maize and Wheat Improvement Center in Mexico, to the International Laboratory for Research on Animal Diseases in Nairobi, Kenya, and the International Center for Agricultural Research in the Dry Areas of West Asia and North Africa in Aleppo, Syria.[81] Among the innovative proposals derived from such research is the idea of combining fish farms and rice paddies on the same plots of land, and of interspersing rows of trees and rows of crops in semiarid tropical areas such as north and central Africa—a form of "agroforestry."

Many of the agencies mentioned above work closely with the Food and Agriculture Organization, along with the World Food Program, which was established by the UN in the 1960s to provide emergency assistance (for example, sending 1,500 tons of food per month to one region of Uganda alone in the early 1980s, and providing sustenance for Kampuchean and Afghan refugees victimized by wars during that decade).[82] Although the World Food Council has held extensive discussions of food problems at its annual meetings, the main action in promoting food production is carried on by FAO, with its relatively extensive staff. Other assorted UN agencies, such as UNICEF, help deal with technical assistance needs, nutritional problems, and other food-related concerns.

Despite all this impressive machinery, implementation of the food regime objectives still has fallen short in many respects. The World Food Council has failed to provide adequate coordination of programs, and FAO has been criticized by many in the North as wasteful and lacking in careful project evaluation.[83] There remains no automatic mechanism for committing accumulated reserve food stocks to needy areas of the world. Food aid in general is controversial—it obviously can help relieve disastrous famines and facilitate long-term development, as in "food-for-work" programs; however, heaping food aid on a stricken country also can undercut the market for that country's own farm products and thus hurt its farmers. The FAO, therefore, has tried to promote greater food exchanges between neighboring LDCs, some of which produce too much and some too little food. The problem of malnutrition is likely to be alleviated only by greater food self-sufficiency and, more importantly, through a greater transfer of purchasing power to the masses of the South.[84]

Northerners have demanded that Southern governments undertake agricultural reforms within their own societies, in conjunction with agricultural development. In particular, the North has urged an end to Southern governments' subsidization of food prices, which keeps food costs artificially low so that they are within reach of the urban masses. It is argued that such subsidies depress the agricultural market, discouraging Southern farmers from producing more food and making needed investments, and that they drain government treasuries, thus ultimately leading to higher prices through inflationary borrowing or printing of money. Yet Southern governments risk urban riots, such as those seen in Jordan in 1996, and risk overthrow if food prices are allowed to skyrocket overnight.

Southerners, in turn, have demanded that the seed banks, supported by the FAO and World Bank to conserve precious plant seed stocks, be administered with greater input from less developed countries. Northerners want to retain patent rights over new seed varieties their laboratories have developed. As plant and animal genetic engineering progresses and becomes commercially rewarding, such battles over "genetic imperialism" are likely to intensify.

Private interests, ranging from domestic farm groups to transnational grain marketeers and food-processing companies, also find their way into the global politics of food. For example, multinational food companies, such as Swiss-based Nestlé, ironically were blamed for contributing to malnutrition by marketing nutritious baby formula in the third world. It seems that mothers, initially given the formula free at maternity centers, stopped breast-feeding their babies and then began diluting the formula, often with polluted water, to cut costs when they discovered they could not afford to buy it. In 1982, the World Health Organization passed a voluntary code of conduct for companies selling such items in the South.[85]

Of more widespread impact on world food concerns is the power of large grain dealers, agribusiness firms, and commodity speculators who have massive effects on markets and prices and control vast food stocks. Along with Northern agricultural and trade ministries, they tend to dominate the terms of international trade in food. For many years, the century-old international grain cartel among five companies owned by seven American and European families—Cargill, Continental, Bunge, Louis Dreyfus, and Andre—held sway at the center of the global trade system. Among their great advantages as conglomerates was that they could control grain as it progressed from the fields to the storage and processing facilities onto the retail shelves all over the world.[86] Greater food self-sufficiency on the part of the South would tend to cut into this corporate leverage.

It has been argued that for more Southern states to become food self-sufficient, a comprehensive approach to nutrition and public health must be adopted. It is not enough, for example to save malnourished and sick babies through oral rehydration if the medical, sanitation, and food systems are insufficient to keep them alive later. There must be follow-up with enlightened public health policies and a flexible approach to selecting the best food production and distribution methods for the particular location, and there must be sufficient capital to bring it all about.[87] All of these issues were debated further at yet another UN-sponsored conference in 1996, the World Food Summit in Rome, with the food prospects of many parts of the developing world remaining uncertain.

Population: Politics and Regimes

At the 1974 **World Population Conference** in Bucharest, Rumania, sponsored by the United Nations, Southern governments generally agreed that attempts to limit population growth were unfairly aimed at the South, where growth rates were highest. They labeled the Northern call for the South to control its numbers a subtle form of racism, noting that high per capita consumption in affluent developed countries was putting at least as much pressure on global resources as growing populations in the third world.

A decade later, however, as 149 countries met at the UN International Conference on Population in Mexico City, many of these same LDC leaders were openly advocating population control, recognizing how serious an impediment to development the population explosion had become. Ironically, at this same time some in the North were reconsidering their traditional support for population control programs. In 1985, in response to domestic anti-abortion groups, the Reagan administration cut off American contributions to the UN Fund for Population Activities (UNFPA), a program begun in the late 1960s under U.S. auspices to deal with the threat of overpopulation. UNFPA had established links with over 130 nations. The administration's position was that UNFPA was overly involved in promoting abortion and coercive birth control measures in China and elsewhere, even though the Fund's primary thrust was in the area of contraceptive education and family planning. American policy reverted mainly to bilateral programs and voluntary agencies stressing child health care and private enterprise–oriented economic development (considered the "best contraceptive"), leaving the UNFPA budget substantially depleted and restoration of American funds a controversial issue in Washington.[88]

By 1994, when the International Conference on Population and Development was held in Cairo (marking the twentieth anniversary of the first UN population conference), a fragile consensus had emerged around the notion that population policy had to be part of a comprehensive program of social and economic development, with cooperation between governments, international agencies, NGOs, and local grassroots groups. Still, conflicts persisted between Western governments promoting women's rights and reproductive rights (supported by feminist groups, the International Planned Parenthood Federation, and other NGOs) and the Vatican, joined by many Islamic states, concerned about upholding traditional values and lifestyles. The 170 national governments in attendance ultimately papered over their differences, allowing for the adoption of a program of action that emphasized linking an individual country's population policy to other aspects of development, such as health policy.[89] UNFPA, along with individual Northern donor nations such as Japan, agreed to aid in Southern population policy initiatives. This led to the adoption of population reform policies in a number of countries, ranging from Egypt to Ethiopia, from Bangladesh to the Philippines, including such measures as establishing programs for reproductive health under ministries of health.

Nongovernmental organizations are joining in these efforts as well, sometimes consulting with provincial and local governments:

> Community organizations, medical associations, scientific institutes and societies, family planning associations, legal organizations, churches, women's groups, youth associations, labour organizations, mothers' leagues, entrepreneurial coalitions, theatre groups, education associations, volunteer groups, child welfare and other social service organizations are advocating and working towards implementing the Programme of Action. Many of these organizations were among the 1,254 officially accredited NGOs at the ICPD.[90]

UN agencies have had interagency task forces working on proposals for creating a global data base related to health concerns, especially dealing with infant, child, and maternal mortality; improving basic education, with special attention to inequalities between the genders; and articulating policy statements on subjects such as women's empowerment and social services. Under the impetus of the General Assembly, reflecting the effort to take the spotlight off population alone and link the issue to development challenges in general, the UN Population Commission was redesignated as the Population and Development Commission. UN agencies involved in the fight against AIDS also consolidated their efforts in the 1990s, with an emphasis on AIDS prevention through "safe sex" and clean blood supplies.[91]

Growing attention also has been paid to urbanization problems. The UN Conference on Human Settlements ("Habitat II"), held in Istanbul, Turkey in 1996, was turned into a sort of "summit on cities." Mayors and representatives of local governmental authorities had a chance to interact with national leaders and IGO bureaucrats; among the ideas developed were plans for a computerized database of "best practices" by cities throughout the world on issues ranging from sewage treatment to preventing graffiti.[92]

One often overlooked aspect of the population problem (and the food problem as well) is the imbalance caused by the migration of *refugees*. Refugees are defined by the UN as persons with "well founded fears" of persecution because of race, religion, nationality, membership in a particular social group, or political views.[93] Worldwide refugee problems, present at least since World War I, have worsened recently with an outpouring of desperate people leaving their homelands because of war, famine, or political repression—being displaced across national boundaries or in some cases forced to relocate within their own country. Estimates have put the refugee population at 20 million internationally and 20 to 25 million internally displaced persons by the mid-1990s.[94]

Refugees, left homeless and often stateless, represent difficult burdens for the countries hosting them. Countries receiving the most refugees often are the destitute neighbors of the countries from which the asylum seekers have fled. Although the UN High Commission for Refugees (UNHCR) has campaigned for better living conditions as well as an easing of repression and an end to wars so that repatriation might be possible, refugee politics is highly controversial. States whose citizens become refugees traditionally have been embarrassed and reluctant to admit that the problem exists. Other governments have argued that UN relief programs as well as those operated by the International Red Cross and other NGOs—as in the case of Palestinian or African refugees or Kurds in northern Iraq—merely perpetuate political conflicts by subsidizing refugee camps and the governments that host them. Still others, including the United States, have become more resistant to accepting refugees in times of budgetary constraints and high unemployment, and have tried to hand the problems over to UN agencies. In many cases the difficulty for policymakers is to distinguish between political and economic refugees, with the latter turned away as merely fleeing to improve their economic lot.[95] The budget for the UNHCR, composed of mainly voluntary governmental contributions, doubled between 1990 and 1995 to approximately $1.2 billion; still this was hardly adequate to keep up with the burgeoning demand.[96]

Numerous actors also are involved in health concerns related to population, including NGOs such as French Doctors Without Borders and IGOs such as UNICEF. The major global institution in the health care field, the World Health Organization (WHO), has become increasingly involved in servicing the needs of the developing world. The North-South battle lines have not been as clearly drawn in WHO as in some other international institutions, partly because it is recognized that killer diseases, such as AIDS, cholera, and the Ebola virus, do not respect national or regional boundaries.[97] Massive global campaigns mounted by WHO and other international organizations have scored remarkable successes, eliminating killers such as smallpox, and reducing the incidence of polio and African tropical diseases such as Guinea worm and river blindness (onchocerciasis).[98]

However, global problem solving in the area of health care has not been as politically noncontroversial as one might hope. Despite its successes, WHO has come up against a variety of political forces that have frustrated its attempts to deal with health concerns. For instance, many governments still are unwilling to notify WHO of outbreaks of cholera and other communicable diseases, lest announcements of local epidemics damage port traffic and tourism and produce other adverse economic consequences. In its efforts to regulate the global marketing of products that it deems dangerous or needlessly expensive, WHO has had to confront MNCs that market pharmaceuticals and other products in LDCs. The same goes for worldwide anti-smoking campaigns. In working with the UN Commission on Narcotic Drugs to counter drug abuse problems, WHO confronts cash-hungry governments and NGOs (drug cartels) reliant on drug sales. Swamp-draining efforts and insecticide-spraying programs to combat malaria also have caused conflicts with environmentalists, in some cases pitting one UN agency (WHO) against another (the UN Environmental Program).[99]

Health care is one area in which regime formation has included the drafting of explicit rules, in the form of conventions and regulatory codes, designed to raise global standards. Central to this effort has been the World Health Assembly, a plenary body of WHO that meets annually to determine the broad policies of the organization, with each of the more than 160 member states having one vote. Among the rules that have been widely accepted are a series of International Sanitary Conventions, covering such matters as what can and cannot be done on ships and aircraft to prevent the spread of diseases. The Assembly also has the power to adopt technical regulations that promote uniform classification of diseases and pharmaceuticals (so that morbidity statistics can be compared and treatment standardized across national boundaries), a uniform code of standards regarding the safety, labeling, and advertising of health products sold internationally, and uniform procedures for reporting and responding to epidemics. Assembly regulations, administered by the WHO secretariat in Geneva, are binding on all member governments except those that, within a specified time, expressly reject the rule in question.[100] Hence, when purchasing drugs from the neighborhood pharmacy, one is receiving products that probably have been subject not only to local, state, and national regulation and testing, but also to international review.

As with population matters in general, the international community has been careful to respect national sovereignty in the health field. WHO, along with UNICEF, FAO, UNDP, and the World Bank, mainly have served as facilitators of improvements in national health care programs rather than acting as supranational agencies. The UN Conference on Human Settlements and the UN Water Conference in the late 1970s set various sanitation priorities. The latter conference designated the 1980s as the International Drinking Water Supply and Sanitation Decade and endorsed the goal—only partially achieved—of adequate drinking water for all people by 1990; it was left to national governments to figure out how to carry out conference recommendations.

In a sense, the world is involved in a population race toward stability. In the long run, improvements in personal income, education, and employment opportunities for women (see Fig. 14.4) and other such progress will tend to reduce birth rates, as improved health care extends life expectancies throughout the world. With global population growth already slowing somewhat, projections are for a "steady-state" global population of approximately double its current number by the end of the twenty-first century. The problem, though, is that this may be too many, depending on the resources available and their cost. Even in Africa there are signs of birth rates slackening, and if global rates can be made to decline faster, the steady-state population, when reached, would be smaller and easier to support (9 billion, for example, if a level of two children per family were reached by the year 2015).[101] World population efforts continue

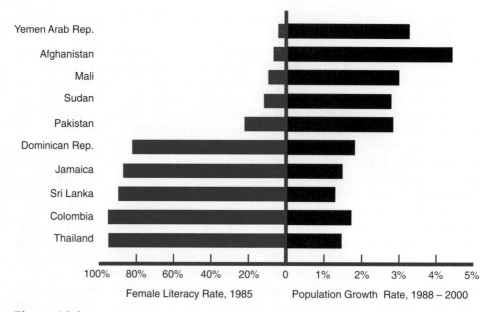

Figure 14.4
WOMEN'S LITERACY AND POPULATION GROWTH: THE MORE FEMALE EDUCA-TION, THE MORE LIKELY THEY ARE TO HAVE SMALLER FAMILIES
Source: John Van Pelt, *The Christian Science Monitor,* July 8, 1992, p. 14. Reprinted by permission from *The Christian Science Monitor.* © 1992 The Christian Science Publishing Society. All rights reserved.

to be hampered, however, by the inability of the world's leaders and citizens to agree on an "optimal" population level and on the means of achieving it.

Transfer of Capital and Technology: Politics and Regimes

Since the NIEO debate of the 1970s, LDC demands have been most pointed in regard to the transfer of capital and technology, and have involved congeries of actors—nation-states, MNCs, global IGOs, and private banks. Specifically, the South has sought reform in the rules governing international trade, aid, and investment, and monetary matters, along with debt relief and the dissemination of information and technology. For example, the International Development Strategy for the Third "Development Decade" (1981–1990), adopted by the UN General Assembly, set targets of an annual 7 percent increase in gross domestic products in the third world, 8 percent annual growth in trade, and .7 percent of the combined GNPs of the developed states to be allocated to development aid (with an additional .15 percent going to the very poorest states).[102] Despite some progress, these targets generally went unfulfilled, and the aid targets essentially were restated at the Social Summit in Copenhagen in 1995.[103]

During the NIEO debate, high on the South's list for trade improvements were (1) commodity agreements to raise and stabilize agricultural and raw material prices and to create "buffer stocks" that could be released in controlled ways on the market; (2) a common fund to back these commodity arrangements financially and to aid against the competition of synthetic products; (3) reductions in Northern tariff and nontariff barriers against Southern products, without necessary reciprocity for Northern products in the South (to stimulate Southern manufacturing and exports); and (4) Northern domestic economic policies to phase out production of goods that the South could produce more cheaply.

However, many of these demands elicited criticism from the North. Increased Southern exports of manufactured goods based on "cheap labor" production were seen as threatening to traditional Northern industries, such as textiles, shoes, and steel. Although many Northern governments were willing to write off such labor-intensive sectors of their economy, most insisted in return that they be given easier access to LDC markets, including banking, transport, and other "service" sectors. Among free trade enthusiasts in the developed countries, it was argued that price stabilization of raw materials and other commodities was contrary to the laws of supply and demand and was likely to result in higher prices for Northern consumers. Hence, most Southern demands in the area of international trade remained unmet through the 1980s and 1990s.[104]

The establishment of the World Trade Organization, discussed in the previous chapter, represents new hope for developing countries. Nevertheless, although four-fifths of WTO members are developing countries, the organization is perceived as Northern-dominated.[105] Moreover, WTO's existence is likely to render the UN Conference on Trade and Development (UNCTAD)—heretofore the third world's preferred trade forum—even less important than in the past. By the time 2,500 people representing 135 states, along with IGOs and NGOs, convened for UNCTAD's ninth session in South Africa in 1996, leaders in the United States and elsewhere were wondering if a "debating society" was needed any longer. There were calls for merging UNCTAD and WTO, both based in Geneva. UNCTAD IX reaffirmed the UN commitment to trade liberalization in light of the continued globalization of the international economy, while at the same time raising concern that the poorest states might be marginalized and left behind by the globalization process. A number of observers also pointed out that many Northern states were circumventing free trade rules and engaging in "neoprotectionist" practices against many LDCs.[106]

In the global trade regime, renewed emphasis has been placed on regional integration of Southern states to generate stronger trading communities; as one newspaper put it, "Though the world economy is globalizing, its trade rules are regionalizing."[107] Regional trade associations have taken hold from South America (Mercosur) to Northeast Asia (APEC), with at least one hundred such associations having notified WTO of their existence by the mid-1990s. Some of these groupings, such as NAFTA, have formal rules and binding regulations, and others, such as APEC, have only vague targets of cooperation.[108] As we noted in Chapter 13, global trade norms, such as continued tariff reduction, could unravel if regional associations do not harmonize their rules with those of WTO; for example, in a 1996 survey of eighty RTAs, only six met basic WTO rules against setting restrictions on and denying reciprocal trade advantages to nonmembers.[109]

In the area of foreign investment, Southern states have tried both for greater access to and control over MNC investment funds. Many have established codes of conduct for MNCs that would limit the profits that could be repatriated and prohibit MNC interference in host country domestic politics while strengthening host country taxing authority and participation in ownership or management. Such rules are based on the central tenets of the 1974 UN General Assembly resolution calling for a **Charter of Economic Rights and Duties of States:**

> Every state has and shall freely exercise full permanent sovereignty, including possession, use, and disposal, over all its wealth, natural resources, and economic activities. [This includes competence] to nationalize, expropriate, or transfer ownership of foreign property.

However, the militant positions reflected in this charter lessened during the 1980s and 1990s, as foreign investment was seen increasingly not so much as a form of imperialism as an alternative to expensive loans for debt-ridden states. The World Bank formed a billion-dollar insurance agency, the Multilateral Investment Guarantee Agency, to promote renewed MNC interest in LDCs.[110]

Southern priorities regarding foreign aid long have included (1) greater efforts by developed states to meet the aid targets set by the UN; (2) increased Northern financial commitments to the various emergency funds set up to deal with problems stemming from famine, wars, disasters, and market downturns; (3) greater Northern willingness to cancel debts of Southern states in serious balance of payments difficulties, or to renegotiate longer repayment schedules; and (4) loans at lower interest rates with fewer strings attached. As noted, the tendency of the World Bank, IMF, and regional lending agencies to require loan recipients to adopt austerity measures in their economies (higher taxes, reductions in government social services, and so forth) has been especially controversial, though more Southern states, as well as former East bloc members, have learned to live within the guidelines. In addition to greater voice in IMF decision making, the South also would like to see higher levels of international currency reserves set aside for developing countries.

In place of wholesale debt forgiveness or moratoriums, which many in the North argue would simply further harm Southern credit ratings, "creditors like the World Bank and IMF have tried to put indebted countries on track to repayment through structural adjustment programs. These modify indebted countries' interest rates, exchange rates, wage, trade policies, and other economic variables in an effort to help them earn cash. To date, their record has been mixed at best, and many countries that accepted adjustment programs are worse off than they were before. Moreover, these programs have been particularly hard on the poorest people in the poorest countries by cutting government subsidies for food and health care. . . . In the meantime, traditional lending continues."[111] Thus, the international debt problem has been handled on a case-by-case basis through negotiations among the World Bank, IMF, regional development banks, consortia of private banks, and lender and debtor governments. In emergencies, such as Mexico's near-default in 1982, the coordinated response among these actors can be swift. Long-term and sustained debt relief is more difficult, however. Other innovative debt reducing schemes are reviewed in the box on pages 546–547.

Thus, international aid agencies have moved toward combinations of public and private enterprise and market-oriented approaches in hopes of eliminating inequities, empowering the poor, and giving them opportunities to support themselves and their families and contribute to their societies' development. World Bank lending, for example, has placed emphasis on projects leading to broad-based economic growth, development of "human capital" (as in education, family planning, health care, sanitation, and nutrition), and social "safety nets" (such as short-term public works job creation) for the most vulnerable groups. Even "mini-credit" loans of as little as $100 or less to rural women and other "microentrepreneurs" in LDCs have been tried successfully (e.g., by the Grameen Bank of Bangladesh) through an international banking network called the International Consultative Group to Assist the Poorest (CGAP) established to spur local economic growth in chronically poor areas.[112]

Conclusion

Although a New International Economic Order has not dawned, economic development concerns have been given somewhat greater visibility on the global agenda through a series of consciousness-raising events and conferences, and through the development of more sober multilateral and bilateral approaches tailored to reaching more of those in need. Increasingly, methods of addressing poverty and development have combined public and private approaches, governments and nongovernmental organizations, the global, regional, and local levels.

We have said very little, however, about a related set of issues that is crowding the global agenda and creating complications for economic development problem solving: the management of energy and nonrenewable resources, and protection of

POSSIBLE REMEDIES FOR INTERNATIONAL DEBT

A number of possible debt remedies have been offered, including U.S. initiatives during the 1980s such as the Baker Plan, in which the Treasury Secretary, James Baker, proposed that commercial and international development banks participate in a multi-year lending program to promote economic growth among the fifteen major debtor states; in return, borrowers would be expected to emphasize private enterprise and market-oriented approaches to development. LDC critics of the proposal, especially those in the Cartegena Group of eleven Latin American debtor states, charged that it did not go far enough to cover issues such as reducing interest rates and improving repayment terms especially for smaller developing states hit by falling commodity markets.

More esoteric approaches have included specific "debt swap" measures, under which debts are written off in return for some concessions by the debtor. The "debt-equity" swap was pioneered in Latin America, and worked as follows:

> An American company planning, for example, a cassette-tape plant in Mexico, purchases $1 million worth of Mexican debt from an American bank that loaned the money to Mexico. The bank sells the $1 million IOU for just $600,000, happy to wipe the shaky loan from its books rather than wait years in hope of repayment. The company then presents the $1 million IOU to the Mexican government, which, after applying a 10 percent discount, "buys" the note for $900,000 worth of pesos to be spent on the new plant.

Other swap plans have included "debt for nature" agreements (e.g., having Madagascar agree to adopt development policies that limit destruction of its tropical rain forests, a valuable global resource, in return for debt buyouts) and "debt for children" agreements (e.g., involving Bolivia in commitments to aid children and preserve Bolivian culture in return for debt-reducing donations by the U.S. Agency for International Development and the private Save the Children Federation and Foster Parents Plan).

The Washington-based Debt-for-Development Foundation has helped arrange such deals, including a $5 million "debt-for-education" swap in Ecuador in the late 1980s, which established an endowment to send Ecuadorian students on scholarship to Harvard University. Such measures, however, do little to relieve the debtor's overall dependence on outside powers and sources of finance. Indeed, as its peso neared collapse in 1995, Mexico was forced essentially to mortgage its oil industry as collateral for Washington loan guarantees, while the U.S.

Congress still felt reluctant to commit to the President's desire to shore up the Mexican economy and help American banks avoid huge losses.

Sources: Howard La Franchi, "U.S. Firms Help Lighten Mexico's Debt," *Christian Science Monitor,* April 13, 1987, p. 3; John Yemma, "FYI: International Debt Crisis," *Christian Science Monitor,* March 19, 1987, pp. 18–19; and James Painter, "Bolivian Debt Swap Hikes Aid to Children," *Christian Science Monitor,* January 28, 1991, p. 6.

the natural environment. Many Northerners in the 1970s were warning of threats posed to human survival by resource scarcities and environmental pollution. While Northerners began to speak of the "limits to growth" in the world economy, arguing the need for altering high-consumption habits represented by gas-guzzling automobiles and all-electric kitchens, Southerners contended that they had yet to enjoy these benefits fully and would continue to seek them. Nevertheless, economic hardship also has forced Southerners to recycle and conserve. In Brazil, for example, citizens of Recife are noted for turning old bottles, cans, tins, and electric light bulbs into salable figurines, lamps, sandals, bed-webbing, and ashtrays. However, elsewhere in Brazil and Latin America, more and more people are buying cars, roads are being carved through once remote Amazon jungles, and the land is being subjected to alarming rates of deforestation and soil erosion.

Many of the North's achievements as well as its problems are being transferred to the South, and many of the South's responses are both creative and destructive. Even international lending agencies have been asking questions about the environmental impact of proposed development projects such as dam and road construction. Earlier in this chapter we alluded to the concept of "sustainable development." A much-publicized study was published in 1987 by the UN-sponsored World Commission on Environment and Development, the Brundtland Commission Report entitled *Our Common Future,* which documented the link between poverty and environmental decay, arguing that poverty-related overpopulation and land degradation in the South were threatening the global ecology no less than affluence and overconsumption in the North; the report's central conclusion was that LDC economic growth was necessary to avoid environmental disaster, but that such development had to be ecologically sound and "sustainable." Based on the Brundtland Commission Report, a UN Conference on Environment and Development was held in 1992 in Brazil, whose tropical rainforests, considered a vital world resource by the scientific community, were gradually being destroyed by the march of civilization. In Chapter 15, we discuss this conference and how developing countries attempted to use the meeting to reopen the NIEO debate and renew pressure on the rich countries to accelerate development assistance, this time in a new context; as one UN official remarked at the time: "The developing countries consider technology transfers and financial aid essential to carrying out plans for environmentally sound development."[113]

Therefore, we turn next to an examination of how modern industrial civilization is putting pressure on the "carrying capacity" of the earth's oceans, air, and land, and how the global political system is attempting to cope with the threat to the global ecosystem.

SUMMARY

1. A rich-poor gap exists both between states (the North versus the South) and within states. Substantial improvement in the lot of the poor depends on economic development, which in turn is associated with a number of interrelated problems, including food supply, population growth, and the transfer of capital and technology. A series of consciousness-raising global conferences have been held in the 1990s to attract the world's attention to these problems, with modest outcomes produced.

2. Although world food production has been growing, periodic downturns and other factors hamper efforts to relieve global hunger. Among these factors are lack of effective food distribution networks along with inadequate water and energy supplies and agricultural research. The "green revolution" has made a substantial dent in the problem of LDC food self-sufficiency, but the impact has been uneven and particularly weak in Africa.

3. Food problems are intimately linked with population problems. Population growth has accelerated since World War II, particularly in the South, though the growth rate has declined recently except in Africa. The North has urged the South to control its numbers; the South has responded with extensive birth control programs. Many analysts note that lower birth rates would occur if Southern standards of living were raised and educational and other opportunities for women were increased.

4. Although medical advances have lowered death rates in the South, serious problems remain, particularly in the areas of health care delivery, nutrition, and sanitation.

5. Although foreign aid and foreign investment as well as funds earned from exports provide important sources of capital for LDCs, these countries point out that existing international economic relationships and rules tend to help the rich more than the poor. Technological advances of the computer era have reached the South, and a few states have achieved the ability to generate new wealth and products on their own. However, the flow of advanced technology still tends to follow mainly a North-North path rather than North-South. Capital also has tended to flow northward in loan repayments and investments, and donor states on the whole have failed to meet foreign aid targets.

6. All of these problems have been closely associated with past demands for a "New International Economic Order" as a way of redistributing wealth more equally between North and South. The South has sought reform in the rules governing international trade, aid and investment, monetary matters, debt, and the dissemination of technology. But Southern demands have met with criticism from Northern states, which have tended to blame corrupt governments and inefficient IGOs for at least part of the South's poverty problem.

7. The two main bargaining groups in the North-South debate have been the Group of 77 (representing the South) and OECD (representing the North), along with several subgroups. Nonstate actors have come to play an increasingly prominent role in this debate, including agribusiness corporations and other MNCs, private banks, local governments and grassroots organizations, and a variety of IGOs and NGOs. The NIEO debate in the 1970s was characterized by considerable Southern solidarity and militancy; in the 1980s and 1990s, NIEO calls became more muted, the Southern bloc more fragmented, and the rhetoric less militant.

8. An international development regime is emerging that partially addresses Southern demands, but with an emphasis on free market domestic reforms demanded by certain Northern states. The regime is strongest on issues jointly benefiting both North and South. Increasingly, proposed remedies for debt and underdevelopment involve a combination of public and private approaches.

9. Among the regime's norms or principles are realizations that malnutrition in the South probably can be alleviated only through greater food self-sufficiency and purchasing power in LDCs; population problems can be solved only within the framework of an overall development strategy that deals with issues such as health care, sanitation, jobs, and education; and effective use of capital depends on reaching and empowering people at the grassroots.

10. Certain aspects of the international development regime have had difficulty or broken down (e.g., some commodity agreements) or are still in transition between case-by-case and comprehensive approaches (e.g., debt relief). Other aspects, such as the World Health Organization's organized disease-fighting campaigns and regulatory codes for health products, have scored major successes, though usually not without political controversies.

SUGGESTIONS FOR FURTHER READING AND STUDY

General works dealing with the problems of economic development include Jan Black, *Development in Theory and Practice: Bridging the Gap* (Boulder, Colo.: Westview Press, 1991); Richard W. T. Pomfret, *Diverse Paths of Economic Development* (New York: Harvester Wheatsheaf, 1992); Bjorn Hettne, *Development Theory and the Three Worlds* (New York: Wiley, 1990); Kathleen Staudt, *Managing Development: State, Society, and International Contexts* (Thousand Oaks, Calif.: Sage, 1991); Kempe R. Hope, *Development in the Third World; From Policy Failure to Policy Reform* (Armonk, NY: M. E. Sharp, 1996); Richard B. Norgaard, *Development Betrayed: The End of Progress and a Coevolutionary Revisioning of the Future* (London: Routledge, 1994); David E. Apter, *Rethinking Development: Modernization, Dependency, and Postmodern Politics* (Newbury Park, Calif.: Sage, 1987); M. V. Naidu, " 'International Development': An Attempt at Conceptualization for Comparative Analysis of Models of Development," *Peace Research* (Canada), 26 (February 1994), pp. 1–17; and Nicholas Kaldor, *Causes of Growth and Stagnation in the World Economy* (Cambridge, Eng.: Cambridge University Press, 1996).

Specific aspects of development are treated in Kartik C. Roy, Clement Allan Tisdell, and Hans C. Blomqvist, eds., *Economic Development and Women in the World Com-*

munity (Westport, Conn.: Praeger, 1996); Janet H. Momsen and Vivian Kinnaird, eds., *Different Places, Different Voices: Gender and Development in Africa, Asia and Latin America* (London: Routledge, 1993); Tariq Banuri, ed., *Economic Liberalization: No Panacea: The Experiences of Latin America and Asia* (Oxford: Clarendon Press, 1991); UNESCO, *The Cultural Dimension of Development: Towards a Practical Approach* (Paris: UNESCO Publishing, 1995); *Development Management in Africa: Toward Dynamism, Empowerment, and Entrepreneurship* (Boulder, Colo.: Westview Press, 1995); Kenneth E. Bauzon, ed., *Development and Democratization in the Third World: Myths, Hopes, and Realities* (New York: Crane Russack, 1992); and Lilia Shevtsova, "Russia Facing New Choices: Contradictions of Post Communist Development," *Security Dialogue* (UK), 25 (September 1994), pp. 321–334.

Works focusing on food, population, capital, and technology include Phillips Foster, *The World Food Problem: Tackling the Causes of Undernutrition in the Third World* (Boulder, Colo.: Lynne Rienner, 1992); Ismail Serageldin and Pierre Landell-Mills, eds., *Overcoming Global Hunger*, Environmentally Sustainable Development Proceedings Series, No. 3 (Washington, D.C.: World Bank, 1994); Michael Dover and Lee Talbot, *To Feed the Earth* (Washington, D.C.: World Resources Institute, 1987); Neal Spivack and Ann Florini, *Food on the Table* (New York: United Nations Association, 1986); Paul and Anne Ehrlich, *The Population Explosion* (New York: Simon and Schuster, 1990); Dennis Pirages, *Global Technopolitics* (Pacific Grove, Calif.: Brooks/Cole, 1989), chs. 6 and 7; James Reed Golden, *Economics and National Strategy in the Information Age: Global Networks, Technology Policy, and Cooperative Competition* (Westport, Conn.: Praeger, 1994); Mark W. Zacher, *Governing Global Networks: International Regimes for Transportation and Communications* (Cambridge, Eng.: Cambridge University Press, 1996); Steve H. Hanke and Alan A. Walters, eds., *Capital Markets and Development* (San Francisco: ICS Press, 1991); Susan George, *The Debt Boomerang: How Third World Debt Harms Us All* (London: Pluto Press, 1992); Edward R. Fried and Philip H. Trezise, eds., *Third World Debt: The Next Phase* (Washington, D.C.: Brookings Institution, 1989); Roger Riddell, *Foreign Aid Reconsidered* (Baltimore, Md.: Johns Hopkins University Press, 1987); and Mark Zacher and Jock Finlayson, *Developing Countries and the Commodity Trading Regime* (New York: Columbia University Press, 1988).

Additional information can be found in the official publications of such UN agencies as the World Bank and IMF, UNESCO and the UN Development Program; in such periodicals as *The Wall Street Journal*, *The Financial Times* (London), *The Economist*, *World Development*, and *Choices: The Human Development Magazine*; in reports and publications of the Overseas Development Council (Washington); and in the *State of the World* series, edited by the staff of the Worldwatch Institute in Washington.

The Management of Resources: Negotiating the World's Troubled Waters, Land, and Air

On December 17, 1970, the United Nations General Assembly passed Resolution 2749 by a vote of 108 yeas, 0 nays, and 14 abstentions. The resolution contained the following statement:

> The sea-bed and the ocean floor, and the subsoil thereof beyond the limits of a national jurisdiction, as well as the resources of the area, are the common heritage of mankind. The area shall not be subject to appropriation by any means by States or persons . . . and no State shall claim or exercise . . . sovereign rights over any part thereof.

The term "common heritage of mankind" included in this resolution potentially has profound implications. The resolution refers specifically to the oceans, which altogether cover 70 percent of the earth's surface. But, in a sense, it might just as well apply to the entire ecosystem on which life on the planet depends: minerals, energy sources, oxygen, plant and animal species, and other natural resources. When viewing photos of the earth taken from outer space, one can appreciate the extent to which human beings all coexist on a lovely and delicate orb and possess a common heritage.

However, as compelling as "Spaceship Earth" imagery is, the view from the ground up looks quite different. Instead of a common heritage, the dominant reality "down here" is that different actors compete to control and exploit the world's natural resources, including outer space itself. Questions about ownership of the world's resources can be treated in the context of what social scientists call *collective goods* and *private goods*. **Collective goods** are those resources that can be used by one party without diminishing the supply available to other parties, i.e., they are *jointly available,* like public parks and clean air. Such goods are *indivisible;* they cannot be parceled out for the benefit of some individuals while being denied to others. In contrast, **private goods** are resources that can be possessed by individuals and can be divided up.

The tension between collective goods and private goods in international relations can be seen in the law of the sea debate. The traditional notion of "freedom of the seas," a fixture of international law over the centuries, implied that the vast stretches of the oceans—unlike land masses and the waters immediately adjacent to them—were to be considered a collective good, a commons subject to no state's ownership or jurisdiction. As the seventeenth-century legal scholar Grotius stated, "The sea, since it is incapable of being seized as the air, cannot be attached to the possessions of any particular nation."[1] The 1970 UN resolution noted above was essentially a reaffirmation of this basic principle.

However, the virtually unanimous vote in support of the resolution disguised some major disagreements. These disagreements surfaced at the **UN Conference on the Law of the Sea** held during the 1970s, which was attended by almost every country in the world, coastal and landlocked states alike. At the conference, the common heritage concept was challenged as many participants proposed to treat the oceans as a private good, i.e., a commodity to be carved up and claimed by individual countries for their own exclusive use— whether in the form of national economic zones (for exploiting offshore oil and gas), fishing zones (for controlling access to nearby fish stocks threatened with depletion), deep-sea mining preserves, or restricted areas of various other sorts. The law of the sea debate continued during the 1980s and 1990s.

Similar conflicts have occurred over whether air space and outer space, as well as Antarctica, are to be considered the "common heritage of mankind" or whether they are to be subject to extended national claims. Even where countries clearly exercise sovereignty, there is some question as to what obligation a state has to refrain from activities within its borders that could have potentially harmful environmental impacts on neighboring states. In this chapter, we examine the politics of global ecology, with reference to management of land-based resources as well as the atmosphere, the oceans, and outer space. In addition to the Law of the Sea Conference, we will look at a number of other efforts to promote cooperation and regime-building, notably the 1992 UN Conference on Environment and Development (UNCED, or the "Earth Summit") held in Rio de Janeiro, where a variety of environmental concerns were discussed. In launching UNCED, the Brundtland Commission Report acknowledged that "the Earth is one but the world is not."[2]

The Nature and Magnitude of the Problem

One way of classifying the world's resources is in terms of **nonrenewable** and **renewable resources.** The former include such raw materials as copper, zinc, and nickel, as well as such energy sources as oil and natural gas, all of which are in finite supply and are capable of being exhausted. Resources that are renewable, such as air and water, are threatened not so much by exhaustion as by pollution and spoilage. Modern industrial civilization—characterized by high technology, energy-intensive means of production, and mass consumption—puts an increased burden on both kinds of resources.

Scientists do not agree on exactly how serious is the threat to global resources. In the early 1970s, doomsday predictions about imminent resource scarcities and environmental decay mounted and produced a movement to limit growth in world population and consumption. Especially provocative was a 1972 study by the Club of Rome entitled *The Limits to Growth*, which concluded that economic growth would have to be halted in the late twentieth century if civilization were to survive.[3] Alarms were sounded at the 1972 UN Conference on the Human Environment that the world would soon be out of fuel and raw materials, if it did not first suffocate from pollution. It now appears that some of the predictions of the **limits to growth school** were erroneous and based on faulty computer models that included exaggerated rates of

FACTORIES NEAR SANTOS, BRAZIL: WHAT CONSTITUTES "SUSTAINABLE DEVELOPMENT" THAT CONTRIBUTES TO BOTH ECONOMIC GROWTH AND ECOLOGICAL BALANCE?

consumption, population growth, industrialization, and pollution. Such models may have underrated such factors as human innovation, economic slowdowns, and the abundance of raw materials available at higher market prices.[4] By the time the Earth Summit was convened in 1992, the call for limits to growth had been replaced with a call for **sustainable development,** which offered a middle path between no economic growth and unrestrained economic growth; it was argued that developed and developing countries alike could continue to expand their economies and avoid environmental disaster as long as they followed environmentally sensitive policies that sustained existing ecosystems. Nevertheless, with continued concerns about toxic waste dumping, global warming, tropical deforestation, energy uncertainties, and other matters, warnings about the finiteness of key resources and the fragility of ecological balances still have validity. We survey major areas of concern below.

THE ATMOSPHERE

Natural pollutants (e.g., smoke from forest fires and ash from volcanoes) have been around since before human memory. Man-made pollution can be traced as far back as ancient Babylon and Rome, with the Industrial Revolution accelerating the phenomenon.[5] Since World War II, the world has seen "killer smogs in London and Los Angeles and the widespread use of gas masks in Tokyo."[6] Although air quality in many industrialized countries has improved somewhat in recent years because of environmental measures taken by governments, pollution in the North remains a serious problem. The problem is worsening in most developing countries; in India, for example, breathing the air in Bombay is said to be equivalent to smoking 10 cigarettes a day, whereas in Mexico City it is the equivalent of smoking two packs a day.[7] Air pollution impairs plant growth, alters climatic conditions, threatens animal and human life, and produces other harmful effects. Atmospheric pollutants become an *international* problem when, as in the case of acid rain and greenhouse gases, they know no national boundaries as they circle a given geographical region and have global implications.

Great cultural monuments of Rome and Venice as well as natural habitats in North America and Europe have been ravaged by *acid rain*, caused mainly by the burning of coal that produces airborne sulfur dioxide and nitrogen oxide emissions, which dissolve in rain droplets and then fall to the ground far from their source. Sweden and Norway have been net importers of such emissions from Germany and other neighboring states, with the resulting deaths of many forests and lakes. Similarly, Canada has complained for years about destruction of woodlands caused by acid rain originating in the northeastern and midwestern United States. China's heavy reliance on coal (for almost three-fourths of its total energy use), combined with its rapid industrialization, is provoking much concern in Japan and other states in the region.[8]

The accumulation of carbon dioxide and other gases caused by the burning of oil and other fossil fuels is thought to produce a *greenhouse effect*, trapping heat and raising the earth's temperature. Although scientists disagree about whether a long-term global warming trend is taking place, there has been a temperature rise of between .3° and .6°C during the twentieth century, coinciding with a steady buildup of CO_2 in the atmosphere. The ten warmest years ever recorded (since record keeping began around 1880) have all occurred since 1980. Projecting from computer models, some expect a further 2.0° rise over the next century, which would raise sea levels (through polar melting) about .5 meters, thus flooding many coastal areas, and at the same time perhaps trigger abnormal droughts in some parts of the world.[9] The buildup of greenhouse gases called chlorofluorocarbons (CFCs) has also been blamed for contributing to a *depletion of the ozone layer*, which shields us from the sun's ultraviolet rays and helps to prevent skin cancer.[10]

LAND

Land-based resources are being threatened partly by changing atmospheric conditions and partly by other factors. Creeping "desertification"—the spread

"The extra fifteen per cent is for the rain forest."

Drawing by Lomez; © 1990 The New Yorker Magazine, Inc.

The greening of the world: environmental consciousness-raising among nonstate actors.

of deserts to previously arable land—has been occurring globally at a rate of 6 million hectares per year (the Sahara alone has increased by over 250,000 square miles in recent years). Desertification has been traced to long-term atmospheric changes as well as overgrazing, overfarming, and deforestation. Deserts now cover one-third of the earth's land area and are encroaching on another 20 percent. In addition, an estimated 26 billion tons of topsoil are eroding and blowing away each year.[11]

It is estimated that 25 to 40 percent of the tropical rain forests that existed before the twentieth century now have been eliminated, and that an area the size of New York state is deforested yearly. As one example, Madagascar has lost half its forests since 1950, and at present rates of destruction may well lose much of the remainder by the year 2015.[12] Special attention has been drawn to Brazil, where the Northwest Brazilian Project in the 1980s (designed to build a 1,000-mile paved highway through the Amazon jungle) resulted in some 20,000 square miles of forests being lost in eight years.[13] Burning of tropical rainforests contributes to the release of CO_2 and, hence, global warming. In addition, because half of all plant and animal species on earth are thought to live in the rainforests, rainforest destruction threatens biodiversity, including the possible extinction of plants that have important potential medical and other applications (e.g., medicines derived from the rosy periwinkle in Madagascar have been used to combat childhood leukemia).[14] Deforestation is also occurring in temperate regions, although the rate of destruction is moderating in some cases where publics and governments are engaging in reforestation programs and taking other corrective actions.[15]

The land, and creatures living on it, are also threatened by deposits of toxic substances, including heavy metals (such as mercury), nuclear wastes, and pesticides. In 1962, Rachel Carson's book, *The Silent Spring*, alerted people to the danger of bird and animal extinction caused by ingested pesticides (which weaken eggshells), expanding cities and industries (which destroy animal habitat), and general pollution. Industrialized countries account for roughly 90 percent of the world's hazardous wastes.[16] Environmental consciousness has increased greatly since Carson's day, particularly in the developed countries of the North and even in the poverty-stricken South, as seen in the refusal of Latin American and African states to serve as the dumping ground for chemical and radioactive wastes exported from advanced industrial economies.[17] Still, some capital-starved governments may be tempted to become "waste havens" out of desperation.

WATER

Although water blankets much of the earth, drinkable water is in short supply. Ninety-nine percent of the world's water is inaccessibly tied up in salty oceans of frozen polar caps; over half of the remaining 1 percent is located more than a mile underground. Hence, lakes and rivers, representing only a tiny fraction (less than 1 percent) of total global water resources, constitute the bulk of available fresh water supplies. The lakes and rivers themselves are being subjected to increased pollution and deterioration of water quality. The "Blue Danube" in Europe, for example, has been referred to as the "Brown Danube." In much of Africa and Latin America, raw sewage is discharged directly into waterways used for drinking. Over 1 billion people lack access to clean water for drinking or sanitation.[18]

With worldwide water demand doubling every 20 years,[19] fresh water could indeed become "the world's scarcest resource, more valuable than petroleum."[20] Noting that 80 countries, most in Africa and the Middle East, are now facing water shortages, a World Bank official has stated that "the wars of the next century will be over water."[21] The potential for international conflict over water is heightened by the fact that 40 percent of the world's population depends for drinking water and irrigation on 214 river systems shared by at least two states; 12 of these are shared by at least five different states.[22] Although disputes may arise over some countries seeking to divert water from their neighbors, such interdependence could also produce pressures for upstream and downstream states to cooperate in preserving a common resource.

Land-based pollutants—industrial effluents, chemical fertilizers, nuclear wastes, pesticides, and raw sewage—that enter rivers and lakes ultimately are fed into the world's oceans, with the potential to cause enormous harm. The oceans serve many functions that are not all completely compatible: as the earth's major source of oxygen, as commercial laboratories for deep-sea mining, as transport lanes for oil tankers and freighters, as food baskets, as industrial wastebins, and as the aquatic home for animals.

The oceans also are a source of mystical beauty providing unique contentment—both quite scarce resources these days. The fact that deserts in the United States and Middle East were once vast seas, that continents still drift apart (or together), that some of the earth's highest mountain peaks are submerged, all testify to the immense natural forces that dwarf the power of nations.

ENERGY

Both the oceans and the land harbor vast energy supplies, but there is concern regarding whether they will be sufficient to meet future global demand. Should developing countries seek to emulate the intensive energy consumption patterns of the industrialized countries of the North, the pressure on nonrenewable resources such as petroleum could become intolerable and could pose a major supply challenge in addition to the problems associated with the burning of fossil fuels.

In the early 1990s, the South, with about three quarters of the world's population, accounted for only about one quarter of its total energy consumption. However, it is estimated that, by 2010, the share of global energy consumption attributable to economically advanced countries will fall below 50 percent for the first time since the Industrial Revolution;[23] by 2010, also, LDC carbon dioxide emissions are expected to be equal to those the entire world produced in 1970.[24] The fifteen major energy-consuming nations in 1996 were still mainly industrial Northern states but included such developing giants as China, India, and Brazil as well. These fifteen states, with about 65 percent of the world's population, consumed roughly 80 percent of the world's commercial energy. The United States alone, with only 6 percent of the world's population, accounted for some 30 percent of annual global energy consumption. Experts now predict that "although in the past, energy consumption was overwhelmingly dominated by the highly industrialized countries, in the next generation most of the increase will be in the developing countries."[25]

However, the energy picture has improved somewhat as the early 1990s saw a slight dip in per capita global energy consumption. Conservation efforts and economic slowdowns (particularly in the former Soviet Union) appear to have at least temporarily curbed the North's rate of resource depletion. China's emergence into the "automotive age" could, however, reverse these gains. Commercial energy price increases have a significant slowdown effect on energy consumption; the oil price "shocks" of the 1970s and a mini-shock in 1990 brought greater conservation. Throughout the industrial era, energy consumption and energy prices have been closely related to the rate of economic growth. Yet, recent conservation efforts have shown that growth does not have to depend so heavily on increased energy consumption, as demonstrated by the significant per capita economic growth in OECD countries between 1973 and 1985 despite a 5 percent per capita reduction in energy use; during the 1990s, the United States continued to register economic growth while somewhat curtailing energy consumption.[26]

The earth's primary power source, the sun, is free, renewable, and nonpolluting. However, it is economically costly and technologically difficult to harness solar energy, whether through solar cells, windmills, or other devices.[27] World shipments of small silicon photovoltaic chips for solar energy collectors, as well as global wind-generating capacity, both rose by some 50 percent in the 1990s; still, reliance on renewable solar energy remained low (e.g., wind power accounted for less than .1 percent of global electricity supplies).[28] Nuclear power, once thought to be an attractive, plentiful energy source, has fallen into disfavor after numerous nuclear plant accidents, notably the Chernobyl reactor explosion in the Ukraine in 1986, although France, Japan, and some other countries continue to rely heavily on nuclear power as part of their overall energy strategy.[29] For the foreseeable future, the developed world will continue to rely primarily on oil, coal, and natural gas, while the developing world increasingly uses these fuels as well, except for the poorest areas, where biomass (such as firewood and animal dung) will remain the dominant energy source.[30]

Among fossil fuels, coal is the most plentiful on the globe, with an estimated 200 years remaining. Although it is especially abundant in North America and Russia, China has led in coal production over the past several years, accounting for almost a quarter of the world total. Serious environmental problems are associated with the expanded use of coal, however, notably, increases in acid rain.[31]

Oil reserves are far more concentrated than coal deposits. The bulk of known oil reserves (perhaps as much as 70 percent) is concentrated in the Middle East, with four states—Saudi Arabia, Kuwait, Iran, and Iraq—controlling over half the proven reserves there. Vast additional quantities are located in the former Soviet Union, with a rush among Western diplomats and oil company executives to establish positive relations with states such as Kazakhstan and Azerbaijan. New petroleum deposits also are suspected to exist off the coast of China. Natural gas tends to be concentrated near oil fields, with the former Soviet Union and the Middle East having the lion's share (approximately two-thirds) of the known reserves.

Petroleum and natural gas markets are expected to encounter problems of political and economic uncertainties more than physical supply exhaustion. Proven reserves appear sufficient to last approximately six decades at current production levels, with the possibility of supplies extending still further if oil shale and other more expensive sources are tapped.[32] However, the "last drop" of oil probably will remain in the ground and never be used because the energy and economic costs required to extract it would be prohibitive; other, cheaper energy alternatives would likely already have supplanted oil as a fuel.[33] In the short term, the political volatility of many oil-producing regions (most conspicuously, the instability in the Middle East) raises concerns that shortages could arise, as occurred during the 1990–1991 Gulf War, with a resultant rise in global energy prices.

The environmental problems of coal, petroleum-based, and nuclear energy, along with oil and gas supply uncertainties, make a *mix* of energy strategies, including greater use of renewable resources, crucial for the future. "Countries situated in the higher latitudes are favored with wind resources; mountainous countries have falling water; tropical countries can produce organic materials for fuel throughout the year, and countries in desert areas have an abundance of sunlight."[34] Such variations leave room for controlled use of nuclear power as well, especially in countries with few energy alternatives and possessing safe geological sites for waste storage.

NONFUEL MINERALS

Turning to the supply of nonfuel minerals, one finds that reserves generally are more widely distributed than fossil fuel reserves, but that many countries are highly dependent on imports of selected raw materials. (See Table 15.1 for the location of major mineral reserves.) The Japanese and West Europeans are particularly short of key minerals, relying on imports to meet over 90 percent of their needs in several raw materials categories (in seventeen of forty-two important categories in the case of the European Union as a whole, and nineteen of forty-two in the case of Japan).[35] Recalling our earlier discussion of trade dependence in the international economy, the United States also has had a heavy "mineral import reliance" despite being blessed with various raw materials found within its own borders.[36]

To judge the potential for mineral supply crises, one must assess many factors: the changing importance of each resource in industry; its abundance in various countries; the likelihood that producers could coalesce politically to restrict supply through a cartel; the availability and price of substitutes; the power of MNCs to control the market and make up for shortages; the effect of price increases on new exploration; and the level of reserves in relation to demand. In the case of lead, for example, environmental concerns (lead poisoning dangers) have led to international efforts to reduce its use in products such as paints, batteries, and auto fuels and to promote substitutes.[37]

Table 15.1
THE WORLD'S MINERAL RESERVES

Mineral	Country	Percentage of World Reserves	Mineral	Country	Percentage of World Reserves
Bauxite			Nickel		
	Australia	24.3		Cuba	38.3
	Guinea	24.3		Russia	14.0
	Brazil	12.2		Canada	13.2
	Jamaica	8.7		New Caledonia	9.6
	India	4.3		Indonesia	6.8
Chromium				South Africa	5.3
	South Africa	83.8		Australia	4.7
	Kazakhstan	8.6	Tin		
	Zimbabwe	3.8		China	22.9
Cobalt				Brazil	17.1
	Zaire	50.0		Malaysia	17.1
	Cuba	25.0		Thailand	13.4
	Zambia	9.0		Indonesia	10.7
	New Caledonia	5.8	Tungsten		
Copper				China	45.7
	Chile	28.4		Canada	12.4
	United States	14.5		Russia	11.9
	Poland	6.5		United States	6.7
	Russia	6.5		Bolivia	2.5
Lead			Zinc		
	Australia	27.9		Canada	15.0
	United States	11.8		Australia	12.1
	China	10.3		United States	11.4
	Canada	5.9		Peru	5.0
Manganese				Mexico	4.3
	South Africa	54.4		China	3.6
	Ukraine	19.9	Iron ore (crude ore)		
	Gabon	6.6		Russia	42.7
	China	5.9		Australia	10.7
Molybdenum				United States	10.7
	United States	49.1		Canada	8.0
	Chile	20.0		Brazil	7.3
	China	9.1			
	Canada	8.2			
	Russia	4.4			

Source: Adapted from *Mineral Commodity Summaries, 1996.* (Washington, D.C.: U.S. Geological Survey, 1996).

Among key commercial raw materials, iron has few substitutes but is abundant and widely distributed across the globe. Bauxite (aluminum) similarly is widely available; during the 1980s, Brazil entered the market as a major new bauxite producer, contributing to a decline in global prices despite the efforts of the International Bauxite Association—a coalition of producing and consuming states—to stabilize them.[38] Manganese, once mined mainly in the Soviet Union, has been found in greater abundance worldwide since World War II. Nickel, used in stainless steel, likewise has been more widely available since the price doubled in the 1970s and discoveries were made on the ocean floor. Conversely, chromium and platinum are available only through a few sources; some of these, such as the former Soviet Union, South Africa, Zimbabwe, and Albania, have in the past been politically volatile locales.[39]

Slowed economic growth in the North, increased conservation and recycling since the 1970s, and new discoveries of mineral reserves have caused doomsday projections about exhaustion of global raw materials to be modified. It does not now appear that any major metals will disappear in the near future.[40] However, the costs of future raw materials, the political developments that could disrupt supplies, and the mix of available alternatives are not fully predictable.

The Politics of Resource Management

Although all human beings seemingly have a common stake in achieving better management of resources, major conflicts nonetheless exist among various actors involved in the global politics of resource management. These actors include not only *nation-states* (ranging from the resource-rich to the resource-starved, industrial to underdeveloped, and coastal to landlocked) but also *non-state* actors, such as subnational interest groups (ranging from conservationist and wildlife groups to mining, timber, and fishing interests within countries), multinational corporations, NGOs (such as Greenpeace, initially organized to protect whales but now engaged in antinuclear protests and other causes), and IGOs (such as the International Whaling Commission and other bodies affiliated with the United Nations).

One can see how global environmental politics has evolved by comparing the **UN Conference on the Human Environment** held in Stockholm in 1972 with the **UN Conference on Environment and Development** (UNCED) held in Rio de Janeiro in 1992. Spurred by the *Limits to Growth* study and other scientific writings warning of impending ecological catastrophe, the Stockholm conference was the first global conference in history to focus on the environment. A total of 114 states attended. The industrialized democracies, among the leading environmental culprits, were concerned enough to take the lead in placing environmental issues on the global agenda. The Soviet bloc boycotted the conference, miffed that East Germany was not invited, and dismissing environmental concerns as relatively unimportant. Many third world states were present but participated halfheartedly, expressing dismay that economic development was taking a backseat to environmental issues. In addition to the national governments that were represented, 250 NGOs also participated. Among the major accomplishments of the conference was the creation of a new IGO, the **UN Environmental Program (UNEP),** which was to serve as the major UN agency responsible for addressing environmental concerns; in an attempt to coopt LDCs into becoming more supportive of global environmental efforts, Nairobi, Kenya was designated as the headquarters of UNEP, the first UN agency to be headquartered in a third world country.[41]

The Stockholm meeting served as an important catalyst in raising environmental consciousness worldwide. In 1972, only a few national governments had a special environmental agency, such as the Environmental Protection Agency in the United States (established in 1970); over the next twenty years, virtually all states, including LDCs and Soviet bloc countries, created such entities.[42] By 1992, when the "Earth Summit" convened in Rio, over 900 international agreements had been entered into relating to the environment. The Rio conference, organized by UNEP, was the biggest international conference in history, attracting 178 governmental delegations (including over one hundred heads of states), hundreds of IGO officials, 25,000 representatives from 1,400 NGOs that had been officially invited to participate (including scientific bodies such as the International Union for the Conservation of Nature and activist groups such as the World Wildlife Fund) along with 500 uninvited groups that staged their own gathering at a parallel "Global Forum," as well as 9,000 journalists (compared with only 1,500 at Stockholm).[43]

Although developing countries had increased their environmental consciousness since the Stockholm conference, they conditioned their participation in the Rio meeting on the promise that the Earth Summit would address both the environment *and* development. As noted in the previous chapter, Northern calls for greater efforts to combat tropical deforestation and other environmental problems were met with Southern demands for greater foreign aid, debt relief, technology transfer, and responsiveness to LDC economic problems.[44] Brazilian leaders, for example, seeking to develop Brazil's rain forests in support of cattle ranchers and other domestic interests, expressed resentment at outside interference by other governments and global environmental interest groups, which invoked the "common heritage" principle to urge rain forest preservation, and requested economic benefits in return.[45] Brazil and other LDCs were quick to accuse the United States and other industrialized states of hypocrisy in exploiting their own forestlands and contributing to greenhouse warming and other environmental problems through their own selfish behavior.

The Rio conference saw environmental NGOs from both the North and the South pressuring governments to take stronger environmental action. Although 70 percent of the accredited NGOs were based in industrialized countries, some developing countries, such as India, the Philippines, and Kenya,

U.S. PRESIDENT BUSH AND MRS. BUSH TAKE TIME OUT FROM THE EARTH SUMMIT TO TOUR AN AMAZON RAIN FOREST. DESTRUCTION OF THE RAIN FORESTS IN BRAZIL AND ELSEWHERE IS CONTRIBUTING TO GLOBAL WARMING AND SPECIES EXTINCTION.

also were heavily represented.[46] Some NGOs at Rio were not environmental groups but business and other groups arguing against excessive new governmental and intergovernmental environmental regulations (although at least one corporate NGO, the Business Council for Sustainable Development—an alliance of Volkswagen, Dow Chemical, Nippon Steel, and some other MNCs—took a pro-environment stance).[47]

One can see that global environmental politics have become increasingly complex. In the remainder of this chapter we will see what has come out of the Earth Summit and other international conferences, as we examine the politics surrounding the formation of regimes governing the world's oceans, air, and outer space, and land-based resources.

The Oceans: Politics and Regimes

The "freedom of the sea" concept goes back a long way in history. Even the ancient Romans spoke of the free, public use of the oceans by all peoples. It is true that a few states in the fifteenth and sixteenth centuries made extravagant claims of ownership of large ocean areas (for example, Spain claimed possession of the Pacific Ocean). However, these claims had been generally discredited by the time Grotius initiated the notion of *mare liberum* (open seas) in his seventeenth-century international law treatises. The British and the Dutch, great seafaring and trading nations, led the way in pushing for universal acceptance of the freedom of the sea doctrine.

The basic principle that became widely accepted was that no state could exercise sovereignty or control over any part of the oceans except for the waters immediately adjacent to its coast—the so-called **territorial sea,** in which the coastal state could regulate navigation and any other activities in the interest of its security. This area was to be distinguished from the **high seas,** where no regulation was permissible. Practically all coastal states established territorial seas three nautical miles in width, based on the prevailing range of seventeenth-century cannon, although a few states did attempt to assert rights of up to twelve miles. Even within a state's territorial sea, where it had sovereign jurisdiction, it could not deny another state's vessels the legal **right of innocent passage** (the right to pass through a state's coastal waters as long as it is done peaceably).

Hence, for centuries the oceans were relatively calm in terms of rule consensus. However, in the mid-twentieth century, the "laissez-faire" approach to managing the oceans came to be challenged for a variety of reasons. First, as land-based resources began to dry up, states intensified their search for ocean-based resources and discovered oil, gas, and mineral deposits in the seabed. Second, with new technologies, such as sonar fishing that could sweep huge expanses of the ocean clean of fish and supertankers that could spill oil over huge stretches of shoreline, humans were faced for the first time in history with the prospect of the oceans becoming depleted and even destroyed if not regulated in some fashion; coastal states suddenly had to be concerned about policing commercial activities not only within their territorial seas but in coastal waters beyond a three-mile limit.

Ironically, it was the United States, a major naval power and long-time champion of the freedom of the sea doctrine, that set a key precedent for expanded national claims on the oceans. With Americans pioneering deep-sea drilling, the Truman administration proclaimed in 1945 the exclusive right of the United States to exploit the oil and other resources on its *continental shelf* to a depth of 200 meters (extending well beyond three miles). This action sparked a wave of new claims to assorted segments of the oceans, with many states claiming twelve-mile territorial seas or even 200-mile limits (as in the case of several Latin American countries seeking to compensate for the fact they had no continental shelf to exploit), others claiming 12- to 200-mile exclusive fishing zones, and still others claiming 12- to 200-mile zones in which they had a right to regulate pollution.

Numerous disputes arose over these claims. Major maritime powers, including the United States, became alarmed that 200-mile zones, especially around such vast island archipelagos as Indonesia, would endanger the principle of the open sea that allowed maximum freedom of operation for their large far-flung navies, scientific research expeditions, and fishing fleets. Coastal states lacking such maritime prowess felt they benefited more from an "enclosure" policy that limited other countries' access to their offshore waters than from an "open sea" policy that gave free rein to anyone who had the capability to exploit the oceans. Smaller, less developed states, then, tended to advocate increased national control over their coastal waters. The latter sought to restrict certain activities on the high seas as well, urging international regulation through the United Nations to ensure that technologically advanced states did not exploit the deep seabed for their exclusive gain. Landlocked states were somewhat wary of all coastal states— big and small alike—and voiced concerns about how they too might share in the riches of the sea.

Law of the sea politics occurred at several levels. Subnational groups, such as hard-pressed U.S. fishermen, waded into the fray and muddied the waters further, often disagreeing among themselves over what legal positions best served the "national interest" of their country. For example, American fishermen on the East Coast, generally operating with small boats in nearby waters and having to compete with mechanized Soviet floating fish factories, favored a 200-mile exclusive fishing zone; in contrast, West Coast tuna fishermen, plying the distant waters off the coasts of Ecuador and Peru, supported the principle of a more limited twelve-mile zone so that they would not be excluded entirely from Latin American waters. Various governmental agencies also often took conflicting positions and engaged in domestic bureaucratic politics to have their particular views accepted as official national policy. American Defense Department officials—concerned primarily about the free passage of U.S. warships on the high seas—sought to retain the narrow three-mile territorial sea, although expressing a willingness to tolerate a twelve-mile territorial limit as long as the principle of "unimpeded transit" applied to international straits falling in the extended band; conversely, Interior Department officials—primarily concerned about managing U.S. coastal resources, including policing would-be polluters and exploiting offshore wealth—were less supportive of the freedom of the sea doctrine and instead wanted to expand the national zone of jurisdiction to 200 miles for certain purposes. Battles between such ministries were fought not only in the United States but in other countries as well.

Despite efforts in the 1950s and 1960s to reconcile differing viewpoints through UN conferences, disagreements persisted. The first UN Conference on the Law of the Sea (UNCLOS I), held in Geneva in 1958 and attended by eighty-six states, managed to produce four conventions that codified some traditional customary rules (e.g., the right of innocent passage in territorial waters) along with some new ones (e.g., the right of coastal states to exploit the continental shelf to a depth of 200 meters). However, UNCLOS I as well as a similar conference held in 1960 (UNCLOS II) failed to reach agreement on several key issues, particularly the width of the territorial sea. Agreement became increasingly difficult as more and more independently minded third world nations entered the United Nations. These states viewed the oceans—particularly the mineral-rich deep seabed—as a means of facilitating a global redistribution of wealth; a 1967 UN agenda item introduced by Malta's UN Ambassador, Arvid Pardo, called for "the use of [seabed] resources in the interest of mankind," i.e., as a "common heritage."[48]

By 1973, however, unilateral claims to expanded territorial seas and other parts of the oceans had reached such proportions that the 65 percent of the oceans that represented an unclaimed "common heritage" in 1958 had shrunk to 35 percent.[49] Almost all the harvestable fish and readily exploitable oil and gas resources were to be found within these newly claimed coastal areas rather than further out to sea in the commons.

Such was the setting for UNCLOS III, as officials from 149 states along with numerous nongovernmental bodies met in Caracas, Venezuela, in 1973 to forge a new regime. The goal was nothing less than producing a *single comprehensive* agreement on the rules governing well over half the earth's surface; the complete spectrum of issues was to be addressed—territorial seas, economic and fishing zones, continental shelves, high seas, the deep seabed and ocean floor, marine pollution, and the transfer of technology. In the words of one writer, UNCLOS III was "the largest single international legal undertaking since the time of Grotius."[50] The agreement was to be based on consensus as much as possible and otherwise by a two-thirds vote. Little did the participants know that UNCLOS III would last over eight years.

By the late 1970s, a virtual consensus had been achieved among all states (including the thirty or so landlocked states) behind a twelve-mile territorial sea with unimpeded transit through international straits, a 200-mile exclusive fishing zone for coastal states, a similar zone covering nonliving resources, and an **International Seabed Authority** for regulating deep-sea mining. A draft convention was finally readied in 1980.

However, the adoption of the draft treaty was delayed when the incoming Reagan administration decided to renounce the product of eight years' labor primarily because of objections to the International Seabed Authority. Two competing positions had emerged at UNCLOS III about the Authority. Technologically advanced Western states wanted the Authority's powers limited to licensing mining enterprises. They argued that a free enterprise and open exploitation system would maximize the economic return to the whole world. In contrast, less developed countries wanted a strong Authority to govern the exploration, extraction, and marketing of seabed mineral resources and to determine how the proceeds were to be distributed, with all states sharing the wealth whether or not they had invested any capital or technological expertise. States that relied on the sale of minerals for the bulk of their export earnings (for example, the so-called three Z's—Zaire, Zambia, and Zimbabwe) were especially concerned that unlimited mining of manganese nodules might produce a world raw materials glut and depress prices. A compromise was finally reached. However, the United States continued to push for modifications in the proposed mining regime to benefit private mining companies. These included more Western voting power in the Authority, with a U.S. veto over proposed amendments to the convention.

When the **Law of the Sea Treaty** finally came to a vote in April of 1982, it was adopted by a margin of 130 to 4, with 17 abstentions. Since then, more than 160 countries have signed the treaty and are in the process of ratifying it. The treaty entered into force in 1994, with the sixtieth ratification (by Guyana). As of 1997, only a few major industrialized powers had ratified the treaty, with Japan and some others inclined to support the agreement but waiting for U.S. approval. A UN Preparatory Commission (PREPCOM) has been charged with implementing UNCLOS III and ironing out remaining problems. In an effort to attract American participation and promote the universality of the accord, it produced a Modification Agreement in 1995, which contained new seabed provisions closer to the American position. The Clinton administration signed the treaty, but it was held up pending the approval of the U.S. Senate.[51]

The United States may well decide ultimately to become a party to the treaty, because it accepts most of the provisions and because there are obvious benefits to be derived from a strong oceans regime. It is estimated that the provisions pertaining to expanded territorial seas and economic zones would confer on the United States—with one of the longest coastlines in the world—clear legal title to some 3 million square miles, the biggest territorial acquisition in American history; other benefits accruing to the United States, as well as to other regime members, would include legal protection against "claim jumping" of deep-sea mining sites, agreed mechanisms for peaceful settlement of ocean disputes, and a stable and predictable framework of ocean law.[52] Without the full participation of the United States and other major actors, implementation of the treaty will be difficult, although there is reason to believe that a consensus will eventually be reached. Most treaty provisions are now so widely accepted as to constitute new customary law.[53]

Less controversial than a Seabed Authority is another body that has been in existence since 1958 and is the major international agency overseeing ocean navigation and pollution today. The International Maritime Organization (IMO) is a UN Specialized Agency with more than 130 members. From its inception, IMO has been charged with facilitating international cooperation on maritime issues, specifically promoting maritime safety, efficiency, and fair practices among shipping interests. The Torrey Canyon tanker disaster, which occurred off the British coast in 1967, added oil pollution to IMO's concerns.

IMO helps formulate rules for preventing collisions at sea, standards for ship construction and safety, as well as pollution safeguards. It is merely an advisory body, having the power only to recommend. Nonetheless, it has had some success in convincing states to ratify conventions and accept uniform practices regarding ship-to-shore communications, minimum standards for ship crews, and handling of dangerous cargoes.[54] IMO has been dominated traditionally by states with significant shipping interests, although recent reforms have permitted broader representation.[55]

The 1973 International Convention for the Prevention of Pollution by Ships sets limits for ship discharges of oil and other pollutants that can threaten marine life. The 1972 Convention on Prevention of Marine Pollution by Dumping of Wastes and Other Matter, along with subsequent agreements, restricts the use of the oceans as a dumping ground for plastics and other debris as well as radioactive and toxic wastes. Although these conventions represent important environmental measures, many countries are not parties to the agreements, and even some parties have not always fully complied. In addition to these global regimes, various Regional Seas Action Plans, such as those for the Mediterranean and for East Asian waters (especially subject to oilspills), have been mounted under UN auspices to help coastal states manage their marine environment.[56]

In addition to the UNCLOS III provisions relating to the right of coastal states to police exclusive fishing zones, the international community has attempted to deal with overfishing through such regional IGOs as the Inter-American Tuna Commission and the International Pacific Halibut Commission, which tries to regulate the fish catch in waters shared by several states. The small boats of the Greenpeace Foundation speeding out to stand between Soviet and Japanese harpoonists and the whales they hunted, in the early 1980s, alerted the world to the politics of another IGO, the International Whaling Commission (IWC). Animal conservationist NGOs had tried futilely at IWC annual meetings in the 1970s to push for a complete ban on whaling. However, as IWC membership gradually expanded to include several non-whaling states willing to support the conservationists, a moratorium on all commercial whaling was adopted in 1982. Japan, Norway, and Iceland, with powerful domestic whaling interests to satisfy, have continued hunting under a provision allowing "scientific" exploitation and have tried to overturn or at least circumvent the commercial ban. Still, the moratorium has reduced the annual whale kill considerably from the 60,000 level of the 1960s.[57] Other IGOs exist to protect seals and other marine wildlife.[58]

Air and Outer Space: Politics and Regimes

Many of the disputes concerning atmospheric and outer space resources are similar to disputes about the oceans, especially those regarding what constitutes the common heritage and what is up for grabs by individual states. Indeed, ocean controversies have been directly related to air space controversies because national sovereignty over a state's territorial sea has—at least since the advent of the airplane—also included sovereignty over the skies above the territorial sea. These skies, along with those above a country's land mass itself, have been considered **national air space**—a column of air in which a state exercises total jurisdiction and can even deny overflight rights to foreign aircraft. Hence, the U.S. Air Force was as concerned as the U.S. Navy about expanded territorial seas.

There has been no attempt to develop a multilateral "Law of the Atmosphere Treaty" akin to the Law of the Sea Treaty. Currently a state has no right to use the national air space of another state unless the latter has granted specific permission through a bilateral agreement. The International Civil Aviation Organization (ICAO) helps to develop uniform air safety standards but has little control over air traffic.

Although it is clear that each state has sovereignty over its air space, there remain conflicts over certain airborne activities such as weather modification and atmospheric pollution. The 1972 UN Conference on the Human Environment in Stockholm articulated the general principle that states "have the responsibility to ensure that activities within their jurisdiction or control do not cause damage to the environment of other States or of areas beyond the limits of national jurisdiction"; states are expected to inform and consult with other states likely to be affected by a pending activity if there is an "appreciable risk of effects on climate." The Soviet Union was widely viewed to have violated the Stockholm principles when it failed to provide prompt and full reports on the damage produced by the Chernobyl nuclear accident in 1986.

Some atmospheric pollution problems, such as acid rain, are relatively localized—transborder or regional—rather than global in scope. Under the 1979 Convention on Long-Range Transboundary Air Pollution, more than thirty signatory states in Western and Eastern Europe committed themselves to reducing air pollution in their region. A subsequent 1985 protocol to the agreement obligated the parties to reduce sulfur emissions by 30 percent over the next decade; within just one year, ten states had met or exceeded the goal.

Still another protocol was signed in 1988, dealing with nitrogen oxides. One writer has suggested that European cooperation in combating acid rain is attributable to "the power of tote-board diplomacy," i.e., "the protocols were tote-boards showing who was responsible [pro-environment] and who was not . . . [as] countries which remained off the tote-board were subject to external pressure and internal pressure."[59] In the case of North America, Canada's repeated but unheeded complaints about half of its acid rain originating across the border in the United States led the Canadian Environment Minister in 1982 to comment that acid rain was the "single most important irritant, or issue, in Canadian-American relations."[60] Finally, pressures from the Canadian government, along with domestic political pressure from environmental groups in the United States, led Washington in 1990 to enact legislation containing stricter emission controls on sulfur dioxide and other pollutants.

Some atmosphere pollution concerns, such as ozone layer deterioration and greenhouse warming, are generally understood to be global in nature. As we have noted, the UN Environmental Program (UNEP) is the major global environmental agency. UNEP's main contribution has been to coordinate the "Earthwatch" network that gathers worldwide data on the environment and monitors any changes in the atmosphere and elsewhere that could pose dangers. In these efforts, UNEP has worked closely with the World Meteorological Organization (WMO), although both agencies remain information-gathering more than rule-making organizations. Under WMO auspices, for example, international weather and climatological data are shared by countries participating in the World Weather Watch program.

UNEP was responsible for organizing a landmark 1987 conference in Montreal to deal with the decay of the ozone layer that protects humanity from the sun's rays. The Montreal conference was preceded by a 1985 Vienna Convention for the Protection of the Ozone Layer that called for general cooperation among the thirty-four participating states—the major producers of chlorofluorocarbons (CFCs) and other ozone-depleting chemicals—in controlling their ozone-related activities but did not set any specific standards or targets. The Montreal meeting resulted in the **Montreal Protocol** signed by twenty-four nations, including the United States, Canada, the Soviet Union, and the members of the European Community, each of which pledged to cut by half the production of CFCs by the end of the century. On learning from scientists that the ozone problem had become more serious, and from industry that chemical substitutes for CFCs were feasible, the parties subsequently agreed to attempt to phase out CFCs totally by 1999. Further alarming evidence moved up the timetable to 1996. As of 1997, more than 140 states had become parties to the Protocol, with China and other developing countries agreeing to join only after they were promised access to economical CFC substitutes for refrigeration and other needs and were granted a ten-year grace period to phase out their own CFCs. NGOs clearly played a critical role in "ozone politics";

among the nonstate actors who shaped the final outcome of the Montreal Protocol were numerous scientific groups ("epistemic communities") that first sounded the alarm, environmental groups such as Greenpeace and Friends of the Earth, which lobbied in Montreal, and E.I. Dupont (the largest CFC producer in the world, which announced plans to curtail all such manufacturing).

There remains some scientific debate over the extent to which the CFCs already present in the atmosphere continue to pose a danger to humanity. In any event, the Montreal Protocol represented a remarkable accomplishment. The head of UNEP described the Protocol as "the beginning of a new era of environmental statesmanship," and the U.S. ambassador to the negotiations suggested it might be "a hopeful paradigm of an evolving global diplomacy, one wherein sovereign nations find ways to accept common responsibility for stewardship of the planet and for the security of generations to come."[61]

It has proved more difficult to achieve international cooperation in combatting greenhouse warming. This issue was hotly debated at the Earth Summit. Germany and Japan were willing to commit to reducing their CO_2 emissions by 25 percent, and other states were willing to have the UN collect a global tax on carbon emissions. However, the United States—the largest single source of greenhouse gas emissions (see Table 15.2)—and Saudi Arabia—the largest source of petroleum reserves—led a coalition to block a strong climate treaty that would have required major cuts in fossil fuel use. The Rio conference ended up producing a modest **Framework Convention on Climate Change,** signed by more than 150 countries (including the United States), which urged states not to exceed their 1990 emission levels but did not contain any binding commitments requiring reductions. The United States argued that, before more drastic steps could be warranted, the international community needed more definitive scientific findings on the extent of the problem and should seek further study by the Intergovernmental Panel on Climate Change established by UNEP in 1988; despite a 1995 IPCC report reiterating greenhouse warming dangers, little further action has been taken.

Consensus on a greenhouse treaty appears more difficult to achieve than the CFC agreement for a variety of reasons: not all states would be equally adversely affected by a global warming trend; the scientific evidence regarding the need to reduce CO_2 and other emissions remains inconclusive; the reduction of greenhouse gases through limiting the use of fossil fuels would require far greater economic changes and sacrifices than in the case of CFC reduction because of the unavailability of ready substitutes; and strong measures have been particularly opposed by the country whose support is most pivotal—the United States, which has played the role of a "veto state."[62]

Much of the earth's atmosphere—all the air over the high seas—remains *terra nullius,* territory belonging to no one. The moon and celestial bodies and outer space as a whole are also considered *terra nullius.* Northern, technologically advanced states, although agreeing that outer space cannot be claimed as sovereign territory by any state, interpret *terra nullius* to mean that it is

Table 15.2

GREENHOUSE INDEX RANKING AND PERCENT SHARE OF GLOBAL EMISSIONS

Rank	Country	Percent
1	United States	18.4
2	USSR	13.5
3	China	8.4
4	Japan	5.6
5	Brazil	3.8
6	Germany	3.6
7	India	3.5
8	United Kingdom	2.4
9	Mexico	2.0
10	Italy	1.8
11	France	1.7
12	Canada	1.7
13	Indonesia	1.6
14	Poland	1.4
15	Thailand	1.4
16	Colombia	1.4
17	Australia	1.1
18	South Africa	1.1
19	Myanmar	1.1
20	Spain	1.1
21	Nigeria	1.1

Source: Data are for 1989. World Resources Institute, *World Resources 1992–93* (New York: Oxford University Press, 1992), p. 208. Note that just twenty-one states are responsible for over 75 percent of all greenhouse gas emissions.

nonetheless open to free use and exploitation on a "first come, first served" basis. Countries lacking space technology, notably less developed countries, have interpreted *terra nullius* to mean that outer space is part of the common heritage, jointly owned by everyone and subject to international regulation (i.e., more properly, *"terra communis"*).

The different perspectives could be seen in disagreements between the Soviet Union and Argentina during negotiations over a Moon Treaty in the 1970s. The Soviets refused to accepted the common heritage notion, insisting that space belonged to *no one* (not everyone) and hence was available for use by any state. Argentina, however, pointed out that when Soviet moon probes brought back samples of moon rocks, Moscow in effect was taking ownership of space property. In an argument reminiscent of the deep seabed debate, Argentina urged that rules be developed for sharing space benefits widely and equitably, especially as future technology would likely enable states to build permanent space stations and to exploit gases, metals, and various other space resources.[63]

In addition to nation-states (the roughly twenty countries currently capable of launching satellites as well as the remaining "have-nots"), the group of actors potentially involved in space politics also includes MNCs and other enterprises that build, launch, and rent satellites or contract for services from space (such as utilizing data gained from remote sensing devices); IGOs such as the International Telecommunications Satellite Consortium (INTELSAT) and International Telecommunication Union (ITU), whose role in regulating the satellite uses of space and allocation of radio frequencies was discussed in Chapter 10; and others involved in TV viewing or telephone, fax, and other forms of communication.

Although air space and outer space are connected, the regimes governing the two domains are quite different. The Outer Space Treaty of 1967 prohibits sovereignty or ownership over any part of outer space. Some states have attempted to restrict the movement of space satellites passing over their territory. Satellites situated in the "geostationary orbit" 22,300 miles directly above the equator travel in a fixed position relative to the earth's surface and have certain advantages over other satellites, so that "parking" rights in such a choice slot are considered valuable. In 1986, the equatorial nations declared in the Bogota Declaration that their sovereignty extended straight upward into space and that any state seeking to occupy an earth-stationary spot above the equator would have to pay an orbiting fee owed to the country below. The international community has refused to recognize this claim.[64]

However, with the growing network of satellites surveying world crop patterns, connecting transoceanic telecommunications, and spying on military installations, states have recognized the need for some degree of coordination and regulation. At its periodic meetings, the ITU's World Radio Conference has attempted to distribute communications frequencies among states in an equitable manner, although some believe the radio spectrum should be treated as a common resource to be "rented" out to users by the UN, with the proceeds shared by all nations.[65] A Unispace Conference, held in 1982, sought to develop rules requiring technologically advanced states to share with LDCs any data on the latter's weather and agricultural conditions derived from remote sensing satellites. States launching satellites into outer space must currently register them with the United Nations and are liable for any damages caused by such objects falling to earth (under the Convention on Liability for Damage Caused by Objects Launched into Outer Space). In addition, there is an Agreement on the Rescue of Astronauts.

The main body responsible for developing space law is the UN Committee on the Peaceful Uses of Outer Space (COPUOS). COPUOS prepared the UN Draft Treaty Relating to the Moon, which was opened for ratification in 1979. This treaty, which the United States has been reluctant to ratify, culminated ten years of debate triggered by man's first steps on the moon in 1969. The treaty augmented the principles of the 1967 Outer Space Treaty and banned the exploitation of moon resources for profit (a blow to private enterprise in space). States would be free to explore the moon and to collect rocks and minerals, however. Stations established on the moon could not interfere with other states' access, and their presence there would not imply permanent ownership. Parties to the agreement also are pledged to establish an international regime to "govern the exploitation of the natural resources of the moon."[66] Although it is difficult to establish such agreements for sharing the common heritage in a world of sovereign states, regime-building efforts continue in regard to outer space as in other domains of human activity.

Land-Based Resources: Politics and Regimes

For a period of years during the 1970s and 1980s, the goal of stabilizing world commodity and fuel prices dominated the global agenda regarding land-based natural resources. Governments wishing to coordinate their policies to push up resource prices or control supplies were pitted against importing countries wanting freer access to raw materials at lower costs. Often in between have been the MNCs that dominate global extraction and distribution of zinc, copper, tin, and other resources. In some cases organizations were established to include both exporter and importer interests and MNCs (e.g., the Uranium Institute), whereas in other cases exporter cartels were established to negotiate common prices with industries and importers (e.g., OPEC or the Intergovernmental Council of Copper Exporting Countries).

However, in many cases the failure to include all relevant producing or exporting states, as well as the availability of alternative substitutes, undercut the unity and effectiveness of supplier agreements. For example, tin's usefulness in manufacturing appears to have diminished over time, thus undermining the International Tin Council (ITC). The growing indebtedness of many less developed countries, along with the sudden emergence of cash-starved former Soviet republics, has added to a general willingness to sell off natural resources without regard for ITC or other umbrella supplier organization efforts to control supply and raise prices.[67] Even OPEC, although technically still negotiating price levels with oil companies, has seen its unity weakened because of a relative glut of oil on the world market and resultant squabbles among its membership as to what countries should withhold supplies to sustain the world price.

Environmentalists have begun to emphasize resource management based on sustainable development. For example, proposals have surfaced calling for "international commodity-related environmental agreements" (ICREAs). Under such agreements, import taxes would be levied if the commodity exporter had not factored environmental costs into the purchase price. The tax revenue generated would then be returned to the exporting country to foster research on alternative, environmentally sound production. The emphasis here would be on interstate agreements linking exporters and importers bilaterally in a series of price and environmental commitments.

Among the many international regimes that have been developed to address land-based environmental problems are agreements that establish global standards for handling hazardous wastes, for managing tropical forests, and for sustaining biodiversity. At a conference in Basel, Switzerland, in 1989, attended by governmental officials from 116 countries along with NGO representatives from chemical industries and environmental groups, a treaty was concluded that placed restrictions on the export of toxic wastes to other states, in particular the use of Africa and other parts of the developing world as hazardous waste dumps. The Rio Earth Summit produced both a Forestry Action Plan as well as a Biodiversity Treaty aimed at managing tropical forests in a sustainable fashion and reducing the rate of species extinction, although critics argued that both papered over the problems and catered to commercial interests.[68]

The management of land-based resources seems to be in a period of transition. In the future, supplies of all types of nonrenewable resources (such as oil) and renewable resources (such as timber) will depend as much on economics and politics as on geological conditions. Companies and governments will decide how much to search for, to drill/mine/cut/, to refine, and to sell; these decisions will tend to be based on the economic return and political leverage that can be generated in the trade on natural resources. Therefore, in the next century, resource politics are likely to involve efforts by MNCs to manage global supplies and negotiate with governments so that prices stay high enough to make exploration and extraction financially worthwhile. Governments of producer and consumer states, often having divergent interests from those of MNCs, might occasionally organize their own enterprises to extract raw materials and compete with MNCs.

One additional consideration for the future of resource politics is the role of culture. For example, under Islam or traditional religions in many parts of the developing world, the meaning and importance of natural resources and the extent to which they should be exploited can be quite different from prevailing Western notions. Competing spiritual and ethical considerations could come into play in determining the rate of resource utilization, as they have in the global debate on whaling.[69] Depending on the level of political power exercised by such cultural groups, and whether their norms clash with or uphold economic and environmental interests, the rules for resource management could change.

Conclusion

Contemporary civilization will be remembered for a variety of good and bad developments, ranging from women's liberation to nuclear explosions.

If one travels through Israel and some other Middle Eastern states and sees thousands of rooftop solar collectors for water heating, giant arrays of photovoltaic receivers for solar electricity, irrigation systems turning deserts green, pools of Dead Sea water drying in the scorching sun for the extraction of minerals, fish farms with self-feeding devices and raceways for trout (and if one remembers that even in biblical times roofs had rainwater catch basins), one realizes how far some countries have gone and how far others must go in adapting to their natural environments and making the best of them.

In addition to national responses to environmental problems, there will be a continued need for international responses. On the eve of his departure from the White House in 1980, outgoing President Jimmy Carter received the results of "The Global 2000 Report to the President," a three-year study he had commissioned. As one news service characterized it, the study was "gloom and doom qualified," since it tended to paint an extremely pessimistic picture of the world resource situation. Although many thought the report exaggerated the severity of global problems, few could quarrel with the general conclusion of the authors:

> The only solutions . . . are complex and long-term. . . . The needed changes go far beyond the capability and responsibility of this or any other single nation. An era of unprecedented cooperation and commitment is essential.[70]

A decade later, in 1992, more than 1,600 scientists, including 102 Nobel laureates, signed a "Warning to Humanity" that stated: "No more than one or a few decades remain before the chance to avert the threats we now confront will be lost and the prospects for humanity immeasurably diminished. . . . A new ethic is required—a new attitude towards discharging our responsibility for caring for ourselves and for the earth. . . . This ethic must motivate a great movement, convincing reluctant leaders and reluctant governments and reluctant peoples themselves to effect the needed changes."[71]

Whether greater international cooperation in managing global resources will be forthcoming remains to be seen. The contest between the private use versus the common heritage perspectives continues. If resources are going to cost much more, and if the environment is increasingly fouled, economic growth may be seriously slowed even if resources are physically available in sufficient supplies. The politics determining "who gets what, when, and how" may become even more hotly contested. Labor union members and other workers will vie for higher wages and jobs; India, Pakistan, China, and Brazil will vie with each other and with the North for affordable energy and other resources vital to their industrialization; tourists will vie for space on a clean beach. Children will vie for survival, and the outcome will depend on the foresight and vision of parents.

SUMMARY

1. Although the earth's natural resources can be viewed as a common heritage (collective goods), different actors compete to control and exploit them (as private goods).

2. Scientists distinguish between renewable resources (e.g., water) and nonrenewable resources (e.g., petroleum). Many have questioned the "limits to growth" thesis that continued economic growth will soon exhaust the earth's nonrenewable resources and destroy renewable resources. Although doomsday predictions seem premature, warnings about the finiteness of key resources and the fragility of ecological balances remain valid. The concept of sustainable development has become generally accepted as a middle position between growth and no-growth ideas.

3. Renewable resources are affected by a number of environmental problems that transcend national boundaries. The atmosphere is subject to deterioration in the form of smog, acid rain, greenhouse warming, and ozone layer depletion. Oceans, lakes, and streams are being polluted by chemical wastes and industrial effluents. Land-based resources are threatened by desertification and deforestation, with tropical deforestation especially threatening biodiversity.

4. These same environmental problems also affect nonrenewable resources such as energy supplies. Although much of the South still relies on such traditional energy sources as wood and dung, the North relies on fossil fuels, including oil, gas, and coal, in addition to nuclear power. Increased pressures on resources are likely to occur as the South shifts to fossil fuels. The environmental problems associated with nuclear energy and fossil fuels, along with some uncertainty over energy supplies, make a mix of energy strategies crucial for the future.

5. Reserves of nonfuel minerals are generally more widely distributed than fossil fuel reserves, making a mineral supply crisis unlikely in the near future, although some countries are heavily dependent on just a few suppliers for imports of certain vital raw materials. Political and economic factors are likely to dominate the minerals situation more than physical scarcities will.

6. Major conflicts surround the global politics of resource management, as seen at the 1972 UN Conference on the Human Environment in Stockholm, the first global environmental meeting, and the "Earth Summit" held in Rio twenty years later. Northern calls for greater efforts to combat tropical deforestation and other environmental problems have been met with Southern demands for greater aid, technology transfer, and responsiveness to LDC economic problems. Many Northern countries themselves, notably the United States, have been ambivalent about taking necessary actions to address environmental concerns. Nonstate actors (IGOs, NGOs, MNCs, and subnational interest groups) also have been involved in environmental politics and shaping international regimes.

7. Among the nonstate actors involved in law of the sea politics, for example, are defense departments and interior departments, multinational mining companies, IGOs such as the UN and the International Whaling Commission, and NGOs such as Greenpeace. Although the success of the Law of the Sea Treaty is uncertain, several new customary rules regarding territorial seas and economic zones have become widely accepted.

8. Some progress has been made in global regulation of atmospheric pollution. Some countries have reached bilateral and regional agreements to deal with acid rain. The Montreal Protocol has resulted in countries worldwide phasing out their production of CFCs thought to deplete the ozone layer. Less progress has been made on greenhouse warming, although the Earth Summit did produce a modest Framework Convention on Climate Change. Scientific NGOs (epistemic communities) have played a key role in getting environmental issues on the global agenda.

9. Under existing treaties, states are prohibited from claiming sovereignty over the moon or any part of outer space. However, just as there are debates over ownership of resources beneath the high seas, there is disagreement regarding outer space and whether it is to be considered *terra nullius*—territory belonging to no one and hence free to be exploited—or *terra communis*—territory belonging to everyone and hence subject to international control.

10. Regimes are also being developed at the global, regional, and bilateral levels to facilitate the management of land-based resources, including efforts to deal with hazardous waste disposal, deforestation, and other forms of land degradation.

SUGGESTIONS FOR FURTHER READING AND STUDY

A classic study of world environmental problems, examining both renewable and nonrenewable resources, is Barbara Ward and Rene Dubos, *Only One Earth: The Care and Maintenance of a Small Planet* (New York: Penguin, 1972). In addition, see Gerald O. Barney, ed., *The Global 2000 Report to the President of the United States: Entering the 21st Century*, vol. 1 (New York: Pergamon Press, 1980); Donella H. Meadows et al., *Beyond the Limits* (Post Mills, Vt.: Chelsea Green, 1992), a sequel to the original 1972 *Limits to Growth* study; Jessica Tuchman Matthews, ed., *Preserving the Global Environment* (New York: W. W. Norton, 1991); Sandra Postel, *Last Oasis: Facing Water Scarcity* (New York: W. W. Norton, 1992); Christopher D. Stone, *The Gnat Is Older than Man* (Princeton, N.J.: Princeton University Press, 1993), which looks at the moral and legal dimensions of global environmental problems; the report of the Brundtland Commission, *Our Common Future* (New York: Oxford University Press, 1987), focusing on the link between environmental and economic development concerns; the annual editions of *Environment*, published by McGraw-Hill; and the annual volumes of *State of the World*, authored by Lester Brown et al. of the Worldwatch Institute and published by W. W. Norton.

Works that focus specifically on the politics and regime-making surrounding the oceans are Robert L. Friedheim, *Negotiating the New Ocean Regime* (Columbia: University of South Carolina Press, 1993); and Clyde Sanger, *Ordering the Oceans: Making of the Law of the Sea* (Toronto: University of Toronto Press, 1987). On air and outer space, see Michael Akehurst, *A Modern Introduction to International Law*, 6th ed. (London: Allen and Unwin, 1987), ch. 14; and M. N. Snow, *International Law* (Cambridge, Eng.: Cambridge University Press, 1991), ch. 9.

On environmental politics and regimes generally, see Kenneth A. Dahlberg et al., *Environment and the Global Arena* (Durham, N.C.: Duke University Press, 1985); Gareth

Porter and Janet Welsh Brown, *Global Environmental Politics*, 2nd ed. (Boulder, Colo.: Westview Press, 1996); Jacqueline V. Switzer, *Environmental Politics: Domestic and Global Dimensions* (New York: St. Martin's Press, 1994); Oran R. Young, *International Cooperation: Building Regimes for Natural Resources and the Environment* (Ithaca, N.Y.: Cornell University Press, 1989); Lawrence E. Susskind, *Environmental Diplomacy* (New York: Oxford University Press, 1994); Tony Brenton, *The Greening of Machiavelli: The Evolution of International Environmental Politics* (London: Earthscan, 1994); Peter M. Haas, Robert O. Keohane, and Marc A. Levy, *Institutions for the Earth* (Cambridge, Mass.: MIT Press, 1995); and The Royal Institute of International Affairs, *The Earth Summit Agreements: A Guide and Assessment* (London: Earthscan, 1993).

An extremely valuable reference work is the volume published biannually by the World Resources Institute on "World Resources," such as *World Resources, 1996–97* (New York: Oxford University Press, 1996), which contains comprehensive coverage of global environmental problems, including a wealth of statistics on the latest trends and elaborate discussion of international responses to such problems. Also see the UN Environmental Program's biannual *Environmental Data Report*. Useful information on recent developments also can be found by reading the following periodicals: *Environment Magazine, The Interdependent, Science, Scientific American,* and the many publications produced by the Worldwatch Institute in Washington, D.C., including the annual editions of *Vital Signs*.

PART
V

Conclusion

The world is unhappy. It is unhappy because it does not know where it is going and because it senses that if it knew, it would discover that it was heading for disaster. VALÉRY GISCARD D'ESTAING, PRESIDENT OF FRANCE, IN A 1974 SPEECH

The age of nations is past; the task before us, if we would survive, is to build the earth. PIERRE TEILHARD DE CHARDIN

I n Part V we offer some concluding observations about the global condition on the eve of the twenty-first century, and where the world seems to be heading. There is room for both pessimism and optimism. We noted near the outset of this book that one can find in international relations over the centuries elements of continuity as well as change. The continuities are such that one well-known writer, reflecting on the persistent theme of interstate competition and conflict that has characterized human affairs since the days of antiquity, asserts: "In honesty, one must question whether or not twentieth century students of international relations know anything that Thucydides and his fifth century [B.C.] compatriots did not know about the behavior of states."[1] Yet another writer, reflecting on political life in the nuclear age, sees at least one fundamental change today from the past that might require a rethinking of world politics: "It has historically been one thing to die *for* your country. It is a different thing [today] to die *with* your country."[2]

In our last chapter (Chapter 16), we attempt to provide some further perspective on the past and, even more, the *future,* as we examine a variety of "alternative world order models." We are interested here not only in how the nation-state system can be made more peaceful (as discussed in Chapter 8), but also in the broader question of whether other systems (such as regional or world government) are possible, and whether they would promote a number of human values in addition to peace.

16

Toward the Year 2001
and Beyond

We have just concluded our discussion of some of the great issues on the global agenda. There are hundreds of other, not-so-great issues that, despite their triviality, can affect the lives of people everywhere in the world. Consider the crusade for a "world plug and socket system," described in the Sidelight below. That a global conference would even be convened to address

SIDELIGHT

GLOBAL PROBLEM SOLVING AND YOU

Travel can be fun. It can also be a nightmare of delays, strikes, lost reservations and an occasional hijacking. But worst of all is the electric plug that won't fit.

Imagine a world in which your electric shaver or hair dryer worked instantly everywhere you went. Well, the idea has been imagined for 74 years now, and the news is bad: It may soon be abandoned.

At a meeting this June, a final attempt will be made to reach agreement on a "world plug and socket system"—familiarly known as "whoops." The meeting, in Rio de Janeiro, is being convened by the International Electrotechnical Commission.

Founded in 1906, the IEC now has 43 member states, including the United States, the Soviet Union, China and India. Members represent 80 percent of the world's population and generate 95 percent of global electric power.

"We dislike puns," says an official at IEC headquarters here, "but it would be fair to say that our members are still poles apart." He adds, "The whole concept of a standard plug and socket may die." In a sense, it already has died: The current (we don't mind puns) proposal by IEC engineers envisions two systems, not one. The proposal, which the IEC likes to describe as a "universal system with two varieties," calls for a 250-volt round-pin plug for most of the world—the plug pictured here—and a 125-volt flat-pin, or rectangular, plug for North America and Japan.

Two varieties would be a great help. There now are hundreds of different plugs and sockets in the world, the IEC says, often as many as 20 different types in one country alone.

such a concern shows how far the world has come in terms of the range of problems now being treated at the global level. That no politically acceptable solutions have yet been found for such a seemingly mundane, technical matter shows how far the world still has to go to become a true global community with effective problem-solving machinery. This example is offered as a hu-

Of course, there are adapters on the market, but they can't allow for the hundreds of different sockets around the world, and there are many countries where adapters simply can't be found—many places in the Third World, for instance. To fit any possible situation anywhere, you would have to lug around a separate suitcase full of adapters.

Governments first began thinking of a universal system in 1908 when national standardization started. But it was only in 1970 that real negotiations were opened within the IEC. At first everyone fully backed the idea of world standardization. When a design was proposed four years later, however, the problems began. Governments promptly said the principle of a global plug and socket was fine *provided* it was based on their own national system.

Mr. Folcker [a Swede, head of IEC] concedes that adoption of a universal system would be extremely expensive. He estimates that it would cost $175 to change all the plugs and outlets in a normal-size home. That would put the total bill at $700 million in Sweden alone.

Voting procedures in the "whoops" committee require approval of draft designs by a four-fifths majority. That has proved impossible.

In 1977, the United States rejected one proposal because it was so unlike the American system that it would have meant rewiring the entire country. A year later, the French had everyone applauding when, after years of opposition, they finally accepted the basic concept of one world, one plug. "On condition it is the French system," the delegate from Paris added when people stopped clapping.

Japan in 1979 produced what it called a prototype world plug. Other committee members were pleased by the design.

"Delight quickly faded when the experts took the plug apart and discovered it wasn't a prototype at all," one IEC official discloses. "It turned out to be a real production model and Japan had production lines all ready to go as soon as the so-called prototype was accepted."

As for the IEC engineers' latest proposal, Britain has already made it known that it will reject a round-pin plug. The British want rectangular pins and say that round pins would give some countries an unfair economic advantage. Countries with round pins say a rectangular system would be unfair to them.

Actually, the IEC people say, the existing round-pin "Europlug" does work in Britain. "But you need a matchstick to make it fit and that's dangerous," a frustrated spokesman says.

Source: Excerpted from John Calcott, "A World-Wide Plug Faces Disconnection After 74-Year Effort," *Wall Street Journal* (April 1, 1982), p. 1. Reprinted by permission of Dow Jones & Company, Inc. © 1982. All rights reserved worldwide.

morous, and also somewhat sad, commentary on the state of the world at the turn of the twentieth century.

In this chapter, we look to the *future* and speculate about how human beings will be organizing themselves to cope with large and small problems in the twenty-first century. We noted in Chapter 2 that the history of humankind could be viewed as the ongoing search for the optimal political unit, with the pendulum swinging between a virtually single universal order (such as the empire of Alexander the Great) and much more fragmented, smaller political communities (such as those that existed in the feudal era). As discussed in the box on "Human Governance" in Chapter 1, and commented on throughout the text, we are witnessing today a peculiar, seemingly paradoxical mix of *both* integrative *and* disintegrative tendencies occurring all at once. There is great uncertainty over how these competing forces will play out. An interesting debate has ensued in the international relations field as to the shape of the "post–Cold War" order, with some arguing that what has transpired is simply an end of the post–World War II bipolar world and a return to the kind of multipolar world that had characterized much of international relations between 1648 and 1945, and others suggesting that humanity is in the midst of a far more profound and fundamental shift away from the Westphalian nation-state system to a completely new "post-international politics."[1]

Some observers argue that just as the nation-state came into being as the primary unit of political organization some 350 years ago, the world today is on the threshold of another great transformation—this one of epic proportions. According to this view,

© 1982, Malcolm Hancock.

Controlling the fate of the earth

the world is at a psychological moment comparable to that time, some 5,000 to 15,000 years past, when human society moved from an essentially nomadic-hunting existence to an essentially territorial-agricultural way of life. Just as the breakdown of old myths and values led to the territorial-agricultural unit . . . , so now . . . the breakdown of statist myths and values, hastened by our growing sensitivity to humankind's ecopolitical interrelatedness, is leading to the long-term emergence of a truly planetary civilization.[2]

Although many other observers reject such Spaceship Earth notions as naive "globaloney," even the realists have acknowledged the strains on the current nation-state system and the pressures for change. The father of the realist school, Hans Morgenthau, lamenting the growing threat to human existence posed by nuclear weapons and other hazards, wrote toward the end of his life that

the technological revolutions of our age have rendered the Nation-State's principle of political organization as obsolete as the first modern industrial revolution of the steam engine did feudalism. The governments of Nation-States are no longer able to perform the functions for the sake of which civilized governments have been instituted in the first place: to defend and promote the life, liberty, and pursuit of happiness of its citizenry. Unable to perform these functions with regard to their own citizens, these governments are incapable of performing them in their relations with each other.[3]

There is admittedly a tendency for every generation to be temporocentric, i.e., to assume that it is living in an era that is at the crossroads of history and that its actions will be the pivotal ones on which the entire future of humanity will hinge. However, the current generation may be more justified in its temporocentrism than past generations, if only because it has only been in the nuclear age that "mankind as a whole has had to live with the prospect of its extinction as a *species*."[4] Whether such awesome responsibility for the fate of the planet requires fundamental changes in the world political order, and whether people are prepared to accept such changes, remains to be seen. One can rightly ask: If not the nation-state, then *what?* How else might, or should, human affairs be organized?

Thinking About the Future

In conjecturing about the world politics of the future, it is helpful to think in terms of **alternative world order models,** ways in which human beings could conceivably organize themselves politically. Scholars who engage in such crystal-ball gazing generally pose two basic questions: (1) What alternative world order models are *possible?* (2) Which are *desirable?* The first is an empirical question, and calls for a judgment about what kind of world one can realistically expect to see in the future. The second is a normative question and calls for a value judgment about what kind of world one would ideally like to see.

Regarding the empirical question, it is almost as difficult today for the average person to envision a world without nation-states as it was for people in an earlier time to envision a world that was round rather than flat. Yet, as we have noted, the nation-state is a human creation that has not always existed and will not necessarily be with us for all time. Indeed, it seems extremely unlikely that the world map in, say, the year 3000 will look even remotely like the world map of today, delineated by nation-state boundaries in dark colors. Although the year 3000 is admittedly too far off to ponder, let us take a more manageable time frame and look ahead to the year 2001 and a generation or two beyond. Given the trends we have described throughout this book, what might the world look like by the mid–twenty-first century?

Regarding the normative question, there is much disagreement over the criteria to be applied in evaluating the merits of alternative world order models. For example, one group of scholars participating in the World Order Models Project has suggested that alternative world order systems be judged in terms of how well they would promote the following four "human" values: peace, individual freedom and dignity, economic justice, and ecological balance.[5] Other people, however, might add such goals as cultural diversity, national unity, or economic efficiency. A world that is conducive to one set of values might well be detrimental to another set of values. What kind of world should we be striving for in the next few years?

Of course, one hopes that the way the world is heading happens to coincide with the direction one wishes to see it take, or that it at least can be moved in that direction. In considering what is possible and desirable, people tend to become either overly cynical and resigned to the present reality or overly optimistic and idealistic about what could be. The former are obsessed with what *is,* and are incapable of opening their minds to new possibilities; the latter are preoccupied with what *ought to be,* to the exclusion of what can practically be attained. The future is difficult to predict, precisely because it partly depends on what we want the future to look like. Within limits, humanity has the ability to shape the future, to continue or to alter the existing course.

We will now examine a number of alternative world order models. In each case, we will attempt to assess the likelihood of the world's resembling that model in the twenty-first century. We will also consider whether the model in question would necessarily represent an improvement on the current international system in terms of various values one might seek to promote.

Alternative World Order Models

THE CONTEMPORARY NATION-STATE SYSTEM

One distinct possibility is that the world will look much as it does today. We have spent virtually this entire book describing the contemporary international system. As we have shown, the dominant feature of this system remains the competition between the governments of sovereign nation-states, although IGOs and other nonstate actors are part of an expanding web of human relationships that cut across state lines and complicate world politics. This is a complex system in terms of not only the congeries of actors involved in world politics but also the range of issues that concern them, with economic and other issues vying for attention with traditional military-security ones. Central guidance mechanisms remain weak despite increased interdependence and attempts at coordination.

Although the pace of change today may be so great that the least likely future is one that resembles the present, there seems to be a strong probability that—barring a nuclear holocaust or some other global cataclysm—the contemporary system will last well into the next century, at least in its basic characteristics. In other words, one would expect nation-states still to be the key units of political organization in the world even if technological and other developments increasingly threaten to undermine their sovereignty. Several variants of the nation-state system are possible, though. For example, interdependence might increase to the point where efforts at regime-building become more intensified, and increased regulatory power is vested in global IGOs such as the United Nations or in regional IGOs. Or just the opposite might occur, as national governments seek to reduce interdependence (say, by restricting transnational activities of their citizens) and to return to a more clearly "state-centric" system. In place of the growing *multipolar* ("polycentric") configuration of power and alignments, a loose or tight *bipolar* system could reemerge; or one might find a *concert of great powers* attempting to exercise a global condominium in the absence of any single hegemonic state or a world government. Alternatively, if more and more states were to develop nuclear weapons, there might be a *unit veto* system in which no one state or group of states could dominate but all would be at a standoff.[6]

It is difficult to say which of these directions the nation-state system might take. Interdependence can possibly be reduced, but it cannot be undone in the modern age. It is difficult to envision a concert of great powers imposing their will on the world when some powers today already have what seem to be unparalleled means of influence at their disposal yet are failing to take advantage of it; although countries such as the United States, Japan, China, Germany, Britain, France, and Russia might have more leverage if they consistently worked together, such "grand coalitions" have a way of falling apart. As for the unit veto system, if it ever did come into being, the number of fingers on the nuclear trigger suggests it would not last very long.

Normatively speaking, a unit veto system would resemble the nineteenth-century American Wild West at High Noon, with each individual living by the gun. Nationalism and cultural diversity would be preserved, but the survival of the human race might be questionable. In fact, as the quotation from Hans Morgenthau on page 587 indicates, some have questioned whether *any* variant of the nation-state system, including the contemporary system, is capable of preventing the destruction of civilization. In the words of Robert North, "One may entertain serious doubts whether the competitive, often violent nation-state system as it now exists is any longer safe for the human race."[7] Perhaps if a concert of great powers that enjoyed unchallenged power and a high degree of cohesiveness could somehow emerge, it might be able to maintain order and minimize violent conflict. To some, the rudiments of such a system showed signs of materializing during the 1990 Iraq-Kuwait crisis, based on the extensive cooperation among the permanent members of the UN Security Council. However, as Robert Johansen points out, "Because such a system would be hierarchical and inequitable, it would doubtless be exploitative. It probably would not attack worldwide poverty, political repression, or ecological decay."[8] If one wishes to maximize the chances not only for peace but for other values to be realized, then maybe the only road open within the framework of a nation-state system is to continue to "muddle along," trying to strengthen regimes as much as possible through negotiation and compromise among multiple actors.

REGIONALISM

An alternative to the nation-state system is a system of regional units. Instead of more than 180 nation-states, the world's people might be organized in five or six region-states—the United States of Europe, the United States of Africa, and so forth. We noted the euphoria that surrounded the creation of the European Community in the 1950s and the predictions by some that it would not only lead to a United States of Europe but would also serve as a model for similar integration movements in other parts of the world. We noted, too, that these predictions have proved erroneous, with regional integration efforts failing in Africa and elsewhere and with the European experiment itself stalling somewhat in recent years. Still, as evidenced by the expansion of the European Union, **regionalism** remains a significant phenomenon in international relations, with regional organizations growing far more rapidly than global organizations. It is not inconceivable that sometime in the future, because of mutual security or economic concerns, national units might merge into larger regional political communities. Such regionalization is likely to be an uneven process, because the transfer of loyalty and authority to regional institutions is likely to occur in some geographical areas sooner than in others. As a world order model, regionalism would still be a decentralized system, with sovereignty residing in the individual regional units.

Would this necessarily be a better world than the current one? Because it would be a somewhat more centralized political system in which agreement would have to be reached among only a few actors rather than many, it would probably be a more manageable world in many respects. Such a system would be particularly effective in dealing with problems that are primarily regional rather than global in scope. Some have also suggested that regional units would represent "stepping stones" toward a global community and world government, or at least would be "islands of peace." There is evidence to suggest that the regional arrangements that have developed thus far, modest as they are, have helped "to control certain types of conflicts among their members and prevent them from spreading."[9]

Others, however, argue that regional units would simply be nation-states writ large, with the same propensity for conflict and with far more firepower with which to pursue their interests. Conflicts that today might be confined to a relatively localized area on the world map would in a future regional system likely pit very large areas of the globe against each other, especially if leaders of regional units believed they could maintain regional cohesion only by inventing external scapegoats. As difficult as it is for many national leaders today to sustain national unity and patriotism among their people, loyalty to a regional state would be even more diluted and difficult to maintain. It is not clear, either, whether regionalism would promote values of economic justice and individual freedom. Even if regional states do not materialize, we have mentioned that there is already mounting concern about the prospect of regional blocs headed by regional hegemons forming in the international economy—a U.S.-led bloc in the Americas, a Japanese-led Asian bloc, and an EU (possibly German)-led European bloc—which might experience increased conflict in trade and other sectors, leading to the kinds of tensions that characterized the interwar period.

WORLD GOVERNMENT

Another world order model is **world government**—a political system in which one central set of institutions would preside over all human beings and political units on the planet. Several variations of this model have been contemplated. The most ambitious proposal calls for nation-states surrendering total sovereignty to a supreme global authority that would rule directly over all citizens of the world. Almost equally ambitious would be a *federation*, in which nation-states would share power and authority with a central world government; the world government would be delegated specific powers in certain areas (e.g., maintenance and deployment of armed forces) and the nation-states allowed to exercise jurisdiction over other areas (e.g., education, health care). This would resemble the model used by the Founding Fathers of the United States in creating a nation in 1787. Another possibility would be a *confederation*, in which a world government would enjoy some limited degree of power and authority but the bulk would be clearly retained by the constituent nation-state units. Still another approach to world government might be the creation of several separate global authorities in different functional areas, along the lines of the International Seabed Authority proposed at UNCLOS III.

Various model constitutions have been drafted over the years to flesh out what the elements of a world government might look like in terms of executive, legislative, and judicial organs. Among the most widely discussed plans is one by Grenville Clark and Louis Sohn who, in *World Peace Through World Law*, envisioned a permanent world police force with a monopoly on the legitimate use of force.[10] A starting point for world government might be a change in UN General Assembly voting procedures whereby each state's voting strength would be based on population or some criterion other than sovereign equality; no state would have a veto, and resolutions would be binding rather than merely advisory.

Notwithstanding the growing "globalization" of the international economy, the spread of the World Wide Web, and other globalizing trends, speculating about the prospects for world government admittedly borders on science fiction. By the year 2500—the setting for *Star Trek*—humankind's sense of the universe may indeed have expanded to the point where earthlings will view each other as one people with a common destiny. However, short of a Martian invasion, the vision of a single supranational community under one roof is not likely to materialize anytime soon. Indeed, as we have noted, there has been a tendency in recent years to experiment increasingly with subglobal forums for problem solving (e.g., the Group of 7) as a supplement to global approaches (e.g., the World Trade Organization).

Even if a world government were possible, though, would it necessarily be a panacea for all our problems? It is true that a centralized system would facilitate a more concerted global effort to deal with environmental and other problems; it would be less possible, for example, for states to offer themselves to multinational corporations as "pollution havens" where few environmental regulations were enforced (as Brazil and some other countries now do to attract foreign industry). Such a system also might allow for a more equitable distribution of wealth, although probably at the expense of some individuals and states that are now in a privileged position. There is serious question whether such a system would promote freedom and democracy. Who would determine the nature of the political institutions? Where would the "capital" be located? There are complaints today that even in a democracy such as the United States the average person has little access to the decision-making centers of power. One would imagine the problem would be greatly magnified with a world government. A world government would be in a better position to enforce the Universal Declaration of Human Rights than the United Nations is today, because national governments that practice repression could not then invoke sovereign privileges against foreign interference in their internal affairs; yet some of the same governments might be the ones controlling the world government and defining the nature of the "rights" enjoyed by Americans and other peoples.

The one value that a world government would most likely maximize, according to conventional wisdom, is peace. However, just as central governments of nation-states today are often incapable of preventing the outbreak of large-scale domestic violence and civil war, there is no reason to assume that a world government could necessarily keep its house in order. In fact, some have suggested that the more "amalgamated" a political community is (in terms of having a common set of governmental institutions), the more prone it can be to instability and disintegration; instead, it might be better to work toward a "pluralistic" community with constituent units sharing common values and interests but not necessarily tied together under one government.[11]

POLIS

Regionalism and world government models are based on increased centralization of the global political system. However, another possibility is increased *decentralization*, with political life on the planet revolving around even smaller and more fragmented units than the current nation-states. It is estimated that there are at least 1,500 distinct nationality or ethnic groups in the world (and over 200 languages spoken).[12] Potentially each of these groups might form its own state. This scenario, unlikely as it is, gained a measure of credibility in the 1990s with the growing ethnic unrest in places as diverse as Canada and Rwanda and the breakup of Yugoslavia and the Soviet Union.

Smaller units might be based not on common ethnicity but on the special needs of local populations. The attempts by the "flower children" in the United States during the 1960s to form relatively isolated, self-sufficient communes represented a desire to "drop out" from both a nation and a world that seemed alien to them. Jackson Davis has noted that

> in the recent past, local governments in the United States have grown faster than the federal government in terms of budget.... A trend toward decentralization is not confined to the United States, nor even to industrial nations; rather it is global in scope. If continued, trends such as these could culminate eventually in a confederacy of small, relatively autonomous local governments, perhaps coordinated and represented internationally by central governments that are vastly reduced from today's unwieldy bureaucracies.[13]

The "states rights" movement in the United States (aimed at giving more power back to states and localities) is paralleled by recent calls for greater regional autonomy on the part of Northern Italians unhappy with the Italian government's tax and other policies that have the effect of redistributing resources from the highly industrialized, wealthy North to the less developed, poorer South.[14] Some observers have noticed a trend toward the evolution of "microregions" springing up not only within national boundaries but in some cases across national boundaries. James Rosenau states:

> [One can see] the emergent role of certain cities and "natural" economic zones as subtle and nascent forms of transnational rule systems that are

not sponsored by states and that, instead, emerge out of the activities of other types of actors. . . . An insightful example along these lines is provided by the developments that have flowed from the success of a cooperation pact signed in 1988 by Lyon [in France], Milan [in Italy], Stuttgart [in Germany], and Barcelona [in Spain], developments that have led one analyst to observe that "a resurrection of 'city states' and regions is quietly transforming Europe's political and economic landscape, diminishing the influence of national governments and redrawing the continental map of power for the twenty-first century." All four cities and their surrounding regions . . . are attracting huge investment and enjoying a prosperity that has led to new demands for greater autonomy. Some argue that, as a result, the emerging urban centers and economies are fostering "a new historical dynamism that will ultimately transform the political structure of Europe by creating a new kind of 'Hanseatic League' that consists of thriving city-states." One specialist forecasts that there will be nineteen cities with at least twenty million people in the greater metropolitan area by the year 2000, with the result that "cities, not nations, will become the principal identity for most people in the world."[15]

Similarly, Seyom Brown speaks of "geographically concentrated clusters of economic activity, which may not fall within the borders of a particular country and in which the major sectors engage in a high degree of coordination to advance the prosperity of the region. . . . Examples of such flourishing regional clusters are the San Diego and Tijuana corridor . . . and the 'growth triangle' linking Singapore and some of the nearby islands of Indonesia."[16]

Although a world order system made up of subnational local entities or transnational microregions as the dominant political units is conceivable, it seems at least as unlikely as world government. The world might be organized in communes after a nuclear war, as Jonathan Schell has suggested in *The Fate of the Earth*.[17] Otherwise, it would seem a utopian idea. As a utopian model, one can again ask whether it would necessarily be an improvement on the current system or any of the other alternative world order models that have been mentioned. Those who believe greater decentralization would be a positive development include "New Left" thinkers who seek greater democracy in the workplace and in other areas, as well as some "limits to growth" thinkers who urge a "small is beautiful" approach to life. The common thread is a concern that the world has become too big and complicated for individuals to relate meaningfully to it, and a resultant desire to return to smaller "human-scale" communities—along the lines of the ancient Greek city-states, which stressed the concept of **polis.**

Although such decentralization might well maximize individual freedom, democracy, and economic justice, some central guidance mechanism would still be needed to address global issues such as ecological problems that are not likely to disappear from the planet. Traditional security concerns would also have to be addressed somehow. The specter of Peoria, Poughkeepsie, and

Portland, or the San Diego-Tijuana corridor, saber rattling with nuclear weapons is hardly any more reassuring than the likes of the United States and Russia doing it. Given the nature of the problems we have discussed in this book, a "stop the world, I want to get off" approach does not seem appropriate. Some degree of decentralization might be both possible and desirable, but only within limits.

OTHER WORLD ORDER MODELS

All of the models we have discussed here tend to assume a *territorial* basis for human organization. Even world government models generally assume that, in addition to a global orientation, people will retain some degree of identity with smaller territorial units, be they regional, national, or subnational. However, other futures are conceivable. Indeed, we noted in Chapter 13 that some observers—certain liberal internationalist and world system theorists—already see the world organized around nonterritorial principles, with transnational economic elites and the pursuit of corporate interests overshadowing national governments and the pursuit of national interests. Although these theorists seem to underestimate the forces of nationalism, it is possible that at some time in the future, if the multinational corporation phenomenon continues to grow, the world political map might consist of units defined more by corporate logos than geographical boundaries. In this world society, human beings would be primarily employees and managers of MNCs rather than citizens of nation-states. The General Motors auto worker in St. Louis would feel a greater bond of community with his fellow GM worker in Brazil than with his next-door neighbor employed by Ford Motors.

Stephen Kobrin argues that the kind of "strategic alliance" that had been discussed in the 1990s between U.S.-based Boeing and the European-based Airbus—which would have merged the world's two biggest civilian aircraft manufacturers—presages a world in which one might not even be able to identify the "home" country of most MNCs, "borders are blurred and ambiguous," and "economic activity is increasingly organized" in terms of "electronic space" rather than "geographic space."[18] Some have gone so far as to talk of the "end of geography."[19]

In a variety of ways, the future world system could be based on "networks" of nongovernmental organizations. Today various groups around the world—not only MNCs and terrorist organizations—already meet and communicate over the heads of or underground from national governments. For example, we have noted the growing interactions of feminist groups and other "transnational interest groups" at UN forums in the 1990s. With the development of instantaneous telecommunications and computer terminal networks, it is becoming increasingly feasible to bring people from remote parts of the globe into direct contact.[20]

It may be that integrative, centripetal forces, such as "globalization" of the international economy, are in an odd sort of way feeding disintegrative, centrifugal forces, such as the "microregion" phenomenon we just mentioned. As one newspaper recently reported:

> In Montreal, Rita Dionne-Marsolais by day plots global energy strategies as a Price Waterhouse consultant. By night, she plots Quebec's independence. "We want to position ourselves in the world market," she says. "The rest of Canada is just another business partner." . . . In Brussels, the capital of economically unified Western Europe, Guy Verhofstadt, a Flemish opposition leader, proposes turning over most of Belgium's social-security system to the nation's three regions—even if the country breaks apart over the issue. "We'd be three independent regions in the European Union," he says.[21]

The reader should recall our box on "The New Feudalism" in Chapter 3, where we alluded to the growing complexity of human relationships, which some see taking humanity back to a pre-Westphalian, medieval-type system of overlapping hierarchies of authority and multiple affiliations and loyalties. Is this the future?

It is not clear what the implications of such a scenario would be for various world order values.[22] In an MNC-centered world, for example, although there would seemingly be less international conflict as we know it, there might be intensified transnational class conflict. Although the drive for profit maximization would presumably contribute to economic growth and some economic efficiencies, concerns about economic justice and environmental protection would probably suffer. How would *government* function? In a world of overlapping hierarchies of authority, the lines of accountability might be so blurred that it might be difficult to hold officials responsible for decisions, and hence democracy would be difficult to sustain. Growing attention is being paid in the international relations literature to the problem of "global governance," i.e. how subnational and transnational actors will relate to existing nation-states in a way that best promotes human values.[23]

Toward the Year 2001: Onward and Upward

There is little doubt that space-age technology will be changing our lives in many ways that will go far beyond microwave ovens and home computers, and that along with improvements in the human condition will also come new, unforeseeable problems. Looking ahead to the twenty-first century, in addition to these unforeseeable problems, we can expect older, more familiar problems to remain on the global agenda. In compiling his "agenda for the twenty-first century," Robert McNamara has listed as the top two concerns the "threat of nuclear war" and the "imbalance of population growth rates on the one hand and social and economic rates of advance on the other"; he also lists as a major concern the need for new global institution building.[24]

This leads us back to our discussion of alternative world order models. All the alternative world order models we have discussed have potential drawbacks. There are no obvious solutions to the human predicament that are both ideally perfect and realistically attainable. It may be that the *present* system, with some tinkering here and there (centralizing some aspects and decentralizing others), could be the best of all possible worlds. We do not want to engage in false optimism, especially given all the global problems we have noted. However, there is reason to be cautiously hopeful. In a world where several human beings have landed on the moon, we do not want to sell future possibilities short. (Even before the winding down of the Cold War, Soviet and Western astronauts had "broken bread" together and dined on creamed crab in a joint space voyage.)[25] Just as certain centuries-old human institutions once thought unchangeable have been changed for the better—for example, the virtual eradication of slavery—other deeply embedded human institutions, such as war, might also become relics of the past. The seemingly impossible occasionally does happen.

At the outset of this book, we distinguished between the differing perspectives of policymakers, scholars, and laymen as observers of international relations. Policymakers and laymen will probably continue to be preoccupied with more immediate, less philosophical and theoretical matters than the futuristic issues discussed above, leaving scholars to ponder the long term. Nevertheless, rather than asking "What has posterity ever done for me?"[26] *all* of us could accept some responsibility for the future world we bequeath to tomorrow's children. For policymakers and laymen, no less than scholars, the starting point in working toward a better world is *understanding* how the world works—overcoming the ignorance that blinds people both to the seriousness of recent developments and to the vision of future possibilities.

As the year 2001 approaches, the current generation is faced with entering not only a new century but a new *millennium*. No generation will experience such a moment for another thousand years. Playing on the symbolism of the moment, it would appear that this is a propitious time to pause and reflect on the global condition and what might be done to improve it. More than ever, the future is now.

SUGGESTIONS FOR FURTHER READING AND STUDY

Among the works that analyze the competing tendencies toward integration (centralization) and disintegration (decentralization) at work in contemporary international relations, explaining these in terms of larger socioeconomic and other changes since World War II and calling for new ways to conceptualize world politics, see James N. Rosenau, *Turbulence in World Politics: A Theory of Change and Continuity* (Princeton, N.J.: Princeton University Press, 1990); Yale Ferguson and Richard Mansbach, *Polities* (Columbia, S.C.: University of South Carolina Press, 1995); and Benjamin R. Barber, *Jihad vs. McWorld* (New York: Random House, 1995).

An excellent general work on thinking about the future is Barry B. Hughes, *International Futures: Choices in the Creation of A New World Order* (Boulder, Colo.: Westview Press, 1993). Among the scholarly works that offer a negative view of the world's future, perhaps the most gloomy is Robert Heilbroner's *An Inquiry Into the Human Prospect,* 2nd ed. (New York: W. W. Norton, 1991); the work that most clearly addresses the issue of human extinction is Jonathan Schell's *The Fate of the Earth* (New York: Knopf, 1982). Also see Robert Kaplan, "The Coming Anarchy," *The Atlantic* (February 1994); Paul Kennedy, *Preparing for the Twenty-First Century* (New York: Random House, 1993); and John Mearsheimer, "Why We Will Soon Miss the Cold War," *The Atlantic* (August 1990), pp. 35–50.

Among those scholars who have been optimistic about recent trends are Julian Simon, *The Ultimate Resource* (Princeton, N.J.: Princeton University Press, 1982); Max Singer and Aaron Wildavsky, *The Real World Order,* rev. ed. (Chatham, N.J.: Chatham House Publishers, 1996); and Allan Goodman, *A Brief History of the Future* (Boulder, Colo.: Westview Press, 1993). Also see Charles Maynes, "The New Pessimism," *Foreign Policy* (Fall 1995), pp. 33–49.

On "global governance," see the Report of the Commission on Global Governance, *Our Global Neighborhood* (New York: Oxford University Press, 1995); Lawrence S. Finkelstein, "What Is Global Governance?" *Global Governance,* 1 (September–December 1995), pp. 367–372; James N. Rosenau, "Governance in the Twenty-First Century," *Global Governance,* 1 (Winter 1995), pp. 13–43; and Karen Knop et al., *Rethinking Federalism: Citizens, Markets, and Governments in A Changing World* (Vancouver: University of British Columbia Press, 1995).

Novels that offer fictitious accounts of future societies, either utopias or dystopias, include the following: George Orwell, *1984* (New York: Harcourt, Brace, 1949); Ernest Callenbach, *Ectotopia* (New York: Bantam, 1975); H. G. Wells, *A Modern Utopia* (1905; reprint, Lincoln: University of Nebraska Press, 1967); and Cecilia Holland, *Floating Worlds* (New York: Knopf, 1976). See also Martin Harry Greenberg and Joseph D. Olander, eds., *International Relations Through Science Fiction* (New York: Franklin Watts, 1978); and Dennis Livingston, "Science Fiction Modes of Future World Order Systems," *International Organization,* 25 (Spring 1971), pp. 254–270.

Notes

PART I. INTRODUCTION

Chapter 1. The Study of International Relations, or Getting a Handle on the World

1. This proverb was uttered as the opening remark by a Soviet diplomat at a meeting of the International Studies Association in Anaheim, California, on March 29, 1986, in a forum in which the Soviet official was engaging in a dialogue with his American counterpart on "The Future of U.S.-Soviet Relations."

2. On the failure of international relations scholars to predict the end of the Cold War, see John Lewis Gaddis, "International Relations Theory and the End of the Cold War," *International Security*, 17 (Winter 1992–93), pp. 5–58. For a post-hoc analysis of the causes of the end of the Cold War, see Charles W. Kegley, Jr., "How Did the Cold War Die?: Principles for An Autopsy," *Mershon International Studies Review*, 38 (April 1994), pp. 11–14.

3. *U.S. Department of State Bulletin*, 88 (November 1988), p. 1.

4. *U.S. Department of State Dispatch*, 4 (September 1993), p. 649.

5. Norman Angell, *The Great Illusion: A Study of the Relation of Military Power in Nations to Their Economic and Social Advantage* (London: W. Heinemann, 1910). Another intellectual of the time, Scott Nearing, included war "among such defunct social practices as cannibalism and chattel slavery," arguing that "all three . . . belong in the past, were being outlived in the present, and would play little or no part in the human future." Scott Nearing, *The Making of a Radical* (New York: Social Science Institute, 1972), p. 177.

6. Address from 10 Downing Street, London, September 30, 1938.

7. Ted Galen Carpenter, "The New World Disorder," *Foreign Policy*, 84 (Fall 1991), pp. 24–39.

8. Alan Durning, *How Much Is Enough?* (New York: W. W. Norton, 1992).

9. For example, see Roger D. Blair and Ronald J. Vogel, "Heroin Addiction and Urban Crime," *Public Finance Quarterly*, 1 (October 1974), pp. 457–466; James C. Weissman, "Understanding the Drugs and Crime Connection," *Journal of Psychedelic Drugs*, 10 (July–September 1978), pp. 171–192; and Stephen Flynn, "Worldwide Drug Scourge: The Expanding Trade in Drugs," *Brookings Review* (Winter 1993).

10. U.S. Bureau of Justice Statistics, *Drugs, Crime, and The Justice System* (Washington, D.C., U.S. Department of Justice, 1992), pp. 36–51.

11. On the American-Soviet arms competition in the 1980s, see Stephanie G. Neuman, "The Arms Market: Who's On Top?," *Orbis*, 33 (Fall 1989), pp. 509–530. On U.S. dominance of the world arms market in the 1990s, see U.S. Arms Control and Disarmament Agency, *World Military Expenditures and Arms Transfers, 1993–94* (Washington, D.C.: U.S. ACDA, 1995), pp. 14–18.

12. *St. Louis Post-Dispatch*, October 31, 1993, p. 8. Also see *St. Louis Post-Dispatch*, July 16, 1995, p. 1E.

13. Ralph M. Doggett, "Defense Expenditures in the 1980s: A Macroeconomic, Interindustry, and Regional Analysis," in F. Gerard Adams, ed., *The Macroeconomic Dimensions of Arms Reduction* (Boulder, Colo.: Westview Press, 1992), pp. 39–50. An excellent discussion of the prospects for reduced global military spending and the implications for the U.S. economy and other economies is Steve Chan, "Grasping the Peace Dividend: Some Propositions on the Conversion of Swords into Plowshares," *Mershon International Studies Review*, 39

(April 1995), pp. 53–95. Chan is skeptical of major reductions in defense spending in the United States and elsewhere.

14. The foreign import share of the U.S. car market peaked at 31 percent in 1987, declining thereafter, mainly because of Japanese and other foreign firms relying more on their transplant operations in the United States than on imports to serve the American market. American Automobile Manufacturers Association, *Motor Vehicle Facts and Figures, 1994* (Washington, D.C.: AAMA, 1994), p. 20. For data on market shares, also see Walter Adams and James Brock, *The Structure of American Industry*, 9th ed. (Englewood Cliffs, N.J.: Prentice Hall, 1995), pp. 68–75.

15. Adams and Brock, *The Structure of American Industry*, p. 70. Trends in the growth of the world auto market are discussed in Lester R. Brown et al., *Vital Signs 1996* (New York: W. W. Norton, 1996), pp. 84–85.

16. Stephen H. Schneider, *Global Warming: Are We Entering the Greenhouse Century?* (New York: Sierra Club Books, 1989); Schneider, "The Changing Climate," *Scientific American,* 261 (September 1989), pp. 70–79; World Resources Institute and International Institute for Environment and Development, *World Resources 1994–95* (New York: Oxford University Press, 1994), pp. 197–212; William Dwyer and Frank Leeming, eds., *Earth's Eleventh Hour* (Boston: Allyn and Bacon, 1995), ch. 2; and Lester R. Brown et al., *Vital Signs 1996* (New York: W. W. Norton, 1996), pp. 66–67.

17. *U.S. News and World Report*, January 2, 1995, p. 76.

18. Commission on Global Governance, *Our Global Neighborhood* (New York: Oxford University Press, 1995), p. 42. The reference to "global village" is from McLuhan's *Understanding Media: The Extension of Man* (New York: McGraw-Hill, 1965), p. 93; the reference to "Spaceship Earth" is from Ward's *The Lopsided World* (New York: W. W. Norton, 1968), p. 26.

19. "Only About Half of Public Knows U.S. Has to Import Oil, Gallup Survey Shows," *New York Times*, June 2, 1977.

20. See the 1981 Washington Post–ABC News poll, reported in *Interdependent*, 7 (November 1981), p. 1; also, the 1983 CBS–New York Times poll cited in *National Journal*, August 8, 1983, p. 1658; and the 1987 Overseas Development Council poll cited in *Interdependent*, 13 (April/May 1987), p. 1.

21. Cited in Bob Herbert "A Nation of Nitwits," *New York Times*, March 1, 1995, p. A-15.

22. John Dillin, "Education's New International Wave," *Christian Science Monitor*, March 1, 1989, p. 8. Another study showed that one-third of the American students surveyed could not identify France or Great Britain on an outline map of Europe, and two-thirds could not identify the United States' enemies during World War II. Richard Wood, "For Americans the World is Terra Incognita," *Christian Science Monitor*, February 28, 1989, p. 19. There is evidence that geographical literacy in the United States is lower today than it was in the 1950s, based on recent surveys done by the National Geographical Society.

23. Reported on CNN on May 29, 1995.

24. Barbara Crossette, "U.S. Foreign Aid Budget: Quick, How Much? Wrong," *New York Times*, February 27, 1995.

25. For a general discussion of the American public's level of knowledge about international affairs, see Charles W. Kegley and Eugene R. Wittkopf, *American Foreign Policy: Pattern and Process*, 4th ed. (New York: St. Martin's Press, 1991), ch. 9.

26. See Ronald Inglehart and J. R. Rabier, "Europe Elects a Parliament: Cognitive Mobilization," *Government and Opposition*, 14 (Autumn 1979), pp. 478–507; *Euro-Barometre*, May 1979, pp. 3–6 and *Euro-Barometre*, December 1983, pp. 63–68 and 85–86. A six-nation study in 1985 found that American university students registered lower scores on a standard foreign affairs test than their counterparts in Canada, West Germany, India, and Brazil. Wayne C. McWilliams, "What University Students Know About Foreign Affairs: A Six-Nation Study," paper presented at Annual Meeting of the International Studies Association, Anaheim, Calif., March 1986.

27. *Merriam Webster's Collegiate Dictionary,* 10th ed. (Springfield, Mass.: G. and C. Merriam Co., 1994), p. 611.

28. James N. Rosenau, ed., *International Politics and Foreign Policy,* rev. ed. (New York: Free Press, 1969), p. 1.

29. Ibid., pp. 1–29.

30. Harold D. Lasswell, *Politics: Who Gets What, When, How?* (Cleveland: World Publishing, 1958).

31. Gerald B. Hellman and Steve R. Ratner, "Saving Failed States," *Foreign Policy* (Winter 1992–1993), pp. 3–20.

32. John Stoessinger, *The Might of Nations,* 9th ed. (New York: McGraw-Hill, 1990), p. 5. Of course, similar struggles go on *within* nations as well, particularly in many less developed countries in Africa, Asia, and elsewhere, where such conflicts can be every bit as violent as conflicts between nations. The main point here, however, is that within nations central authoritative institutions do exist, however weakly they may actually function in many instances. For a discussion comparing the stability of international and intranational politics, see Fred W. Riggs, "International Relations as a Prismatic System," *World Politics,* 14 (October 1961), pp. 141–181. Also, see Hedley Bull, *The Anarchical Society* (New York: Columbia University Press, 1977).

33. There has been debate in the international relations field over the question of whether interdependence has in fact been increasing and is undermining the viability of nation-states. The standard view that interdependence is increasing and poses challenges to the functioning of the state system is expressed in Mark W. Zacher, "The Decaying Pillars of the Westphalian Temple: Implications for International Order and Governance," in James N. Rosenau and Ernst-Otto Czempiel, eds., *Governance Without Government* (Cambridge, Eng.: Cambridge University Press, 1992). A few scholars (such as Kenneth Waltz) argue that it has actually been *decreasing,* and others (such as Richard Rosecrance and Stephen Krasner) argue that there is at least contradictory evidence to be found and that the phenomenon is more complex than commonly conceived. See Kenneth N. Waltz, "The Myth of National Interdependence," in Charles P. Kindleberger, ed., *The International Corporation: A Symposium* (Cambridge, Mass.: MIT Press, 1970), pp. 205–223; Richard N. Rosecrance and Arthur Stein, "Interdependence: Myth or Reality?" *World Politics,* 26 (October 1973), pp. 1–27; and Janice E. Thomson and Stephen D. Krasner, "Global Transactions and the Consolidation of Sovereignty," in James N. Rosenau and Ernst-Otto Czempiel, eds., *Global Changes and Theoretical Challenges* (Lexington, Mass.: Lexington Books, 1989), pp. 195–220. We will discuss the various arguments and evidence in detail in later chapters. Suffice it to say at this point that the weight of the evidence would seem to justify the minimal assertion that "we live in an era of interdependence." Robert O. Keohane and Joseph S. Nye, *Power and Interdependence,* 2nd ed. (Boston: Scott Foresman, 1989), p. 3.

34. Robert C. Angell, *Peace on the March: Transnational Participation* (New York: Van Nostrand Reinhold, 1969); Allen Goodman, *A Brief History of the Future* (Boulder, Colo.: Westview Press, 1993).

35. Paul Kennedy, *Preparing for the Twenty-First Century* (New York: Random House, 1993); Robert Kaplan, "The Coming Anarchy," *The Atlantic,* 273 (February 1994), pp. 44 ff.

36. Keohane and Nye, *Power and Interdependence,* p. 5, define regimes as "governing arrangements" among nation-states.

37. For an elaborate discussion of the meaning of the term, see Thomas S. Kuhn, *The Structure of Scientific Revolution* (Chicago: University of Chicago Press, 1962).

38. See J. Martin Rochester, "The Paradigm Debate in International Relations and Its Implications for Foreign Policy Making," *Western Political Quarterly,* 31 (March 1978), pp. 48–58.

39. Dante Alighieri, *On World Government,* trans. Herbert W. Schneider, 2nd rev. ed. (New York: Liberal Arts Press, 1957). Dante's horizons at the time essentially were limited to Europe, where he hoped a "Christian commonwealth" would emerge.

40. Albert Fried, ed., *A Day of Dedication: The Essential Writings and Speeches of Woodrow Wilson* (New York: Macmillan, 1965).

41. R. S. Baker, *Woodrow Wilson and World Settlement* (Gloucester, Mass.: P. Smith, 1922), p. 93. Wilson's statement also points to a seedier side of idealism, i.e., the sometimes fanatical missionary zeal with which idealists attempt to reform the world, even to the point of producing the very conflict they ostensibly seek to avoid. Wilson's own "messianic liberalism" is discussed in Alexander L. George and Juliette George, *Woodrow Wilson and Colonel House* (New York: John Day, 1956).

42. E. H. Carr, *The Twenty Years' Crisis, 1919–1939* (London: Macmillan, 1939).

43. Hans J. Morgenthau, *Politics Among Nations* (New York: Knopf, 1948). Other "realist" works include George F. Kennan, *American Diplomacy, 1900–1950* (Chicago: University of Chicago Press, 1951); Arnold Wolfers, *Discord and Collaboration* (Baltimore: Johns Hopkins University Press, 1962); and Henry A. Kissinger, *American Foreign Policy: Three Essays* (New York: W. W. Norton, 1969).

44. See, for example, Robert G. Gilpin, *War and Change in World Politics* (Cambridge, Eng.: Cambridge University Press, 1981); and Kenneth N. Waltz, *Theory of International Politics* (Reading, Mass.: Addison-Wesley, 1979). For a general discussion of neorealism, see Robert O. Keohane, ed., *Neorealism and Its Critics* (New York: Columbia University Press, 1986); and the "Symposium on the New Realism," in *International Organization*, 38 (Spring 1984). Also see Joseph Grieco, "Anarchy and The Limits of Cooperation: A Realist Critique of the Newest Liberal Institutionalism," *International Organization*, 42 (Summer 1988), pp. 486–507.

45. See Keohane and Nye, *Power and Interdependence*; Richard W. Mansbach, Yale G. Ferguson, and Donald E. Lampert, *The Web of World Politics: Nonstate Actors in the Global System* (Englewood Cliffs, N.J.: Prentice-Hall, 1976); and Richard Rosecrance, *The Rise of the Trading State* (New York: Basic Books, 1986). A variation of the "globalist" paradigm is the "world society" approach, as represented by John W. Burton, *World Society* (Cambridge, Eng.: Cambridge University Press, 1972).

46. Robert O. Keohane and Joseph S. Nye, eds., *Transnational Relations and World Politics* (Cambridge, Mass.: Harvard University Press, 1971). Among the precursors of the globalists was John Herz, who in the 1950s already pointed to the increased "permeability" of national boundaries and envisioned the "demise of the territorial state," although he later had second thoughts about the latter prediction. See John Herz, *International Politics in the Atomic Age* (New York: Columbia University Press, 1959).

47. Realists acknowledge the existence of actors other than the nation-state but consider them to be relatively peripheral to international politics. See Wolfers, *Discord and Collaboration*, pp. 3–24. The key assumptions of the globalist paradigm are summarized in Paul R. Viotti and Mark V. Kauppi, *International Relations Theory: Realism, Pluralism, Globalism*, 2nd ed. (New York: Macmillan, 1993), pp. 5–7 and 35–228; what we call the globalist paradigm, however, is labeled "pluralism" by Viotti and Kauppi.

48. See Michael Doyle, "Liberalism and World Politics," *American Political Science Review*, 80 (December 1986), pp. 1151–1169; and Zacher, "The Decaying Pillars."

49. See Charles W. Kegley, ed., *Controversies in International Relations Theory: Realism and the Neoliberal Challenge* (New York: St. Martin's Press, 1995). Even realists and neorealists have found themselves reexamining their assumptions somewhat; see Fareed Zakaria, "Is Realism Finished?," *The National Interest*, 30 (Winter 1992–1993), pp. 21–32.

50. James Rosenau has argued that the notion of "international politics" or "international relations" seems "obsolete when so many of the interactions that presently sustain world politics do not unfold directly between nations or states." "Global Changes and Theoretical Challenges: Toward a Postinternational Politics for the 1990s," in Rosenau and Czempiel, *Global Changes*, p. 2. See Rosenau's *Turbulence in World Politics* (Princeton, N.J.: Princeton University Press, 1990).

51. See Immanuel Wallerstein, *The Capitalist World-Economy* (Cambridge, Eng.: Cambridge University Press, 1979); and Thomas Shannon, *An Introduction to the World-System Perspective* (Boulder, Colo.: Westview Press, 1989).

52. For post-modern perspectives, see the special issue of *International Studies Quarterly* entitled "Speaking the Language of Exile Dissidence in International Studies," 34 (September 1990). Feminist perspectives are discussed in V. Spike Peterson, ed., *Gendered States: Feminist (Re)Visions of International Relations Theory* (Boulder, Colo.: Lynne Rienner, 1992).

53. For an excellent discussion of methodological issues, see Klaus Knorr and James N. Rosenau, eds., *Contending Approaches to International Politics* (Princeton, N.J.: Princeton University Press, 1969). For a discussion of both methodological and paradigmatic issues, see James E. Dougherty and Robert L. Pfaltzgraff, *Contending Theories of International Relations*, 3rd ed. (New York: Harper and Row, 1990); and Hayward R. Alker and Thomas J. Biersteker, "The Dialectics of World Order: Notes for a Future Archaeologist of International Savior Faire," *International Studies Quarterly*, 28 (June 1984), pp. 121–142.

54. Some behavioralists such as Deutsch urged *both* "quantitative" and "qualitative" analysis, whereas others such as Singer were more unequivocal in their criticism of traditional approaches and in their use of quantitative techniques. See, for example, Karl W. Deutsch, "Toward an Inventory of Basic Trends and Patterns in Comparative and International Politics," *American Political Science Review*, 54 (March 1960), pp. 34–57; J. David Singer, "The Behavioral Science Approach to International Relations: Payoff and Prospect," *SAIS Review*, 10 (Summer 1966), pp. 12–20; and James N. Rosenau, *The Scientific Study of Foreign Policy* (New York: Free Press, 1971).

55. Even though Hans Morgenthau's work has been called "the first 'scientific' treatment of world politics," in the sense that he did attempt to develop an explicit empirical theory, his methods were still essentially traditionalist ones. See Stanley Hoffmann, "An American Social Science: International Relations," *Daedalus*, 106 (Summer 1977), p. 43.

56. Charles A. McClelland, "International Relations: Wisdom or Science?," in James N. Rosenau, ed., *International Politics and Foreign Policy*, rev. ed. (New York: Free Press, 1969), p. 4.

57. See Benjamin Jowett, trans., *The Republic of Plato*, 4th ed. (Fair Lawn, N.J.: Oxford University Press, 1953); Niccolo Machiavelli, *The Prince*, T. G. Bergin, trans. and ed. (New York: Appleton-Century-Crofts, 1947).

58. For a discussion of the relationship between the scholarly community and the policymaking community, see Raymond Tanter and Richard H. Ullman, eds., *Theory and Policy in International Relations* (Princeton, N.J.: Princeton University Press, 1972); of particular interest is the article by Allen S. Whiting entitled "The Scholar and the Policy-Maker," pp. 229–247.

59. Much of this discussion owes a debt to William Coplin. See William D. Coplin and Charles W. Kegley, eds., *A Multi-Method Introduction to International Politics* (Chicago: Markham Publishing, 1971). The discussion also relates to the taxonomy of cognitive skills developed by Benjamin S. Bloom et al., *Taxonomy of Educational Objectives, Handbook I: Cognitive Domain* (New York: McKay, 1956). The latter suggests that there is a certain hierarchy of skills that build on each other, ranging from the most basic skill of factual literacy to more sophisticated skills that include comprehension and ultimately evaluation and application. In our scheme of things in this section, factual literacy is roughly related to description, comprehension to what we call explanation, evaluation to what we call normative analysis, and application to what we call prescription.

60. A country's per capita gross national product equals its gross national product (i.e., the total value of all goods and services produced in the national economy over a given time period) divided by its total population. The distribution of wealth in the world is skewed by the fact that two countries—China and India, each with a PGNP of under $500—together constitute roughly one third of humanity. With its rapid GNP growth in the 1990s, along with a reduced population growth rate, China's PGNP will undoubtedly soon exceed the $500 threshold. It should be added that PGNP is only one of several indicators that one might use to measure national wealth. The data were obtained from the *World Bank Atlas*, 1995 (Washington, D.C.: World Bank, 1994), pp. 18–20.

Chapter 2. A Glimpse into the Past: The Historical Development of the International System

1. Barbara W. Tuchman, "Is This the Summer of 1914?" *Washington Post*, May 11, 1980, p. C-7. It should be noted that Tuchman has often strayed into the *déjà vu* school, such as in *A Distant Mirror* (New York: Knopf, 1978), where she draws a sweeping parallel between the economic dislocation and political chaos of the fourteenth century and the troubles of the twentieth century.
2. Alvin Toffler, *Future Shock* (New York: Bantam Books, 1970), p. 17.
3. Kenneth N. Waltz, *Theory of International Politics* (Reading, Mass.: Addison-Wesley, 1979), pp. 65–66.
4. George Santayana, *Life of Reason*, I (New York: Scribner's, 1954), p. 12. A more extreme version of this *déjà vu* view was offered by the historian Crane Brinton, who once remarked that "while those who do not know history are bound to repeat it, those who know it are bound to repeat it as well." Cited in Jagdish Bhagwati, "Economics and World Order from the 1970s to the 1990s: The Key Issues," in *Economics and World Order*, J. Bhagwati, ed. (London: Macmillan, 1972), p. 4.
5. F. S. Northedge and M. J. Grieve, *A Hundred Years of International Relations* (New York: Praeger, 1971), p. 351. On the general theme of continuity and change in international relations, see George Liska, "Continuity and Change in International Systems," *World Politics*, 16 (October 1963), pp. 118–136.
6. For example, see Morton A. Kaplan, *System and Process in International Politics*, science ed. (New York: John Wiley, 1964); William D. Coplin, *Introduction to International Politics*, 3rd ed. (Englewood Cliffs, N.J.: Prentice-Hall, 1980), pp. 23–52; K. J. Holsti, *International Politics: A Framework for Analysis*, 4th ed. (Englewood Cliffs, N.J.: Prentice-Hall, 1983), pp. 57–94; Richard Rosecrance, *Action and Reaction in World Politics* (Boston: Little, Brown, 1963); Geoffrey Barraclough, *An Introduction to Contemporary History* (Baltimore: Penguin Books, 1967), ch. 1; and Evan Luard, *Types of International Society* (New York: Free Press, 1976).
7. In previous editions of this textbook, the authors suggested that the transformation of the Post–World War II system was already well underway by 1973. While we still believe this to be historically accurate, in this new edition we have adopted the more conventional position held by most observers, i.e. the postwar system ended with the end of the Cold War, symbolized by the fall of the Berlin Wall in 1989.
8. The concept of "interconnectedness" as one aspect of interdependence is discussed by Alex Inkeles in "The Emerging Social Structure of the World," *World Politics*, 27 (July 1975), pp. 468–495. The concept of "mutual sensitivity and vulnerability" as another aspect of interdependence is discussed by Robert O. Keohane and Joseph S. Nye, *Power and Interdependence*, 2nd ed. (Boston: Little, Brown, 1989), pp. 11–22. Other "properties" of the international system can be identified. For a discussion of some of the difficult conceptual problems involved in defining what an "international system" is and in distinguishing between different international systems, see Dina A. Zinnes, "Prerequisites for the Study of System Transformation," in Ole R. Holsti et al., eds., *Change in the International System* (Boulder, Colo.: Westview Press, 1980), pp. 3–21.
9. Trends toward "universalism" and "particularism" are discussed in Richard W. Mansbach et al., *The Web of World Politics* (Englewood Cliffs, N.J.: Prentice-Hall, 1976), ch. 1. For a survey of various historical state systems, including the city-state systems of Ancient Greece and Renaissance Italy, see Martin Wight, *Systems of States* (London: Leicester University Press, 1977).

10. Some monarchs were more assertive of their authority than others, notably Elizabeth I of England, who warned "my dogs shall wear no collars but mine own." Still, all monarchs encountered difficulty in enforcing their will. England actually possessed many attributes of a territorial state as early as 1400.

11. For a discussion of the feudal era and the emergence of nation-states, see Charles Tilly, *Coercion, Capital and European States A.D. 900–1990* (Cambridge, Eng.: Basil Blackwell, 1990); and Gianfranco Poggi, *The Development of the Modern State* (Palo Alto, Calif.: Stanford University Press, 1978).

12. For a detailed discussion of how the "balance of power" operated in the seventeenth and eighteenth centuries, see John B. Wolf, *Louis XIV* (New York: W. W. Norton, 1968). The "balance of power" notion was not identified solely with the classical era but was to be applied to international politics in subsequent eras as well.

13. The conceptual problems surrounding the term "balance of power" are discussed by Ernst Haas in "The Balance of Power: Prescription, Concept, or Propaganda?" *World Politics*, 5 (July 1953), pp. 442–477; and by Dina A. Zinnes, "An Analytical Study of the Balance of Power Theories," *Journal of Peace Research*, 4 (1967), pp. 270–288.

14. The term "prismatic" was used originally by Fred Riggs to describe developing *countries* that were passing through an intermediate stage from traditional to modern societies in which old and new cultures collided. See Fred W. Riggs, *Administration in Developing Countries: The Theory of Prismatic Society* (Boston: Houghton Mifflin, 1964).

15. "Universal adult suffrage" (at least among males) was not to be achieved in most European countries until the late nineteenth and early twentieth centuries, whereas in many other countries voting was rendered meaningless by either the persistence of monarchical rule or the emergence of "one-party" regimes.

16. For example, by 1990, Switzerland's per capita income exceeded that of Mozambique by a ratio of 480:1. See World Bank, *World Development Report 1993* (Oxford: Oxford University Press, 1993), pp. 238–239. Also, see UN Development Program, *Human Development Report 1994* (Oxford: Oxford University Press, 1994), p. 35. It should be added that there were a few exceptions to the concentration of poverty in the Southern Hemisphere, notably Australia and South Africa. For a discussion of the historical development of the rich-poor gap, see Patrick J. McGowan, "Imperialism in World-System Perspective," *International Studies Quarterly*, 25 (March 1981), pp. 45–46; and Immanuel Wallerstein, *The Modern World-System* (New York: Academic Press, 1974).

17. Waltz's listing in Table 2.1 conforms roughly to the listings compiled by many other scholars. See J. David Singer, ed., *The Correlates of War I* (New York: Free Press, 1979), p. 241; and Charles F. Doran and Wes Parsons, "War and the Cycle of Relative Power," *American Political Science Review*, 74 (December 1980), p. 953.

18. Barraclough, *Introduction to Contemporary History*, pp. 110–111. See Barraclough, chs. 2–5, for general historical background on political, economic, and social trends affecting international relations during the nineteenth and early twentieth centuries.

19. Many observers had anticipated the emergence of the United States and Russia as "superpowers" well before 1945. As early as 1835, Alexis de Tocqueville had written that "there are, at the present time, two great nations in the world which seem to tend toward the same end. . . . I allude to the Russians and the Americans . . . each of which seems to be marked out . . . to sway the destinies of half the globe." *Democracy in America*, part I, Henry Reeve, trans. (New York: J. H. G. Langle, 1841), pp. 470–471. Likewise, Sir John Seeley noted in 1883 that the United States and Russia were "enormous political aggregations" that would eventually "completely dwarf such European states as France and Germany and depress them into a second class." Cited in Richard J. Barnet, *The Giants* (New York: Simon and Schuster, 1977), p. 14.

20. Mass democracy in countries such as England and France meant that the public had to be consulted or at least mobilized in support of foreign policy decisions; the new military

technology meant that alliances had to be more institutionalized and defense planning among allies more coordinated. Despite the rigidity that these elements tended to introduce, Britain was almost prepared to ally with Germany at "the eleventh hour" in 1914. See Northedge and Grieve, *A Hundred Years of International Relations*, ch. 5.

21. For a discussion of the new military technology, see David W. Ziegler, *War, Peace, and International Politics*, 4th ed. (Boston: Little, Brown, 1987), pp. 14–19.

22. "[Of 1,300,000 French troops initially put into combat] they suffered in August 1914 alone 600,000 casualties. . . . On one day alone, July 1, 1916, the British attacked with 140,000 troops and suffered 60,000 casualties. On another occasion it cost the French 160,000 casualties to gain 7,000 yards. At Passchendaele it cost the British 370,000 casualties for no gain at all." Ibid., p. 20.

23. It is estimated that a total of 30 million combatants and civilians died in World War I, and twice as many died during World War II.

24. As noted by Hornell Hart, "In 1944 [the 'killing area' within which people could be killed from a given base] . . . surpassed the size of the largest governing area ever attained. . . . The development of refueling in the air . . . [has] extended the potential killing radius to globe-encircling dimensions." Hornell Hart, "The Hypothesis of Cultural Lag," in Francis R. Allen et al., *Technology and Social Change* (New York: Appleton-Century-Crofts, 1957), p. 428.

25. Waltz especially stressed the fact that the two major powers in the post–World War II era—the United States and the Soviet Union—had little to do with each other economically compared with the intricate economic ties that the European powers had in the late nineteenth and early twentieth centuries. See Waltz, *Theory of International Politics*, pp. 138–160.

26. Asa Briggs, "The World Economy: Interdependence and Planning," in C. L. Mowat, ed., *The New Cambridge Modern History*, vol. 12 (Cambridge, Eng.: Cambridge University Press, 1968); cited in Waltz, *Theory of International Politics*, p. 140.

27. Erich Marcks, *Manner and Zeiten* (Leipzig, 1911); cited in Barraclough, *Introduction to Contemporary History*, p. 53.

28. For long-term trends in world trade, see Simon Kuznets, *Modern Economic Growth* (New Haven, Conn.: Yale University Press, 1966), pp. 306–307. More recent data are found in John Sewell et al., *Growth, Exports, and Jobs in a Changing World Economy: Agenda 1988* (New Brunswick, N.J.: Transaction Books, 1988), p. 207; Shahrokh Fardoust and Ashok Dhareshwar, *A Long-Term Outlook for the World Economy: Issues and Projections for the 1990s* (Washington, D.C.: World Bank, 1990), pp. 5–6 and 29–30; and Maurice D. Levi, *International Finance: The Markets and Financial Management of Multinational Business* (New York: McGraw-Hill, 1990), p. 3.

29. Although the number of people *immigrating* to one country from another never again reached the high pre–World War I levels (due to stricter immigration barriers imposed by governments), the number of people *traveling* across national boundaries increased enormously after World War II (as personal mobility was increased by improved transportation technology). Transborder movement of people has also increased with a growing number of refugees and illegal aliens relocating across national boundaries. For data on these and other trends related to interdependence, see Mark W. Zacher, "The Decaying Pillars of the Westphalian Temple: Implications for International Order and Governance," in James N. Rosenau and Ernst-Otto Czempiel, eds., *Governance Without Government* (Cambridge, Eng.: Cambridge University Press, 1992); and Inkeles, "The Emerging Social Structure." Inkeles notes that "recent decades reveal a general tendency for many forms of human interconnectedness across national boundaries to be doubling every ten years." Ibid., p. 479. For a contrary analysis that shares Waltz's skepticism about growing human interconnectedness, see Janice E. Thomson and Stephen D. Krasner, "Global Transactions and the Consolidation of Sovereignty," in James N. Rosenau and Ernst-Otto Czempiel, eds., *Global Changes and Theoretical Challenges* (Lexington, Mass.: Lexington Books, 1989), pp. 195–220.

30. Although it was not until much later, well into the post–World War II era, that Jean-Jacques Servan-Schreiber was to write *The American Challenge*, in which he warned of

the challenges posed by American corporations establishing marketing and manufacturing facilities throughout Western Europe, F. A. MacKenzie had anticipated the scale of the MNC phenomenon as early as 1902 in his *The American Invaders* (London: Oxford, 1902).

31. We will discuss these different types of international organizations in Chapter 10. NGOs are sometimes referred to as INGOs (international nongovernmental organizations).

32. As Inis Claude suggests, the Hague Conferences of 1899 and 1907, convened to discuss ways of settling disputes peacefully, symbolized the shifting nature of the international system at the turn of the century: "Whereas the first conference was attended by only twenty-six states and was preponderantly European in composition, the second involved representatives of forty-four states, including the bulk of the Latin American republics [as well as Asian states]." Inis L. Claude, *Swords Into Plowshares*, 4th ed. (New York: Random House, 1971), p. 29.

33. Barbara Ward, *The Lopsided World* (New York: W. W. Norton, 1968).

34. For a discussion of the impact of nuclear weapons on various aspects of world politics, see Michael Mandelbaum, *The Nuclear Revolution: International Politics Before and After Hiroshima* (New York: Cambridge University Press, 1981). For an unconventional view, which argues that the effects of nuclear weapons on world politics have been exaggerated, see A. F. K. Organski, *World Politics*, 2nd ed. (New York: Knopf, 1968), pp. 313–335.

35. The United States actually enjoyed an atomic monopoly until 1949, when the Soviet Union acquired its first atomic weapons and along with the United States developed massive military superiority in the international system.

36. Charles W. Maynes and Richard H. Ullman, "Ten Years of Foreign Policy," *Foreign Policy*, Fall 1980, p. 5.

37. The United States helped to launch the postwar independence boom by granting the Philippines independence on July 4, 1946. Fifteen new nations, almost entirely in the Middle East and Asia, came into being between 1945 and 1955. The big wave of independence, however, was to occur in the 1960s, when forty-four states (including seventeen in 1960 alone), mostly in sub-Saharan Africa, were created.

38. Soviet territorial annexation ceased with the absorption of Estonia, Lithuania, and Latvia at the very end of World War II. Although territorial issues were not important to the superpowers, they were still of concern to other lesser states (e.g., the disputes between Morocco, Mauritania, and Algeria over the Spanish Sahara, between Argentina and Chile over the Beagle Channel and other border areas, and between Israel and various Arab states over lands controlled by Israel after its achieving statehood).

39. The Suez crisis was sparked when Egypt's President Nasser seized the Suez Canal from the British, who had administered the Egyptian waterway since the nineteenth century. The British responded by launching air attacks to recapture the Canal, joined by the French (who were angered by Nasser's assistance to Algeria in the latter's struggle for independence), and by the Israelis (who were concerned about threats posed by Nasser to Israeli shipping and other interests). The United States and Soviet Union joined with Canada and others to organize a United Nations peacekeeping force, which helped to defuse the crisis. On the Suez crisis, see Kennett Love, *The Twice-Fought War* (New York: McGraw-Hill, 1969).

40. The Hungarians were not seeking to overturn the Communist regime in Budapest but rather to adopt a more independent posture vis-à-vis Moscow, along the lines of Communist Yugoslavia. For a discussion of the Hungarian Revolution and its implication for Eastern solidarity, see Ghita Ionescu, *The Break-up of the Soviet Empire in Eastern Europe* (Baltimore: Penguin Books, 1965), pp. 68–86.

41. Ronald Steel, *The End of Alliance: America and the Future of Europe* (New York: Viking Press, 1964). With regard to the Western alliance, in particular, U.S. allies expressed doubts about the reliability of the American guarantee to use nuclear weapons to counter a possible Soviet aggression in Western Europe, given the fact the Soviet ICBMs might then be aimed directly at the U.S. homeland.

42. France remained in the North Atlantic Treaty Organization (NATO) alliance, but withdrew from the military command structure in 1966. Rumania remained in the Warsaw Pact, the Eastern European counterpart to NATO, but refused to allow joint military maneuvers on Rumanian soil.

43. The five states that had exploded bombs by the early seventies were the United States, the Soviet Union, the United Kingdom, France, and Communist China; India had for all intents and purposes joined the club also by detonating a nuclear device, but officially denied it had "gone nuclear." The United States and the Soviet Union remained far superior in terms of numbers of weapons and types of delivery systems.

44. The *Pueblo* was an American naval vessel seized by North Korea on the grounds that it was spying in North Korean waters. Despite U.S. denials and demands that the ship be released, the North Koreans kept the eighty-three-man crew for almost a year before setting the group free (which included one deceased crewman) after a formal American apology.

45. The Soviet Union had helped arm and train the Egyptian military personnel against Israel. However, Anwar Sadat, Nasser's successor as president of Egypt, became suspicious of Soviet motives in the Middle East and ordered Soviet advisers out of the country. He was to use Soviet help again during the Arab-Israeli war of 1973, only to move closer to the United States later.

46. OPEC included several Arab states in the Middle East (Algeria, Iraq, Kuwait, Libya, Qatar, Saudi Arabia, and the United Arab Emirates), a non-Arab Middle East state (Iran), two African states (Nigeria and Gabon), an Asian state (Indonesia), and two from Latin America (Ecuador and Venezuela). The "Seven Sisters" included, in addition to Exxon and Shell, Mobil, Texaco, Gulf, Chevron, and British Petroleum. Excellent accounts of the oil embargo episode are provided in Leonard Mosley, *Power Play: Oil in the Middle East* (Baltimore: Penguin Books, 1974); and Raymond Vernon, ed., *The Oil Crisis* (New York: W. W. Norton, 1976).

47. The Arab oil "weapon" remained an uncertain one, and indeed diminished in importance along with OPEC in the 1980s. After a second price surge in 1979, the combination of increased energy conservation efforts in the Western industrialized states, increased petroleum supplies from non-OPEC sources (including newly opened British oil fields in the North Sea as well as expanded Mexican and Soviet exports), and overproduction by many OPEC members themselves in violation of OPEC production quotas all resulted in a world oil glut in the 1980s and a rollback in prices (from a high of $34 a barrel in 1981 to $15 by the end of the decade). However, the Gulf War in 1990, when Iraq invaded Kuwait and attempted to take over its oil fields, for awhile was to restore OPEC in general and the Persian Gulf oil-producing states in particular to prominence in international politics, as concern over disruption of key oil supplies led to oil prices more than doubling at one point to over $40 a barrel. For trends after the 1970s, see Mohammed E, Ahari, *OPEC: The Falling Giant* (Lexington: University of Kentucky Press, 1986), and Daniel Yergin, "Energy Security in the 1990s," *Foreign Affairs*, 67 (Fall 1988), pp. 110–128.

48. World Bank, *World Development Report 1988* (New York: Oxford University Press, 1988), p. 4.

49. Despite President Carter calling the 1979 Soviet invasion of Afghanistan "the greatest threat to peace since World War II," he was unable to convince many U.S. allies to join Washington in protest by boycotting the 1980 Olympic games held in Moscow. Even Puerto Rico sent a team to the Olympic Games.

50. The term "bimultipolar" was first coined by Richard Rosecrance in 1966 to describe a hypothetical system that he thought might exist in the future but did not yet exist at the time. See Richard N. Rosecrance, "Bipolarity, Multipolarity, and the Future," *Journal of Conflict Resolution*, 10 (September 1966), pp. 314–327. John Spanier used similar terminology to describe the international system in the 1980s, calling it "bipolycentric." See John Spanier, *Games Nations Play*, 4th ed. (New York: Holt, Rinehart and Winston, 1981), p. 273.

51. The "Group of 77" is a term that began to be used in the 1960s to refer to the 77 less developed countries that formed the United Nations Conference on Trade and Development in

1964 in an early attempt to press economic demands against developed countries. The term continued to be used throughout the postwar period even though by 1980 the ranks of the less developed countries had swelled to over 100.

52. George F. Will, "Europe's Second Reformation," column in *Newsweek*, November 20, 1989, p. 90.

53. Francis Fukuyama, "The End of History," *The National Interest*, 16 (Summer 1989), pp. 3–16.

54. John G. Ruggie, "Territoriality and Beyond: Problematizing Modernity in International Relations," *International Organization*, 47 (Winter 1993), p. 149; and John Agnew, "The Territorial Trap: The Geographical Assumptions of International Relations Theory," *Review of International Political Economy*, 1 (Spring 1994), pp. 53–80.

55. John J. Mearsheimer, "Why We Will Soon Miss The Cold War," *The Atlantic Monthly* (August 1990), pp. 35–50.

Chapter 3. A Bird's-Eye View of the Present: The Contemporary International System

1. Cited in Henry A. Kissinger, "We Live In An Age of Transition," *Daedalus*, 124 (Summer 1995), p. 99.

2. On the end of the Cold War, see Michael J. Hogan, ed., *The End of The Cold War: Its Meaning and Implications* (Cambridge, Eng.: Cambridge University Press, 1992), and John Lewis Gaddis, *The United States and the End of the Cold War* (Oxford University Press, 1992), along with the correspondence between Gaddis and Ted Hopf in *International Security*, 18 (Fall 1993), pp. 202–210. On the shape of the "new world order" in the post–Cold War era, see Sean M. Lynn-Jones, ed., *The Cold War and After: Prospects for Peace* (Cambridge, Mass.: MIT Press, 1991); Barry Buzan, *People, States and Fear: An Agenda for International Security*, 2nd ed. (Boulder, Colo.: Lynne Rienner, 1991); Seyom Brown, *New Forces, Old Forces, and the Future of World Politics: Post–Cold War Edition* (New York: Harper Collins, 1995); Max Singer and Aaron Wildavsky, *The Real World Order* (Chatham, N.J.: Chatham House, 1993); the symposium on "The Quest for World Order" in *Daedalus*, 124 (Summer 1995); the symposium on "A World Transformed," in *Foreign Affairs*, 69 (Fall 1990), including Robert Tucker's "1989 and All That" and Stanley Hoffmann's "A New World"; and the symposium on "Shaping the New World Order," *International Security*, 17 (Summer 1992).

3. This school of thought is represented by John J. Mearsheimer, "Why We Will Soon Miss the Cold War," *The Atlantic Monthly* (August 1990), pp. 35–50; and "Back To The Future: Instability in Europe after the Cold War," *International Security*, 15 (Summer 1990), pp. 5–56.

4. See Mark Zacher, "The Decaying Pillars of the Westphalian Temple: Implications for International Order and Governance," in James N. Rosenau and Otto-Ernst Czempiel, eds., *Governance Without Government: Order and Change in World Politics* (Cambridge, Eng.: Cambridge University Press, 1992); and Singer and Wildavsky, *The Real World Order*.

5. Kenneth N. Waltz, "Nuclear Myths and Political Realities," *American Political Science Review*, 84 (September 1990), p. 744. Waltz himself is associated with the realist school. The phrase "long peace" is credited to John Lewis Gaddis; see his "The Long Peace: Elements of Stability in the Postwar International System," in Jones, *The Cold War and After*. We discuss the "long peace" and the future of war at great length in Chapter 8.

6. Henry Kissinger has cautioned that "in the long interval of peace [between the 1815 Congress of Vienna and the onset of World War I in 1914, a period in which a few dyadic great power wars occurred but no terribly destructive systemwide war was fought], the sense of the tragic was lost." Cited in George Will, "Defense Cuts Reflect Liberals' Blind Optimism in Lasting Peace," *St. Louis Post-Dispatch*, July 17, 1995, p. 6B.

7. Steven L. Burg, *Conflict and Cohesion in Socialist Yugoslavia: Political Decision Making Since 1966* (Princeton, N.J.: Princeton University Press, 1983), p. 9.

8. Alex N. Dragnich, "The West's Mismanagement of the Yugoslav Crisis," *World Affairs*, 156 (Fall 1993), p. 63.

9. On the workings of the federal system under Tito and after his death, see Dennison Rusinow, ed., *Yugoslavia: A Fractured Federalism* (Washington, D.C.: Woodrow Wilson Center Press, 1988); and Susan Woodward, *Balkan Tragedy* (Washington, D.C.: Brookings Institution, 1995).

10. One writer notes: "The proportion of the population that declared itself to be 'Yugoslav' rather than an ethnic identity in the national census, for example . . . [was only] 5.4 percent in 1981. For the vast majority of the population, distinct ethnic or national identities continued to command emotional loyalties and provide the most powerful bases for political mobilization." Steven L. Burg, "Why Yugoslavia Fell Apart," *Current History* (November 1993), p. 357.

11. Woodward, *Balkan Tragedy*, p. 225. In a lecture at the University of Missouri–St. Louis on May 12, 1993, Dennison Rusinow also stressed that the average Yugoslav citizen—while having a strong ethnic identity—had learned to overcome ethnic separatism and was prepared to live alongside fellow Yugoslavs of different ethnic origin until, in the late 1980s, nationalistic leaders in Serbia, Croatia, and elsewhere in the Federal Republic began playing up their differences rather than commonality.

12. Excellent narratives that trace the disintegration of Yugoslavia are Woodward, *Balkan Tragedy*, and Burg, "Why Yugoslavia Fell Apart."

13. Woodward, *Balkan Tragedy*, p. 97.

14. Ibid., p. 120.

15. Charles G. Boyd, "Making Peace With The Guilty," *Foreign Affairs*, 74 (September/October 1995), p. 24.

16. Woodward, *Balkan Tragedy*, p. 148.

17. The disagreements among the United States and its European allies over recognizing the former Yugoslav republics are discussed in Dragnich, "The West's Mismanagement of the Yugoslav Crisis," and Woodward, *Balkan Tragedy*.

18. One of the more creative proposals came from the Vance-Owen peace mission in 1993 (headed by former U.S. Secretary of State Cyrus Vance and Lord David Owen of the United Kingdom), which envisioned Bosnia becoming a confederation divided into ten cantons— three made up predominantly of Muslims, three made up mainly of Bosnian Serbs, three made up mainly of Bosnian Croats, and one centered in the Bosnian capital of Sarajevo— that would be a multicultural ethnic entity. A good discussion of the diplomatic efforts surrounding the Bosnian conflict is found in Robert Hayden, "The Partition of Bosnia, 1990–1993," Radio Free Europe/Radio Free Liberty Research Report, 2, no. 22, May 28, 1993, pp. 1–15.

19. There is considerable controversy over whether the Bosnian Serbs were responsible for firing the mortar round into the marketplace and were responsible for other alleged attacks on "safe havens." Although there is general agreement that the Bosnian Serbs were guilty of numerous atrocities, some observers have noted that the Bosnian Muslims had to share the blame because they committed numerous atrocities themselves. Indeed, it has been argued that the Sarajevo government purposely stationed its troops in safe havens so as to invite Serb military attacks and then be in a position to attract world attention to their cause, scoring propaganda victories in the public opinion battle waged on CNN and in other media. See Woodward, *Balkan Tragedy*, pp. 320–324; Boyd, "Making Peace With the Guilty"; David Binder, "Bosnia's Bombers," *The Nation*, October 2, 1995, pp. 336–337; Peter Brock, "Dateline Yugoslavia: The Partisan Press," *Foreign Policy*, no. 93 (Winter 1993–94), pp. 152–172; and Yohanan Ramati, "Stopping the War in Yugoslavia," *Midstream*, 40 (April 1994), pp. 2–3. For another view, stressing Serb atrocities, see Albert Wohlstetter, "Chirac's Challenge on Bosnia," *Wall Street Journal*, July 20, 1995; and Anthony Lewis, "Serbs Must Be Called to Account for Their Atrocities," *New York Times*, November 14, 1995.

20. Boyd, "Making Peace With the Guilty," p. 27.

21. William Safire, "Clinton Flinched from Bosnia Duty," *St. Louis Post-Dispatch*, July 16, 1995.

22. Jonathan Clarke and James Clad, *After the Crusade: American Foreign Policy for the Post-Superpower Age* (New York: Madison Books, 1995); also, see Aaron L. Friedburg, "The Future of American Power," *Political Quarterly*, 109 (September 1994), pp. 1–22.

23. In particular, see Paul Kennedy, *The Rise and Fall of the Great Powers* (New York: Random House, 1987), especially pp. 514–535.

24. Charles W. Maynes and Richard H. Ullman, "Ten Years of Foreign Policy," *Foreign Policy* (Fall 1980), p. 6.

25. U.S. Arms Control and Disarmament Agency, *World Military Expenditures and Arms Transfers, 1993–1994* (Washington, D.C.: USACDA, 1995), pp. 2–3; and U.S. Central Intelligence Agency, *Handbook of International Economic Statistics, 1992* (Washington, D.C.: CIA, 1992), p. 14.

26. "The U.S.—Decline or Renewal?," *Foreign Affairs*, 67 (Winter 1988/89), pp. 76–96; Henry R. Nau, *The Myth of America's Decline* (New York: Oxford University Press, 1990); and Joseph S. Nye, *Bound to Lead: The Changing Nature of American Power* (New York: Basic Books, 1990).

27. Earl Fry, *America the Vincible* (Englewood Cliffs, N.J.: Prentice-Hall, 1994). Insofar as U.S. indebtedness to foreigners is a function of increased foreign investment in the United States, and hence reflects the basic soundness and attractiveness of the American economy, this could be taken as a source of strength rather than of weakness.

28. To be a member of the "nuclear club," a state must conduct a test explosion of a nuclear bomb. For a list of those states that are thought to presently have such a capability or to be on the brink of acquiring a capability, see Leonard S. Spector, *Nuclear Proliferation Today* (New York: Random House, 1984); Spector, "Proliferation: The Silent Spread," *Foreign Policy* (Spring 1985), pp. 53–78; Gary T. Gardner, *Nuclear Nonproliferation: A Primer* (Boulder, Colo.: Lynne Rienner, 1994), ch. 9; and *Newsweek*, July 24, 1995, pp. 36–37.

29. Statement by Madeleine Albright, reported in *St. Louis Post-Dispatch*, August 4, 1995, p. 8.

30. Kenneth N. Waltz, "The Emerging Structure of International Politics," *International Security*, 18 (Fall 1993), p. 54; also see Colin Gray, *War, Peace, and Victory: Strategy and Statecraft for the Next Century* (New York: Simon and Schuster, 1990).

31. One of the best statements on the changed role of military power in the nuclear age is found in Klaus Knorr's *On the Uses of Military Power in the Nuclear Age* (Princeton, N.J.: Princeton University Press, 1966). Richard Rosecrance, in *The Rise of the Trading State: Commerce and Conquest in the Modern World* (New York: Basic Books, 1986), presents the provocative thesis that trade has replaced military strength and territorial expansion as the route to world power.

32. Kissinger, "We Live in An Age of Transition," p. 102. Theodore Moran, in "An Economic Agenda for Neorealists," *International Security*, 18 (Fall 1993), p. 211, states that economic power is "probably the most important source of power, and in a world in which military conflict between major states is unlikely, economic power will be increasingly important in determining the primacy or subordination of states."

33. See Charles Krauthammer, "The Unipolar Moment," *Foreign Affairs*, 70, no. 1 (1991), pp. 23–33; remarks of U.S. Secretary of Defense Richard Cheney, entitled "The United States as a Superpower," made before the National Newspaper Association, Washington, D.C., March 16, 1990, published in *Defense Issues*, 5 (May 7, 1990), pp. 5–8; and Robert W. Tucker and David C. Hendrickson, *The Imperial Temptation: The New World Order and America's Purpose* (New York: Council on Foreign Relations, 1993). Susan Strange, writing in 1995, noted that "five years of post–Cold War 'order' have only confirmed what I have always believed: there is only one superpower, the U.S." "ISA As A Microcosm," *International Studies Quarterly*, 39 (September 1995), p. 293. Earl Ravenal, in a lecture at the University of Missouri-St. Louis on November 17, 1995, stated that "the U.S. is the only country on earth whose foreign policy choices are still determinative of the shape of the in-

ternational system," although Ravenal also argued that America's triple deficits made it unlikely the U.S. could sustain a superpower role in the future. The "sheriff of the posse" analogy is taken from Joseph Nye, "Conflicts After the Cold War," *Washington Quarterly* (Winter 1996), p. 2; he acknowledges that the United States in many respects remains a superpower in a privileged position in the post–Cold War era, but feels Washington will need to act through building coalitions rather than alone if it is to exercise power successfully.

34. Henry Kissinger, *American Foreign Policy*, 3rd ed. (New York: W. W. Norton, 1977), p. 416, alluded to the emergence of multiple power centers before the "decline of hegemony" literature started appearing in the 1980s; Kissinger most recently has added India as a sixth power center, suggesting "we are now living in a world composed of six or seven major global players." Kissinger, "We Are Living in An Era of Transition," p. 102. In Kennedy, *The Rise and Fall*, ch. 8, the author speculates about the United States, the former Soviet Union, the European Union, China, and Japan assuming leadership roles in the twenty-first century. On the unlikelihood of a unipolar system, especially one led by the United States, see Christopher Layne, "The Unipolar Illusion: Why New Great Powers Will Rise," *International Security*, 17 (Spring 1993), pp. 5–51. In response to Layne's suggestion that Japan might overtake the United States in the twenty-first century, see Michael May, "Japan As A Superpower?," *International Security*, 18 (Winter 1993–1994), pp. 182–187.

35. For example, see Brown, *New Forces, Old Forces*, pp. 152–153; Donald J. Puchala and Roger A. Coate, *The Challenge of Relevance: The United Nations in a Changing World Environment* (Hanover, N.H.: Academic Council on the UN System, 1989), pp. 31–32; and Richard A. Higgott and Andrew F. Cooper, "Middle Power Leadership and Coalition-Building," *International Organization*, 44 (Autumn 1990), pp. 589–632. On the search for #1 status, see the articles by Robert Jervis, "International Primacy: Is the Game Worth the Candle?," and Samuel Huntington, "Why International Primacy Matters," in *International Security*, 17 (Spring 1993).

36. J. David Singer, "Reconstructing the Correlates of War Data Set on Material Capabilities of States, 1816–1985," paper presented to the Annual Meeting of the International Studies Association, Washington, D.C., April 1987; see also Richard L. Merritt and Dina A. Zinnes, "From National Capabilities to National Power: Indicators and Indices," paper presented to the Annual Meeting of the International Studies Association, Washington, D.C., April 1987; and Steven L. Spiegel, *Dominance and Diversity* (Boston: Little, Brown, 1972), pp. 93–96.

37. At least one analyst suggests that "will" can be measured with some degree of precision. See Ray Cline, *World Power Assessment: A Calculus of Strategic Drift* (Washington, D.C.: Georgetown University Center for Strategic and International Studies, 1975).

38. "I still believe he [President Lyndon Johnson] found it viscerally inconceivable that what Walt Rostow [Johnson's chief national security adviser] kept telling him was 'the greatest power in the world' could not dispose of a collection of night-riders in black pajamas." Quoted from Arthur Schlesinger, Jr., "The Quagmire Papers," *New York Review of Books*, December 16, 1971, p. 41.

39. On the anti-statist tradition of the United States and its "weak state" characteristics, see Andrew Shonfield, *Modern Capitalism* (New York: Oxford University Press, 1965); Stephen Krasner, *Defending the National Interest: Raw Materials, Investments, and U.S. Foreign Policy* (Princeton, N.J.: Princeton University Press, 1978); and Strange, "ISA As A Microcosm," p. 293.

40. See Nye, *Bound to Lead*. The quotation is from G. John Ikenberry and Charles A. Kupchan, "Socialization and Hegemonic Power," *International Organization*, 44 (Summer 1990), p. 284.

41. In other words, power is not completely "fungible" in terms of being equally usable and effective for a variety of purposes. Although power in international relations has always been "issue-specific" in a sense, it is especially the case today with so many variables being relevant to the power equation. The notion that power is issue-specific and, hence, that identifying a single power hierarchy in a political system is somewhat simplistic has been discussed by several scholars in the context of both domestic politics and international

politics. See Robert Dahl, *Who Governs: Democracy and Power in an American City* (New Haven, Conn.: Yale University Press, 1961), in which the notion of "polyarchy" is developed; William D. Coplin and Michael K. O'Leary, *Everyman's Prince* (North Scituate, Mass.: Duxbury Press, 1972); and Robert O. Keohane and Joseph S. Nye, *Power and Interdependence* (Boston: Little, Brown, 1977). The concept of "issue-area" was first developed in the international relations field by James Rosenau. See his article "Pre-Theories and Theories of Foreign Policy," in R. Barry Farrell, ed., *Approaches to Comparative and International Politics* (Evanston, Ill.: Northwestern University Press, 1966), pp. 27–92.

42. Marian Miller, in *The Third World in Global Environmental Politics* (Boulder, Colo.: Lynne Rienner, 1995), p. 24, notes that "despite decades of 'development,' the gap between the industrialized countries and the Third World is growing rather than decreasing. . . . In 1960 the average income for a Third World country was 17 percent of the industrialized world average; 30 years later it had declined to 15 percent. Only 20 of the 86 [developing states surveyed in a UN study] showed a relative increase in income, whereas some experienced a precipitous decline."

43. Paul Kennedy, *Preparing for the Twenty-First Century* (New York: Random House, 1993); and Claire Sjolander, "Multilateralism, Regionalism, and Unilateralism: International Trade and the Marginalization of the South," in *The State of the United Nations, 1993: North-South Perspectives* (Providence: Academic Council on the UN System, 1993), pp. 83–101.

44. The United Nations Development Program's annual *Human Development Report* examines rich-poor gaps both between and within states. For example, in the mid-1990s, it identified Egypt, South Africa, Nigeria and Brazil as countries having among the widest income gaps between different sections of their populations. See Paul Lewis, "UN List Four Lands At Risk Over Income Gaps," *New York Times*, June 2, 1994, p. A7. We will discuss the rich-poor gap between and within societies at greater length in Chapter 14 when we focus on economic development.

45. As can be seen in *World Development Report 1995* (New York: Oxford University Press, 1995), the World Bank classifies the countries of the world as "low-income economies," "lower middle-income economies," "upper middle-income economies," and "high-income economies." Singapore is listed as a high-income economy based on its per capita income, but is nonetheless labeled "developing."

46. Richard Barnet and John Cavanaugh, *Global Dreams* (New York: Simon and Schuster, 1994), pp. 284–285. J. Ravenhill, in "The North-South Balance of Power," *International Affairs*, 66, no. 4 (1990), pp. 745–746, distinguishes between five categories of "developing" states seeking to join the ranks of the First World: (1) industrializing economies with strong states and relatively low levels of indebtedness (e.g., Singapore); (2) industrializing economies with internal political or debt problems (e.g., Poland and Argentina); (3) high-income oil-exporting countries (OPEC members); (4) next NICs (e.g., Malaysia and Thailand); and (5) countries whose economies are based on primary commodities (e.g., in sub-Saharan Africa).

47. *World Bank Atlas 1995* (Washington, D.C.: World Bank, 1995), pp. 18–19.

48. Ibid., p. 20. Sub-Saharan Africa has been called "the third world's third world." D. E. Duncan, "Africa: The Long Good-bye," *The Atlantic Monthly*, 266 (July 1990) p. 20.

49. Miller, *Third World in Global Environmental Politics*, p. 25.

50. The Overseas Development Council has pioneered this concept. See Morris D. Morris, *Measuring the Condition of the World's Poor: The Physical Quality of Life Index* (Washington, D.C.: Overseas Development Council, 1979).

51. *See United Nations Development Report, 1994* (New York: Oxford University Press, 1994), pp. 90–91, and Table 1. Also, see Howard Handelman, *The Challenge of Third World Development* (Englewood Cliffs, N.J.: Prentice-Hall, 1996), pp. 3–7.

52. Mearsheimer, "Why We Will Soon Miss the Cold War," p. 35.

53. Abba Eban, "The UN Idea Revisited," *Foreign Affairs*, 74 (September/October 1995), p. 50.

54. Cited in Dragnich, "The West's Mismanagement of the Yugoslav Crisis," p. 65.

55. See James G. Blight and Aaron Blekin, "USSR's Third World Orphans: Deterring Desperate Dependents," *Third World Quarterly*, 13, no. 4 (1992), pp. 715–726; and Mark Webber, "The Third World and the Dissolution of the USSR," *Third World Quarterly*, 13, no. 4 (1992), pp. 691–713.

56. We alluded to the "end of history" phrase at the end of Chapter 2. A controversial essay on this theme was written by Francis Fukuyama of the U.S. State Department. See *New York Times*, August 27, 1989, IV, p. 5. The full article entitled "The End of History?" appears in *The National Interest* (Summer 1989), pp. 3–16.

57. Nicholas Kristof, "China Sees 'Market-Leninism' As Way to Future," *New York Times*, September 6, 1993. Some wags have said that Marxism in China today looks more like Groucho than Karl.

58. See Mark T. Berger, "The End of the 'Third World'?," *Third World Quarterly*, 15 (June 1994), pp. 257–275; Vicky Randall, "Third World: Rejected or Rediscovered?" *Third World Quarterly*, 13, no. 4 (1992), p. 730; R. Galli, ed., *Rethinking the Third World* (New York: Crane, Russak, 1992); and the special issue of *Third World Quarterly* entitled "The South in the New World (Dis) Order," 15 (March 1994), especially Timothy M. Shaw's article on "Beyond Any New World Order: The South in the Twenty-first Century," pp. 139–146.

59. John Stoessinger, *The Might Of Nations*, 9th ed. (New York: McGraw-Hill, 1990), p. 5.

60. See Sjolander, "Multilateralism, Regionalism, and Unilateralism," pp. 91–93; Louis Emmerij, "Globalization, Regionalization, and World Trade," *Columbia Journal of World Business*, 27 (Summer 1992), p. 11; and "Everybody's Favorite Monsters," *The Economist*, March 27, 1993, pp. 12–13.

61. Samuel P. Huntington, "The Clash of Civilizations?," *Foreign Affairs*, 72 (Summer 1993), p. 48. Also see the special forum on the Huntington article in *Foreign Affairs*, 72 (September/October 1993) as well as Huntington's response in the November/December issue; and Eisuke Sakakibara, "The End of Progressivism," *Foreign Affairs*, 74 (September/October 1995), pp. 8–20. The Huntington article has been expanded into a book-length work, *The Clash of Civilizations and the Remaking of World Order* (New York: Simon and Schuster, 1996).

62. Myron Weiner, "Peoples and States In A New Ethnic Order?," *Third World Quarterly*, 13 (1992), pp. 317–333.

63. Earl C. Ravenal, "The Regionalization of Power: General Unalignment in the Future International System," paper delivered at Annual Meeting of International Studies Association, Washington, D.C., April 14, 1990.

64. See Michael T. Klare and Daniel C. Thomas, eds., *World Security: Challenges for A New Century* (New York: St. Martin's Press, 1994); Sean M. Lynn-Jones and Steven E. Miller, eds., *Global Dangers: Changing Dimensions of International Security* (Cambridge: MIT Press, 1995); and Buzan, *People, States, and Fear*, pp. 19–20.

65. Stanley Hoffmann, "Choices," *Foreign Policy* (Fall 1993), p. 5.

66. Henry A. Kissinger, "A New National Partnership," *U.S. Department of State Bulletin*, February 17, 1975, p. 199.

67. The quote is from Daniel Bell in the Fall 1990 issue of *Dissent*, cited in Samuel P. Huntington, "Why International Primacy Matters," p. 81. Huntington does not see economic conflict as benign.

68. See notes 4 and 5. These statements are from Singer and Wildavsky, *The Real World Order*, James Lee Ray, "The Abolition of Slavery and the End of International War," *International Organization*, 43 (Summer 1989), pp. 405–439. Also, see John Mueller, *Quiet Cataclysm: Reflections on the Recent Transformation of World Politics* (New York: Harper Collins, 1995).

69. Cited in Peter W. Rodman, "Points of Order," *National Review*, May 1, 1995, p. 37.

70. The phrase "teacup wars" is from Leslie Gelb, "Teacup Wars," *Foreign Affairs* (November 1995).

71. Rodman, "Points of Order," p. 37.

72. Clayton Jones, "Paradise Islands Or An Asian Powder Keg?," *Global Issues, 1994/95* (Sluice Dock, Conn.: Dushkin, 1994), pp. 109–110.

73. See Brown, *New Forces, Old Forces*, pp. 144–148, on how traditional "sphere of influence" politics still play a role in Russian, Chinese, and Japanese foreign policy. Similar remarks about the continued importance of military-strategic issues in international affairs were made by Earl Ravenal in a lecture at the University of Missouri-St. Louis on November 17, 1995. Also see Mearsheimer, "Why We Will Soon Miss The Cold War."

74. Commission on Global Governance, cited in Emma Rothschild, "What Is Security?," *Daedalus*, 124 (Summer 1995), pp. 55–56.

75. Alex Inkeles, "The Emerging Social Structure of the World," *World Politics*, 27 (July 1975), p. 479.

76. Michael Stewart, *The Age of Interdependence* (Cambridge: MIT Press, 1986), p. 26.

77. Zacher, "The Decaying Pillars," provides a wealth of data.

78. John Herz was among the first to call attention to this "permeability" in his *International Politics in the Atomic Age* (New York: Columbia University Press, 1959).

79. Inkeles, "Emerging Social Structure," p. 84; and William Cummings, "Global Trends in Overseas Study," in Crauford D. Goodwin, ed., *International Investment in Human Capital: Overseas Education for Development* (New York: Institute of International Education, 1993), p. 31.

80. Janice E. Thomson and Stephen D. Krasner, "Global Transactions and the Consolidation of Sovereignty," in Ernst-Otto Czempiel and James N. Rosenau, eds., *Global Changes and Theoretical Challenges* (Lexington, Mass.: Lexington Books, 1989), pp. 203–204.

81. Of the top ten trading partners of the United States, six are developing countries, all in southeast Asia except for Mexico. See Michael Kidron and Ronald Segal, *The State of the World Atlas*, 5th ed. (London: Penguin, 1995), pp. 35–36; *Direction of Trade Statistics Yearbook, 1995* (Washington, D.C.: International Monetary Fund, 1995), pp. 2 and 10; and John Sewell et al. *Growth, Exports, and Jobs in a Changing World Economy: Agenda 1988* (New Brunswick, N.J.: Transaction Books, 1988), pp. 214–224.

82. Kjell Skjelsbaek, "The Growth of International Nongovernmental Organization in the Twentieth Century," in Robert O. Keohane and Joseph S. Nye, eds., *Transnational Relations and World Politics* (Cambridge, Mass.: Harvard University Press, 1971), p. 82; Harold K. Jacobson, *Networks of Interdependence* (New York: Knopf, 1984), pp. 53–54.

83. Harold K. Jacobson et al., "National Entanglements in International Governmental Organizations," *American Political Science Review*, 80 (March 1986), p. 141.

84. Jeffrey Frieden, *Banking on the World: The Politics of American International Finance* (New York: Random House, 1987), p. 116.

85. An example of such havoc is discussed in an article on the "shadow bankers" in *Newsweek*, October 23, 1989, p. 47. Also, see *Newsweek*, March 20, 1995, pp. 23–24; and *Newsweek*, March 13, 1995, pp. 37–39.

86. See Keohane and Nye, *Transnational Relations*; Kenneth A. Dahlberg, et al., *Environment and the Global Arena* (Durham, N.C.: Duke University Press, 1985); Barry B. Hughes et al., *Energy in the Global Arena* (Durham, N.C.: Duke University Press, 1985); Jonathan Aronson, "Multiple Actors in the Transformation of the International Monetary System," paper presented at the Annual Meeting of the International Studies Association, Toronto, February 25, 1976; David P. Forsythe, "The Red Cross as Transnational Movement: Conserving and Changing the Nation-State System," *International Organization*, 30 (Autumn 1976), pp. 608–630; Kenneth P. Thomas, "Auto Bargaining in Canada," in Steve Chan, *Foreign Direct Investment in A Changing Global Political Economy* (London: Macmillan, 1995), pp. 7–24; and Vicki Golich, "The Metamorphosis of Global Corporations from Servants of the State to Servants of the Market: The Case of Commercial-Class Aircraft Manufacturing," paper presented at Annual Meeting of International Studies Association, Chicago, February 24, 1995. For a systematic empirical analysis that attempts to assess the relative significance of state and nonstate actors, see Richard W. Mansbach et al., *The Web of World Politics* (Englewood Cliffs, N.J.: Prentice-Hall, 1976).

87. Charles Kindleberger, *American Business Abroad* (New Haven, Conn.: Yale University Press, 1969), p. 207.

88. George W. Ball, "The Promise of the Multinational Corporation," *Fortune,* June 1, 1967, p. 80. George Ball was a U.S. Assistant Under Secretary of State during Lyndon Johnson's administration.

89. Zbigniew Brzezinski, *Between Two Ages: America's Role in the Technotronic Era* (New York: Viking, 1970), p. 275. Brzezinski had to change his orientation toward the world somewhat when he found himself in the position of chief U.S. national security adviser to President Carter in the late 1970s. On the staying power of nationalism, see William Pfaff, *The Wrath of Nations* (New York: Simon and Schuster 1994).

90. Lucian Pye, "Political Science and the Crisis of Authoritarianism," *American Political Science Review,* 84 (March 1990), p. 6.

91. One study finds that "data from 1986 on 166 countries show only a third to be ethnically homogeneous (where one group constituted at least 90 percent of the population)." Bruce Russett and Harvey Starr, *World Politics: The Menu for Choice,* 3rd ed. (San Francisco: W. H. Freeman, 1989), p. 54. Another study reports that "only one in ten of the world's countries are ethnically homogeneous; three-quarters of the countries have ethnic minorities that make up over 5 percent of the population; and in one-tenth of the countries at least 40 percent of the population is distinct from the dominant ethnic group." Brown, *New Forces, Old Forces,* p. 237, based on Gunnar P. Nielson, "States and 'Nation-Groups': A Global Taxonomy," in Edward A. Tiryakian and Ronald Rogowski, *New Nationalisms of the Developed West* (Boston: Allen and Unwin, 1985), pp. 27–56. Also see Ted Robert Gurr, *Minorities At Risk* (Washington, D.C.: U.S. Institute of Peace Press, 1993), pp. 3–10.

92. James N. Rosenau, "Governance in the Twenty-First Century," *Global Governance,* 1 (Winter 1995), p. 13.

93. A 1985 study found only 53 countries that could be called "free," compared with 59 that were "partly free" and 55 labeled "not free," and noted that "since the first survey [of freedom] published in . . . 1973, . . . worldwide the percentage of people living in freedom or the percentage of free nations has not changed noticeably." Raymond G. Gastil, *Freedom in the World: Political Rights and Civil Liberties* (Westport, Conn.: Greenwood Press, 1985), pp. 11 and 25. However, according to a more recent survey, the events of the late 1980s and early 1990s have set in motion a process whereby "free" nations are soon likely to outnumber "not free" nations. See *Comparative Survey of Freedom* (New York: Freedom House, 1990).

94. See Pye, "Political Science," for an excellent discussion of recent democratization trends. Pye, on p. 6, notes that "in some respects we live in a more nation-bound, less internationalized world than did the Europeans of the nineteenth century. It is, for example, astonishing that it was not considered odd for the tsarist government [in Russia] to raise the funds for fighting the Crimean War [against Britain] by floating bonds on the London market, the same market that the British government was using to cover its own expenses in the same war."

95. James N. Rosenau, "Patterned Chaos in Global Life: Structure and Process in Two Worlds of World Politics," mimeo, Institute for Transnational Studies, University of Southern California, April 1987, pp. 3 and 6; and *Turbulence in World Politics* (Princeton, N.J.: Princeton University Press, 1990); also see Seyom Brown's concept of "polyarchy" in Brown, *New Forces, Old Forces.*

PART II. NATIONAL ACTORS AND INTERNATIONAL INTERACTIONS

1. Hedley Bull, *The Anarchical Society: A Study of Order in World Politics* (New York: Columbia University Press, 1977), p. 8.

2. One attempt to develop a "standardized" list was undertaken by Bruce Russett, J. David Singer, and Melvin Small. See "National Political Units in the Twentieth Century: A Stan-

dardized List," *American Political Science Review*, 62 (September 1968), pp. 932–952. For a more current listing of "independent territorial units," see Harold K. Jacobson, *Networks of Interdependence*, 2nd ed. (New York: Knopf, 1984), Appendix C.

Chapter 4. Describing Foreign Policy Behavior: What Is It Nation-States Do?

1. Richard Sisson and Leo Rose, *War and Secession: Pakistan, India and the Creation of Bangladesh* (Berkeley: University of California Press, 1990); Wayne Wilcox, *The Emergence of Bangladesh: Problems and Opportunities for a Redefined American Policy in South Asia* (Washington, D.C.: American Enterprise Institute, 1973).

2. See S. M. Burke, *Pakistan's Foreign Policy: An Historical Analysis*, 2nd ed. (Karachi: Oxford University Press, 1990); Robert Wirsing, *Pakistan's Security Under Zia, 1977–88: The Policy Imperatives of a Peripheral Asian State* (New York: St. Martin's, 1991): Robert J. McMahon, *The Cold War on the Periphery: The United States, India, and Pakistan* (New York: Columbia University Press, 1994); and *South Asia and the United States After the Cold War* (New York: The Asia Society, 1994).

3. John Battersby, "Israel Reaps Benefits from Asian Trade as Arab Boycott Frays," *Christian Science Monitor*, March 30, 1995, p. 9.

4. ABC-TV interview by Peter Jennings, April 20, 1994.

5. Arnold Wolfers, *Discord and Collaboration* (Baltimore: Johns Hopkins University Press, 1962), pp. 81–102.

6. On alliance concepts and policies, see Edwin H. Fedder, "The Concept of Alliance," *International Studies Quarterly*, 12 (March 1978); George Liska, *Nations in Alliance* (Baltimore: Johns Hopkins University Press, 1962); Charles W. Kegley and Gregory A. Raymond, *When Trust Breaks Down: Alliance Norms and World Politics* (Columbia, S.C.: University of South Carolina Press, 1990); and Stephen M. Walt, *The Origins of Alliance* (Ithaca, N.Y.: Cornell University Press, 1987).

7. See Edwin H. Fedder, *NATO: The Dynamics of Alliance in the Postwar World* (New York: Dodd, Mead, 1973).

8. On neutrality concepts and practice, see Cecil V. Crabb, Jr., *The Elephants and the Grass: A Study of Nonalignment* (New York: Praeger, 1965); John F. L. Ross, *Neutrality and International Systems: Sweden, Switzerland and Collective Security* (New York: Praeger, 1989); and Efraim Karsh, *Neutrality and Small States* (London: Routledge, 1988).

9. The Swiss position on neutrality is a complicated one. Over the years, the Swiss have joined certain specialized UN agencies, such as the Universal Postal Union and World Health Organization, and even Western-oriented economic organizations such as the Organization for Economic Cooperation and Development. In a 1986 national referendum, 75 percent of Swiss voters opposed Switzerland joining the UN. On the viability of neutrality as a post–Cold War diplomatic strategy, see Josef Binter, "Neutrality in a Changing World: End or Renaissance of a Concept?," *Bulletin of Peace Proposals*, 23 (June 1992), pp. 213–218.

10. Israel and the United States, which are not formal treaty allies, frequently have sided with each other on a variety of issues; France, America's oldest ally (dating back to the Revolutionary War era), frequently has disputed American policy, and in the mid-1990s was charged by the United States with spying concerning industrial secrets. For contrasting views on the post–Cold War options of Third World states, see K. P. Misra, "Nonaligned Movement Back on the Rails: A Study of the Jakarta Summit," *International Studies*, 30 (January-March 1993), pp. 1–14; and James G. Blight and Thomas G. Weiss, "Must the Grass Still Suffer? Some Thoughts on Third World Conflict after the Cold War," *Third World Quarterly*, 13, no. 2 (1992), pp. 229–253.

11. The Burmese case is a curious one because it was during the height of their isolation that a Burmese citizen, U Thant, happened to become head of the United Nations, serving as Secretary-General of the world organization between 1962 and 1972.

12. Michael Hirsh, with Ron Moreau, "Making it in Mandalay," *Newsweek*, June 19, 1995, p. 46.

13. In 1995, Washington and Tokyo went to the brink of a trade war, threatening sanctions against each other's products, in discussing American demands for specific increases in Japanese auto-related imports from the United States. The concessions that Japan offered caused Western European states to insist that they too be given such assurances for their own auto exports to Japan. Principles were built into the U.S.-Japanese agreement, which required that the provisions apply to other states.

14. See K. J. Holsti, "National Role Conceptions in the Study of Foreign Policy," *International Studies Quarterly*, 14 (September 1970), pp. 233–309; and Naomi B. Wish, "Foreign Policy Makers: Their National Role Conceptions," *International Studies Quarterly*, 24 (December 1980), pp. 532–554. See also the distinctions between active versus passive, planned versus opportunistic, and uncompromising versus bargaining leadership styles made by Harold and Margaret Sprout in their classic *Toward a Politics of the Planet Earth* (New York: Van Nostrand Reinhold, 1971), p. 161.

15. Frederic S. Pearson, Robert A. Baumann, and Jeffrey J. Pickering, "Military Intervention and Realpolitik," in Frank W. Wayman and Paul F. Diehl, eds., *Reconstructing Realpolitik* (Ann Arbor: University of Michigan Press, 1994), pp. 205–225. Also, see Isabell Duyvesteyn, "Wars and Military Interventions Since 1945: Some Observations on Patterns, Regions, Actors, and Duration," (Hamburg, Germany: University of Hamburg, Unit for Study of Wars, Armaments, and Development, Working Paper 88, 1995).

16. Martha Finnemore, "Changing Patterns of Military Intervention," paper presented to the Annual Meeting of the International Studies Association, Chicago, February 23, 1995, pp. 3 and 26.

17. One should not conclude, however, that strategic motives are completely divorced from humanitarian or peacekeeping interventions. Syria, for example, was authorized by the League of Arab States in the late 1970s to intervene to settle the Lebanese civil war; Syrian troops remained in Lebanon for the next twenty years, effectively taking control of much of the country and exercising control over the Lebanese government.

18. For an assessment of the impacts of military intervention, humanitarian intervention in particular, see Patrick Regan, "Third Party Intervention in Intrastate Conflicts: Identifying Strategies for Stopping the Violence," paper presented to the Annual Meeting of the International Studies Association, Chicago, February 23, 1995; and, concentrating on the case of the Ethiopian civil and international wars of the 1970s and 1980s, William DeMars, "Does International Humanitarian Action Prolong or Resolve Civil Wars?," paper presented to the Annual Meeting of the International Studies Association, Chicago, February 23, 1995; and Finnemore, *op. cit.*, p. 18.

19. We will discuss this matter in our focus on international law and international organization in Chapters 9 and 10.

20. The term "new nation" refers to the fact that the United States was the first major colony to break away from colonial rule and achieve sovereign independence. See Seymour Martin Lipset, *The First New Nation* (New York: W. W. Norton, 1979). For a discussion of American foreign policy in the early years of the nation, see Alexander De Conde, *A History of American Foreign Policy*, vol. 1, 3rd ed. (New York: Scribner's, 1978).

21. Some historians see American expansion as planned and imperialistic, whereas others see it as somewhat reluctant, defensive, or idealistic. Reality may have been a mixture of both. See William A. Williams, *The Contours of American History* (Chicago: Quadrangle, 1966) and *The Tragedy of American Diplomacy* (New York: Dell, 1962); Richard Van Alstyne, *The Rising American Empire* (Oxford: Quadrangle, 1960); Sidney Lens, *The Forging of the American Empire: A History of American Imperialism from the Revolution to Vietnam* (New York: Thomas Y. Crowell, 1974); Amy Kaplan and Donald E. Pease, eds., *Cultures of United States Imperialism* (Durham, N.C.: Duke University Press, 1993); and Robert Leckie, *From Sea to Shining Sea: From the War of 1812 to the Mexican War, the Saga of America's Expansion* (New York: Harper-Collins, 1993).

22. The moralistic-legalistic thread running through much of U.S. foreign policy history is ably discussed by George F. Kennan in *American Diplomacy 1900–1950* (Chicago: University of Chicago Press, 1951). See also Stanley Hoffmann, *Gulliver's Troubles, or The Setting of American Foreign Policy* (New York: McGraw-Hill, 1969), ch. 5; and G. John Ikenberry, ed., *American Foreign Policy: Theoretical Essays* (Glenview, Ill.: Scott, Foresman, 1989), Parts 4 and 8.

23. The mix of principles and interests was especially evident in U.S. participation in World War I. Washington insisted at the outset that its neutral status entitled it to freedom of the seas. Neutrality was difficult, however, because Germany and England sought to blockade each other's ports. Pro-British sentiment in the United States increased with German attacks on American shipping, and when the United States finally entered the war, President Woodrow Wilson justified the cause moralistically with statements about a war "to end war" and to "make the world safe for democracy." Pragmatically, he was concerned as well about Europe coming under the domination of a single empire centered in Berlin. Although none of the conservative blood-related European monarchies resembled what we now think of as totalitarian despotisms, raising issues of democracy and national self-determination could help sell the war at home and distinguish the American cause from the sordid balance of power dealings that characterized Europe.

24. During the 1990s, similar conceptions were reflected at least rhetorically in President George Bush's call for another new world order stemming from the coalition of states assembled to defeat Saddam Hussein's Iraq in the Gulf War, as well as in Bill Clinton's stress on promoting democracy and free trade abroad through the North American Free Trade Agreement (NAFTA) and the World Trade Organization. See Philip Abbott, *The Exemplary Presidency: Franklin Delano Roosevelt and the American Political Tradition* (Amherst: University of Massachusetts Press, 1990), chs. 1–3.

25. The United States was faced with increasing Japanese warfare in China throughout the thirties. President Roosevelt had to decide whether to recognize or resist Japanese gains; in holding out for China's "territorial integrity," he finally employed trade sanctions against Tokyo, then as now one of America's leading trade partners. The cutoff of oil supplies to resource-starved Japan led eventually to the desperation attack to oust U.S. forces from the western Pacific. On Pearl Harbor, see Herbert Feis, *The Road to Pearl Harbor* (Princeton, N.J.: Princeton University Press, 1950); and William Neumann, *America Encounters Japan* (New York, Harper, 1965), chs. 10–13.

26. Recent literature has debated the degree of President Roosevelt's efforts to involve America in the war. See Warren F. Kimball, *The Juggler: Franklin Roosevelt as Wartime Statesman* (Princeton, N.J.: Princeton University Press, 1991); and Thomas Parrish, *Roosevelt and Marshall: Partners in Politics and War* (New York: William Morrow, 1989), pp. 188–191.

27. Stephen Ambrose has noted that in 1939, the United States had an army of 185,000, no overseas bases, and a defense budget of less than $500 million. With the impetus of World War II and the Cold War, the army was to grow to millions—stationed in numerous foreign as well as domestic bases—and the budget to hundreds of billions. See Ambrose, *America's Rise to Globalism: American Foreign Policy Since 1938,* 7th rev. ed. (New York: Penguin, 1993), p. xi. For an overview of American foreign policy in the postwar period, through several administrations, see James E. Dougherty and Robert L. Pfaltzgraff, Jr., *American Foreign Policy: FDR to Reagan* (New York: Harper and Row, 1986).

28. Aside from security needs, there were other reasons the Soviets thought that U.S. and British concessions were called for. The Soviet Union had allowed the Western allies to enter Berlin and share the occupation of Germany even though allied troops had not arrived in the German capital during the war. The Stalin government in Moscow had already accumulated grievances against the West, including the failure to open a full second fighting front in Europe until 1944 (the Normandy invasion). From Stalin's viewpoint, the Soviet Union had been bled of nearly twenty million lives before Britain and American forces ventured onto the European continent. Of course, from the Western viewpoint, it was neces-

sary to be sure Moscow would stay in the war before risking troops in an offensive against Germany. Stalin also was irritated by American-British cooperation in atomic bomb research and President Truman's use of the bomb to end the Pacific war before Russia could become involved. For one version of atomic diplomacy, see Gar Alperovitz, *Atomic Diplomacy: Hiroshima and Potsdam* (New York: Vintage, 1967).

29. Washington's failure to understand local or regional issues was typified by American policy regarding the Greek Civil War in 1947. The Truman administration moved to oppose the Communist-supported side in that war, yet also aided Stalin's main Communist rival, Marshal Tito of Yugoslavia, on the mistaken assumption that Stalin, not Tito, was behind the leftist insurgency in Greece. Thus, U.S. leaders unwittingly aided both sides in the Greek war.

30. In October 1944, near the end of World War II, Churchill himself had sat across a conference table from Stalin passing slips of paper on which were written the names of certain Southern and Eastern European countries together with the proposed percentage of British or Soviet influence over those countries. After checking off approval on each slip, Churchill asked if the slips should not be burned. Stalin replied, "No, you can keep them." So descended the "Iron Curtain" in the Balkan countries. See Winston Churchill, *Triumph and Tragedy* (Boston: Houghton Mifflin, 1953), pp. 226 ff. On the origins of the Cold War, see Walter LaFeber, *America, Russia, and the Cold War, 1945–1967,* 2nd ed. (New York: John Wiley, 1972); Daniel Yergin, *Shattered Peace: Origins of the Cold War and the National Security State* (Boston: Houghton Mifflin, 1978); Adam Ulam, *The Rivals: America and Russia Since World War II* (New York: Penguin, 1976); and John Lewis Gaddis, *The United States and the Origins of the Cold War, 1941–1947* (New York: Columbia University Press, 1972).

31. Kennan argued that if the Soviets were prevented from expanding in Europe or the Mediterranean areas, their top-heavy political system would collapse, a prediction somewhat similar to Lenin's observations about Western imperialist states. In later years, Mr. X argued that he never meant containment to be a worldwide concept, as it came to be viewed by subsequent U.S. administrations, or, especially, to involve the U.S. in Asian land wars. But the "logic" of *extended* containment was difficult to avoid once the containment concept itself was accepted.

32. Although NATO committed all members to consider an attack on one equivalent to an attack on all, members promised only to consult together and take such action as was "constitutionally appropriate" in response. Originally, the European states desired an alliance to guard against a resurgent Germany as much as against the Soviet Union. By 1960, the United States had a network of alliances in addition to NATO, including SEATO (Southeast Asia Treaty Organization, now lapsed), ANZUS (a treaty with Australia and New Zealand), and the OAS (Organization of American States), with the NATO commitment remaining the strongest. The United States had moved firmly from neutrality to alliance in world affairs. See Fedder, *NATO, op. cit.*

33. As it turned out, both the U.S. and Soviet interventionist efforts produced mixed results in terms of successes. For example, a U.S.-backed "contra" attack on Fidel Castro's Cuba in 1961, the famous Bay of Pigs invasion (by anti-Castro Cuban exiles trained by the United States), failed, with lasting embarrassment for the Kennedy administration. Although technically a success, U.S. support for the anti-Soviet "mujihadeen" rebel fighters in Afghanistan during the 1980s tended to reinforce the strength of Islamic militants throughout the region, groups not always favorable to continued American influence.

34. Taken from the documentary film, *I.F. Stone's Weekly,* directed by Jerry Bruch. Further studies of the Vietnam involvement include Paul Kattenburg, *The Vietnam Trauma in American Foreign Policy, 1945–75* (New Brunswick, N.J.: Transaction Books, 1980); George McT. Kahin, *Intervention: How America Became Involved in Vietnam* (New York: Knopf, 1986); Anthony Short, *The Origins of the Vietnam War* (London: Longman, 1989); and Stanley Karnow, *Vietnam: A History* (New York: Viking, 1983).

35. The SALT and other arms control agreements will be discussed in Chapter 11. On Kissinger's designs, see Henry A. Kissinger, *American Foreign Policy,* 2nd and 3rd eds.

(New York: W. W. Norton, 1974 and 1977); and *The White House Years* (Boston: Little, Brown, 1979).

36. This visit, between one of America's chief anti-communists and one of the world's most noted revolutionaries, was so striking and evocative that a grand opera was written on the subject during the 1980s.

37. His pragmatism notwithstanding, Kissinger also could be as anti-communist as John Foster Dulles. He reportedly asked a meeting of the U.S. National Security Council dealing with nationalization of American corporate property by the Allende government in Chile, "Why should we stand by and watch a country go Communist merely because of the irresponsibility of its own people?" Cited in James A. Nathan and James K. Oliver, *United States Foreign Policy and World Order* (Boston: Little, Brown, 1976), p. 496.

38. After his presidency, Mr. Carter went on to play an independent negotiator's role in world politics, engaging in mediation and anti-poverty programs through his Carter Center in Atlanta. He played an effective, though sometimes controversial role in defusing crises in Haiti, the Balkans, and Africa during the Clinton administration.

39. Studies have shown mixed findings regarding the actual relationship of U.S. aid policies and recipients' human rights records across various U.S. administrations. Some have determined that human rights practices influence aid decisions at early stages of policymaking (in Congress and the State Department), but not necessarily when aid money is actually appropriated. Furthermore, the rights record may affect military aid decisions more than economic aid decisions, as they seemed to do for both the Carter and Reagan administrations. Others have found no clear overall pattern. See Simon Payaslian, *Human Rights and United States Distribution of Foreign Economic and Military Assistance*, Ph.D. dissertation (Ann Arbor: University of Michigan microfilm, 1992).

40. Despite expectations of massive "peace dividends" with the end of the Cold War in 1989, U.S. defense spending and military preparedness in the 1990s, though reduced, remained well above 1939 levels. This validates Bruce Russett's contention that security policy has a "ratcheting effect"; after each major war, military effort stays above the level before the war. See Bruce M. Russett, *What Price Vigilance? The Burdens of National Defense* (New Haven, Conn.: Yale University Press, 1970), chs. 5–6.

41. For example, consensus was reached that aid should be offered the faltering Russian economy, at least to avert a renewed hostile dictatorship in Moscow and to prevent Russian officials and scientists from selling their services and weapons to other states. In 1993, President Clinton campaigned successfully with U.S. allies for a $28 billion joint aid package. However, in contrast to the Marshall Plan in the 1940s, heavy reservations were placed on the timing, amount, and conditions required for such assistance. Among the requirements were progress in privatizing the Russian economy and controlling inflation. Pressures ultimately were applied also to oppose certain exports of Russian technology such as nuclear plants for Iran. See "Western Creditors to Reschedule Russia's Debt," *New York Times*, June 5, 1994, p. 4. The resultant policy drew criticism from some as overcommitted to the potentially unstable and repressive Russian government, and from others as inadequate and inappropriate to the evolving needs of the former Soviet Union. Similarly, despite the successful use of force against Iraq in 1990, American security doctrines continued to reflect the nagging legacy and questions of Vietnam and the Cold War. Although President Bush had spoken in Wilsonian terms of a "new world order," realities were far from fully amenable to multilateral agreements and governing coalitions of states. In Washington, although it was still assumed that the American public would not stand for long, stalemated wars of attrition such as Vietnam or Korea, or even for long peacekeeping involvements, defense plans continued to stress being able to fight at least two "major regional conflicts" at the same time should the need arise. See the "Bottom Up Review" conducted by the Secretary of Defense in 1993 and enshrined in legislation passed by the U.S. Senate in 1995.

42. *Newsweek*, February 1, 1993, p. 45. Also, see Kissinger's "We Live In An Age of Transition," *Daedalus*, 124 (Summer 1995), p. 101.

43. On the similarities between the Soviet state and old Muskovy, see Roman Sporluk, "Soviet Domestic Foreign Policy: Universal Ideology and National Tradition," *Nationalities Papers*, 22 (Spring 1994), pp. 195–208.

44. One indication of pragmatism and power balancing was Soviet willingness to allow German troops to train in Russia while the Versailles treaty still outlawed German rearmament. For an exhaustive discussion of early Soviet foreign policy, see Adam Ulam, *Expansion and Coexistence: A History of Soviet Foreign Policy 1917–1973*, 2nd ed. (New York: Praeger, 1974). On the later years, see Joseph L. Nogee and Robert H. Donaldson, *Soviet Foreign Policy Since World War II*, 3rd ed. (Oxford: Pergamon Press, 1988); and Alvin Z. Rubinstein, *Soviet Foreign Policy Since World War II*, 3rd ed. (Glenview, Ill.: Scott, Foresman, 1989).

45. Ulam, *Expansion and Coexistence*, pp. 250–279.

46. In comparison, the United States suffered 405,000 casualties during World War II. See Martha Boyd Hoyle, *A World in Flames* (New York: Atheneum, 1970).

47. A unique commentary on Khruschev's political initiatives is provided by his son Sergei in *Khrushchev on Khrushchev, An Inside Account of the Man and His Era* (Boston: Little, Brown, 1990).

48. In an effort to preclude Germany's NATO membership, Moscow had offered in 1952 to allow a reunified but neutral Germany. See Richard J. Barnet, *The Giants* (New York: Simon and Schuster, 1977), p. 17.

49. Recent works on the Cuban missile crisis, based on more complete documentation and "reunions" of American and Soviet decision makers, have produced more balanced and sober assessments. See, for example, Dan Caldwell, *The Cuban Missile Crisis Affair and the American Style of Crisis Management* (Santa Monica: Rand, 1989); James A. Nathan, ed., *The Cuban Missile Crisis Revisited* (New York: St. Martins, 1992); Dino A. Brugioni, *Eyeball to Eyeball: The Inside Story of the Cuban Missile Crisis* (New York: Random House, 1991); Robert Smith Thompson, *The Missiles of October: The De-classified Story of John F. Kennedy and the Cuban Missile Crisis* (New York: Simon and Schuster, 1992); James G. Blight, *On the Brink: Americans and Soviets Reexamine the Cuban Missile Crisis* (New York: Hill and Wang, 1989); Raymond L. Garthoff, *Reflections on the Cuban Missile Crisis*, rev. ed. (Washington, D.C.: Brookings Institution, 1989); and Richard Ned Lebow, *We All Lost the Cold War* (Princeton, N.J.: Princeton University Press, 1994).

50. Much of this consultation took place in the Conference on Security and Cooperation in Europe (CSCE), which was renamed the Organization for Security and Cooperation in Europe (OSCE) in 1994. CSCE had been formed during the détente period of the Cold War as a vehicle for stabilizing East-West relations, but took on unexpected added meaning by legitimizing human rights concerns in the East and as a joint Euro-security organization once the USSR collapsed.

51. Wendy Sloane, "Yeltsin Finds Himself on Edge of World Sandbox," *Christian Science Monitor*, June 16, 1995, p. 6.

52. The brutal response also could spur the opposite effect, i.e., to strengthen regional autonomy movements. Exchange of correspondence with Moscow anthropologist Algis Prazauskas, March 1995. See also Marjorie Mandelstam Balzer and Harley D. Balzer, "Yeltsin's Chechen Move—A Massive Backfire," *Christian Science Monitor*, January 12, 1995, p. 19.

53. On the developing Russian foreign policy, see Milton Kooner, "Russia in Search of a Foreign Policy," *Comparative Strategy*, 12 (July-September 1993), pp. 307–320; Robert V. Barylski, "The Russian Federation and Eurasia's Islamic 'Crescent,' " *Europe-Asia Studies*, 46, no. 3 (1994), pp. 389–416; Rodric Braithwaite, "Russian Realities and Western Policy," *Survival*, 36 (Autumn 1994), pp. 11–27; and Neal Malcolm, "The New Russian Foreign Policy," *The World Today*, 50 (February 1994), pp. 28–32.

54. On Chinese Development strategies, see Harry Harding, *China's Second Revolution: Reform After Mao* (Washington, D.C.: Brookings Institution, 1987). The basic tendency of

Asian "miracle states" such as South Korea, Taiwan, and Singapore, has been to organize specifically for export, to hold down domestic consumption through relatively high prices, encourage saving and investment, and stimulate the production of high-quality goods at low prices for export. Democratic reforms and much improved living standards have taken place in these states, but with a certain tolerance for authoritarian security practices to underwrite "economic stability."

55. A. Doak Barnett, *China and the Major Powers in East Asia* (Washington, D.C.: Brookings Institution, 1977).

56. Samuel Kim, *China, the United Nations, and World Order* (Princeton, N.J.: Princeton University Press, 1979).

57. In a sense, Chiang and Mao competed over who would inherit the "mandate of heaven." For insight into the imperial past, as well as the turbulent reform years, see the popular film "The Last Emperor."

58. Documents released after the fall of the USSR lent greater insight into the distrustful early relations between the People's Republic and Stalin's government, especially relating to issues such as the Korean War.

59. Kim, *China, the United Nations, and World Order*, p. 24.

60. Samuel Kim, "Thinking Globally in Post-Mao China," *Journal of Peace Research*, 27 (May 1990), p. 196. As Chinese forces mobilized in response to Moscow, two clashes occurred along the Ussuri River in 1969, the scene of Sino-Russian skirmishes as far back as the turn of the century.

61. China came out of the UN "closet" in July of 1978, casting a vote in the UN Security Council in favor of a Western-sponsored proposal for a peacekeeping force in Namibia (South-West Africa); Beijing had been recorded as "not participating" ever since assuming China's UN membership seat in place of Taiwan in 1971.

62. Michael Brzoska and Frederic S. Pearson, "The Prospect for Post–Cold War Arms Markets," *Annals of the Academy of Political and Social Sciences*, (July 1994), pp. 59–72.

63. See "China: New Reforms, Old Politics," *Great Decisions* (Washington, D.C.: Foreign Policy Association, 1993), pp. 37–44; Qingshan Tan, "Chinese Foreign Policy After Tianamen and Beyond," *Asian Profile*, 21 (April 1993), pp. 87–99; Michael B. Yahuda, "Chinese Foreign Policy and the Collapse of Communism," *SAIS Review* 12 (Winter-Spring 1992), pp. 125–137; Quansheng Zhao, "Patterns and Choices of Chinese Foreign Policy," *Asian Affairs*, 20 (Spring 1993), pp. 3–15; Pi Ying-hsien, "Peking's Foreign Relations in the New International Situation," *Issues and Studies*, 28 (May 1992), pp. 13–28.

64. The political intrigues of the warlords, as well as their views of foreigners as barbarians, are vividly and entertainingly portrayed in the novel *Shogun*, by Richard Clavell.

65. Linda S. Wojtan, *Introduction to Japan* (Washington, D.C.: Youth for Understanding, 1992), pp. 2–4.

66. Ibid., p. 4.

67. The United States, under President Theodore Roosevelt, stepped in as mediator during peace talks, assisting the Russians in maintaining face in view of the embarrassing defeat.

68. W. R. Nester, *Japan and the Third World* (London: Macmillan, 1992).

69. Over 90 percent of Japanese foreign aid went to valuable potential Asian markets, helping make recipients dependent on Japanese products and technology in much the same way that U.S. aid did for U.S. products in other regions.

70. See Aurelia George, "Japan's Participation in UN Peacekeeping Operations: Radical Departure or Predictable Response?" *Asian Survey*, 33 (June 1993), pp. 560–575.

71. One who argues that economic factors are not as decisive in Japanese foreign policymaking as often thought is Bill Emmott, "The Economic Sources of Japan's Foreign Policy," *Survival*, 34 (Summer 1992), pp. 50–70. For new directions in Japanese foreign policy, see Yoshinobu Yamamoto, "Japan's Security Policies in the Post–Cold War Era, *Australian Journal of International Affairs*, 47 (October 1993), pp. 286–298.

72. Nester, *Japan and The Third World*, pp. 17–18.

73. Edith Terry, "China Checks Japan's Power in Asia," *Christian Science Monitor*, January 10, 1995, p. 7.

Chapter 5. Explaining Foreign Policy Behavior: Why Do Nation-States Do What They Do?

1. Winston Churchill, radio broadcast, London, October 1, 1939.

2. As with Hans Morgenthau's and Arnold Wolfers' use of the term, "national interests" are sometimes referred to as the "core values" held by a national society. Not all analysts agree on the exact identity of these values, but the three mentioned here are the most often cited. See Morgenthau, "Another Great Debate: The National Interest of the United States," *American Political Science Review*, 46 (December 1952), pp. 961–988; and Wolfers, *Discord and Collaboration* (Baltimore: Johns Hopkins University Press, 1962), pp. 67–80.

3. Charles A. Beard, *The Idea of National Interest* (New York: Macmillan, 1934), p. 4.

4. On such debates, see Stephanie G. Neuman, "The Defense Sector and Economic Development: A Survey and Debate," paper presented at the workshop on Arms Trade and Arms Control in the Post–Cold War World: Future Trends and Developments, Center for War/Peace Studies, Columbia University, New York, November 1993.

5. See, for example, Samuel J. Raphalides, "Rethinking Security: The Environmentalist Dimension and the Third World in the Post–Cold War Era," *Journal of Asian and African Affairs*, 5 (Fall 1993), pp. 21–29.

6. For a discussion of the problems and usefulness of the national interest concept, see J. Martin Rochester, "The 'National Interest' and Contemporary World Politics," *The Review of Politics*, 40 (January 1978), pp. 77–96; and Alexander L. George and Robert O. Keohane, "The Concept of National Interests: Uses and Limitations," in George, ed., *Presidential Decisionmaking in Foreign Policy* (Boulder, Colo.: Westview Press, 1980), pp. 217–237.

7. This list of factors corresponds essentially to other lists developed by scholars. Some have adopted a simpler scheme, noting that one can view states as actors from two vantage points— either from "inside out" or "outside in," i.e., looking at how foreign policy is shaped either by factors within the state or by factors external to the state. Others broaden levels of analysis to include individual, role, governmental, societal, bilateral, or interstate and global levels. The three levels of analysis used here embrace all of these. Much work in this area of inquiry owes an intellectual debt to James Rosenau, who developed an early "pre-theory" of foreign policy behavior. See Rosenau, "Pre-Theories and Theories of Foreign Policy," in R. Barry Farrell, ed., *Approaches to Comparative and International Politics* (Evanston, Ill.: Northwestern University Press, 1966), pp. 27–92; Rosenau, *The Scientific Study of Foreign Policy*, rev. ed. (London: Frances Pinter, 1980), ch. 6; and Rosenau, "A Pre-Theory Revisited: World Politics in an Era of Cascading Interdependence," *International Studies Quarterly*, 28 (September 1984), pp. 245–305. For a discussion of "levels of analysis" and the relative merits of "inside-out" vs. "outside-in" perspectives, see J. David Singer, "The Level-of-Analysis Problem in International Relations," in Klaus Knorr and Sidney Verba, eds., *The International System: Theoretical Essays* (Princeton, N.J.: Princeton University Press, 1961), pp. 77–92; Kenneth N. Waltz, *Theory of International Politics* (Reading, Mass.: Addison-Wesley, 1979), especially ch. 4; and Robert C. North, *War, Peace, Survival* (Boulder, Colo.: Westview Press, 1990).

8. Trudy Rubin, "Why Sadat, Begin Plan Summit," *Christian Science Monitor*, May 29, 1981, p. 13.

9. Two influential theorists, one American and one British, have stressed the importance of controlling particular sealanes or land masses. Late in the nineteenth century, U.S. Admiral Alfred Thayer Mahan identified control of the seas as the key to world power. World leaders from Teddy Roosevelt to Leonid Brezhnev seem to have been influenced by this notion.

However, British geographer Sir Halford J. MacKinder later disputed the importance of naval strength, and worried about potential German or Russian domination of the key Eurasian land mass, or "world island," which included Africa as well. Athough many observers argue that modern technology has greatly diminished the importance of geography, some still stress geographical factors as key elements in foreign policy; for example, see Colin S. Gray, *The Geopolitics of the Nuclear Era: Heartland, Rimlands, and the Technological Revolution* (New York: National Strategy Information Center, 1977); Francis P. Sempa, "The Geopolitics of the Post–Cold War World," *Strategic Review*, 20 (Winter 1992), pp. 9–17; and Michael P. Gerace, "Transforming the Pattern of Conflict: Geopolitics and Post–Cold War Europe," *Comparative Strategy*, 11 (October-December 1992), pp. 373–407.

10. John Vasquez is among the scholars who point to the continued importance of territorial competition as a prime cause of war. See Vasquez, "Why Do Neighbors Fight—Proximity, Interaction, or Territoriality?," paper presented to the annual meeting of the Peace Science Society (International), Urbana, Ill. (November 1994).

11. See Harvey Starr and Benjamin A. Most, "Contagion and Border Effects on Contemporary African Conflict," *Comparative Political Studies*, 16 (April 1983), pp. 92–117; and Starr and Most, "The Forms and Processes of War Diffusion: Research Update on Contagion in African Conflict," *Comparative Political Studies*, 18 (July 1985), pp. 206–227.

12. On the importance of geography in conflictual interactions, see John A. Vasquez: "Why do Neighbors Fight? Proximity, Interaction, or Territoriality," *Journal of Peace Research*, 32 (August 1995), pp. 277–293; Lewis F. Richardson, *Statistics of Deadly Quarrels* (Pittsburgh: Boxwood, 1960), pp. 176–177; Quincy Wright, *A Study of War* (Chicago: University of Chicago Press, 1965), p. 1240, ch. 46, appendix 5; Frederic S. Pearson, "Geographic Proximity and Foreign Military Intervention," *Journal of Conflict Resolution*, 18 (September 1974), pp. 432–460; and Harvey Starr and Benjamin Most, "Diffusion, Reinforcement, Geo-Politics and the Spread of War," *American Political Science Review*, 74 (December 1980), pp. 932–946. On geography and cooperative interactions, see Richard L. Merritt, "Distance and Interaction Among Political Communities," *General Systems Yearbook*, 9 (1964), pp. 255–263; Bruce M. Russett, *International Regions and the International System* (Westport, Conn.: Greenwood Press, 1975); Peter J. Taylor, *Political Geography: World-Economy, Nation-State, and Locality*, 2nd ed. (London: Longman, 1989); and Patrick O'Sullivan, *Geopolitics* (London: Croom Helm, 1986).

13. In the latter days of the Soviet Union, efforts were made to defuse some of the tension along the Chinese border. Since Russia has reemerged onto the scene, the two states have continued this "détente," which has included basic Chinese acceptance of changes in the Russian border since the nineteenth century. Full agreement on all such changes is still to be achieved, however.

14. This notion was developed in the pioneering work of Quincy Wright, *A Study of War*, 2 vols. (Chicago: University of Chicago Press, 1942). Also, see Rudolph J. Rummel, *The Dimensions of Nations* (Beverly Hills: Sage, 1972), ch. 16.

15. On the democracy-peace nexus, see the work of Rudolf J. Rummel, summarized in "Questions and Answers on the Fact that Democracies Do Not Make War on Each Other," Peacenet (Internet), September 2, 1994; and *Death by Government* (New York: Transaction Books, 1994). See also William J. Dixon, "Democracy and the Peaceful Settlement of International Conflict," *American Political Science Review*, 88 (March 1994), pp. 14–32; Dixon, "Democracy and the Management of International Conflict," *Journal of Conflict Resolution*, 37 (March 1993), pp. 42–68; John A. Vasquez, *War Puzzles* (Cambridge, Eng.: Cambridge University Press, 1993); Bruce Russett, *Grasping the Democratic Peace* (Princeton, N.J.: Princeton University Press, 1993); Bruce Bueno de Mesquita and David Lalman, *War and Reason* (New Haven, Conn.: Yale University Press, 1993); and Joe D. Hagan, "Domestic Political Systems and War Proneness," *Mershon International Studies Review*, 38 (October 1994), pp. 183–207.

16. See Zeev Maoz and Bruce Russett, "Normative and Structural Causes of Democratic Peace, 1946–1986," *American Political Science Review,* 87 (September 1993), pp. 624–638; Max Singer and Aaron Wildavsky, *The Real World Order* (Chatham, N.J.: Chatham House, 1993), pp. 20–22; and Michael W. Doyle, "Kant, Liberal Legacies, and Foreign Affairs," *Philosophy and Public Affairs,* 12 (1983), pp. 205–235. For a counter viewpoint stressing the close connection of liberal democracy and militarism, see Robert Latham, "Democracy and War-Making: Locating the International Liberal Context," *Millennium,* 22 (Summer 1993), pp. 139–164. See also Harvey Starr, "Why Don't Democracies Fight One Another? Evaluating the Theory-Findings Feedback Loop," *Jerusalem Journal of International Relations,* 14 (December 1992), pp. 41–59.

17. Bueno de Mesquita, *War and Reason,* p. 272.

18. Jack Levy, "The Causes of War: A Review of Theories and Evidence," in Philip E. Tetlock et. al., eds., *Behavior, Society, and Nuclear War,* vol. 1 (New York: Oxford University Press, 1989), p. 270.

19. In research reported to the Annual Meeting of the Peace Science Society (International) in Champaign, Illinois, in November 1994, Paul Senese from the State University of New York, Binghamton, found evidence of correlations between democratic pairs of states and the resort to violence that fell short of bilateral war. Patrick James of the University of Florida and Murray Wolfson of Iowa State University have reported similar findings. See David P. Forsyth, "Democracy, War, and Covert Action," *Journal of Peace Research,* 29 (November 1992), pp. 385–395, where it is argued that the United States frequently has resorted to "covert force" or hostile violent intelligence operations against other freely elected governments, actions that fell short of war but nonetheless raise questions about the "democratic peace."

20. See A.F.K. Organski, *World Politics,* 2nd ed. (New York: Knopf, 1968), pp. 293–295; and Organski and Jacek Kugler, *The War Ledger* (Chicago: University of Chicago Press, 1980).

21. See Kenneth N. Waltz, "The Stability of a Bipolar World," *Daedalus,* 93 (Summer 1964), pp. 881–909, and "International Structure, National Force, and the Balance of Power," *Journal of International Affairs,* 21 (1967), pp. 215–231.

22. See Karl W. Deutch and J. David Singer, "Multipolar Power Systems and International Stability," *World Politics,* 16 (April 1964), pp. 390–406; and Richard N. Rosecrance, "Bipolarity, Multipolarity, and the Future," *Journal of Conflict Resolution,* 10 (September 1966), pp. 314–327.

23. Instead of assuming that polarity alone influences system stability or war, some have argued for a more refined view of the power balance of offensively versus defensively oriented states in the system. Others try to link the existence of unstable systems, such as the multipolar period of the seventeenth and early twentieth centuries, to the scarcity of desired international resources. See Manus I. Midlarsky and Ted Hopf, "Polarity and International Stability," *American Political Science Review,* 87 (March 1993), pp. 173–180.

24. Brian Pollins, "Systemic Model Specification of Interstate Armed Conflict, 1495–1995," presentation to Correlates of War Project, Ann Arbor, The University of Michigan, July 1995.

25. See George Modelski and William R. Thompson, *Leading Sectors and World Powers: The Coevolution of Global Politics and World Economics* (Columbia, S.C.: University of South Carolina Press, 1995); Thompson, *On Global War: Historical-Structural Approaches to World Politics* (Columbia, S.C.: University of South Carolina Press, 1988); Thompson, "Systemic Leadership and Growth Waves in the Long Run," *International Studies Quarterly,* 35 (March 1992), pp. 25–48.

26. See Jonathan Friedman, "Order and Disorder in Global Systems: A Sketch," *Social Research,* 60 (Summer 1993), pp. 205–234; Patrick James and Michael Brecher, "Stability and Polarity: New Paths for Inquiry," *Journal of Peace Research,* 25 (1988), pp. 31–42; and John Gerard Ruggie, "International Structure and International Transformation: Space, Time and Method," in *Global Changes and Theoretical Challenges: Approaches to World Politics for the 1990s,* ed. by Ernst-Otto Czempiel and James N. Rosenau (Lexington, Mass.: Lexington Books, 1989), pp. 21–35. Neorealist, "structuralist" theorists, such as Kenneth

Waltz, look at system change in terms of the evolving global power hierarchy among states. Waltz, in "The New World Order," *Millennium*, 22 (September 1993), pp. 187–195, has argued that the immediate post–Cold War situation—with the United States alone at the top of the power hierarchy—would be unstable and likely to develop into a multipolar system. Neo-Marxist or "world system" theorists, such as Immanuel Wallerstein, view system change in terms of evolving capitalist dominance over the world's poor; see Christopher Chase-Dunn and Thomas D. Hall, "The Historical Evolution of World Systems" *Social Inquiry*, 64 (Summer 1994), pp. 257-280. One school thus stresses order and stability in a disorderly world, whereas the other stresses change in the direction of greater equity. See also Yale H. Ferguson and Richard W. Mansbach, *The Elusive Quest: Theory and International Politics* (Columbia: University of South Carolina Press, 1988), pp. 196–197. For a set of four potential future scenarios involving "benign hegemony," "coercive hegemony," "concert of great powers," and "regional rivalry" as possible international systems, see David Skidmore, "Teaching About the Post–Cold War World: Four Future Scenarios," *International Studies Notes*, 20 (Winter 1995), pp. 1–8. On the benefits and limitations of the concert system, see Robert Jervis, "A Political Science Perspective on the Balance of Power and the Concert," *American Historical Review*, 97 (June 1993), pp. 716–724; and Wolf D. Gruner, "Was there a Reformed Balance of Power System or Cooperative Great Power Hegemony?," *American Historical Review*, 97 (June 1993), pp. 725–732.

27. For a historical account of such struggles, see Malcolm Kerr, *The Arab Cold War* (New York: Oxford University Press, 1971).

28. See Nazli Choucri and Robert C. North, *Nations in Conflict* (San Francisco: W. H. Freeman, 1975); and North, *War, Peace, Survival*.

29. War-making decisions ordinarily will be based not only on one's own capabilities but also on an assessment of the comparable capabilities and attitudes of one's adversaries and allies. Hence, national attributes also must be seen in relation to those of others. See Harvey Starr and Benjamin Most, *Inquiry, Logic and International Politics* (Columbia, S.C.: University of South Carolina Press, 1989), ch. 4; and North, *War, Peace, Survival*, pp. 22–24.

30. Governments can become paranoid about dissident ethnic groups, especially in wartime. Thousands of loyal Americans of Japanese descent were interned in camps and lost their property during World War II in the United States because it was assumed that they represented a "fifth column" for Japanese infiltration and because of racist attitudes in certain parts of the country. Restitution payments were later made to the victims of this ethnic repression. See Bill Hosokawa, *The Quiet Americans* (New York: Morrow, 1969); Roger Danuiels, *Concentration Camps U.S.A.: Japanese Americans and World War II* (New York: Holt, Reinhart and Winston, 1972). On the challenge of ethnic issues in international relations, see Anthony D. Smith, "The Ethnic Sources of Nationalism," *Survival*, 35 (Spring 1993), pp. 48–62. In the case of prejudice against Japanese, the issue of race arose, as it sometimes does in relation to ethnic conflict. Race is generally an ascribed rather than objective difference among people, but because physical differences are noticeable, various groups can seize on them to victimize others, increase power, and gain political support through the manipulation of fear and hatred. On the general question of race in world politics, see Roxanne Lynn Doty, "The Bounds of 'Race' in International Relations," *Millennium*, 22 (Winter 1993), pp. 443–461.

31. On models of ending conflict in such divided societies as Lebanon, see John Coakley, "The Resolution of Ethnic Conflict: Towards a Typology," *International Political Science Review*, 13 (October 1992), pp. 343–358; and Sammy Smooha and Theodor Hanf, "The Diverse Modes of Conflict-Regulation in Deeply Divided Societies," *International Journal of Comparative Sociology*, 33 (January–April 1992), pp. 26–47. Essentially there are four types of solutions: "ethnic democracy" (where one group dominates the government); partition (where incompatible nationalities and groups are largely separated, each on their own lands); consociational democracy (where groups share power, with equal status and built-in safeguards and veto powers; and liberal democracy (where ethnic differences tend to be ho-

mogenized and people are treated as individuals rather than as members of "tribal" groupings). The appropriate pattern varies according to history and international pressures.

32.   We are not reviving here the traditional and largely discredited notion of "national character." Although it is possible that at certain times a country's population has certain clear preferences about, for example, the use of force, there is no evidence that certain nations are inherently more peaceloving or warlike, more practical or romantic, more cowardly or courageous than others. Commentators may sometimes refer to "naive Americans," "brutal Russians," "inscrutable Chinese," "fun-loving Italians," or "militaristic Germans," but societies are far too complex and individuals far too diverse for such oversimplifications. When governments develop behavior patterns such as the "m.o.'s" described in Chapter 4, they usually are reacting to historical and cultural experience rather than genetic traits.

33.   See Chapter 3 for our discussion of Samuel P. Huntington's "The Clash of Civilizations?" *Foreign Affairs*, 72 (Summer 1993), pp. 22–49. Also, see Yosef Lapid and Friedrich Kratochwil, eds., *The Return of Culture and Identity in IR Theory* (Boulder, Colo.: Lynne Reinner, 1995); Errol A. Henderson and J. Scott DeSonia, "Cultural Differences and War in the Interstate System, 1816–1989," paper presented to the Annual Meeting of the International Studies Association, Washington, D.C., March 1995; Richard W. Drislin, *Understanding Culture's Influence on Behavior* (Fort Worth: Harcourt, Brace, Jovanovich, 1993); and D. Jacquin, A. Oros, and M. Verweij, "Culture in International Relations—An Introduction to the Special Issue," *Millennium* (Winter 1993), pp. 375–377.

34.   Religious cultural impacts become important for foreign policy mainly if the state in question adopts religious rather than secular law in government. Most Islamic states and Israel remain essentially in the secular tradition, but growing efforts by religious revivalists have injected religious law into foreign policy controversies in states as diverse as Algeria and Iran. One striking and controversial example in 1995 concerned a group of Orthodox rabbis in Jerusalem who called for resistance and disobedience in the armed forces to Israeli government efforts to return parts of the occupied West Bank of the Jordan River to local Palestinian control. For a greater understanding of Islamic cultural views of world politics, see Ghassan Salame, "Islam and the West," *Foreign Policy*, 90 (Spring 1993), pp. 22–37; Bassam Tibi, "Islamic Law/Shari'a, Human Rights, Universal Morality, and International Relations," *Human Rights Quarterly*, 16 (May 1994), pp. 277–299; and Sohail H. Hashmi, "Is there an Islamic Ethic of Humanitarian Intervention?" *Ethics and International Affairs*, 7 (1993), pp. 55–73. On religion and ethnicity generally, see Alexander Shtromas, "Religion and Ethnicity in World Order," *International Journal on World Peace*, 9 (June 1992), pp. 33–45.

35.   In the history of U.S.–Japanese relations, cultural misunderstandings have abounded. Japan's treatment of war prisoners and conquered peoples, for example, was at least partially conditioned by Japanese disdain for being taken prisoner and their assumptions that foreigners are barbarian. The former beliefs allowed hundreds of Japanese to commit suicide rather than be taken prisoner in World War II, and the latter beliefs mean that Japanese have difficulty accepting that foreigners could ever truly understand their civilization. Getting beyond such cultural assumptions, biases, and obstacles is one of the key difficulties in developing a set of principles under which all nations can live tolerably. See Stella Ting–Toomey, "Managing Intercultural Conflicts Effectively," Larry A. Samovar and Richard Porter, eds., *Intercultural Communication* (Belmont, Calif.: Wadsworth, 1994), pp. 360–372; and Edward T. Hall, *Beyond Culture* (New York: Doubleday, 1976).

36.   Robert C. North, Nobutake Ike, and Jan F. Triska, *The World of Superpowers*, rev. ed. (Stanford, Calif.: Notrik Press, 1985), ch. 1.

37.   Gross domestic product (GDP), which measures only the domestic aspects of production, is at times used in place of GNP as a size indicator.

38.   Harold K. Jacobson, *Networks of Interdependence*, 2nd ed. (New York: Knopf, 1984), p. 50.

39.   See Walter Russell Mead, "An American Grand Strategy: The Quest for Order in a Disordered World," *World Policy Journal*, 10 (Spring 1993), pp. 9–37; and Aaron L. Friedburg, "The Future of American Power," *Political Quarterly*, 109 (Spring 1994), pp. 1–22.

40. For a discussion of these claims and counterclaims, see Bernard S. Morris, *Imperialism and Revolution* (Bloomington: Indiana University Press, 1973). See also, Frederic S. Pearson, "American Military Intervention Abroad: A Test of Economic and Noneconomic Explanations," in *The Politics of Aid, Trade, and Investment,* ed. by Satish Raichur and Craig Liske (New York: John Wiley, 1976), ch. 2.

41. Katherine Barbier, "Economic Interdependence and Dyadic Dispute Proneness, 1873-1939," paper presented to the Annual North American Meeting of the Peace Science Society (International), Pittsburgh, November 1992.

42. They have been generally less involved in foreign trade and investment activities than capitalist states, and hence are less dependent on states outside the Communist bloc.

43. See Daniel Hewitt, "Military Expenditures Worldwide: Determinants and Trends," *Journal of Public Policy,* 12 (April–June 1992), pp. 105–152.

44. See Pearson, *The Weak State,* ch. 3.

45. See Chapter 8 for a discussion of which variables tend to be the best predictors of ultimate military success in war.

46. Of course, one must also factor in the competition with Pakistan. See Ido Oren, "The Indo-Pakistani Arms Competition: A Deductive and Statistical Analysis," *Journal of Conflict Resolution,* 38 (June 1994), pp. 185–214.

47. See Jack S. Levy and Michael M. Barnett, "Alliance Formation, Domestic Political Economy, and Third World Security," *Journal of International Relations,* 14 (December 1992), pp. 19–40.

48. George F. Kennan, *Memoirs, 1925–1950* (Boston: Little, Brown, 1976), p. 53.

49. Kennan in fact compared democracies to a gigantic, pinheaded prehistoric monster wallowing in the mud unaware of the environment until some enemy finally whacks his tail off: "Once he grasps this, he lays about with such blind determination that he not only destroys his adversary but largely wrecks his native habitat." See George F. Kennan, *American Diplomacy, 1900–1950* (Chicago: University of Chicago Press, 1951), p. 59.

50. See Richard D. Anderson Jr., Margaret G Hermann, and Charles F. Hermann, "Explaining Self-Defeating Foreign Policy Decisions: Interpreting Soviet Arms for Egypt in 1973 through Process or Domestic Bargaining Models," *American Political Science Review,* 86 (September 1992), pp. 759–766.

51. Critics of democratic foreign policy processes note that the strong roles of the legislature and the press can jeopardize the discretion and state secrecy that are often deemed essential to the conduct of foreign policy. Those heading the Nixon administration were extremely concerned about information "leaks," and even authorized burglaries by "plumbers" to stop the leaks. Yet discretion is a matter of law, ethics, and competent administration as much as a product of strict control. President Nixon himself taped supposedly confidential conversations with foreign leaders in the Oval Office; confidence in U.S. discretion had to be shaken when these leaders found out about the recordings. In fact, journalists long have claimed that most leaks are planted by government officials themselves for political impact. Differences between political systems in maintaining secrecy should not be overdrawn. Despite Nazi totalitarianism, Hitler's entire strategy for the 1939 invasion of Western Europe was leaked in advance to disbelieving foreign officials by a high-ranking informant in the German army. See Henry L. Mason, "War Comes to the Netherlands: September 1939-May 1940," *Political Science Quarterly,* 78 (1963), pp. 548–580.

52. See Charles W. Kegley and Eugene R. Wittkopf, eds., *The Domestic Sources of American Foreign Policy: Insights and Evidence* (New York: St. Martin's, 1988); Barry B. Hughes, *The Domestic Context of American Foreign Policy* (San Francisco: W. H. Freeman, 1978); and Lloyd Jensen, *Explaining Foreign Policy* (Englewood Cliffs, N.J.: Prentice-Hall, 1982), ch. 5.

53. See Morton H. Halperin, *Bureaucratic Politics and Foreign Policy* (Washington, D.C.: Brookings Institution, 1974).

54. Both Japan and Italy in particular have seen their political party systems come apart amidst corruption scandals during the 1990s, and have relied on the bureaucracy to maintain policy direction. For Japan this came at a time of delicate trade negotiations with the United States.

55. Some analysts maintain that geographical as well as partisan splits in the United States impact heavily on policy coherence. Since at least the 1970s, congressional representatives of the American South have differed in foreign policy positions from their northeastern colleages. See Peter Trubowitz, "Political Conflict and Foreign Policy in the United States: A Geographical Interpretation," *Political Geography*, 12 (March 1993), pp. 121–135.

56. See Deborah Gerner, "Foreign Policy Analysis: Renaissance, Routine, or Rubbish?" in William Crotty, ed., *Political Science: Looking to the Future*, vol. 2 (Evanston, Ill.: Northwestern University Press, 1990).

57. See Karl W. Deutsch, *The Analysis of International Relations*, 3rd ed. (Englewood Cliffs, N.J.: Prentice-Hall, 1988), ch. 10; and Russell Neuman, *The Paradox of Mass Politics: Knowledge and Opinion in the American Electorate* (Cambridge, Mass.: Harvard University Press, 1986).

58. The President also avoided raising taxes during the war years in order to avert a public debate on the wisdom and costs of the war; some economists blamed this strategy for spurring wartime inflation. See James A. Nathan and James K. Oliver, *United States Foreign Policy and World Order*, 4th ed. (Boston: Little, Brown, 1989), pp. 270–300; and *The Pentagon Papers*, Gravel Edition, vol. 3 (Boston: Beacon Press, 1971), pp. 180–192.

59. For specific examples of idiosyncratic analysis, see Raymond Birt, "Personality and Foreign Policy: The Case of Stalin," *Political Psychology*, 14 (December 1993), pp. 607–625; and Robert G. Kaufman, "Winston S. Churchill and the Art of Statecraft: The Legacy of Principled Internationalism," *Diplomacy and Statecraft*, 3 (July 1992), pp. 159–187.

60. Blaise Pascal, *Lettres Provinciales, 1656–1956*, no. 162; and Ronald Steele, interview with Robert F. Kennedy, *New York Review of Books* (March 13, 1963), p. 22. For exploratory discussions of individual leaders' impact on foreign policy behavior, see Margaret G. Hermann, "Effects of Personal Characteristics of Political Leaders on Foreign Policy," in Maurice A. East et al., eds., *Why Nations Act: Theoretical Perspectives for Comparative Foreign Policy Studies* (Beverly Hills: Sage, 1978), pp. 49–68; see also, Philip E. Tetlock, "Good Judgment in International Politics: Three Psychological Perspectives," *Political Psychology*, 13 (September 1992), pp. 517–539; Arye L. Hillman, "International Trade Policy: Benevolent Dictators and Optimizing Politicians," *Public Choice*, 74 (July 1992), pp. 1–15; Brian L. Crowe, "Foreign Policy-Making: Reflections of a Practitioner," *Government and Opposition*, 28 (September 1993), pp. 174–189; and Michael D. Yaffe, "Realism in Retreat? The New World Order and the Return of the Individual to International Relations Studies," *Perspectives on Political Science*, 23 (Spring 1994), pp. 79–88.

61. On the importance of Gorbachev in changing basic Soviet core beliefs, see Douglas W. Blum, "The Soviet Foreign Policy Belief System: Beliefs, Politics, and Foreign Outcomes," *International Studies Quarterly*, 87 (December 1993), pp. 373–394; and Jeff Checkel, "Ideas, Institutions, and the Gorbachev Foreign Policy Revolution," *World Politics*, 45 (January 1993), pp. 271–300.

62. For a chilling account of the lethal effects of individual dictatorial personality in crisis, see Jerrold M. Post's discussion of Saddam Hussein, "Current Concepts of the Narcissistic Personality: Implications for Political Psychology," *Political Psychology*, 14 (March 1993), pp. 99–121.

63. Harold and Margaret Sprout, "Man-Milieu Relationship Hypotheses in the Context of International Politics," Center for International Studies, Princeton University, research monograph (Princeton, N.J.: 1956); and "Environmental Factors in the Study of International Politics," *Journal of Conflict Resolution*, 1 (December 1957), pp. 309–328.

64. Kenneth Boulding, "National Images and International Systems," *Journal of Conflict Resolution*, 3 (June 1959), p. 120.

65. See Bruce Bueno de Mesquita, *The War Trap* (New Haven: Yale University Press, 1981), pp. 34 and 124; and Bueno de Mesquita and Lalman, *War and Reason*.

66. Alexander L. George and Juliette George, *Woodrow Wilson and Colonel House* (New York: John Day, 1956). For further discussion of the role of personality in shaping foreign policy, see Post, *op. cit.* 1993; Stephen G. Walker, "The Motivational Foundations of Political Be-

lief Systems: A Reanalysis of the Operational Code Construct," *International Studies Quarterly*, 27 (June 1983), pp. 179–202; Lloyd S. Etheredge, "Personality Effects on American Foreign Policy, 1898–1968: A Test of Interpersonal Generalization Theory," *American Political Science Review*, 72 (June 1978), pp. 435–436; Etheredge, *A World of Men: The Private Sources of American Foreign Policy* (Cambridge: MIT Press, 1979); and William D. Davidson and Joseph V. Montville, "Foreign Policy According to Freud," *Foreign Policy*, 45 (Winter 1981–92), pp. 145–157.

67. Lecture by Paul M. Kattenburg at the University of Missouri-St. Louis on March 30, 1978, and his book, *The Vietnam Trauma in American Foreign Policy, 1945–75* (New Brunswick, N.J.: Transaction Books, 1980), pp. 113–115. See also, Richard E. Neustadt and Graham T. Allison, "Afterword," in Robert F. Kennedy, *Thirteen Days* (New York: W. W. Norton, 1971), p. 123.

68. See, for example, V. Spike Peterson and Anne Sisson Runyan, "The Radical Future of Realism: Feminist Subversion of IR Theory," paper presented at the Annual Meeting of the International Studies Association, Washington, D.C., April 1990, as part of a panel on "Sex, Strategy, Security, and the Sovereign State"; and Lise Togeby, "The Gender Gap in Foreign Policy Attitudes," *Journal of Peace Research*, 31 (November 1994), pp. 375–392.

69. See V. Spike Peterson and Anne Sisson Runyan, *Global Gender Issues* (Boulder, Colo.: Westview Press, 1993), chs. 2–3.

70. Interesting arguments have been made by ecologists and ethologists concerning sex roles and politics. One study maintained that women are rarely national leaders because their biological roles, stressing the survival of offspring instead of mating success (as for men), lend themselves to less assertive public competition, and to a different sort of bonding. Where success in breeding is less important, as when a society becomes monogamous, or when female dominance would allow their offspring more success, more women leaders tend to emerge. See, for example, Bobbi S. Low, "Sex, Coalitions, and Politics in Preindustrial Societies," *Politics and the Life Sciences*, 11 (February 1992), pp. 63–80. See also, Sarah Blaffer Hardy, *The Woman that Never Evolved* (Cambridge, Mass.: Harvard University Press, 1981); and Ruth Bleir, *Science and Gender: A Critique of Biology and its Theories on Women* (New York: Pergamon Press, 1984).

71. "Strong Words from Serb General," *New York Times*, July 28, 1995, p. A4.

72. It is intriguing that in South Asia especially—known for a culture emphasizing male dominance in public life—India, Pakistan, Sri Lanka, and Bangladesh all have had female leaders since World War II. Globally, although constituting one-half the world's population, and accounting for two-thirds of the world's work hours, women constitute only 5 percent or less of national leaders, cabinet members, and senior policymakers, and hold roughly 10 percent of national legislative seats and 5 percent of senior positions in intergovernmental organizations. See Peterson and Runyan, *Gender Issues*, pp. 5–6 and 46–49.

73. Indira Gandhi pursued the Bangladesh war against Pakistan in 1971; Golda Meir defended against Syria and Egypt in 1973; and Margaret Thatcher dispatched a naval armada against Argentina in the Falklands War in 1982.

74. Indeed, women frequently compete and fight for highly valued interests in everyday life. This can be seen to a certain, and evidently growing, degree in American adolescent and gang-related violence, for example. It appears that the issues at stake are the key to understanding female aggression. See Glenn E. Weisfeld, "Teaching About Sex Differences in Human Behavior and the Biological Approach in General," *Politics and the Life Sciences*, 5, no. 1 (1986), pp. 36–43.

75. A good illustration of this interaction is provided by Michael Ng-Quinn in his attempt to explain Chinese foreign policy behavior using a framework similar to that used in this chapter. See "The Analytic Study of Chinese Foreign Policy," *International Studies Quarterly*, 27 (June 1983), pp. 203–224.

76. Jerry Hough, "Gorbachev's Politics," *Foreign Affairs*, 68 (Winter 1989/90), p. 27.

77.   Quote of Donna Stath, by Sara Rimer, "Bosnian War Bewilders a Midwestern Town," *New York Times*, July 24, 1995, p. 1.

Chapter 6. The Foreign Policy Process: A View from the Inside

1.   Graham T. Allison, "Conceptual Models and the Cuban Missile Crisis," *American Political Science Review*, 63 (September 1969), p. 689. For more recent reflections on the Cuban missile crisis, see the works cited in Note 49 in Chapter 4.
2.   *St. Louis Post-Dispatch*, June 14, 1981, p. 1.
3.   *Time*, January 1, 1990, p. 20.
4.   *Harpers*, 288 (January 1994), pp. 57–64.
5.   Henry A. Kissinger, "Bureaucracy and Policymaking: The Effects of Insiders and Outsiders on the Policy Process," in Morton H. Halperin and Arnold Kanter, eds., *Reading in American Foreign Policy: A Bureaucratic Perspective* (Boston: Little, Brown, 1973), p. 85. The essay originally appeared in a 1968 volume shortly before Kissinger became the chief foreign policy adviser to Richard Nixon.
6.   For example, see discussions of "the new world order" in *Foreign Policy* (Summer 1991); Anthony Lake, "From Containment to Enlargement," address to SAIS, Washington, D.C., September 21, 1993; and William Safire, "The En-En Document," *New York Times*, August 25, 1994, p. A17.
7.   Roger Hilsman, *To Move a Nation: The Politics of Foreign Policy in the Administration of John F. Kennedy* (Garden City, N.Y.: Doubleday, 1967), p. 5.
8.   One set of authors has developed a fourfold issue-area typology: military-security, economic-developmental, political-diplomatic, and cultural-status. See Michael Brecher et al., "A Framework for Research on Foreign Policy Behavior," *Journal of Conflict Resolution*, (March 1969), pp. 75–101. Also, see William C. Potter, "Issue Area and Foreign Policy Analysis," *International Organization*, 34 (Summer 1980), pp. 405–427.
9.   Linda B. Brady, "The Situation and Foreign Policy," in Maurice A. East, Stephen A Salmore, and Charles F. Hermann, *Why Nations Act: Theoretical Perspectives for Comparative Foreign Policy Studies* (Beverly Hills, Calif.: Sage, 1978), pp. 173–190.
10.   K. J. Holsti, *International Politics: A Framework for Analysis*, 7th ed. (Englewood Cliffs, N. J.: Prentice-Hall, 1995), p. 267, based on testimony from U. S. State Department officials. Similar estimates are reported in Lincoln P. Bloomfield, *The Foreign Policy Process: A Modern Primer* (Englewood Cliffs, N. J.: Prentice-Hall, 1982), p. 143.
11.   Charles F. Hermann, "International Crisis as a Situational Variable," in James N. Rosenau, ed., *International Politics and Foreign Policy*, rev. ed. (New York: Free Press, 1969), pp. 409–421.
12.   See Charles F. Hermann, *International Crisis: Insights from Behavioral Research* (New York: Free Press, 1972). Also, see Hermann, "International Crises and National Security," in Edward A. Kolodziej and Patrick Morgan, eds., *International Security and Arms Control* (Westport, Conn.: Greenwich Press, 1990).
13.   Michael Brecher and Jonathan Wilkenfeld, "Crises in World Politics," *World Politics*, 34 (April 1982), p. 381. For a fuller discussion of crises, see Brecher et al., *Crises in the Twentieth Century*, 2 vols. (Oxford: Pergamon, 1988), and Brecher and Wilkenfeld, vol. 3 (1989).
14.   The term "billiard ball" was coined by Arnold Wolfers. See his chapter "The Actors in International Politics" in *Discord and Collaboration* (Baltimore: Johns Hopkins University Press, 1962), pp. 3–24.
15.   Graham T. Allison, *Essence of Decision* (Boston: Little, Brown, 1971), pp. 4–5.
16.   The so-called "decision-making approach" to the study of foreign policy was pioneered by Richard C. Snyder, H. W. Bruck, and Burton M. Sapin in *Foreign Policy Decision Making: An Approach to the Study of International Politics* (New York: Free Press, 1962). Snyder,

Bruck, and Sapin were criticized for giving too much attention to idiosyncratic factors to the exclusion of other factors in their study.

17. Allison, *Essence of Decision*. For additional models, see Barbara Kellerman, "Allison Redux: Three More Decision-Making Models," *Polity*, 15 (Spring 1983), pp. 351–367. A critique of Allison's approach is Stephen D. Krasner, "Are Bureaucracies Important (or Allison's Wonderland)," *Foreign Policy*, 7 (Summer 1972), pp. 159–179.

18. Some analysts argue that in certain welfare areas, such as trade policy, the central institutions of a state are able to insulate themselves somewhat from interest groups and domestic political forces, even in the case of a country like the United States, which does not have a strong "statist" tradition. See Judith Goldstein and Stephanie Ann Lenway, "Interest or Institutions: An Inquiry into Congressional-ITC Relations," *International Studies Quarterly*, 33 (September 1989), pp. 304–327. Also, see Wendy L. Hansen and Kee Ok Park, "Nation-State and Pluralistic Decision Making in Trade Policy: The Case of the International Trade Administration," *International Studies Quarterly*, 39 (June 1995), pp. 181–211. Most observers, however, point to the important role played by domestic interest groups in affecting foreign economic policy generally and trade policy in particular. See Jeff Frieden, "Sectoral Conflict and U. S. Foreign Economic Policy, 1914–1940," *International Organization*, 42 (Winter 1988), pp. 59–90, and other writings in this special journal volume devoted to "The State and Foreign Economic Policy"; and I. M. Destler, *Making Foreign Economic Policy* (Washington, D. C.: Brookings Institution, 1980).

19. Abram Chayes and Antonia Chayes, "On Compliance," *International Organization*, 47 (Spring 1993), pp. 180–181.

20. Robert Putnam in "Diplomacy and Domestic Politics: The Logic of Two-Level Games," *International Organization*, 42 (Summer 1988), pp. 427–460, examines "domestic-international entanglements" and attempts to demonstrate "the inevitability of domestic conflict about what the 'national interest' requires." Putnam is among those who argue that the dynamics of decision making in the traditional military-security area are essentially similar to the dynamics of nonsecurity decision making in terms of the need for "central decision makers" to play to both a domestic audience as well as an external audience in most situations. Also, see Chayes and Chayes, "On Compliance," p. 180; and Phillip R. Trimble, "Arms Control and International Negotiation Theory," *Stanford Journal of International Law*, 25 (Spring 1989), pp. 543–574.

21. Selective attention and rationalization are devices for avoiding or resolving "cognitive dissonance," the tension we can experience between our existing view of the world and our exposure to stimuli that are at odds with the latter. See Leon Festinger, *A Theory of Cognitive Dissonance* (Stanford, Calif.: Stanford University Press, 1962).

22. See Robert Jervis, "Hypotheses on Misperception," *World Politics*, 20 (April 1968), pp. 454–479.

23. The "spiral of misconceptions" is discussed in John G. Stoessinger, *Nations in Darkness: China, Russia, and America*, 5th ed. (New York: Random House, 1990), chs. 11 and 12. Empirical evidence supporting the contention that both the United States and Soviet Union misperceived each other's behavior after World War II can be found in William A. Gamson and Andre Modigliani, *Untangling the Cold War* (Boston: Little, Brown, 1971), p. 108. Also, see Richard Herrmann, "The Power of Perceptions in Foreign Policy Decision Making: Do Views of the Soviet Union Determine the Policy Choices of American Leaders?," *American Journal of Political Science*, 30, no. 4 (1986), pp. 841–875; and Herrmann, *Perceptions and Behavior in Soviet Policy* (Pittsburgh: University of Pittsburgh Press, 1985).

24. J. David Singer, "Threat Perception and the Armament-Tension Dilemma," *Journal of Conflict Resolution*, 2 (March 1958), pp. 90–105. See also Dean G. Pruitt, "Definition of the Situation as a Determinant of International Action," in Herbert C. Kelman, ed., *International Behavior* (New York: Holt, Rinehart and Winston, 1965), pp. 393–432.

25. U.S. leaders realized the Japanese might attack somewhere, but *not* Pearl Harbor, See Roberta Wohlstetter, *Pearl Harbor: Warning and Decision* (Stanford, Calif.: Stanford Uni-

versity Press, 1962). Another study, on the decisions leading up to World War I, indicates that the flurry of messages exchanged between Berlin, Vienna, St. Petersburg, London, and Paris on the eve of World War I was characterized by overestimation of the threat by one side and underestimation by the other side. See Ole R. Holsti et al., "Perception and Action in the 1914 Crisis," in J. David Singer, ed., *Quantitative International Politics* (New York: Free Press, 1968), p. 157. Jack Levy has noted the tendencies to underestimate or overestimate an adversary's hostile intentions and capabilities. See Jack S. Levy, "Misperception and the Causes of War," *World Politics*, 36 (October 1983), pp. 76–99.

26. On the Netherlands, see Frederic S. Pearson, *The Weak State in International Crisis: The Case of the Netherlands in the German Invasion of 1939–1940* (Washington, D. C.: University Press of America, 1981).

27. Joseph de Rivera, *The Psychological Dimensions of Foreign Policy* (Columbus, Ohio: Charles E. Merrill, 1968), p. 133. See also Glenn D. Paige, *The Korean Decision* (New York: Free Press, 1968).

28. Ernest R. May, *"Lessions" of the Past: The Use and Misuse of History in American Foreign Policy* (New York: Oxford University Press, 1973), p. 52. On Korea, see ibid., ch. 3, and Marshal D. Shulman, *Stalin's Foreign Policy Reappraised* (New York: Atheneum, 1966), ch. 6. On Vietnam, see May, *"Lessons,"* ch. 4, and James C. Thomson, "How Could Vietnam Happen? An Autopsy," in Halperin and Kanter, *Readings,* pp. 98–110. On the role of historical analogies in contributing to the Cold War, see Deborah W. Larson, *Origins of Containment: A Psychological Explanation* (Princeton, N.J.: Princeton University Press, 1985).

29. Kenneth Boulding, "National Images and International Systems," *Journal of Conflict Resolution,* 3 (June 1959), pp. 120–131.

30. On the Russo-Chinese relationship, see Stoessinger, *Nations in Darkness,* ch. 15. On the Franco-German relationship, see G. P. Gooch, *Franco-German Relations, 1871–1914* (New York: Russell and Russell, 1967). Gooch, writing after World War I, noted: "The story of Franco-German relations since 1871 is the record of France's endeavor to regain her lost territories and of Germany's attempt to retain them. The one [Germany] remembered the aggression of 1870, the other [France] the settlement of 1871; and the writers of schoolbooks took good care that the children should inherit the passions of their elders. There were pauses between the rounds, but the wrestlers never left the arena" (p. 5).

31. On culture, see Valerie M. Hudson, "Culture and Foreign Policy: Developing a Research Agenda," paper presented at Annual Meeting of the International Studies Association, Chicago, February 23, 1995; Marijke Breuning, "Culture, History, and Role: How the Past Shapes Foreign Policy Now," paper presented at Annual Meeting of the International Studies Association, Chicago, February 23, 1995; and Alexander Wendt, "Collective Identity Formation and the International State," *American Political Science Review,* 88 (June 1994), pp. 384–396. On the power of ideas and ideology, as opposed to raw calculation of self-interests, see Peter A. Hall, *The Political Power of Economic Ideas: Keynesianism Across Nations* (Princeton, N.J.: Princeton University Press, 1989); Wendt, "Anarchy Is What States Make of It: The Social Construction of Power Politics," *International Organization,* 46 (Spring 1992), pp. 392–403; Douglas W. Blum, "The Soviet Foreign Policy Belief System: Beliefs, Politics, and Foreign Policy Outcomes," *International Studies Quarterly,* 37 (December 1993), pp. 373–394; and Judith Goldstein and Robert O. Keohane, *Ideas and Foreign Policy: Beliefs, Institutions, and Political Change* (Ithaca, N.Y.: Cornell University Press, 1993).

32. McNamara contended that the placement of intermediate-range ballistic missiles in Cuba created no new dramatic threat to U.S. security that was not already posed by existing Soviet intercontinental ballistic missiles based in the Soviet Union. McNamara's argument was summed up by his statement that "a missile is a missile." Hilsman, *To Move a Nation,* p. 195. For the different perceptions of U.S. officials involved in the Cuban missile crisis decision, see ibid., ch. 15, and Allison, "Conceptual Models and the Cuban Missile Crisis," p. 712–715.

33. There is some disagreement over Kennedy's motive for discontinuing U-2 flights over the western half of the island. Some analysts argue it had as much to do with Kennedy's desire

to avoid a diplomatic incident over a possible shooting down of an American plane as with his subconscious desire to avoid information that might disturb his image. For discussion of this question, see Hilsman, *To Move a Nation*, ch. 14; Alexander George and Richard Smoke, *Deterrence in American Foreign Policy: Theory and Practice* (New York: Columbia University Press, 1974), pp. 472–491; and Roberta Wohlstetter, "Cuba vs. Pearl Harbor: Hindsight and Foresight," *Foreign Affairs*, 43 (July 1965), pp. 691–707.

34. Allison, *Essence of Decision*, pp. 176–178. Also, see Morton H. Halperin, *Bureaucratic Politics and Foreign Policy* (Washington, D.C.: Brookings Institution, 1974); and Jerel A. Rosati, "Developing a Systematic Decisionmaking Framework: Bureaucratic Politics in Perspective," *World Politics*, 33 (January 1981), pp. 234–252.

35. Les Aspin, "Misreading Intelligence," *Foreign Policy*, Summer 1981, p. 168.

36. Ole R. Holsti, "The Belief System and National Images: A Case Study," *Journal of Conflict Resolution*, 6 (September 1962), pp. 248–249.

37. Ole R. Holsti, "The 1914 Case," *American Political Science Review*, 59 (June 1965), pp. 375–376; Hermann, *International Crisis*; and Pearson, *The Weak State in International Crisis*.

38. Irving L. Janis, *Groupthink*, 2nd ed. (Boston: Houghton Mifflin, 1982). Also see G. M. Herek, Irving L. Janis, and Paul Huth, "Decision Making During International Crises: Is Quality of Process Related to Outcome?," *Journal of Conflict Resolution*, 31 (1987), pp. 203–226; and Paul 't Hart, *Groupthink in Government* (Amsterdam: Swets and Zetlinger, 1990).

39. See Margaret G. Hermann, Charles F. Hermann, and Joe D. Hagan, "How Decision Units Shape Foreign Policy Behavior," in Charles F. Hermann et al., eds., *New Directions in the Study of Foreign Policy* (Boston: Allen and Unwin, 1987), pp. 309–338.

40. Patrick J. McGarvey, "DIA: Intelligence to Please," in Halperin and Kanter, *Readings*, p. 325; reprinted from *The Washington Monthly*, July 1970. For a look at organizational routines and information processing problems in a country such as India, see Yaacov Vertzberger, "Bureaucratic-Organizational Politics and Information Processing in a Developing State," *International Studies Quarterly*, 28 (March 1984), pp. 69–95.

41. Cited in Allison, *Essence of Decision*, p. 193.

42. Theodore Sorenson, *Kennedy* (New York: Harper and Row, 1965), p. 675. Also see Fen Osler Hampson, "The Divided Decision-Maker: American Domestic Politics and the Cuban Crisis," *International Security*, Winter 1984–85, pp. 130–165.

43. The remark has been attributed to James F. Byrnes, Secretary of State under President Truman.

44. Cited in David V. Edwards, *The American Political Experience* (Englewood Cliffs, N.J.: Prentice-Hall, 1979), p. 223.

45. Edward L. Katzenbach, "The Horse Cavalry in the Twentieth Century," *Public Policy*, 8 (1958), pp. 120–149.

46. Deborah Shapley, "Technological Creep and the Arms Race: ICBM Problem a Sleeper," *Science*, 201 (September 22, 1978), p. 105. For a discussion of the impact of bureaucractic pressures on Soviet perceptions of international reality, see Vernon V. Aspaturian, "The Soviet Military-Industrial Complex: Does It Exist?" in Steven Rosen, ed. *Testing the Theory of the Military-Industrial Complex* (Lexington, Mass.: Lexington Books, 1973), pp. 103–134; and Andrew Cockburn, *The Threat: Inside the Soviet Military Machine* (New York: Random House, 1983). On the reasons behind past U.S. and Soviet weapons procurement policies, see James Kurth, "Why We Buy the Weapons We Do," *Foreign Policy*, 11 (Summer 1973), pp. 33–56; and Matthew A. Evangelista, "Why the Soviets Buy the Weapons They Do," *World Politics*, 36 (July 1984), pp. 597–618. Interestingly, Russia continued to have a penchant for developing missiles in fours even in the 1990s, as reported in the *St. Louis Post-Dispatch*, October 18, 1990, p. 14A.

47. Robert Kennedy, for example, commenting on the necessity of a U.S. naval blockade during the Cuban missile crisis, said, "I just don't think there was any choice." Robert F. Kennedy, *Thirteen Days* (New York: W. W. Norton, 1971), p. 45.

48. See L. L. Farrar, "The Limits of Choice: July 1914 Reconsidered," *Journal of Conflict Resolution*, 16 (March 1972), pp. 1–23.

49.   James C. March and Herbert A. Simon, *Organizations* (New York: John Wiley, 1958); and Herbert A. Simon, *Administrative Behavior*, 2nd ed. (New York: Free Press, 1957).

50.   De Rivera, *Psychological Dimension*, p. 139.

51.   Janis, *Groupthink*, p. 3.

52.   See Hannes Adomeit, *Soviet Risk-Taking Behavior: A Theoretical and Empirical Analysis* (London: George Allen and Unwin, 1982), pp. 44–49.

53.   For a discussion of implementation problems, see Michael Clarke, "Foreign Policy Implementation: Problems and Approaches," *British Journal of International Studies*, 5 (1979), pp. 112–128; and Halperin, *Bureaucratic Politics*, chs. 13–15. A number of interesting case studies are contained in Steve Smith and Michael Clarke, eds., *Foreign Policy Implementation* (London: Allen and Unwin, 1985).

54.   Richard E. Neustadt, *Presidential Power*, 2nd ed. (New York: John Wiley, 1976), p. 77.

55.   Hilsman, *To Move a Nation*, p. 221.

56.   The complete incident is discussed in Allison, *Essence of Decision*, pp. 131–132.

57.   See Dan Caldwell, "The Cuban Missile Affair and the American Style of Crisis Management," *Parameters*, 19 (March 1989), pp. 49–60, drawing on information in Raymond L. Garthoff, *Reflections on the Cuban Missile Crisis* (Washington, D.C.: Brookings Institution, 1987), pp. 62–63, and J. Anthony Lukas, "Class Reunion: Kennedy's Men Relive the Cuban Missile Crisis," *New York Times Magazine* (August 30, 1987), p. 51.

58.   An excellent examination of the "lessons" seemingly learned by American leaders from the Vietnam experience, based on a "foreign policy leadership" opinion survey, can be found by Olé R. Holsti and James N. Rosenau, "Cold War Axioms in the Post-Vietnam Era," in Olé R. Holsti et al., eds., *Change in the International System* (Boulder, Colo.: Westview Press, 1980), pp. 263–301. On lessons from the Cuban missile crisis, see James G. Blight, Joseph S. Nye, and David A. Welch, "The Cuban Missile Crisis Revisited," *Foreign Affairs*, 66 (Fall 1987), pp. 170–188.

59.   In an extensive discussion of the Strategic Bombing Surveys, Bernard Brodie notes that the aerial bombing of German cities did lower German morale somewhat but did not have much effect on the ability of the German economic and military machine to continue functioning. See Bernard Brodie, *Strategy in the Missile Age* (Princeton, N.J.: Princeton University Press, 1959), pp. 131–138. In a personal account, John Kenneth Galbraith reports similar conclusions and notes that the Air Force attempted to summarize the USSBS in a way that inflated the success of their bombing missions. See *A Life in our Times: Memoirs* (Boston: Houghton Mifflin, 1982), chs. 13 and 14.

60.   Janis, *Groupthink*, p. 157. Robert Kennedy was further quoted as saying "my brother is not going to be the Tojo of the 1960s," referring to the Japanese commander who ordered the Pearl Harbor attacks; cited in Ronald Steel, "The Kennedys and the Missile Crisis," in Halperin and Kanter, *Readings*, p. 205. According to Theodore Sorenson, Robert Kennedy had intended to address the general question of morality in international relations in his memoirs, before his life was abruptly ended by assassination in 1968; see Kennedy, *Thirteen Days*, p. 106.

61.   James Lee Ray, "The Abolition of Slavery and the End of International War," *International Organization*, 43 (Summer 1989), pp. 405–439. Also see Note 31.

62.   See Paul A. Anderson, "Justification and Precedents as Constraints in Foreign Policy Decision-Making," *American Journal of Political Science*, 25 (November 1981), pp. 738–761.

63.   There have been many different interpretations of the A-bomb decision and why U.S. leaders felt it necessary to use such a weapon. For various views on this, see Len Giovannitti and Fred Freed, *The Decision to Drop the Bomb* (New York: Coward-McCann, 1965). One can also read the many retrospectives published in major newspapers in 1995, on the occasion of the fiftieth anniversary of the A-bomb decision.

64.   In one conventional bombing raid on Tokyo, only a few months before Hiroshima, over 80,000 persons died. This was less than the number of Japanese deaths reported at Hiroshima in 1945. It must be noted, however, that not all Hiroshima casualties have been

accounted for. Additional casualties beyond those originally counted are still being uncovered because of the long-term effects of radiation causing cancer and other diseases. The Hiroshima victims would have been more numerous had the atomic bomb exploded at ground level rather than as an air burst.

65. On this point, see Herek, Janis, and Huth, "Decision Making During International Crises," p. 203.

66. Quoted by Allison, *Essence of Decision*, p. 131.

Chapter 7. Playing the Game of International Relations: Diplomacy before Force

1. Patrick James, Eric Solberg, and Murray Wolfson, "An Identified Systemic Test of the Democracy-Peace Nexus," paper presented at the Annual Meeting of the Peace Science Society (international), Columbus, Ohio, October 1995, p. 9.

2. J. David Singer, "Accounting for International War: The State of the Discipline," *Annual Review of Sociology*, 6, (1960), p. 353. War is defined and identified according to type of combat, participants, and number of battle-related casualties. Put a bit differently, between 1816 and 1976, states involved in serious international disputes, including at least the threatened use of force, pulled back from the brink of war in nine of ten cases. See Charles S. Gochman and Zeev Moas, "Militarized Interstate Disputes, 1816–1976," in *International War: An Anthology and Study Guide*, Melvin Small and J. David Singer, eds. (Homewood, Ill: Dorsey Press, 1985), pp. 27–36. Other researchers have found many more major-power incidents, though not necessarily "serious" ones, and a considerable frequency of wars involving minor powers, especially in the twentieth century. See Barry M. Blechman and Stephen S. Kaplan, *Force Without War* (Washington, D.C.: Brookings Institution, 1978); Istvan Kende, "Twenty-five Years of Local Wars," *Journal of Peace Research*, 8, no. 1 (1971), pp. 5–22; and Kende, "Wars of Ten Years," *Journal of Peace Research*, 15, no. 3 (1978), pp. 227–241.

3. See Roger Fisher, William Ury, and Bruce Patton, *Getting to Yes: Negotiating Agreement Without Giving In*, 2nd ed. (New York: Penguin, 1991); and Roger Fisher and Scott Brown, *Getting Together: Building Relationships As We Negotiate* (New York: Penguin, 1989).

4. Sir Harold Nicolson, *Diplomacy* (1939; reprint, New York: Oxford University Press, 1964), pp. 4–5.

5. Sir Harold Nicolson, *The Evolution of Diplomacy* (London: Constable, 1956), pp. 50–51.

6. Ibid., p. 63

7. *Washington Post*, April 13, 1990, p. A7.

8. George Ball, *Diplomacy for a Crowded World* (Boston: Little, Brown, 1976), pp. 35–36. To these summit pitfalls, one should add the possibility of mistaken identity, as when President Bush evidently spoke by telephone in 1990 to a man impersonating Iranian president Ali Akbar Hashami Rafsanjani in a conversation about international hostages. *Washington Post*, April 13, 1990, p. A7.

9. Canadian Prime Minister Lester Pearson once suggested that the best formula is "open covenants secretly arrived at." See Abba Eban, "The UN Idea Revisited," *Foreign Affairs* (September/October 1995), p. 48.

10. Patrick J. McGowan and Howard B. Shapiro, *The Comparative Study of Foreign Policy* (Beverly Hills, Calif.: Sage, 1973), p. 140. For research studies, see Michael K. O'Leary, "Linkages Between Domestic and International Politics in Underdeveloped Nations," in James N. Rosenau, ed., *Linkage Politics* (New York: Free Press, 1969), pp. 324–326; and Elmer Plishke, *Microstates in World Affairs* (Washington, D.C.: American Enterprise Institute, 1977), ch. 4.

11. See Jacob Bercovitch and Jeffrey Z. Rubin, eds., *Mediation in International Relations* (New York: St. Martin's Press, 1992); Jacob Bercovitz and Jeffrey Langley, "The Nature of the Dispute and the Effectiveness of International Mediation," *Journal of Conflict*

Resolution, 37 (December 1993), pp. 670–691; and Jacob Bercovitch and James W. Lamare, "The Process of International Mediation: An Analysis of the Determinants of Successful and Unsuccessful Outcomes," *American Journal of Political Science, 28* (July 1993), pp. 290–305.

12. On negotiations in general, see Linda P. Brady, *The Politics of Negotiation: America's Dealings With Allies, Adversaries, and Friends* (Chapel Hill: University of North Carolina Press, 1991).

13. Robert D. Putnam, "Diplomacy and Domestic Politics: The Logic of Two-Level Games," *International Organization, 42* (Summer 1988), p. 434.

14. Robert S. Strauss, "Foreword," in Joan E. Twiggs, *The Tokyo Round of Multilateral Trade Negotiations: A Case Study in Building Domestic Support for Diplomacy* (Washington, D.C.: Georgetown University Institute for the Study of Diplomacy, 1987), p. vii; cited in Putnam, "Diplomacy," p. 433.

15. From Howard Raiffa, *The Art and Science of Negotiation* (Cambridge, Mass.: Harvard University Press, 1982), p. 166; cited in Putnam, "Diplomacy," p. 433.

16. Maria Cowles, *The Politics of Big Busines in the European Community,* Ph.D. dissertation. The American University, 1994. Also see Vivien Schmidt, "The New World Order, Incorporated," *Daedalus, 124* (Spring 1995), pp. 75–106.

17. Putnam believes the prevalence of "two-level games" in international negotiations can be found in bargaining over security as well as nonsecurity issues and is nothing new. He attempts to show how game-playing at one level affects game-playing at the other level. See also Peter B. Evans, Harold K. Jacobson, and Robert D. Putnam, *Double-Edged Diplomacy: International Bargaining and Domestic Politics* (Berkeley: University of California Press, 1993).

18. Indeed, an organization called "Search for Common Ground," based in Washington, D.C., has been at work for a number of years seeking informal dialogue among conflicting parties all over the world—even opening operations in Moscow after the fall of the Soviet Union and running television documentaries on the virtues of peaceful bargaining. One definition of conflict sees it as "perceived divergence of interests, or a belief that the parties' current aspirations cannot be achieved simultaneously." Jeffrey Z. Rubin, Dean G. Pruitt, and Sung Hee Kim, *Social Conflict: Escalation, Stalemate, and Settlement,* 2nd ed. (New York: McGraw-Hill, 1994), p. 5.

19. On the potential role of emotions, see Steven Brams, "Game Theory and Emotions," paper presented at Annual Meeting of the Peace Science Society (International), Columbus, October 1995.

20. Raiffa, *The Art and Science of Negotiation,* pp. 176-177.

21. Rubin, Pruitt, and Kim, *Social Conflict,* pp. 5–6 and chs. 2–3.

22. This point is made very well in regard to international bargaining by Christopher Dupont and Guy-Olivier Favre, "The Negotiation Process," in Victor A. Kremenyuk, ed., *International Negotiation* (San Francisco: Jossey-Bass, 1991), ch. 3. If the players expect that bargaining is not a one-shot exercise but will occur over an extended period with a series of moves and countermoves, this will affect behavior. Frank C. Zagare, "Nonmyopic Equilibria and the Middle East Crisis of 1967," *Conflict Management and Peace Science, 5* (Spring 1981), pp. 139–162; Zagare, *The Dynamics of Deterrence* (Chicago: University of Chicago Press, 1987); and Steven J. Brams and Donald Wittman, "Nonmyopic Equilibria in 2 x 2 Games," *Conflict Management and Peace Science, 6* (Fall 1982), pp. 39–62.

23. The bargaining that occurred over Berlin is discussed among many other examples and cases in Glenn H. Snyder and Paul Diesing, *Conflict Among Nations* (Princeton, N.J.: Princeton University Press, 1977), p. 69.

24. Thomas C. Schelling, *The Strategy of Conflict* (New York: Oxford University Press, 1960), pp. 55–56.

25. The distinction between compellence and deterrence is discussed in Thomas C. Schelling, *Arms and Influence* (New Haven, Conn.: Yale University Press, 1966), pp. 69–78. One

would ordinarily expect states to exploit the possibilities of promises and threats before employing rewards and punishments. It would seem logical to provide rewards only *after* some *desired* behavior has taken place, either to fulfill an earlier promise or to reinforce continuation of the desired behavior. Likewise, punishments would seem appropriate only *after* some *undesired* behavior persists. However, states do not always follow the logic of delaying rewards and punishments until promises and threats have been tried. Sometimes punishment is meted out early in the bargaining process, when it is thought that mere threats will be insufficient; sometimes rewards are bestowed early also, as bribes to induce cooperation.

26. Henry A. Kissinger, *American Foreign Policy* (New York: W. W. Norton, 1974), p. 61.

27. John P. Lovell, *Foreign Policy in Perspective* (New York: Holt, Rinehart, and Winston, 1970), p. 80.

28. See Schelling, *Arms and Influence*, especially ch. 2 on "The Art of Commitment" as well as his *Strategy of Conflict.*

29. The literature has ranged from Anatol Rapoport's *Fights, Games, and Debates* (Ann Arbor: University of Michigan Press, 1960) and John von Neumann and Oscar Morgenstern's *Theory of Games and Economic Behavior* (Princeton, N.J.: Princeton University Press, 1964) to Steven Brams' "Game Theory and Emotions." Latest developments in game theoretical analysis are presented in the *Journal of Conflict Resolution.*

30. See Snyder and Diesing, *Conflict Among Nations*, ch. 2.

31. On such constructive solutions and the need to keep future plays of the game in mind, see Robert Axelrod, *The Evolution of Cooperation* (New York: Basic Books, 1985); Charles E. Osgood, *An Alternative to War or Surrender* (Urbana: University of Illinois Press, 1962); and Dupont and Olivier-Favre, "The Negotiation Process." Steven Brams has noted that emotions such as anger or frustration may be integral parts of game structures and bargaining; as such, they influence the utilities or values attached to various moves. This means that instead of eliminating emotions in negotiation, one should study them because they affect the potential for mutual satisfaction in game outcomes. See Brams, "Game Theory and Emotions."

32. Among those questioning military power has been Richard Rosecrance, *The Rise of the Trading State: Commerce and Conquest in the Modern World* (New York: Basic Books, 1986). Among those more sure of its continued relevance, see Robert J. Art, "To What Ends Military Power?," *International Security*, 4 (Spring 1980), pp. 3–35; also see the works cited in Note 30 in Chapter 3.

33. See Klaus Knorr, *The Power of Nations: The Political Economy of International Relations* (New York: Basic Books, 1975), pp. 7–8; and Andrew J. Pierre, *The Global Politics of Arms Sales* (Princeton, N.J.: Princeton University Press, 1982).

34. Throughout history, and particularly in the twentieth century, militarily superior states have sometimes failed to deter attacks from weaker states. See Raoul Naroll, *Military Deterrence in History* (Albany: State University of New York Press, 1974), p. 328; Bruce M. Russett, "The Calculus of Deterrence," *Journal of Conflict Resolution*, 7 (June 1963), pp. 97–109; and Russett, *The Prisoners of Insecurity: Nuclear Deterrence, the Arms Race, and Arms Control* (San Francisco: W. H. Freeman, 1983).

35. Russett, "Calculus," pp. 106–108. See also Paul Huth and Russett, "What Makes Deterrence Work?," *World Politics*, 36 (July 1984), pp. 496–526; Huth and Russett, "Deterrence Failure and Crisis Escalation," *International Studies Quarterly*, 32 (March 1988), pp. 29–45; and Clinton Fink, "More Calculations about Deterrence," in Naomi Rosenbaum, ed., *Readings on the International Political System* (Englewood Cliffs, N.J.: Prentice-Hall, 1970), p. 191.

36. Richard Ned Lebow, *Between Peace and War: The Nature of International Crisis* (Baltimore: Johns Hopkins University Press, 1981), pp. 274–275.

37. See David A. Baldwin, *Economic Statecraft* (Princeton, N.J.: Princeton University Press, 1985).

38. Knorr, *The Power of Nations*, pp. 134–138; and Knorr, "International Economic Leverage and Its Uses," in Knorr and Frank N. Trager, eds., *Economic Issues and National Security* (Lawrence, Kans.: Regents Press of Kansas, 1977), ch. 4.

39. Knorr, "Economic Leverage," p. 103.

40. This relates to earlier comments in Chapter 3. See Robert O. Keohane and Joseph S. Nye, *Power and Interdependence*, 2nd ed. (Boston: Little, Brown, 1989), pp. 12–19.

41. Roy Licklider, "The Power of Oil: The Arab Oil Weapon and the Netherlands, the United Kingdom, Canada, Japan, and the United States," *International Studies Quarterly*, 32 (June 1988), p. 207.

42. Peter Wallensteen, "Characteristics of Economic Sanctions," *Journal of Peace Research*, 5, no. 3 (1968), pp. 248–267; such findings are further substantiated by Magaret P. Doxey, *Economic Sanctions and International Enforcement*, 2nd ed. (New York: Oxford University Press, 1980), ch. 2.

43. Knorr, *The Power of Nations*. One study of 103 cases of economic sanctions since 1914 identifies certain "limited circumstances" in which they can work; see Gary Hufbauer and Jeffrey Schott, *Economic Sanctions in Support of Foreign Policy Goals* (Washington, D.C.: Institute for International Economics, 1983). James T. Lindsay has shown that while trade sanctions usually fail if the goal is compliance, subversion, or deterrence, they retain great appeal as international and domestic political symbols. See Lindsay, "Trade Sanctions as Policy Instruments: A Reexamination." *International Studies Quarterly*, 30 (June 1986), pp. 153–173. See also Lori Fisler Damrosch, "The Collective Enforcement of International Norms Through Economic Sanctions," *Ethics and International Affairs*, 8 (1994), pp. 59–75; and Li Chien-Pin, "The Effectiveness of Sanction Linkages: Issues and Actors," *International Studies Quarterly*, 37 (September 1993), pp. 349–370.

44. On the 1973 Arab oil embargo and the attempted use of the "oil weapon" against the United States and Western States, see Stephen D. Krasner, "The Great Oil Sheikdown," *Foreign Policy*, no. 13 (Winter 1973–74), pp. 123–138; Hanns Maull, "Oil and Influence: The Oil Weapon Examined," in Knorr and Trager, *Economic Issues*, ch. 10; also, Knorr, "The Limits of Economic and Military Power," in Raymond Vernon, ed., *The Oil Crisis* (New York: W. W. Norton, 1976), pp. 229–243; and Licklider, "The Power of Oil."

45. As with trade, the effectiveness of cutting off capital also depends on the availability of other states to fill the breach as aid donors or investors. On the relationship of aid to influence, see Joan M. Nelson, *Aid, Influence, and Foreign Policy* (New York: Macmillan, 1968); and Philip G. Roder, "The Ties that Bind: Aid, Trade, and Political Compliance in Soviet-Third World Relations," *International Studies Quarterly*, 29 (June 1985), pp. 191–216. On the relationship between capital investment and influence, see Keohane and Nye, *Power and Interdependence*, ch. 7.

46. See Richard S. Olson, "Economic Coercion in World Politics," *World Politics*, 31 (July 1979), pp. 471–494.

47. The definition has been attributed to Sir Henry Wooten, an ambassador of King James I of England in the seventeenth century; cited in Arthur Lall, *Modern International Negotiation* (New York: University Press, 1966), p. 151.

48. Cited in David J. Dallin, *Soviet Foreign Policy After Stalin* (Philadelphia: J. B. Lippincott, 1961), p. 9.

49. Nicolson, *Diplomacy*, pp. 55–67.

50. Off the record briefing by an American diplomatic negotiator, Council on Foreign Relations meeting, Detroit, October 1995.

51. Willem F. G. Mastenbroek, "Development of Negotiating Skills," in Kremenyuk, ed., *International Negotiation*, p. 382.

52. Roger Fisher, *International Conflict for Beginners* (New York: Harper and Row, 1969).

53. Ibid., p. 11.

54. Raiffa, *The Art and Science of Negotiation*, pp. 209–219.

55. Miles Copeland, *The Game of Nations: The Amorality of Power Politics* (London: Weidenfeld and Nicolson, 1969).

56. Ibid., p. 9.

Chapter 8. Breakdown in the Game: The Resort to Armed Force

1. Claudio Cioffi-Revilla, "Origins and Evolution of War and Politics," *International Studies Quarterly*, 40 (March 1996), pp. 1–22.

2. The quote, based on the findings of Norman Cousins, is from Francis A. Beer, *Peace Against War: The Ecology of International Violence* (San Francisco: W. H. Freeman, 1981), p. 20.

3. Anthony Sampson, "Want to Start a War?" *Esquire* (March 1978), p. 60.

4. Stockholm International Peace Research Institute (SIPRI), *Yearbook of World Armaments and Disarmament* (Stockholm: Almqvist and Wiksell, 1976), p. 48.

5. Peter Wallensteen and Karin Axell, "Major Armed Conflicts," *SIPRI Yearbook 1994* (Oxford: Oxford University Press, 1994), ch. 2.

6. See James Lee Ray, "The Abolition of Slavery and the End of International War," *International Organization*, 43 (Summer 1989), pp. 405–439; Werner Levi, *The Coming End of War* (Beverly Hills, Calif.: Sage, 1981); John Mueller, *Retreat from Doomsday: The Obsolescence of Major War* (New York: Basic Books, 1989), and *Quiet Cataclysm* (New York: Harper Collins, 1995); and Carl Kaysen, "Is War Obsolete? A Review Essay," *International Security*, 14 (Spring 1990), pp. 42–64. See also R. C. Smith, "After Van Creveld: The Moral Future of War," *Political Science*, 44 (July 1992), pp. 47–56. Note, as well, that some forms of involuntary servitude resembling slavery still exist in some parts of the world, especially among women and children.

7. Karl von Clausewitz, *On War*, Anatol Rapoport, ed. (Baltimore: Penguin, 1968), p. 410.

8. Albert Einstein, correspondence with Sigmund Freud, in Robert Goldwin and Tony Pearce, eds., *Reading in World Politics* (New York: Oxford University Press, 1970), p. 125.

9. They were both members of OPEC, and continued to conduct diplomacy on the issue of oil supply and pricing.

10. See Bruce Bueno de Mesquita, *The War Trap* (New Haven: Yale University Press, 1981); Bueno de Mesquita, "*The War Trap* Revisited," *American Political Science Review*, 79 (March 1985), pp. 156–177; Bueno de Mesquita and David Lalman, "Reason and War," *American Political Science Review*, 80 (December 1986), pp. 1113–1129; and *Reason and War* (New Haven: Yale University Press, 1992).

11. Lloyd Jensen, *Explaining Foreign Policy* (Englewood Cliffs, N.J.: Prentice-Hall, 1982), p. 217. Premises of *The War Trap* are also questioned in Stephen J. Majeski and David J. Sylvan, "Simple Choices and Complex Calculations: A Critique of *The War Trap*," *Journal of Conflict Resolution*, 28 (June 1984), pp. 316–340; Harrison Wagner, "War and Expected Utility Theory," *World Politics*, 36 (September 1983), pp. 407–432; and Michael Nicholson, "The Conceptual Bases of *The War Trap*," *Journal of Conflict Resolution*, 31 (June 1987), pp. 346–359.

12. Of course, wars also can end in deadlock or stalemate without being won or lost. On war settlement, see Robert F. Randle, *The Origins of Peace: A Study of Peacemaking and the Structure of Peace Settlements* (New York: Free Press, 1973); and Sydney D. Bailey, *How Wars End: The United Nations and the Termination of Armed Conflict, 1946–1964*, 2 vols. (Oxford: Clarendon, 1982). For a fuller classification of more or less complex wars, see also, Manus I. Midlarsky, *On War: Political Violence in the International System* (New York: Free Press, 1975), pp. 8–14.

13. Randolph M Siverson, "Thinking about Puzzles in the Study of International War," Presidential Address, Annual Meeting of Peace Science Society (International), Columbus, Ohio, October 1995; see also Bruce Bueno de Mesquita and Randolph Siverson, "War and the Survival of Political Leaders," *American Political Science Review*, 89 (December 1995), pp. 841–855. In his presidential address (p. 5), Siverson went on to argue that "the expansion of a war beyond the original parties significantly decreases the probability that the initiator will win when compared with a baseline of the outcomes found in wars that do not expand."

14. See Siverson, "Puzzles," p. 11. Using game theory analysis, Bueno de Mesquita and Kim maintain that misperception can, depending on circumstances, lead either to peace or war; see Woosang Kim and Bruce Bueno de Mesquita, "How Perceptions Influence the Risk of War," *International Studies Quarterly*, 39 (March 1995), pp. 51–65. On war as a test of uncertainty about overall superiority, and the optimism unaccountably shared by all sides in many wars, see Geoffrey Blainey, *The Causes of War* (New York: Free Press, 1973).

15. On such distortions, see Dagobert L. Brito and Michael D. Intrilligator, "Conflict, War, and Redistribution," *American Political Science Review*, 79 (December 1985), p. 945; and Jack S. Levy, "Misperception and the Causes of War: Theoretical Linkages and Analytical Problems," *World Politics*, 36 (October 1983), pp. 76–99.

16. See Albert Einstein and Sigmund Freud, "Why War?," *International Journal for the Reduction of Group Tensions*, 1 (January–March 1971), pp. 9–25; Freud, *Civilization and Its Discontents*, J. Strachey, ed. and trans. (New York: W. W. Norton, 1962), p. 58; and *The Standard Edition of the Complete Psychological Works of Sigmund Freud*, J. Strachey, ed. (London: Hogarth Press, 1953–54), vols. 14 and 22, for a comparison with Freud's early, more pessimistic views on controlling or abolishing war.

17. See the work of Konrad Lorenz, *On Aggression* (New York: Bantam, 1967).

18. See Ivo K. Feierabend, Rosalind J. Feierabend, and Ted R. Gurr, eds., *Anger, Violence, and Politics* (Englewood Cliffs, N.J.: Prentice-Hall, 1972); Gurr, ed., *Handbook of Conflict Theory and Research* (New York: Free Press, 1980); and John Burton, ed., *Human Needs Theory* (New York: St. Martin's Press, 1990).

19. See Ted R. Gurr and V. F. Bishop, "Violent Nations and Others," *Journal of Conflict Resolution*, 20 (March 1976), pp. 79–110; and Frank Klingberg, "The Historical Alteration of Moods in American Foreign Policy," *World Politics*, 4 (March 1952), pp. 239–273.

20. See D. Fabbro, "Peaceful Societies: An Introduction," *Journal of Peace Research*, 15, no. 1 (1978), pp. 67–83; and Ashley Montagu, *The Nature of Human Aggression* (New York: Oxford University Press, 1976). Those who claim that some societies are entirely peaceful have been challenged by others who attribute pacification largely to outside powers forcing local tribes to settle disputes.

21. The disease analogy is fully explored in Beer, *Peace Against War*, esp. ch. 1; and criticized by Urs Luterbacher, "Last Words About War? A Review Article," *Journal of Conflict Resolution*, 28 (March 1984), pp. 165–182.

22. See Philip D. Zelikow, "Force Without War, 1975–82," *The Journal of Strategic Studies*, 7 (March 1984), pp. 29–54.

23. George Will, "Defense Cuts Reflect Liberals' Blind Optimism in Lasting Peace," *St. Louis Post-Dispatch*, July 17, 1995, p. 6B, citing Kagan, *On the Origins of War*.

24. Joseph S. Nye, Jr., "Conflicts after the Cold War," *The Washington Quarterly* (Winter 1996), p. 5.

25. See Melvin Small and J. David Singer, "Patterns in International Warfare, 1816–1980," in Small and Singer, eds., *International War: An Anthology and Study Guide* (Homewood, Ill.: Dorsey Press, 1985); Small and Singer, "Conflict in the International System, 1816–1977: Historical Trends and Policy Futures," in Charles W. Kegley, Jr. and Patrick J. McGowan, eds., *Challenges to America: United States Foreign Policy in the 1980s* (Beverly Hills, Calif.: Sage, 1979), pp. 89–115; and Ray, "Abolition of Slavery," p. 426. The problems involved in developing an operational definition of war and measuring its occurrence are discussed in Singer and Small, *The Wages of War, 1816–1965: A Statistical Handbook* (New York: John Wiley, 1972), pp. 1–39.

26. Figures are derived from Jack S. Levy and T. Clifton Morgan, "The Frequency and Seriousness of International War: An Inverse Relationship," *Journal of Conflict Resolution*, 28,

(December 1984), p. 742. On increased casualties, see also Beer, *Peace Against War*, ch. 2; and Gwynn Dyer, *War* (Homewood, Ill.: Dorsey Press, 1985). It is important to note that so-phisticated weaponry is not the only reason for high war casualties; in some cases, wanton killing has taken place with relatively primitive arms, such as the use of machetes in the Honduras–El Salvador "football" war of the 1960s and in the repeated ethnic bloodbaths in-side Rwanda and Burundi in Africa.

27. See Harold K. Jacobson, *Networks of Interdependence*, 2nd ed. (New York: Knopf, 1984), p. 192; and Small and Singer, "Conflict in the International System," pp. 97–99.

28. See Beer, *Peace Against War*, p. 41. In the study of 118 wars from 1816 to 1980, Melvin Small concludes that "international war appears to be neither on the rise or the decline." Small and Singer, "Patterns in International Warfare, 1816–1980," p. 13.

29. Jack Levy, *War in the Modern Great Power System, 1495–1975* (Lexington, Ky.: University of Kentucky Press, 1983), p. 130.

30. See Charles W. Kegley, Jr., "The Long Postwar Peace During the Cold War: Some New Con-ventional Wisdoms Reconsidered," *Jerusalem Journal of International Relations*, 14 (De-cember 1992), pp. 1–18.

31. Nye has noted that "conflicts with the greatest potential for devastation—great power con-flicts over the global balance of power"—have become least likely; "regional balance of power conflicts like the Persian Gulf War are more probable than world wars," and inter-nal, or "communal" conflicts within states "are likely to be the prevalent form of con-flict." See Nye, "Conflicts after the Cold War," p. 6.

32. Barry M. Blechman and Stephen S. Kaplan, *Force Without War: U. S. Armed Forces as a Po-litical Instrument* (Washington, D.C.: Brookings Institution, 1979); and Kaplan, *Diplomacy of Power: Soviet Armed Forces as a Political Instrument* (Washington, D.C.: Brookings In-stitution, 1981).

33. William Eckhardt and Edward A. Azar, "Major World Conflicts and Interventions, 1945–1975," *International Interactions*, 5 (1978), pp. 78–83.

34. Andrew Selsky, "Peru-Ecuador Feud Dates Back A Half-Century," *St. Louis Post-Dispatch*, February 1, 1995.

35. The concept of "diplomacy of violence" is developed by Thomas Schelling in *Arms and In-fluence* (New Haven: Yale University Press, 1966), ch. 1. The concept of "coercive diplo-macy" is developed by Alexander L. George, David K. Hall, and William R. Simons in *The Limits of Coercive Diplomacy* (Boston: Little, Brown, 1971). See, also, *Forceful Persuasion: Coercive Diplomacy as an Alternative to War* (Washington, D.C.: United States Institute of Peace Press, 1991).

36. This tactic might have chastened Libya's Mohammar Qadaffi and reduced his support of in-ternational terrorists, but it also evidently resulted in the killing of some of his family members, thus undoubtedly increasing his bitterness and unwillingness to cooperate diplo-matically with the United States subsequently—for example, as Washington sought to ob-tain the release of individuals accused in the bombing of a Pan-Am flight over Lockerbie, Scotland.

37. Glen H. Snyder and Paul Diesing, *Conflict Among Nations: Bargaining, Decision Making, and System Structure in International Crises* (Princeton, N.J.: Princeton Uniiversity Press, 1977), pp. 453–455. See, also, Stephen Blank, "Afghanistan and Beyond: Reflections on the Future of Warfare," *Small Wars and Insurgency*, 3 (Winter 1993), pp. 217–240.

38. Roy L. Prosterman, *Surviving to 3000* (Belmont, Calif.: Duxbury Press, 1973), p. 33.

39. See Project Ploughshares, *Armed Conflicts Report 1995* (Waterloo, Canada: Institute of Peace and Conflict Studies, Spring 1995), p. 4; and Peter Wallensteen and Karin Axell, "Major Armed Conflicts," pp. 81–83. On general trends in civil war, see Melvin Small and J. David Singer, *Resort to Arms: International and Civil Wars, 1816–1980* (Beverly Hills, Calif.: Sage, 1982); Eckhardt and Azar, "Major World Conflict"; and Eckhardt, "Wars Started in the 1980s," St. Louis: Lentz Peace Research Laboratory monograph (1990).

40. "The World's Wars," *The Economist*, March 12, 1988, pp. 19–20.

41. *Armed Conflicts Report,* p. 3.

42. Small and Singer, "Conflict in the International System," p. 100. See also, Istvan Kende, "Twenty-Five Years of Local Wars," *Journal of Peace Research,* 8, no. 1 (1971), pp. 5–22; and Herbert Tillema, "Foreign Overt Military Intervention, International Armed Conflict, and Contemporary International War," unpublished manuscript.

43. Ted Gurr argues that "the post–Cold War surge in so-called tribal conflict is . . . the continuation of a trend that began in the 1960s." See his "Peoples Against States: Ethnopolitical Conflict and the Changing World System" *International Studies Quarterly,* 38 (September 1994), p. 347. The latter article contains an analysis of ethnopolitical conflict between 1945 and 1994.

44. Michael Brecher and Jonathan Wilkenfeld, "The Ethnic Dimension in Twentieth-Century Crises," paper presented at the Annual Meeting of the International Studies Association, Chicago, February 1995, p. 2; and David Carment, "The International Dimensions of Ethnic Conflict: Concept, Indicators, and Theory," *Journal of Peace Research,* 30, no. 2 (1993), pp. 137–150. The latter argues that ethnic conflict "is an important explanatory variable in analyzing levels of interstate violence" (p. 145). Also, see Joane Nagel, "Ethnic Nationalism: Politics, Ideology, and the World Order," *International Journal of Comparative Sociology,* 34 (January–April 1993), pp. 103–121.

45. In Rwanda, for example, people evidently were threatened by militia forces with death unless they in turn participated in mass killings of their neighbors. On the processes whereby ethnic grievances are formed and expressed, see Ted Robert Gurr, "Why Minorities Rebel: A Global Analysis of Communal Mobilization and Conflict Since 1945," *International Political Science Review,* 14 (April 1993), pp. 161–201; and Klaus Schlichte, "Is Ethnicity a Cause of War?," *Peace Review* 6 (Spring 1994) pp. 59–65.

46. *Armed Conflicts Report 1995,* p. 3.

47. Wallensteen and Axell, "Major Armed Conflicts," p. 82. See also, Schlichte, "Is Ethnicity a Cause of War?, pp. 59–65.

48. Carment, "The International Dimensions of Ethnic Conflict." Carment points out that ethnicity can be a changing attribute, often self-ascribed to people or ascribed to them by others. (Race is especially dependent on subjective definitions, because there is very little difference detectable in genetic or physical structure among groups of people). In addition, he notes that ethnic motives have long been part of international warfare, under the heading of "irredentist" efforts to reunite ethnically similar peoples and reclaim their territories across national borders. Among those who have classified ethnic groups as people "at risk," see Ted Robert Gurr, *Minorities at Risk: Origins and Outcomes of Ethnopolitical Conflicts* (Washington, D.C.: U.S. Institute of Peace, 1993).

49. Between 1989 and 1992, only three of the eighty-two armed conflicts underway, as identified by the United Nations, were cross-border conflicts between countries. John G. Mason, "Failing Nations: What U.S. Response?," *Great Decisions* (Washington, D.C.: Foreign Policy Association, 1996) p. 52. In another study, the authors found relatively few interstate wars occurring between 1989 and 1995, although there was at least one such war annually with the exception of 1993 and 1994; Peter Wallenstein and Margareta Sollenberg, "The End of International War? Armed Conflict 1989–95," *Journal of Peace Research,* 33, no. 3 (1996), pp. 353–370. Among those who conclude that patterns of international violence have shown little pronounced change in the immediate post–Cold War period are Peter Wallensteen and Karin Axell, "Armed Conflict at the End of the Cold War, 1989–92," *Journal of Peace Research,* 30 (August 1993), pp. 331–346.

50. Mason, "Failing Nations," p. 53.

51. *Armed Conflicts Report 1995,* p. 4; see also, Ruth L. Sivard, *World Military and Social Expenditures,* 1995 (Washington, D.C.: World Priorities, 1995).

52. To be technically accurate, it is best to speak of "antecedents" or "predictors" of war, because one can hardly know "first causes"—for example, what "caused" the components of the human brain involved in making political decisions? For one of the earliest efforts to

explain war, see Thucydides, *History of the Peloponnesian War*, R. Warner, trans. (Harmondsworth, Eng: Penguin, 1972). On philosophical approaches, see Keith L. Nelson and Spencer C. Olin, Jr., *Why War? Ideology, Theory and History* (Berkeley: University of California Press, 1979). A penetrating historical analysis is presented by Blainey, *The Causes of War.* The scientific approach is epitomized by the work of J. David Singer, *Correlates of War*, 2 vols. (New York: Free Press, 1979 and 1980).

53. Such relief becomes more difficult in the modern age with large populations. It is estimated that neither major diseases, such as AIDS, nor warfare, unless it is of truly global destructive proportions using nuclear or biological weapons, will have much impact on the levels of human population in the twenty-first century. Population growth was discussed by demographer Joel Cohen on National Public Radio, January 22, 1996. See also Andrew P. Vayda, *War in Ecological Perspective: Persistence, Change, and Adaptive Processes in Three Oceanic Societies* (New York: Plenum, 1976).

54. William Eckhardt, "Civilizations, Empires, and Wars," *Journal of Peace Research*, 27 (February 1980), pp. 9–24.

55. Kenneth N. Waltz, *Man, the State and War: A Theoretical Analysis* (New York: Columbia University Press, 1959).

56. Benjamin A. Most and Harvey Starr, *Inquiry, Logic and International Politics* (Columbia, S.C.: University of South Carolina Press, 1989). In their review of methods of theory-building, Most and Starr criticize the tri-level approach, and instead call for the construction of a unified "grand theory" of warfare, which accounts for both its occurrence and nonoccurrence in various contexts.

57. In animals, instincts are identified when individuals raised apart from others of their species nevertheless display behavior typical of that species; i.e., the behavior occurs without having been *taught* by a parent or other species member. See Lorenz, *On Aggression*, and Robert Ardry, *The Territorial Imperative* (New York: Antheneum, 1966). Because such experiments are nearly impossible to conduct on humans, human instincts are more difficult to demonstrate. Researchers argue that if a behavior is found in all countries, regardless of culture, it can be assumed to result from instincts. Although warfare is not found in all cultures, some still argue that it is known in all, and that its nonoccurrence is attributable to various pacification schemes sometimes imposed on a culture from the outside.

58. See our discussion of idiosyncratic factors in Chapter 5. An author who has argued emphatically that individual personalities have had a major impact on the outbreak of war is John C. Stoessinger, in *Why Nations Go to War*, 4th ed. (New York: St. Martin's Press, 1985), p. 206.

59. See Ralph K. White, *Nobody Wanted War* (Garden City, N.Y.: Doubleday, 1968); Ole R. Holsti, Robert C. North, and Richard A. Brody, "Preception and Action in the 1914 Crisis," in J. David Singer, ed., *Quantitative International Politics: Insights and Evidence* (New York: Free Press, 1968), pp. 123–158; and Levy, "Misperceptions and the Causes of War."

60. Gurr has applied such reasoning to the outbreak of rebellion and domestic political violence such as rioting. See Gurr, *Why Men Rebel.* An interesting case is made that such basic emotions are part of what might be termed "basic human needs" that require satisfaction, either through nonviolent or violent means. See Burton, *Conflict: Human Needs Theory.*

61. Bueno de Mesquita and Lalman, *War and Reason*, pp. 13–19.

62. Ibid., p. 156. On the "democratic peace," also see Steven Chan, "Mirror, Mirror on the Wall . . . Are the Free Countries More Pacific?," *Journal of Conflict Resolution*, 28 (December 1984), pp. 617–648; David A. Lake, "Powerful Pacifists: Democratic States and War," *American Political Science Review*, 86 (March 1992), pp. 24–37; and the writings cited in Notes 15 and 16 of Chapter 5.

63. Erich Weede, "Economic Policy and International Security: Rent-Seeking, Free Trade and Democratic Peace," *European Journal of International Relations*, 1 (December 1995), p. 520. Even greater stress is laid on free trade as an economic incentive for cooperation among democracies by Solomon W. Polachek, "Cooperation and Conflict Among Democra-

cies: Why Do Democracies Cooperate More and Fight Less?," paper presented to the Peace Science Society (International), Champaign-Urbana, Ill., November 1994.

64. As we noted in Chapter 5, though, much of this theory's validity rests on definitions of democracy and on the number of opportunities for war among democracies (on their relative number in the international system). On definitional and philosophical treatments of the problem, see Roslyn Simowitz and William S. Ward, "War and Democracy: What Have We Learned?" paper presented to the Peace Science Society (International), Champaign-Urbana, Ill., November 1994. One study which found that democracies may be as likely or even more likely than autocracies to escalate disputes is Paul Senese, "Democracies and the Use of Force: Surprising Findings from the Updated Militarized Interstate Dispute Data Set," paper presented to the Peace Science Society (International), Champaign-Urbana, Ill., November 1994.

65. See Richard Tucker, "Revolutionary Regimes: Conditions Affecting the Likelihood of Their Offensive or Defensive Involvement in International Conflict," paper presented to the Peace Science Society (International), Champaign-Urbana, Ill., November 1994; Joseph M. Scolnick, Jr., "An Appraisal of Studies of the Linkage Between Domestic and International Conflict," *Comparative Political Science*, 6 (January 1974), pp. 485–509; Arthur Stein, "Conflict and Cohesion: A Review of the Literature," *Journal of Conflict Resolution*, 20 (March 1976), pp. 143–172; and Francis W. Hoole and Chi Huang, "The Global Conflict Process," *Journal of Conflict Resolution*, 33 (March 1989), pp. 143–163.

66. Errol A. Henderson and J. Scott DeSonia, "Cultural Differences and War in the Interstate System, 1816–1989," unpublished paper using data from the Correlates of War Project, Ann Arbor: The University of Michigan, 1994.

67. Stuart A. Bremer, "National Capabilities and War Proneness," in J. David Singer, ed., *Correlates of War II: Testing Some Realpolitik Models* (New York: Free Press, 1980); Nazli Choucri and Robert C. North, *Nations in Conflict* (San Francisco: W. H. Freeman, 1975); and Charles F. Doran, "War and Power Dynamics: Economic Underpinnings," *International Studies Quarterly*, 27 (December 1983), pp. 419–441.

68. Beer, *Peace Against War*, pp. 49–51. Doubt about the effect of war weariness on subsequent wars, at least for democracies, is expressed in the findings of David Garnham, "War-Proneness, War-Weariness and Regime Type: 1816–1980," *Journal of Peace Research*, 23 (September 1986), pp. 279–289.

69. See Jack S. Levy, "Theories of General War," *World Politics*, 37 (April 1985), pp. 344–374.

70. George Modelski, "Long Cycles of Global Politics and the Nation-State," *Comparative Studies in Society and History*, 20 (April 1978), pp. 214–235; Modelski, *Long Cycles in World Politics* (Seattle: University of Washington Press, 1987); William R. Thompson and Karen A. Rasler, "War and Systemic Capability Reconcentration," *Journal of Conflict Resolution*, 32 (June 1989), pp. 335–366; Thompson, "Cycles of General, Hegemonic, and Global War," in Urs Luterbacher and Michael D. Ward, eds., *Dynamic Models of International Conflict* (Boulder, Colo.: Lynne Rienner, 1985); and Charles W. Kegley and Gregory A. Raymond, "The Long Cycle of Global War and the Transformation of Alliance Norms," *Journal of Peace Research*, 26 (August 1989), pp. 265–284. Diana Richards has claimed that there have been no regular cycles since 1494, and that cyclical theory is less adequate as an explanation of behavior in the international system than a model based on notions of "chaos" (as expressed in mathematical terms). See Richards, "A Chaotic Model of Power Concentration in the International System," *International Studies Quarterly*, 37 (March 1993), pp. 55–72.

71. See Inis Claude, *Power and International Relations* (New York: Random House, 1962), p. 56.

72. See J. David Singer, "Accounting for International War: The State of the Discipline," *Journal of Peace Research*, 18, no. 1 (1981), p. 10.

73. See Michael P. Sullivan, *International Relations: Theories and Evidence* (Englewood Cliffs, N.J.: Prentice-Hall, 1976), pp. 179–189; for a review of research findings on power relationships generally, see also Singer, "Accounting for International War," pp. 10–11.

74. See A. F. K. Organski, *World Politics*, 2nd ed. (New York: Knopf, 1968), ch. 14; Organski and Jacek Kugler, *The War Ledger* (Chicago: University of Chicago Press, 1980); Urs Luterbacher, "Last Words About War?"; and Hank Houweling and Jan G. Siccama, "Power Transitions as a Cause of War," *Journal of Conflict Resolution*, 32 (March 1988), pp. 87–102.

75. For a review of empirical research in this area, see Sullivan, *International Relations*, pp. 189–199; and Singer, "Accounting for International War," pp. 8–10. See also Jack S. Levy, "Alliance Formation and War Behavior: An Analysis of the Great Powers, 1495–1975," *Journal of Conflict Resolution*, 25 (December 1981), pp. 581–613; Woosang Kim, "Power, Alliances, and Major Wars: 1816–1975," *Journal of Conflict Resolution*, 33 (June 1989), pp. 255–273; Tom Walker, "Do States Make Efforts to Balance? Strategic Interaction and War Between Major Power Rivals, 1816–1980," paper presented at the Annual Meeting of the American Political Science Association, Chicago, September 1995; Douglas M. Gibler and John A. Vasquez, "Testing an Empirical Typology of Alliances: Avoiding War Versus Preparing for War, 1495–1980," paper presented to the Annual Meeting of the Peace Science Society (International), Columbus, Ohio, October 1995; Frank Wayman, "Bipolarity and War: The Role of Capability Concentration and Alliance Patterns Among Major Powers, 1816–1965," *Journal of Peace Research*, 21, no. 1 (1984), pp. 61–77; Alan Ned Sabrosky, ed., *Polarity and War: The Changing Structure of International Conflict* (Boulder, Colo.: Westview Press, 1985); and Randall Schweller, "Tripolarity and the Second World War," *International Studies Quarterly*, 37 (March 1993), pp. 73–103.

76. Karl W. Deutsch and J. David Singer, "Multipolar Power Systems and International Stability," *World Politics*, 16 (April 1964), pp. 881–909. See also Manus Midlarsky, "A Hierarchical Equilibrium Theory of Systemic War," *International Studies Quarterly*, 30 (March 1986), pp. 75–105; and Midlarsky and Ted Hopf, "Polarity and International Stability," *American Political Science Review*, 87 (March 1993), pp. 173–180, which reiterated the importance of distinguishing offensive from defensive power balances and examining the linkage of polarity and war through such factors as scarcity of desired resources.

77. Patrick James, "Structural Realism and the Causes of War," *Mershon International Studies Review*, 39 (October 1995), pp. 199–200.

78. Most and Starr, *The Logic of Inquiry*, ch. 6.

79. John A. Vasquez, "Why Do Neighbors Fight—Interaction Proximity or Territoriality?," paper presented to the Peace Science Society (International), Champaign-Urbana, Ill., November 1994. See also Most and Starr, *The Logic of Inquiry*, ch. 4.

80. Hidemi Suganami, "Bringing Order to the Causes of War Debates," *Millennium*, 19, no. 1 (1990), pp. 19–35.

81. Richard Ned Lebow, *Between Peace and War: The Nature of International Crisis* (Baltimore: Johns Hopkins University Press, 1981), preface and ch. 1.

82. Suganami, "Bringing Order"; and Davis B. Bobrow, "Stories Remembered and Forgotten," *Journal of Conflict Resolution*, 33 (June 1989), pp. 187–209.

83. Stanley Milgram, "Some Conditions of Obedience and Disobedience to Authority," *Human Relations*, 18 (February 1965), pp. 57–75; reprinted in Prosterman, *Surviving to 3000*, p. 85.

84. Ibid., p. 101.

85. S. L. A. Marshall, *Men Against Fire* (New York: Morrow, 1947).

86. On the important distinction between "necessary" and "sufficient" causes, see Most and Starr, *The Logic of Inquiry*, chs. 1–3.

87. Dwight D. Eisenhower, "Farwell Radio and Television Address to the American People," January 1961. *Public Papers of the President of the United States, Dwight D. Eisenhower, 1960–1961* (Washington, D.C.: U.S. Government Printing Office, 1961) p. 1037; reprinted in Carroll W. Purcell, Jr., ed., *The Military-Industrial Complex* (New York: Harper and Row, 1971), p. 206.

88. Clearly, it is not only the United States and other capitalist societies that would seem susceptible to the development of such complexes. In varying degrees, all modern societies have well-developed linkages between their industrial and defense establishments.

89. See Michael Wallace, "Armaments and Escalation: Two Competing Hypotheses," *International Studies Quarterly*, 26 (March 1982), pp. 37–56; and Lewis F. Richardson, *Arms and Insecurity* (Pittsburgh: Boxwood, 1960). On the possibilities of cooperative solutions to arms races, see Stephen J. Majeski, "Technological Innovation and Cooperation in Arms Races," *International Studies Quarterly*, 30 (June 1986), pp. 175–191.

90. Lewis F. Richardson, *Statistics of Deadly Quarrels* (Pittsburgh: Boxwood, 1960). See also Richardson, *Arms and Insecurity*, chs. 2 and 3, for an analysis of arms races in contexts such as World War I, which his model of escalation fits quite well, and World War II, which, despite significant arms build-ups, fits less well.

91. Wallace, "Armaments and Escalation."

92. Samuel Huntington, "Arms Races: Prerequisites and Results," in John Mueller, ed., *Approaches to Measurement in International Relations* (New York: Appleton-Century-Crofts, 1969), pp. 15–33. See also, Carlos Seiglie, "International Conflict and Military Expenditures," *Journal of Conflict Resolution*, 32 (March 1988), pp. 141–161.

93. On the benefits of armament vs. alliance in defense policy, see James D. Morrow, "Arms Versus Allies: Trade-offs in the Search for Security," *International Organization*, 47 (Spring 1993), pp. 207–233.

94. For discussions of the beginnings of World War I, see Holsti, et al., "Perception"; Holsti, *Crisis, Escalation, War* (Montreal: McGill University Press, 1972); L. L. Farrar, Jr., "The Limits of Choice: July 1914 Reconsidered," *Journal of Conflict Resolution*, 16 (March 1972), pp. 1–23; and Paul Schroeder, "World War I as Galloping Gertie," *Journal of Modern History*, 44 (September 1972), pp. 319–345. See also Jack S. Levy, "Organizational Routines and the Causes of War," *International Studies Quarterly*, 30 (June 1986), pp. 193–222.

95. See Lebow, *Between Peace and War*; and Michael Brecher, ed., *Studies in Crisis Behavior* (Jerusalem: Hebrew University, 1978).

96. Frustration-aggression and "relative deprivation" explanations have been applied to all types of violence, ranging from murder to urban riots to terrorism and international warfare. See Anatol Rapoport, *The Origins of Human Violence* (Toronto: University of Toronto Press, 1989).

97. On this point, see Midlarsky, *On War*, chs. 2 and 3.

98. It is often argued that relative deprivation—the gap between one's current situation and one's aspirations or expectations—is a more important trigger of violence than one's absolute condition. See, for example, Gurr, *Why Men Rebel*, ch. 2.

99. See Johan Galtung, " A Structural Theory of Aggression," *Journal of Peace Research*, 1, no. 2 (1964), pp. 95–119; Midlarsky, *On War*, ch. 5; Michael D. Wallace, "Power, Status, and International War," *Journal of Peace Research*, 8, no. 1 (1971), pp. 23–35; and Maurice East, "Status Discrepancy and Violence in the International System: An Empirical Analysis," in Vincent Davis, et al., eds., *The Analysis of International Politics* (New York: Free Press, 1972), pp. 299–319.

100. Bueno de Mesquita, *The War Trap*, ch. 5.

101. Paul Kennedy, *The Rise and Fall of the Great Powers* (New York: Random House, 1987); Wayman, "Bipolarity and War"; Steven Rosen, "War, Power and the Willingness to Suffer," in Bruce M. Russett, ed., *War, Peace and Numbers* (Beverly Hills: Sage, 1972), pp. 167–183; and A. F. K. Organski and Jacek Kugler, "The Costs of Major Wars: the Phoenix Factor," *American Political Science Review*, 71 (December 1977), pp. 1347–1366.

102. Rosen, "War, Power, and the Willingness to Suffer." See also, David W. Ziegler, *War, Peace and International Politics* (Boston: Little, Brown, 1977), p. 1; and Dyer, *War*, photo caption facing p. 101.

103. On the "phoenix factor," see Organski and Kugler, *The War Ledger* and "Costs of Major Wars"; and Organski, *World Politics*, pp. 207–215.

104. Randolph M. Siverson, "War and Change in the International System," in Ole R. Holsti, et al., eds., *Change in the International System* (Boulder, Colo.: Westview Press, 1980), pp. 216–217.

105. See the works of F. Scott Fitzgerald and historians such as Frederick Lewis Allen, *Only Yesterday: An Informal History of the 1920s* (New York: Harper and Row, 1964).

106. Although most economic recessions in the United States have occurred during periods of peace, so have most economic booms—perhaps because most years have been spent at peace. See J. A. Thornton, "Wars, Peace, and Prosperity," in L. L. Farrar, ed., *War: A Historical, Political, and Social Study* (Santa Barbara: ABC-CLIO, 1978), p. 195; see also Harvey Starr, et al., "The Relationship Between Defense Spending and Inflation," *Journal of Conflict Resolution,* 28 (March 1984), pp. 103–122.

107. Major wars generally seem to lead to the growth of government bureaucracies and the expansion of the size and power of the central government. See Karen A. Rasler and William R. Thompson, "War Making and State Making: Governmental Expenditures, Tax Revenues, and Global Wars," *American Political Science Review,* 79 (June 1985), pp. 491–507.

108. Richard E. Neustadt and Graham T. Allison, "Afterword," in Robert F. Kennedy, *Thirteen Days* (New York: Norton, 1971), p. 115.

109. Ray, "Abolition of Slavery," pp. 429–430.

110. On this point, see Frederic S. Pearson and Michael Brzoska, *Arms and Warfare: Escalation, Deescalation, Negotiation* (Columbia, S.C.: University of South Carolina Press, 1994), ch. 4.

111. I. William Zartman, ed., *Elusive Peace: Negotiating an End to Civil Wars* (Washington, D.C.: Brookings Institution, 1995), p. 3.

112. Ibid., p. 18.

113. Duncan Keith Shaw, *Prime Minister Neville Chamberlain* (London: Wells Gardner, updated), pp. 111–112, as quoted by Siverson, "War and Change," p. 216.

114. Some have proposed merely the absence of war and violence as a working definition, whereas others insist that true peace is impossible without "justice," or without satisfaction of "basic human needs." See Ronald J. Glossop, *Confronting War: An Examination of Humanity's Most Pressing Problem,* 2nd ed. (Jefferson, N.C.: McFarland, 1987), pp. 10–20.

115. A good comparison of the balance of power and concert of powers approaches to world order is presented by Robert Jervis, "From Balance to Concert: A Study of International Security Cooperation," *World Politics,* 38 (October 1985), pp. 58–79.

116. On the theory of hegemonic stability, see Robert G. Gilpin, *War and Change in World Politics* (Cambridge, U.K.: Cambridge University Press, 1981); and G. John Ikenberry and Charles A. Kupchan, "Socialization and Hegemonic Stability," *International Organization,* 44 (Summer 1990), pp. 283–316. A good overview of this literature is provided in Richard Rosecrance, "Long Cycle Theory and International Relations," *International Organization,* 41 (Spring 1987), pp. 283–301.

117. Paul Kennedy, *Rise and Fall.*

118. See Robert O. Keohane, *After Hegemony: Cooperation and Discord in World Political Economy* (Princeton, N.J.: Princeton University Press, 1984).

119. The success record of conversion attempts has been mixed, however. See Frederic S. Pearson, *The Global Spread of Arms: The Political Economy of International Security* (Boulder, Colo.: Westview Press, 1994).

120. Hans J. Morgenthau, *Politics Among Nations,* 5th ed. (New York: Knopf, 1973), p. 400.

121. Inis L. Claude, Jr., *Swords into Plowshares,* 3rd ed. (New York: Random House, 1964), p. 197.

122. The general problem of achieving cooperation in an anarchy-prone international system, and the role international institutions can play in conflict resolution, are discussed by Robert Axelrod and Robert O. Keohane, "Achieving Cooperation Under Anarchy: Strategies and Institutions," *World Politics,* 38 (October 1985), pp. 226–254.

123. The actual plebiscite was long delayed because of procedural disagreements, however. On the settlement strategy, see Marion Houk, "Western Saharan Peace Prospects Improve, UN Says," *Christian Science Monitor,* July 3, 1990, p. 6.

124. For a variety of war termination and settlement approaches, see Randle, *Origins of Peace*, especially ch. 2.
125. Karl W. Deutsch, et al., "Political Community and the North Atlantic Area," *International Political Communities: An Anthology* (Garden City, N.Y.: Doubleday, 1966), pp. 1–91.
126. Kenneth E. Boulding, *Stable Peace* (Austin: University of Texas Press, 1978), ch. 2.

PART III. INTERNATIONAL INSTITUTIONS

Chapter 9. International Law: Myth or Reality?

1. Lincoln P. Bloomfield, *The Foreign Policy Process: A Primer* (Englewood Cliffs, N.J.: Prentice-Hall, 1982), p. 139.
2. Paul Martin, Canadian Secretary of State for External Affairs, cited in *External Affairs*, 16 (1964).
3. This definition is based on a discussion by William D. Coplin in *The Functions of International Law* (Chicago: Rand McNally, 1966), pp. 1–3.
4. This is the traditional notion of law attributed primarily to John Austin, a British writer in the nineteenth century; cited in Edward Collins, Jr., ed., *International Law in a Changing World* (New York: Random House, 1970), p. 2. For a discussion of how law and order can exist in a decentralized political system such as the international system, see Hedley Bull, *The Anarchical Society: A Study of Order in World Politics* (New York: Columbia University Press, 1977).
5. There is some disagreement over the consensual nature of customary international law, particularly as it applies to states that have just achieved independence and joined the international community. For a discussion of this issue, see Michael Akehurst, *A Modern Introduction to International Law*, 6th ed. (London: Allen and Unwin, 1987), pp. 31–33.
6. Richard Bilder, *Managing the Risks of International Agreement* (Madison: University of Wisconsin Press, 1981), p. 5.
7. Ibid., pp. 6 and 233, notes that of more than 15,000 treaties in force in the 1980s, bilateral agreements far exceeded multilateral ones. The same can be said for the 1990s. For data on the growth of multilateral treaty-making, see John King Gamble, "Reservations to Multilateral Treaties: A Macroscopic View of State Practice," *American Journal of International Law*, 74 (April 1980), pp. 372–394.
8. Based on University of Washington Treaty Research Center Studies, reported in Bilder, *Managing the Risks*, p. 232. Some international agreements take the form of "executive agreements" rather than treaties. These have the same binding character in international law as treaties but are not subject to the same ratification procedures domestically. The United States in particular has relied heavily on executive agreements more so than treaties.
9. Akehurst, *Modern Introduction*, p. 25.
10. Mark W. Janis, *An Introduction to International Law* (Boston: Little, Brown, 1988) p. 11. Most treaties today are registered with the United Nations and can be found in the UN Treaty Series.
11. On trends in codification of international law and other aspects of lawmaking in the international system, see Nicholas G. Onuf, ed., *Law Making in the Global Community* (Durham, N.C.: Carolina Academic Press, 1982); and Onuf, "International Codification: Interpreting the Last Half-Century," in Richard Falk et al., eds., *International Law: A Contemporary Perspective* (Boulder, Colo.: Westview Press, 1985), pp. 264–279.
12. For a discussion of law observance, see Louis Henkin, *How Nations Behave*, 2nd ed. (New York: Columbia University Press, 1979), pp. 46–47; Bull, *Anarchical Society*, p. 137; Bilder,

Managing the Risks, pp. 7–11. Oran Young, *Compliance and Public Authority* (Baltimore: Johns Hopkins University Press, 1977) offers a conceptual treatment of the problem of compliance in decentralized systems.

13. David V. Edwards, *The American Political Experience*, 4th ed. (Englewood Cliffs, N.J.: Prentice-Hall, 1988), pp. 372–373. Law enforcement is not much better in the British criminal justice system, with only 22 percent of the robberies committed in England and Wales solved by the police according to a recent annual survey. Akehurst, *Modern Introduction*, p. 2.

14. Data on the caseload of the Court, including a listing of the individual cases, can be found in A. LeRoy Bennett, *International Organizations*, 6th ed. (Englewood Cliffs, N.J.: Prentice-Hall, 1995), pp. 188–194; also see *UN Chronicle*, 20, no. 11 (1983), pp. 47–53.

15. J. Alan Beesley, *New Frontiers of Multilateralism* (Hanover, N.H.: Academic Council on the UN, 1989), p. 9.

16. On the tendency of defendant states to refuse to participate in ICJ proceedings despite court rulings that the court has jurisdiction, see Dana D. Fischer, "Decisions to Use the International Court of Justice," *International Studies Quarterly*, 26 (June 1982), pp. 251–277.

17. These are the words of Benjamin Civiletti, former U.S. Attorney General, in his oral argument presented before the World Court on December 10, 1979, during the proceedings of the *US Diplomatic and Consular Staff in Tehran* case; cited in U.S. Department of State, Bureau of Public Affairs, Current Policy No. 118 (December 1979), p. 1.

18. The term "allocation of legal competences" is borrowed from Coplin, *Functions of International Law*. See ch. 2 of his book for a discussion of the way in which international law performs this function.

19. One of the best statements of the relationship between law and politics in international relations is found in Morton A. Kaplan and Nicholas DeB. Katzenbach, *The Political Foundations of International Law* (New York: John Wiley, 1961).

20. On cultural differences pitting "the West vs. the rest," see Samuel P. Huntington, "The Clash of Civilizations?," *Foreign Affairs*, 72 (Summer 1993), pp. 22–49. During the Cold War, most international law texts distinguished between Western, communist, and third world views of international law, as seen in Akehurst, *Modern Introduction*, ch. 2, and A. Sheikh, *International Law and National Behavior* (New York: John Wiley, 1974), especially ch. 11.

21. In the case of the League of Nations Covenant, the only obligation of states to refrain from war was that they at least exhaust all peaceful settlement procedures first. For a discussion of the Covenant and the Kellogg-Briand Pact, see Bennett, *International Organizations*, ch. 2.

22. One of the most widely accepted definitions of "self-defense" was offered by U.S. Secretary of State Daniel Webster in condemning British actions in the Caroline case during the nineteenth century. Webster argued that the use of force in self-defense was permissible "only when the necessity for action is instant, overwhelming and leaving no choice of means, and no moment for deliberation." See Collins, *International Law*, pp. 336–337.

23. Going back to St. Augustine and later Grotius, the use of violence was considered "just" as long as the purpose was not self-aggrandizement or revenge but rather correction of some larger evil, and as long as the means used were proportionate to the provocation. The "just war" tradition is discussed in Michael Walzer, *Just and Unjust Wars: A Moral Argument with Historical Illustrations* (New York: Basic Books, 1977); Louis Henkin et al., *Right vs. Might: International Law and the Use of Armed Force*, 2nd ed. (New York: Council on Foreign Relations, 1991); and William V. O'Brien, *The Conduct of Just and Limited War* (New York: Praeger, 1981).

24. Henkin, *How Nations Behave*, p. 146.

25. Article 3 of the 1949 Geneva Convention dealt with treatment of prisoners in civil wars, but only weakly.

26. Lori Fisler Damrosch, *Enforcing Restraint: Collective Intervention in Internal Conflicts* (New York: Council on Foreign Relations, 1993), p. 12.

27. See ibid.; Abiodun Williams et al., *Article 2 (7) Revisited* (Providence: Academic Council on the United Nations System, 1994); and Anthony Clark Arend and Robert J. Beck, *International Law and the Use of Force* (London: Routledge, 1993), ch. 8. Arend and Beck dis-

cuss not only humanitarian intervention but also other "challenges to the Charter paradigm" posed by the fact that most episodes of planetary violence today are not of the interstate war variety the framers had in mind when they designed the UN Charter.

28. See Michael Bothe et al., ed., *New Rules for Victims of Armed Conflicts* (The Hague: Martinus Nijhoff, 1982); William R. Slomanson, *Fundamental Perspectives on International Law*, 2nd ed. (St. Paul: West Publishing, 1995), ch. 10; and Ray August, *Public International Law* (Englewood Cliffs, N.J.: Prentice-Hall, 1995), ch. 10.

29. See Collins, *International Law*, p. 254; and Akehurst, *Modern Introduction*, pp. 92–97.

30. For a discussion of the "minimum international standard" issue in general and the expropriation issue in particular, see Akehurst, *Modern Introduction*, ch. 7; and August, *Public International Law*, pp. 348–360.

31. Rhoda E. Howard and Jack Donnelly, eds., *International Handbook of Human Rights* (New York: Greenwood Press, 1987), p. 1.

32. Gidon Gottlieb, *Nation Against State* (New York: Council on Foreign Relations, 1993), p. 21.

33. Bilahari Kausikan, "Asia's Different Standard," *Foreign Policy* (Fall 1993), pp. 28–34, cited in Samuel P. Huntington, "If Not Civilizations, What?," *Foreign Affairs*, 72 (November/December 1993), p. 193. Also see Note 20.

34. *Freedom in the World* (London: Freedom House, 1993), p. 4.

35. Ibid. See Lucia Monat, "Abuse of Human Rights Continuing Worldwide," *Christian Science Monitor*, July 20, 1990, p. 7, citing figures on detention, torture, and other violations released by Amnesty International.

36. For data on compliance, see David L. Banks, "Patterns of Oppression: An Explanatory Analysis of Human Rights Data," *Journal of the American Statistical Association*, 407 (September 1989), pp. 674–681; and Charles Humana and *The Economist*, *World Human Rights Guide* published by Facts on File.

37. Louise I. Shelly, "Human Rights as an International Issue," *Annals of the American Academy of Political and Social Science*, 506 (November 1989), pp. 42–56. On enforcement machinery, see W. B. Ofuatey-Kodjoe, "Human Rights and Humanitarian Intervention," in Albert Legault et al., eds., *The State of the United Nations 1992*, (Providence: Academic Council on the UN System, 1992), pp. 33–47.

38. Jarat Chopra, "The New Subjects of International Law," *Brown Foreign Affairs Journal* (Spring 1991), pp. 27–30.

Chapter 10. International Organizations: Links Between Governments and Between Peoples

1. Based on a comparison of GNP data from *World Bank Atlas, 1995* (Washington, D.C.: World Bank, 1995), pp. 18–19, and gross sales of industrial firms from *Fortune*, August 7, 1995, pp. 123 ff.

2. *Yearbook of International Organizations, 1995/1996*, 32nd ed. (Brussels: Union of International Associations, 1995), Table 1 in Appendix 7 of Vol. 1.

3. Neill Nugent, *The Government and Politics of the European Union*, 3rd ed. (Durham: Duke University Press, 1994), p. 404.

4. Kjell Skjelsbaek, "The Growth of International Nongovernmental Organization in the Twentieth Century," *International Organization*, 25 (Summer 1971), pp. 435–436.

5. For example, see James N. Rosenau, "Governance in the Twenty-First Century," *Global Governance*, 1 (Winter 1995), pp. 13–43; Ronnie Lipschutz, "Reconstructing World Politics: The Emergence of Global Civil Society," *Millennium*, 21 (1992), pp. 389–420; and Paul Ghils, "International Civil Society: International Nongovernmental Organizations in the International System," *International Social Science Journal*, 133 (1992), pp. 417–429. See our box on "Human Governance in the Post–Cold War Era" in Chapter 1.

6. Harold K. Jacobson, *Networks of Interdependence*, 2nd ed. (New York: Knopf, 1984), p. 14.

7. Depending on the criteria used, one might find well over 300 IGOs and 10,000 NGOs. The *Yearbook of International Organizations* counts over 1,000 and 11,000, respectively, if one includes "nonconventional" organizations. Rosenau, "Governance in the Twenty-First Century," p. 24, counts over 17,000 NGOs; Ghils, "International Civil Society," p. 419, counts over 23,000; The Commission on Global Governance, *Our Global Neighborhood* (Oxford: Oxford University Press, 1995) p. 32, counts over 28,000. For a discussion of membership classification, see Jacobson, *Networks*, ch. 1; and Werner J. Feld and Robert Jordan, *International Organizations: A Comparative Approach*, 3rd ed. (Westport, Conn.: Praeger, 1994), ch. 1.

8. For comparison of regional and global IGO growth, see Feld and Jordan, *International Organizations*, pp. 16–18; Jacobson, *Networks*, pp. 47–50; and Jacobson et al., "National Entanglements in International Governmental Organizations," *American Political Science Review*, 80 (March 1986), pp. 145–147.

9. Jacobson et al., "National Entanglements," p. 149. Also, see *Yearbook of International Organizations*, Vol. 2, p. 1671.

10. *Our Global Neighborhood*, p. 33. Africa now accounts for 16 percent of all NGO memberships, and Asia 17 percent. For trends in NGO growth, see Feld and Jordan, *International Organizations*, pp. 25–26; and Jacobson, *Networks*, pp. 50–53.

11. Feld and Jordan, *International Organizations*, p. 18.

12. Jacobson, *Networks*, p. 49.

13. Ibid.

14. James A. Field, Jr., "Transnationalism and the New Tribe," *International Organization*, 25 (Summer 1971), pp. 355–356.

15. As indicated in Note 7, tracking the growth of NGOs depends on the definitions and counting procedures used. The historical data cited here are from Jacobson, *Networks*, p. 10. Feld and Jordan, *International Organizations*, p. 17, limiting the analysis to "conventional" organizations, find explosive growth of NGOs tapering off after 1985. Others, using different measures, such as the authors of *Our Global Neighborhood*, note explosive growth continuing in the 1990s.

16. Robert C. Angell, *Peace on the March: Transnational Participation* (New York: Van Nostrand Reinhold, 1969). Included in his definition of "transnational participation" are activities engaged in by representatives of national governments, such as U.S. Peace Corps volunteers and delegates to IGOs, although most of his study focuses on nongovernmental actors.

17. A. LeRoy Bennett, *International Organizations*, 6th ed. (Englewood Cliffs, N.J.: Prentice-Hall, 1995), p. 275.

18. Remarks of a UN official, cited in Donald Puchala and Roger Coate, *The Challenge of Relevance: The United Nations in a Changing World Environment* (Hanover, N.H.: Academic Council on the UN, 1989), p. 95.

19. Joseph S. Nye, Jr., and Robert O. Keohane, "Transnational Relations and World Politics: A Conclusion," *International Organization*, 25 (Summer 1971), p. 723.

20. Jacobson, *Networks*, pp. 9 and 48; and *Yearbook of International Organizations*.

21. Craig N. Murphy, *International Organization and Industrial Change* (Oxford: Oxford University Press, 1994), especially ch. 2.

22. Inis L. Claude, *The Record of International Organizations in the Twentieth Century*, Tamkang Chair Lecture Series, Tamkang University, January 1986, p. 2.

23. In *After Hegemony: Cooperation and Discord in the World Political Economy* (Princeton, N.J.: Princeton University Press, 1984), pp. 85–102, Robert Keohane explains why states, acting as rational actors, participate in international "regimes" (including not only treaties but organizations).

24. Joseph S. Nye, *Peace in Parts* (Boston: Little, Brown, 1971), p. 169. The OAS was the most successful, followed by the OAU and Arab League.

25. The classic formulation of functionalist theory is David Mitrany, *A Working Peace System: An Argument for the Functional Development of International Organization* (London: Royal Institute of International Affairs, 1943). An analysis of Mitrany is provided by James P. Sewell, *Functionalism and World Politics* (Princeton, N.J.: Princeton University Press, 1966), pp. 28–72.

26. For the "neofunctionalist" viewpoint and discussion of the "spillover" concept, see Ernst B. Haas, "International Integration: The European and the Universal Process," in *International Political Communities* (New York: Doubleday Anchor, 1966), pp. 93–130; and Leon N. Lindberg and Stuart A. Scheingold, *Europe's Would-Be Polity* (Englewood Cliffs, N.J.: Prentice-Hall, 1970), pp. 117–120 especially.

27. James A. Caporaso, *Functionalism and Regional Integration: A Logical and Empirical Assessment* (Beverly Hills, Calif.: Sage, 1972). See also Peter Wolf, "International Organization and Attitude Change: A Re-Examination of the Functionalist Approach, *International Organization*, 27 (Summer 1973), pp. 347–371.

28. Jacobson et al., "National Entanglements," p. 152. Jacobson and his co-authors acknowledge that IGO growth is not the only explanation for the drop in interstate wars since World War II, but they argue that it has been a contributing factor.

29. *U.S. Department of State Bulletin*, 12 (April 29, 1945), p. 789.

30. Cited in Abba Eban, "The UN Idea Revisited," *Foreign Affairs*, 74 (September/October 1995), pp. 39–40.

31. Ibid., p. 39.

32. On the use of the veto, see Robert E. Riggs and Jack C. Plano, *The United Nations: International Organization and World Politics*, 2nd ed. (Belmont, Calif.: Wadsworth, 1994), pp. 57–59.

33. Karen A. Mingst and Margaret P. Karns, *The United Nations in the Post–Cold War Era* (Boulder, Colo.: Westview Press, 1995), pp. 23–24.

34. Riggs and Plano, *The United Nations*, pp. 66–69. Also, see Richard Bernstein, "The UN Versus the U.S.," *The New York Times Magazine*, January 22, 1984.

35. Christopher S. Wren, "U.S., A Prominent Founder, Is Now Biggest UN Debtor," *New York Times*, October 21, 1995, p. 4.

36. The UN system as a whole, including such entities as UNICEF, the World Bank, and the World Health Organization, employs over 50,000 people.

37. For a general discussion of the "loyalty" question and other issues related to the UN Secretariat, see Bennett, *International Organizations*, ch. 16.

38. Cited in *Chronicle*, published by the Dag Hammarskjold Information Centre on the Study of Violence and Peace, 2 (March 1982), p. 12.

39. For a good discussion of these and other UN missions, see Bennett, *International Organizations*, ch. 7; John F. Murphy, *The United Nations and the Control of International Violence* (Totowa, N.J.: Allanheld, Osmun, 1983); and Riggs and Plano, *The United Nations*, chs. 5 and 6.

40. Ernst B. Haas, "Regime Decay, Conflict Management and International Organizations, 1945–1981," *International Organization*, 37 (Spring 1983), pp. 189–256. In many of these cases, however, the UN contribution was judged to be "limited" rather than "great." Also see Jonathan Wilkenfeld and Michael Brecher, "International Crises 1945–1975: The UN Dimension," *International Studies Quarterly*, 28 (March 1984), pp. 45–67.

41. Ernst B. Haas, *Why We Still Need the UN* (Berkeley: University of California Press, 1986), p. 20.

42. The UN revival in peacekeeping is discussed in Thomas G. Weiss, David P. Forsythe, and Roger A. Coate, *The United Nations and Changing World Politics* (Boulder, Colo.: Westview Press, 1994), ch. 3; Puchala and Coate, *Challenge of Relevance*, ch. 2; and George L. Sherry, *The United Nations Reborn: Conflict Control in the Post–Cold War World* (New York: Council on Foreign Relations, 1990).

43. Mandatory economic sanctions previously had been taken under Chapter VII of the UN Charter against Rhodesia in 1966 and South Africa in 1977 (the latter in the form of an

arms embargo). The effectiveness of UN economic sanctions is discussed in Riggs and Plano, *The United Nations*, pp. 109–111.

44. See notes 26 and 27 in Chapter 9. Also, see Weiss et al., *The United Nations*, chs. 3 and 4.

45. *An Agenda for Peace*, UN Doc. A/47/277 and S/24111, 1992. The rapid deployment force is discussed in Joseph S. Nye, "What New World Order?," *Foreign Affairs* (Spring 1992), pp. 83–96.

46. Over $3 billion in annual assessments are owed to the UN by member states, with the U.S. being the prime delinquent. Wren, "U.S. Now Biggest UN Debtor."

47. In Puchala and Coate, *Challenge of Relevance*, pp. 102–106, the authors speak of "the decline of globalism" and "the limits of intergovernmentalism." Also, see Robert O. Keohane and Joseph S. Nye, "Two Cheers for Multilateralism," *Foreign Policy*, (Fall 1985), pp. 155–159, where in arguing against global unilateralism of the type practiced by the Reagan administration in the early 1980s, the authors appear to be urging instead nonglobal multilateralism.

48. J. Martin Rochester, "Global Policy and the Future of the United Nations," *Journal of Peace Research*, 27 (May 1990), p. 141.

49. Technically, since 1993 the EEC has been renamed the European Community.

50. Lindberg and Scheingold, *Europe's Would-Be Polity*, p. 2.

51. See Maria Cowles, "Multinationals, Two-Level Games and the European Community," paper presented at Annual Meeting of the International Studies Association, Chicago, February 24, 1995.

52. An excellent discussion of the formal structure as well as the political process of the European Union can be found in Nugent, *Government and Politics of the European Union*, and Desmond Dinan, *Ever Closer Union?* (Boulder, Colo.: Lynne Rienner, 1994).

53. This quote is attributed to Geoffrey Ripon, a chief negotiator representing Britain when it entered the Community in 1972; cited in *New York Times*, March 21, 1982, p. 6.

54. Puchala and Coate, *Challenge of Relevance*, p. 36.

55. On the prospects of the CFSP, see "The European Union's Security and Defense Policy," *NATO Review* (November 1995), pp. 3–9.

56. Nugent, *Government and Politics of the European Union*, p. 65.

57. The British and Danes are among the least supportive of the idea of a United States of Europe, and tend to favor widening the membership. States that are the most supportive of increased integration, such as Italy and the Netherlands, tend to be more cautious about enlarging the Union lest it undermine "deepening." For public opinion surveys in the member states, see Richard C. Eichenberg and Russell Dalton, "Europeans and the European Community: The Dynamics of Public Support for European Integration," *International Organization*, 47 (Autumn 1993), pp. 507–534.

PART IV. THE GLOBAL CONDITION: THE POLITICS OF GLOBAL PROBLEM SOLVING

1. Oran R. Young, "International Regimes: Problems of Concept Formation," *World Politics*, 32 (April 1980), pp. 332–333.

2. Robert O. Keohane and Joseph S. Nye, *Power and Interdependence* (Boston: Little, Brown, 1977), p. 5. On the concept of regimes, see Stephen D. Krasner, ed., *International Regimes* (Ithaca, N.Y.: Cornell University Press, 1983); and the review essay by Oran R. Young, "International Regimes: Toward a New Theory of Institutions," *World Politics*, 39 (October 1986), pp. 104–122.

3. See James N. Rosenau and Ernst-Otto Czempiel, eds., *Governance Without Government* (Cambridge, Eng.: Cambridge University Press, 1992). For examples of regimes in specific issue-areas, see Mark W. Zacher and Brent A. Sutton, *Governing Global Networks: Interna-*

tional Regimes for Transportation and Communications (Cambridge, Eng.: Cambridge University Press, 1996).

Chapter 11. The Control of Violence: Arms Races and Arms Control in the Nuclear Age

1. Soadet Deger, "World Military Expenditures," in Stockholm International Peace Research Institute, *The SIPRI Yearbook, 1989: World Armaments and Disarmament* (Oxford, Eng.: Oxford University Press/ SIPRI, 1989), ch. 5; and Nicole Ball et al., "World Military Expenditure," *The SIPRI Yearbook, 1994: World Armaments and Disarmament* (Oxford: Oxford University Press/ SIPRI, 1994), ch. 12.

2. Michael Renner, "Converting to a Peaceful Economy," in Lester R. Brown et al, eds., *State of the World 1990* (New York: W. W. Norton, 1990), p. 155.

3. Philip Finnegan, "CIA Says China to Lift Defense Spending 15 Percent," *Defense News,* July 9, 1990, p. 8; Frederic S. Pearson, *The Global Spread of Arms: The Political Economy of International Security* (Boulder, Colo.: Westview Press, 1994).

4. Tim Weiner, "Weapons of Mass Destruction Are Spreading, Pentagon Warns," *New York Times,* April 12, 1996, p. 4.

5. Stockholm International Peace Research Institute, *SIPRI Yearbook 1995: Armaments, Disarmament and International Security* (Oxford, Eng.: Oxford University Press, 1995), pp. 8 and 317.

6. Weiner, "Weapons," p. 4.

7. Despite military spending cuts, the U.S. defense budget of some $270 million in 1994 was over five times greater than of its nearest competitor, Russia. See Randall Forsberg, "Force Without Reason," *Boston Review,* 20, no. 3 (Summer 1995), p. 4.

8. For descriptions of the "weapons game," see Pearson, *The Global Spread of Arms;* Helena Tuomi and Raimo Vayrynen, *Transnational Corporations, Armaments and Development* (London: Gower, 1982); Christian Catrina, *Arms Transfers and Dependence* (New York: Taylor and Francis, and UNIDIR, 1988); Michael Brzoska and Thomas Ohlson, eds., *Arms Production in the Third World* (London: Taylor and Francis and SIPRI, 1986); and Herbert Wulf, ed., *Arms Industry Limited* (New York: Oxford University Press/SIPRI, 1993).

9. Edward J. Laurance, Siemon T. Wezeman, and Herbert Wulf, *Arms Watch: SIPRI Report on the First Year of the UN Register of Conventional Arms,* SIPRI Research Report No. 6 (Oxford: Oxford University Press/Stockholm International Peace Research Institute, 1993).

10. *The Defense Monitor* (September/October 1995), p. 1. The quotation is from U.S. Secretary of State Warren Christopher.

11. International Institute for Strategic Studies, *Military Balance: 1985–1986* (London: 1985).

12. See Emil Benoit, "Growth Effects of Defense in Developing Countries," *International Development Review,* 14, no. 1 (1972), pp. 2–10; Benoit, *Defense and Economic Growth in Developing Countries* (Lexington, Mass.: Lexington Books, 1973); and Benoit, "Growth and Defense in Developing Countries," *Economic Development and Cultural Change,* 26 (January 1978), pp. 271–280.

13. Alex Mintz, "Guns Versus Butter: A Disaggregated Analysis," *American Political Science Review,* 83 (December 1989), pp. 1285–1293; also see Bruce M. Russett, "Defense Expenditure and National Well Being," *American Political Science Review,* 76 (December 1982), pp. 767–777.

14. See, for example, Jogat S. Mehta, ed., *Third World Militarization: A Challenge to Third World Diplomacy* (Austin: L. B. Johnson School, University of Texas, 1985); Seymour Melman, *The Permanent War Economy: American Capitalism in Decline,* rev. ed. (New York: Simon and Schuster, 1985); and Melman, *Profits Without Production* (New York: Knopf, 1983).

15. See Lisa M. Grober and Richard C. Porter, "Benoit Revisited: Defense Spending and Economic Growth," *Journal of Conflict Resolution,* 33 (March 1989), pp. 318–345; and Robert

E. Looney, "The Political Economy of Third World Military Expenditures: Impact of Regime Type on the Defense Allocation Process," *Journal of Political and Military Sociology*, 16 (Spring 1988), pp. 21–29.

16. *World Military Expenditures and Arms Transfers, 1993–1994* (Washington, D.C.: U.S. Arms Control and Disarmament Agency, 1995), Table 1.

17. *World Military Expenditures and Arms Transfers 1993–1994*, p. 4.

18. Pearson, *Global Spread of Arms*, p. 29.

19. Keith Krause, *Arms and the State: Patterns of Military Production and Trade* (Cambridge, Eng.: Cambridge University Press, 1992), p. 168.

20. Ruth L. Sivard, *World Military and Social Expenditures*, 1985 (Washington, D.C.: World Priorities, 1983), and also the 1987–88 volume. Also, see Michael Renner, "Enhancing Global Security," in Lester R. Brown et al., *State of the World 1989* (New York: W. W. Norton, 1989), pp. 132–153.

21. These trends in arms transfers are discussed by Andrew J. Pierre, *The Global Politics of Arms Sales* (Princeton, N.J.: Princeton University Press, 1982). On one of the world's most famous private used arms dealers, see Patrick Brogan and Albert Zacha, *Deadly Business: Sam Cummings, Interarms, and the Arms Trade* (New York: W. W. Norton, 1983).

22. *SIPRI Yearbook, 1989*, p. 195; *The SIPRI Yearbook, 1990: World Armaments and Disarmament* (Oxford: Oxford University Press, 1990); and Richard F. Grimmett, *Trends in Conventional Arms Transfers to the Third World by Major Supplier, 1981–1988* (Washington, D.C.: Congressional Research Service, August 1989), p. 27.

23. On arms import trends, see *World Military Expenditures and Arms Transfers, 1993–1994*, pp. 9–14.

24. Charles Sennott, "Armed for Profit," *The Boston Globe*, February 11, 1996, p. B2.

25. For arms export trends, see *World Military Expenditures and Arms Transfers, 1993–1994*, pp. 14–21.

26. *Arming the World: An Introduction to the International Arms Trade and Alternatives* (London: Campaign Against Arms Trade, 1980), pp. 15–17. On the distinction between "gray" and "black" markets in arms supply, see *SIPRI Yearbook, 1989*, pp. 190–192.

27. Colin Smith and Shyam Bhatia, "Proliferation: Atoms for War," *The Observer* (London), December 16, 1979.

28. Jocelyn Boryczka, M.K. Mohanan, Frederic Pearson, and Jeffrey Weigand, "Cultural and Strategic Factors in South Asian Arms Control," paper presented to the Annual Meeting of the International Studies Association, San Diego, April 18, 1996.

29. SIPRI, *Armament or Disarmament? The Crucial Choice* (Stockholm: SIPRI, 1979), p. 15.

30. Cited by Thomas Stock and Anna de Geer, "Chemical and Biological Weapons: Developments and Destruction" *SIPRI Yearbook, 1995*, p. 340. Among the suspected chemical weapons states were Afghanistan, Burma, China, Egypt, Ethiopia, Israel, Kazakhstan, North Korea, Syria, Taiwan, Ukraine, Vietnam, Chile, Cuba, France, South Korea, Libya, Pakistan, Somalia, South Africa, and Thailand. Suspected of possessing biological weapons were China, India, Iran, North Korea, Pakistan, Syria, Taiwan, Egypt, and Libya, with Iraq showing a "clear intent."

31. Deger, "World Military Expenditures," p. 171.

32. David C. Gompert, "Introduction: Nuclear Proliferation and the 1980s Project," in Ted Greenwald, Harold Feiveson, and Theodore B. Taylor, eds., *Nuclear Proliferation: Motivations, Capabilities, and Strategies for Control* (New York: McGraw-Hill, 1971), p. 1.

33. See Leslie H. Gelb, "Arms Sales," *Foreign Policy*, no. 25 (Winter 1976–77), pp. 3–23.

34. Thomas Ohlson, ed., *Arms Transfer Limitations and Third World Security* (Oxford, Eng.: Oxford University Press/SIPRI, 1988).

35. Klare, "Who's Arming Who?"; and *Fact Sheet: U.S.-Soviet Regulations: Arms Control Negotiations* (Washington, D.C.: U.S. Department of State, 1990). See also *Conventional Arms Transfer Restraint in the 1990s* (Washington, D.C.: Center for Defense Information, November 1994).

36. For an exploration of some of these motives and patterns, see William W. Keller, *Arm in Arm: The Political Economy of the Global Arms Trade* (New York: Basic Books, 1995); and Pearson, *The Global Spread of Arms.*

37. Pierre, *Global Politics of Arms Sales*, pp. 14–38; and Neuman, "The Arms Market," p. 521.

38. In this case, the U.S. administration evidently looked the other way while Islamic states sympathetic to the government side, such as Iran, shipped weapons, some of which also got into the hands of the Bosnian Croats during their alliance with the government.

39. On bureaucratic politics within the U.S. Defense Department, see Asa Clark, "Armies Walk, Air Forces Fly, Navies Sail . . . Military Services Compete: Interservice Competition and U.S. Defense Policy," paper delivered at Annual Meeting of the International Studies Association, Cincinnati, Ohio, March 1982.

40. Anthony Sampson, *The Arms Bazaar* (London: Hodder and Stoughton, 1977), pp. 23–30; see also Brogan and Zacha, *Deadly Business.*

41. Over 700 citizens groups from around the world sent the Court boxloads of "Declarations of Public Conscience" from over 3.5 million people. Anabel Dwyer, "The Nuclear States vs. Humanity!" *Peace and Freedom*, Women's International League for Peace and Freedom (January–March 1996), pp. 12–13. On the split decision, see Roger K. Smith, "World Court's Historic Opinion on Nuclear Weapons," *Disarmament Times*, 19 (September 1996), p. 1.

42. The apparent imbalance of conventional forces, and the sense that nuclear threats enhanced extended deterrence, were the main reasons why the United States refused to accept Soviet offers of a "no first use of nuclear weapons" pledge. After 1990, at Washington's urging, NATO adopted the principle of "last resort" in the use of nuclear forces, and both Washington and Moscow claimed to have ended targeting of missiles at each other's territory.

43. See Boryczka, Pearson, and Weigand, "Cultural Factors."

44. The statement was made by William Epstein, cited in *Progress in Arms Control?* (San Francisco: W. H. Freeman, 1978), p. 183.

45. The U.S. position also has reflected concern about being able to modernize and assure the reliability of existing weapons and to develop very small nuclear explosives if need be. China has advocated possible nuclear testing for major construction projects and to intercept "killer asteroids" in space. In accepting the principle of a comprehensive test ban, Beijing advocated reconsideration of peaceful testing in ten years and a ban on the use of advanced monitoring technologies for verification of the agreement—technologies which they argued would give major powers such as the United States too much ability and advantage in spying. Barbara Crossette, "In Concession, China Is Ready to Ban A-Test," *New York Times*, June 7, 1996, pp. 1 and 4.

46. Virginia I. Foran, "Preventing the Spread of Arms: Nuclear Weapons," in Jeffrey A. Larsen and Gregory J. Rattray, eds., *Arms Control: Toward the 21st Century*, (Boulder, Colo.: Lynne Rienner, 1996), pp. 186–188.

47. The SALT II Treaty was never ratified by the U.S. Senate and hence never entered into force, although the Reagan administration for several years honored the informal understandings contained in the treaty.

48. *SIPRI Yearbook, 1995*, p. 871; and Forrest Waller, "Strategic Offensive Arms Control," in *Arms Control: Toward the 21st Century*, p. 106.

49. John Pike, "Military Uses of Outer Space," *SIPRI Yearbook, 1989* (Oxford: Oxford University Press, 1989), ch. 3.

50. Commission on Global Governance, *Our Global Neighborhood* (Oxford, Eng.: Oxford University Press, 1995), p. 121.

51. IAEA inspection procedures frequently have been criticized as inadequate to the task of preventing nuclear proliferation. However, the system was never designed to be foolproof. IAEA has been unable to inspect nuclear facilities in states that have not ratified NPT. Although nuclear fuels have been largely accounted for by the agency, small amounts of weapons-grade materials have disappeared over the years; and some states, such as Israel, have acquired nuclear supplies through unknown channels. Although the "nightwatch-

man" can "blow the whistle" on an apparent nuclear violation or discrepancy in nuclear supply totals, it has little or no enforcement power. It can only refer matters to the UN Security Council, call for the return of material and technical assistance already supplies, or suspend the offending state from IAEA membership.

52. Joseph F. Pilat, "Arms Control Verification and Transparency," in *Arms Control: Toward the 21st Century*, pp. 84–85; and James A. Schear, "Arms Control and Verification: Learning from Experience," paper presented to the Seminar on Arms Control Verification, University of Lancaster, England, April 1982, pp. 16–17; and William H. Kincaide, "Challenge to Verification: New and Old," Seminar on Arms Control Verification.

53. Foran, "Nuclear Weapons," pp. 179 and 189.

54. Thomas C. Schelling, "Thinking About Nuclear Terrorism," *International Security*, 6 (Spring 1982), p. 76.

Chapter 12: The Control of Violence: Confronting Terrorism and Unorthodox Violence

1. U.S. Department of State, *Patterns of Global Terrorism, 1995* (Washington, D.C.: April 1996) and *Patterns of Global Terrorism, 1993* (Washington, D.C.: April 1994).

2. See also, *The Economist*, July 26, 1986, p. 44.

3. The authors are grateful for the advice and comment of Dr. Richard J. Chasdi, who has examined in great detail the patterns and trends of Middle Eastern terrorism over the past thirty years.

4. This is a finding of Dutch political scientist Alex Schmid, reported and elaborated on by Anthony Clark Arend and Robert J. Beck, *International Law and the Use of Force* (London: Routledge, 1993), p. 140.

5. Leonard B. Weinberg and Paul B. Davis, *Introduction to Political Terrorism* (New York: McGraw-Hill, 1989), p. 3.

6. The Irgun, for example, was responsible for blowing up Jerusalem's King David Hotel, killing many British soldiers as well as bystanders in the name of liberating the Jewish homeland from British rule and creating the state of Israel. See Thurston Clarke, *By Blood and Fire: The Attack on the King David Hotel* (New York: Putnam, 1981).

7. One observer who argues that the line between terrorists and freedom fighters is very clear is James Q. Wilson in "Thinking About Terrorism," *Commentary*, 72 (July 1981), pp. 34–39. For a different view, see Benjamin B. Ferencz, "When One Person's Terrorism is Another Person's Heroism," *Human Rights*, 9 (Summer 1981), pp. 39–43.

8. Richard J. Chasdi, "Terrorism: Stratagems for Remediation from an International Law Perspective," *Shofar: An Interdisciplinary Journal of Jewish Studies*, 12 (Summer 1994), p. 77. This definition is derived by combining elements in the legal discussions of Louis Rene Beres, "Confronting Nuclear Terrorism," *The Hastings International and Comparative Law Review*, 14, no. 1 (1990), pp. 130, 132, 133; *America Outside the World: The Collapse of US Foreign Policy* (Lexington, Mass.: D.C. Heath, 1987); "Terrorism and International Law," *Florida International Law Journal*, 3, no. 3 (1988), p. 293 and p. 299, note 14; "Genocide Law and Power Politics," *Whittier Law Review*, 10, no. 2 (1988), p. 335. Beres tells us that "insurgent violence without just cause (*jus ad bello*) and/or insurgent violence which falls outside of justice in war (*jus in bello*) is terrorism." See also, Christopher L. Blakesley, *Terrorism, Drugs, International Law and the Protection of Human Liberty: A Comparative Study of International Law, Its Nature, Rule and Impact in Matters of Terrorism, Drug Trafficking, War and Extradition* (New York: Transnational Publishers, 1992), pp. 35–37; and Alex P. Schmid, *Political Terrorism: A Research Guide to Concepts, Theories, Data Bases and Literature* (Amsterdam: Transaction Books, 1983), pp. 119–158.

9. Frank H. Perez, Deputy Director, Office for Combatting Terrorism, U.S. State Department, cited in U.S. State Department Bureau of Public Affairs, *Current Policy* No. 402 (June 10,

1982). Similar definitions are offered in Timothy B. Garrigan and George A. Lopez, *Terrorism: A Problem of Political Violence* (Columbus, Ohio: Consortium for International Studies Education, 1978), pp. 1–2; Michael Stohl and George A. Lopez, *The State as Terrorist* (Westport, Conn.: Greenwood Press, 1984); Andrew J. Pierre, "The Politics of International Terrorism," *Orbis,* 19 (Winter 1976), pp. 1251–1270; Alan D. Buckley, "Editor's Foreword," *Journal of International Affairs,* 32 (Spring–Summer 1978); and Arend and Beck, *International Law and the Use of Force,* p. 141.

10. See Walter Laqueur, *Terrorism* (London: Weidenfeld and Nicolson, 1977).

11. On this point, see Ted Robert Gurr, "Some Characteristics of Political Terrorism in the 1960s," in Michael Stohl, ed., *The Politics of Terrorism,* 3rd ed. (New York: Marcel Dekker, 1988).

12. Arend and Beck, *International Law and the Use of Force,* p. 141.

13. See Edward Luttwak, *Coup d'Etat: A Practical Handbook* (Cambridge, Mass.: Harvard University Press, 1979).

14. See Serge Schmemann, "Israeli Forces Seal Off Big Parts of West Bank," *New York Times,* March 6, 1996, pp. 1 and 6A; and Youssef M. Ibrahim, "Hamas Chief Says He Can't Curb Terrorists," *New York Times,* March 9, 1996, p. 5A.

15. "Paradoxically terrorism which must appear irrational and unpredictable, in order to be effective, is an eminently rational strategy, calculated in terms of predictable costs and benefits." See Jorge Nef, "Some Thoughts on Contemporary Terrorism: Domestic and International Perspectives," *Terrorism in Theory and Practice: Proceedings of a Colloquium,* ed. by John Carson (Toronto: The Atlantic Council of Canada, 1978), p. 20. See also, Jerrold M. Post, "Notes on a Psychodynamic Theory of Terrorist Behavior," *Terrorism: An International Journal,* 7, no. 3 (1984), pp. 241–256; Abraham Kaplan, "The Psychodynamics of Terrorism," *Terrorism: An International Journal,* 1, no. 3/4 (1978), pp. 237–254; and Irving Goldaber, "A Typology of Hostage-Takers," *The Police Chief,* 46, no. 6 (1979), pp. 21–23.

16. For a view that states commit terrorist acts no less than nonstate actors, see Michael Stohl and George A. Lopez, eds. *The State as Terrorist: The Dynamics of Governmental Violence and Repression* (Greenwood, Ill.: Greenwood Press, 1984).

17. See Claire Sterling, *The Terror Network* (New York: Holt, Rinehart and Winston, 1981).

18. U.S. Department of State, *Patterns of Global Terrorism, 1995,* p. 71. Some underreporting of events may plague these data since only "international" events were counted and since regions such as Africa may have been underrepresented.

19. "International Terrorism," *GIST* (Washington, D.C.: U.S. Department of State, April 1989). The findings of several studies of terrorism reveal that, despite the rising violence potential of remote-control bombing devices and other technologies, such as the poison gas which injured 5,500 on the Tokyo subway, most terrorist events have caused relatively few casualties when compared with the casualties caused by other forms of political violence. For example, see David E. Long, *The Anatomy of Terrorism* (New York: The Free Press, 1990), p. 1; Gurr, "Some Characteristics of Political Terrorism in the 1960s," pp. 45–46; Edward F. Mickolus, *Transnational Terrorism: A Chronology of Events 1968–1979.* (Westport, Conn.: Greenwood, 1980), pp. xxii–xxiii; Peter A. Flemming, *Patterns of Transnational Terrorism in Western Europe, 1968–1987: A Quantitative Perspective,* Ph.D. dissertation (Lafayette, Ind.: Purdue University, 1992), pp. 164, 180, 194–195, 203–204; and Richard J. Chasdi, *The Dynamics of Middle Eastern Terrorism, 1968–1993; A Functional Typology of Terrorist Group-Types,* Ph.D. dissertation (Lafayette, Ind.: Purdue University, 1995).

20. U.S. Department of State, *Patterns of Global Terrorism, 1993* and *Patterns of Global Terrorism, 1995.*

21. Arend and Beck, *International Law and the Use of Force,* p. 140.

22. U.S. Department of State, *Patterns of Global Terrorism, 1989* (Washington, D.C.: 1990), pp. 1–5; and *Patterns of Global Terrorism, 1990* (Washington, D.C.: 1991), p. 37. Even where Western Europe or some region other than the Middle East has been the site of terrorist incidents, there often is a Middle Eastern connection. One rather unusual international terrorist episode was the death sentence in absentia pronounced in 1989 by Iran's Ayatollah

Khomeini on British-Indian Muslim novelist Salman Rushdie for perceived slights to the Islamic faith in Rushdie's novel, *The Satanic Verses*. Bookstores in many countries carrying Rushdie's book were firebombed, and a Muslim leader critical of the threat was assassinated in Belgium. Some observers speculate that Europe is the scene for so much terrorism because of the large number of politically open societies there that permit freedom of travel. See *The Americana Annual, 1990* (Danbury, Conn.: Grolier, 1990), p. 515.

23. David L. Milbank, "International and Transnational Terrorism: Diagnosis and Prognosis" (Washington, D.C.: U.S. Central Intelligence Agency, April 1976); and Chalmers Johnson, "Perspectives on Terrorism, Summary Report of the Conference on International Terrorism" (Washington, D.C.: U.S. Department of State, 1976). Both are cited in Garrigan and Lopez, *Terrorism: A Problem of Political Violence*, pp. 5–6.

24. Laqueur, *Terrorism*, p. 221. Also, see Laqueur, "The Futility of Terrorism," *Harper's* (March 1976). Political scientist Ted Gurr examined 87 countries between 1960 and 1976, and found measurable changes made in the political systems traceable to terrorism in only a half-dozen cases; cited in Neil C. Livingston, "Is Terrorism Effective?," *International Security Review* (Fall 1981), pp. 387–409.

25. Youssef M. Ibrahim, "In Debris of Bombing, Manchester Carries On," *New York Times*, June 17, 1996, p. A5.

26. On "how good things do not all necessarily go together," and how democratization and economic growth in the short-term can be associated with increased societal disorder, see Lucian W. Pye, "Political Science and the Crisis of Authoritarianism," *American Political Science Review*, 84 (March 1990), p. 3–19; Samuel P. Huntington, "The Goals of Development," in Myron Weiner and Samuel P. Huntington, eds., *Understanding Political Development* (Boston: Little, Brown, 1987), p. 3–32; Manus I. Midlarsky, "Rulers and the Ruled: Patterns of Inequality and the Onset of Mass Political Violence," *American Political Science Review*, 82 (June 1988), pp. 491–509; Richard E. Rubenstein, "Rebellion in America: The Fire Next Time?" in Ted Robert Gurr, ed., *Protest, Rebellion, Reform, Violence in America*, vol. 2 (Newbury, Calif.: Sage, 1989), p. 308–309; Hugh Davis Graham, "Violence, Social Theory, and the Historians: The Debate Over Consensus and Culture in America," in *Protest, Rebellion, Reform*, pp. 334–338; and Chasdi, *Dynamics of Terrorism*, p. 95. See also, Noemi Gal-Or, *International Cooperation to Suppress Terrorism* (New York: St. Martins, 1985), p. 136.

27. See Robert Katz, *Days of Wrath: The Ordeal of Aldo Moro, the Kidnapping, the Execution, the Aftermath* (New York: Doubleday, 1980); and Daniela Salvoni and Anders Stephanson, "Reflections on the Red Brigades," *Orbis*, 29 (Fall 1985), pp. 489–506.

28. John Newhouse, "A Freemasonry of Terrorism," *The New Yorker* (July 8, 1985), pp. 55–58.

29. See J. D. Zawodny, "Infrastructures of Terrorist Organizations," in Lawrence Z. Freedman and Yonah Alexander, eds., *Perspectives on Terrorism* (Wilmington, Delaware: Scholarly Resources, Inc., 1983), pp. 61–70; Martha Crenshaw, "An Organizational Approach to the Analysis of Political Terrorism," *Orbis*, 29 (Fall 1985), pp. 465–489; and As'as AbuKhalil, "Ideology and Practice of Hizballah in Lebanon: Islamization of Leninist Organizational Principles," *Middle Eastern Studies*, 27, no. 3 (1991), pp. 390–403.

30. The term is borrowed from John Newhouse, "A Freemasonry of Terrorism," *The New Yorker* (July 8, 1985), pp. 55–58.

31. Buckley, "Foreword." For a good survey of terrorist groups operating during the Cold War era in different regions of the world, see Michael Stohl, ed., *The Politics of Terrorism*, 2nd ed. (New York: Marcel Dekker, 1983), pt. 2.

32. Chasdi, *The Dynamics of Middle Eastern Terrorism*.

33. There is no single comprehensive treaty covering all varieties of terrorism; one such treaty was established under the League of Nations in 1937—the Convention for the Prevention and Punishment of Terrorism—but received only one ratification and lapsed. (See Arend and Beck, *International Law and the Use of Force*, pp. 144–145.) Instead, there are many different treaties addressing specific dimensions of terrorism, such as skyjacking.

34. See Garrigan and Lopez, *Terrorism: A Problem of Political Violence*, pp. 14–15. On the problems associated with developing a legal antiterrorism regime, see Harry H. Almond, Jr., "The Legal Regulation of International Terrorism," *Conflict*, 3, no. 2 (1981), pp. 144–165.

35. Alona Evans, "Aerial Hijacking," in M. Cherif Bassionni, ed., *International Terrorism and Political Crimes* (Springfield, Ill.: Charles C. Thomas, 1974), p. 247.

36. See Phil Williams and Paul N. Woessner, "Nuclear Material Trafficking: An Interim Assessment," *Ridgway Viewpoints*, No. 95-3 (Pittsburgh: Matthew B. Ridgway Center for International Security Studies, University of Pittsburgh, 1995), pp. 10–11.

37. See Paul A. Tharp, Jr., "The Laws of War as a Potential Legal Regime for the Control of Terrorist Activities," *Journal of International Affairs*, 32 (Spring–Summer 1978), pp. 94–97; and Juliet Lodge, "The European Community and Terrorism: Establishing the Principle of Extradite or Try," in Lodge, ed., *Terrorism: A Challenge to the State* (Oxford: Martin Robertson, 1981), pp. 164–194.

38. Stephen Sloan, "International Terrorism: Academic Quest, Operational Art and Policy Implications," *Journal of International Affairs*, 32 (Spring–Summer 1978), p. 3; and Abraham H. Miller, *Terrorism and Hostage Negotiations* (Boulder, Colo.: Westview Press, 1980).

39. Livingston, "Is Terrorism Effective?," p. 409.

40. Anti-terrorist attacks, such as Israeli kidnappings or assassinations of militant Palestinian leaders, or the KGB's kidnapping and mutilation of a relative of Hizballah terrorists holding three Soviet diplomats during the 1980s, can resemble the very acts they are meant to eliminate. The three Russian diplomats were released in the incident, seemingly validating Moscow's hard line response. See James Der Derian, "The Terrorist Discourse: Signs, States, and Systems of Global Political Violence," in Michael T. Klare and Daniel C. Thomas, eds., *World Security: Trends and Challenges at Century's End* (New York: St. Martin's Press, 1991), pp. 253–255. See also, Robert W. White and Terry Falkenberg White, "Repression and the Liberal State: The Case of Northern Ireland, 1969–1972," *Journal of Conflict Resolution*, 39 (June 1995), pp. 330–352.

41. The fact that bombings and assassinations have increased as hijackings and hostage-taking have decreased seems to fit a cyclical pattern observed by political scientists Eric Im and Todd Sandler. See their "Cycles and Substitutions in Terrorist Activities," *Kyklos* 40, no. 2 (1987), pp. 238–254. Other research has related the rate of terrorism to changes in types of governments prevalent in world politics, and particularly to shifts to and from democracy, with some arguing that shifts toward democracy actually increase the probability of terrorism. See Joseph Eyerman, "The Price of Peace: Regime Type, Transitions, and Terrorism," paper presented to the 29th Peace Science Society Meeting, Columbus, Ohio, October 1995.

Chapter 13. The Promotion of Prosperity: Keeping the World Economy Running

1. Richard J. Barnet and John Cavanaugh, *Global Dreams: Imperial Corporations and The New World Order* (New York: Simon and Schuster, 1994), p. 161.

2. *World Factbook 1995* (Washington, D.C.: U.S. Central Intelligence Agency, 1995), p. 464.

3. *Newsweek*, August 13, 1990, p. 60.

4. Charles Lipson, "International Cooperation in Economic and Security Affairs," in *World Politics*, 37 (October 1984), p. 12. A similar observation is made by Robert Jervis in "Security Regimes," *International Organization*, 36 (Spring 1982), pp. 357–378.

5. Economic trends can be found in Joan E. Spero, *The Politics of International Economic Relations*, 4th ed. (New York: St. Martin's Press, 1990), p. 76; *World Factbook 1995*, p. 463; Lester R. Brown, et al., *Vital Signs 1995* (New York: W. W. Norton, 1995), pp. 16 and 70; World Bank, *World Development Report 1992* (New York: Oxford University Press, 1992), pp. 32–33 and 196; Ray Marshall, "The Global Jobs Crisis," *Foreign Policy*, no. 100 (Fall 1995), pp. 50–68; and UNDP, *Human Development Report 1994* (New York: Oxford University Press, 1994), p. 26.

6. On the long-term decline of median family income in the United States, see U.S. Council of Economic Advisors, *Economic Report of the President, 1996* (Washington, D.C.: Council of Economic Advisors, 1996) p. 330; and Lester Thurow, "Falling Wages, Struggling Families," *St. Louis Post-Dispatch,* September 10, 1995.

7. For one of the best statements of the mercantilist view, see Jacob Viner, "Power Versus Plenty as Objectives of Foreign Policy in the Seventeenth and Eighteenth Centuries," *World Politics,* 1 (October 1948), pp. 1–29. A classic text in the mercantilist tradition, first written in 1841, is Friedrich List, *The National System of Political Economy* (Philadelphia: J. B. Lippincott, 1956).

8. Robert Gilpin, "Three Models of the Future," *International Organization,* 29 (Winter 1975), p. 42. Gilpin, a critic of the liberal school, believes such a scenario is unrealistic.

9. One of the foremost proponents of the liberal internationalist school is Harry Johnson. See his *Economic Policies Toward Developed Countries* (Washington, D.C.: Brookings Institution, 1967) and "The Probable Effects of Freer Trade on Individual Countries," in C. Fred Bergsten, ed., *Toward a New World Policy: The Maidenhead Papers* (Lexington, Mass.: D.C. Heath, 1975). Also representative of this school, but stressing the need for a substantial degree of inter-governmental management of international economic affairs, is Richard Cooper. See Richard N. Cooper et al., *Towards a Renovated International System* (New York: The Trilateral Commission, 1977). The tendency of twentieth-century liberals to support an enhanced role for the state in promoting national economic growth and social welfare and at the same time to support cooperative multilateral coordination in facilitating market-oriented international economic activity has been called "the compromise of embedded liberalism" (or the "Keynesian compromise") by John Ruggie. See his "International Regimes, Transactions, and Change: Embedded Liberalism in the Postwar Economic Order," *International Organization,* 36 (Spring 1982), pp. 379–415.

10. Representative of the *dependencia* school are Gabriel Kolko's *The Limits of Power* (New York: Harper and Row, 1972); Johan Galtung's "A Structural Theory of Imperialism," *Journal of Peace Research,* 8, no. 2 (1971), pp. 81–117; and Susanne Bodenheimer, "Dependency and Imperialism: The Root of Latin American Underdevelopment," in K. T. Fann and D. C. Hodges, eds. *Readings in U.S. Imperialism* (Boston: Porter Sargent Publisher, 1971), pp. 155–182.

11. The world system approach can be found in Immanuel Wallerstein's *The Modern World-System II: Mercantilism and the Consolidation of the European World-Economy, 1600–1750* (New York: Academic Press, 1980) and *The Capitalist World-Economy* (Cambridge, Eng.: Cambridge University Press, 1979). Also see "World System Debates," a special issue of *International Studies Quarterly,* 25 (March 1981), devoted to discussion of the world system approach.

12. See Stephen Hymer, "The Multinational Corporation and the Law of Uneven Development," in Jagdish N. Bhagwati, ed., *Economics and World Order: From the 1970s to the 1990s* (New York: Macmillan, 1972), pp. 113–140; and Christopher K. Chase-Dunn, "The System of World Cities," mimeo, Johns Hopkins University, Department of Social Relations, May 1981.

13. For a critique of both liberal and Marxist ideas from a realist perspective, see Stephen D. Krasner, *Structural Conflict: The Third World Against Global Liberalism* (Berkeley: University of California Press, 1985); and Robert Gilpin, *The Political Economy of International Relations* (Princeton, N.J.: Princeton University Press, 1987), esp. ch. 2.

14. Ibid., pp. 33–34.

15. An overview of "liberal," "radical," and other perspectives on international political economy is provided in David H. Blake and Robert S. Walters, *The Politics of Global Economic Relations,* 4th ed. (Englewood Cliffs, N.J.: Prentice-Hall, 1992,) ch. 1.

16. D. Held and A. McGrew, "Globalization and The Liberal Democratic State," in Y. Sakamoto, *Global Transformation: Challenges to the States System* (New York: United Nations Press, 1994), p. 66.

17. For different views on the shape of the international economy in the post–Cold War era, see C. Fred Bergsten, "The World Economy After the Cold War," *Foreign Affairs,* 69 (Summer 1990), pp. 96–112; Benjamin Cohen, "Toward A Mosaic Economy: Economic Relations in the

Post–Cold War Era," in Steven L. Spiegel and David Pervin, eds., *At Issue: Politics in the World Arena*, 7th ed. (New York: St. Martins Press, 1994), pp. 471–486; and Michael Borrus et al., "Mercantilism and Global Security," in Spiegel and Pervin, *At Issue*, pp. 504–515.

18. This framework follows that suggested by William D. Coplin in his *Introduction to International Politics: A Theoretical Overview* (Chicago: Markham, 1971), pp. 194–200.

19. For world trade statistics and patterns, see Blake and Walters, *The Politics of Global Economic Relations*, ch. 2; Spero, *The Politics of International Economic Relations*, chs. 3, 7, and 10; World Bank, *World Tables 1995* (Baltimore: Johns Hopkins University Press, 1995), pp. 34–35; International Monetary Fund, *Direction of Trade Statistics Yearbook 1995* (Washington, D.C.: IMF, 1995).

20. *Atlas of the Soviet Union* (Washington, D.C.: U.S. State Department, September 1987), p. 14; *Atlas of United States Foreign Relations* (Washington, D.C.: U.S. State Department, December 1985), p. 53; *Selected Countries' Trade with the USSR and Eastern Europe* (Washington, D.C.: U.S. Central Intelligence Agency, 1990); and *Handbook of Economic Statistics 1989* (Washington, D.C.: U.S. Central Intelligence Agency, 1989), tables, section 12.

21. *The Economist*, July 7, 1990, pp. 52ff.

22. *Direction of Trade Statistics Yearbook*, p. 16. In the case of the U.S., reliance on LDCs as export markets was on the increase in the 1990s, in the vicinity of 40 percent. See p. 438.

23. On the continued reliance of most developing countries on primary products for the bulk of their export revenues, see Blake and Walters, *The Politics of Global Economic Relations*, ch. 2; Dennis Pirages, *Global Technopolitics* (Pacific Grove, Calif.: Brooks/Cole, 1989), p. 152; and *Handbook of International Economic Statistics, 1992* (Washington, D.C.: U.S. Central Intelligence Agency, 1992), p. 170.

24. *Direction of Trade Statistics Yearbook*, p. 24.

25. These trends are discussed in John W. Sewell et al., *Agenda 1988* (New Brunswick, N.J.: Transaction Books, 1988), especially Ray Marshall's article on "Jobs: The Shifting Structure of Global Employment"; Brundtland Commission, *Our Common Future* (New York: Oxford University Press, 1987), pp. 207–208; Raj Aggarwal, "The Strategic Challenge of the Evolving Global Economy," *Business Horizons* (July/August 1987), pp. 38–44; and Barnet and Cavanaugh, *Global Dreams*.

26. Aggarwal, "Strategic Challenge," p. 41.

27. Spero, *The Politics of International Economic Relations*, p. 90; Sewell et al., *Agenda 1988*, p. 153.

28. Spero, *The Politics of International Economic Relations*, pp. 219–220. Interestingly, one of the "Asian tigers" is a state so small it is often referred to as a "city-state" (Singapore); another is one-half of a "divided nation" (South Korea); a third is technically not recognized as a sovereign state by most countries (Taiwan). Hong Kong, often referred to as a fourth "Asian tiger," reverts to Chinese sovereignty in 1997 under an agreement between the United Kingdom and the People's Republic of China ending its status as a British "crown colony."

29. In order, the top ten are Canada, Japan, Mexico, China, United Kingdom, Germany, South Korea, Taiwan, Singapore, and Malaysia.

30. GDP refers to the total value of goods and services produced during a given period by all factors of production that earn income within a particular country. See Mark Gasiorowski, "The Structure of Third World Interdependence," paper delivered at Annual Meeting of the International Studies Association, Cincinnati, Ohio, March 26, 1082, p. 30; Spero, *The Politics of International Economic Relations*, pp. 74 and 225; Brundtland Commission, *Our Common Future*, p. 79; and *World Tables*.

31. See Pirages, *Global Technopolitics*, ch. 5; Raymond Mikesell, *Nonfuel Minerals: Foreign Dependence and National Security* (Ann Arbor: University of Michigan Press, 1987); Phillipe Chalmin, ed., *International Commodity Markets Handbook 1993* (New York: Woodhead, 1992), parts VI–VIII; and U.S. Department of the Interior, Bureau of Mines, *Mineral Commodities Summaries*, 1990, p. 3.

32. *World Development Newsletter*, 4 (March 4, 1981), p. 1; Aggarwal, "Strategic Challenge"; and Earl H. Fry, Stan A. Taylor, and Robert J. Wood, *America the Vincible* (Englewood Cliffs, N.J.: Prentice-Hall, 1994), p. 312–313. Also, see Heidi Hobbs, *City Hall Goes Abroad* (Beverly Hills: Sage, 1994).

33. Remarks by Sir Roy Denman, head of the European Community Mission to U.S.; cited in *Washington Post National Weekly Edition*, September 22, 1986, p. 19.

34. Michael Aho and Bruce Stokes, "Managing Economic Interdependence: The European Challenge," U.S. Congress, House Committee on Foreign Affairs, *Europe and the United States*, p. 350.

35. It is not only explicit governmental policies and regulations that work against foreign imports, but also the informal Japanese business culture, notably the *keiretsu*, the network of banking, manufacturing, and other interests that have incestuous relations and dominate the Japanese economy. See Bruce Moon, *Dilemmas of International Trade*, (Boulder, Colo.: Westview Press, 1996), ch. 5. Although it is difficult for outsiders to break into this network, big U.S. retailers have been increasingly successful.

36. See James A. Dunn, "Automobiles in International Trade," *International Organization*, 41 (Spring 1987), pp. 225–252. Pressures on the EU to open its markets are discussed in "Now Japan's Autos Push into Europe," *Fortune*, January 29, 1990, pp. 96ff. On the "new protectionism" generally (especially the use of nontariff barriers), see Spero, *The Politics of International Economic Relations*, pp. 85–90; and Claire Sjolander, "Multilateralism, Regionalism, and Unilateralism: International Trade and the Marginalization of the South," in *State of the United Nations 1993: North-South Perspectives* (Providence: Academic Council of the UN, 1993), pp. 84–91.

37. See *The Economist*, April 21, 1990; and the "Survey of World Trade" in *The Economist*, September 22, 1990.

38. *Christian Science Monitor*, January 4, 1989, p. 1.

39. *Christian Science Monitor*, May 18, 1990, p. 6.

40. *Christian Science Monitor*, November 6, 1989, p. 10. The United States was invited to participate in this group despite the misgivings of some Asian states.

41. The rates quoted above were as of June 4, 1996; for other selected currencies and exchange rates that day see *New York Times*, June 15, 1996, p. C13.

42. Norman Lewis, "Globalization and the End of the Nation-State," paper delivered at Annual Meeting of the International Studies Association, San Diego, April 18, 1996, p. 16.

43. The quote was from futurist Hazel Henderson, in the *St. Louis Post-Dispatch*, June 6, 1996, p. C1.

44. Vincent Cable, "The Diminished Nation-State: A Study in the Loss of Economic Power," *Daedalus* (Spring 1995), p. 27.

45. See Benjamin J. Cohen, "A Brief History of International Monetary Relations," in Jeffrey A. Frieden and David A. Lake, eds. *International Political Economy*, 2nd ed. (New York: St. Martin's Press, 1991), pp. 234–254.

46. Data are from World Bank, *World Development Report 1994* (New York: Oxford University Press, 1994), p. 196; Spero, *The Politics of International Economic Relations*, pp. 176–177; and Sewell et al., *Agenda 1988*.

47. Spero, *The Politics of International Economic Relations*, p. 176; and Sewell et al, *Agenda 1988*, p. 40.

48. World Resources Institute, *World Resources 1994–95* (New York: Oxford University Press, 1994), p. 255.

49. *Handbook of Economic Statistics 1989* (Washington, D.C.: Central Intelligence Agency, 1989), pp. 180–181.

50. On recent foreign aid trends, see Thomas Omestad, "Foreign Aid Budget Stuck in a Time Warp," *St. Louis Post-Dispatch*, July 5, 1990; *Newsweek*, April 16, 1990, p. 23; *New York Times*, April 20, 1990; and *Christian Science Monitor*, April 23, 1990.

51.   On the ebb and flow of foreign aid, including discussion of "donor fatigue" and "privatization," see Blake and Walters, *The Politics of Global Economic Relations*, ch. 5; and Spero, *The Politics of International Economic Relations*, ch. 6.

52.   Sources and targets of direct foreign investment are discussed in Spero, *The Politics of International Economic Relations*, pp. 106 and 250–251; and Blake and Walters, *The Politics of Global Economic Relations*, p. 93. For the latest trends, also see World Bank, *Financial Flows and the Developing Countries* (May 1996), p. 14.

53.   Lewis, "Globalization and the End of the Nation-State," p. 24.

54.   *Fortune*, July 30, 1990, p. 268.

55.   *Human Development Report 1994*, p. 61.

56.   *World Development Report 1994*, p. 92.

57.   Lewis "Globalization and the End of the Nation-State," p. 29. Also see *Human Development Report 1994*, p. 62; John Stopford and Susan Strange, *Rival States, Rival Firms* (Cambridge, Eng.: Cambridge University Press, 1991), p. 18; *Finance and Development* (March 1996), p. 32, and *Financial Flows and the Developing Countries*, p. 14.

58.   J. W. Vaupel and J. P. Curhan, *The Making of Multinational Enterprise* (Boston: Harvard Business School, 1969).

59.   The definition is attributed to David Lilienthal; cited in Yair Aharoni, "On the Definition of a Multinational Corporation," in Ashok Kapur and Phillip D. Grub, eds., *The Multinational Enterprise in Transition* (Princeton, N.J.: Darwin Press, 1972).

60.   Raymond Vernon, "Economic Sovereignty at Bay," *Foreign Affairs*, 47 (October 1968), p. 114.

61.   An excellent discussion of definitional problems surrounding MNCs is provided by Aharoni, "On the Definition of a Multinational Corporation."

62.   Historical background on the evolution of MNCs is furnished in ch. 1 of *The New Sovereigns*, Abul A. Said and Luiz R. Simmons, ed. (Englewood Cliffs, N.J.: Prentice-Hall, 1975).

63.   Spero, *The Politics of International Economic Relations*, p. 106; and Kenneth Thomas, *Capital Beyond Borders* (New York: Macmillan, 1997).

64.   Duane Kujawa, "International Business Education and International Studies: A Multinational Enterprise Perspective on the Development of a Convergence Theorem," paper presented at Annual Meeting of the International Studies Association, Cincinnati, Ohio, March 25, 1982.

65.   Susan Strange, "The Defective State," *Daedalus* (Spring 1995), p. 59, based on data from the UN Center on Transnational Corporations, *World Investment Report 1993*. Also, see Lewis, "Globalization and the End of the Nation-State," p. 15; and Stephen Gill, "Globalization, Market Civilization, and Disciplinary Neoliberalism," *Millennium*, 24, no. 3 (1995), p. 405.

66.   Gill, "Globalization, Market Civilization, and Disciplinary Neoliberalism," p. 405.

67.   *Fortune*, 132 (August 7, 1995), pp. 123ff. This issue was the first in which *Fortune's* Global 500 combined industrial and service companies.

68.   Aggarwal, "Strategic Challenge."

69.   On comparison of MNC annual sales with country GNPs, see UN Center on Transnational Corporations, *Transnational Corporations in World Development: Third Survey* (New York: United Nations, 1983), p. 46.

70.   D. Korten, *When Corporations Rule the World* (West Hartford: Kumarian Press, 1995), p. 124; and K. Watkins, "The Foxes Take Over the Hen House," *The Guardian*, July 16, 1992, p. 27.

71.   "A Survey of Multinationals," *The Economist*, March 27, 1993.

72.   Richard Barnet and Ronald Muller, *Global Reach* (New York: Simon and Schuster, 1974), p. 15.

73.   Louis Turner, *Invisible Empires* (New York: Harcourt Brace Jovanovich, 1971).

74.   Said and Simmons, *The New Sovereigns*.

75.   Raymond Vernon, *Sovereignty at Bay: The Multinational Spread of U.S. Enterprise* (New York: Basic Books, 1971). Vernon revisited this question in "Sovereignty At Bay: 20 Years After," *Millennium*, 20 (Summer 1991), pp. 191–195.

76. See Richard D. Robinson, *National Control of Multinational Corporations: A Fifteen Country Study* (New York: Praeger, 1976), and the works cited in Note 13; also, see Borrus et al., "Mercantilism and Global Security."

77. See Spero, *The Politics of International Economic Relations*, p. 237.

78. Richard S. Newfarmer, "Multinationals and Marketplace Magic in the 1980's," in Jeffry A. Frieden and David A. Lake, eds., *International Political Economy*, 2nd ed. (New York: St. Martin's Press, 1991), p. 199.

79. There is disagreement in the scholarly literature as to whether MNCs or national governments have the upper hand. See Thomas, *Capital Beyond Borders* for the view that MNCs, due to capital mobility, tend to dominate the relationship. For the opposite view, see Theodore H. Moran, *Multinational Corporations and the Politics of Dependence: Copper In Chile* (Princeton, N.J.: Princeton University Press, 1974). Also see Moran, ed., *Governments and Transnational Corporations* (London: Routledge, 1993).

80. K. J. Holsti, "Change in the International System: Interdependence, Integration, and Fragmentation," in Olé R. Holsti et al., eds., *Change in the International System* (Boulder, Colo.: Westview Press, 1980), p. 37.

81. Peter Kresl, "Canada-United States Investment Linkages," paper delivered at Annual Meeting of the International Studies Association, Cincinnati, Ohio, March 26, 1982, p. 6.

82. Rick Salutin, "Keep Canadian Culture Off the Table—Who's Kidding Who," in Laurier LaPierre, ed., *If You Love This Country* (Toronto: McClelland and Stewart, 1987), pp. 205–206; cited in Moon, *Dilemmas of International Trade*, p. 141.

83. "The Buying of America," featuring a hypothetical "For Sale" sign on the Statue of Liberty, was the cover story of the November 27, 1978 issue *of Newsweek*. See Earl H. Fry, *Financial Invasion of the U.S.A.* (New York: McGraw-Hill, 1980); and Fry et al., *America the Vincible*.

84. UN Center on Transnational Corporations, *Foreign Direct Investment, the Service Sector and International Banking* (New York: United Nations, 1987), pp. 5–6; also, see *Economic Report of the President 1990* (Washington, D.C.: U.S. Government Printing Office, 1990), pp. 125ff; and Spero, *The Politics of International Economic Relations*, p. 113.

85. By 1985, the combination of a growing trade deficit along with increased funds owed to foreign investors had resulted in the United States becoming a "net debtor" nation for the first time since 1914. See ibid.; *Foreign Direct Investment in a Global Economy* (Washington, D.C.: U.S. State Department, March 1989); and *UN Watch* (February/March 1996), p. 8. An excellent review essay examining recent writings on the theme of increased foreign penetration of the U.S. economy is Robert Kudrle, "Good for the Gander? Foreign Direct Investment in the United States," paper presented at the Annual Meeting of the International Studies Association, Washington, D.C., April 13, 1990.

86. Excerpted material taken from Earl Fry, "Foreign Direct Investment in the United States: Public Policy Options," paper presented at the Annual Meeting of the International Studies Association, Washington, D.C., April 13, 1990, pp. 1–2.

87. For a summary of empirical studies generally supporting the view that MNCs on balance produce positive benefits in developed states that play host to them, see Spero, *The Politics of International Economic Relations*, p. 115. Regarding the MNC impacts produced in host developing countries, the evidence is more mixed; see ibid., pp. 240–241, and Sayre P. Schatz "Assertive Pragmatism and the Multinational Enterprise," in Frieden and Lake, *International Political Economy*, pp. 179–191. A decidedly negative view of MNC impacts on developing countries is presented by the Newfarmer article in Frieden and Lake, "Multinationals," pp. 192–207.

88. On host government concerns, see Robert Kudrle, "The Several Faces of the Multinational Corporation: Political Reaction and Policy Response," in W. Ladd Hollist and F. Lamond Tullis, eds., *An International Political Economy* (Boulder, Colo.: Westview Press, 1985), pp. 175–197.

89. Lewis, "Globalization and the End of the Nation-State," p. 24, reports excellent data on this point, based on W. Ruigrok and R. Van Tuldr, *The Logic of International Restructuring* (London: Routledge, 1995).

90. Ibid., p. 24.
91. Ibid., p. 25–26.
92. For a discussion of these and other examples, see Jack N. Berhman, *National Interests and the Multinational Enterprise: Tensions Among the North Atlantic Countries* (Englewood Cliffs, N.J.: Prentice-Hall, 1970). For the role of ITT in Chile, see Richard W. Mansbach et al., *The Web of World Politics* (Englewood Cliffs, N.J.: Prentice-Hall, 1976), pp. 175–176.
93. Raymond Vernon, "The Multinationals: No Strings Attached," *Foreign Policy*, 33 (Winter 1978–79), p. 121.
94. Kathryn J. Ready, "NAFTA: Labor, Industry and Government Perspectives," in Mario Bognanno and Kathryn J. Ready, *The North American Free Trade Agreement* (Westport, Conn.: Praeger, 1993), p. 12.
95. See Barnet and Müller, *Global Reach*, pp. 77 and 87–89, for discussion of several such incidents.
96. Raymond Vernon, "The Role of U.S. Enterprise Abroad," *Daedalus*, 98 (Winter 1969), p. 129.
97. On the growing complexity of "strategic alliances," see Stephen J. Kobrin, "Strategic Alliances and State Control of Economic Actors," paper delivered at Annual Meeting of International Studies Association, Chicago, February 24, 1995.
98. Cable, "The Diminished Nation-State," p. 31.
99. Cited in Barnet and Muller, *Global Reach*, p. 16.
100. Robert B. Reich, *The Work of Nations: Preparing Ourselves for 21st Century Capitalism* (New York: Knopf, 1991), p. 8. Also see William J. Holstein, "The Stateless Corporation," *Business Week*, 14 (May 1990), pp. 98–100.
101. Korten, *When Corporations Rule the World*, p. 125.
102. Barnet and Muller, *Global Reach*, p. 16.
103. Gilpin, *The Political Economy of International Relations*, p. 379.

Chapter 14. Economic Development: Bridging the Rich-Poor Gap

1. "Summit of Hope Ends Without Progress," *Peace Courier* (March–April 1995), p. 1.
2. Barbara Crossette, "Why the U.N. Became the World's Fair," *New York Times*, March 12, 1995, p. 4–1.
3. As one Cameroon delegate put it, "We are not satisfied. We hoped that the industrial countries would give us more. Before I came to Copenhagen, I hoped this summit would be the best thing for my country in 20 years, but now I'm disappointed." See David Rohde, "Poverty Summit Falters in Giving a Map of Future," *Christian Science Monitor*, March 13, 1995, pp. 1 and 7; Barbara Crossette, "World Leaders Confer on Aid for Very Poor," *New York Times*, March 12, 1995; and "Summit of Hope Ends Without Progress," p. 14.
4. These trends actually can be traced at least to the 1980s with the North-South summit of 1981 in Cancun, Mexico, the "Live Aid" rock concerts for African famine relief in London and Philadelphia in 1985, and the G-15 gathering of less developed states in Kuala Lumpur, Malaysia, in 1985.
5. An unlikely coalition of Britian, Sweden, and some poorer states opposed the "20:20 principle" in foreign aid, causing it to be watered down and made voluntary. Such states feared being forced into rigid quotas in various budget categories. All of the specific timetables for reforms, such as the goal of having 80 percent of the world's children complete primary school by the year 2000, were ultimately voluntary. See Rohde, "Poverty Summit Falters," p. 7; "Summit of Hope Ends Without Progress," p. 14; and Crossette, "World Leaders Confer on Aid for Very Poor."
6. See Howard Handelman, *The Challenge of Third World Development* (Englewood Cliffs, N.J.: Prentice-Hall, 1996).

7. *North-South: A Program for Survival,* Report of the Independent Commission on International Development Issues (Cambridge, Mass.: MIT Press, 1980), pp. 48–49.

8. The sustainable development concept first appeared in 1987 with the report of the World Commission on Environment and Development, chaired by Norway's then Prime Minister Gro Harlem Brundtland, entitled *Our Common Future.* The concept was pushed forward by the 1992 UN Conference on Environment and Development (UNCED). See Shareen Hertel, *The World Economy in Transition: Prospects for Sustainability, Equity, and Prosperity* (New York: United Nations Association of America, 1993), ch. 4. We discuss sustainable development in Chapter 15.

9. Argument rages about whether governments must be democratic in the western liberal mode to be effective, but it appears minimally necessary that governments be well organized and motivated enough to reach outlying districts and the entire national population with effective basic services (such as health care, schools, and police), with a minimum of corruption and disruptive violence. See Handelman, *The Challenge,* p. 7.

10. Lester R. Brown, "The Acceleration of History," *State of the World 1996* (New York: W. W. Norton, 1996), p. 3.

11. United Nations Development Program, *Human Development Report 1994* (New York: Oxford University Press/UN, 1994, p. 35.

12. Ishrat Husain, "Global Experience is Bringing Better Anti Poverty Programs," *Christian Science Monitor,* July 1, 1996, p. 19.

13. Brown, "The Acceleration of History," p. 3.

14. *Human Development Report 1994,* pp. 130–131; and Handelman, *The Challenge,* p. 6.

15. One study notes: "Despite all our technological breakthroughs, we still live in a world where a fifth of the developing world's population goes hungry every night, a quarter lacks access even to a basic necessity like safe drinking water, and a third lives in a state of abject poverty." See *Human Development Report 1994,* p. 2.

16. Other estimates put it slightly differently, noting that "the richest billion people command 60 times the income of the poorest billion." See *Human Development Report, 1994,* p. 2; see also, *North-South,* p. 32; United Nations Development Program, *UNDP and World Development by the Year 2000,* Draft (April 17, 1989), pp. 1 and 3; and World Bank, *World Development Report 1988* (Oxford: Oxford University Press, 1988), pp. 13–39.

17. *UN Development Report 1994,* p. 2; and Barbara Crossette, "In Low-Key Denmark, U.N. Talks Will Discuss All the Ways the World Hurts," *New York Times,* March 6, 1995.

18. *North-South,* pp. 48–51.

19. In the words of the Brandt Commission, "Women participate in development everywhere. But they are not equal participants because very frequently their status prevents them from having equal access to education, training, jobs, land ownership, credit, business opportunities, and even (as mortality statistics show in some countries) to nutritious food and other necessities for survival." *Ibid.,* pp. 59–60.

20. See Atul Kohli, Michael F. Altfeld, Saideh Lotfian, and Russell Mardon, "Inequality in the Third World: An Assessment of Competing Explanations," in Edward Weisband, ed., *Poverty Amidst Plenty: World Political Economy and Distributive Justice* (Boulder, Colo.: Westview Press, 1989), p. 74.

21. Lester R. Brown et al., *Vital Signs 1995* (Washington, D.C.: W. W. Norton 1995), pp. 144–145.

22. Norman Lewis, "Globalization and the End of the Nation-State," paper presented to the Annual Meeting of the International Studies Association, San Diego, March 1996, p. 30.

23. Handelman, *The Challenge,* pp. 4–5. There are, of course, sharp differences even within rich countries such as the United States, where the percentage of African American men in Harlem, New York, living to age 40 is the same as in Bangladesh.

24. Ray Marshall, "The Global Jobs Crisis," *Foreign Policy,* no. 100 (Fall 1995), p. 50. Some estimates have the percentage even higher. See United Nations Development Program, *Human Development Report 1992* (New York: Oxford University Press, 1992); and Crossette, "World Leaders Confer on Aid for Very Poor."

25. UN estimates cited by Richard Barnet and John Cavanaugh, *Global Dreams* (New York: Simon and Schuster, 1994), p. 294.

26. Interestingly, social policies more than wealth alone appear to influence this rates, as Saudi Arabia, with an average income of about $7,000 per person, has a life expectancy (69) roughly equal to that of Sri Lanka, with its average income of $500 per person. Lester R. Borwn et al., *Vital Signs 1994* (New York: W. W. Norton, 1994), pp. 134–135.

27. Stuart A. Bremer and Barry B. Hughes, *Disarmament and Development: A Design for the Future?* (Englewood Cliffs, N.J.: Prentice-Hall, 1990), p. 177.

28. Some expect that the search for cheap labor will lead MNCs to Africa, for example, just as it did to East Asia. Others, however, note that advanced cutting edge technologies may well restore cost advantages to northern industry in key economic sectors, and that only a few LDCs—the most advanced among them—will be positioned to compete in in this modern global economy, with continued large wealth gaps inside most states. See Manuel Castells and Laura D'Andrea Tyson, "High-Technology Choices Ahead: Restructuring Interdependence," in John W. Sewell et al., eds., *Growth, Exports and Jobs in a Changing World Economy, Agenda 1988* (New York: Transaction Books, 1988), pp. 55–95; and Raj Aggarwal, "The Strategic Challenge of the Evolving Global Economy," *Business Horizons* (July/August 1987), pp. 38–44.

29. *World Development Report 1992* (Oxford: Oxford University Press, 1991), p. 29.

30. Among the things that can happen to slow the pace are increased labor cost demands, resource depletion or price increases, war or revolution, disease or natural disasters, policy blunders, increased corruption, and market downturns. As noted in our discussion of national power in Chapter 3, levels of population size and skill can greatly affect a country's growth rates and the tendency to sustain them.

31. Ruth Sivard, *World Military and Social Expenditures, 1985* (Washington, D.C.: World Priorities, 1985), p. 27. In 1974, then Secretary of State Henry Kissinger had addressed the historic United Nations World Food Conference promising that "in ten years not one child shall go to bed hungry." See Joseph Collins, "World Hunger: A Scarcity of Food or a Scarcity of Democracy?," in Michael T. Klare and Daniel C. Thomas, eds., *World Security: Risks and Challenges at Century's End* (New York: St. Martin's, 1991), p. 345.

32. Estimates vary between 550 million and more than 1 billion hungry. See Collins, "World Hunger," p. 345, quoting World Bank and UN Food and Agriculture Organization calculations in 1988. See also, the Brundtland Commission, *Our Common Future* (New York: Oxford University Press, 1987), p. 118.

33. Many suspected that corporate price manipulations were behind the grocery inflation, but predictions of such price impacts were seen at scientific conferences such as the American Association for the Advancement of Science meetings in early 1995. See Robert C. Cowen, "Food Storage in US? Global Population Rise Could Drain US Markets," *Christian Science Monitor*, February 23, 1995, p. 3. See also, Hertzel, *The World Economy in Transition*, p. 3.

34. Brown, "Acceleration of History," p. 8.

35. Global food production trends are discussed in Brown et al., *Vital Signs* 1995, pp. 26–27.

36. Lester R. Brown, "A False Sense of Security," in Brown et al., *State of the World 1985* (New York: W. W. Norton, 1985), ch. 1.

37. Jennifer Seymour Whitaker, "Africa: Should the U.S. Care?" *Great Decisions*, 1996 edition (New York: Foreign Policy Association, 1996), p. 65. One is tempted to speculate about the relationship between this deterioration and the frustrations it generated and the subsequent genocidal violence that befell Rwanda, but one must note too that earlier ethnic fighting occurred in more prosperous times as well.

38. Collins, "World Hunger," p. 346.

39. The stored food could not find buyers on the world market. Neal Spivak and Ann Florini, *Food on the Table* (New York: United Nations Association, 1986), p. 28. "Ground-breaking historical research carried out in the 1970s and 1980s revealed that frequently there have

been major famines in which millions of people died while local food output and availability remained high and undiminished." Collins, "World Hunger," p. 349.

40. Robert Holden, "The Hamburger Connection," *St. Louis Post-Dispatch*, November 18, 1981.

41. Phillips Foster, *The World Food Problem: Tackling the Causes of Undernutrition in the Third World* (Boulder, Colo.: Lynne Rienner, 1992), p. 289.

42. See Brundtland Commission, *Our Common Future*, ch. 5; Lester Brown and John E. Young, "Feeding the World in the Nineties," in Lester Brown et al., *State of the World 1990* (New York: W. W. Norton, 1990), ch. 4; and Lester Brown, "Reexamining the World Food Prospect," in Lester Brown et al., *State of The World 1989* (New York: W. W. Norton, 1989) ch. 3.

43. Collins, "World Hunger," p. 346.

44. Brown, "Reexamining the World Food Prospect," pp. 43–44.

45. Joel Cohen, interview, National Public Radio, January 22, 1996; and Peter McPherson, Lecture on Foreign Assistance, Wayne State University Center for Peace and Conflict Studies, July 18, 1996. In some cases, of course, groups of people may have to adjust their culturally determined appetites for certain types of food to make more efficient use of available supplies.

46. For details on the origin of the green revolution, see Lester R. Brown, *By Bread Alone* (New York: Praeger, 1974), especially ch. 10.

47. The "oil crises" of the 1970s were particularly hard on Indian farmers who needed fuel for their irrigation pumps.

48. Ann Scott Tyson, "Budget Cuts Jeopardize Discovery of Better Seeds," *Christian Science Monitor*, June 29, 1994, p. 8.

49. Brundtland Commission, *Our Common Future*, p. 99. Such estimates both of the actual and sustainable global population are based on alternate assumptions of high, medium, or low fertility. Many are centered on medium projections; under high projections, population could go as high as 28 billion by 2150; under low projections—if the whole world emulated the low and stabilized rates seen in the North—the population would dip to less than its current 5 billion. See "World Population," *Christian Science Monitor*, July 8, 1992, quoting UN Population Fund estimates.

50. There is some disagreement about what constitutes urban areas, as some point out that "a significant proportion of the world's 'urban' population live in small market towns and administrative centers rather than cities." Fred Pearce, "Apocalypse Postponed?," *New Scientist* (London), June 1, 1996, quoting a study by the United Nations Center for Human Settlements, and reprinted in *World Press Review*, August 1996, p. 8.

51. Roger D. Hansen, *Beyond The North-South Stalemate* (New York: McGraw Hill, 1979), pp. 94 and 117.

52. Howard LaFranchi, "Mexico Curbs Birth Rate, Yet Jobless on Rise," *Christian Science Monitor*, May 10, 1996, p. 1.

53. The relief organization also addresses the criticism that offering more aid to destitute, overcrowded hordes makes the population problem worse by letting more survive. Noting that again this is "rehashed Malthusianism," relying on famine, poverty, and war to control population, they point out that population is not really exploding, and in fact is following the course predicted by "demographic transition theory" from one balanced or stabilized period to another. See Francois Jean, ed., *Populations in Danger: Medecins San Frontieres* (London: John Libbey/Medicins Sans Frontieres, 1992), pp. 9 and 145–150.

54. See *Christian Science Monitor*, July 8, 1992, p. 14; and Amy Kaslow, "Helping Women Seen as Boosting World Prosperity," *Christian Science Monitor*, August 24, 1995, p. 1.

55. Lucia Mouat, "Global Population Growth Begins to Brake, Slowly," *Christian Science Monitor*, September 17, 1991, p. 12; and Brown, "Acceleration of History," pp. 12–14.

56. See Brown, "The Acceleration of History," p. 14.

57. See Brown, "The Acceleration of History, p. 13. It has been argued that Asian states base their social structures more on ancient principles of discipline and order, such as confucianism, than on Western conceptions of individualism, freedom, and democracy. For

years, China officially encouraged late marriages, and more recently, adopting a goal of one-child families, imposed heavy financial penalties on couples having more than two children. Experiments with mandatory sterilization also have been tried in India, along with mass birth control campaigns and education programs, but with mixed results, depending on the region of the country. See Mouat, "Global Population Growth," p. 12; Werner Fornos, *Gaining People, Losing Ground* (Washington, D.C.: Population Institute, 1987), p. 45; John Dillin, "Birth Control Lags, Report Warns," *Christian Science Monitor*, February 26, 1990, p. 8; and John Gray, "The Hubris is Staggering," *The Guardian*, reprinted in *World Press Review*, August 1994, p. 50.

58. William Stevens, "3rd World Gains in Birth Control: Development Isn't Only Answer," *New York Times*, January 2, 1994.

59. Mouat, "Global Population Growth," p. 12.

60. It has been estimated that for the richest fifth of the world's population, public spending on health care averages about $600 per person, compared with about $2 per person among the world's poorest fifth. In the United States there was one doctor for every 460 persons in 1986, whereas in the African nation of Burkina Faso there was one for every 54,000. Doctors in the developing world as well as the United States tend to be concentrated in cities, leaving the rural population especially vulnerable. See Ruth L. Sivard, *World Military and Social Expenditures, 1989* (Washington, D.C.: World Priorities, 1989), pp. 24–33.

61. "Update: AIDS," *Great Decisions 1992* (New York: Foreign Policy Association, 1992). Despite the alarm raised by the spread of communicable diseases such as AIDS and TB, some experts claim that health care successes are raising the probability that noncommunicable diseases and accidents will become the chief causes of premature death and disability. See Barbara Crossette, "Noncommunicable Diseases Seen As a World Challenge," *New York Times*, September 16, 1996, p. A4.

62. Brown et al., *Vital Signs 1995*, p. 72.

63. Brown et al., *Vital Signs 1994*, p. 74.

64. For foreign aid trends, see Organization of Economic Cooperation and Development, "Aid from DAC Countries to Least Developed Countries," 1996, Table 39, Internet.

65. The quotation is found in Karin Lissakers, "Dateline Wall Street: Faustian Finance," *Foreign Policy*, no. 51 (Summer 1983), p. 160. On international bank lending practices, see Anthony Sampson, *The Money Lenders: The People and Politics of the World Banking Crisis* (New York: Penguin, 1981). Note that non-U.S. Banks, especially those in Europe and Japan, held two-thirds of the debt of the four largest Latin American debtors—Argentina, Brazil, Mexico, and Venezuela. See Steward Fleming, "Baker Banks on Non-U.S. Creditors," *Financial Times* (London), October 28, 1985, p. 3.

66. Hertel, *The World Economy in Transition*, p. 3.

67. Copper accounted for 98 percent of Zambia's export earnings; cocoa for 59 percent of Ghana's; natural gas for 49 percent of Bolivia's. Such countries' economies saw their export revenues decline by 40 to 60 percent in the falling commodity markets of the 1980s. See U.S. Central Intelligence Agency, *Handbook of International Economic Statistics* (Washington, D.C.: U.S. Government, 1992), Figure 46; Barnet and Cavanaugh, *Global Dreams*, p. 286; Raymond F. Mikesell, "The Changing Demand for Industrial Raw Materials," in Sewell et al., *Growth, Exports and Jobs in a Changing World Economy, Agenda 1988* (New York: Transaction Books, 1988), p. 155. Again, it may be no accident that a country such as Liberia, traditionally nearly totally dependent on rubber exports, stumbled badly on the road to democracy, suffering a horrific civil war in the 1990s.

68. Edward A. Gargan, "A Boom in Malaysia Reaches for the Sky," *New York Times*, February 2, 1996, p. C1.

69. "Morning Edition," National Public Radio, August 19, 1996.

70. *Our Global Neighborhood*, p. 31.

71. Donald J. Puchala and Roger A. Coate, *The Challenge of Relevance: The UN in a Changing World Environment* (Hanover, N.H.: Academic Council of UN, 1989), p. 47.

72. There have been at least two main factions within the Group of 77: (1) radicals (at various times including such states as Cuba, Algeria, and Benin), who have called for complete overhauling of the international economic system; and (2) moderates (including richer LDCs such as South Korea, Singapore, and the Ivory Coast), who have supported some NIEO proposals but have leaned more toward making practical reforms within existing institutions rather than necessarily seeking drastic change. As part of its policy reappraisal during the 1980s, the G-77 as a whole gravitated toward the moderates' position, recognizing the political and economic infeasibility of many of the NIEO demands advanced by the radicals. The G-77 continued to speak for "the South" in the 1990s despite growing diversity among LDCs. Michael W. Doyle, "Stalemate in the North-South Debate: Strategies and the NEIO," *World Politics* 35 (April 1983), pp. 426–464; "Tone is Mild at UN Session for Aid to the Third World," *New York Times*, April 24, 1990, p. A15; and Gerald Dirks et al., *The State of the United Nations, 1993: North-South Perspectives* (Providence: Academic Council on the United Nations System, 1993).

73. For a general discussion of NIEO bargaining into the 1970s, see Robert Rothstein, *Global Bargaining: UNCTAD and the Quest for a New International Economic Order* (Princeton, N.J.: Princeton University Press, 1979), pp. 23–24. The minimal role of the developed Communist states in that earlier NIEO debate is discussed in Robert M. Culter, "East-South Relations at UNCTAD: Global Political Economy and the CMEA," *International Organization*, 31, (Winter 1983), pp. 121–142.

74. Hansen, *Beyond the North-South Stalemate*, p. 216.

75. China has been singled out for criticism on the last score, for example in reproducing music and software CDs and written material with little regard for copyrights.

76. See Ernst Haas, "Why Collaborate? Issue-Linkage and International Regimes, "*World Politics*, 32 (April 1980), pp. 364–365. See also, Hayward Alker, "Dialectical Foundations of Global Disparities," *International Studies Quarterly*, 25 (March 1981), pp. 69–98.

77. See Hans-Henrik Holm, *The Game is Up: The North-South Debate Seen Through Four Different Perspectives* (Aarhus, Denmark: Institute of Political Science, University of Aarhus, 1982); and Thomas Franck and Mark M. Munansangu, *The New Order: International Law in the Making?* (New York: UNITAR, 1982).

78. Brundtland Commision, *Our Common Future*, p. 119. The world grain market also is discussed in Dennis Pirages, *Global Technopolitics* (Pacific Grove, Calif.: Brooks/Cole, 1989), ch. 4.

79. Peter G. Brown and Henry Shue, eds., *Food Policy: The Responsibility of the United States in the Life and Death Choices* (New York: Free Press, 1977), p. 2.

80. On the growing role of NGOs in economic development generally, see *Our Global Neighborhood*, pp. 198–200.

81. Foster, *The World Food Problem*, pp. 314–316. See also, Barbara Crossette, "U.N. Meeting Plans to Discuss Crisis in World Food Supply," *New York Times*, February 5, 1995, p. 12.

82. *The Economist*, December 26, 1981, pp. 79–80.

83. Spivack and Florini, *Food on the Table*, pp. 51–52.

84. Indeed it has been argued that certain aid philosophies and policy reforms work better than others. For example, land reform—taking acreage away from relatively wealthy elites and giving it to poor peasants—while well-intentioned, may deprive the agricultural sector of investment capital. Similarly, credit subsidies can deprive the poor of income because the credits tend to go to the most creditworthy, thus wealthy, farmers; minimum wage laws, if they lead to the substitution of more machines for workers, may also depress farm incomes and increase unemployment among the poor, compounding the malnutrition problem. Conversely, progressive taxation which redistributes wealth, transportation subsidies to get people to places of employment, and population services such as health care, fertility control, and public education have clearly beneficial income effects, which then improve people's nutrition. The cost of sending food subsidies or shipments to needy areas may be greater, when transportation and storage charges are figured in, than would be a compre-

hensive system of rural health services, which might save more lives, especially among children. See Foster, *The World Food Problem*, pp. 257–266.

85. The United States was the only country to vote against the code, based on the argument that it represented overregulation of the private sector. Nestlé, seeking to end a consumer boycott of its products, promised to comply.

86. See Dan Morgan, *The Merchants of Grain* (New York: Viking, 1980). See also Wendy L. Wall, "World's Grain Output Surges as Nations Seek Food Self-Sufficiency," *Wall Street Journal*, April 6, 1987, pp. 1 and 12.

87. Foster, *The World Food Problem*, chs. 11–13. It is also very difficult for countries to undergo the types of civil wars and violent disruptions seen during the 1980s and 1990s and maintain food production/distribution networks; the Sudan, for example, which had been making strides toward food self-sufficiency, was set back badly by its prolonged north-south conflict.

88. See Michael J. Berlin, "The Politics of Population," *Interdependent*, 12 (September–October 1986), p. 5; David K. Willis, "Population Growth: A Critical North-South Issue?" *Christian Science Monitor*, March 5, 1985, pp. 20–21. Despite its publicized opposition to family planning during the 1980s, in 1989 Washington joined seventy-eight other countries in signing the "Amsterdam Declaration," which called for making contraceptives available to an additional 209 million couples and set a goal of $9 billion in annual population-related spending by the year 2000.

89. The UNFPA executive director at the 1994 UN population conference was from Pakistan, a Muslim state. Nafis Sadik strongly favored government support for family planning. See Mouat, "Global Population Growth," p. 12. In addition to family planning, increased emphasis has been placed on rights and conditions of children once they are born. This has been enunciated in the United Nations convention on the Rights of the Child, which grew out of the 1979 UN Year of the Child observance, and was unanimously adopted by the General Assembly in 1989. The Convention emphasizes rights and responsibilities of both children and parents. After long delay, caused by factors such as fear of children suing parents, the U.S. signed the convention in 1995, though Senate ratification was further delayed by domestic political wrangling. See George Moffett, "US Signs Treaty on Child Rights as Critics Cringe," *Christian Science Monitor*, February 17, 1995, p. 3.

90. United Nations Population Fund, *The State of World Population 1995*, Internet, 1996, Chapter IV.

91. Ibid. See also, Paul Lewis, "U.N. Agencies to Combine Efforts Against AIDS," *New York Times*, January 23, 1994, p. 7.

92. Meghan Cox Gurdon, "UN Tries New Tack At Summit on Cities," *Christian Science Monitor*, June 3, 1996, p. 6; and "The Megacity Summit," *New York Times*, April 8, 1996, p. A14. See also, "Megacities: Bane or Boon?" *World Press Review*, August 1996, pp. 8–13.

93. "Refugees Knock, but US Doors Are Closing," *Christian Science Monitor*, March 1, 1995, p. 10.

94. Peter Hansen, "Humanitarian Aid on an International Scope," *Christian Science Monitor*, August 15, 1995, p. 18.

95. Indeed, forms of economic oppression, such as systematically denying regions of a country basic investments, have been used by political authorities against opponents, so that the concepts of political and economic repression are inherently related.

96. Lucia Mouat, "As Doors Slam in the Faces of Millions of Refugees, UN Searches for Answers," *Christian Science Monitor*, July 13, 1994, p. 7. It has been argued that getting at the causes of refugee problems, i.e., repressive governments and disruptive violence, is more effective than treating the symptoms. For example, the UN World Food Program is forced to raise its charges to donors for food shipped to refugees in war zones, from the normal $30 to $80 per metric ton to as much as $500 to $1,000 per ton because of problems of shipment and storage. Thus, preventive investments in peacekeeping forces for conflict zones such as Rwanda and Burundi would be far more cost-effective for major powers than trying to grapple with the consequences of these wars later—the massive outflow of desperate people.

See Hansen, "Humanitarian Aid," p. 18; and "Refugees Knock," p. 10. Yet sovereignty norms and deciding how to change them in the future complicate such potential remedies. Who should intervene in humanitarian emergencies—a neighboring state, a major power, a multilateral force (regional or global)? How long should they stay? What should be done to reestablish governmental authority in a chaotic situation in such a way that minorities and dissidents will be safe? See John G. Mason, "Failing Nations: What U.S. Response?" *Great Decision 1996* (Washington, D.C.: Foreign Policy Association, 1996), p. 60; "Changing Sovereignty Games and International Migration," Internet, August 1996; and Mouat, "As Doors Slam," p. 7.

97. The WHO/UNICEF International Conference on Primary Health Care, held at Alma-Ata in the Soviet Union in 1978, identified a number of health needs and objectives, including provision for primary health care in national rural and urban development plans, stress on education and prevention, community-oriented medical services, improved training and incentives for medical workers in the field, and international assistance for needy countries.

98. Warren E. Leary, "With One Disease Defeated, Another Is Attacked," *New York Times*, December 6, 1995, p. A10.

99. William J. Broad, "Is Man Losing Battle with Mosquito?" *International Herald Tribune*, July 24, 1984.

100. See *Handbook on the United Nations*, 7th ed. (New York: John Wiley, 1988), pp. 146–155. See also, Kathryn Sikkink, "Codes of Conduct for Transnational Corporations: The Case of the WHO/UNICEF Code," *International Organization*, 40 (Autum 1986), pp. 815–840.

101. Dillin, "Birth Control Lags," p. 8; and Brundtland Commission, *Our Common Future*, pp. 101–102.

102. For discussion of the UN Development Decades, see Robert E. Riggs and Jack C. Plano, *The United Nations*, 2nd ed. (Chicago: Dorsey Press, 1994), pp. 281–282.

103. The nonbinding target of aid for the poorest states was raised to 20 percent of all foreign assistance, with the 20:20 principle referred to earlier in this chapter. Also, as previously noted, increased emphasis, especially from the United States, was put on the use of private charities and organizations for aid to avoid expanding IGO bueaucracies. See "Poverty's Cure Eludes Leaders," *St. Louis Post-Dispatch*, March 13, 1995, pp. 1 and 5.

104. A Common Fund for Commodities was established in the 1980s, with over twenty states participating, including major industrial nations. At the regional level, the EU committed itself in the Lome Convention to assist former dependencies through a system called STABEX. However, specific commodity agreements, such as those in tin, rubber, and bauxite, have tended to unravel, as states become tempted to ignore provisions or withdraw over differences, leaving prices to collapse periodically, as with the International Tin Agreement in 1985. At its 1994 Uruguay Trade Round meetings, GATT reiterated its agreement that special and flexible advantages should be afforded to LDCs in trade, including extension of "most favored nation" principles. See *WTA/GATT 1994 Table of Contents*, Internet, August 1996.

105. Approximately thirty more LDCs were applying for membership in the late 1990s. See Cathryn J. Prince, "World Trade Chief Praises Expanding Global Market," *Christian Science Monitor*, April 26, 1996, p. 8.

106. One writer notes that "approximately seventy-five percent of all VERs [Voluntary Export Restraints] and OMAs [Orderly Marketing Arrangements] negotiated and imposed on exporters in the 1980s were directed toward developing countries; most were aimed at the countries of Southeast Asia by countries of the G-7. Many of these were . . . [aimed at] textiles in the cases of Bangladesh, Columbia, Egypt, Guatemala, Haiti, Mexico, and Uruguay." Clair Sjolander, "Multilateralism, Regionalism, and Unilateralism: International Trade and the Marginalization of the South," *State of The UN, 1993: North-South Perspectives* (Providence: Academic Council on the UN System, 1993), p. 88.

107. In fact, observers have noted that enthusiasm for regional trade arrangements seems to outshine that for the World Trade Organization itself, as global agreements on tariff reduction

stall. Edith Terry, "Regional Trade Blocs Are In; Global Group Draws Yawns," *Christian Science Monitor*, May 1, 1996, p. 7.

108. Despite its lack of formal structure, however, APEC has set ambitious goals, such as the complete elimination of trade and investment restrictions between members by the year 2020. Among its LDC or NIC members are China, Indonesia, Malaysia, Papua New Guinea, Philippines, South Korea, Thailand, Brunei, Chile, Hong Kong, Mexico, Singapore, and Taiwan. Its industrialized members include Canada, New Zealand, Japan, and the United States. Together it accounts for about half of the world's economic output. See Guy de Jonquieres, "Apec 'Road Map' Sets out Path to Free Trade," *Financial Times*, (London), August 31, 1995, p. 3.

109. Terry, "Regional Trade Blocs," p. 7; and Sjolander, *"Multilateralism, Regionalism, and Unilateralism."* Among other potential impediments to WTO success are the delayed entry of China and Russia into the organization, the need to settle over thirty cases of trade disputes brought before the organization, resolution of the debate over free trade vs. cheap labor, and economic corruption in many countries. Those optimistic about WTO, however, point to the fact that ten African states had 3 to 6 percent growth rates in the mid-1990s, and that non-OECD growth rates tended to outpace OECD rates in many parts of the world during those years. Prince, "World Trade Chief." p. 8.

110. Christian Tyler, "Billion-Dollar Boost for Third World," *Financial Times* (London), April 24, 1986. The UN Centre for Transnational Corporations, created to deal with foreign investment issues, had difficulty producing a uniform code of conduct beyond the Charter of Economic Rights and Duties of States. OECD members formulated a set of guidelines reflecting increased sensitivity to Southern concerns about MNC business practices.

111. Brown et al., *Vital Signs 1994*, p. 74.

112. New World Bank "global bonds" traded on world markets have helped finance some of these initiatives. Beginning in 1989, lending rates have been adjusted every six months to reflect weighted average costs of borrowing. See World Bank, "Strategy to Reduce Poverty," Internet, 1996; and Ishrat Husain, "Global Experience is Bringing Better Antipoverty Programs," *Christian Science Monitor*, July 1, 1996, p. 19.

113. Cited in *The Interdependent*, 16, no. 2 (1990), p. 5.

Chapter 15. The Management of Resources: Negotiating the World's Troubled Waters, Land, and Air

1. See Oscar Schachter, *Sharing the World's Resources* (New York: Columbia University Press, 1977), pp. 38–39.

2. Brundtland Commission, *Our Common Future* (New York: Oxford University Press, 1987), p. 27.

3. See Donnella H. Meadows et al., *The Limits to Growth* (Washington, D.C.: Potomac Associates, 1972). Meadows et al. reiterated their concern in their sequel, *Beyond the Limits* (Post Mills, VT.: Chelsea Green, 1992).

4. For an extremely optimistic view that rejects the doomsday perspective, see Julian Simon, *The Ultimate Resource* (Princeton, N.J.: Princeton University Press, 1981).

5. In 61 A.D., Seneca wrote of "the heavy air of Rome." In 1659, one observer wrote that London was enveloped in "such a cloud of sea-coal, as if there be a resemblance of hell on earth." Cited in Jacqueline V. Switzer, *Environmental Politics: Domestic and Global Dimensions* (New York: St. Martin's, 1994), p. 191, and Adam Markham, *A Brief History of Pollution* (New York: St. Martin's Press, 1994), p. 10.

6. W. Jackson Davis, *The Seventh Year: Industrial Civilization in Transition* (New York: W. W. Norton, 1979), p. 109.

7. Hilary F. French, "Clearing the Air," in Lester R. Brown et al., *State of the World 1990* (New York: W. W. Norton, 1990), p. 98; and Pete Hamill, "Where the Air Was Clear," *Audubon*, 95 (January–February 1993), p. 39. Also, see Gregg Easterbrook "Forget PCBs," *New York Time Magazine*, September 11, 1994, p. 60.

8. See Switzer, *Environmental Politics*, ch. 12; and World Resources Institute, *World Resources 1992–93* (New York: Oxford University Press, 1992), pp. 197–198.

9. See World Resources Institute, *World Resources 1996–97* (New York: Oxford University Press, 1996), p. 317; and Lester R. Brown et al., *Vital Signs 1996* (New York: W. W. Norton, 1996), pp. 66–67. Great uncertainties remain regarding greenhouse warming. See Wallace S. Broeker, "Global Warming on Trial," *Natural History* (April 1992), pp. 6–14; and Stephen H. Schneider, *Global Warming: Are We Entering the Greenhouse Century?* (New York: Sierra Club Books, 1989).

10. Cynthia Shea, "Protecting the Ozone Layer," in Lester R. Brown et al., *State of the World 1989* (New York: W. W. Norton, 1989), pp. 77–96. For statistics on ozone depletion and other atmospheric pollution trends, see International Institute for Environment and Development, *World Resources 1988–89* (New York: Basic Books, 1988), chs. 10 and 23; and *Vital Signs 1996*, pp. 64–71.

11. On desertification trends, see Brundtland Commission, *Our Common Future*, pp. 34 and 127–128; and "Stopping the Dry Destruction," in John Allen, ed., *Environment 1995/96* (Sluice Dock, Conn.: Dushkin, 1995), pp. 170–174.

12. Based on presentation by Glenn Green at Conference on the Global Environment, St. Louis, May 17, 1990.

13. Comments of Dennis Mahar, a World Bank official, at Conference on The Global Environment, St. Louis, May 17, 1990. In "Instant Trees," *The Economist*, April 28, 1990, p. 93, it was reported that the most recent satellite photos showed considerably less loss of the Brazilian rain forests than previously thought, though they still showed a damaged area about the size of the western half of Germany. Also, see Switzer, *Environmental Politics*, ch. 14.

14. Species extinction is discussed in Brundtland Commission, *Our Common Future*, ch. 6; *World Resources 1987*, ch. 6; and Edward G. Wolf, "Avoiding a Mass Extinction of Species," in Lester R. Brown et al., *State of the World 1988* (New York: W. W. Norton, 1988), pp. 101–117.

15. On deforestation trends, see Lester R. Brown and Christopher Flavin, "The Earth's Vital Signs," in *State of the World 1988*, pp. 3–21; *Vital Signs 1996*, pp. 122–123; Norman Myers, *The Primary Source* (New York: W. W. Norton, 1992); and John F. Richard and Richard P. Tucker, eds., *World Deforestation in the Twentieth Century* (Durham, N.C.: Duke University Press, 1988).

16. Brundland Commission, *Our Common Future*, pp. 226–232, discusses hazardous wastes. Also, see Switzer, *Environmental Politics*, ch. 5.

17. Marian A. L. Miller, *The Third World in Global Environmental Politics* (Boulder, Colo.: Lynne Rienner, 1995), ch. 5.

18. Sandra Postel, "Managing Freshwater Supplies," in Lester R. Brown et al., *State of the World 1985* (New York: W. W. Norton, 1985), ch. 3; and Easterbrook, "Forget PCBs."

19. "Next Wars Over Water," *World Press Review* (November 1995), p. 8.

20. Andre van Dam, "The Future of Waste," *International Studies Notes*, 4 (Winter 1977), p. 17.

21. Cited in "Next Wars Over Water," p. 8. Another author counts only 26 "Water Scarce" countries; see Sandra Postel, "Facing A Future of Water Scarcity," in Allen, *Environment 1995/96*, pp. 177–180. In the same volume, also see Peter H. Gleick, "Water, War, and Peace in the Middle East," pp. 181–195. "Water wars" are further discussed in *Foreign Policy* (Summer 1991).

22. Michael G. Renner, "Shared Problems, Common Security," in Charles W. Kegley and Eugene Wittkopf, eds., *Global Agenda* (New York: St. Martin's, 1992), p. 337.

23. LDC shares will rise from today's 27 percent to 40 percent, with the former Soviet bloc ac-
     counting for another sixth. See "Energy Survey: Power to the People," *The Economist*, June
     18, 1994, pp. 3–18.

24. Ibid., p. 3. See also Joshua S. Goldstein, Xiaoming Huang, and Burcu Akan, "Energy in the
     World System, 1950–1992," unpublished paper, August 1995, p. 5.

25. Gareth Porter and Janet Welsh Brown, *Global Environmental Politics*, 2nd ed. (Boulder,
     Colo.: Westview Press, 1996) p. 6. Traditionally, the South has been a net energy exporter,
     and every Northern region except the former Soviet Union has been an energy importer.
     This complex energy trade has highlighted the importance of the Middle Eastern oil econ-
     omy and has related strongly to the use of force, as in the Persian Gulf.

26. Even with these changing energy consumption patterns, the growth in overall world energy
     demand led the International Energy Agency (IEA) to predict in 1995 that without new
     policies, world emissions of carbon would exceed 1990s levels by 30 to 40 percent in the
     year 2010. See Christopher Flavin, "Facing Up to the Risks of Climate Change," in Lester
     R. Brown, et al., *State of the World 1996* (New York: W. W. Norton, 1996), p. 37.

27. The verdict is still out on whether the shift to renewable and solar energy will fulfill the vi-
     sion that "the world energy system in the year 2030" will "no longer be dominated by fos-
     sil fuels [but] will be run by solar resources daily replenished by incoming sunlight and by
     geothermal energy." Lester R. Brown et al., "Picturing a Sustainable Society," in *State of
     the World 1990*, p. 176. See also, "Research Goal: Solar-Powered 21st Century," *Christian
     Science Monitor*, June 19, 1990, p. 15.

28. Hal Kane, "Shifting to Sustainable Industries," in Lester R. Brown et al., *State of the World
     1996* (New York: W. W. Norton, 1996), p. 154; also see Christopher Flavin, "Harnessing the
     Sun and the Wind," in *State of the World 1995* (New York: W. W. Norton, 1995), pp. 58–75.

29. See *Vital Signs 1995*, pp. 52–53. The nuclear industry relies on fuels derived from finite,
     nonrenewable supplies of uranium. Using uranium 235, a fission process (which involves
     the splitting of atoms) creates both usable heat and dangerous radioactive waste products.
     To compensate for limited supplies of U235, "fast breeder" reactors have been developed to
     convert more plentiful U238 to plutonium, a highly toxic fuel that is also useful for pro-
     ducing nuclear weapons. In the future, nuclear engineers hope to perfect safer breeder reac-
     tors and to solve the waste disposal problem. They also continue work on perfecting a prac-
     tical commercial "fusion" reactor, using various forms of plentiful hydrogen to fuse, rather
     than split, atoms. The process, similar to the sun's own type of energy output, would lead
     to cleaner emissions but requires containment facilities capable of housing reactions as hot
     as those on the sun or in a thermonuclear blast. See Davis, *The Seventh Year*, p. 64.

30. See Barry D. Hughes et al., *Energy in the Global Arena* (Durham: Duke University Press,
     1985), p. 6; *World Resources 1992–1993* (New York: Oxford University Press, 1993), ch. 10;
     and UN Environmental Program, *UN Environmental Report 1993–94* (Oxford: Blackwell
     Publishers, 1993), pp. 271–294.

31. Although some scrubbing techniques and use of cleaner varieties have improved coal's en-
     vironmental record, the most abundant and easily reached supplies remain the dirtiest.
     Until coal liquefaction and gasification technologies are further developed, coal will have
     only limited utility in the transportation sector.

32. See "Power to the People." Some economists detect trends toward a long-term stabilization
     or possible "equilibrium" of oil prices around $30 dollars per barrel. See Goldstein, Huang,
     and Akan, "Energy in the World Systems."

33. The "political ecology" as well as political economy of energy, and especially petroleum,
     are discussed in Dennis Pirages, *Global Technopolitics* (Pacific Grove, Calif.: Brooks/Cole,
     1989), ch. 3.

34. Lester R. Brown, *The Twenty-Ninth Day* (New York: W. W. Norton, 1978), p. 126.

35. Pirages, *Global Technopolitics*, ch. 5.

36. See, for example, Raymond Mikesell, *Nonfuel Minerals: Foreign Dependence and National
     Security* (Ann Arbor: University of Michigan Press, 1987).

37. Australia and Canada, leading international lead producers, have fought U.S. proposals for a binding agreement, though hope remains for a formal UN treaty. Lead use has declined somewhat in advanced industrial economies, but in developing countries such as China and India, its use has continued to mount. Marlise Simmons, "Rich Nations Urge Action to Cut Danger from Lead," *New York Times*, February 23, 1996, p. A5.

38. See Joan E. Spero, *The Politics of International Economic Relations*, 4th ed. (New York: St. Martin's Press, 1990), pp. 292–294.

39. Pirages, *Global Technopolitics*, ch. 5; *Americana Annual 1990* (Danbury, Conn: Grolier, 1990), p. 580.

40. For some assessments, see Kenneth A. Dahlberg et al., *Environment and the Global Arena: Actors, Values, Policies and Futures* (Durham, N.C.: Duke University Press, 1985), chs. 5 and 6.

41. The Stockholm Conference is discussed in David A. Kay and Eugene B. Skolnikoff, eds., *World Eco-Crisis: International Organizations in Response* (Madison: University of Wisconsin Press, 1972).

42. Peter Haas notes that "the number of developing countries with environmental agencies grew from 11 in 1972 to 110 in 1982." "The Future of International Environmental Governance," paper presented at Annual Meeting of International Studies Association, San Diego, April 17, 1996, p. 28.

43. The Rio Conference is discussed in Michael Grubb et al., *The Earth Summit Agreements: A Guide and Assessment* (London: Earthscan Publications, 1993).

44. On third world views of global environmental issues, see Miller, *The Third World in Global Environmental Politics*; and Roberto P. Guimaraes, *The Ecopolitics of Development in the Third World: Politics and Environment in Brazil* (Boulder, Colo.: Lynne Rienner, 1991).

45. On tropical deforestation in Brazil, see ibid. and Rachel M. McCleary, *Development Strategies in Conflict: Brazil and the Future of the Amazon* (Washington, D.C.: Pew Case Studies Center, Georgetown University, 1990).

46. Haas, "The Future of International Environmental Governance," p. 16. Also, see Robert Livernash, "The Growing Influence of NGOs in the Developing World," *Environment*, 34 (June 1992); Thomas Princen and Matthias Finger, eds., *Environmental NGOs in World Politics* (London: Routledge, 1994); and Ken Conca, "Greening the UN: Environmental Organizations in the UN System," in Thomas E. Weiss and Leon Gordenker, eds., *NGOs, The UN, and Global Governance* (Boulder, Colo.: Lynne Rienner, 1996), pp. 103–119.

47. In 1995, the Business Council for Sustainable Development merged with the World Industry Council for the Environment to form the World Business Council for Sustainable Development, made up of many of the biggest MNCs in the world. Some observers question the degree to which these MNCs are truly pro-environment. See Matthias Finger and James Kilcoyne, "Multinationals Organizing to 'Save' the Global Environment," paper presented at Annual Meeting of International Studies Association, San Diego, April 16, 1996.

48. UN General Assembly, 22nd Regular Session, Document A/16695 (August 17, 1967).

49. *The Law of the Sea* (New York: United Nations. 1973), pp. 2–5; and David L. Larson, ed., *Major Issues of the Law of the Sea* (Durham: University of New Hampshire, 1976).

50. Ibid., p. 10.

51. See David L. Larson, "Will There Be an UNCLOS IV?," paper presented at Annual Meeting of the International Studies Association, Washington, D.C., April 1990; and Larson et al., "An Analysis of the Ratification of the UN Convention of the Law of the Sea," paper presented at Annual Meeting of International Studies Association, Washington, D.C., April 1, 1994.

52. Schachter, *Sharing*, p. 43.

53. Also see Clyde Sanger, *Ordering the Oceans* (Toronto: University of Toronto Press, 1987), for an overview of how various actors viewed various issues during the UNCLOS III negotiations.

54. A special issue that has plagued the IMO is the "flags of convenience" problem. The international shipping industry is split between those countries and companies that adhere to strict regulatory practices and those countries offering, and companies seeking, "flags of

convenience." Flags of convenience are registration and licences issued by states, such as Liberia and Panama, which enforce fewer safety and personnel standards and, hence, require less financial investment or ship upkeep.

55. Seyom Brown et al., *Regimes for Ocean, Outer Space, and Weather* (Washington, D.C.: Brookings Institution, 1977), pp. 38–40.

56. The Regional Seas Program and other efforts to curb ocean pollution are discussed in *World Resources 1986*, pp. 154ff. The East Asia Plan is examined in *World Resources 1988–89*, pp. 152–154.

57. Paul Mackay, "Whaling and Dealing," *Christian Science Monitor*, July 12, 1990, p. 19; and Gareth Porter and Janet Brown, *Global Environmental Politics*, 2nd ed. (Boulder, Colo.: Westview Press, 1996), pp. 77–81.

58. See. M. J. Peterson, "International Fisheries Management," in Peter M. Haas, Robert O. Keohane, and Marc A. Levy, *Institutions for the Earth* (Cambridge: MIT Press, 1993), pp. 249–305.

59. Marc A. Levy, "European Acid Rain: The Power of Tote-Board Diplomacy," in Haas, Keohane, and Levy, *Institutions for the Earth*, pp. 75–132. The author notes that, even with significant interstate cooperation, acid rain remains a serious problem in Europe.

60. Cited in *St. Louis Post-Dispatch*, September 16, 1982, p. 6A.

61. Richard E. Benedick, "Ozone Diplomacy," *Issues in Science and Technology* (Fall 1989), p. 50. Benedick, the U.S. ambassador to the Montreal negotiations, provides a fuller discussion in *Ozone Diplomacy: New Directions in Safeguarding the Planet* (New York: World Wildlife Fund and the Conservation Foundation, 1990). Also see Edward A. Parson, "Protecting the Oxone Layer," in Haas, Keohane, and Levy, *Institutions for the Earth*, pp. 27–73.

62. Benedick, "Ozone Diplomacy," notes the special circumstances that contributed to the success of the Montreal Protocol, although he argues that progress was made in responding to the ozone problem despite initial "ambiguity" surrounding the scientific evidence. On the responses of the international community to the global warming concern, see *World Resources 1988–89*, chs. 10 and 13; Switzer, *Environmental Politics*, ch. 13; and *The Earth Summit Agreements*, ch. 6.

63. Sylvia M. Williams, "International Law Before and After the Moon Agreement," *International Relations* (London), 7 (November 1981), pp. 1170–1171.

64. Christopher D. Stone, *The Gnat Is Older Than Man* (Princeton: Princeton University Press, 1993), p. 36.

65. Ibid., pp. 210–211.

66. Cited in Williams, "International Law," p. 1187. On development of an outer space regime, see Brown et al., *Regimes for the Ocean, Outer Space, and Weather*; and William R. Slomanson, *Fundamental Perspectives on International Law*, 2nd ed. (Minneapolis: West, 1996), pp. 266–269.

67. Consultation on international policy economy with Robert Packer, Wayne State University, October 1996.

68. See Porter and Brown, *Global Environmental Politics*, pp. 45 and 138–139. Also see Helmut Breitmeier, "Opportunities and Limitations for Ecological Regimes in the International System," paper presented to the 22nd Colloquium of the German Association of Peace and Conflict Research, Arnoldshaim, Schmitten, Germany, February 1994; S. M. Mhod Idris, "UN Treaty on Toxic Waste Legalizes Dumping in the Third World," *Peace Research*, 21 (November 1989), pp. 70–71; *World Resources 1988–89*, chs 13, 16, 18, and 19; Juli Abouchar, "Canada and the Biodiversity Convention," *Alternatives* (Canada), 20 (November-December 1993), p. 20.

69. See, for example, Safei El-Deen Hamed, "Seeing the Environment Through Islamic Eyes: Application of Shariah to National Resources Planning and Management," *Journal of Agricultural and Environmental Ethics*, 6, no. 2 (1993), pp. 145–164. Note, though, that certain similarities of viewpoint also prevail cross-culturally, for example, in the Islamic presumption that though the world's resources belong to God, they are here for people's enlightened use, transformation, and enjoyment.

70. Cited in *The Interdependent*, 7 (January–February 1981), p. 2.
71. Cited in Sandra Postel, "Carrying Capacity: Earth's Bottom Line," in Lester R. Brown et al., *State of the World 1994* (New York: W. W. Norton, 1994), p. 19.

PART V. CONCLUSION

1. Robert G. Gilpin, *War and Change in World Politics* (Cambridge, Eng.: Cambridge University Press, 1981), p. 227.
2. Remark by Governor Richard Lamm of Colorado, cited in *Christian Science Monitor*, April 24, 1985, p. 5.

Chapter 16. Toward the Year 2001 and Beyond

1. James Rosenau is among those who have called for a new "postinternational politics" paradigm as a framework for understanding the latest trends. This debate is discussed in Ernst-Otto Czempiel and Rosenau, eds., *Global Changes and Theoretical Challenges: Approaches to World Politics for the 1990s* (Lexington, Mass.: Lexington Books, 1989).
2. This excerpt is from Burns H. Weston, Richard A. Falk, and Anthony D'Amato, *International Law and World Order: A Problem-Oriented Casebook* (St. Paul, Minn.: West Publishing, 1980), p. 1032; these international lawyers acknowledge that this view of the world is not widely shared and is open to serious question.
3. Hans J. Morgenthau, "The New Diplomacy of Movement," *Encounter*, 43 (August 1974), p. 57.
4. Arthur Koestler, "Janus: A Summing Up," *The Bulletin of the Atomic Scientists*, 35 (March 1979), p. 4.
5. For the WOMP point of view, see Richard A. Falk, *This Endangered Planet* (New York: Random House, 1972); Rajni Kothari, *Footsteps into the Future: Diagnosis of the Present World and a Design for an Alternative* (New York: Free Press, 1974); and Saul H. Mendlovitz, *On the Creation of a Just World Order: Preferred Worlds for the 1990s* (New York: Free Press, 1975).
6. The "unit veto system" and other variants of the state system are discussed in Morton A. Kaplan's *System and Process in International Politics* (New York: John Wiley, 1957), ch. 2.
7. Robert C. North, *The World That Could Be* (New York: W. W. Norton, 1976), p. 136.
8. Robert C. Johansen, *The National Interest and the Human Interest* (Princeton, N.J.: Princeton University Press, 1980), p. 29.
9. Joseph S. Nye, *Peace in Parts* (Boston: Little, Brown, 1971), p. 199. Nye is more skeptical about the possibility that regional organizations will lead to regional governments or a world government.
10. For a discussion of approaches to world government, see Louis Renes Beres and Harry R. Targ, *Reordering the Planet: Constructing Alternative Futures* (Boston: Allyn and Bacon, 1974), ch. 6.
11. See Karl W. Deutsch et al., *Political Community and the North Atlantic Area* (Princeton, N.J.: Princeton University Press, 1957).
12. Citing Ted Gurr's definition of a "communal group," one writer notes that "if a nation is defined as a population with a 'distinctive and enduring collective entity based on cultural traits and lifeways that matter to them and to others with whom they interact,' then by some counts the world contains anywhere from 3000 to 5000 nations." Seyom Brown, *New Forces, Old Forces, and the Future of World Politics*, post–Cold War ed. (New York: Harper Collins, 1995), p. 162.
13. W. Jackson Davis, *The Seventh Year: Industrial Civilization in Transition* (New York: W. W. Norton, 1979), p. 276.

14. Celestine Bohlen, "Italy's Northern League Exploits a Growing Army of Malcontents," *New York Times*, June 11, 1996, p. A1.

15. James N. Rosenau, "Governance in the Twenty-first Century," *Global Governance*, 1 (Winter 1995), pp. 25–26. Also, see Saskia Sassen, *The Global City: New York, London, Tokyo* (Princeton, N.J.: Princeton University Press, 1991); and Earl H. Fry et al., *The New International Cities Era: The Global Activities of North American Municipal Governments* (Provo, Utah: Brigham Young University Press, 1989).

16. Brown, *New Forces, Old Forces*, pp. 154–155. Also, see Kenichi Ohmae, "The Rise of the Region-State," *Foreign Affairs*, 72 (Spring 1993), pp. 78–87; and Ohmae, "The New World Order: The Rise of the Region-State," *Wall Street Journal*, August 16, 1994.

17. Jonathan Schell, *The Fate of the Earth* (New York: Knopf, 1982).

18. Stephen J. Kobrin, "Strategic Alliances and State Control of Economic Actors," paper presented at annual meeting of the International Studies Association, Chicago, February 24, 1995.

19. See Richard O'Brien, "Global Financial Integration: The End of Geography," in Royal Institute of International Affairs, *Chatham House Papers* (London: Pinter, 1992). Also see John G. Ruggie, "Territoriality and Beyond: Problematizing Modernity in International Relations," *International Organization*, 47 (Winter 1993), pp. 139–154; John Agnew and Stuart Corbridge, *Mastering Space* (London: Routledge, 1995); and Agnew, "The Territorial Trap: The Geographical Assumptions of International Relations Theory," *Review of International Political Economy*, 1 (Spring 1994), pp. 53–80.

20. On the emergence of "global civil society," see Ronnie D. Lipschutz, "Reconstructing World Politics: the Emergence of Global Civil Society," *Millennium*, 21, no. 3 (1992), pp. 389–420.

21. Bob Davis, "Growth of World Trade Binds Nations, But It Also Can Spur Separatism," *Wall Street Journal*, June 20, 1994, p. 1.

22. "Nonterritorial actors" and their relationship to world order values is discussed in Richard A. Falk, "A New Paradigm for International Legal Studies: Prospects and Proposals," in Falk et al., eds., *International Law: A Contemporary Perspective* (Boulder, Colo.: Westview Press, 1985), pp. 651–702.

23. See, for example, the new journal *Global Governance*; and the Report of the UN Commission on Global Governance, entitled *Our Global Neighborhood* (New York: Oxford University Press, 1995).

24. Remarks in an interview by Rushworth M. Kidder, cited in *Christian Science Monitor*, December 16, 1986, p. 20.

25. In June of 1982, French and Soviet cosmonauts dined on French "haute cuisine" in space, eating tube-fed creamed crab, paté and other items. *St. Louis Post-Dispatch*, June 25, 1982, p. 11A.

26. This line is taken from Robert Heilbroner's *An Inquiry Into the Human Prospect* (New York: W. W. Norton, 1975), p. 169.

Glossary

Alien.   A person traveling or residing within a state who is either a citizen of another state or stateless.

Alliance.   A formal agreement to provide mutual military assistance in time of war.

Alternative world order models.   Alternative political systems into which human beings could conceivably organize themselves.

Ambassador.   A high-level diplomatic official appointed as a representative by one government to another.

Anti-ballistic missile (ABM).   A defensive missile system designed to stop an enemy nuclear attack by destroying incoming missiles before they hit their targets.

Arms control.   Agreements to limit the development, stockpiling, or use of certain types of weapons, or the deployment of weapons in certain areas.

Arms race.   Competitive armament by two or more countries seeking security and protection against each other.

Arms transfers.   Sales and gifts across national boundaries of weapons systems, support services, spare parts, and designs.

Autarky.   National economic self-sufficiency.

Balance of payments.   A financial statement of a country's economic transactions with the rest of the world, taking into account both outflows and inflows of money (e.g., foreign aid given and received, imports and exports, foreign investment funds spent abroad or received from abroad).

Balance of power.   A basis for maintaining order among states, whereby aggressive-minded states are to be deterred by the prospect of coming up against a coalition of states having equal or superior power.

Balance of trade.   A country's annual net trade surplus or deficit, based on the difference in the value of its total exports and imports.

Bargaining.   A means of resolving differences over priorities between contestants through an exchange of proposals containing mutually acceptable terms.

Behavioralists.   International relations theorists who use rigorous social science methods, such as collection and analysis of quantitative data, to develop and test theories explaining the behavior of international actors.

Bilateral.   Pertaining to relations between pairs of countries.

Bilateral diplomacy.   Diplomatic negotiations between two countries.

Bimultipolar system.   An international system in which two major powers predominate but in which other powers have significant freedom of action. (Sometimes called a loose bipolar system.)

Biological weapons.   Toxic substances that can create diseases and epidemics when launched against enemy troops or populations.

Biological Weapons Convention of 1972. An agreement forbidding not only the use of biological weapons but also their production and stockpiling.

Bipolar system.   An international system in which countries align themselves into two cohesive blocs.

Boycott.   The refusal of one country to purchase goods from another country.

Brain drain.   The loss of native third

world technicians, engineers, and scientists to the more technically advanced countries.

Brezhnev Doctrine. A Soviet policy, established in 1968, stipulating that communist countries can intervene in those states (such as Czechoslovakia) where "capitalist circles" threaten to topple an established communist government.

Bureaucratic politics. The infighting between various agencies of a government which in the process of pursuing organizational interests often produce a foreign policy based more on domestic politics than on national interest or national security.

Capitalism. An economic system that stresses private property and the accumulation of private wealth, based on laissez-faire free enterprise principles (a market economy as opposed to an economy stressing a high level of central governmental planning and control).

Capital sector. In the international economy, the flow of foreign aid and foreign investment funds across national boundaries.

Charter of Economic Rights and Duties of States. A resolution passed by the UN General Assembly in 1974 recognizing the right of every state to exercise full permanent sovereignty over all its wealth, natural resources, and economic activities.

Chemical weapons. Gases, herbicides, and other chemical substances that can kill or paralyze enemy troops or populations.

Chemical Weapons Convention of 1993. A treaty that went beyond the Geneva Protocol of 1925, in banning not only the use of chemical weapons but also their production and stockpiling.

Civil war. Sustained violent conflict between organized political forces within a state.

Collective goods. Goods that are jointly available and indivisible, which no individuals can be deprived of even if they did not contribute to the production of the goods.

Collective security. A system of world order in which the weight of the entire international community would be thrown against any state committing aggression, as provided for in the UN Charter.

Commerce. In the international economy, imports and exports of commodities and products that flow across national boundaries; international trade.

Common market. A stage in economic integration, as envisioned in the European Community plan, in which not only goods and services but workers and capital are able to move freely across national boundaries.

Communism. A political ideology and movement which, since Lenin, has advocated the use of a single mass-based party vanguard leadership to bring about a workers' and peasants' revolution, leading to first a socialist society based on central government planning along with state ownership of property, and ultimately, to a stateless and classless society.

Comparative foreign policy analysis. A body of research that attempts to examine systematically the foreign policy behavior patterns that states exhibit and the determinants of these patterns.

Compellence. The attempt by one state to persuade another state to do something the latter generally does not wish to do.

Concert of Europe. Nineteenth-century system of "great power" consultation, created by Britain, Prussia, Russia, and other European powers at the 1815 Congress of Vienna, after the Napoleonic Wars, designed to resolve international problems whenever a dispute threatened to erupt into war.

Congress of Vienna. The 1815 peace conference after the Napoleonic Wars, which created the Concert of Europe and produced one of the first sets of rules governing exchange of ambassadors and other diplomatic relations among states.

Containment. A major theme running through American foreign policy after World War II, involving the establishment of alliances by the United States to halt the expansion of Communism.

Convention. See Treaty.

Conventional weapons. Non-nuclear weapons.

Counterinsurgency. Tactics used to combat revolutionaries engaged in guerrilla warfare, stressing combat in rugged terrain, intelligence operations to identify and destroy guerrilla sanctuaries, and inducements to civilians to report guerrillas to government authorities.

Credibility. The extent to which one state's threats or promises are believed by another state.

Crisis decision. A foreign policy decision made in situations normally characterized by a sense of high threat and potential gravity, an element of surprise, a short time frame, and involvement of the highest level of the foreign policy establishment.

Cultural Revolution. The internal upheaval in the People's Republic of China that occurred in the late 1960s and early 1970s in which the regime of Chairman Mao Tse-tung undertook to rekindle revolutionary fervor in the masses and prevent a technologically elitist society.

Currency. Any form of money used as a medium of exchange in domestic and international economic transactions.

Customary rules. Those practices that have been widely accepted as legally binding by states over a period as evidenced by repeated usage.

Customs union. A stage in eco-nomic integration, as envisioned in the European Community plan, in which all member states impose a common external tariff on goods entering the union from nonmember states.

Democracy. An open, pluralistic governmental system, allowing for free expression and the flow of ideas and for rival political groupings.

***Dependencia* school.** An international economic perspective that sees the international economy as consisting of two sets of states, the dominant North and the dependent South, resulting in pervasive poverty in the South and great wealth in the North.

Détente. The relaxation of tensions between adversaries; applied in the 1970s to the United States and the Soviet Union.

Deterrence. The attempt by one state to dissuade another state from doing something, particularly an act of military aggression.

Devaluation. The lowering of the value of a country's currency relative to other national currencies.

Dictatorship. A closed, authoritarian governmental system in which free expression and the flow of ideas are severely curtailed and political opposition severely restricted.

Diplomacy. The formal practices and methods whereby states conduct their foreign relations, including the exchange of ambassadors; the general process whereby states seek to communicate, to influence each other, and to resolve conflicts through bargaining.

Diplomatic immunity. The freedom from arrest or prosecution enjoyed by foreign diplomats in a host country, based on the Vienna Convention on Diplomatic Relations.

Disarmament. The decision by one or more states to destroy weapons in their possession and to acquire no others.

East-West conflict. The conflict between the two major competing blocs that had formed after World War II—the "First World" (the United States and the economically developed capitalist democracies of Western Europe, Japan, Canada, Australia, and New Zealand) and the "Second World" (The Soviet Union and its communist allies in Eastern Europe and elsewhere).

Economic and monetary union. A stage in economic integration, as envisioned in the European Community, in which all member states harmonize their economic policies and introduce a common currency.

Economic and Social Council (ECOSOC). The UN organ charged with offering recommendations, issuing reports, organizing conferences, and coordinating the activities of various UN agencies in the economic and social field.

Economic development. The improvement of techniques of production and distribution of goods and services, with less waste of resources or human energy, in order to establish conditions that enable the average person to attain a decent standard of living.

Embargo. The refusal of one country to sell goods to another country.

Embassy. A permanent mission established by a government in a foreign country to represent its interests in that country.

Ethnopolitical conflicts. Violent conflicts, either within or across nation-state boundaries, involving competing ethnic groups seeking self-determination or pressing other grievances.

European Union. A regional body consisting of over a dozen Western European states collaborating in the European Coal and Steel Community, the European Economic Community (the Common Market), and the European Atomic Energy Community; created after World War II (originally called the European Community) to promote economic efficiency, free trade, and prosperity among its members.

Exchange rate. The value of one country's currency in terms of another's, in trade and other transactions.

Export. To sell goods to another country in international trade.

Expropriation. Government seizure of foreign-owned property or assets.

Fascism. A political system, such as existed in Mussolini's Italy or Franco's Spain, with a single-party dictatorship ruling and representing interests of the Church, large landholders, the military, and the wealthy industrial classes.

Food and Agriculture Organization (FAO). The UN Specialized Agency that engages in research, technical assistance, and financial support aimed at improving agricultural production and addressing the food needs of less developed countries.

Force without war. The use of armed force in some fashion short of war, e.g., border skirmishes, raids, interventions, and other acts of violence used in limited or low-intensity conflict situations.

Foreign aid. The transfer of resources between governments on generous terms, in the form of grants, loans, export credits, or technical and military assistance; sometimes channeled through NGOs.

Foreign investment. The transfer of funds into a country, by a foreign government or by private parties, for the purchase of property, production facilities, or dividend-bearing securities in that country.

Foreign Policy. A set of priorities and guides for action in certain circumstances that underlies a country's behavior toward other states and includes both the basic goals a national government seeks to pursue in the international arena and the instruments used to achieve those goals.

Foreign policy behavior. The specific actions states take toward each other.

Fourth World. Approximately forty of the world's poorest nation-states, designated by the United Nations as "least developed countries."

Framework Convention on Climate Change. A treaty produced at the Earth Summit in Rio de Janeiro that created modest obligations for states in committing them to aim for reduction of greenhouse gases and to monitor greenhouse warming and other atmospheric changes thought to pose environmental threats.

Free trade. The practice of encouraging as much international trade as possible by removing government-imposed tariff and nontariff barriers between states.

Free trade area. A stage in economic integration, as envisioned in the European Community plan, in which all tariff barriers are eliminated in trade among member states.

Functionalist school. A school of thought arguing that as states collaborate on specific noncontroversial or technical issues, their governments will learn habits of cooperation and will find reason to collaborate on politically more sensitive issues as well, leading gradually to surrender of sovereignty and ultimately a possible supranational community.

Game theory. A branch of social science analysis that uses game models to explain and predict human behavior, and bases those predictions on mathematical probabilities and the values people attach to various outcomes possible in the game.

General Agreement on Tariffs and Trade (GATT). An intergovernmental organization established in 1947 to serve as a global forum for multilateral negotiations aimed at reducing tariff and non-

tariff barriers to trade, replaced by the World Trade Organization in 1995.

General Assembly. The main deliberative body of the United Nations, representing the entire UN membership and authorized by the Charter to deal with a broad range of political, economic, and social issues.

Geneva Protocol of 1925. An agreement prohibiting the first use of lethal biological and chemical weapons by the signatories against each other.

Genocide. The mass extermination of a group of people based on their ethnic or some other group characteristic.

Global actors. States whose interests and activities are global in scope, manifested by widespread diplomatic, commercial, and other ties outside their region.

Globalist school. A major school of international relations, which argues that the struggle between national governments competing for power and security is only one aspect of world politics and that a fuller understanding of world politics requires one to look also at nonstate actors and at economic and nonsecurity issues in an interdependent world.

Globalization. The internationalization of production, finance, and exchange—a process involving the growth of multinational corporations and other relationships that is increasing economic interdependence among states.

Great man theory. The belief that a single individual is capable of shaping great events.

Greenhouse effect. An overall rise in the earth's temperature resulting from the accumulation of carbon dioxide caused by the burning of coal and other fossil fuels.

Green revolution. The introduction of high-yielding "miracle" seeds, along with the heavy application of chemical fertilizer and extensive irrigation, in order to bring about higher agricultural production in less developed countries.

Group of Seven.   The major industrialized democracies (the United States, Canada, France, Germany, Britain, Italy, and Japan) which hold annual economic summits and consult regularly on economic and other matters.

Group of 77.   A group of more than 100 third world countries that in the UN and other forums has sought to promote an overhauling of the international economic order aimed at redistributing wealth from the North to the South.

Groupthink.   A social-psychological phenomenon whereby the pressures for group conformity may lead individual members of a decision-making group to suppress any personal doubts they may have about the emerging group consensus.

Guerrilla warfare.   "Hit-and-run" tactics used by small bands of irregular forces against an invading army or in rebellion against established authorities.

Hague Convention of 1970.   A treaty requiring signatories to extradite or prosecute air hijackers in their custody.

High politics.   Issues that involve the most crucial interests of states and are the most controversial in nature, such as national security issues.

High seas.   Waters beyond the control or sovereignty of any state.

Home government.   The government of the country in which a multinational corporation is headquartered.

Host government.   The government of a country in which a foreign-based multinational corporation operates subsidiaries.

Human rights.   The set of privileges supposedly enjoyed by all human beings, defined in various treaties and declarations, including the Universal Declaration of Human Rights.

Idealist school.   A major school of international relations, focusing on the role of international law and international organization as well as morality in international affairs.

Ideology.   A relatively inflexible set of beliefs regarding the nature of political, economic, and social relations.

Idiosyncratic factors.   The characteristics of individual leaders and groups of decision makers, which can affect a state's foreign policy.

Image.   An individual's view of the world that tends to color, and sometimes distort, perceptions of reality.

Imperialism.   The policy of acquiring foreign territory through force; associated especially with the building of colonial empires during the nineteenth century.

Import.   To purchase goods from another country in international trade.

Influence.   The process whereby one political actor seeks to get another actor to conform to the former's preferences.

Integration theory.   A theory explaining how political units tend to merge together and transfer loyalty to a larger community.

Inter-continental ballistic missiles (ICBMs).   Electronically guided land-based rockets able to deliver nuclear payloads at distances of over 3,000 miles.

Interdependence.   The interrelatedness of national societies, which are in varying degrees sensitive and vulnerable to each other's policies.

Intergovernmental organizations (IGOs).   International organizations that have national governments as members and are created through treaties among states.

International Atomic Energy Agency (IAEA).   The UN Specialized Agency responsible for maintaining safeguards on the use of nuclear fuels and disposal of wastes associated with the Non-Proliferation Treaty and other nuclear arms control agreements.

International Bank for Reconstruction and Development (IBRD). See World Bank.

International Civil Aviation Organization (ICAO). The UN Specialized Agency responsible for establishing uniform practices and standards of international air safety.

International Court of Justice. See World Court.

International Labor Organization (ILO). The UN Specialized Agency responsible for monitoring working conditions worldwide and improving the general standard of living of the world's workers through the drafting of an international labor code and other activities.

International law. The body of rules governing relations between states, derived mainly from custom and treaties.

International Maritime Organization (IMO). The UN Specialized Agency responsible for managing international maritime traffic.

International Monetary Fund (IMF). The UN Specialized Agency responsible for promoting international monetary cooperation, stabilizing exchange rates, and providing foreign exchange funds for needy states so that the maximum amount of world trade can occur.

International organizations. Intergovernmental and nongovernmental organizations, established on a regional or global basis in response to problems that transcend national boundaries.

International political economy. The study of the interplay between economics and politics in world affairs.

International relations. The study of who gets what, when, and how in the international arena; primarily deals with relations between nation-states but includes nonstate actors also.

International Seabed Authority. An organization proposed by the Law of the Sea Conference in 1982, designed to regulate deep seabed mining and to distribute resultant revenues between private investors and developing countries.

International system. The general pattern of political, economic, social, geographical, and technological relationships in world affairs; the general setting in which international relations occur at any point in time.

International Telecommunication Union (ITU). The UN Specialized Agency responsible for managing the flow of telegraph, radio, and television communications across the globe.

Intervention. Military, economic, or diplomatic interference by one country in another country's territory or internal affairs.

Isolationism. A national policy advocating aloofness from political or economic entanglements with other countries.

Kellogg-Briand Pact. A multilateral treaty concluded in 1928 that attempted to outlaw war as a means of settling disputes between members of the international community.

Law of the Sea Treaty. The document drafted at the UN Conference on the Law of the Sea in 1982, aimed at establishing a single set of rules governing the use of territorial waters, economic zones, and all other parts of the oceans.

League of Nations Covenant. The charter establishing a global intergovernmental organization after World War I, the precursor of the United Nations.

Liberal internationalist school. An international economic perspective, widely held in developed capitalist societies, according to which consumers in all nations can expect to benefit from an international economy based on the most efficient allocation and use of resources, competition, and free trade among countries.

Limited war. Violent conflict involving the controlled use of military force, with participants refraining from using their entire arsenals.

Limits to growth school. A school of thought predicting imminent resource scarcities and environmental decay and arguing that economic growth had to be halted in the late twentieth century if civilization were to survive.

Low politics. Issues that are relatively narrow, technical, and noncontroversial in nature.

Macro-decision. A foreign policy decision that involves relatively large, general concerns (e.g., the composition of the defense budget) and is designed to establish guidelines to be applied later to specific situations as they arise.

Marshall Plan. An American foreign aid program that helped to rebuild the war-torn economies of Western Europe following World War II.

Marxist school. A major school of thought that views international relations as a struggle between rich and poor classes rather than as a contest between national governments or nation-states.

Massive retaliation. A U.S. strategic doctrine enunciated during the Eisenhower administration threatening large-scale nuclear retaliation for Soviet-sponsored aggression in Europe or other regions.

Mediation. A form of peaceful settlement of disputes in which a third party is involved in seeking a resolution to the conflict.

Mercantilism. An economic philosophy advocating the use of protective tariffs and other economic measures to be taken by a state to expand national power.

Micro-decision. A foreign policy decision involving concerns that are relatively narrow in scope, that are low threat in nature, and that tend to be handled at the lower levels of the government bureaucracy.

Military-industrial complex. A mutually supportive ongoing relationship between a nation's defense-related industries and its military forces.

Monroe Doctrine. A statement issued by President James Monroe in 1823 opposing European intervention in the Western Hemisphere and promising to refrain from intervention in Europe; the Doctrine has continued to be the basis for American opposition to foreign intervention in Latin America.

Montreal Convention of 1971. A treaty requiring signatories to prosecute or extradite anyone committing acts of sabotage against airports or aircraft on the ground, with the ICAO empowered to suspend air travel to states that fail to comply.

Montreal Protocol of 1987. An agreement among those states which are major producers of ozone-depleting CFC chemicals to eliminate CFC production by the end of the twentieth century.

Most favored nation principle. The principle, adopted by GATT, that whenever one member state lowers tariffs on certain kinds of imports from another member state, all member states are entitled to the same favorable treatment with regard to their goods.

Multilateral. Involving several countries.

Multilateral diplomacy. Diplomatic negotiations between several countries.

Multinational corporation (MNC). A corporation having branch operations abroad that are connected with and subordinate to a headquarters office in another country.

Multipolar system. An international system characterized by multiple power centers and very flexible alignments.

Munich Pact. A 1938 pact whereby Britain and France abandoned their Czech allies and appeased Hitler's territorial demands; became a symbol after World War II of the need to "fight force with force" in order to deter aggression.

Municipal law.   Law within a national political system (domestic law), as opposed to international law.

Mutual assured destruction (MAD). A strategic doctrine of deterrence under which each adversary preserves the capability to absorb a first nuclear attack by the other and still retaliate with devastating nuclear force—inflicting unacceptable damage on the attacker.

Nation.   A cultural or social entity whose members have some sense of shared historical experience as well as shared destiny, based on common language or other ties.

National.   A person owing permanent allegiance to a particular state, either through birth or through naturalization; a citizen.

National air space.   The air above a country's land mass and its territorial sea in which that country exercises sovereignty and can exclude foreign aircraft.

National attribute factors.   The demographic, economic, military, and governmental characteristics of a nation-state, which can affect the foreign policy of that state.

National interests.   The fundamental interests, defined by the government, that a nation's foreign policy is geared to achieve, ordinarily including a nation's physical survival, economic well-being, and self-determination.

National Socialism.   The political system in Germany from 1932 to 1945, commonly called "Nazism," with a single party dictatorship exercising total control of the society and economy based on racial superiority theories, anti-communism, anti-Semitism, and ultranationalism.

Nationalism.   The determination of a group of people to establish or preserve themselves as a nation and to achieve or maintain statehood.

Nation-state.   A national political unit; a term often used by scholars as a synonym for "state." See *State*.

NATO.   See North Atlantic Treaty Organization.

Negotiation.   A form of diplomacy in which bargaining occurs through formal, direct discussion between parties.

Neocolonialism.   The subtle domination of another country, through economic penetration rather than through outright takeover by force.

Neofunctionalist school.   A branch of the functionalist school that identifies certain sectors of intergovernmental cooperation as more likely to lead to further cooperation, or "spillover," than others.

Neomercantilist school.   An international economic perspective that argues that the world economy remains driven by the pursuit of national interests and mercantilist tendencies among states.

Neutrality.   A stance of formal nonpartisanship in world affairs; a refusal to join alliances.

New International Economic Order (NIEO).   A new set of trade, aid, and investment relationships demanded by third world countries during the 1970s and subsequently modified somewhat, intended to produce a more even distribution of wealth between the generally rich North and the generally impoverished South.

NICs.   Newly industrializing countries, such as South Korea, Singapore, and Brazil.

Nixon Doctrine.   An American policy during the Nixon administration, stressing military self-help by third world states, assisted by transfers of U.S. military equipment.

Nonalignment.   A policy of asserting independence from and nonattachment to competing blocs of states, especially as regards the East-West conflict during the Cold War.

Nongovernmental organizations (NGOs). International organizations composed of private individuals or groups.

Nonrational behavior. The failure of a decision maker to specify goals clearly, to consider every possible alternative, and to choose that option calculated to maximize the achievement of goals.

Nonrenewable resources. Raw materials that are in finite supply and capable of being exhausted.

Nonstate actor. An actor other than a national government that has an impact on international relations (e.g., IGOs and NGOs).

North Atlantic Treaty Organization (NATO). A military alliance established in 1949 by fifteen countries in North America and Western Europe, in which the members pledge that an attack on one will be considered equivalent to an attack on all.

North-South conflict. The conflict between the largely well-to-do states of the Northern Hemisphere and the generally poverty-stricken states of the Southern Hemisphere.

Nuclear deterrence. A form of military dissuasion in which a nuclear-armed nation threatens to use nuclear weapons if an adversary initiates a nuclear strike or commits a conventional aggression.

Nuclear Non-Proliferation Treaty (NPT) of 1970. An agreement in which the signatory nuclear states are pledged not to transfer nuclear weapons to nuclear have-nots, while the have-nots are pledged not to attempt to acquire nuclear weapons.

Nuclear proliferation. The acquisition of nuclear weapons by states that formerly did not have them.

Nuclear weapons. High-explosive bombs, operating through atomic fusion reactions, that are capable of producing destructive force up to the equivalent of millions of tons of TNT.

Nuremberg Trials. The trials following World War II of those leaders of Nazi Germany charged with committing war crimes and crimes against humanity.

Optional Clause. A clause in the International Court of Justice Statute giving the Court compulsory jurisdiction in certain kinds of disputes.

Organization of Economic Cooperation and Development (OECD). A key institution through which the industrialized democracies—the United States, Japan, Canada, and the Western European states—promote mutual economic cooperation and plan common strategies to address the demands of less developed countries.

Organization of Petroleum Exporting Countries (OPEC). An organization of less developed countries that together account for a major portion of the world's oil exports.

Outer Space Treaty of 1967. A treaty banning the placement of "mass destruction" weapons in orbit around the earth or on celestial bodies.

Pacta sunt servanda. The fundamental principle of international law stipulating that treaties are to be obeyed.

Paradigm. An intellectual framework that structures one's thinking about a set of phenomena.

Partial Test Ban Treaty of 1963. A treaty banning nuclear testing in the atmosphere by the signatories; was followed up in 1996 with a Comprehensive Test Ban Treaty.

Peaceful settlement procedures. Procedures, such as mediation and adjudication, that are outlined in Chapter VI of the UN Charter and are designed to forestall the use of military force in disputes between states.

Peace of Westphalia. The treaty ending the Thirty Years' War in 1648, widely accepted as marking the origin of the nation-state system.

Peacekeeping. A function performed by the UN when it sends troops into a conflict not to punish or confront an aggressor but to provide a neutral buffer between warring sides.

Polis. A human-scale community, modeled after the ancient Greek city-states.

Potency. The importance of a promise or a threat—in terms of either attraction or potential harm—as perceived by the other side, an essential ingredient in bargaining.

Power. The ability to get others to do something they would not otherwise do; in international relations, a country's existing strength or relative capabilities and the manner in which one state seeks to control the behavior of another state.

Preventive diplomacy. A UN peacekeeping role, often involving multinational forces, whereby local conflicts are kept from escalating into larger conflagrations directly involving major powers.

Primary resources. The main elements—in land, air, and water—that sustain life on earth.

Private goods. Goods that can be possessed by individuals and can be divided and consumed, as opposed to collective goods.

Prominent solution. In international bargaining, an alternative that is so self-evidently better than others, even if not optimal, that all parties are inclined to settle on it.

Promise. In international bargaining, a statement of intent to reward acceptable or desired behavior.

Punishment. In international bargaining, a penalty imposed on actors whose behavior is considered unacceptable or undesired.

Quota. A method of protecting domestic producers from foreign competition by imposing a limit on the maximum volume of allowable imports.

Rational actor model. A model of decision making whereby one carefully defines the situation, specifies goals, weighs all conceivable alternatives, and selects that option most likely to achieve the goals.

Reagan Doctrine. A policy associated with the Reagan administration in the 1980s, declaring the intention of the United States not only to contain the further spread of communist governments around the world but also to "roll back" communism by supporting insurgency movements against Marxist regimes thought to be aligned too closely with the Soviet Union.

Realist school. A major school of international relations that views international relations as a struggle for power between nation-states whose ultimate goal is security in a hostile, anarchic environment.

Rebus sic stantibus. A legal basis for termination of a treaty obligation on the grounds that present conditions are so radically different from those existing at the outset of the treaty as to render it impossible to continue honoring the terms of the pact.

Regimes. Widely accepted practices, rules, and institutional arrangements governing relations between states in various issue-areas.

Regional actor. A state that interacts primarily with neighboring states in the same geographical area, except for interactions with global actors in economic and other affairs.

Regionalism. The growth of international organizations and other kinds of ties among countries at the regional level.

Renewable resources. Resources such as air and water that are in infinite supply or are constantly renewed by natural processes.

Reprisals. Actions taken by a state that would ordinarily be considered a violation of international law but that are rendered legal when done in retaliation for a prior illegal act committed by another state.

Reward. In international bargaining, a benefit afforded to actors whose behavior is considered acceptable or desirable.

Right of innocent passage. The right of foreign vessels to pass through a state's coastal waters as long as it is done peaceably.

SALT. See Strategic Arms Limitation agreements.

Secondary resources. Resources such as minerals, vegetables, and animals that are derived from primary resources.

Secretariat. The administrative arm of the United Nations.

Secretary-General. The chief administrative officer of the United Nations.

Security community. A group of states among which war is no longer a serious option for pursuing goals or resolving differences.

Security Council. The UN organ with primary responsibility in the area of peace and security, consisting of fifteen states, including five permanent members (China, France, United Kingdom, Russia, and the United States).

Security dilemma. A condition commonly experienced by states because of the anarchic nature of the international system, where there is a felt need to acquire more weapons and other elements of national power to increase national security, yet which ultimately leads to mutual paranoia and increased feelings of insecurity.

Sensitivity. The degree of one country's concern about another country's actions.

Sovereignty. Supreme decision-making authority within the boundaries of a territorial unit and acknowledging no higher authority outside those boundaries.

Specialized Agencies. A group of intergovernmental organizations that are affiliated with the UN but have their own memberships, budgets, secretariats, and decision-making machinery.

Spillover. The process whereby one type of international cooperation might lead to or create needs for other types of international cooperation.

State. A legal-political entity with a sovereign government exercising supreme authority over a relatively fixed population within well-defined territorial boundaries and acknowledging no higher authority outside those boundaries.

State-centric. A focus on nation-states and their national governments as the major actors in world politics.

Strategic Arms Limitation (SALT) agreements. Bilateral agreements between the United States and the Soviet Union during the 1970s setting limits on the number and types of strategic nuclear weapons (e.g., ICBMs) the two sides could possess.

Strategic Arms Reduction Talks (START). A series of bilateral negotiations undertaken between the United States and the Soviet Union/Russia in the 1980s and 1990s, designed to go beyond the SALT process and result in actual elimination of certain categories of nuclear weapons.

Strategic weapons. Large-scale, long-range nuclear weapons.

Submarine-launched ballistic missiles (SLBMs). Sea-based rockets able to deliver nuclear payloads at long or short distances.

Summitry. Direct, personal contact and negotiation between heads of state.

Supranational. A type of organization or community in which nation-states surrender sovereignty to a higher authority.

Sustainable development. A concept that stresses the importance of economic growth but managed in a manner that is sensitive to one's environment.

Systemic factors. External factors such as geography, international interactions and links, and international system structure, which affect a state's foreign policy.

Tacit diplomacy. Informal, indirect communications through words and actions designed to signal intentions or the importance one attaches to some issue.

Tariff. An import tax imposed on foreign products entering a country.

Territorial sea. Waters immediately adjacent to a country's coast, over which that country exercises sovereignty and regulates navigation and other activities in its own interest.

Terrorism. The use or threat of violence for purposes of political extortion, coercion, or publicity for a political cause.

Tertiary resources. Secondary resources that have been processed by humans into other usable forms.

Theory of hegemonic stability. The theory that throughout history large-scale wars involving major powers have tended to produce among the victors one dominant state (a "hegemon") capable of maintaining a degree of world order, and that this order gradually tends to break down as the hegemon suffers decline due to the draining costs of maintaining large armed forces and extensive economic commitments, finally leading to the rise of new hegemonic challengers and a new cycle of war and postwar reconstruction of world order.

Third world. The less developed countries (LDCs), mainly located in the Southern Hemisphere.

Threat. In international bargaining, a statement of intent to penalize unacceptable or undesired behavior.

Threat perception. One nation's estimate of another country's capability and intent to do harm.

Tokyo Convention of 1963. A treaty obligating signatory states to effect the safe release of hijacked aircraft, passengers, and crews entering their borders.

Trade dependence. The extent to which a country's economy requires external trade, reflected in the sum of a country's imports and exports as a percentage of its gross national product (or gross domestic product).

Traditionalists. International relations scholars who base their analysis not on scientific methods but on insights gained from first-hand participant observation and practical experience or second-hand immersion in the great works of diplomatic history, statesmen's memoirs, international law treatises, and philosophical writings.

Transnational relations. Interactions between private individuals and groups across national boundaries.

Treaty. A formal written agreement or convention between states that creates legal obligations for the governments that are parties to it.

Treaty on European Union (Maastricht Treaty). Adopted by members of the European Union in 1993, designed to take Western European integration to the next level in terms of consolidating the common internal market and establishing a single currency and monetary system.

Truman Doctrine. A 1947 declaration promising U.S. assistance against Soviet aggression in Greece and Turkey and in other parts of the world where communist expansion threatened to occur.

Trusteeship Council. A UN organ charged with facilitating the dismantling of colonial empires.

United Nations (UN). A global intergovernmental organization formed in 1945 to promote peace and international security as well as cooperation in the economic and social field.

United Nations Charter. The document enumerating the powers of the

United Nations and its various organs and specifying the rights and obligations of member states.

United Nations Conference on Environment and Development. The "Earth Summit" held in Rio de Janeiro in 1992, which sought to address a wide range of global environmental issues along with economic development concerns.

United Nations Conference on the Human Environment. A 1972 UN-sponsored conference in Stockholm, Sweden that was a landmark attempt to address environmental problems at the global level.

United Nations Conference on the Law of the Sea. A UN conference convened in 1958 and in subsequent years to codify rules governing the oceans.

United Nations Conference on Trade and Development (UNCTAD). A UN General Assembly organization established in 1964 to supplement GATT as a world trade forum; relied on primarily by less developed countries.

United Nations Educational, Scientific and Cultural Organization (UNESCO). The UN Specialized Agency responsible for improving literacy rates in less developed countries, promoting scientific and cultural exchanges, and facilitating the dissemination of information by drafting universal copyright conventions and related rules.

UN Environmental Program (UNEP). The major global environmental agency, established after the 1972 Conference on the Human Environment.

Universal Postal Union (UPU). The UN Specialized Agency responsible for facilitating the flow of mail across national boundaries.

Variable-sum game. In game theory, a type of game in which both parties can simultaneously win something, even though one might benefit more than the other.

Vulnerability. The degree of harm or damage that one country might suffer from another country's actions.

War. Sustained armed combat between the organized military forces of at least two nation-states.

Warsaw Pact. An alliance formed in 1955 by the Soviet Union and Eastern European countries after West Germany's entry into NATO; was terminated in the early 1990s at the end of the Cold War.

World Bank (International Bank for Reconstruction and Development). The UN Specialized Agency responsible for providing loans to less developed countries to finance the building of bridges, dams, roads, and other developmental needs.

World Court (International Court of Justice). A global institution for adjudicating international disputes, located in The Hague, Netherlands.

World Food Conference of 1974. A UN-sponsored conference in Rome whose purpose was to recommend ways to improve the supply and distribution of food in the world.

World government. A political system in which one central set of authoritative institutions would preside over all human beings and political units on the planet.

World Health Organization (WHO). The UN Specialized Agency responsible for controlling communicable diseases and promoting health education and public health services in less developed countries.

World Meteorological Organization (WMO). The UN Specialized Agency responsible for collecting and exchanging global weather forecasting data and monitoring conditions relating to the global environment and climate change.

World Population Conference of 1974. A UN-sponsored conference in Bucharest, organized to address global population issues and resulting in a World Population Plan of Action.

World system school. Similar to the *dependencia* school, an international economic perspective that focuses on interactions between nonstate actors and argues that the international economy is driven by the interests of economic elites—residing mainly in the North—who compete with each other in accumulating wealth.

World Trade Organization. Created in 1995 to replace GATT and to promote global free trade.

Zero-sum game. In game theory, a type of game in which whatever one party wins the other party automatically loses; in other words, conflict is total.

Photo Credits

3 (Bernard Shaw, CNN news anchor, sitting at the CNN "World News" set.) Courtesy of CNN; 5 Robert Wallis/Sipa Press; 37 (Napoleon directing battle. [Painting by G. Chambord.]) Corbis-Bettmann; 73 AP/Wide World Photos; 74 Christopher Morris/Black Star; 79 (Vietnamese, former U.S. enemies, welcome American foreign investment, as evidenced by signs on the road to the Ho Chi Minh City airport.) © Jeffrey Aaronsen/Network Aspen; 89 © Robin Graubard; 108 © Patrick Aventurier/Gamma Liaison; 125 (Richard Nixon and Chou En-lai review an honor guard marking the American president's arrival in Beijing, China, in 1972.) UPI/Corbis-Bettmann; 142 U.S. Department of Defense; 155 AP/Wide World Photos; 163 Charlie Cole/Sipa Press; 175 ("The Big Three" [Winston Churchill, Franklin Roosevelt, and Josef Stalin] at the Yalta Conference in 1945.) U.S. Department of Defense; 176 Consulate General of Israel; 208 Corbis-Bettmann; 219 (President John Kennedy in the Oval Office during the Cuban missile crisis in October 1962.) AP/Wide World Photos; 226 Bill Fitz-Patrick/The White House; 253 (Anwar Sadat, Jimmy Carter, and Menachem Begin clasp hands as they finalize the peace treaty between Israel and Egypt at Camp David in 1979.) AP/Wide World Photos; 263 John Ficara/Woodfin Camp & Associates; 293 (Korean families weep as they identify the dead, casualties of the Korean War in 1950.) Courtesy of Defense Audio Visual Agency, 1950; 303 UPI/Corbis-Bettmann; 304 Mark Peters/Sipa Press; 320 U.S. Department of Defense; 333 (The World Court sitting in The Hague in 1976. The judges shown in this photograph, seated from left to right, are from Syria, West Germany, United Kingdom, United States, France, India, Uruguay, Senegal, Poland, Soviet Union, Argentina, Nigeria, and Japan.) Courtesy of the United Nations; 335 U.S. Department of Defense; 365 (The United Nations headquarters in New York City, lighted up in 1995 in celebration of the UN's fiftieth anniversary.) UN/DPI Photo by E. Schneider; 387 Jim Estrin; 396 UN/DPI Photo; 413 (The second atomic bomb test at Bikini, July 24, 1946.) Photo by Joint Army-Navy Task Force One; 439 Reuters/Mikhail Chernichkin/Archive; 445 (A scene from the Lebanese civil war in the 1980s: yet another terrorist bombing in Beirut.) AP/Wide World Photos; 453 AP/Wide World Photos; 467 (A young boy sipping Coca-Cola at the Great Wall of China.) James Andanson/Sygma; 475 © Jeffrey Aaronson/ Network Aspen; 513 (In a remote area of northern Kenya, a Samburu warrior uses a cellular telephone to make a call.) © Sally Wiener Grotta/The Stock Market; 518 Robert Grossman/New York Times Pictures; 529 David Portnoy/ New York Times Pictures; 551 (A photo of the earth, taken by weather satellite on May 28, 1974, showing the Western Hemisphere and the west coast of Africa.) Courtesy NASA; 554 Robert Harbison-Staff/Christian Science Monitor; 564 AP/Wide World Photos; 583 (A rising sun illuminates the windows of an office building in Cambridge, Massachusetts, as a full moon sets slowly in the background.) John Tlumacki/Globe Photos.

Name Index

Allison, Grahm:
  on Cuban missile crisis, 227
  on foreign policy process, 220
Ambrose, Stephen:
  on U.S. military, growth of, 619n
Angell, Robert:
  on transnational participation, 6

Baker, James, U.S. Treasury Secretary:
  on debt solutions, 546-547
Ball, George:
  on summitry, 260-261
Barber, Benjamin:
  on Post–Cold War era, 26
Barnet, Richard J.:
  on economic levels of countries, 99-100
  on multinational corporations, 506-507
Barr, Cameron:
  on Japanese foreign policy, 167-168
Barraclough, Geoffrey:
  on Euruopean Civilization, 56
Barry, John:
  on nuclear weapons of former Soviet Union, 427
Beard, Charles:
  on national interests, 178
Begin, Menachem, Israeli Prime Minister:
  as Israeli leader, 211, 259
Bhatia, Shyam:
  on nuclear proliferation, 424
Bonapart, Napoleon:
  as French nationalist, 53
  war activities, 135
Boulding, Kenneth:
  on decision making, 207
Boutros-Ghali, Boutros, UN Secretary-General:
  on new world order, 24
  on Post–Cold War era, 20-22
  as UN leader, 389-390
  on UN peacekeeping reform, 397
Bradsher, Keith:
  on world economy, 62-63

Brandt, Willy, West German Chancellor:
  on economic development, 516
Brezhnev, Leonid:
  as Soviet leader, 153-154
Brown, Seyom:
  on microregions, 494
Bush, George, U.S. President:
  foreign policy of, 147
  negotiations of, 259
  on New World Order, 4, 147, 619n, 621n

Cable, Vincent
  on "new feudalism," 115-117
Carr, E.H.:
  on roots of realism, 22-23
Carter, Jimmy, U.S. President:
  environmental resource management of, 577
  foreign policy of, 146, 154, 248, 429, 608n
  Iranian hostage crisis, 225
  peace work after presidency, 621n
  on war, prevention of, 30
Castro, Fidel, Cuban President:
  U.S., relations with, 153, 620n
Carson, Rachel:
  on future of physical environment, 557
Cavanaugh, John:
  on economic levels of countries, 99-100
  on multinational corporations, 506-507
Chamberlain, Neville, U.K. Prime Minister:
  on peace prospects with Nazi Germany, 6, 322
Chasdi, Richard J.:
  on terrorism, 448
Chayes, Arbram and Antonia:
  on U.S. foreign policy, 233
Churchhill, Winston:
  demise of, 319
  on the Soviet Union, 143, 176
  on unification with France, 399
Clark, Grenville:
  on world government, 592

Claude, Inis:
  on IGOs, 325
  on international conferences, 607n
Clinton, William J., U.S. President:
  on end of Cold War, 4
  foreign policy of, 147, 180, 221-222, 279
  diplomacy of, 259, 621n
  Yugoslavia breakup, response to, 89
Copeland, Miles:
  on CIA, 287-288
Crosette, Barbara:
  on NGOs, 376-377
  on UN summits, 514

Dahl, Robert:
  on power, 48
Davis, Jackson:
  on decentralization, 593
de Gaulle, Charles, French President:
  demise of, 319
  on unification with Great Britain, 399
de Mesquita, Bueno:
  on war, nature of, 295-296
de Tocqueville, Alexis:
  on superpowers, 605n
  on war-proneness, 30
Dulles, John Foster, U.S. Secretary of State:
  on communism, 144
Dunlop, John, U.S. Secretary of Labor:
  on negotiating, 266

Edwards, David V.:
  on American legal system, 343-344
Einstein, Albert:
  on politics, complexities of, 2
Eisenhower, Dwight, U.S. President:
  on military-indutrial complexes, 313
Esquivel, Adolfo Perez:
  on world priorities, 411

Subject Index

Note: *f*, *n*, and *t* following a page number indicate figure, note, and table, respectively.